Seattle & King County

Gateway to the Pacific Northwest

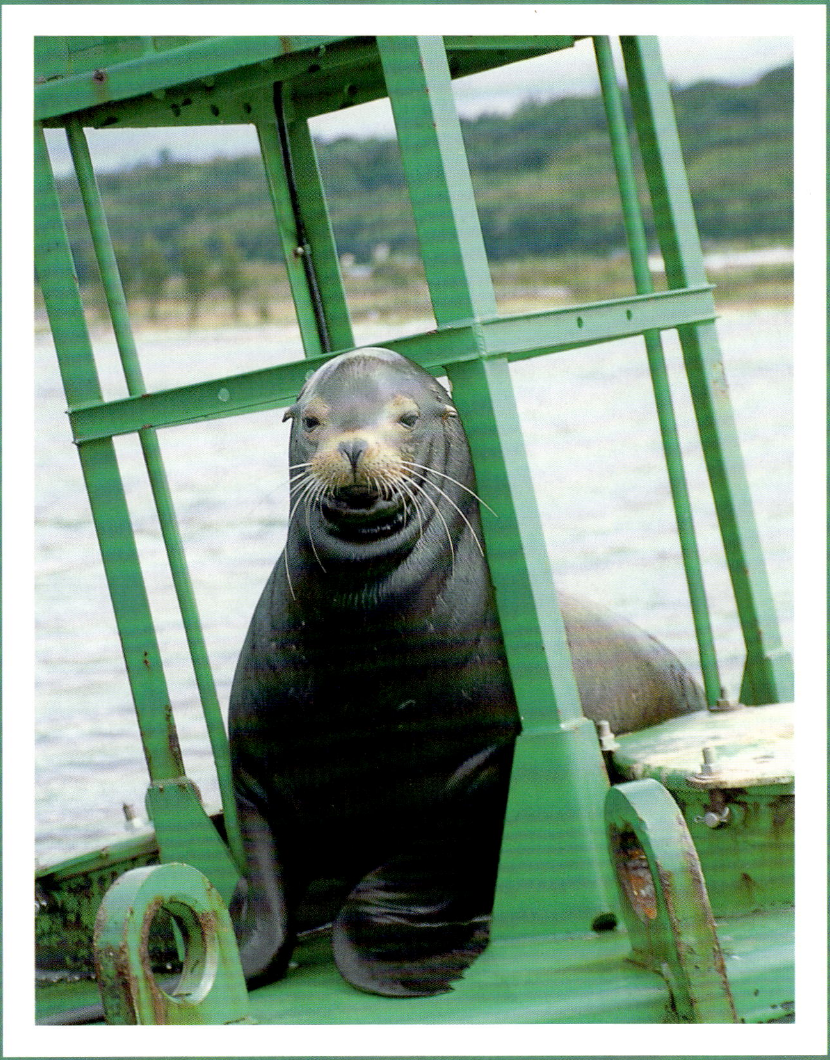

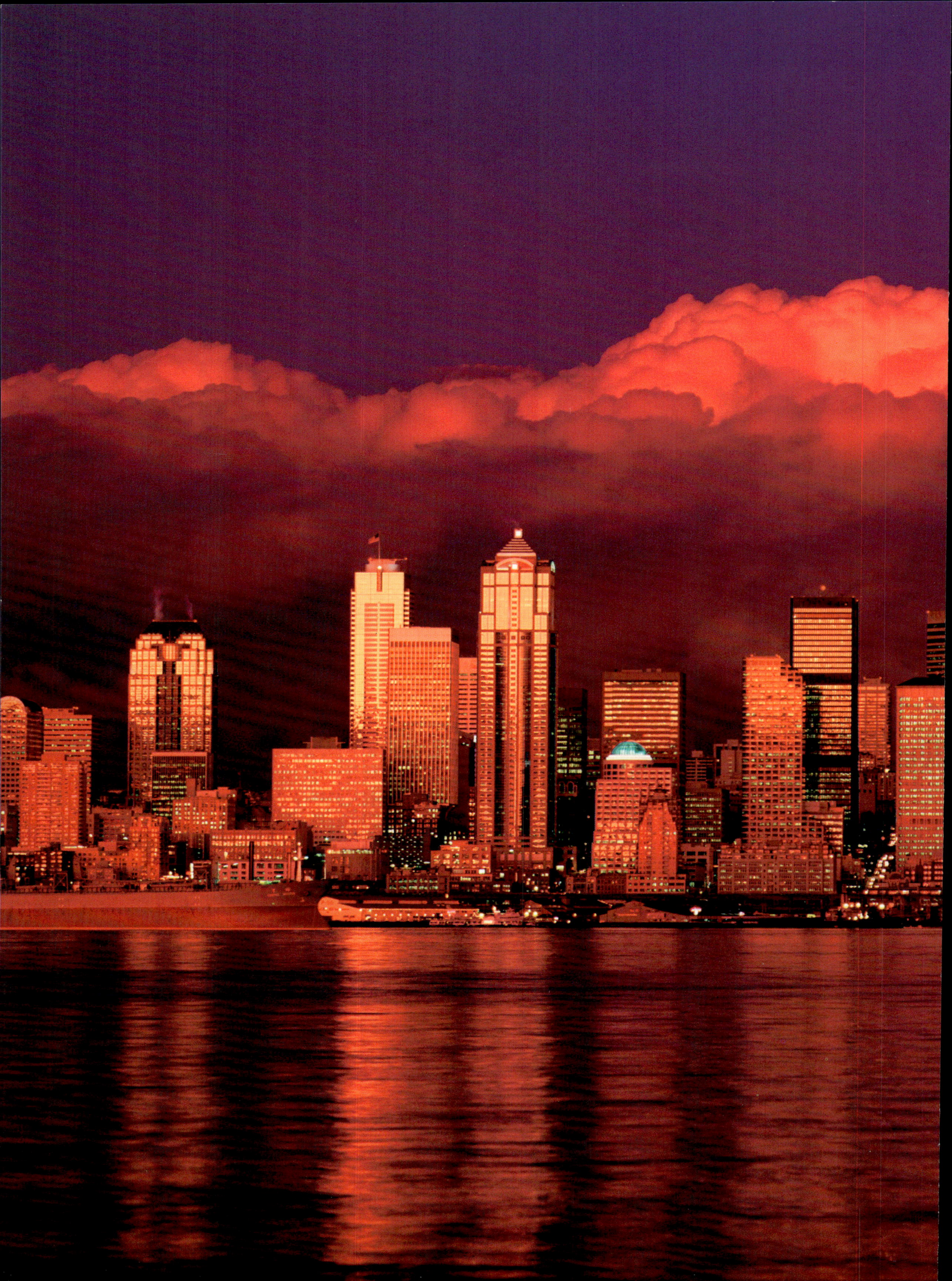

Seattle & King County

Gateway to the Pacific Northwest

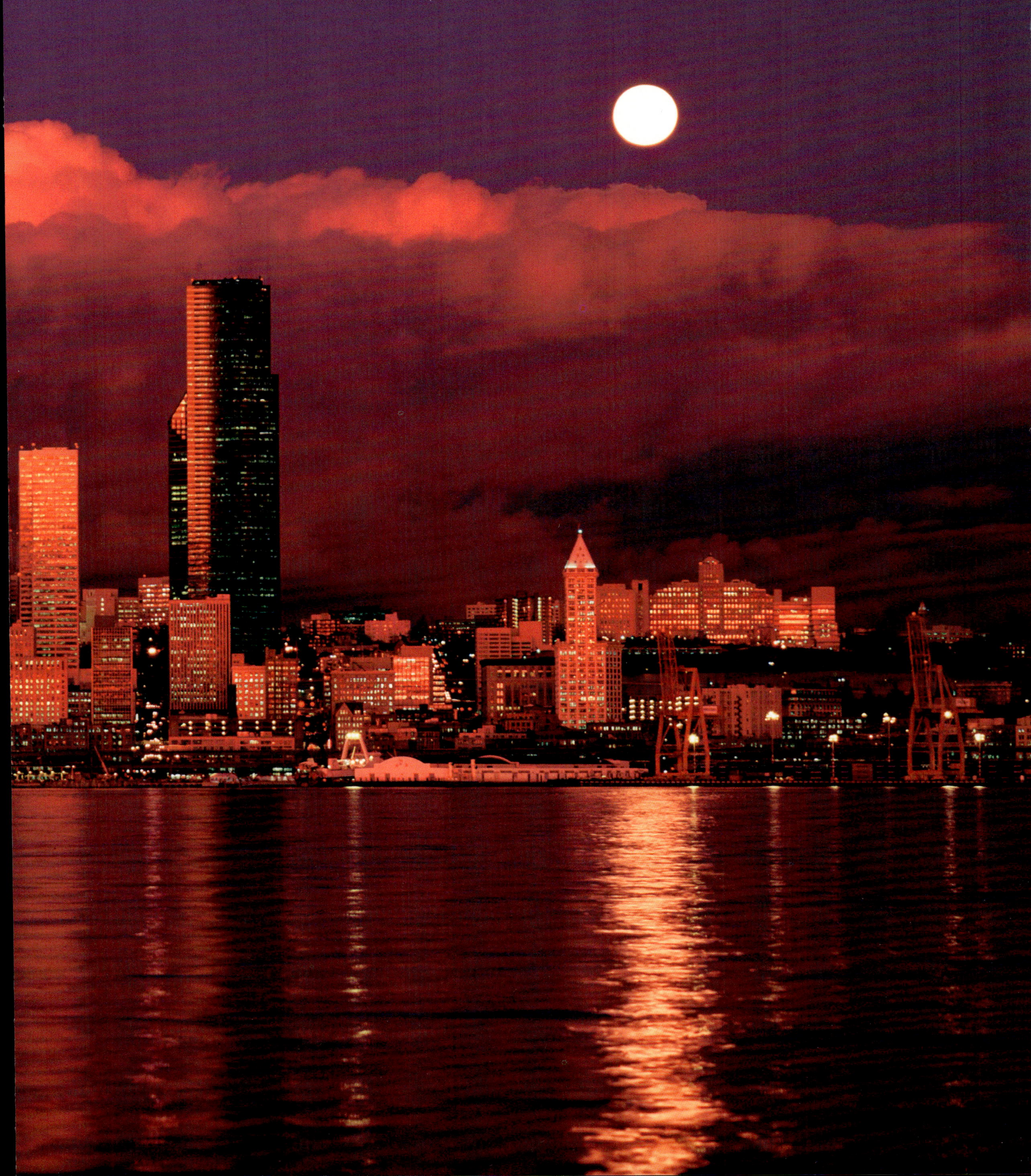

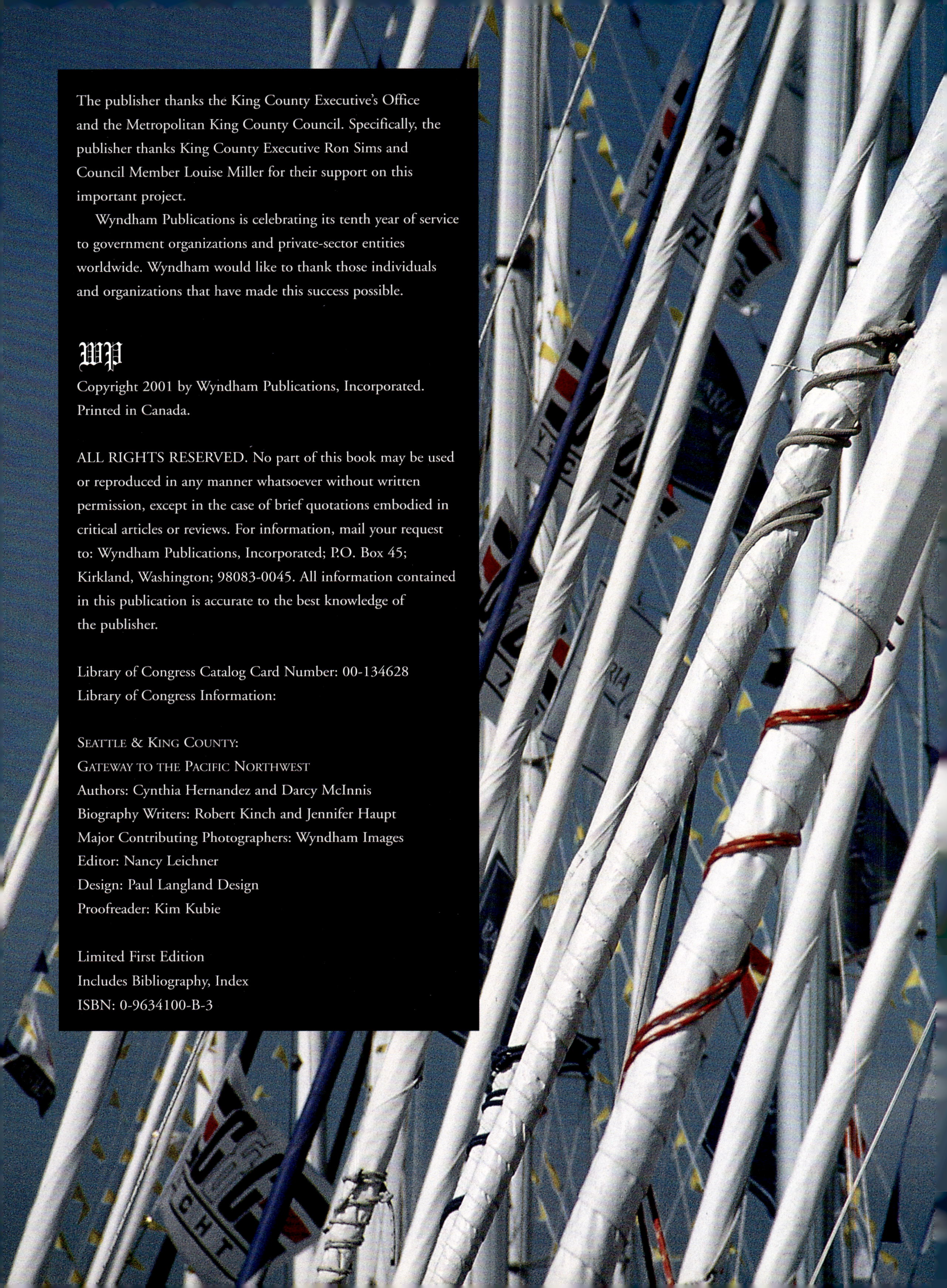

The publisher thanks the King County Executive's Office and the Metropolitan King County Council. Specifically, the publisher thanks King County Executive Ron Sims and Council Member Louise Miller for their support on this important project.

Wyndham Publications is celebrating its tenth year of service to government organizations and private-sector entities worldwide. Wyndham would like to thank those individuals and organizations that have made this success possible.

Library of Congress Catalog Card Number: 00-134628
Library of Congress Information:

SEATTLE & KING COUNTY:
GATEWAY TO THE PACIFIC NORTHWEST
Authors: Cynthia Hernandez and Darcy McInnis
Biography Writers: Robert Kinch and Jennifer Haupt
Major Contributing Photographers: Wyndham Images
Editor: Nancy Leichner
Design: Paul Langland Design
Proofreader: Kim Kubie

Limited First Edition
Includes Bibliography, Index
ISBN: 0-9634100-B-3

Table Of Contents

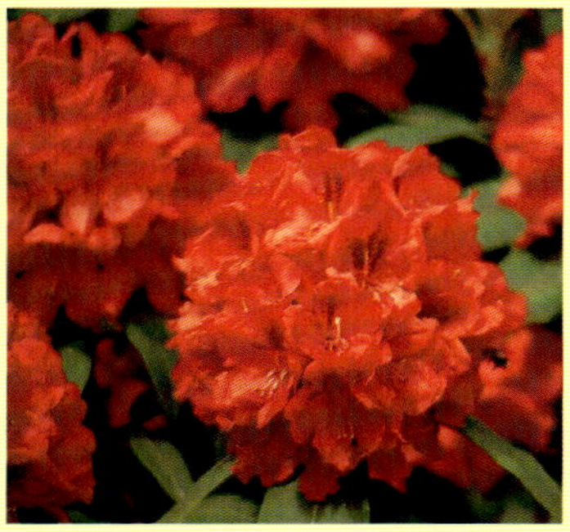

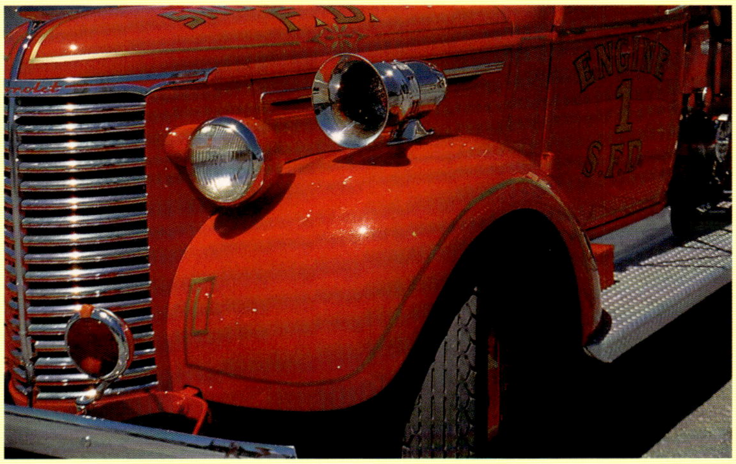

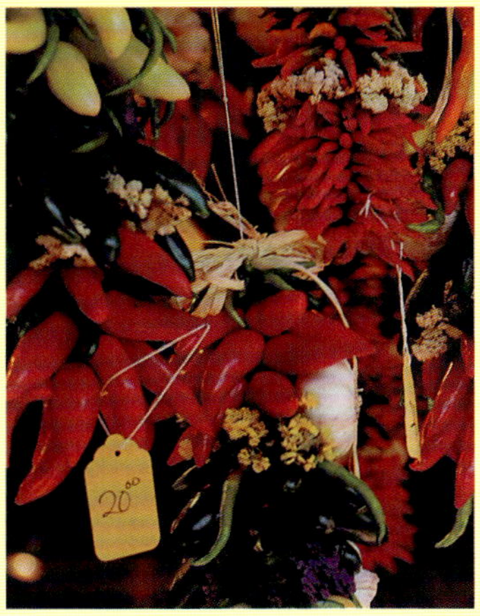

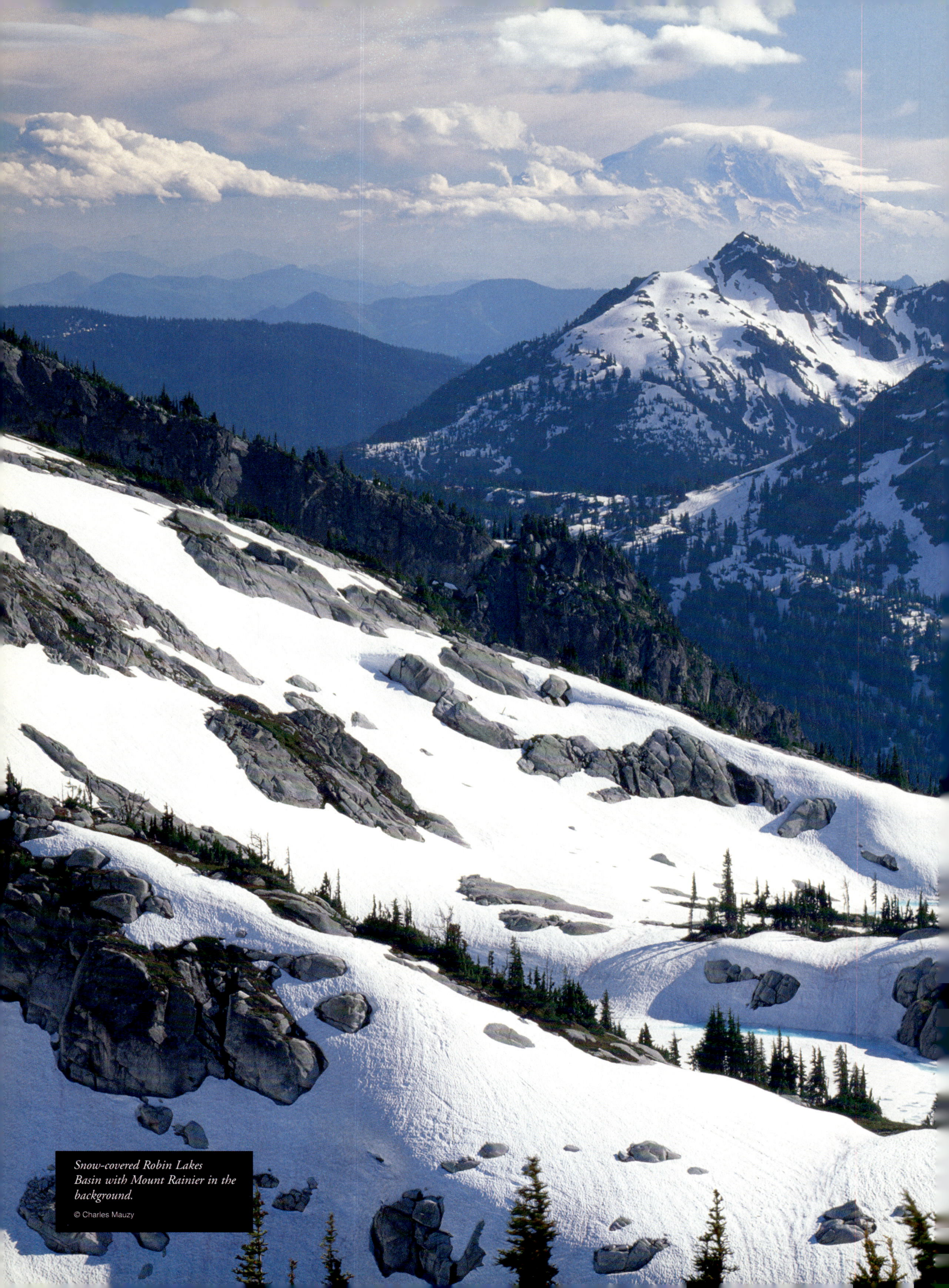

Snow-covered Robin Lakes Basin with Mount Rainier in the background.

© Charles Mauzy

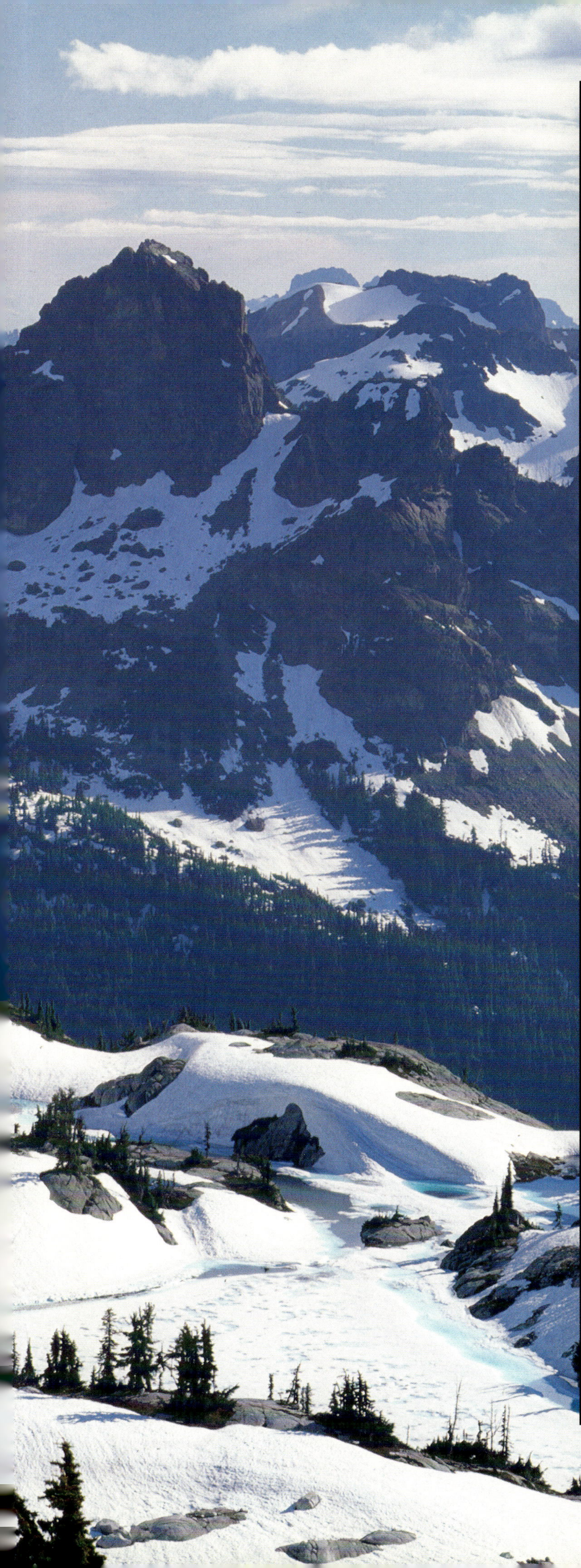

Foreword

Welcome to King County! I consider King County to be one of the most naturally beautiful places on earth. From the crest of the Cascades, through prized, protected rolling farmlands and open spaces, to our bustling cities, King County is a great place to live, work and visit. Home to nearly 1.7 million residents, King County covers over 2,134 square miles, in 39 cities and all unincorporated areas, and has almost 60,000 businesses here that provide more than one million jobs.

In addition to the mountains, forests, wildlife and bodies of water, I also appreciate the people who make King County their home. We are a vibrant international community and I feel privileged to live and work in a community that embraces diversity and cherishes the artistic and social customs and traditions of many cultures. This only adds richness to the communities where we live, learn and grow.

King County is home to many international corporations, including industry giants such as Microsoft, Boeing, Starbucks, Nordstrom, Weyerhaeuser and many more. As King County Executive, I have worked diligently to balance continued economic growth with environmental safeguards to ensure that every resident of King County benefits in the changing economic landscape.

This book represents the best of King County. I hope that you enjoy it as much as I have. From the green trees and clean water to the diverse people who call this region home, King County truly is a beautiful place.

Ron Sims
King County Executive

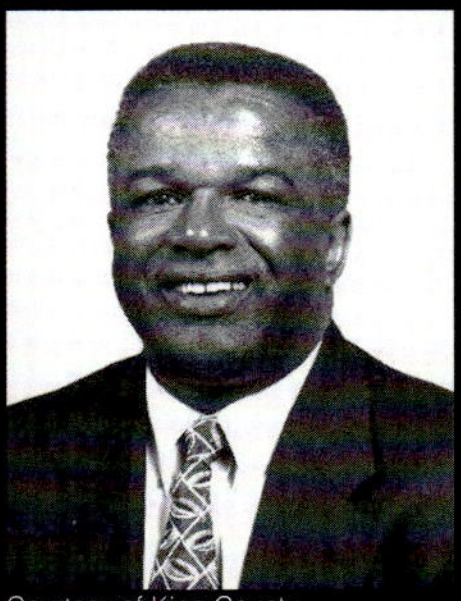

Courtesy of King County

A Legendary Legacy

Long before the legendary Denny Party landed at Alki Beach in what is now known as King County, the land belonged to the Coast Salish Indians. The Duwamish, Snoqualmie, Muckleshoot, Puyallup, and Skykomish tribes—the Southern Coast branch of the Coast Salish Indians—hunted, fished, and gathered food throughout the hills and valleys of this beautiful region. Although historians are not sure how many Native Americans called the area home, it is estimated that several thousand Native Americans spent at least part of each year living near the many rivers, lakes, and saltwater beaches of central Puget Sound.

Several of the larger tribes, such as the Duwamish, Snoqualmie, and Muckleshoot, built year-round villages and permanent structures. Often, these villages included a large building, called a longhouse, that served as communal living quarters. These longhouses could house up to several hundred people. Longhouses were also used as gathering places for the various tribal communities. Here, friends, relatives, and visitors from other groups gathered to share the ancient (and often spiritual) songs, dances, and legends passed down from generation to generation. This sharing of tradition and ceremony served to bond tribal members together and to impart the power and mysticism of their culture.

The abundance of food and natural building materials made this area a natural home for the Native American tribes. Fish, waterfowl, small game, shellfish, berries, and lush forests were all at the disposal of the native peoples. Dugout canoes were built from the large stands of timber, and baskets and mats were woven from natural raw materials.

Legend has it that it was Chief Seattle (also known as Chief Sealth), beloved leader of the Duwamish and Suquamish Tribes, who met the schooner *Exact* on November 13, 1851, when it landed on Alki Beach in what is now West Seattle (a marker at Alki Beach commemorates the event). Aboard were Arthur Denny, nine other adults, and twelve children. Although this land was already home to the native peoples, this event is widely regarded in King County history as the birth of the territory.

Courtesy of Wyndham Images

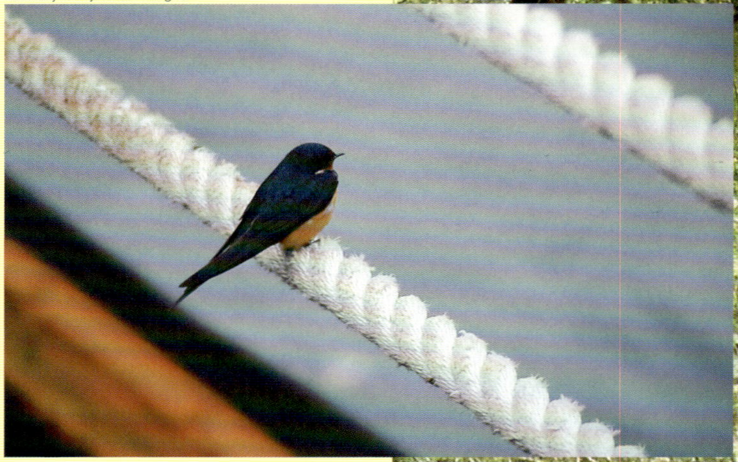

A swallow perches on the moorage line of a yacht.

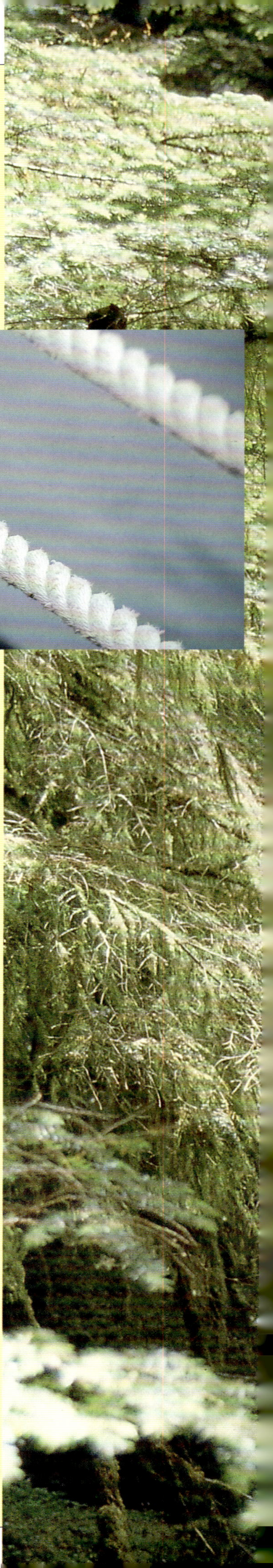

The temperate climate of the Pacific Northwest gives rise to lush, green forests. The abundance of food and building materials made this environment a natural home for Native American tribes.

Courtesy of Wyndham Images

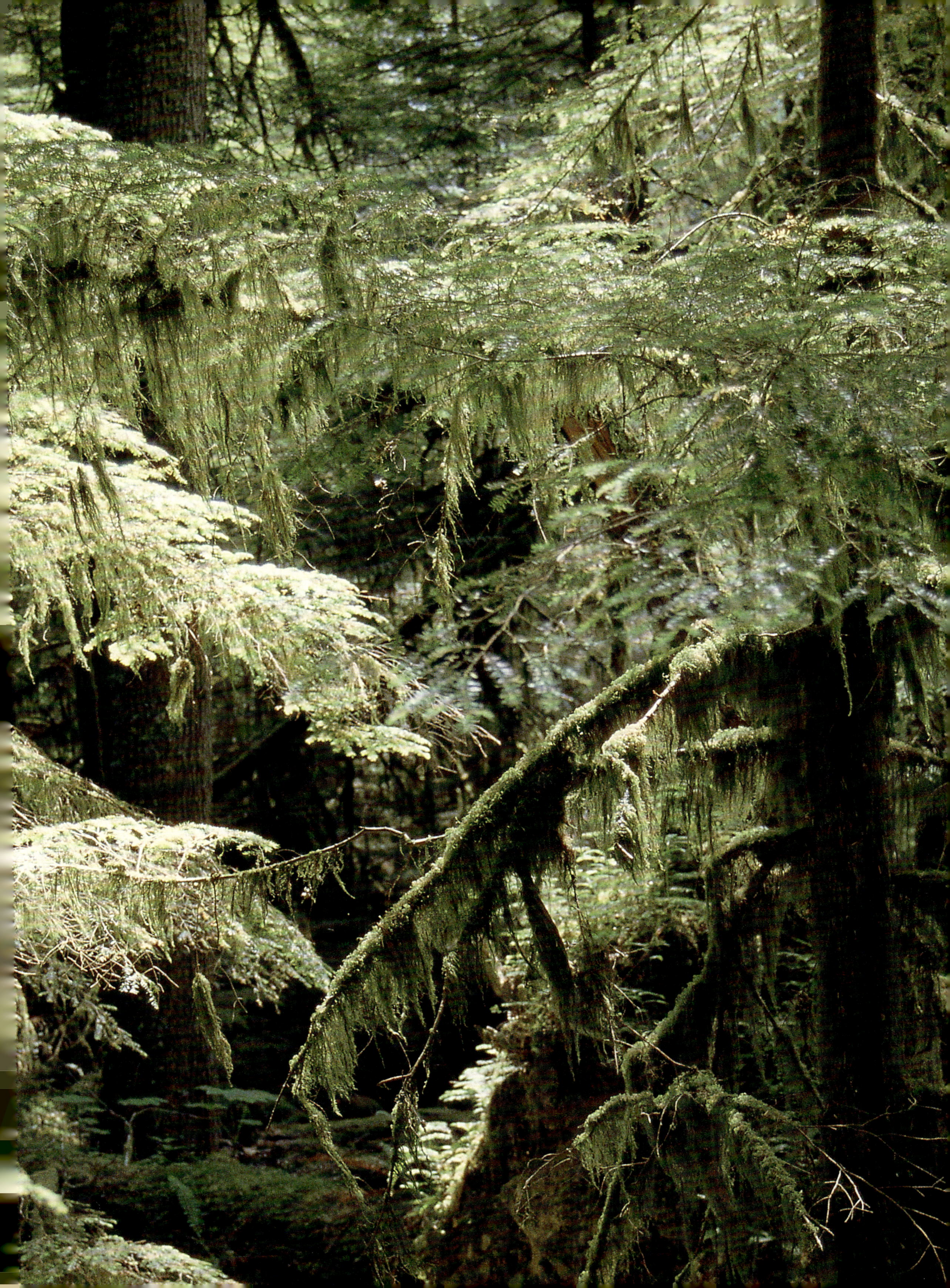

This well-known painting of the 1889 Great Seattle Fire is on display at the Museum of History & Industry.

Courtesy of Museum of History & Industry, Photo by Howard Gisk Photographs

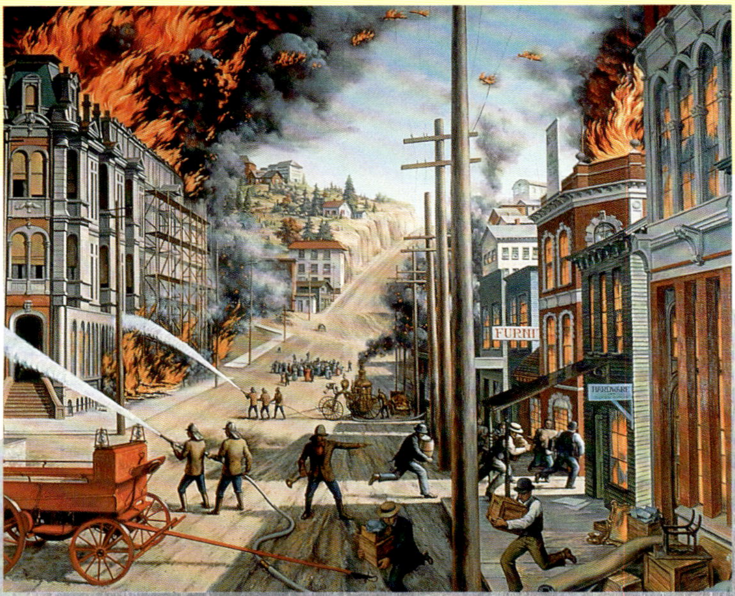

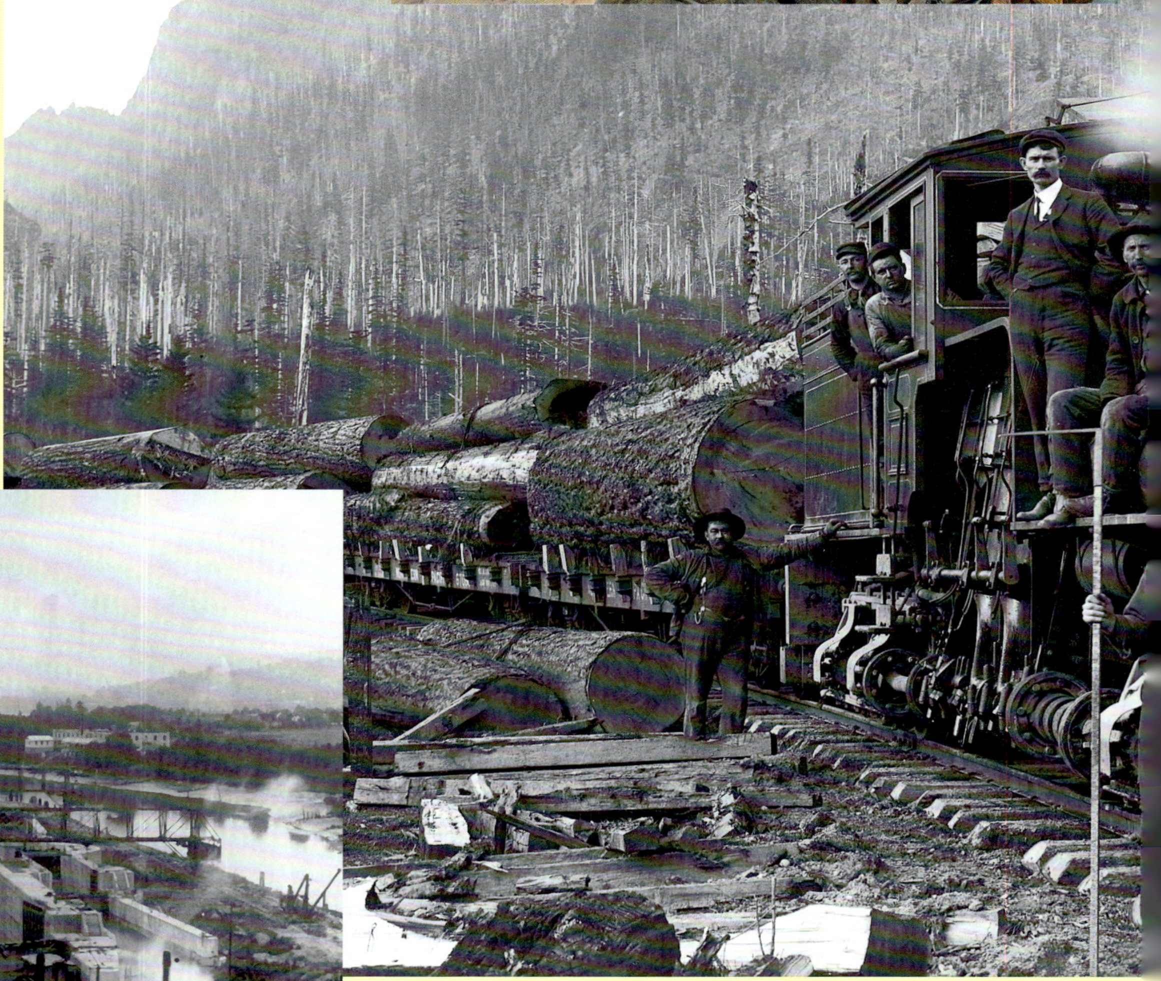

Ground was broken for the Lake Washington Ship Canal locks in 1911, and the first concrete was poured for the lock chambers in 1913. This photo, taken in 1915, shows the two lock chambers under construction. A steam dredge digs a channel (foreground) near a temporary dam built to keep the tide from flooding the unfinished locks. The main waterway has been diverted around the construction site. The first ship traveled through the locks in 1916.

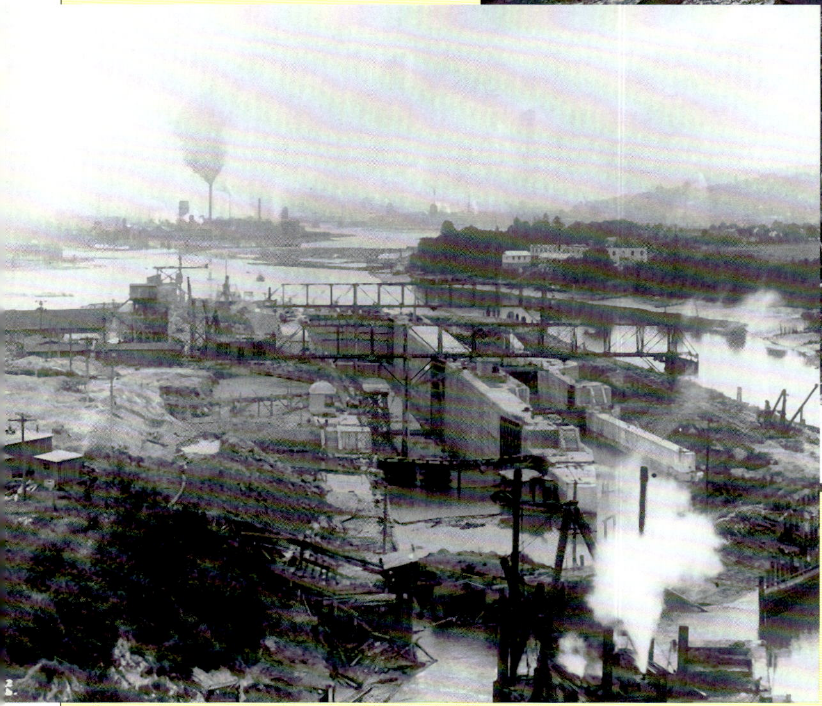

Courtesy of Museum of History & Industry, PEMCO Webster & Stevens Collection

The Denny Party did not find the Alki area to be hospitable and before long most of them relocated to Elliott Bay, in and around the region now called Pioneer Square. Word of this new and beautiful country quickly spread, and by 1852 pioneers began streaming into the territory.

In December of that same year, the county was officially named "King" in honor of William R. King, a former U.S. diplomat, Senator, and Vice President (on February 24, 1986, the King County Council, in a 5-to-4 vote, renamed the county in memory of Dr. Martin Luther King, Jr.). Also in 1852, the first industry began with the construction of the Yesler Sawmill; and by 1853, settlements throughout King County began forming. In March 1853, U.S. President Filmore signed a bill establishing the Washington Territory.

Settlement of King County was slow due to the thick underbrush and heavy forests that covered much of the area. However, residents made use of the many rivers and waterways, and used ingenuity and sheer will to transport goods from one place to another. Coal was discovered in east King County in 1853, and enormous effort was made to transport the coal along waterways to Seattle, although the output was small compared to the work involved.

Expansion continued throughout the 1860s. On November 4, 1861, the Territorial University in downtown Seattle (which later became the University of Washington) opened its doors with one teacher, Asa Mercer, and 30 students. The University taught primary grades and other general subjects. The school eventually did away with these basic subjects 40 years later and became a school of higher learning.

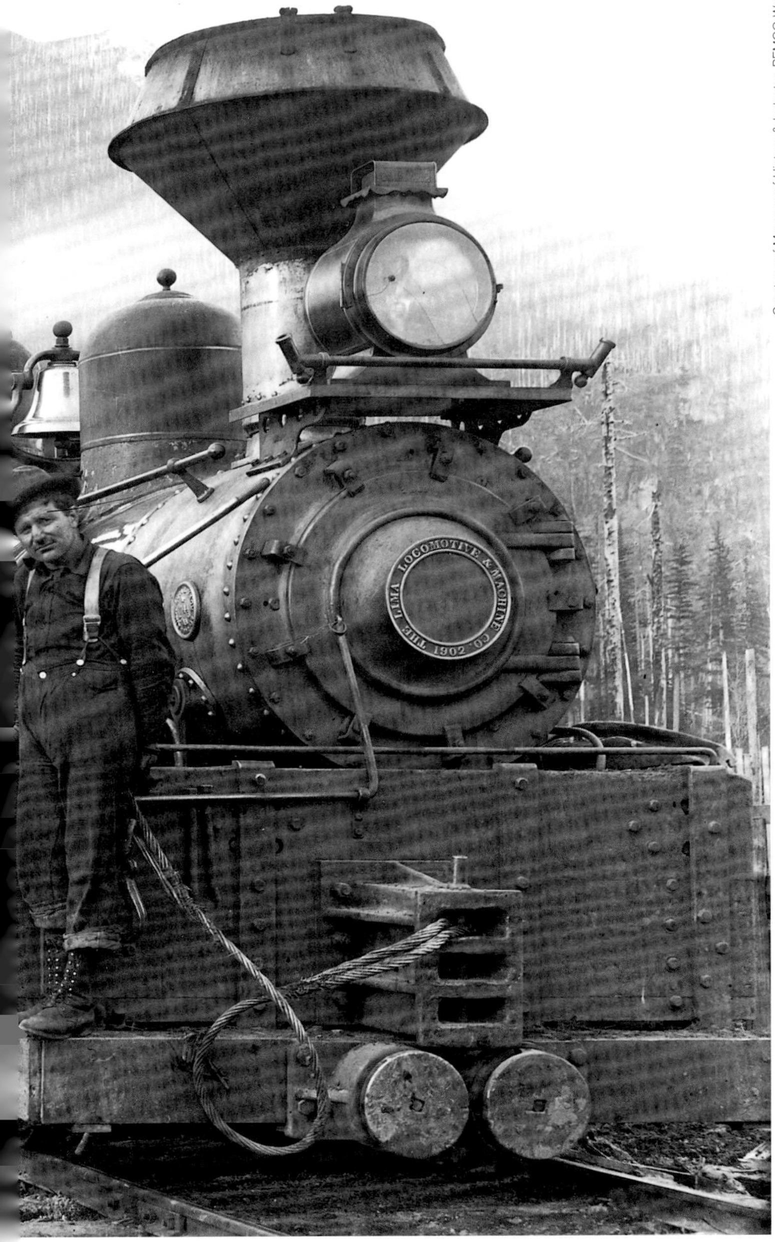

Courtesy of Museum of History & Industry, PEMCO Webster & Stevens Collection

At first, logging companies cut trees along rivers and other bodies of water. They floated the logs downstream to the sawmill. After these areas were logged over, companies began using railroads to haul logs to a river or directly to the mill. The tracks could be moved as needed. This photo was taken sometime between 1903 and 1905, near North Bend, Washington. Mt. Si is in the background.

NOAA ships Rainier *and* Miller *Freeman pass through the Hiram M. Chittendon Locks, Lake Washington Ship Canal.*

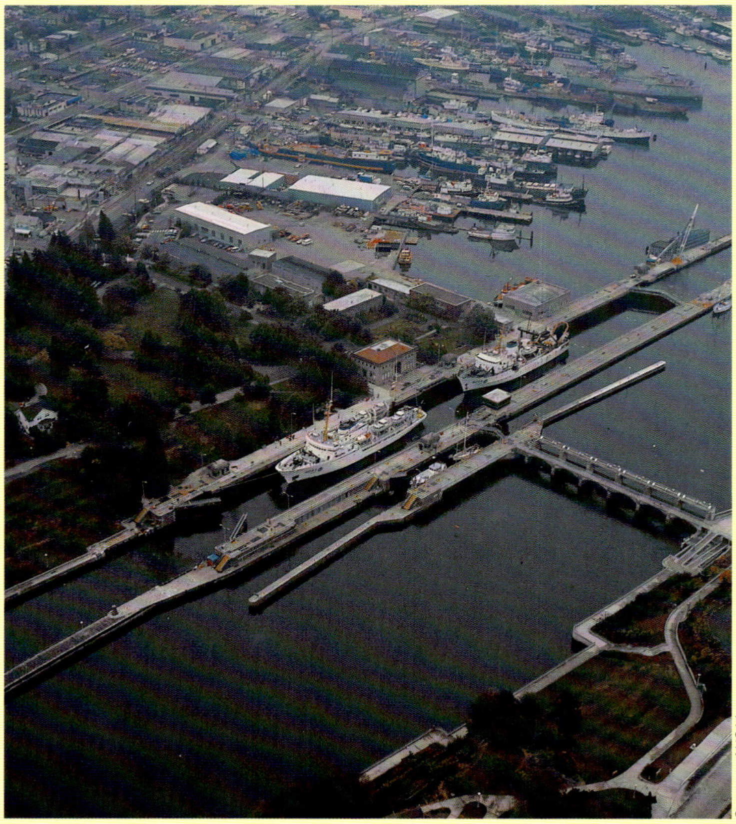

Courtesy of NOAA

Simultaneously, small businesses, such as breweries and metal foundries, flourished. Unfortunately, because of the geography of the county and the lack of railroads, trade with the outside world was virtually non-existent. Because of its geography and its abundance of timber, salmon, and coal, King County had the potential to be a natural exporter of goods to the rest of the country. However, lack of railway connections was a significant problem. In 1873, the Northern Pacific Railroad chose neighboring Tacoma over Seattle as the terminus for its west coast operation, and for the next 20 years, getting railroad service to King County would prove to be a frustrating enterprise.

It was this frustration that led several local residents to privately finance the Seattle and Walla Walla Railroad, which was used to transport coal from the Black River and Newcastle coal mines. Trade routes to San Francisco and other cities commenced, making the dream of a lucrative export market a reality. In 1880, the railroad enterprise was turned over to interests outside the county and its name was changed to Columbia and Puget Sound Railway.

Seattle's growth during the 1880s was remarkable. During that decade, the population rose meteorically from 3,500 to over 40,000 residents. New buildings were constructed and the city's various industries became increasingly important. A dramatic setback occurred in 1889 when a pot of glue exploded in a basement shop in downtown Seattle, starting what came to be known as the Great Seattle Fire. The fire quickly spread to other wood-frame structures, and by nightfall an estimated 64 acres had been destroyed. As it happened, this event was a blessing in disguise because it spurred the townspeople to rebuild the city with bricks and mortar. A testament to this effort is still seen today in the architecture of Pioneer Square.

Throughout the 1890s, additional coal fields were discovered in east King County, but connecting railway service to the rest of the United States was still a problem. Once again, several local citizens banded together to finance their own railroad, this time calling it the Seattle, Lakeshore and Eastern Railroad (SLS&E). The railroad, which followed the shoreline of Lake Washington, spurred the growth of small towns such as Woodinville, Redmond, Bothell, Squak (later renamed Issaquah), North Bend, and Snoqualmie along the route.

Local financing for the railroad ran into trouble over the next several years, which led to its failure and ultimate incorporation into the Northern Pacific. Although local citizens lost control of the SLS&E, it was a fortunate turn of events for the residents of King County—at last, the Northern Pacific began service to Seattle in 1896. Export of lucrative goods such as timber, coal, and agricultural products, soon followed.

For years, there was no easy or cheap way to move logs, coal, and other resources directly from the east side of Lake Washington to Elliott Bay until the Lake Washington Ship Canal was built. The Hiram Chittenden Locks are still a vital part of the canal's operation. They allow boats and ships from Lake Union and Lake Washington to be lowered to the level of Puget Sound and vice versa. This 1916 photo was taken while the Hiram M. Chittenden Locks were still under construction.

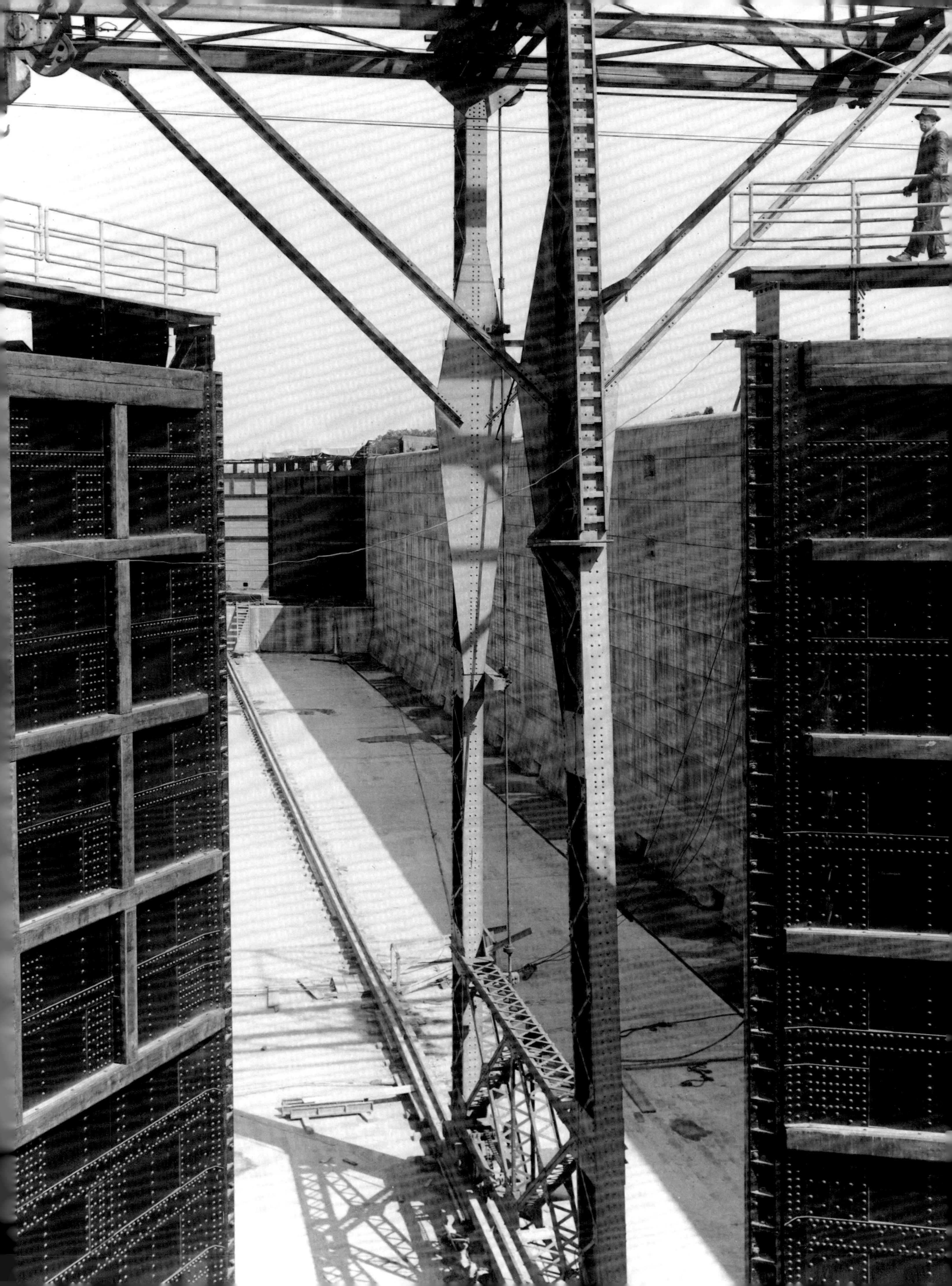

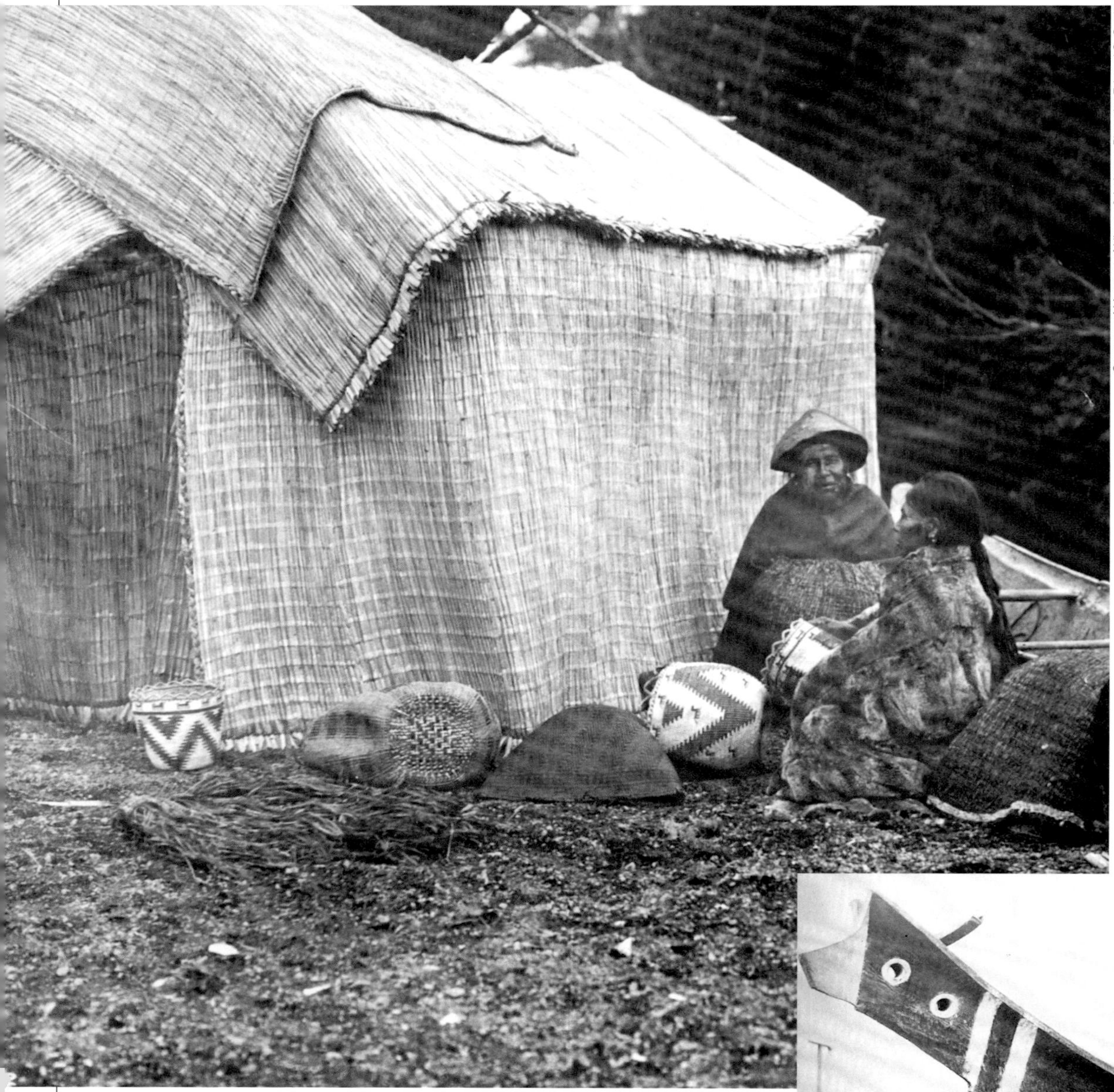

Courtesy of Museum of History & Industry, Photo by Edward S. Curtis

The Skokomish people have traditionally lived along Hood Canal. They moved to the nearby Skokomish Reservation after the Treaty of Point-No-Point (1855). Like other Puget Sound tribes, their lives centered around the water. The Skokomish are known for their fine cedar baskets. In this 1912 photo, two Skokomish women sit by a summer shelter covered with cattail mats and by a cedar canoe.

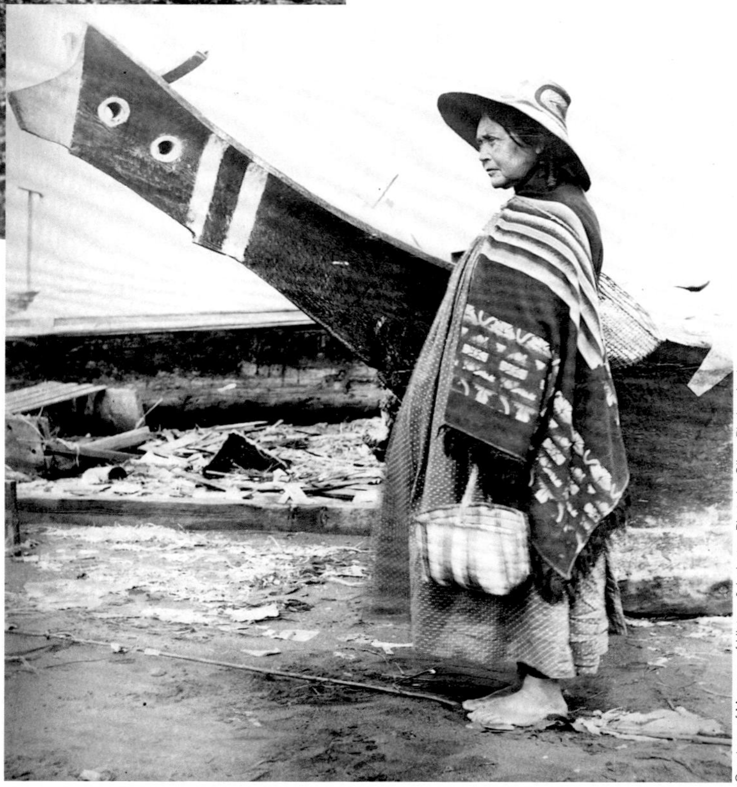

Courtesy of Museum of History & Industry, Photo by Oliver Phelps Anderson

Native people from many parts of Puget Sound came to Seattle to trade and buy supplies. In this 1898 photo, a Native American woman stands by a canoe at the Seattle waterfront. The tall prow of the canoe and the design of her hat suggest that she is from Vancouver Island or some other part of coastal Canada. The photo was taken two blocks south of King Street, near First Avenue.

Other communities, such as Vashon, Kirkland, Mercer Island, Bellevue, Des Moines, Renton, and Maple Valley, also began to emerge around this time, their progress encouraged by the dramatic increase in trade. Growth continued throughout the 1890s, culminating at the close of the decade with the opening of the Carnation Dairy in Kent and the construction of a hydroelectric power-generating station at Snoqualmie Falls, both of which continue to be large industries for King County today.

As the twentieth century dawned, trade was booming. Travel throughout the county was becoming increasingly easy, and the logging industry was proving to be quite lucrative. Agriculture also continued to be a major industry, and in 1907, the Pike Place Public Market opened. Farmers from throughout the county traveled to the market, located at the foot of Pike Street, to sell an assortment of locally grown fruits, vegetables, eggs, and poultry. The Pike Place Market, despite efforts to close it in the 1970s, is still a vibrant and popular downtown destination where one can buy fresh, local produce, fruit, and seafood.

The population of Seattle and King County continued to spiral upward. By 1910, there were over 237,000 people living in the city and another 47,000 living in other areas of King County. Many small communities began to incorporate during this time, and by 1910, there were 22 incorporated towns thriving throughout the county.

Trade continued to be a major economic force for the county through the first 20 years of the new century. The dairy industry was now nationally recognized, and specialty agricultural markets were prospering. Timber and other exports also began to be shipped to new markets in California, Alaska, and Asia. This increased activity led to the institution of the Port of Seattle in 1911 and the opening of the Hiram Chittenden locks in Ballard in 1917. The locks, which still operate today, connect Puget Sound with Lake Union. At approximately the same time, construction on the Ship Canal began,

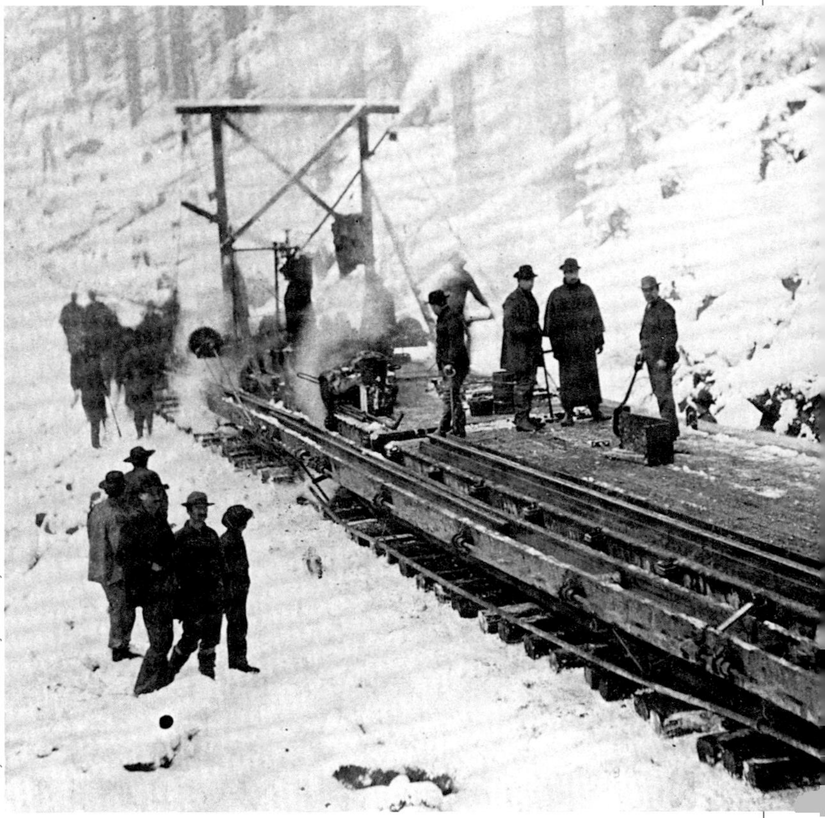

Courtesy of Museum of History & Industry

Great Northern Railroad workers lay the last rail on the main line west of the summit in the Cascade Mountains on December 10, 1892.

eventually connecting Lake Washington with Lake Union. The result was a shipping waterway that connected the salt waters of Puget Sound to inland waters of Lake Union and Lake Washington. This achievement was vital to the prosperity of inland businesses and communities and crucial to the evermore ambitious trade efforts taking place.

In 1910, an airplane took off for the first time from the Meadows, the current site of the King County International Airport, and a new regional industry emerged. Six years later, the first airplane was constructed by the Pacific Aero Products Company, known just one year later as the Boeing Aircraft Company.

The invention of the automobile in the 1900s led the county to turn its attention to transportation. Roadways were improved, and consideration was given to easing travel. Before long, a network of surfaced roadways were running north, east, and south throughout the county. This, coupled with the improved inter-county railway lines and ferry service, led to the emergence of still more residential communities, such as Burien, Shoreline, and the Green River Valley. In 1924, the East Channel Bridge to Mercer Island was opened, and four years later the King County Airport began operations.

Growth continued over the next decade, albeit slowed somewhat in the 1930s by the Great Depression. During the Roosevelt era, numerous projects commenced which resulted in the construction or improvement of roads, bridges, airport facilities, and parks. The Boeing Company, along with several other companies, weathered the Depression years remarkably well—so much so that Boeing produced the revolutionary "monomail" aircraft that was the first large-capacity, single-wing aircraft of its type.

Following World War II, the economy of King County suffered temporarily, but by the late 1940s, the regional expansion resumed. Seattle's suburban areas—Shoreline, Bellevue, White Center, Kirkland, Kent, and Auburn—began growing by leaps and bounds.

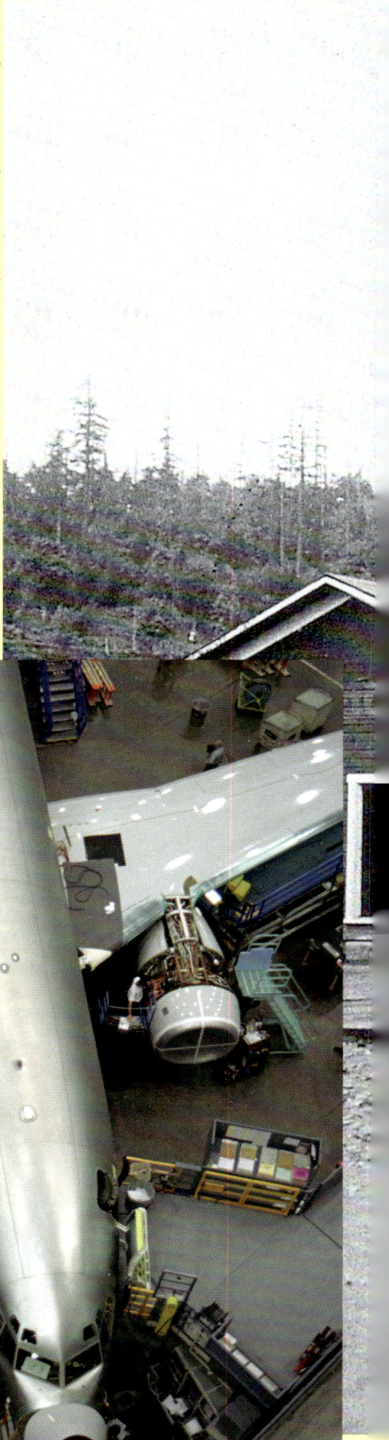
Courtesy of Museum of Flight and The Boeing Company

Boeing's 747 manufacturing facility in Everett, Washington, 30 miles north of Seattle.

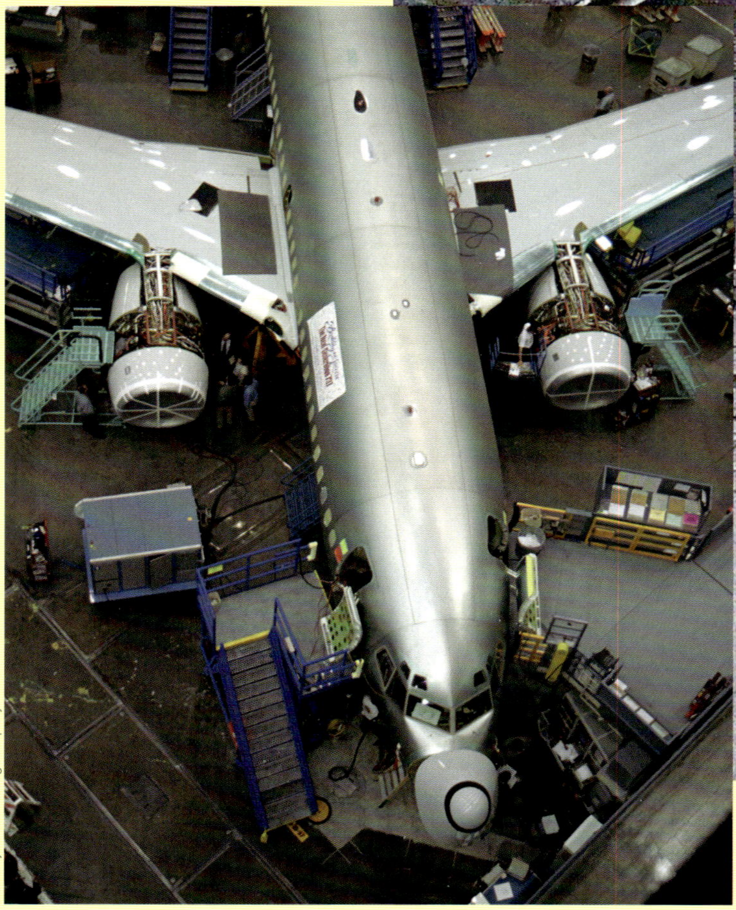
Courtesy of The Boeing Company

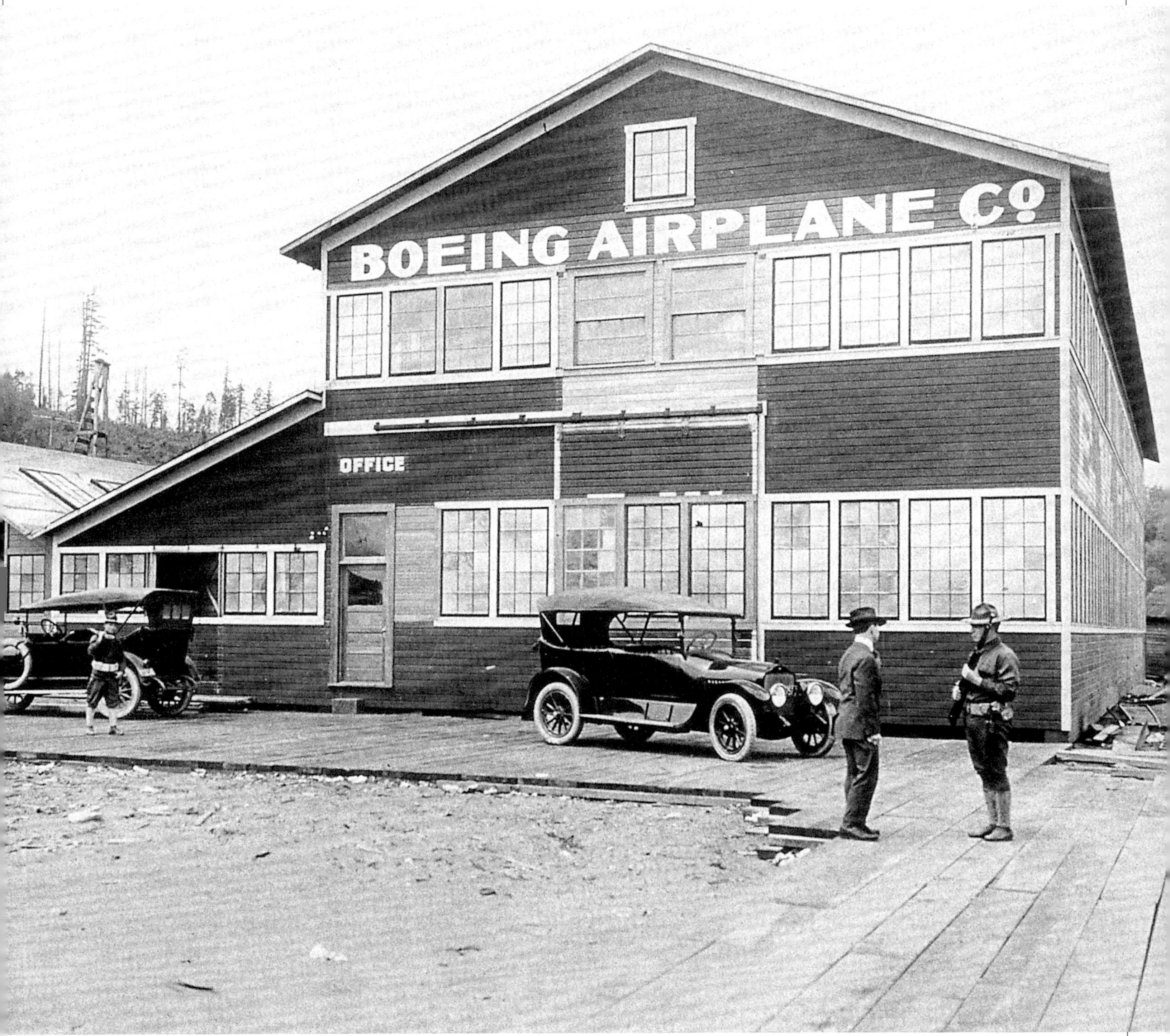

The Boeing Red Barn, shown here circa 1917, was the original manufacturing facility for The Boeing Company.

The clock on the Public Market sign at Pike Place Market is, in itself, a symbol of the market.

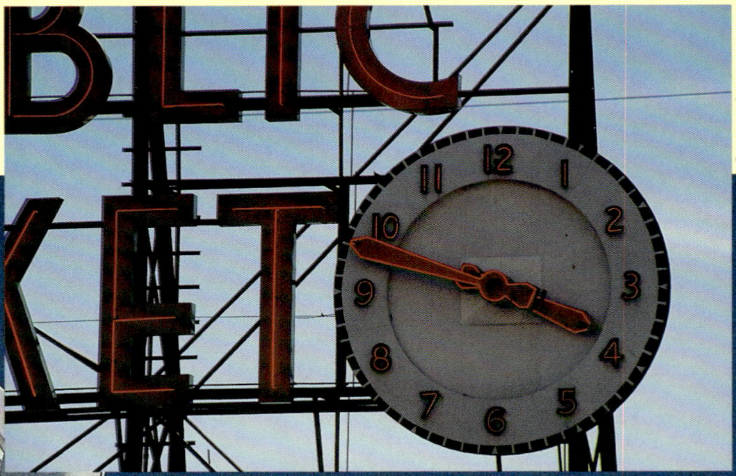

Courtesy of Wyndham Images

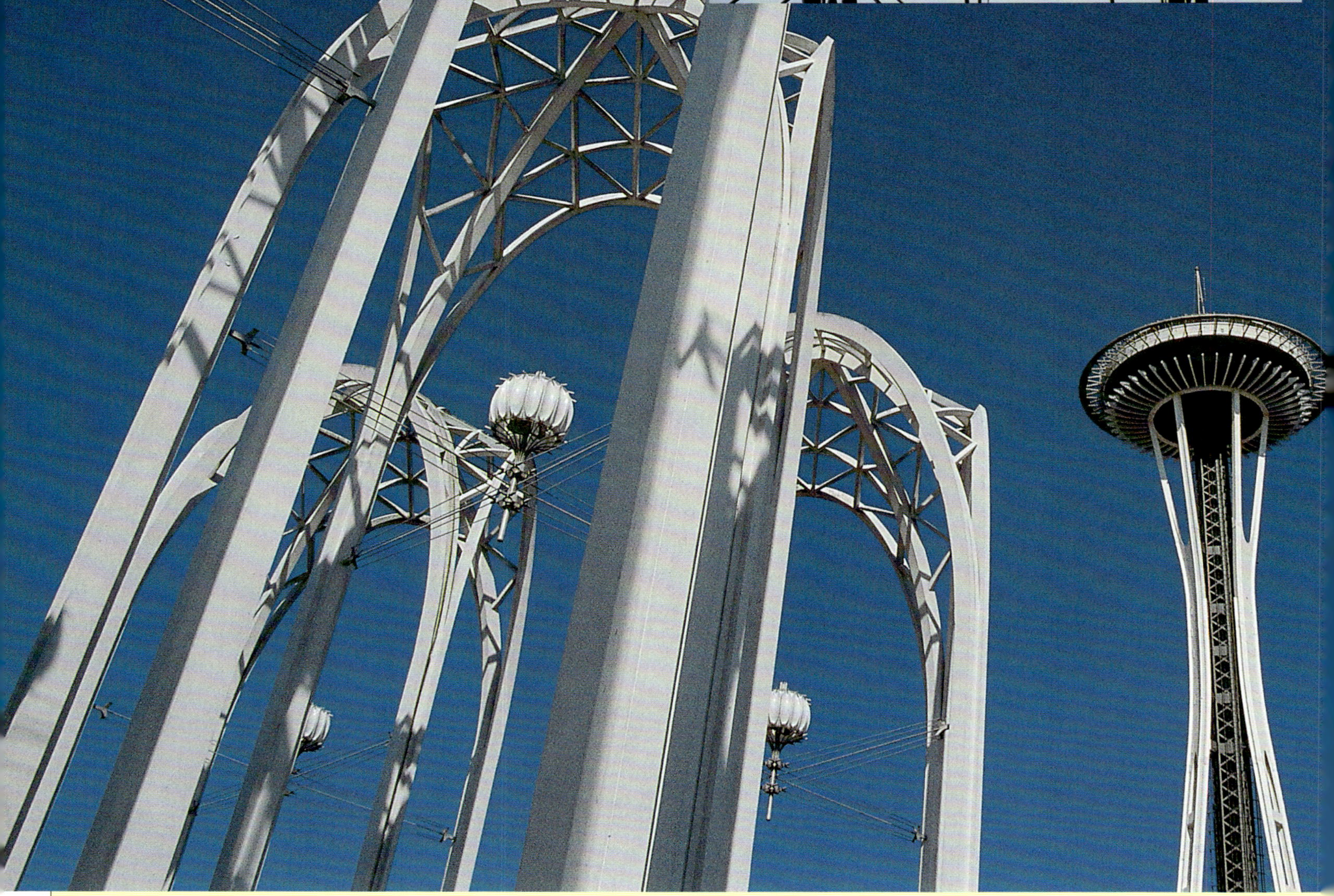

A view of the Space Needle through the arches of the Pacific Science Center in Seattle Center.

This trend continued throughout the 1940s and 1950s. By 1947, operations at the Seattle-Tacoma International Airport were in full swing, and the Port of Seattle expanded its operations. In 1962, Interstate 5, the area's first major north-south freeway, was opened. One year later, the completion of the Evergreen Point Bridge and Interstate 405 brought about major shifts in the industry and demography of the county.

The Century 21 Exposition (Seattle World's Fair) in 1962 cemented Seattle's reputation as a world-class city. Monuments to this event can still be seen at the Seattle Center grounds, with the most well-known landmarks being the Space Needle, the Pacific Science Center, and the Monorail.

Today, King County is one of the world's leaders in computer technology, aerospace, biotechnology, and a wide variety of other industries and businesses. The Boeing Company and Microsoft, two of the area's largest employers, sit side by side with the flagship stores of Seattle's Best Coffee, Starbucks, The Bon Marché, REI, and Nordstrom. The development of these businesses and industries, coupled with the natural beauty of the area, has fostered incredible growth. King County's population today is estimated at 1,677,000 and is expected to increase to over 1,800,000 by 2010.

World-class restaurants, shopping, performing arts, and sporting events abound, not only in Seattle, but also throughout the county. King County is truly a cornucopia of sights, sounds, and delights. From the dense forests to the saltwater beaches, there is truly something for everyone.

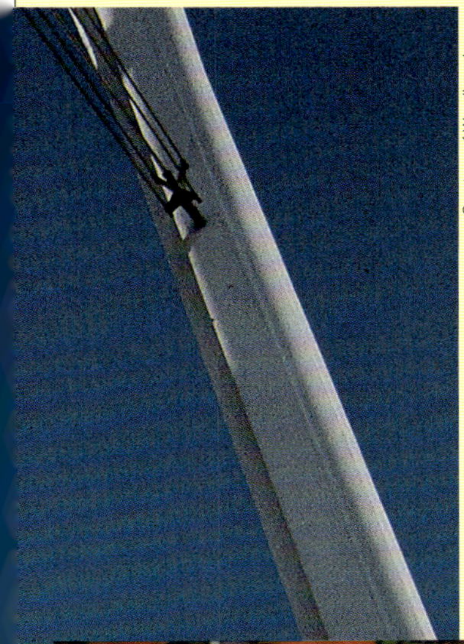

Courtesy of Wyndham Images

Pike Place Market boasts a huge assortment of colorful displays of everything from fresh-cut flowers to geoducks (pronounced "gooey duck," the geoduck is the largest clam in North America).

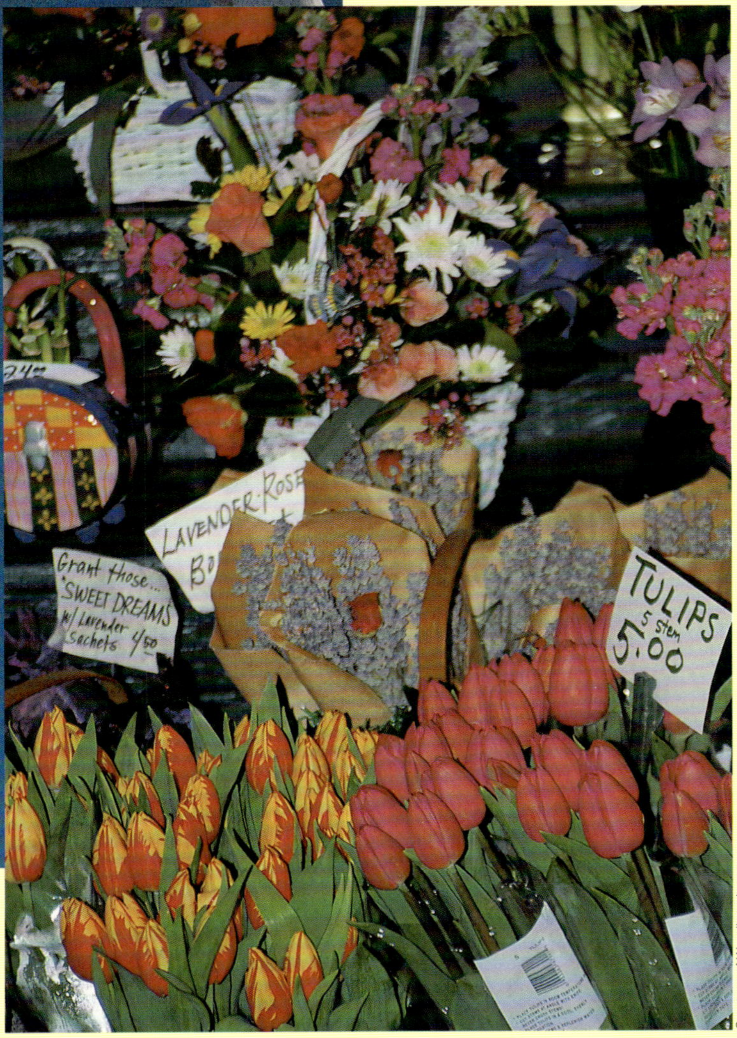

Courtesy of Wyndham Images

Chief Seattle

Chief Seattle, the namesake of Washington State's largest city, was born on the Kitsap Peninsula sometime in the 1780s. There has always been some controversy concerning the correct spelling and pronunciation of Chief Seattle's name, with some insisting the name is "Sealth" (rhyming with "wealth"). However, as the Chief's native Lushootseed language has no th *sound, this is unlikely. The final judges on this matter are Chief Seattle's descendents, who continue to pass down his name as si?al, which is most closely approximated in English as "Seattle." (It is interesting to note that Catholic missionaries baptized Chief Seattle as "Noah.")*

Chief Seattle warmly welcomed the white settlers into this region he loved so much and was largely regarded with respect among them. In his lifetime, Chief Seattle signed several treaties with white leaders, the most famous being the Point Elliott (Mukilteo) Treaty of 1855 that handed over tribal claims to much of the Puget Sound area. Chief Seattle was an intelligent, strong, courageous, and peace loving leader who deeply respected all human beings.

Chief Seattle eventually retired to the Suquamish Reservation, where he died in June of 1866. A stone marker, erected in about 1890, was placed on Chief Seattle's grave on the Port Madison Reservation (near Poulsbo, Washington). On one side, the marker reads "Seattle, Chief of the Suquamps and Allied Tribes, Died June 7, 1866. Firm Friend of the Whites, and For Him the City of Seattle was Named by Its Founders." On the reverse is inscribed: "Baptismal Name: Noah Sealth, Age probably 80 years."

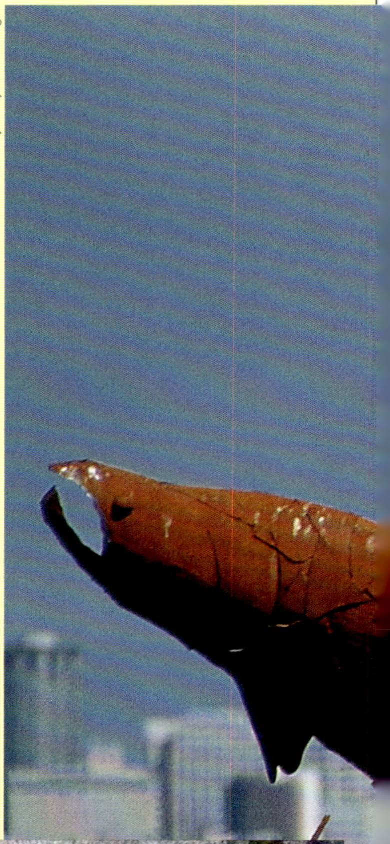
Courtesy of Wyndham Images

Chief Seattle—The Native American leader for whom Seattle was named.

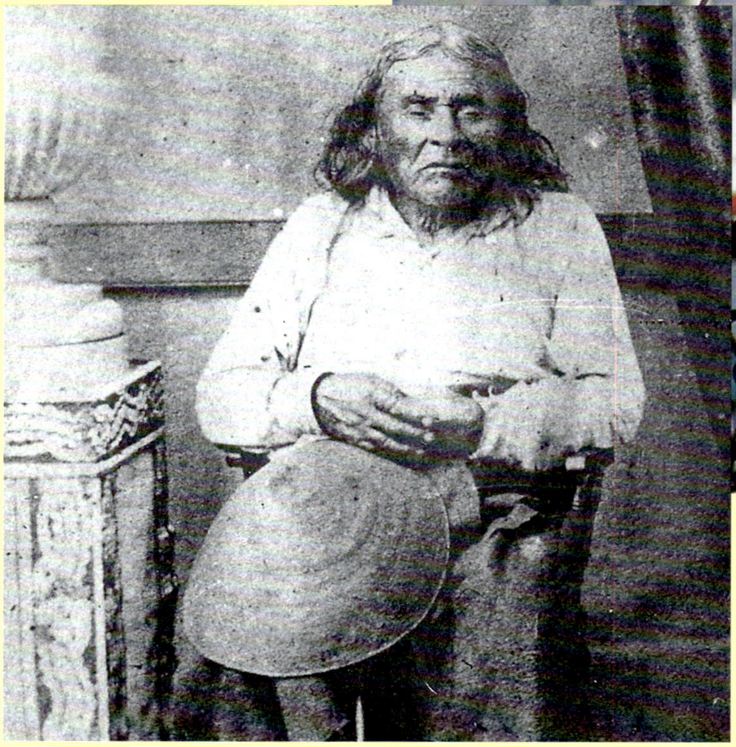
Courtesy of Museum of History & Industry

Cargo ships wait to be loaded.

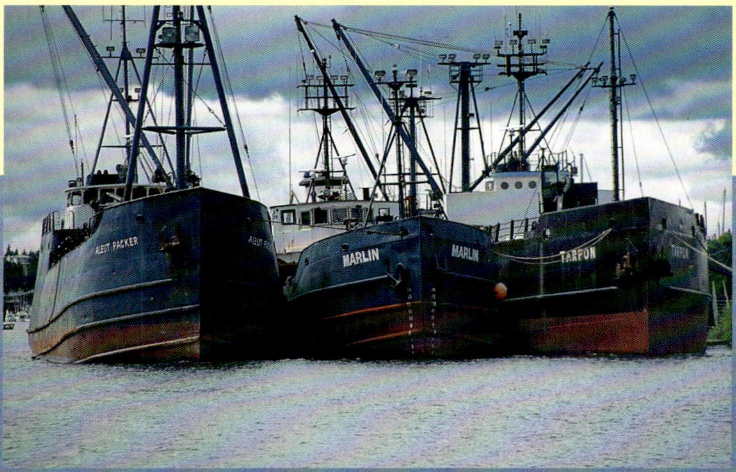

Courtesy of Wyndham Images

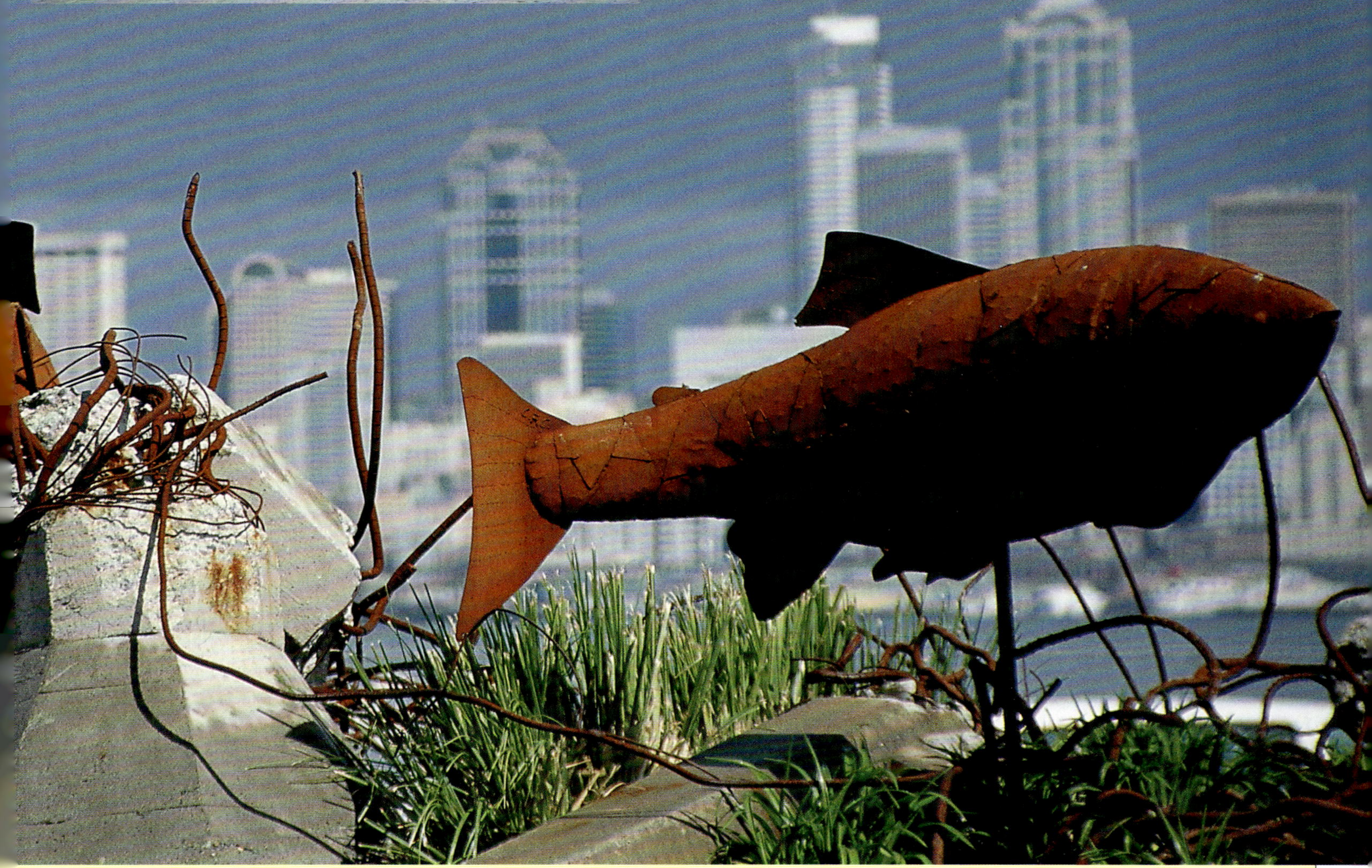

No, this is not a fish tank! It is a view of the Seattle skyline through a lifelike sculpture near Alki Beach in West Seattle.

Leaders in Business and Industry

The business and industry of King County really is a reflection of the region's culture. Pacific Northwesterners are well known as casual, book-reading intellectuals who like nothing more than to venture out on a rainy Sunday and hole up in their favorite coffee house. It is not surprising then that Seattle's Best Coffee, Starbucks, Eddie Bauer, and Amazon.com got their start here—these big businesses serve more to support the lifestyle than to define it.

So many national and international businesses call King County home that it is sometimes difficult to keep up with them all. In fact, with the recent proliferation of e-commerce businesses, it is rather dizzying to keep track. Yes, business is booming in King County. Here, in a nutshell, are the businesses and industries that flourish here in this land of plenty.

The Boeing Company

The world's largest aerospace company got its modest start in 1910, when an airplane took off for the first time from the Meadows, the current site of the King County International Airport. Aboard was William Boeing. It was six years later that the Pacific Aero Products Company built the first airplane. One year later, the Pacific Aero Products Company changed its name to the Boeing Aircraft Company.

Today, The Boeing Company operates a booming commercial airplane division. In addition, Boeing designs and produces military defense systems and is the nation's largest NASA contractor. The company, which in 1918 employed 337 people, today boasts a workforce of well over 200,000. Boeing corporate headquarters are located in Seattle, with major operations in southern California, Kansas, and Missouri.

For all that success, though, Boeing has not forgotten about giving back to the community. Boeing is legendary for its philanthropy. The company is a major contributor to non-profit organizations and places a high value on volunteerism. In addition, the employee-owned Boeing Employees Good Neighbor Fund is the largest employee-owned charitable fund in the world. And if that were not enough, Boeing also loans its executives out to organizations through the Boeing Loaned Executive program.

Courtesy of The Boeing Company

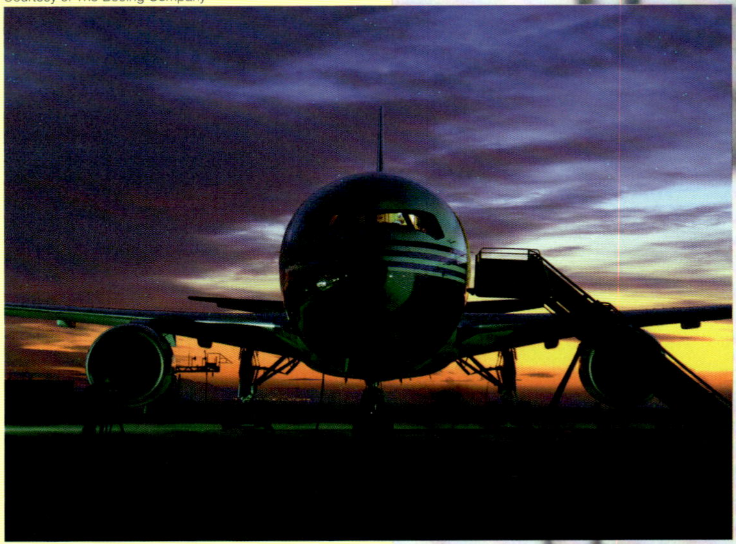

A Boeing 767-300 at sunset.

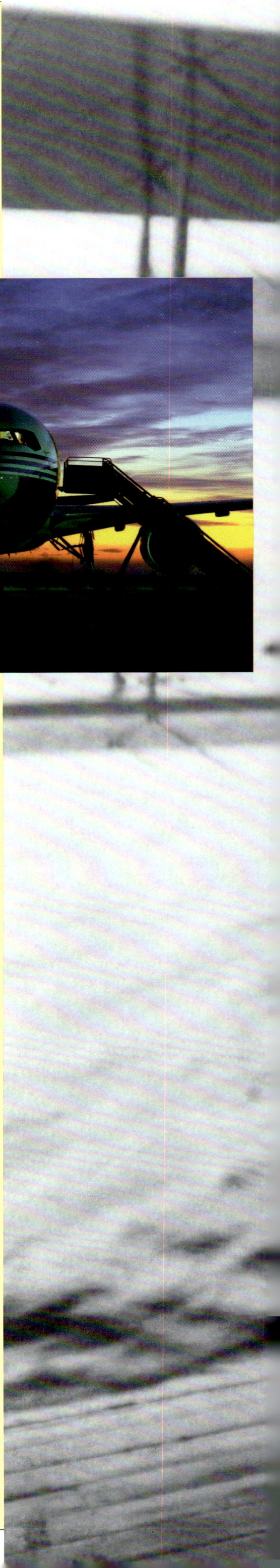

Prior to the late 1920s, most aircraft, including those manufactured by Boeing, were used primarily to deliver mail.

Courtesy of King County

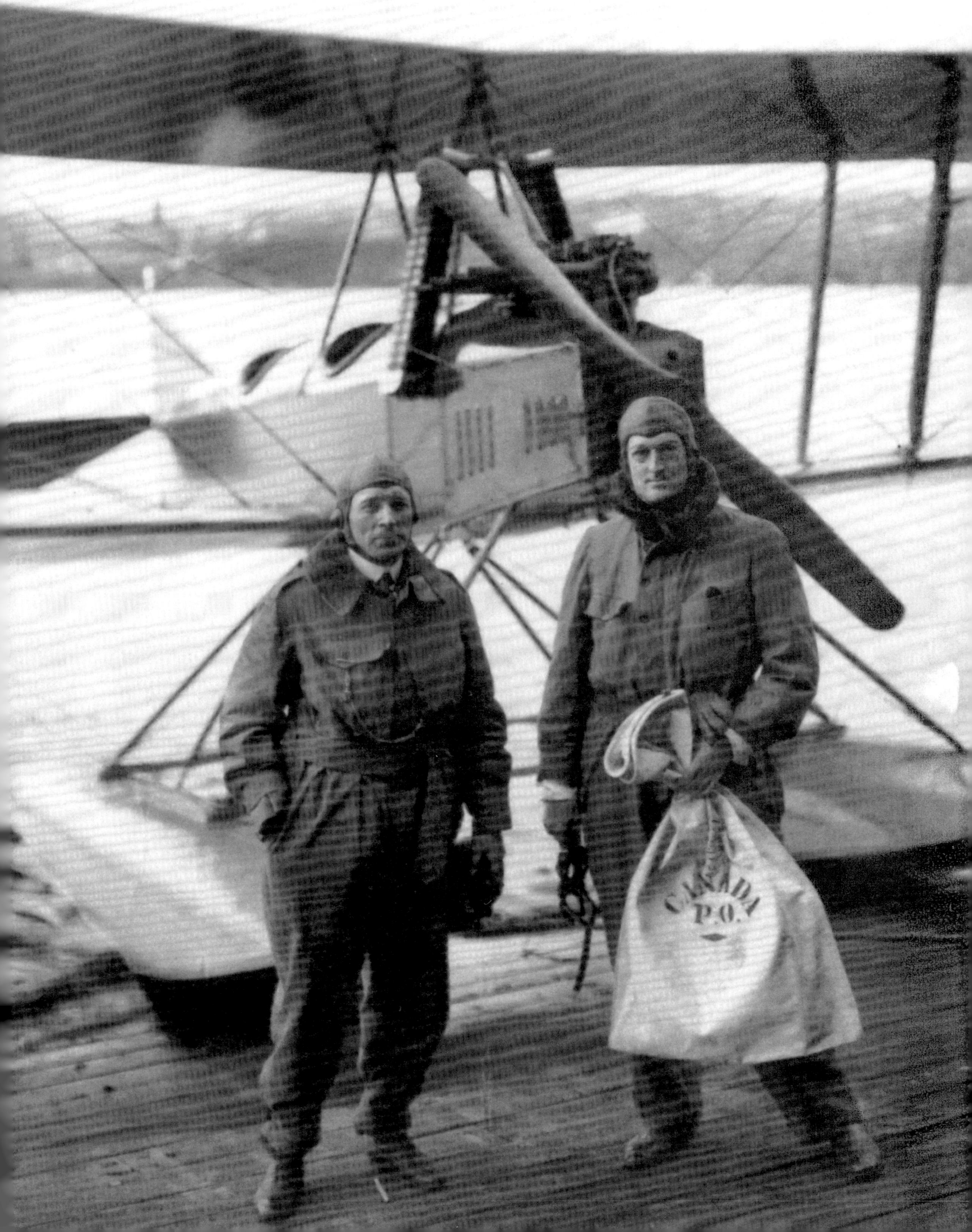
CANADA
P.O.

To accompany its fine coffee, Torrefazione Italia specializes in fine Italian desserts, pastries, and panini.

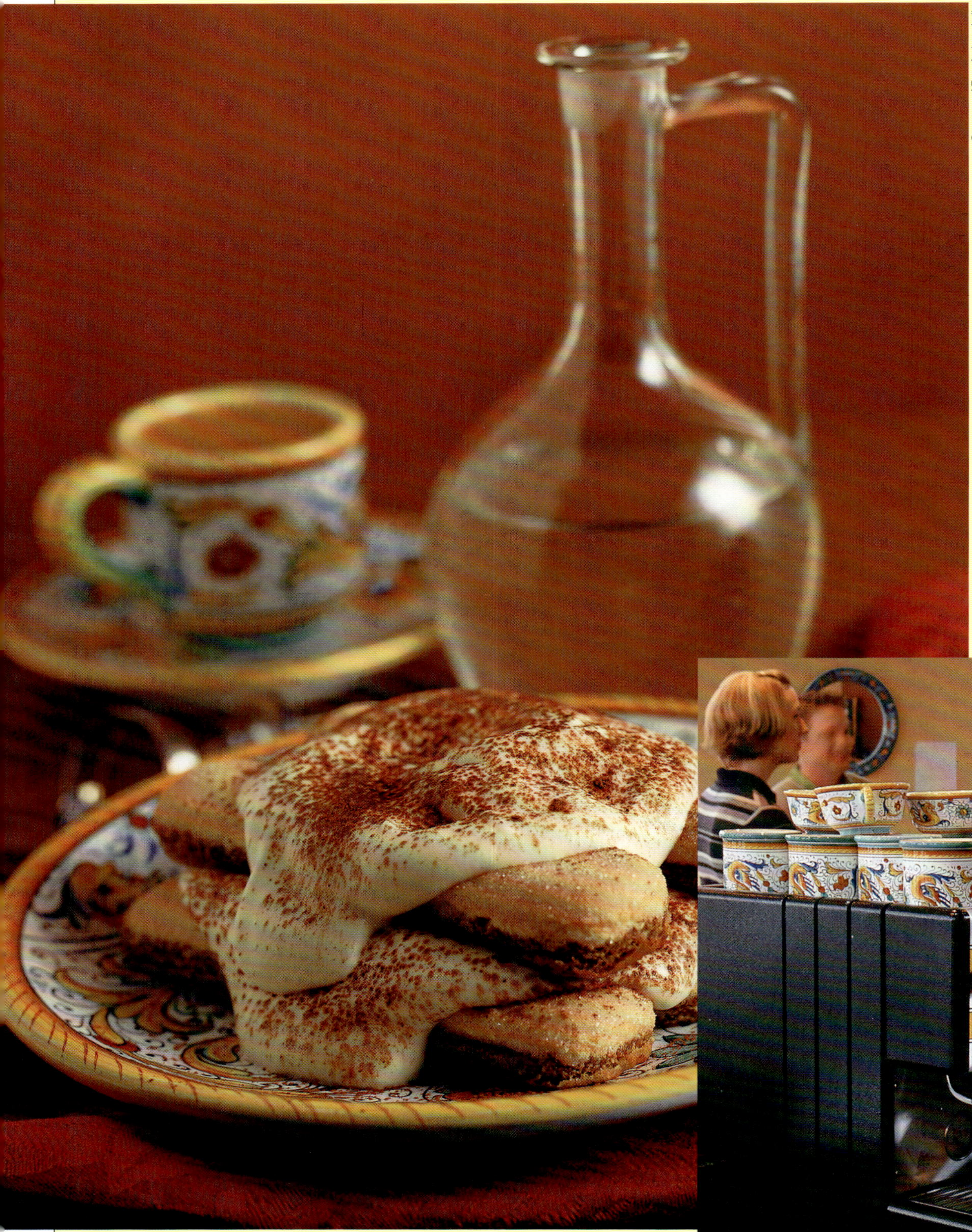

Courtesy of Torrefazione Italia

The deft hands of the Torrefazione Italia barista create the perfect coffee drink exactly to the customer's liking.

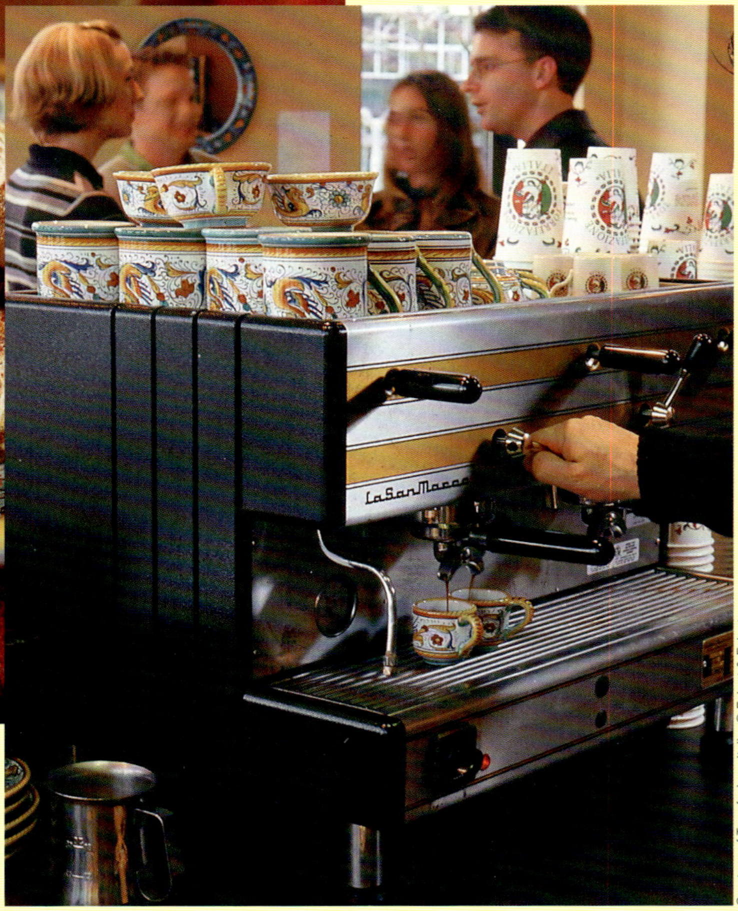

Courtesy of Torrefazione Italia, © Eckert & Eckert

Coffee Culture

When one thinks about it, it makes sense that the coffee craze would have its start in King County. The winter months, which are cool and damp, may seem to go on endlessly, and the comfort of a hot, fragrant cup of joe seems especially appealing when January rolls around. Or it could just be that great minds think alike: two of King County's best known coffee merchants, Seattle's Best Coffee and Starbucks, got their starts at roughly the same time.

To be fair, however, Seattle's Best Coffee, or just SBC as its followers affectionately know it, was actually the first by a few years. SBC's founder, Jim Stewart, opened his first store in Coupeville, Washington in the summer of 1968. Stewart sold that store two years later and moved on to Seattle where he opened a new store, called Stewart Brothers Coffee, on Pier 70. The shop was extremely popular, most likely because the coffee was unlike anything known to most Americans.

In 1971, Stewart Brothers Coffee opened a second store in the Pike Place Market, and his two stores continued to thrive for many years. In 1988, the name was shortened to SBC since that is what most people called it anyway. That same year, SBC won the coveted title of "Seattle's Best Coffee," and the name just stuck.

Ten years later, Atlanta, Georgia-based AFC Enterprises purchased Seattle's Best Coffee. AFC is the parent company for several establishments, including Torrefazione Italia, another gourmet coffee company. Today, under the AFC umbrella, Seattle's Best Coffee has stores in Washington, Oregon, California, Colorado, Illinois, Maryland, Massachusetts, and Georgia, and distributes its beans throughout the world.

The company is also well known for its philanthropic work, including contributions to the Water Keepers Alliance. There are 40 Water Keepers programs throughout the U.S. and Central America, all dedicated to making sure that pure, clean water remains a reality. With each organic coffee purchase, Seattle's Best Coffee makes a donation to the alliance.

In downtown Seattle, one can literally walk in any direction and find a Starbucks. The original Starbucks was a small, unassuming coffeehouse in the Pike Place Market. It continued on as a fairly small operation until 1982, when Howard Shultz was hired as director of retail operations and marketing.

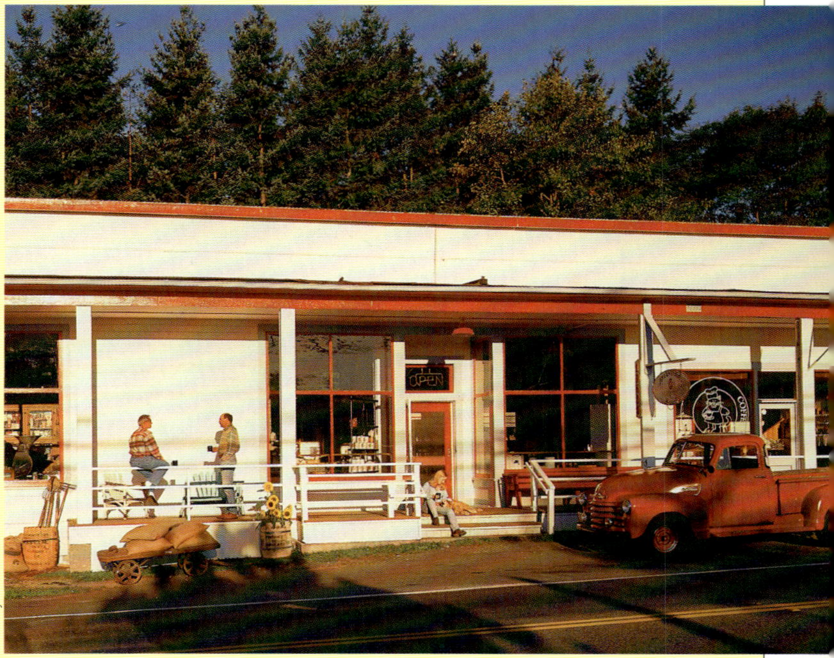

Courtesy of Seattle's Best Coffee

SBC's Vashon Island café and roasting facilities have been serving specialty coffees to the public since 1983.

Upon returning from a trip to Italy in 1983, Shultz pitched the idea of European-style coffee bars to the owners of Starbucks. The following year, the concept was tried in a new Starbucks store in downtown Seattle. Of course Shultz was right—the concept took off. In 1985, Shultz founded his own coffee bar called Il Giornale, and two years later acquired the assets, and the name, of Starbucks. The rest, as they say, is history.

The most recent upstart in the King County coffee wars is Tully's Coffee, which got its start in 1992. Tully's roasts and sells gourmet coffee blends to discerning coffee drinkers and is rapidly expanding, with 81 retail locations, and more sure to come.

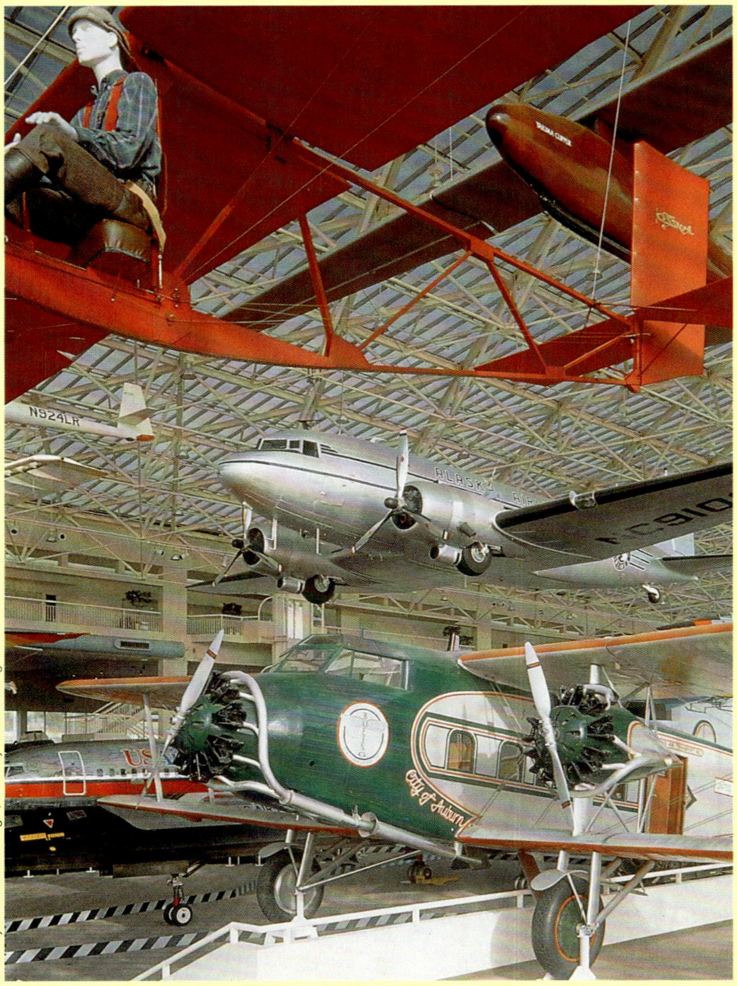

Courtesy of Museum of Flight, Photo by Steve Keating

A Boeing 80A and CG-2 Glider are exhibited in the Great Gallery at the Museum of Flight. In the late 1920s, Boeing's Model 80A was among the new breed of passenger aircraft. This 80A that is on display at the museum is the only surviving example of the Model 80 series. The CG-2 glider, created by Cessna in 1930, could be purchased from a catalog.

Microbreweries

Although coffee is undoubtedly the drink of choice in King County, beer certainly runs a close second. The last decade or so has seen a proliferation of small, independent microbreweries that concoct creative and delicious ales, lagers, and porters that are smooth, satisfying, and flavorful—and that bear little resemblance to their mass-produced cousins. Redhook Ale Brewery is the best known of the King County microbreweries. Founded in 1981, Red Hook produces a number of beers, including Ballard Bitter and Redhook ESB. Other microbreweries also abound throughout the county, including Pyramid Breweries, makers of Hefeweizen and Espresso Stout, Maritime Pacific Brewing Company, Hales Ales, Pike Brewing Company, and Seattle Brewers.

E-Commerce

Ten years ago, who would have believed that one day personal computers would allow people to shop from the comfort of their homes. Yet, it is so. Today, the Internet is the gateway to the world. First used as an educational tool, the Internet is now the platform for endless e-commerce businesses that offer the opportunity to purchase virtually anything desired at the click of a mouse.

King County is no stranger to e-commerce. Each week sees the start of some new Internet business. Some succeed and some fail, but few can boast the staying power and ingenuity of Amazon.com.

Seattle-based Amazon.com blazed on the Internet scene in July of 1995 as the world's first on-line bookseller. The concept proved brilliant. Customers flocked to the virtual bookstore and ate up what Amazon had to offer—popular as well as hard-to-find fiction and non-fiction, available at the click of a mouse and often at a discount. Amazon.com grew rapidly, and soon began selling music, videos, electronics, toys, and games. On-line auctions soon followed. Yet, for all that growth, Amazon.com still manages to deliver top-notch customer service and a truly enjoyable on-line shopping experience.

Boeing built primary structural components of the B-2 stealth bomber, namely the outboard and aft-center sections of the bomber's fuselage. Boeing also supplied the bomber's fuel systems, weapons delivery system, and landing gear. Both the 50-foot-long aft-center sections and the 65-foot-long outboard sections were assembled at Boeing facilities in Seattle.

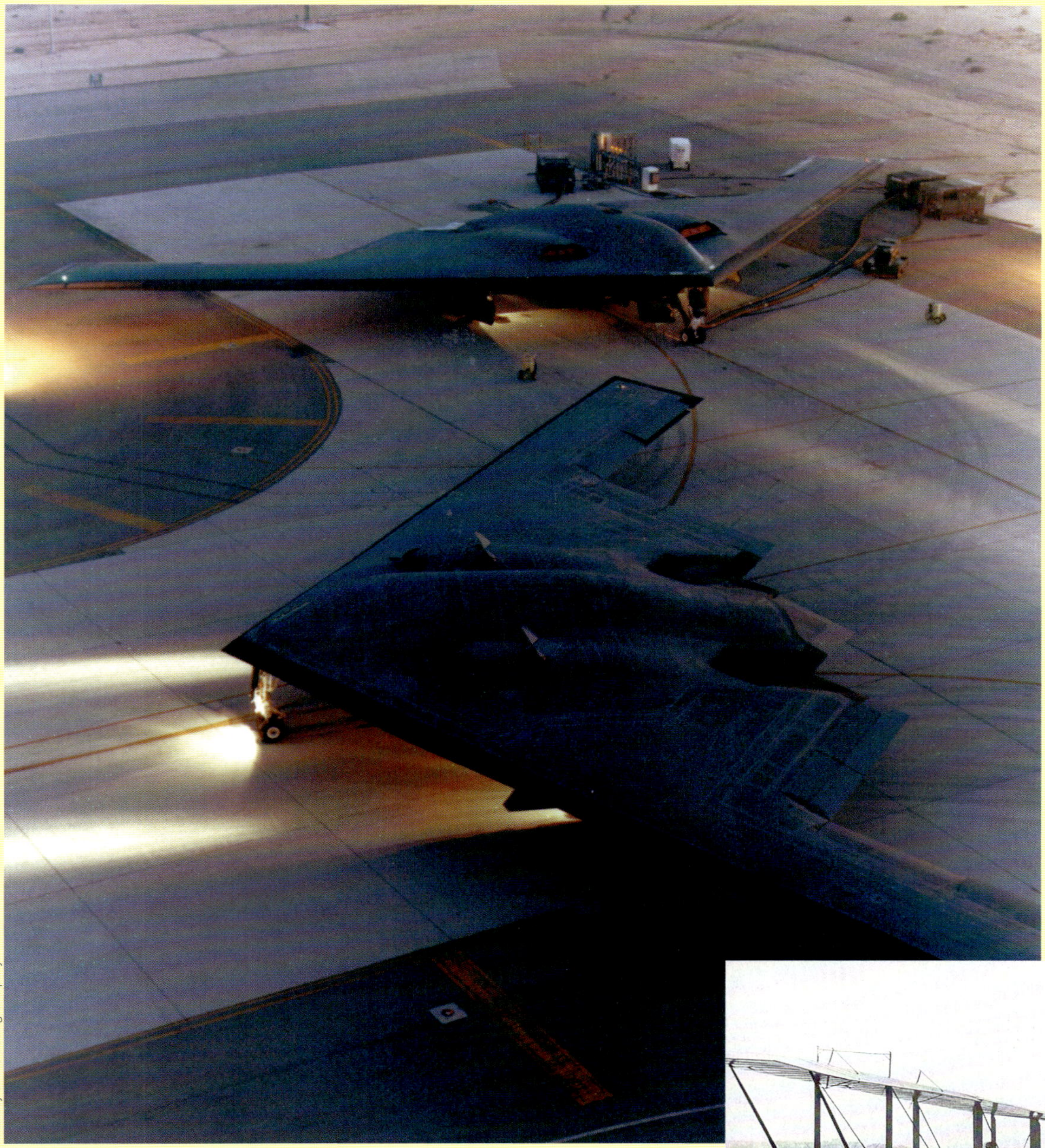

Courtesy of The Boeing Company

The seaplane known as the B&W was the first airplane designed and built by Boeing in 1916.

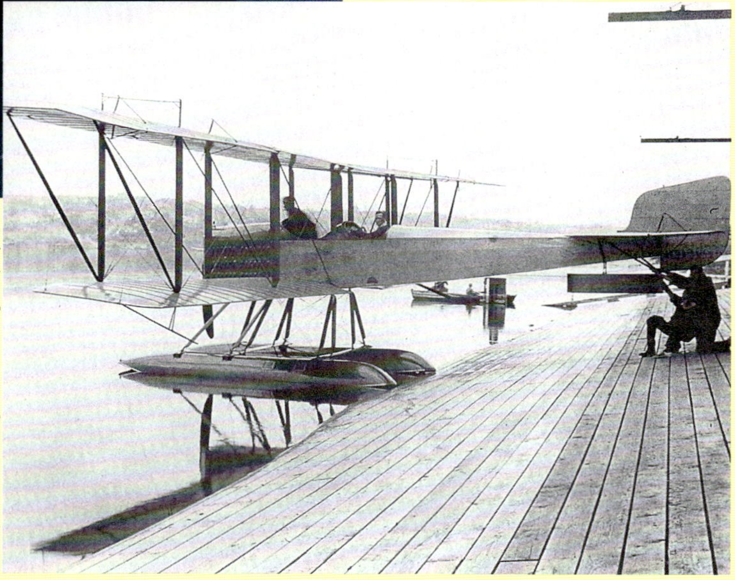

Courtesy of Museum of Flight and The Boeing Company

Seattle skyline as seen from a Washington State ferry.

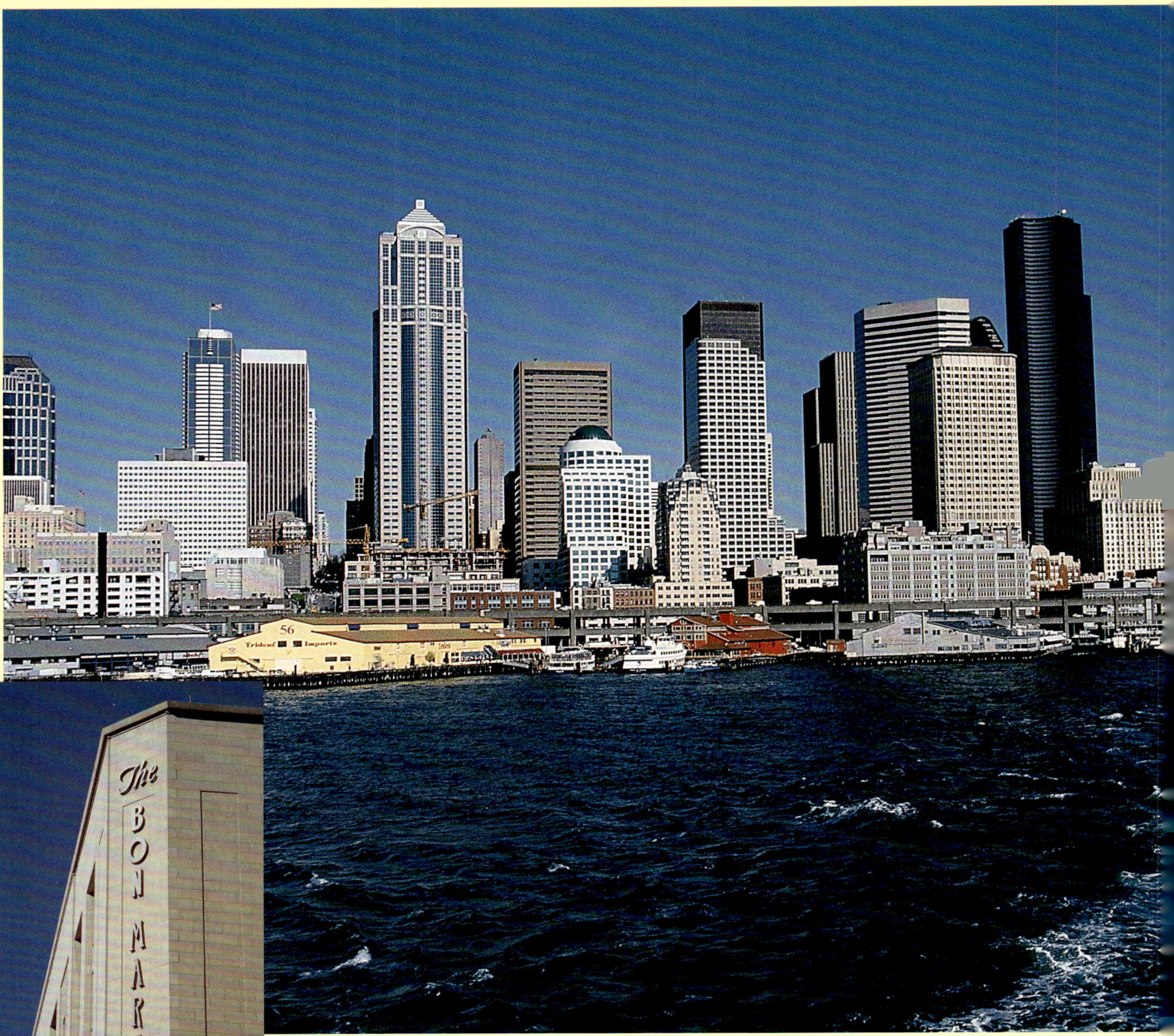

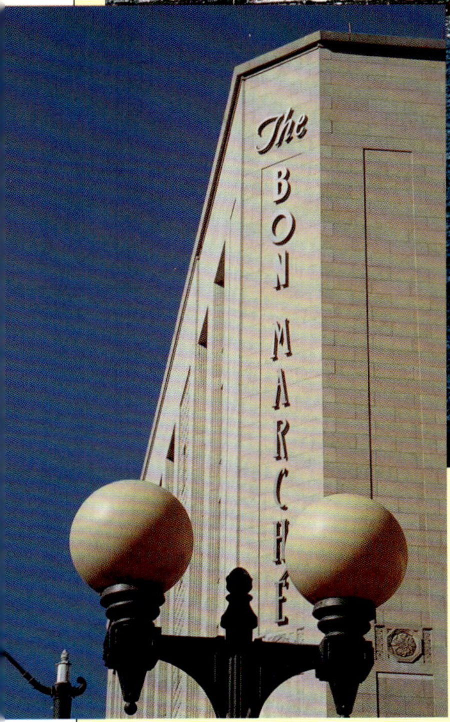

Courtesy of Wyndham Images

Founded in 1889 when Josephine and Edward Nordhoff came to Seattle, The Bon Marché now boasts 42 stores in five northwest states.

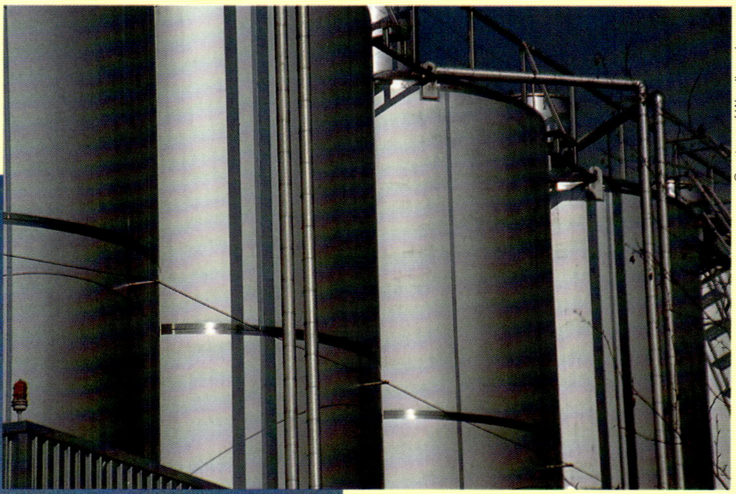

Courtesy of Wyndham Images

Fermentation tanks at the Redhook Ale Brewery in Woodinville.

Courtesy of Wyndham Images

Wholesale, Retail, and Casual Chic

Lots of retail-oriented companies have their corporate homes in King County. Again, maybe it is the weather. Do those endless, cool, cloudy days inspire one to shop? Perhaps so. In any case, the cool and rainy climate, coupled with the awe-inspiring natural beauty, most likely had a lot to do with the success of two of King County's most famous retailers—the Bon Marché and Nordstrom.

The Bon Marché, now owned by Federated Department Stores in Cincinnati, boasts 42 stores in five northwest states, 6,900 employees, and annual sales of $975 million in 1999. The present-day success of this corporate giant belies its modest beginnings. It was 1889 when Josephine and Edward Nordhoff came to Seattle and opened a small retail store they called the Bon Marché. The store started humbly but grew steadily over the next several years. Between 1900 and 1923, the Bon Marché moved locations several times while annual sales concurrently grew from $338,000 to $8 million. Eventually, the Bon Marché was sold to Hahn Stores of Chicago (now known as Allied Stores), which began to expand the department stores into new markets throughout the Pacific Northwest.

In 1949, the Bon Marché became the mainstay retail store in the world's first modern shopping center, Northgate Mall. Today, the Bon Marché is still the cornerstone of this popular mall and one of the most well known retailers in the region.

Nordstrom got its start in 1901 when John W. Nordstrom opened a small shoe store in Seattle with proceeds from his Alaska gold-rush stake. That small store led to a national chain of over 100 stores throughout America. Nordstrom's hallmark is their uncompromisingly gracious customer service, which is legendary in the retail industry. Nordstrom recently opened their 380,000-square-foot flagship store in downtown Seattle.

Other retailers who have done their part to define that signature northwest style are Eddie Bauer and REI.

In 1920, Eddie Bauer opened his first store in downtown Seattle. Since then, the company has grown to more than 500 stores in the U.S. and Canada. Eddie Bauer offers that casually chic clothing that is so undeniably northwestern. REI, which stands for Recreational Equipment Incorporated, has called King County home since 1938. REI specializes in recreational equipment such as climbing and camping supplies and also sells clothing for those excursions. Reportedly, REI is also a great place to work. *Fortune* magazine named REI one of the "100 Best Companies to Work for in America" in both 1998 and 1999.

The last notable retailer, which could also be called a wholesaler, is Costco. Costco, with corporate headquarters in Issaquah, pioneered the membership warehouse concept in the early 1980s. It was an ingenious idea: buy goods in incredible bulk, keep overhead low, and pass on the savings to members. Today, Costco, which merged with the Price Company in 1993, is phenomenally successful. With hundreds of stores in the United States, and others opening throughout the world, Costco is a force to be reckoned with.

Forestry

Lush forests surround the county on three sides, and not surprisingly timber is one of the area's biggest industries. The two largest timber companies in King County are Weyerhaeuser and Plum Creek Timber.

Frederick Weyerhaeuser and a group of investors incorporated Weyerhaeuser in 1900. Today, the company owns 5.3 million acres of timberland, 2 million of which are in the northwest, and employs over 35,000 people. With corporate headquarters in Federal Way, Weyerhaeuser grows and harvests trees, distributes and sells forest products such as logs, wood chips, pulp, and paper, and develops and constructs real estate. The company is also strongly committed to recycling efforts and makes great efforts to protect water quality and fish and wildlife habitats. Weyerhaeuser is the leading exporter of forest products in the United States.

Although smaller than Weyerhaeuser, Plum Creek Timber is also a major timberland owner in the United States. A subsidiary of Burlington Northern Railroad, Plum Creek was born from the Federal Land Grant that gave tracts of land to railroads. Northern Pacific Railroad sold most of its land to start in business, but Burlington Northern did not. Plum Creek Timber is the result. Today, Plum Creek owns 7.9 million acres of timberland (3.3 million acres before the merger with The Timber Company in July 2000). Plum Creek Timber also is strongly committed to protecting the environment.

Conspicuously absent from this chapter are the many King County-based high-tech and biotech companies such as Microsoft and Immunex. Not to worry however. These powerhouse companies are so big that they qualify for their own chapter.

In the early 1890s, about a third of Washington's population worked in logging camps, sawmills, shingle mills, and in factories making wooden doors and window sashes. Nearly 1.2 billion board feet of lumber and almost 1.9 billion shingles were shipped from the state in 1892. Huge trees still filled the coastal forests, and no one thought the supply would ever run out. This 1890s photo shows a giant fir log at the Huron Lumber Company in Bothell. The town got its start in 1886, when David Bothell started a lumber camp and shingle mill in the area.

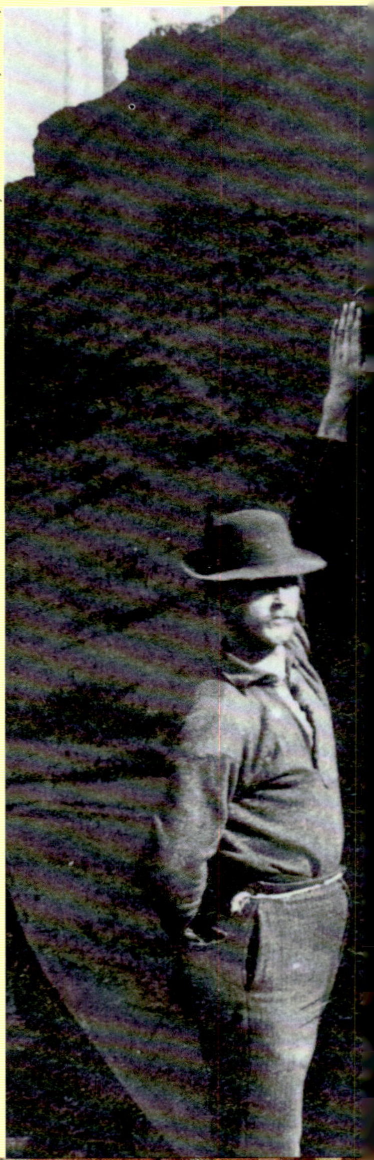

Courtesy of Museum of History & Industry

Although the timber industry does not command as large a portion of the economy as it did in the 1890s, it is still one of the area's biggest industries.

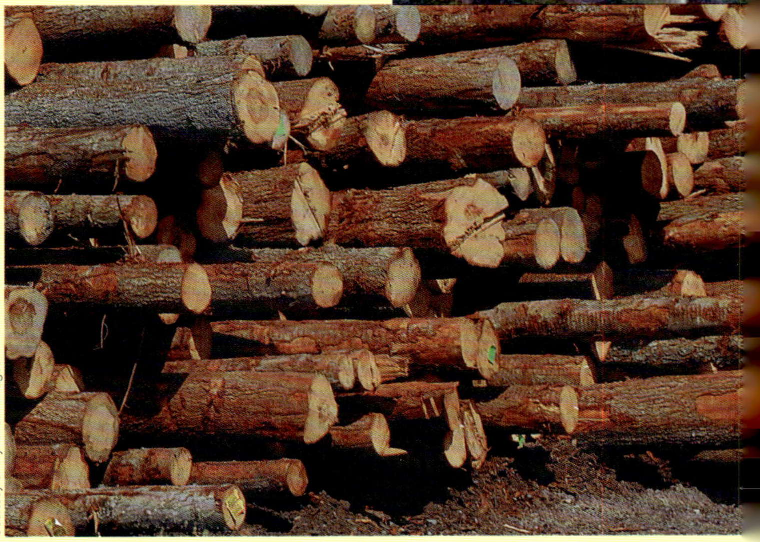

Courtesy of Wyndham Images

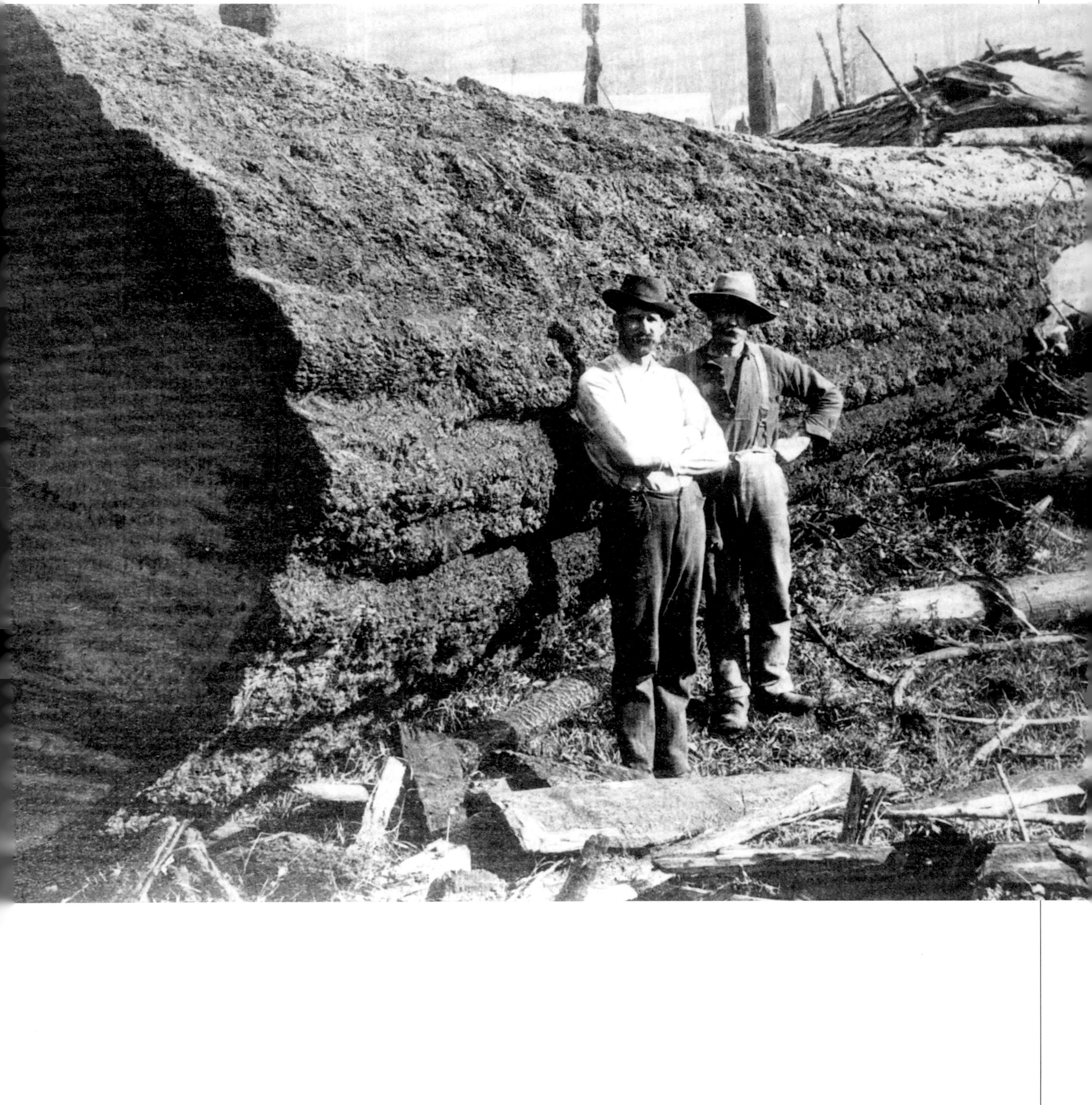

Moving at the Speed of Light

It is interesting to contemplate the question of why the high-tech and biotech industries have flourished in King County. Is there something in the water or the air that attracts some of the best and brightest to this area? Probably not. More practically, King County is a beautiful region, flanked on three sides by lush forests and mountains and on the fourth side by the Puget Sound. In short, it is just a great place to live. Those high-tech and biotech CEOs just want to be amidst all this splendor, and the employees who want to work for them must follow.

However it happened, high technology and biotechnology are two of the fastest-growing and most fascinating industries in the area.

Biotechnology

Quick, which is the younger industry, high tech or biotech? Although the biotech industry has gotten a lot of press in recent years and thus seems newer, it really is the older of the two. The twentieth century era of biotechnology got its start back in 1953 when scientists James Watson and Francis Crick presented the double-helix model of DNA. Today, biotechnology is used in an ever-burgeoning list of industries such as waste management, mining, and medicine.

In King County, the focus is undoubtedly on medicine. King County has the greatest concentration of biotechnology firms in the nation. Most of these companies are engaged in research and development, or R & D as it is known in the field, using their expertise and innovation to create the medical breakthroughs of the twenty-first century. Most of these firms specialize in finding viable treatments for diseases such as cancer, AIDS, arthritis, and diabetes.

King County's largest biotechnology firm is the Immunex Corporation, located in a beautiful state-of-the-art facility overlooking Elliott Bay in Seattle. Immunex, founded in 1981, is one of the top ten biotechnology companies in the United States. Immunex focuses on the science of the human immune system, which has led to exciting discoveries of possible treatments for some of our most insidious diseases such as cancer, asthma, AIDS, rheumatoid arthritis, and heart disease.

Courtesy of VA Puget Sound Health Care System

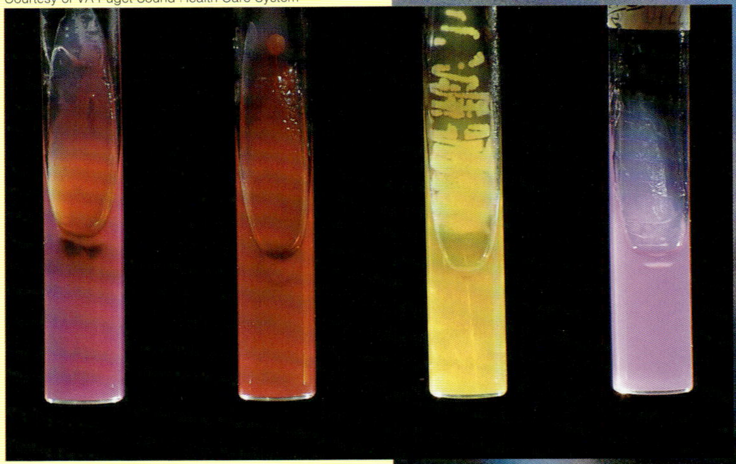

King County has the greatest concentration of biotechnology firms in the nation. Regional medical institutions are also deeply involved in such research. For example, internationally known investigators affiliated with the VA Puget Sound Health Care System are working to unravel the mysteries of aging and dementia and are also working to identify genetic markers for Multiple Sclerosis, Huntington's Disease, and other genetically based diseases.

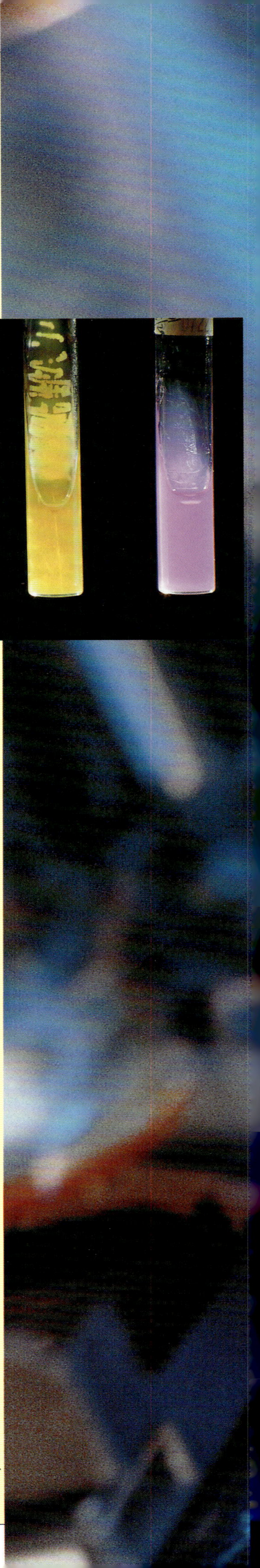

Sophisticated surface-mount technology is used in manufacturing circuit boards for ATL Ultrasound systems.

Courtesy of ATL Ultrasound

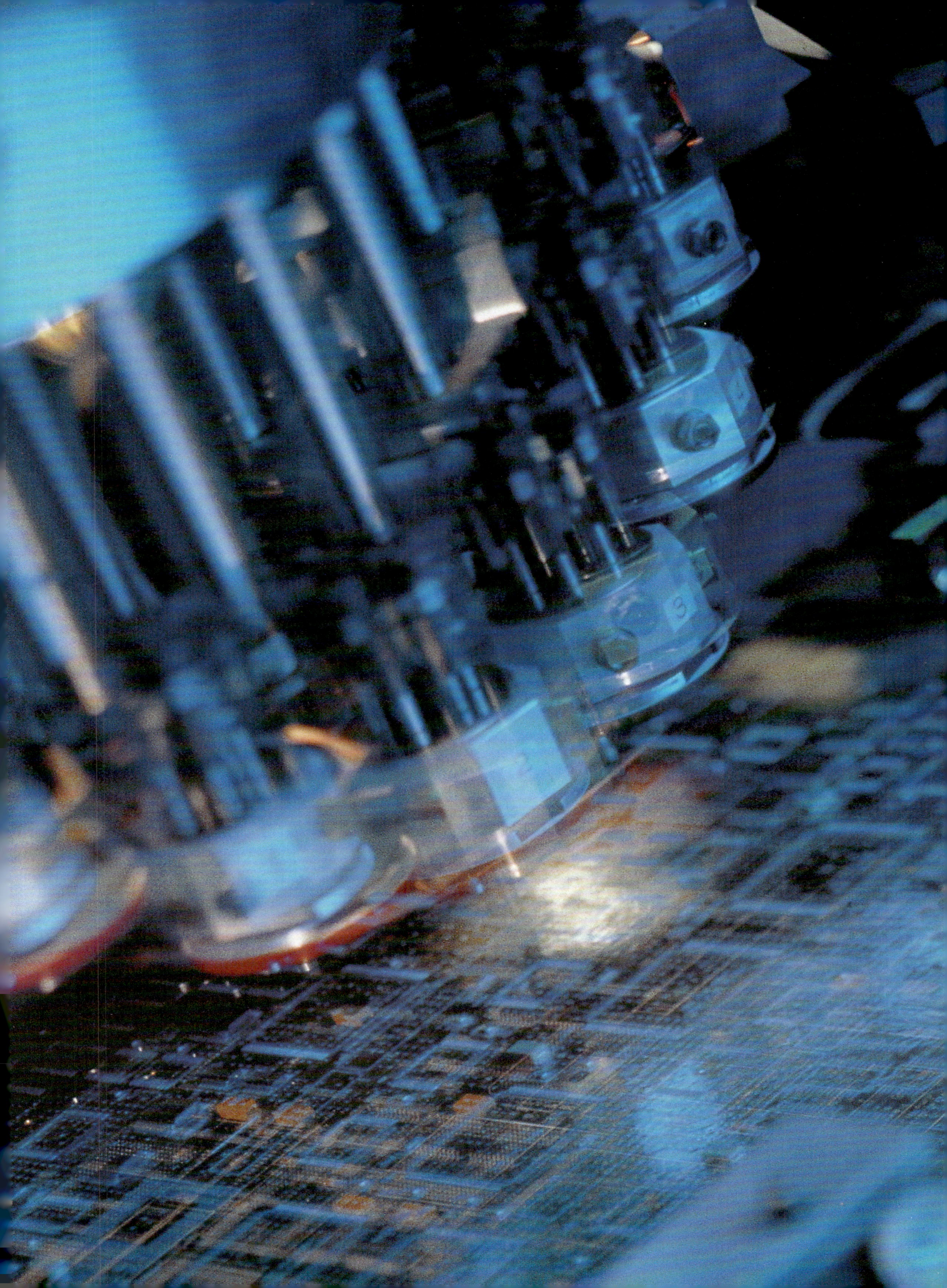

The NOAA Doppler weather radar system provides detailed weather information to the Puget Sound region.

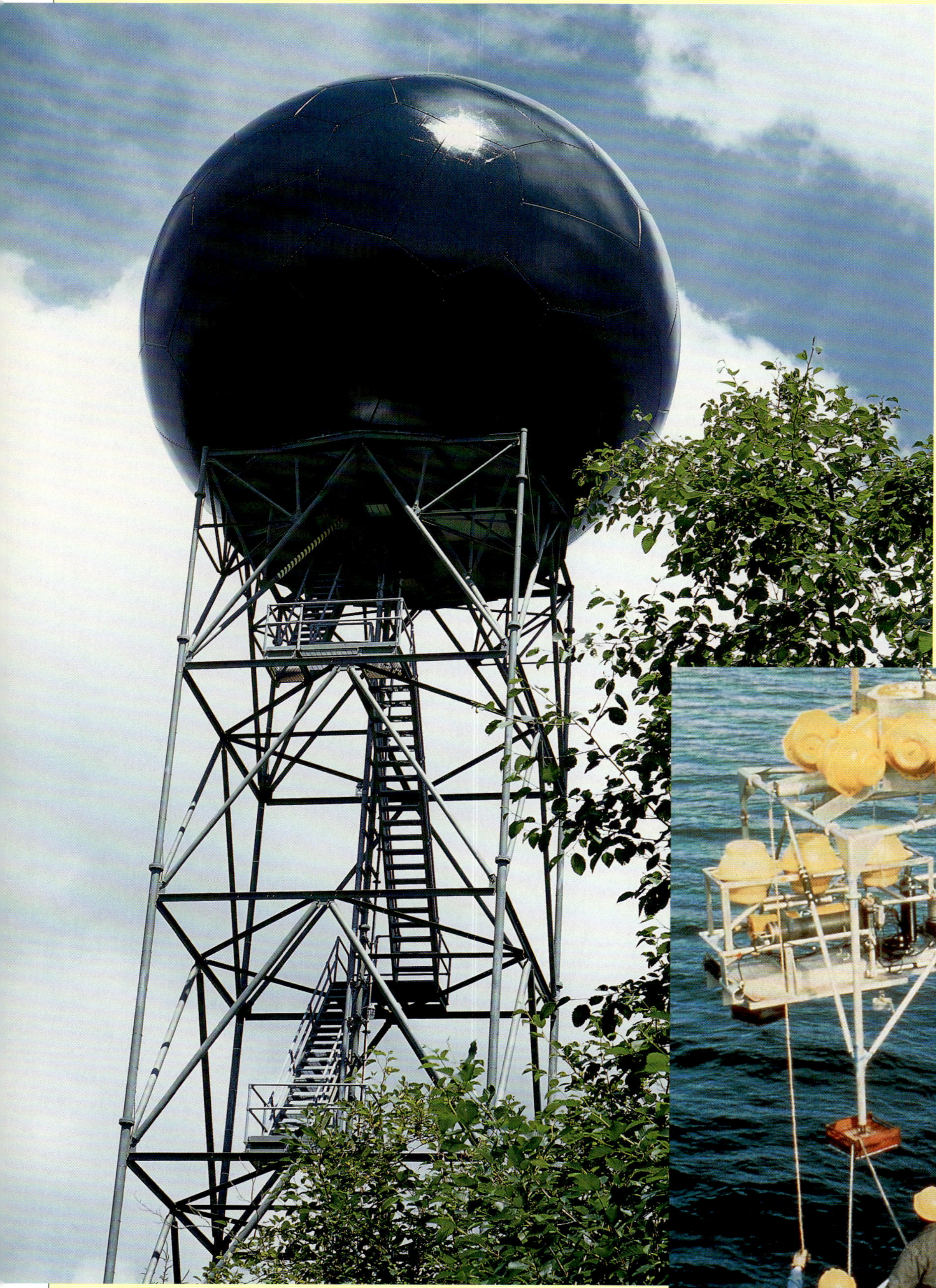

Courtesy of NOAA

The NOAA ship McArther *takes researchers out to the waters of Puget Sound in order to participate in bottom-sediment transport studies.*

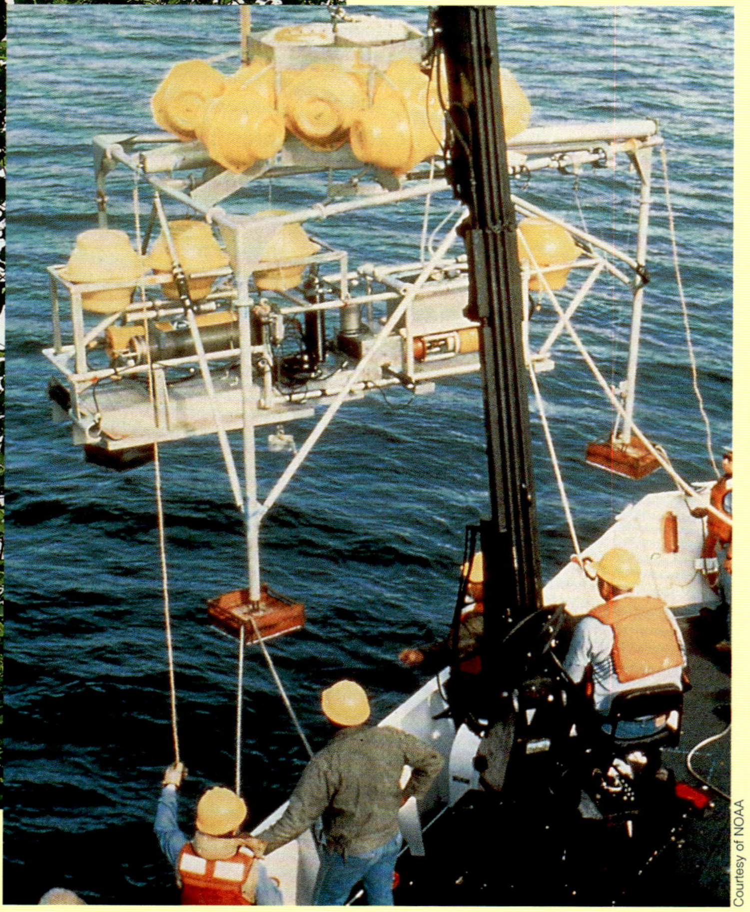

Courtesy of NOAA

Zymogenetics, located on South Lake Union in Seattle, is the fastest growing biotechnology firm in the area. Owned by Danish company Novo Nordisk, Zymogenetics, focuses on the development of genetically engineered active compounds for wound healing, hard and soft tissue repair, hemophilia, and diabetes.

Located in Bothell is ICOS, the third largest biotechnology firm in the region. ICOS conducts research into pharmaceuticals that treat inflammatory diseases and other serious medical conditions. Approximately 87 percent of ICOS's employees work in research and development. Redmond-based Sanofi Diagnostics Pasteur, a subsidiary of Sanofi Diagnostics of France, specializes in blood virus, autoimmune, infectious disease, and clinical microbiology diagnostics.

At Seattle's PathoGenesis Corporation, the specialty is the development of pharmaceuticals to treat infectious diseases, especially those involving the lungs. PathoGenesis is largely known for its development of TOBI, an inhaled antibiotic solution used for the treatment of cystic fibrosis. TOBI has shown great promise for the thousands of people around the world who suffer from the chronic lung infections that often accompany this disease.

Cancer, autoimmune, and other diseases are the specialty of many of King County's other biotechnology firms. Seattle-based Xcyte Therapies, founded in 1996, develops new therapies that use the immune system to treat a host of medical disorders including cancer and infectious diseases. Cell Therapeutics Incorporated, also in Seattle, focuses on small-molecule drugs used in the treatment of cancer and immune diseases.

Several well-known medical devices also got their start in King County. Agilent Technologies' Heartstream, Inc. develops automatic external defibrillators to treat sudden heart attack, Physio-Control Corporation is the world leader in the manufacture of defibrillators, and Redmond-based Heart Technology develops and manufactures equipment used to remove plaque from arteries. In Bothell, ATL Ultrasound is a recognized leader in the manufacture, distribution, and service of diagnostic medical ultrasound systems; and in Issaquah, the Siemens Medical Systems' Ultrasound Group produces state-of-the-art ultrasound equipment.

A NOAA satellite image shows the 1997-1998 El Niño event. NOAA also uses an array of 71 buoys to detect and predict El Niño events.

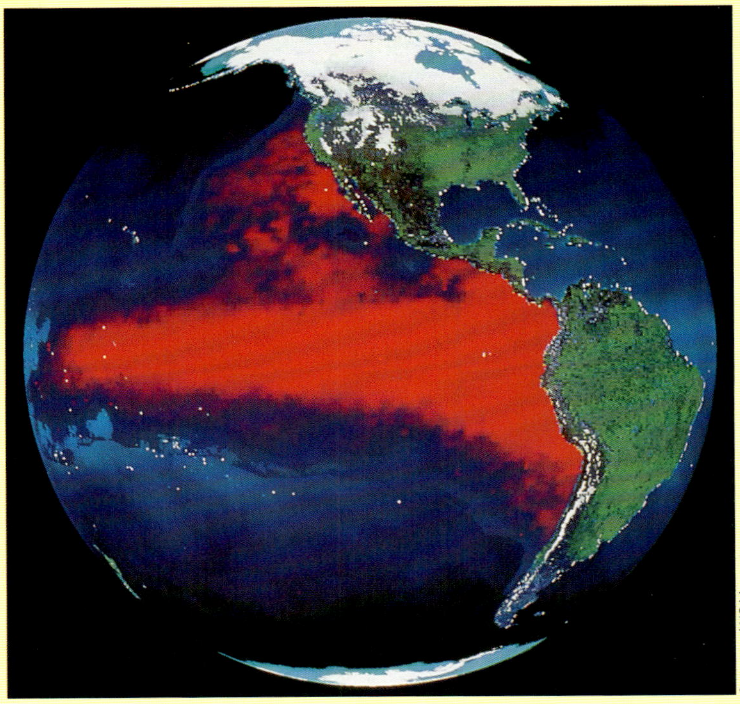

Courtesy of NOAA

High Technology

According to a recent survey, over 40 percent of Americans have a computer in their homes, and 25 percent have modems. In King County, the numbers are even higher, with over 50 percent of King County adults on-line at home. Even more astounding are the numbers of Washingtonians affected by the high-tech industry; one out of every three adults in Washington State works in the high-tech field. There is no doubt that it is an industry that has profoundly affected the culture and economy of the region.

So how did it happen? Without a doubt, the success of Microsoft has much to do with it.

It was the MITS Altair 8800, a special kit computer, that really provided the spark for what would later become the Microsoft Corporation. In 1975, two young men, Bill Gates and Paul Allen, saw the MITS Altair on the cover of *Popular Electronics* and decided to write a language called BASIC for the computer. A month later, Gates and Allen licensed the language to MITS of Albuquerque, New Mexico.

In early 1976, Gates and Allen sold their BASIC language to several other companies, including General Electric and Citibank. In November of that same year, the trade name "Microsoft" was registered with the Secretary of State's Office in New Mexico, and three months after that, an official partnership between Gates and Allen was executed.

By the end of 1998, two more computer languages, FORTRAN and COBOL-80, had been written and year-end sales exceeded the one million dollar mark. Things were definitely heating up.

The next several years brought a lot of change to the budding software company. In 1979, corporate headquarters were moved to Bellevue, and two years later, Microsoft was reorganized into a privately held company with Bill Gates at the helm and Paul Allen as second in command. Four years later, following the success of Microsoft's Disk Operating System (DOS) designed for the IBM personal computer, Paul Allen resigned as Executive Vice President.

In 1985, the first version of Windows was shipped, heralding a new era for Microsoft. The years that followed saw the release of a number of new and very popular software programs, such as Excel, Word, Access, and PowerPoint, growing Microsoft's capital beyond what anyone ever would have guessed.

With the introduction of Windows 95, 98, and 2000, the popularity of Microsoft's products seems to know no bounds. By the end of 1999, the software giant reported revenue in excess of $19 billion, and a workforce of more than 31,000. In fact, the success of Microsoft has much to do with the current high-technology explosion. Microsoft has really changed the landscape, not only in King County, but throughout the world. Pretty good for two guys who thought they would take a crack at writing a computer language.

Microsoft is certainly a hard act to follow, but many other King County companies have also made their mark on the high-tech industry. For example, in Redmond, one can find the American headquarters of Nintendo, the operation center for all of Nintendo's business in the Western Hemisphere. Nintendo, of course, is the maker of some of the world's most popular video games such as Mario and Donkey Kong. In fact, over 40 percent of American households are reported to have a Nintendo game system.

Another major high-tech company in King County is Bellevue-based Attachmate. Attachmate is a world leader in the supply of business software and services. In fact, 80 percent of Fortune 500 and Global 2000 companies trust Attachmate for their database and secure data needs. Like Microsoft, Attachmate has been around a long time. It was founded in 1982, and today employs over 1,900 employees worldwide.

Courtesy of Microsoft

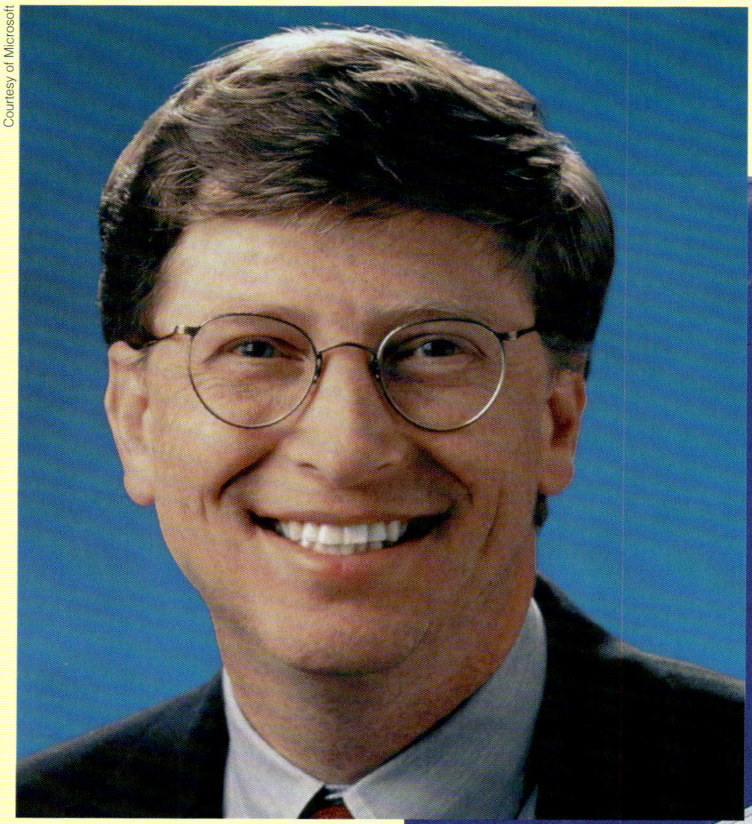

Bill Gates, Microsoft's Chairman and Chief Software Architect.

Courtesy of The Boeing Company

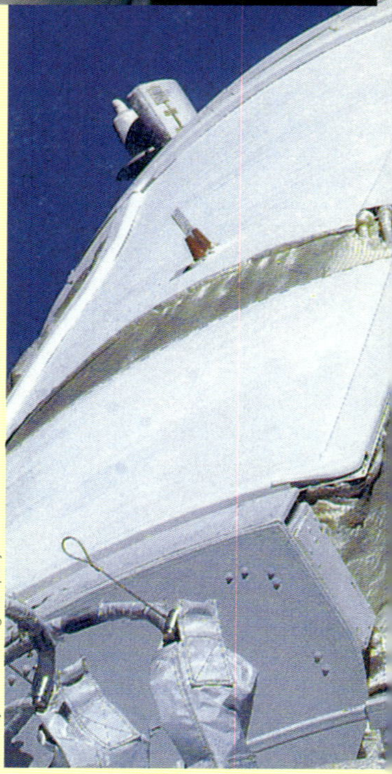

NASA STS-88 Mission specialist Jim Newman performs one of three space-walks to assemble the U.S.-built Unity *connecting module to Russia's* Zarya *during the first International Space Station (ISS) assembly mission. ISS will require 36 shuttle flights through assembly completion. Afterward, shuttles will perform logistics missions.*

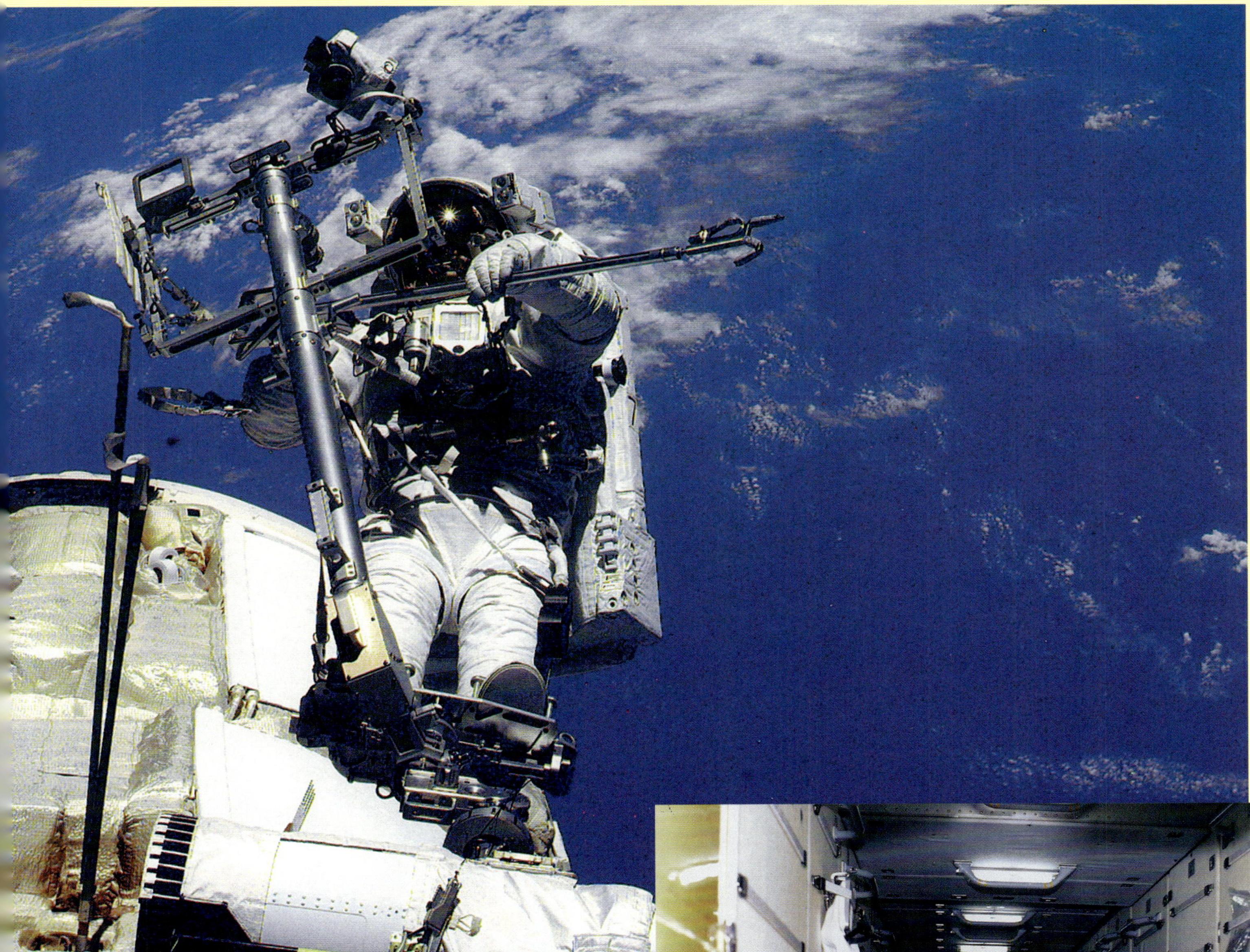

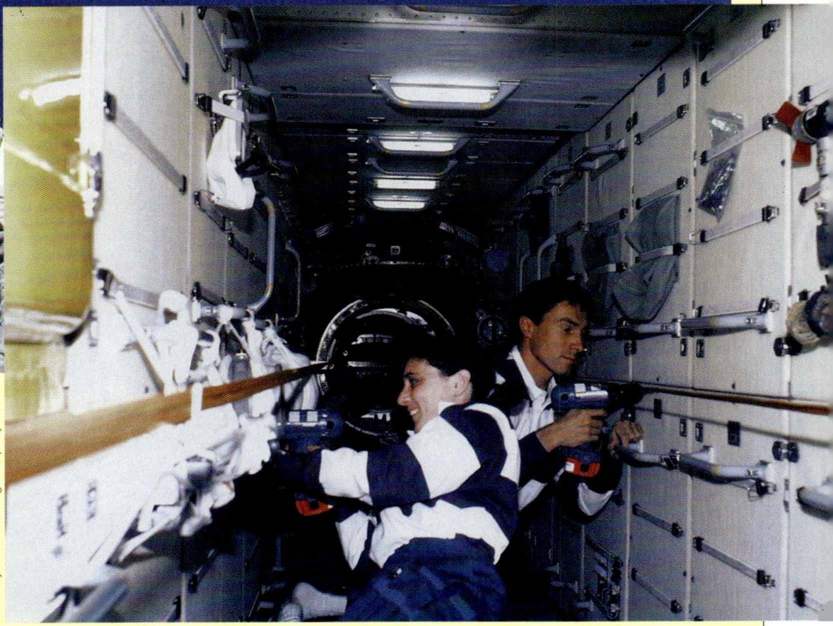

Astronaut Nanacy J. Currie and Cosmonaut Sergei Krikalev on board the International Space Station.

Courtesy of The Boeing Company

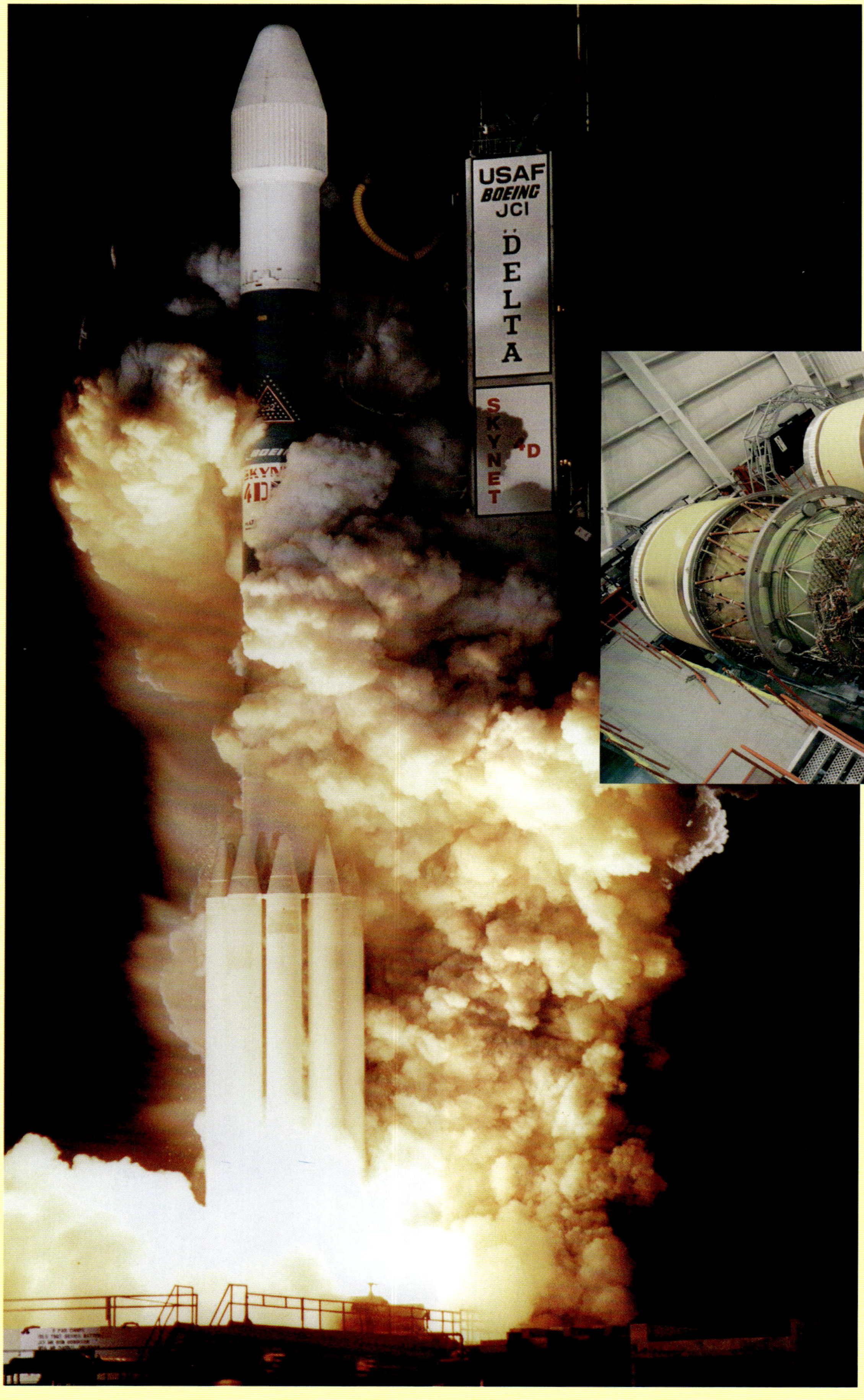

Courtesy of The Boeing Company

A Boeing Delta II model 7426 rocket lifts off, carrying NASA's STARDUST spacecraft on the first leg of a galactic search and recovery mission. During its seven-year mission, the STARDUST spacecraft will collect interstellar and cometary dust from the comet known as Wild 2, returning samples to Earth in 2006.

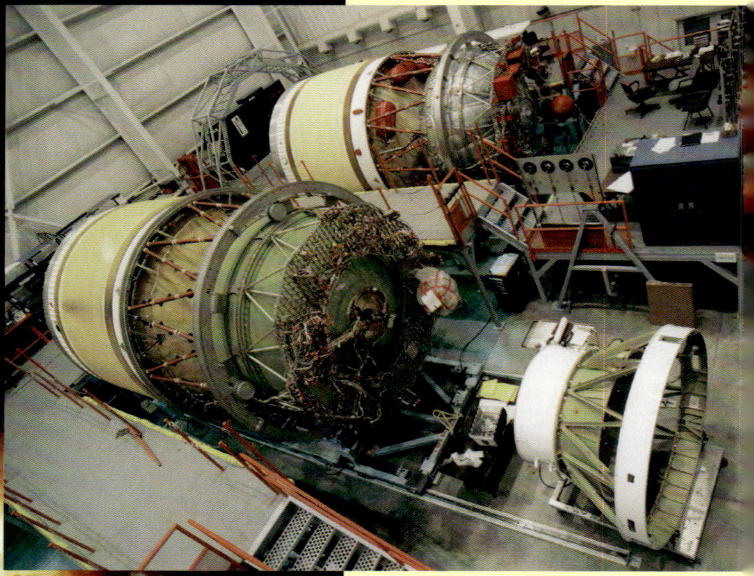

Manufacturing facility for Boeing's Delta III rocket.

Another cutting-edge Seattle-based company is ConneXt. ConneXt develops and delivers powerful and integrated Customer Information System (CIS) software to large utility companies. The software, called ConsumerLinX, is the first of its kind in the utility industry.

Internet High Technology has exploded as well and has changed the way we do business. Seattle-based RealNetworks, led by CEO Rob Glaser, is a global leader in software products that allow "real time" media to be sent and received via the Internet. In fact, each week, over 145,000 hours of sights and sounds are broadcast over the Internet using technology developed by RealNetworks.

Several other King County companies are major players in the ever-evolving Internet information industry. Headquartered here are Onvia.com Inc., a leader in business-to-business (or B2B, as it is known) exchange. Offering everything from website design and hosting to on-line auctions, Onvia.com boasts over 725,000 registered users and in the third quarter of 2000 reported revenue in excess of $45 million.

Another King-County-based B2B is Aventail.com. Founded in 1996, Aventail.com operates business networks that facilitate business-to-business collaboration over the Internet. With its Aventail.Net™ system, Aventail.com helps companies manage their people, policies, and infrastructures.

Also located in this area is Pro2Net. Pro2Net (originally known as AccountingNet Solutions Inc.) was founded in 1995 as an information source for accounting professionals wanting to adapt their businesses to the Internet. Since then, Pro2Net has expanded to include financial services, human resources, insurance, and legal professionals.

In Bothell is LapLink.com Inc. (formerly known as Traveling Software, Inc.). LapLink.com Inc. is best known for its groundbreaking software that enables users to remotely access individual PCs and public and private computer networks. Over 7 million global IT and end users benefit from LapLink.com's file-transfer and synchronization technology.

Without a doubt, King County is home to some of the world's most innovative and competitive biotechnology and high-technology firms. As the Internet gains popularity, and technology continues to move at the speed of light, the twenty-first century will no doubt see the development of technologies that can scarcely be imagined today.

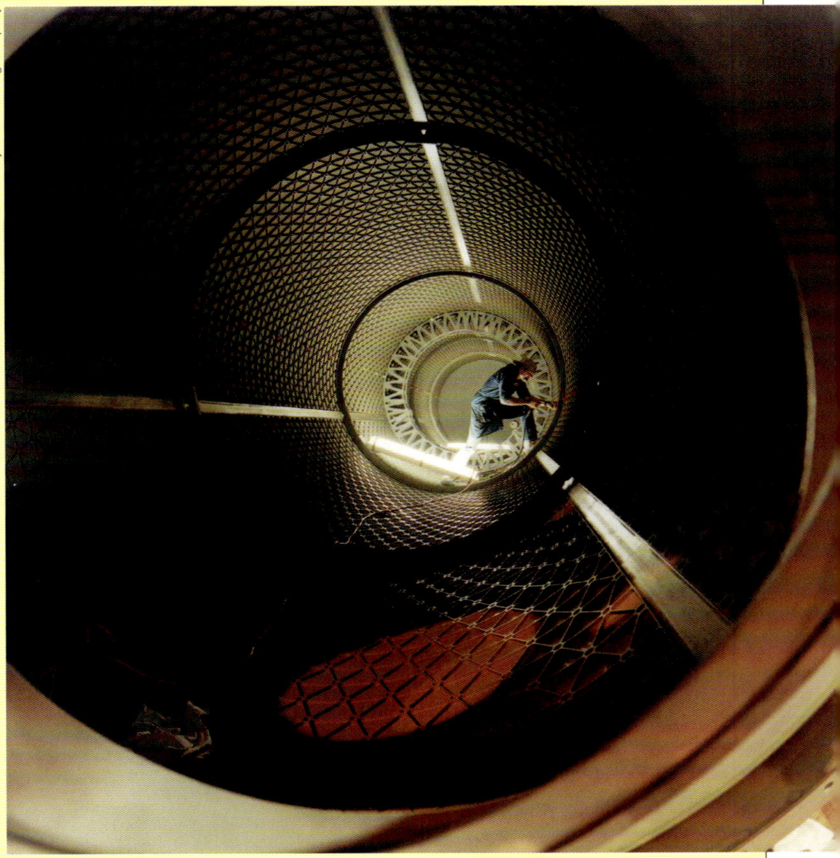

Courtesy of The Boeing Company

A technician inside the Delta II first-stage liquid oxygen tank drills holes for attaching tunnel-clip brackets to support the electrical wiring on the outside of the rocket that is required for data transmission during launch.

The Gateway

From the time the first settlers arrived in the early 1850s, the economic prosperity of King County has been dependent on the ability of the region's people to transport goods and services. In fact, many of the earliest settlers were drawn here because they saw the deep harbor of the Puget Sound as ideally situated for movement of freight and people by boat. At that time, the settlers were primarily interested in moving and selling timber products. Though the harbor did provide excellent access to other key ports along the West Coast, the land transportation required to get the products to the harbor presented significant challenges, especially since local rail service was not available until 1883. By the time that Seattle became the western terminus of the Great Northern Railroad in 1893, the variety of products being transported included coal, hay, dairy goods, and other farm produce, in addition to timber products. Finally able to transport goods efficiently on both land and water, Seattle began to establish important trade relationships that would shape the region's future. As a key outfitter and processor for the Alaska Gold Rush of 1897, the Seattle area became a leading trade center almost overnight. In what would prove to be a major turning point in the history of trade relations in this region, Seattle hosted the 1909 Alaska-Yukon-Pacific Exposition to showcase and celebrate its new relationship with Alaska and to firmly establish itself as a key trade center in the country.

Just two years later, in 1911, the Washington State Legislature passed the Port District Act, sanctioning an independent port authority, and King County voters established a central port authority, now known as the Port of Seattle, later that same year. During World War I, the United States government relied heavily on the warehouses, wharves, and storage facilities that were built in the first years of the port's existence. At the end of the war, Seattle's port had emerged as the second most active port in the country. The Port of Seattle was again instrumental during World War II, as battleships, cruise ships, carrier ships, and other war vehicles were mass-produced in the region's public and private shipyards. The port also served as a pass-through point for the aircraft that were being developed and manufactured for the war by the Boeing Company.

Courtesy of Wyndham Images

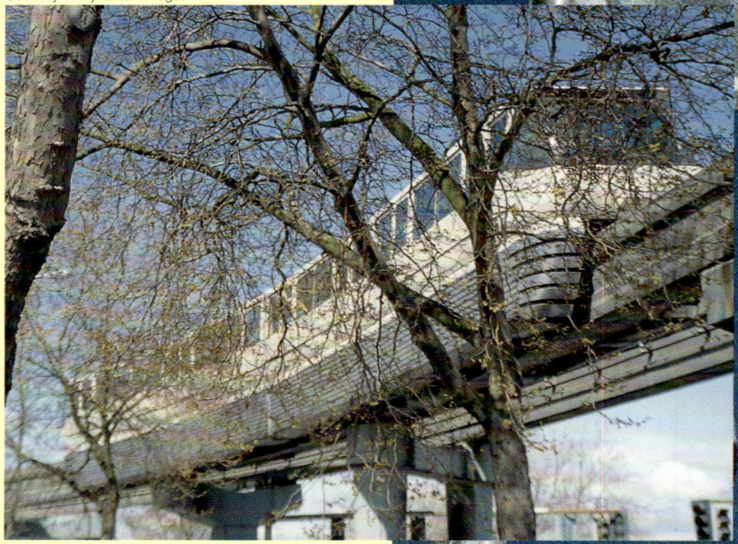

The Seattle Center Monorail travels every 10 minutes to Westlake Center, located in the heart of Downtown's shopping district.

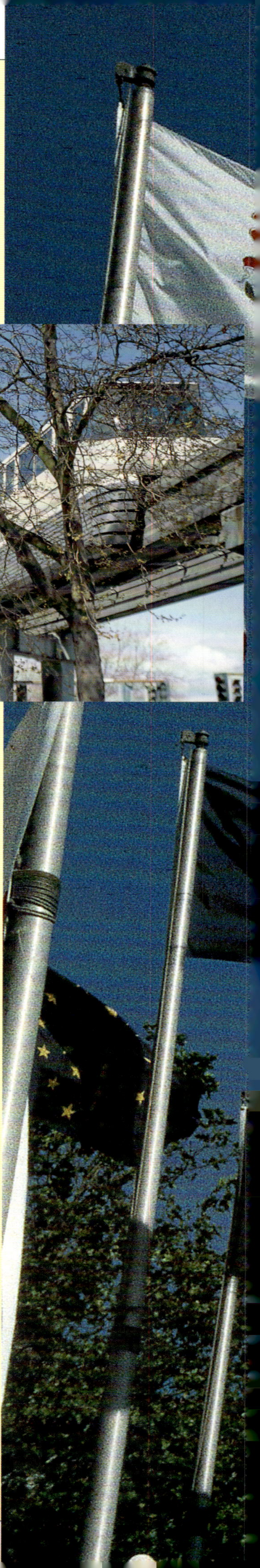

The Space Needle as viewed from the Flag Terrace in Seattle Center.

Courtesy of Wyndham Images

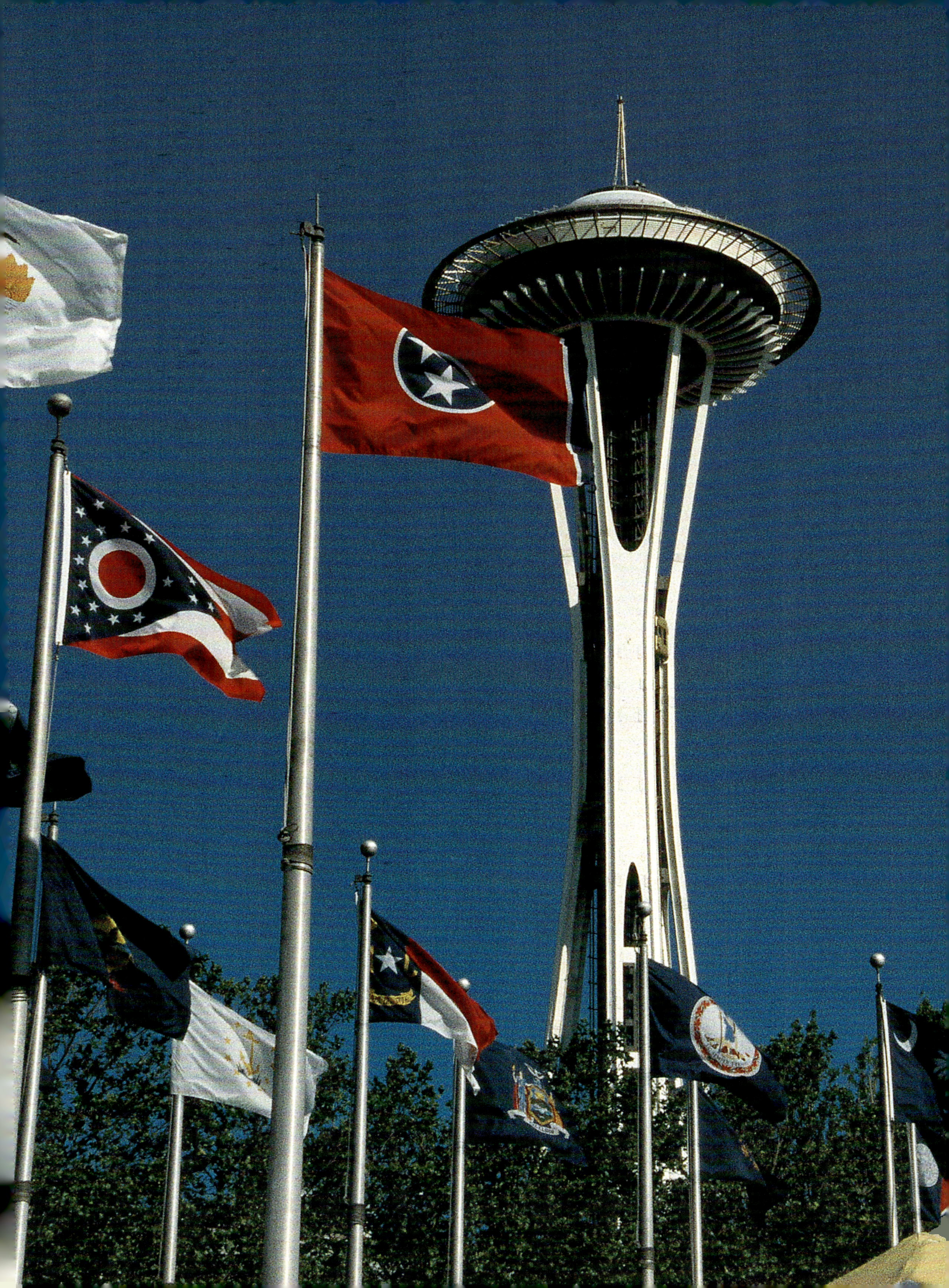

The B-1 Floatplane was Boeing's first commercial plane. Built in 1919 and put into service on the first international airmail flight between Seattle and Victoria, BC, this B-1 is on permanent display at the Museum of History & Industry.

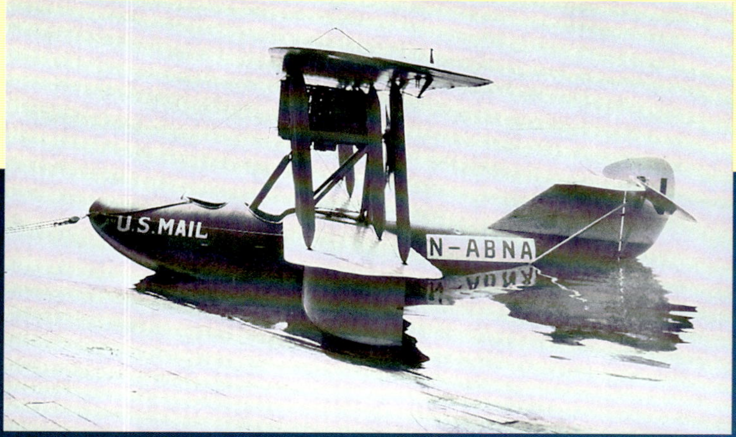

Courtesy of Museum of History & Industry, Photo by Howard Gisk Photographs

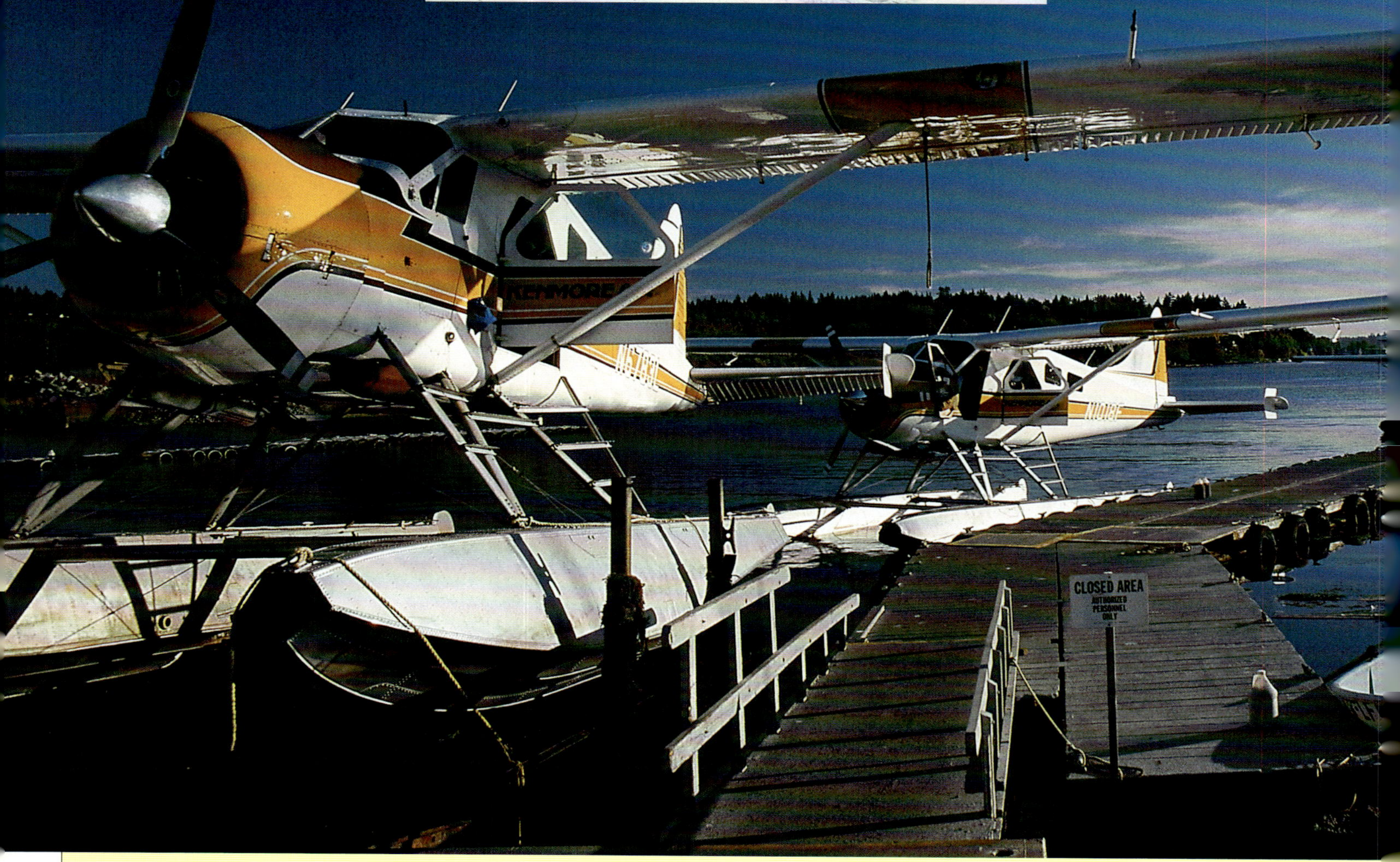

Floatplanes docked at a marina in Kenmore on Lake Washington.

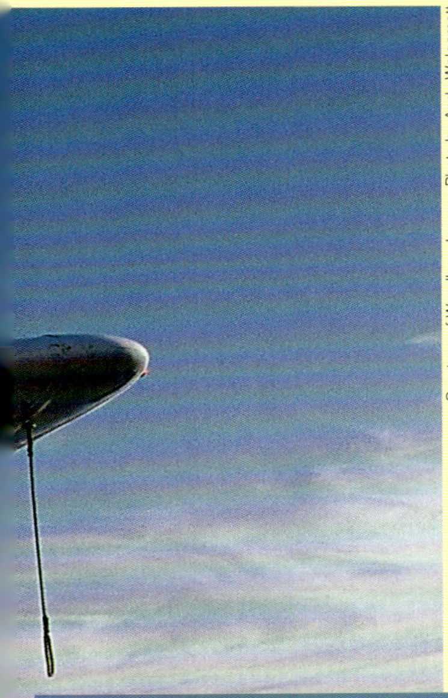

Courtesy of Wyndham Images Photo by Andy Wolgamott

Known around the world as "the birthplace of modern aviation," King County International Airport/Boeing Field offers a wide variety of aircraft services, uses, and facilities for business, government, commercial, personal, and recreational flying.

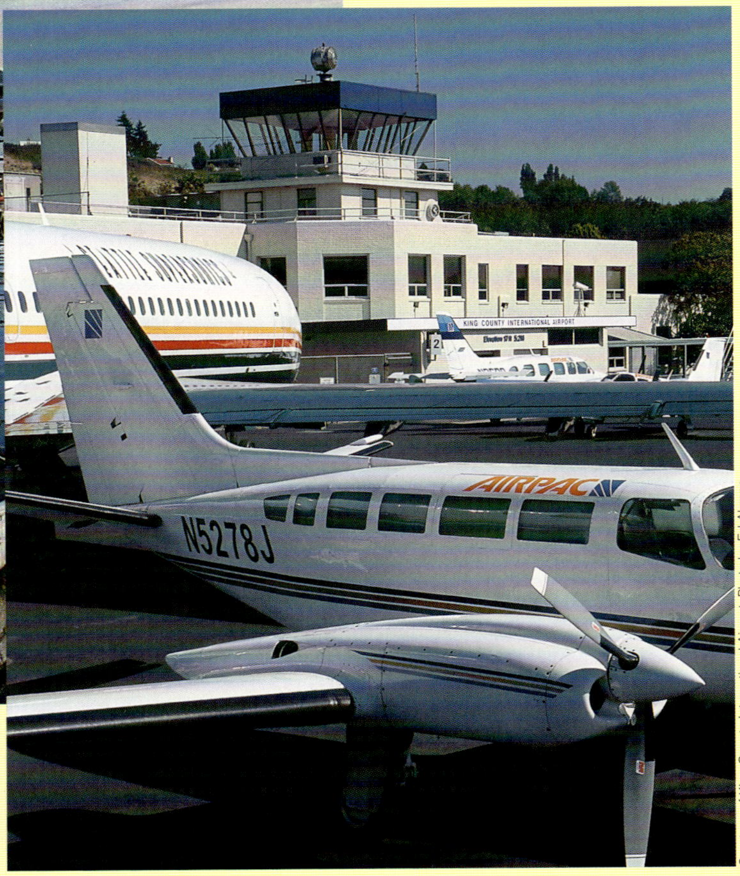

Courtesy of King County International Airport, Photo by Ed Ahrens

During a brief downturn in the peacetime years that followed the wars, shipbuilding and aerospace industries reinvented themselves to serve a mix of commercial and defense activities. In the 1960s, in perhaps the single most significant decision they would ever make, the Port of Seattle's commissioners invested in a new technology called containerization. The port did not have a single client for movement of containerized cargo when construction began on the infrastructure to support the new technology. Fortunately, the risk paid huge dividends in 1970, when six major Japanese shipping companies purchased their first container ships and began to use the Port of Seattle as their point of entry into the Pacific Northwest. Among the greatest attributes of the containerization technology is that the cargo containers are designed to work with multiple modes of transportation, stacking equally well on freight ships, train beds, and truck-and-trailer rigs. Intermodal transportation has set the global standard for moving goods on land and sea, and the Port of Seattle's intermodal transportation, distribution, and warehousing system is the largest port-owned system in the nation.

Building on the strength of its past, today the Port of Seattle is the nation's fifth largest container port and ranks twenty-fifth in the world. Served by more than 100 trucking companies, 3 railroad routes, and 27 regularly scheduled container cargo ships, the Port of Seattle sees $36 billion worth of goods move through its operation centers each year. Located equidistant from Tokyo and London, Japan and the United Kingdom are the port's top two export destinations; other major export partners include Canada, South Korea, China, Germany, Malaysia, Singapore, and Saudi Arabia. Not surprising for the region that is home to The Boeing Company, transportation equipment is far and away the leading export. Other top exports that reflect the area's rich geography and abundant resources include agricultural products, lumber and other wood products, industrial machinery and computer equipment, food, electronics and electrical equipment; and paper and related products. The region's top imports are much more diversified. Leading the list is apparel, which is often manufactured abroad for local clothing purveyors such as The Bon Marché, Nordstrom, Eddie Bauer, REI, and Brittania. Other products that are imported from chief foreign suppliers Japan, Canada, China, and Taiwan, include automobiles, high-tech equipment, aircraft motors, and forest products. As impressive as the county's trade statistics are, they do not account for the service sector production, such as software products and legal and financial services. Statewide, even the addition of software products would have increased the state's export earnings by $5 billion in 1997 alone.

An aerial view of Interstate 5 as it enters Seattle.

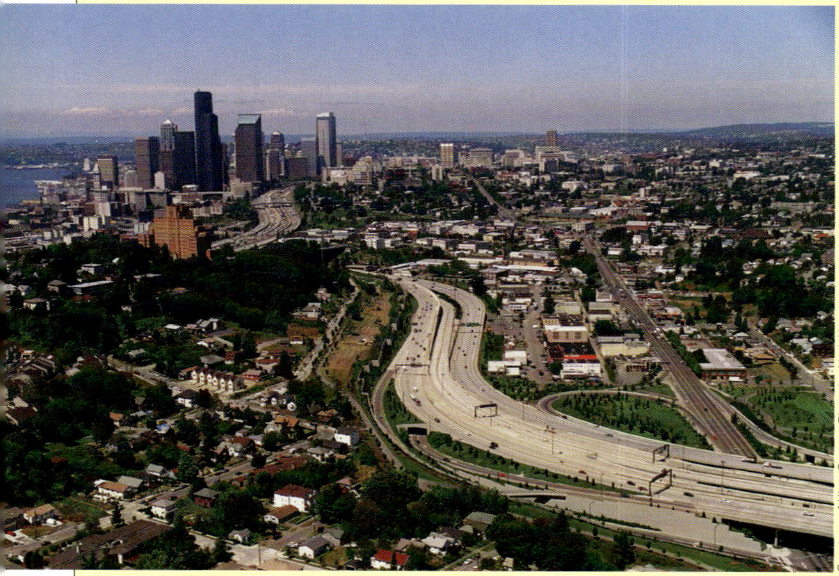

Courtesy of King County, Photo by Ned Ahrens

Seattle-Tacoma International Airport (Sea-Tac), operated by the Port of Seattle's Aviation Division, also plays a critical role in trade and transportation in King County, the state of Washington, and the Pacific Northwest. Located just 14 miles south of the port's harbor facilities, the airport is the eighteenth busiest passenger airport and the twentieth busiest cargo airport in the United States. Served by 41 airlines—including 15 international carriers and 17 cargo carriers—nearly 26 million passengers and approximately 400,000 metric tons of airfreight are flown in and out of Sea-Tac Airport each year. Just nine hours to Tokyo, Sea-Tac Airport is closer to Asia than any other airport in the continental United States. And with direct flights to major international cities in Holland, Japan, Russia, Korea, Scotland, Mexico, England, China, and Canada, Sea-Tac serves as a gateway between King County and the rest of the world. The future of the Seattle-Tacoma International Airport promises phenomenal growth; forecasts indicate that by 2006, air travel will increase as much as 75 percent, and cargo traffic is expected to see growth at a rate of 6.6 percent per year. To accommodate this growth, the airport will invest over a billion dollars in construction and operational improvements in the next decade, including completion of a new 8,500–foot third runway. Between the airport and the harbor facilities, the Port of Seattle is an international leader of sea-air cargo transport.

The King County International Airport, commonly known as Boeing Field also supports the vicinity's trade and transportation industries. After a landslide approval by King County voters in 1928, the county invested $900,000 toward land acquisition, construction, and equipment for the airport, which served both as a production facility for Boeing and as a municipal airport until December 6, 1941, when the United States Army commandeered the airport for production and strategic purposes. The airport remained under the jurisdiction of the military through the end of World War II, during which time the Boeing Company produced more than 10,000 bombers that were critical in efforts to end the war. After the end of the war, the airport resumed its role as the region's primary hub for passenger and commercial traffic until the Seattle-Tacoma International Airport was opened in 1947. Today, the King County International Airport is one of the busiest general aviation airports in the nation, serves as a major freight center for local industries, and remains the Boeing Company's headquarters for testing and delivering airplanes. To stimulate and support international trade, the airport is also home to the King County Office of Trade, Commerce, and International Affairs.

In a state where as many as one in four jobs is dependent on trade, the importance of the Port of Seattle, King County International Airport, and other local trade and transportation systems cannot be overstated. With new communications, production, and infrastructure technologies constantly emerging, King County will need to stay on the cutting edge to compete in the global marketplace. As the region continues to grow and traffic congestion worsens, the greatest challenge will again be land transportation. With more than a billion dollars worth of capital improvements planned for their waterfront facilities alone, and the ability to provide a broad range of cargo and trade services, the Port of Seattle is well positioned to meet these challenges.

Just as the Alaska-Yukon-Pacific Exposition heralded great progress at the beginning of the century, the 1999 World Trade Organization (WTO) Ministerial Conference extended the promise of continued leadership and prosperity into the twenty-first century. The largest trade event ever held in the United States, the 1999 WTO Ministerial Conference joined President Clinton with other leaders and delegates from around the globe to discuss the future of international trade. Though the gathering was not without controversy, it cemented King County's legacy as one of the most influential and important partners in global commerce.

A cargo ship loads at the Port of Seattle.

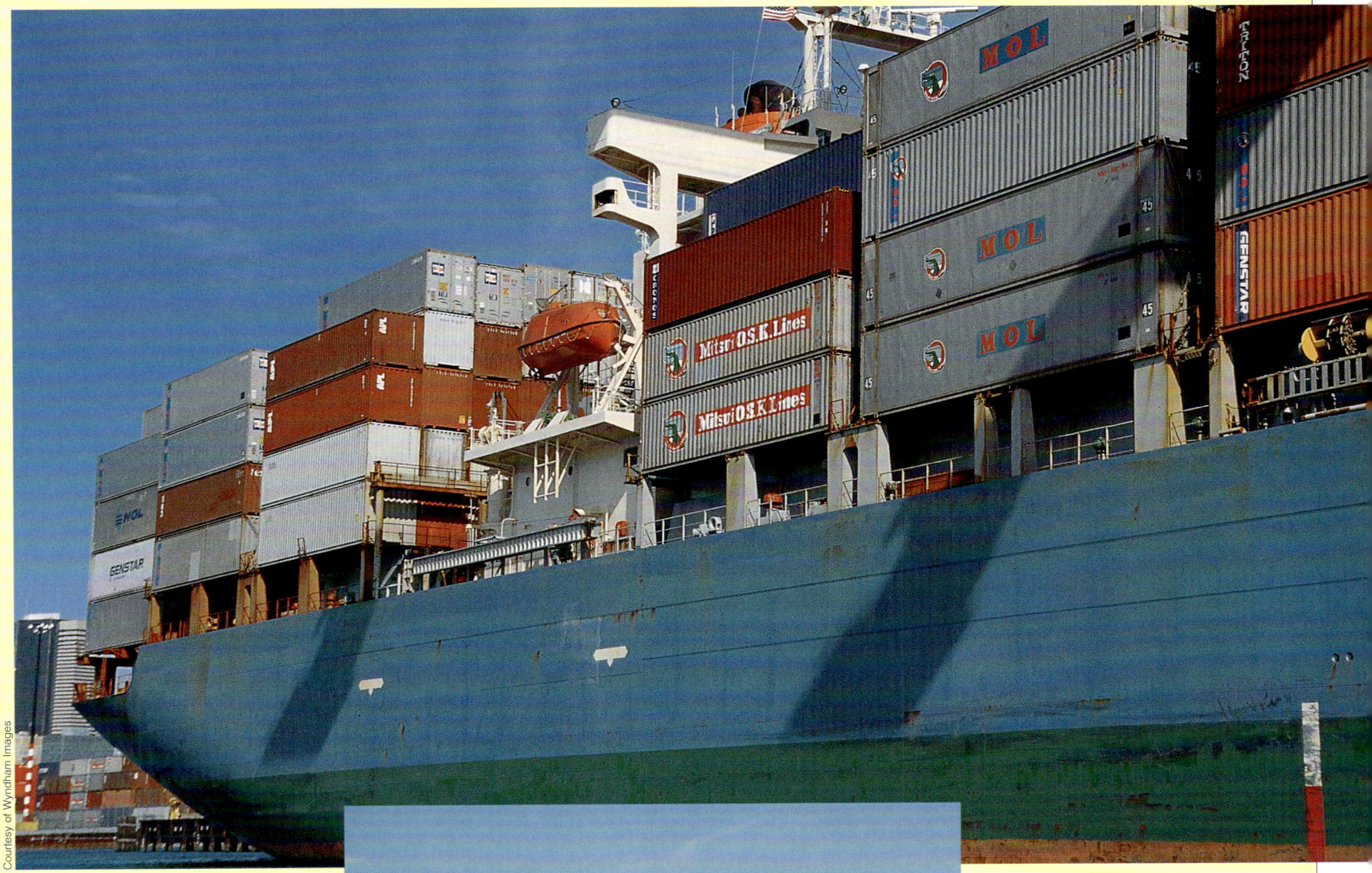

Courtesy of Wyndham Images

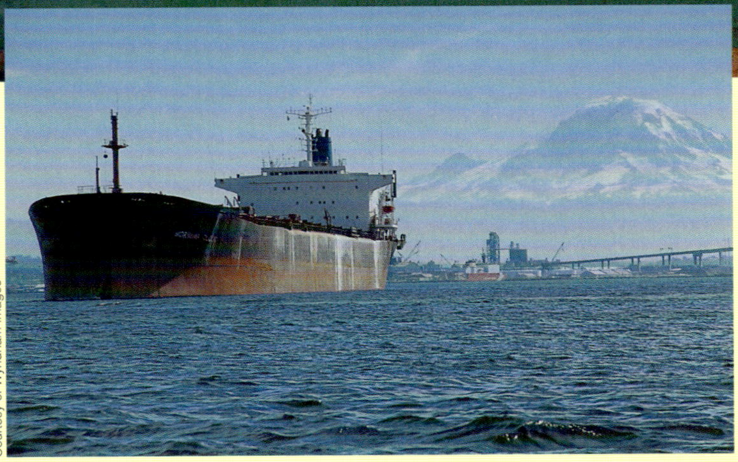

Courtesy of Wyndham Images

A cargo ship gets underway in Elliott Bay. Mount Rainier is in the background.

Courtesy of Museum of History & Industry, Photo by Anders B. Wilse

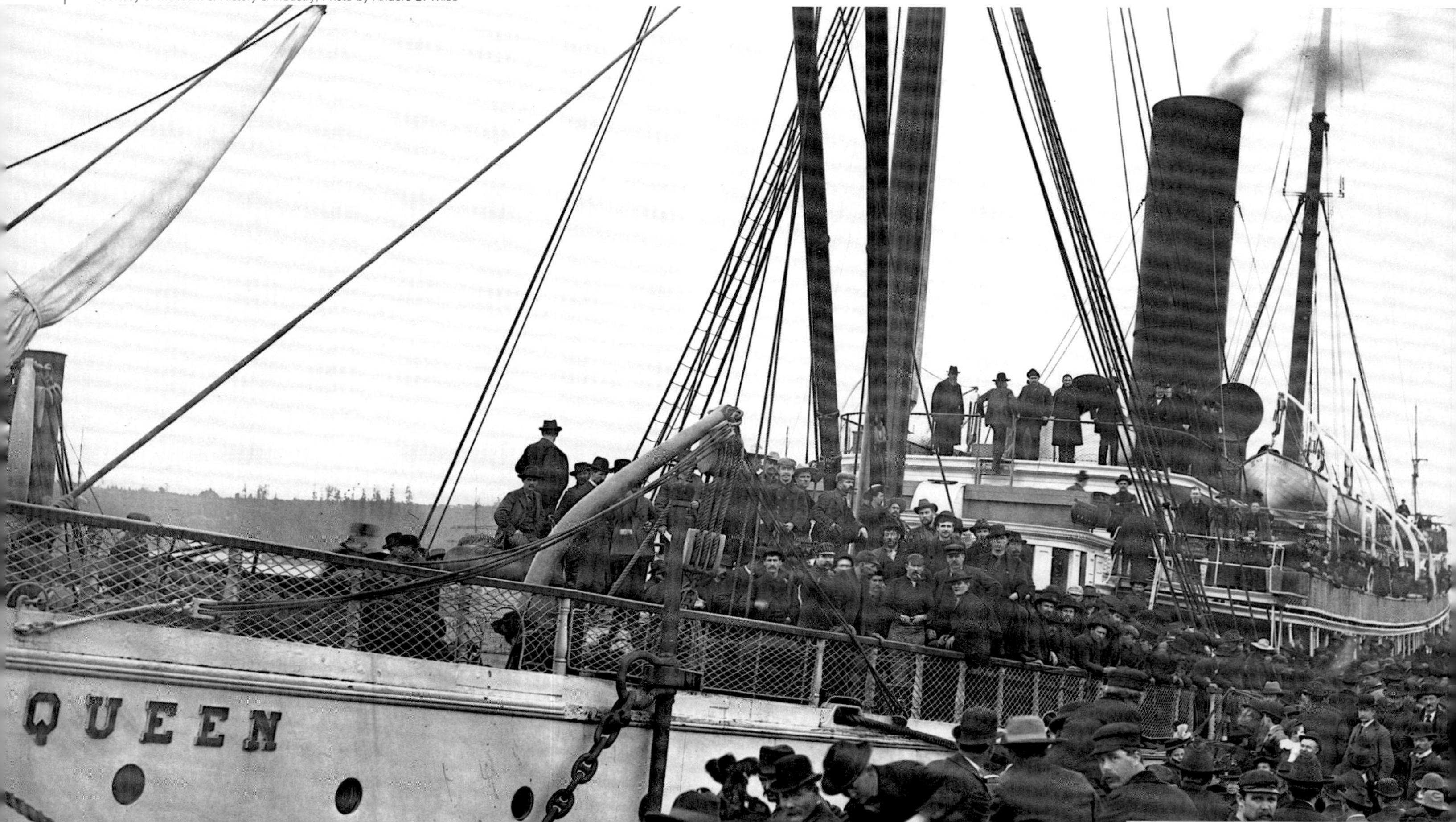

During the spring and summer of 1898, the steamer Queen, *was very busy carrying people between Seattle and southeastern Alaska. The ship passage was only the first part of the long voyage to the Klondike gold fields.*

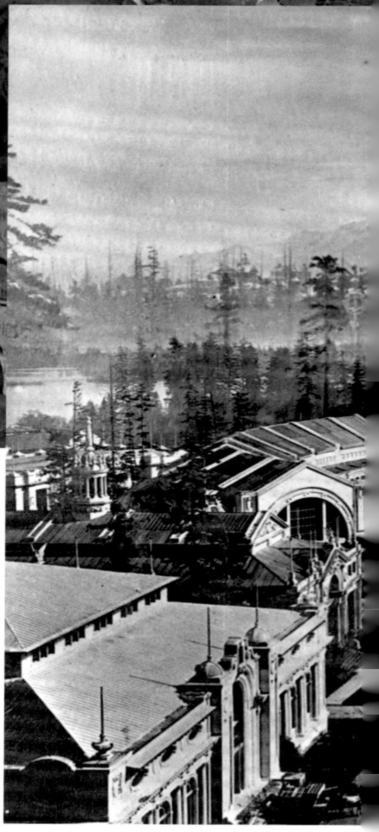

Klondike Fever

One of King County's most defining moments occurred on July 17, 1897, when the steamship Portland *arrived in Seattle carrying over two tons of gold that had been discovered in the Yukon territory. Even before the ship arrived, word had begun to spread, and by 9 o'clock the next morning, the rush was on!*

Before the cries of "Gold!" rang out through Seattle's streets, the region and the rest of the country had been suffering from a depressed economy. Soon after the Portland *docked in Seattle, however, people showed up in droves with visions of striking it rich. Thanks to a stipulation set by the Royal Canadian Mounted Police requiring every passenger to bring a year's worth of provisions, Seattle-area merchants were soon inundated with business. Hotels that had previously been empty and in danger of closing were soon bursting at their seams with travelers stopping by along their path to the Klondike. An economic boom erupted unlike any that local residents had experienced before, and in just a few short years the area grew dramatically. In just one year—from June 1898 to June 1899—more than $6.5 million worth of gold was handled by Seattle's assay office. It has been estimated that area merchants and outfitters did more than $10 million worth of business in that same year. Perhaps most importantly, however, the Klondike Gold Rush helped to establish Seattle and King County's relationships with both Canada and Alaska, setting the stage for the prominence in international trade that the region enjoys to this day.*

The Alaska-Yukon-Pacific Exposition ran through the summer of 1909 on the campus of the University of Washington. This photo of the fairgrounds shows the view along Rainier Vista towards Mount Rainier. Rainier Vista and the fountain, now called Drumheller Fountain, are still part of the campus scene.

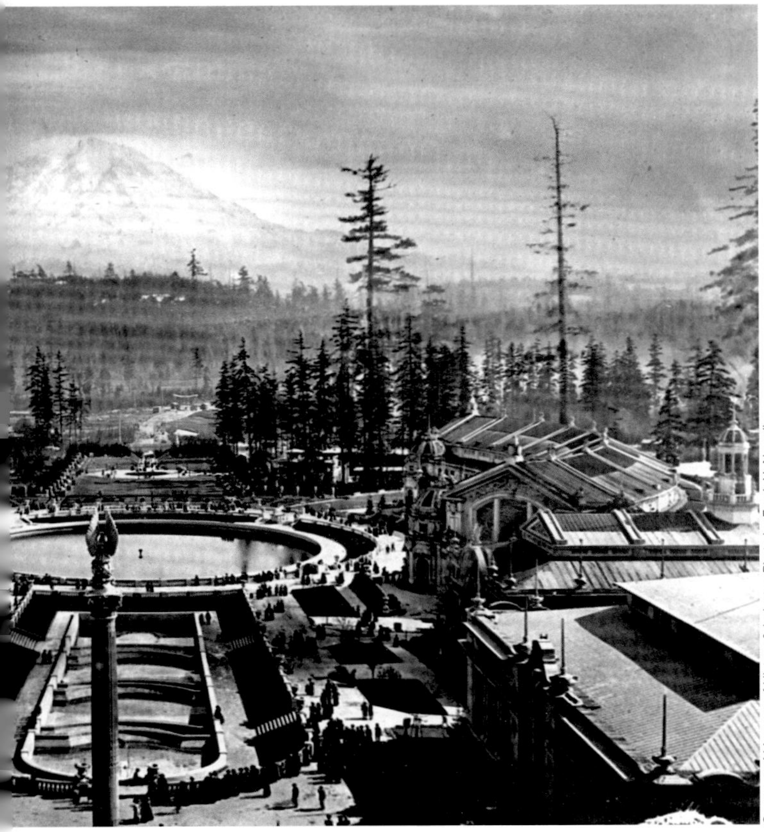

Courtesy of Museum of History & Industry. Photo by Frank H. Nowell

The Bounty of the Land and Sea

King County's first settlers were drawn to this region by the abundance of natural resources that were available from the land and waters. Thanks to the region's mild climate, rich soils, and numerous fish-bearing bodies of water, industries such as fishing, agribusiness, timber, and mining have always been important to King County's economic prosperity.

Fishing

Much of Washington State's thriving fishing industry is centered in Seattle. Fisherman's Terminal in Seattle's Ballard district serves as a central facility for commercial workboats and is the homeport for the United States' North Pacific fishing fleet. Owned and operated by the Port of Seattle, Fisherman's Terminal offers moorage and support services to as many as 700 sea vessels. The Maritime Industrial Center, which is located nearby, provides additional moorage, storage, and maintenance and repair facilities for fishing and other commercial and recreational vessels.

Fisherman's Terminal and other local marinas serve as the business centers for many of the largest fishing companies both in the United States and in foreign nations. The sea bounties that are harvested by these companies represent half of the world's seafood, which is preserved and packaged for global distribution. Fish that are most commonly caught for processing include salmon, crab, and bottom fish. Frozen fish that are exported from Seattle rank in the top twenty of all local exports to other countries and account for more than $200 million worth and nearly 62,000 metric tons worth of exported goods.

Recreational fishing is also important to the economic vitality of this region's fishing industry. The Northwest Marine Trade Association estimates that recreational fishing represents an annual boost of as much as $98 million and thousands of jobs to Washington's economy. Similar research that was conducted by Southwick and Company concluded that in 1991 all sport fishing in the state of Washington had a total economic impact of $1.4 billion.

Courtesy of Wyndham Images

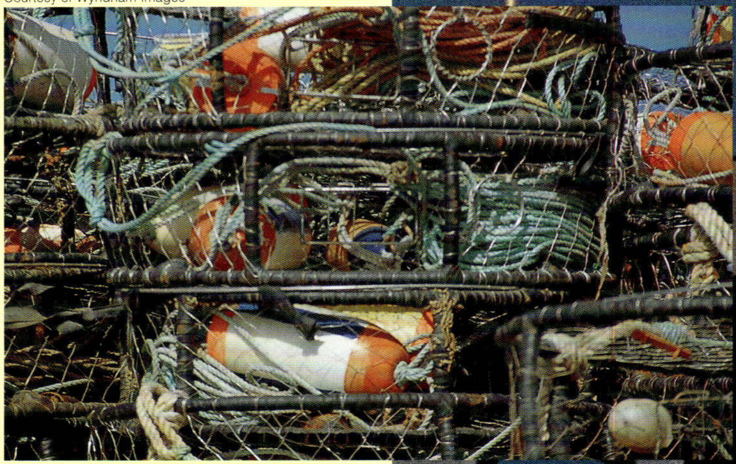

Crab pots are stacked and waiting at Fisherman's Terminal.

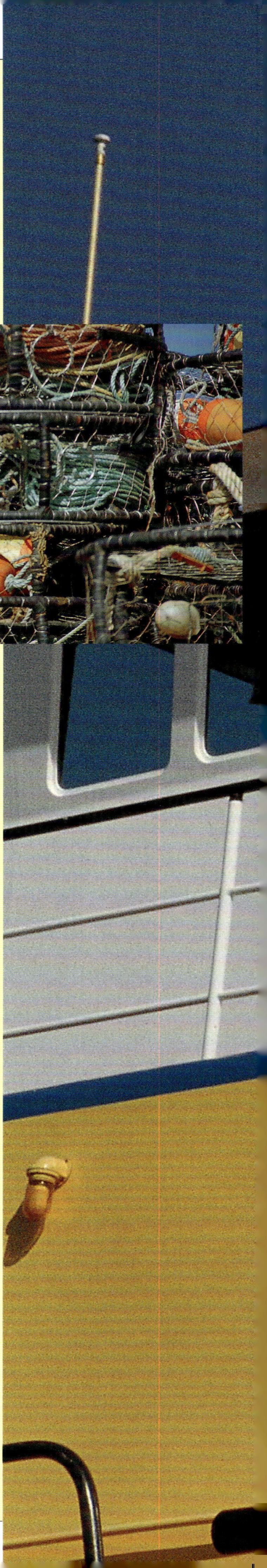

Fisherman's Terminal is the homeport for the United States' North Pacific fishing fleet.

Courtesy of Wyndham Images

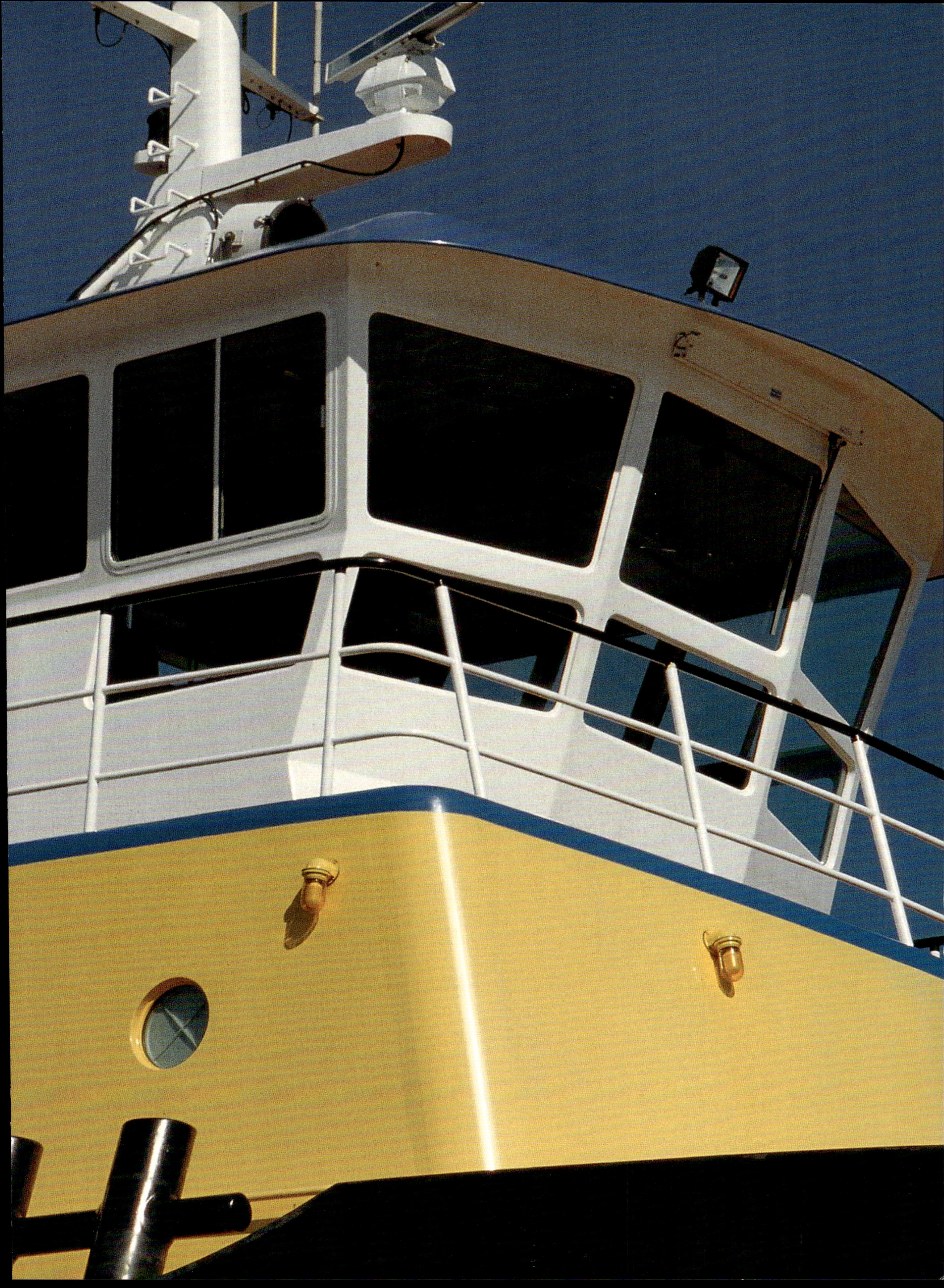

King County ranks third in the state for pumpkin acreage.

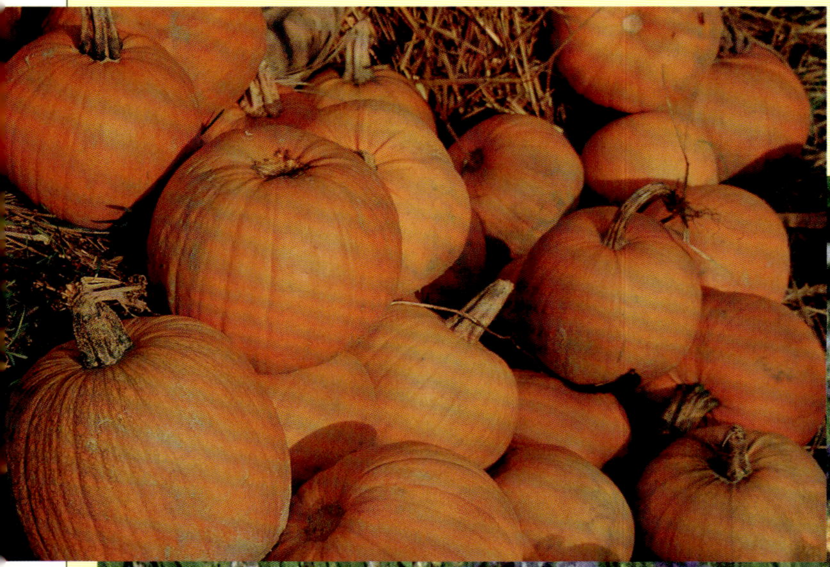

Courtesy of Wyndham Images

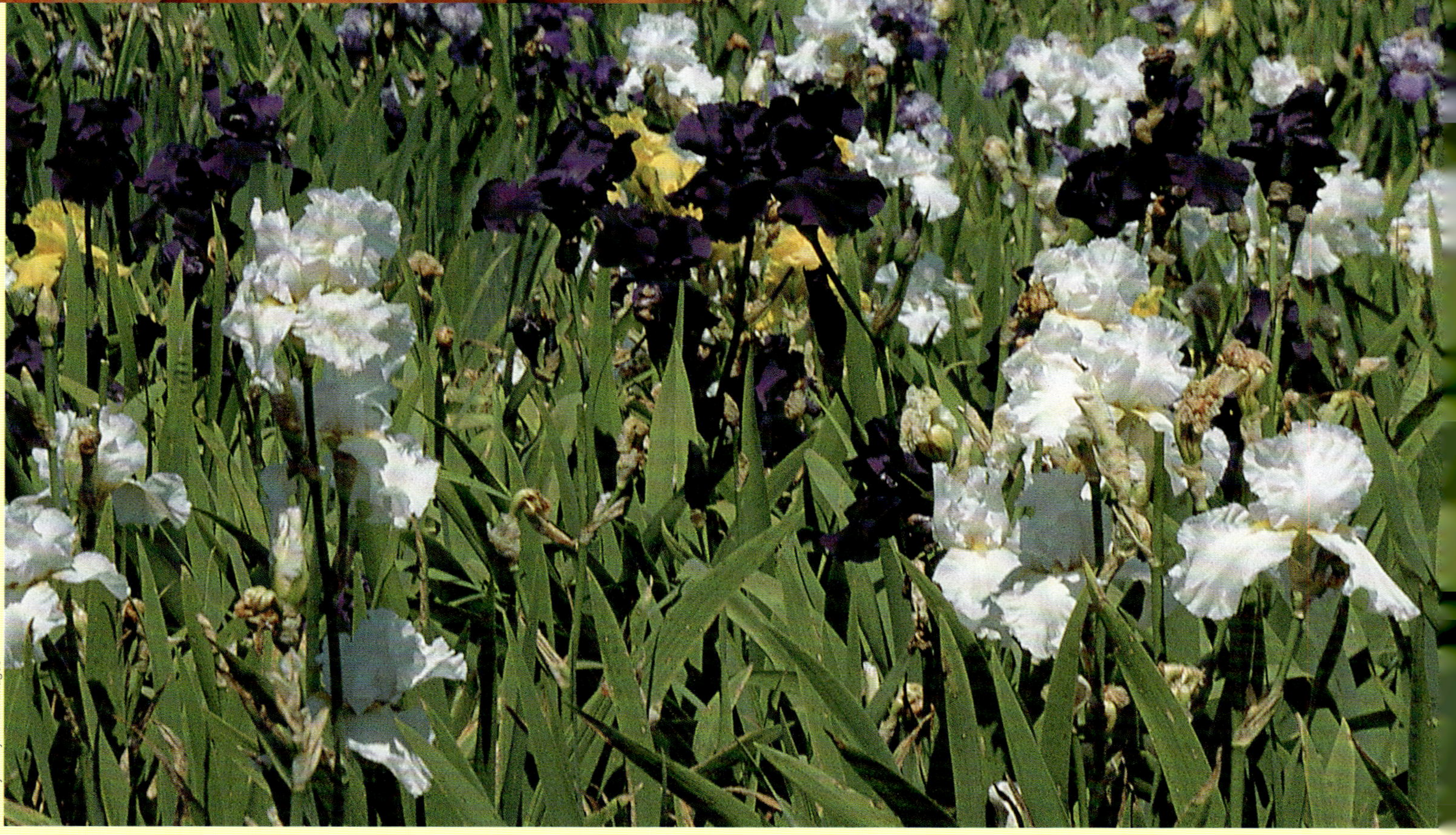

Courtesy of Wyndham Images

Despite fishing's strong cultural, recreational, and economic importance to King County and the Pacific Northwest, the industry is currently facing a number of environmental and operational challenges. In 1999, the Puget Sound Chinook salmon—a Pacific Northwest icon and spiritual symbol for Native tribes—was listed as "endangered" under the Endangered Species Act, and the Bull Trout was listed as "threatened." Both of these listings served as strong reminders about the need to protect fish habitat and recover salmon and trout stocks. In response to these listings, commercial fishers implemented changes and restrictions to assist in the recovery effort, and local governments collaborated on a variety of efforts to save the fish.

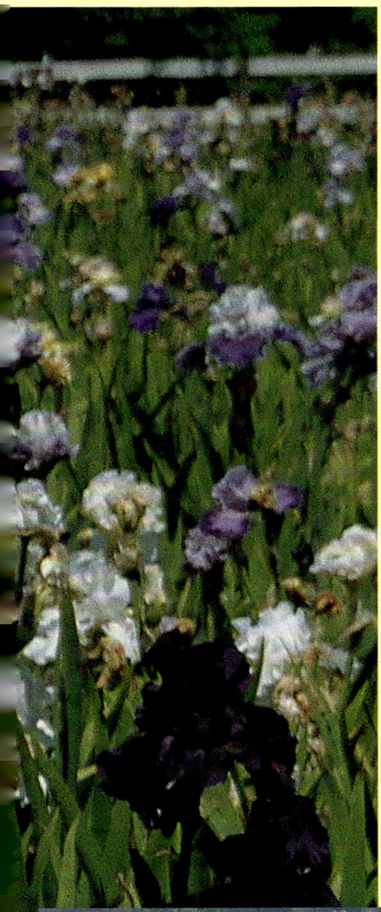

Much of King County's farm acreage is devoted to the flower industry, like this iris farm in Maltby. King County ranks second in the state in the cut-flower industry.

Farming

At one time, farmland represented nearly 80 percent of all the land in King County. Today, farmland accounts for just three percent of the county's land, and many farmers are struggling to survive. Still, there are over a thousand farms operating in King County—and roughly 25 of those were established before 1900.

The largest and most prosperous farming operations in the county are dairy farms. The town of Carnation, in northeast King County, is home to both the Vitamilk Dairy and the Carnation Dairy Farm. The Carnation Dairy Farm, which was once a family-owned operation, was acquired by Nestle's in 1985, in one of the largest food industry takeovers of the 1900s. To preserve the history of dairy farming in this region and to provide visitors an inside look at current-day dairy operations, the Nestle's Carnation Dairy Farm offers daily guided tours and the Nestle Museum.

Founded in 1937, the neighboring Vitamilk Dairy began as a shoestring operation that was inspired by ingenuity born of necessity during the Great Depression. Edwin Teel, the founder of Vitamilk Dairy Products (which includes Vitarich ice cream), possessed great resourcefulness, a commitment to quality, and a vision to improve and expand his operation. Today, the Vitamilk Dairy is one of the best dairies in the nation, serving as the "Quality Check'd Dairy" for Washington State—an honor that indicates Vitamilk's commitment to improving and maintaining higher standards for milk processing than those required by the United States government. These and other smaller dairy farms that operate throughout King County produce over 35 million gallons of milk each year, with the average farm annually producing enough milk to feed 30,000 people.

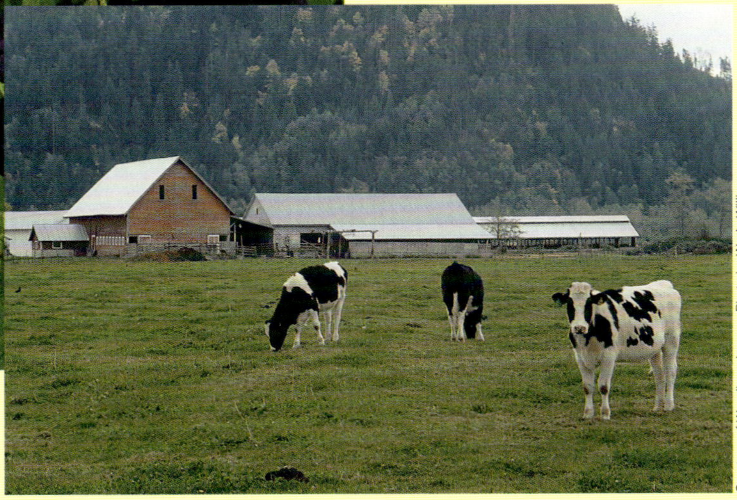

Courtesy of Wyndham Images Photo by Wade Williams

Farmland accounts for three percent of the total acreage in King County today.

Twenty-five percent of the approximately 1,000 farms in King County were established before 1900.

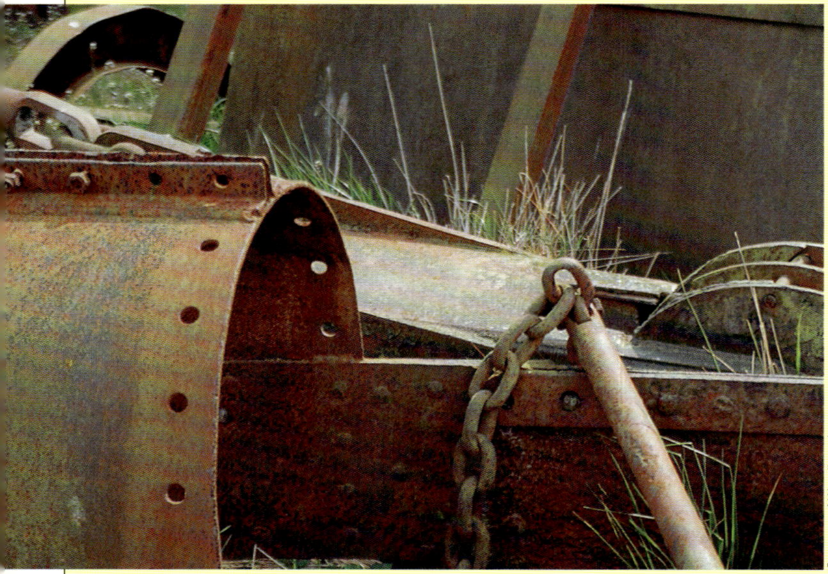

Most of King County's 42,000 acres of farmland produces fruits, vegetables, herbs, and other crops. One of the largest vegetable farms in the region is Carpinito Brothers Farm in Kent. The farm, which began in the late 1960s as a small roadside pumpkin patch, now produces lettuce, corn, cabbage, kale, spinach, greens, and over 1,000 tons of pumpkins. Many other local farms grow similar crops because these are best suited for the climate. Boasting lettuce and celery production in excess of a million cases per year, King County ranks third in the state for production of these vegetables. So many King County farms grow pumpkins that the county ranks third in the state for pumpkin acreage. Other popular crops include radishes, rhubarb, and raspberries. Many of King County's farms are family operations that sell their produce and other goods on site and offer their customers an option to pick their own fruits or vegetables. One of the most popular of these family operations is Remlinger Farms in Carnation.

Began in 1953 as a strawberry farm for the wholesale market, today Remlinger Farms grows a variety of fruits and vegetables for "u-pick" and direct farm sales. The large farm store, which sells seasonal fruits and vegetables—including strawberries, raspberries, blueberries, rhubarb, corn, cucumbers, and pumpkins—also offers other edible delicacies such as seasoned pistachios, specialty olives, and individually quick-frozen fruits. In addition to the farm store, Remlinger Farms features down-on-the-farm fun activities to delight visitors of all ages—from pony trail rides and an authentic steam train to an animal petting barn and a covered hay maze. The crisp cool airs of autumn draw thousands of youngsters who want to witness the top ten giant pumpkins or pick their own perfect carving gourd. During the winter months, Remlinger Farms welcomes visitors to the Christmas Tree Forest. Whatever the season, there is always something to celebrate at Remlinger Family Farms.

While most farmers grow fruits, vegetables, and other edible delicacies, others opt to raise cattle, sheep, alpacas, horses, or even flowers. King County ranks second in the state for cut-flower production. Aptly named Dazzling Dahlias in Auburn is just one of many of the region's flower farms to offer "u-pick" flowers, farm tours, and growing demonstrations. Many people are drawn to the farms by the glorious colors and subtle fragrance of the flowers; others, who have seen the full splendor of the blooming beauty, return year after year as a tradition to mark the seasons. Surprisingly, there are more horses in King County than in any other county in the state of Washington. Some local horse farms and ranches breed, raise, and sell horses, while others organize trail rides, teach riding lessons, or provide boarding and care for other people's horses. The Red Gate Farm and the Witch Creek Farm, both in southeast King County, are model farms that teach environmental sensitivity through demonstrations and farm tours.

Although most of the vineyards are located 200 miles away in Eastern Washington, wineries have emerged as a key agribusiness industry in King County. With nearly a dozen wineries scattered around the county, there are ample opportunities for wine lovers to sample their favorite wine varieties—from Chardonnay to Merlot and everything in between. Chateau Ste. Michelle, Washington's oldest winery, is located in the northeast King County community of Woodinville. Chateau Ste. Michelle is known around the world for its classic European varietal wines and is a clear favorite among locals, who visit the winery for tasting, tours, or summer concerts and outings on the sprawling, lush grounds of the property. Columbia Winery is just across the street from Chateau Ste. Michelle, and Paul Thomas Winery, which is operated by Columbia, is located nearby, making Woodinville the most popular destination in King County for wine aficionados.

The grapes for Chateau Ste. Michelle's acclaimed wines are grown in Eastern Washington.

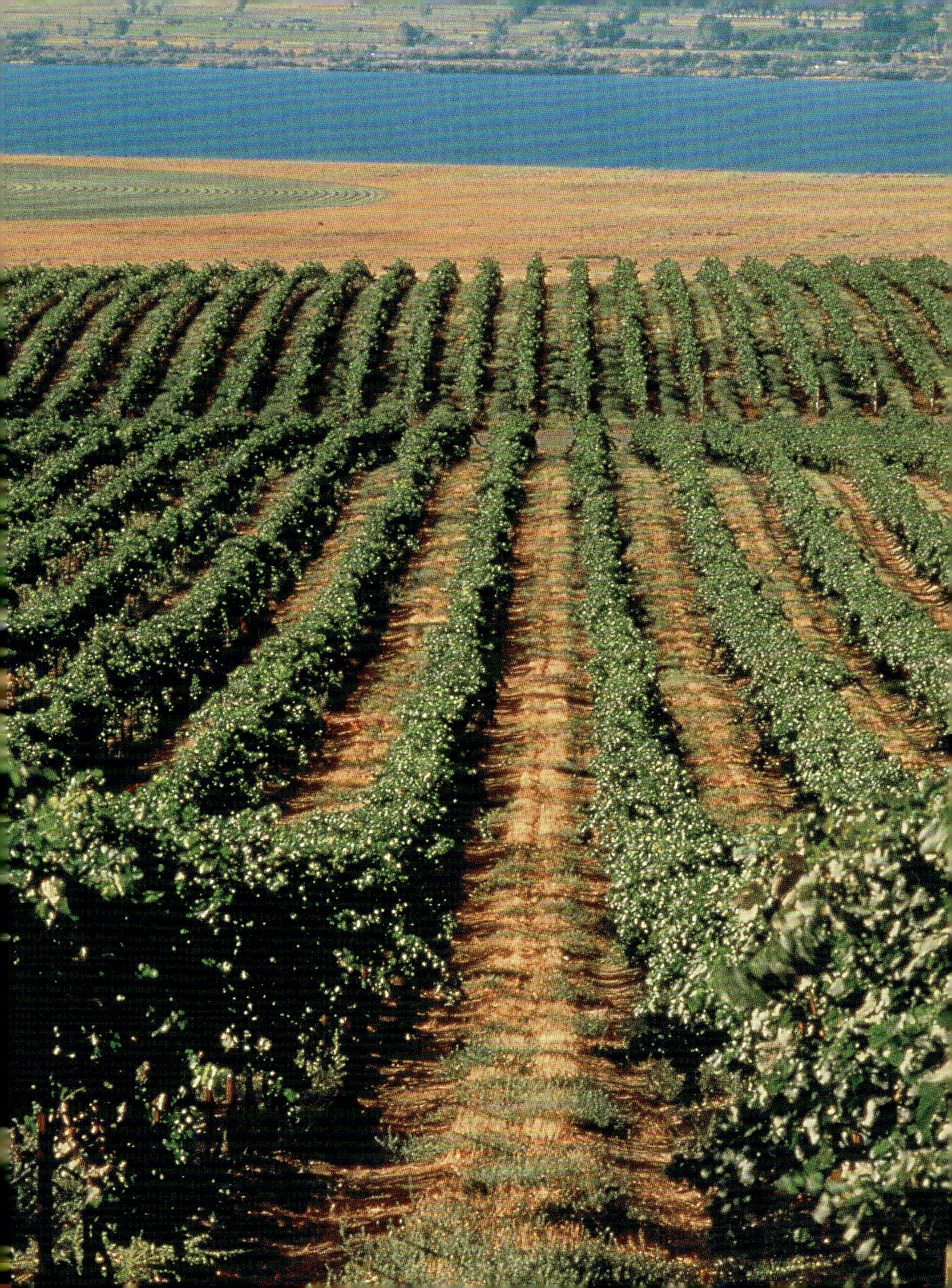

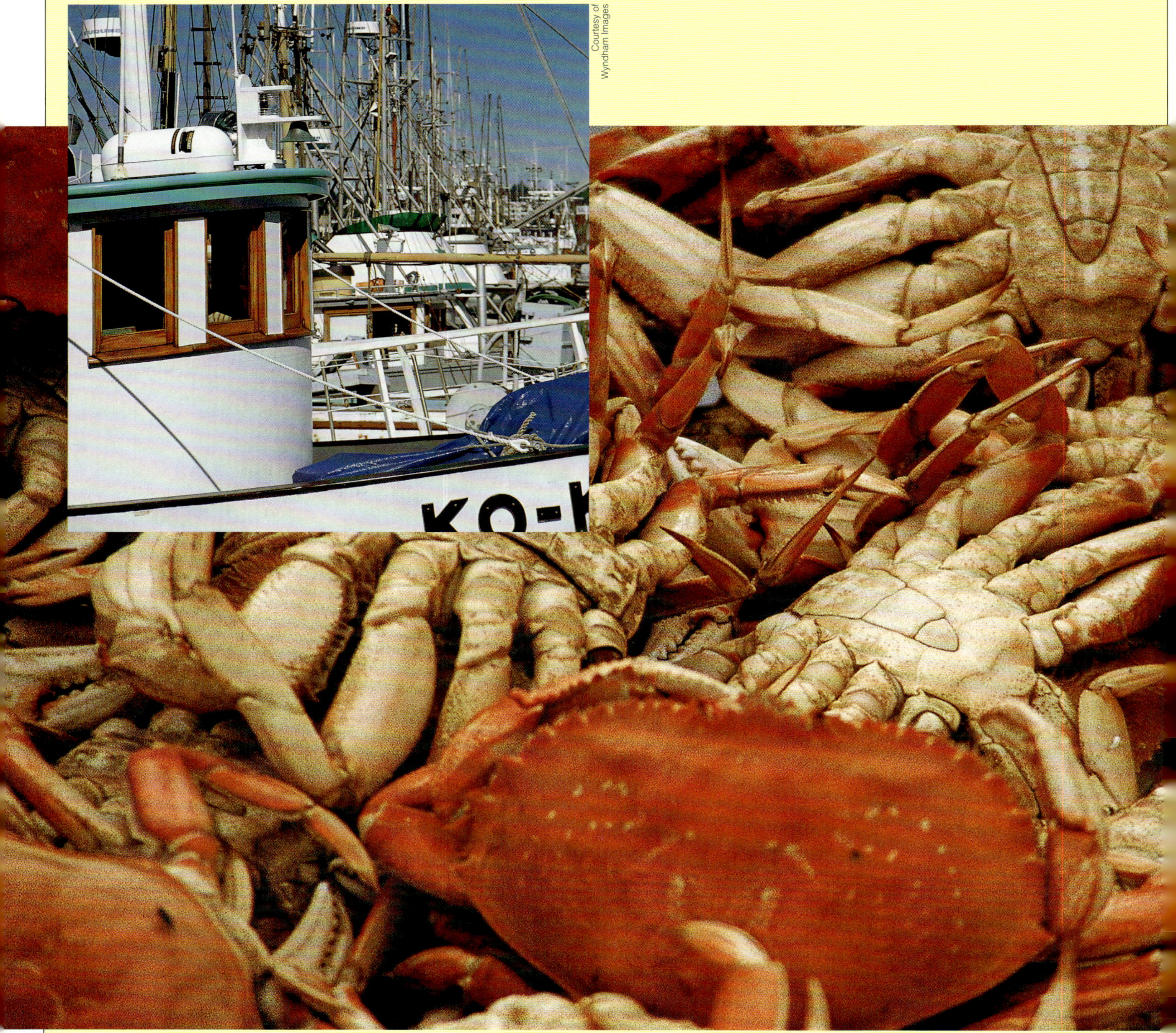

Courtesy of Wyndham Images

The sea bounties harvested by the fishing companies that are served by Fisherman's Terminal and other local marinas as business centers represent approximately half of the world's seafood that is preserved and packaged for global distribution.

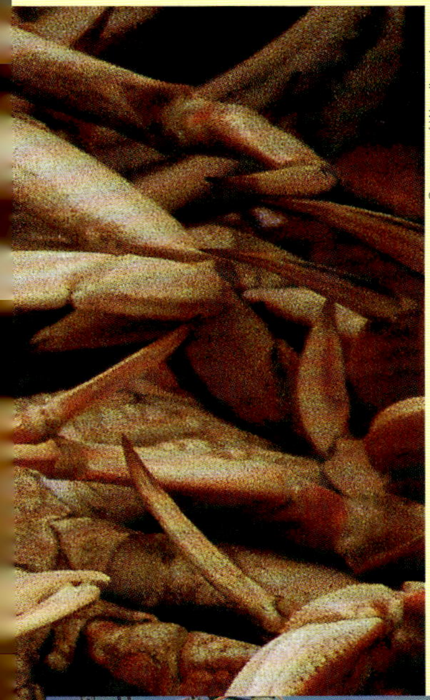

Courtesy of Wyndham Images

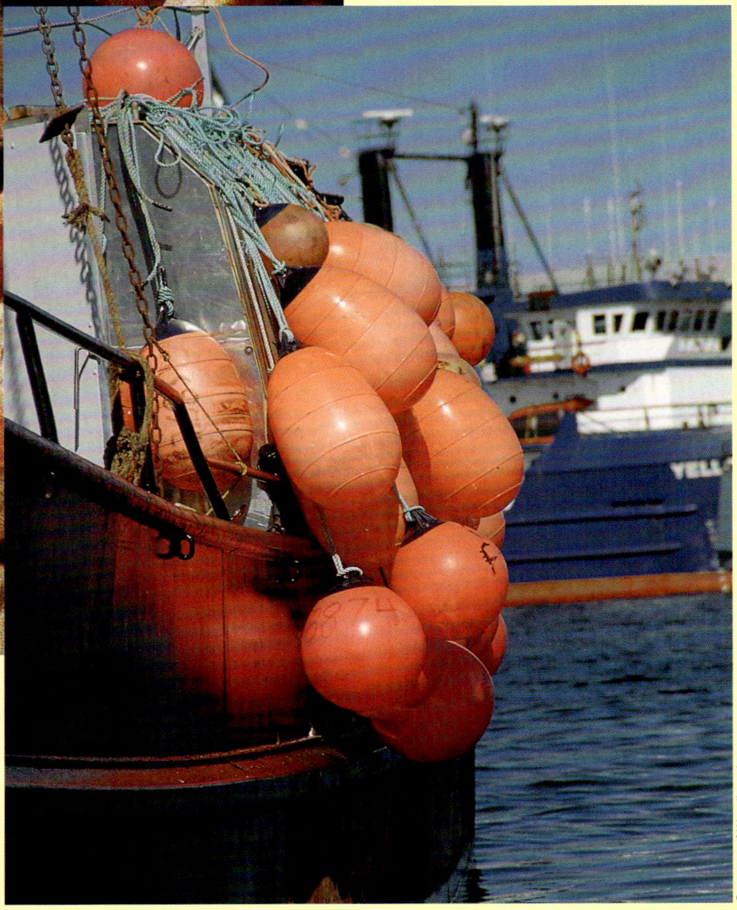

Courtesy of Wyndham Images

King County's increasing growth and prosperity have created serious challenges for the future of farming in this region. In fact, as of 1999, the Puget Sound region was identified as the fifth most threatened farming region in the country. To respond to these increasing challenges, local farmers have been working with government officials for over 20 years to protect the county's remaining farmlands. After suffering a 75 percent decrease in farmland between 1945 and 1994, the amount of farmland has stabilized. The Farmland Preservation program, which was established in 1979, was the first voter-approved measure in the nation to protect farmland in a metropolitan area. Since 1979, the Farmland Preservation program has preserved over 12,800 acres of King County's richest agricultural lands for use as farms and open spaces. These properties are now used as dairies, nurseries, tree farms, and animal farms.

Another government-private effort to support local farming is Puget Sound Fresh, a marketing campaign aimed at promoting locally grown produce in supermarkets and restaurants. It is hoped that the public and private partnerships that were formed to respond to the challenges facing the fishing and farming industries will help them to survive and thrive in the future.

Timber and Mining

Many of the white settlers were drawn to this region in the mid 1800s not by fishing or farming opportunities, but with visions of wealth created though mining or timber, and many succeeded. In fact, the very evolution of the Pacific Northwest's economic prosperity and rugged identity owe much to these industries. Over time, however, environmental impacts have dramatically altered these enterprises. Coal, which was once widely used by homes and businesses as a primary energy source, has been replaced by more environmentally friendly energy alternatives, such as clean-burning natural gas or hydroelectric power. Once one of the area's top exports and a leading source of employment, today coal mining has become virtually obsolete in King County.

In the early days of forestry, little thought was given to how the "harvesting" of trees would impact the rest of the environment, and timber business leaders judged their success more on production and dollars earned than on any other concern. After some painful results over the years, that has all changed now. Today's timber businesses are leaders in environmental forestry, and they judge success not just by profit, but by environmental sustainability.

Two national leaders in timber harvest and forestry practice are based in King County. Weyerhaeuser, the first and still the largest timber company in the state of Washington, has a history in this region dating back to January 3, 1900. Today, the people behind Weyerhaeuser are as proud of the company's environmental stewardship as they are of their product lines.

Plum Creek Timber Company, which has its headquarters in Seattle, merged in July 2000 with the Georgia-Pacific Corporation's The Timber Company. As a result, Plum Creek now owns and manages 7.9 million acres of timberland across the United States, making the corporation the second largest private owner of timberland in the nation. Plum Creek Timber Company is also well established as a leader in environmental forestry.

Thanks to the leadership of these forestry companies, heightened public awareness, and environmental protection policies and initiatives, much is being done to ensure that timber and other environmentally-dependent industries include land management, habitat protection, and species protection measures. As the people of King County have seen with declining salmon runs, endangered species listings, and the loss of ancient forestlands, such measures are long overdue and greatly needed.

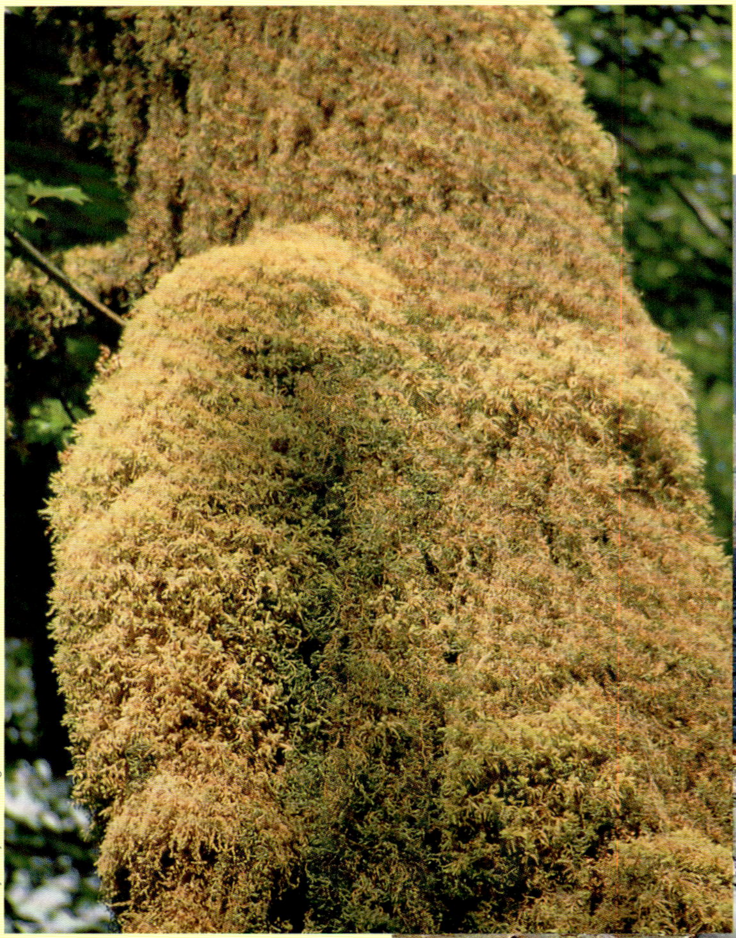
Courtesy of Wyndham Images

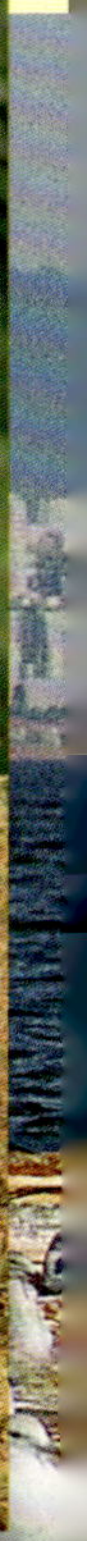

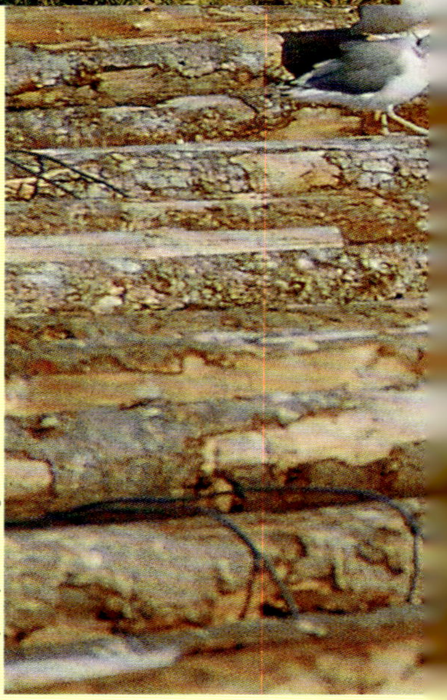
Courtesy of Wyndham Images

Weyerhaeuser and Plum Creek Timber Company, two national leaders in forest products, are based in King County. Both companies are also leaders in environmental stewardship of the timberlands they control.

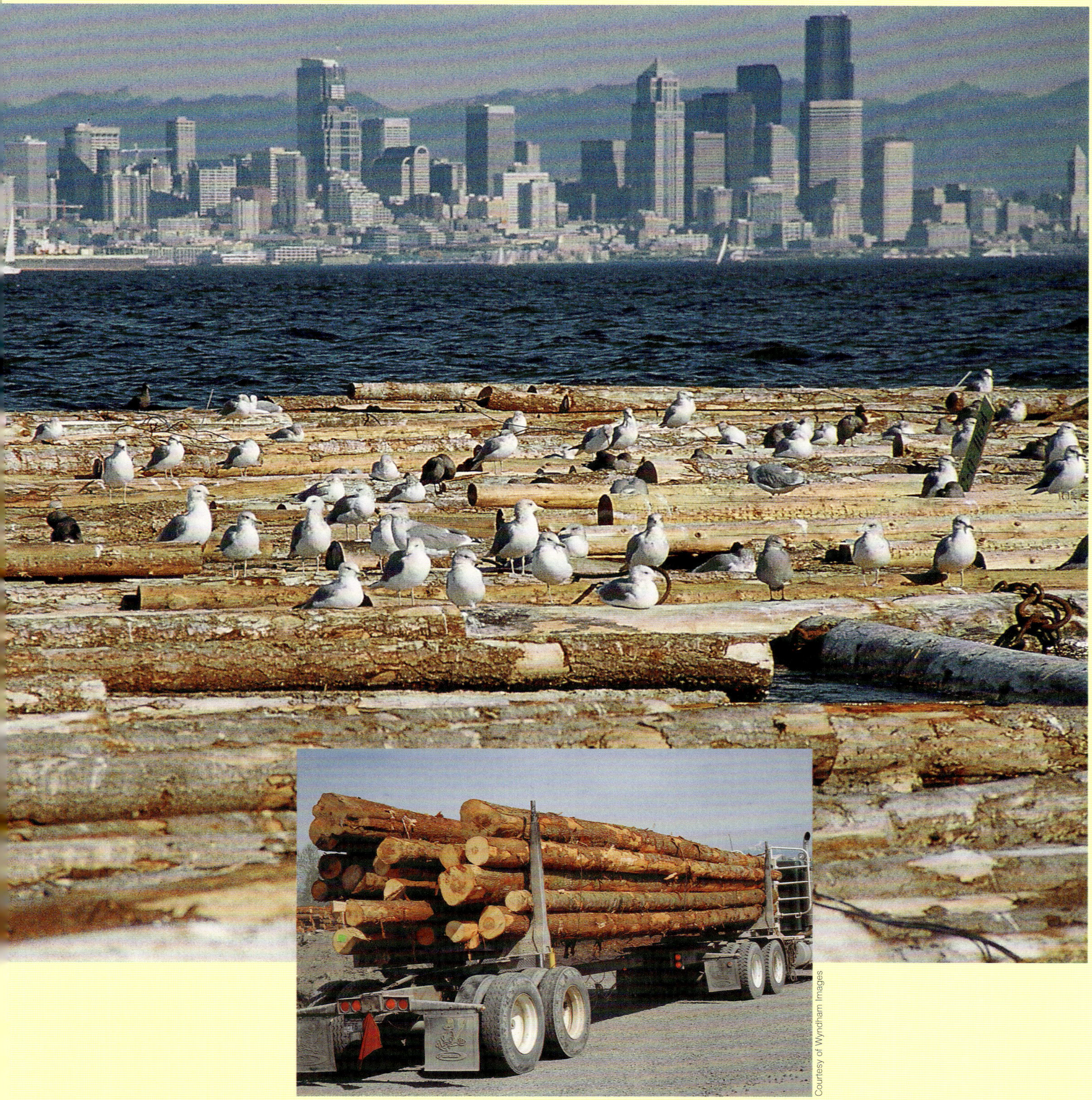

Courtesy of Wyndham Images

Mind and Body

Colleges and Universities

King County is well-known for its knowledge-based economy, and the plethora of top-notch colleges and universities only serve to prove this. Three of the state's largest universities are located in King County, with eight more colleges and universities calling our county home.

The largest university both in the state and in the county is of course the University of Washington. The University of Washington, known to locals as the "U Dub", occupies 703 acres in north-central Seattle. The University of Washington is home to more than 35,000 students, and boasts a faculty of more than 3,500.

The University, which was founded in 1861 as one of the area's first schools, today offers some of the finest academic programs in the nation. Undergraduate degrees are offered in a number of majors ranging from Engineering to Ethnic Studies, and graduate and Doctoral programs are among the most highly-respected in the country.

The University is probably best known for its research. Research is conducted in a variety of areas, including health sciences, engineering, aerospace, forestry, and marine sciences. In 1997 alone, the University of Washington received over $557 million in research grants, and since 1974 has been the leading recipient of federal research and training funds. Research funding supports more than 5,200 campus jobs.

City University is the third largest institute of higher learning and the largest private university in Washington state. City University, located in Bellevue, targets working professionals who wish to earn a bachelor's or master's degree while continuing to work. The University has been a mainstay in the area for more than 20 years, and boasts a student population of nearly 13,000 adults. The University offers more than 50 undergraduate and graduate programs in areas such as business administration, counseling, teacher preparation, and social sciences.

Courtesy of Wyndham Images

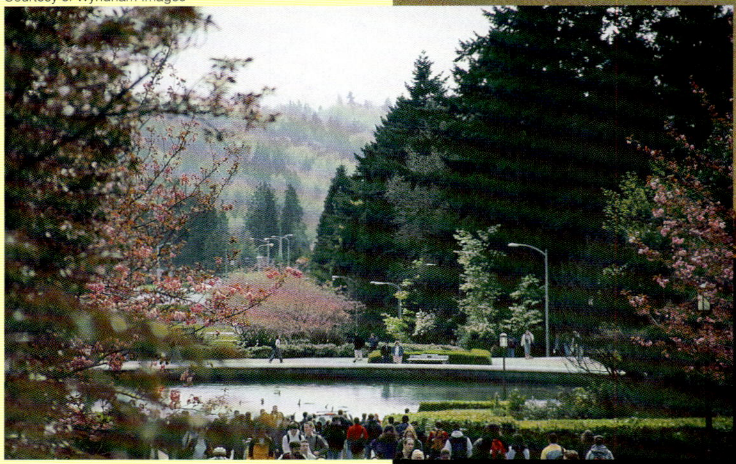

The grounds of the University of Washington are lushly landscaped.

Husky Stadium is silhouetted in the last rays of the afternoon sun.

Courtesy of Wyndham Images

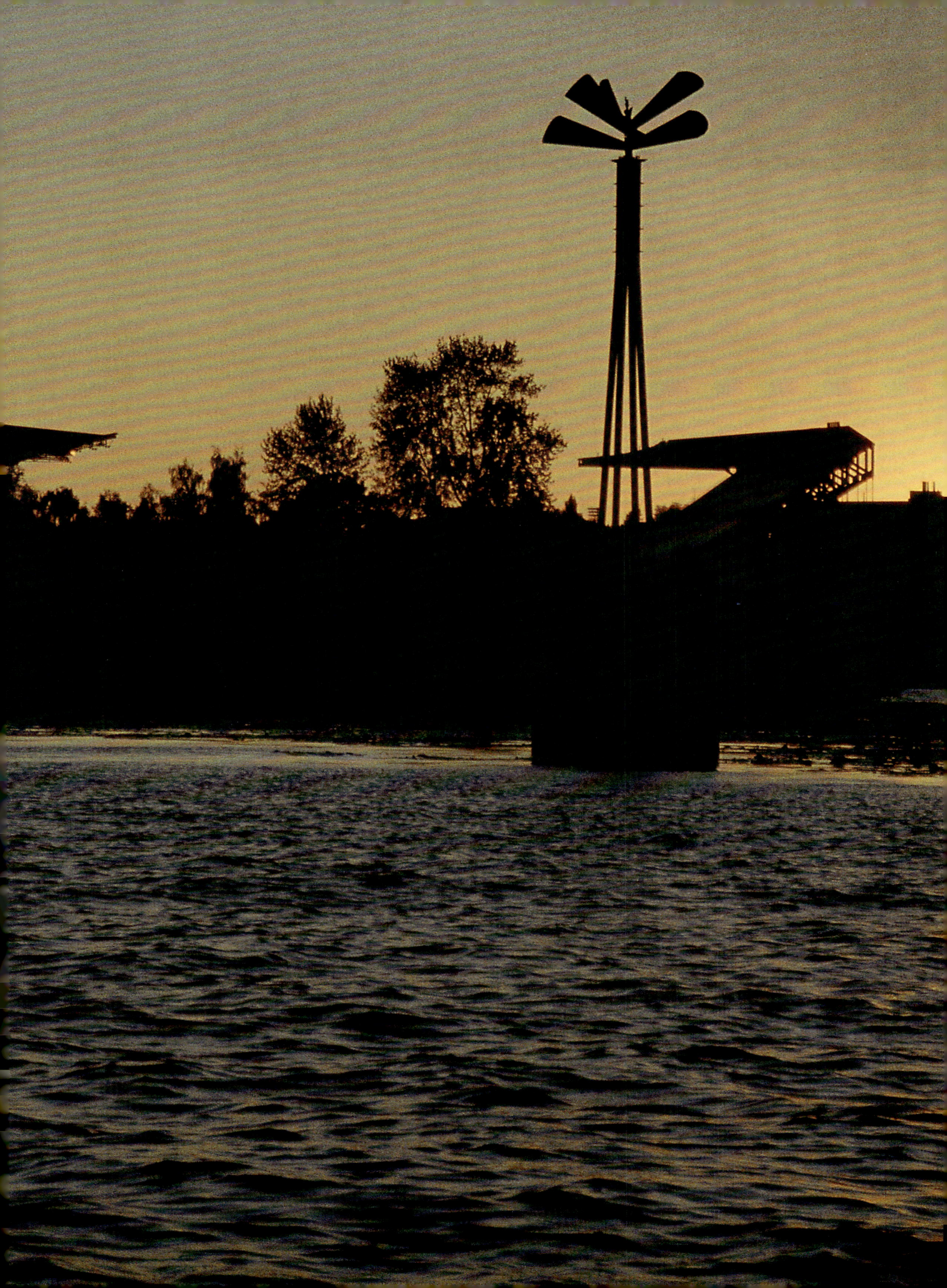

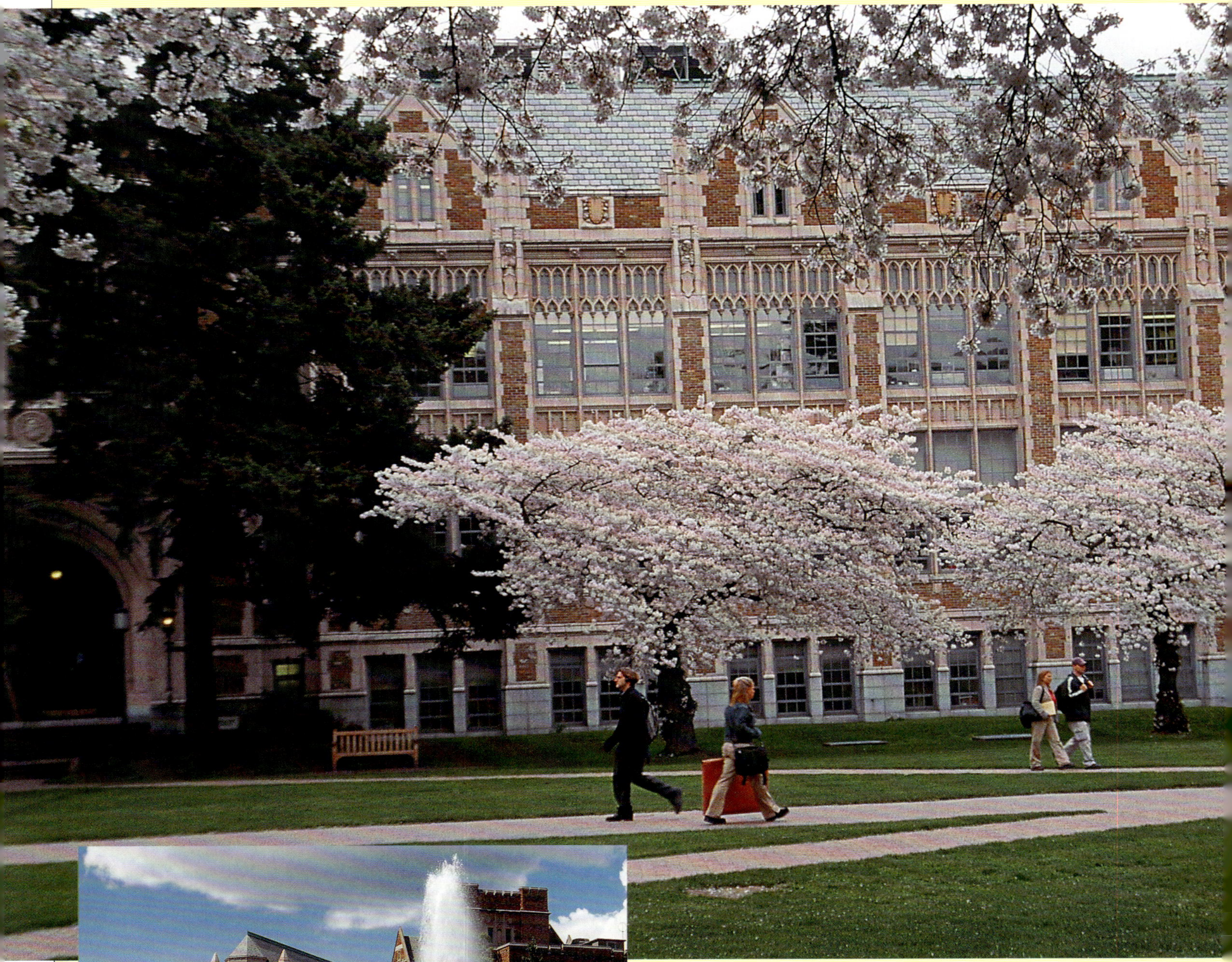

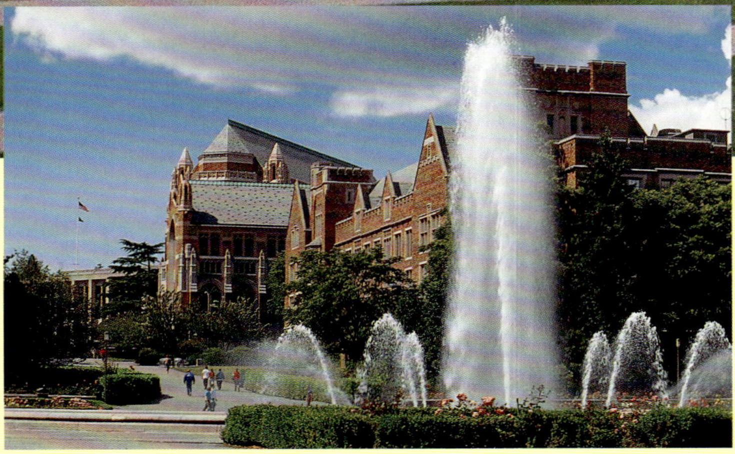

Photo by Barry Provorse

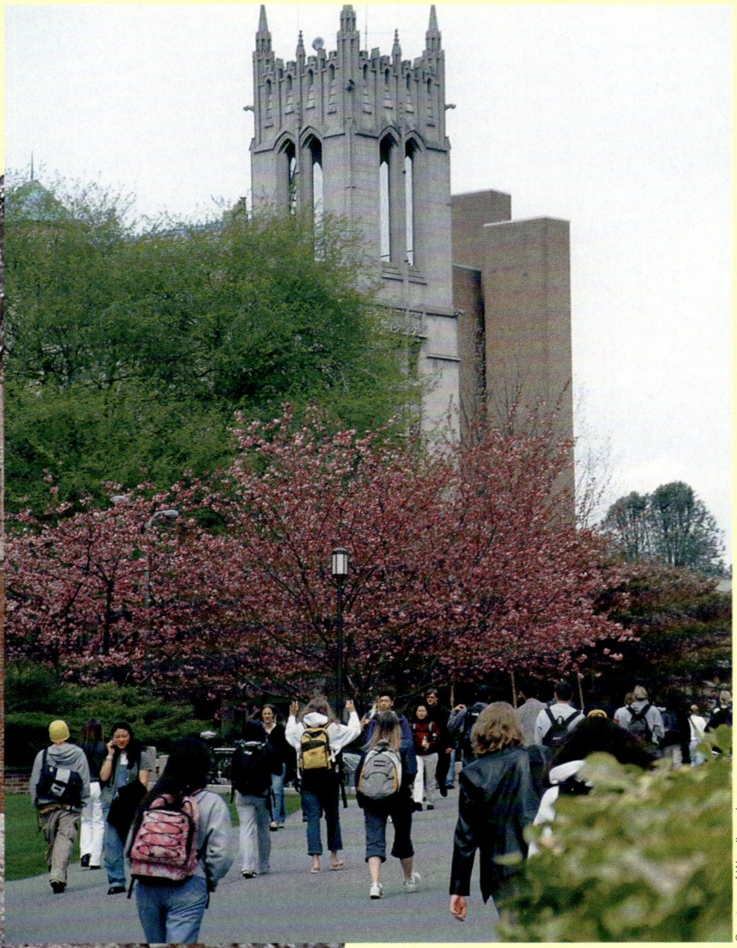

Courtesy of Wyndham Images

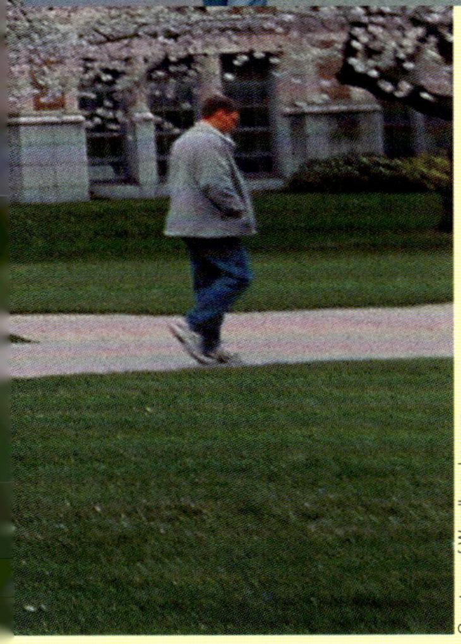

Courtesy of Wyndham Images

The University of Washington is a major research institution with more than 35,000 students and over 3,500 faculty members. The chance to work on the cutting edge of scientific and scholarly research draws almost 8,000 graduate students to UW programs, which include more than 90 special research centers and 25 field sites.

Seattle University, also a private college, is located in the heart of Seattle. The University was founded in 1891 by two Jesuit Priests—Father Victor Garrand and Father Adrian Sweere—from Yakima (Washington) who came here to establish a school for boys. Their efforts eventually gave rise to Seattle University. The University, with a student population of nearly 5,000 undergraduate and graduate students from around the globe, offers a multitude of programs, including pre-medical, pre-law, and a variety of theology and ministry programs. *News and World Report* recently ranked Seattle University as the 11th best regional university in the western states.

King County is also home to two other religious universities, Seattle Pacific University in the Queen Anne/Fremont area of Seattle, and Northwest College located in Kirkland. Combined enrollment for both school is over 4,000.

In downtown Seattle is Antioch University, a school that prides itself on being different. At Antioch Seattle, the emphasis is on progressive education. Students earn credit for life experience, and letter grades do not exist here. Antioch Seattle, one of five Antioch Universities in the nation, offers one bachelor's program, and a handful of graduate programs.

In Bothell, about 12 miles north of Seattle, is Bastyr University, the area's premier alternative health training institute. Bastyr offers an eclectic menu of degree programs such as naturopathic medicine, acupuncture, behavioral science, and psychology. Bastyr University, founded in 1978, also researches the effects of natural treatments on disease, and boasts the largest natural health care facility in the state. Bastyr University is home to 1,500 students.

On Seattle's Capitol Hill is the Cornish College of the Arts, a performing and visual arts school. Cornish, with an enrollment of about 700 students, offers programs in art, dance, design, humanities, music, performance, and production.

Harborview houses more than 60 different clinics to care for a wide variety of illnesses and diseases.

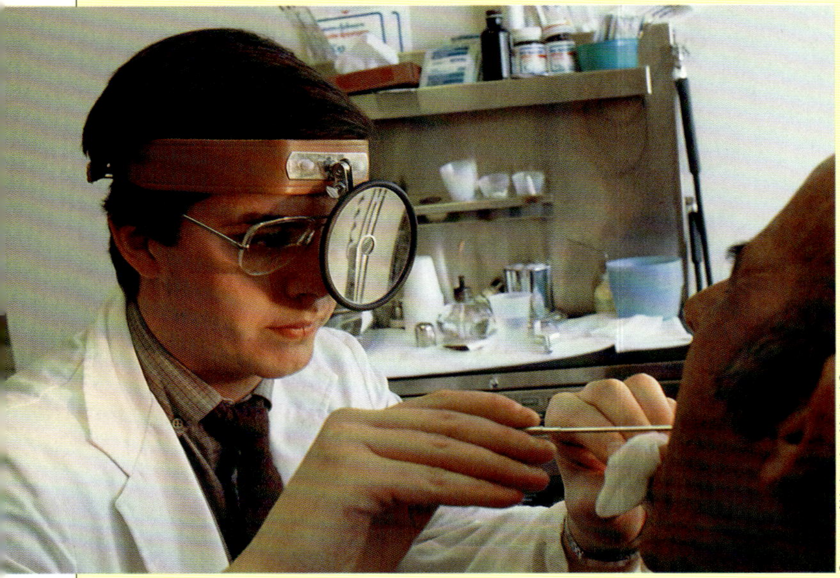

Courtesy of Harborview Medical Center

Community Colleges

King County is home to a number of excellent community colleges. A community college education—whether used as a starting point for admission to a university or an end in itself—offers students the flexibility and accessibility that many four-year institutions cannot. Admissions standards are often less stringent, and a degree or certificate can be earned in much less time.

The Seattle Community College District, made up of three separate community colleges, has the second highest enrollment of all institutes of higher learning in the state: over 28,000 students attend classes at one of the three Seattle Community Colleges. Campuses are located in Central Seattle on Capitol Hill, South Seattle, and North Seattle near Northgate Mall. The Seattle Community Colleges offer 135 academic and technical programs.

The largest single community college in King County is the Bellevue Community College, established in 1966. With an impressive enrollment of over 18,000 students, Bellevue Community College offers Associate's degrees in the arts and sciences. Programs are diverse, and range from radiation therapy to interior design.

Another well-respected community college is Highline, located in Des Moines in South King County. Highline has a student enrollment of approximately 10,000 students, with about half attending classes during the day, and the other half attending evening classes. The college, established in 1961, has a faculty of 120 full-time instructors, and 300 part-time instructors.

Hospitals

King County is renowned for its state-of-the art medical facilities. People come here from all over the world to be treated at the Fred Hutchinson Cancer Research Center, and trauma victims from every corner of the Pacific Northwest are air-lifted to Harborview Medical Clinic in Seattle. Locals jokingly call Seattle's First Hill neighborhood "Pill Hill" because of the profusion of hospitals and other medical facilities.

Seattle's Fred Hutchinson Cancer Research Center is arguably one of the best known cancer research facilities in the world. The story of the Center began in 1960 when its founder, Dr. William Hutchinson, realized his dream of a cancer research foundation. Originally called the Pacific Northwest Research Foundation, the center initially focused on cancer, endocrine disease and heart surgery. Four years later, after Dr. Hutchinson's much-loved brother Fred died of cancer, the Fred Hutchinson Cancer Center was born.

Today, the Fred Hutchinson Cancer Research Center employs more than 2,300 staff dedicated to understanding, preventing, treating, and one day finding a cure for cancer. Although the Center focuses its research primarily on bone marrow transplant, it also conducts research related to the transplantation of stem cells from circulating blood to treat other diseases such as AIDS, ovarian cancer, and sickle cell anemia. Each year, the Fred Hutchinson Cancer Research Center performs about 400 transplants.

Harborview Medical Center, which began in 1877 as a six-bed welfare hospital in south Seattle, is the area's premier trauma hospital. In fact, about 70% of the 15,000 patients admitted to Harborview each year are trauma patients. As the only Level 1 trauma center in the area, Harborview admits trauma victims from Washington, Alaska, Montana and Idaho, many of whom are transported there via Airlift Northwest.

With 16 schools and colleges located on its main campus in Seattle and new campuses in Bothell and Tacoma, the University of Washington has many programs that are among the best in the country.

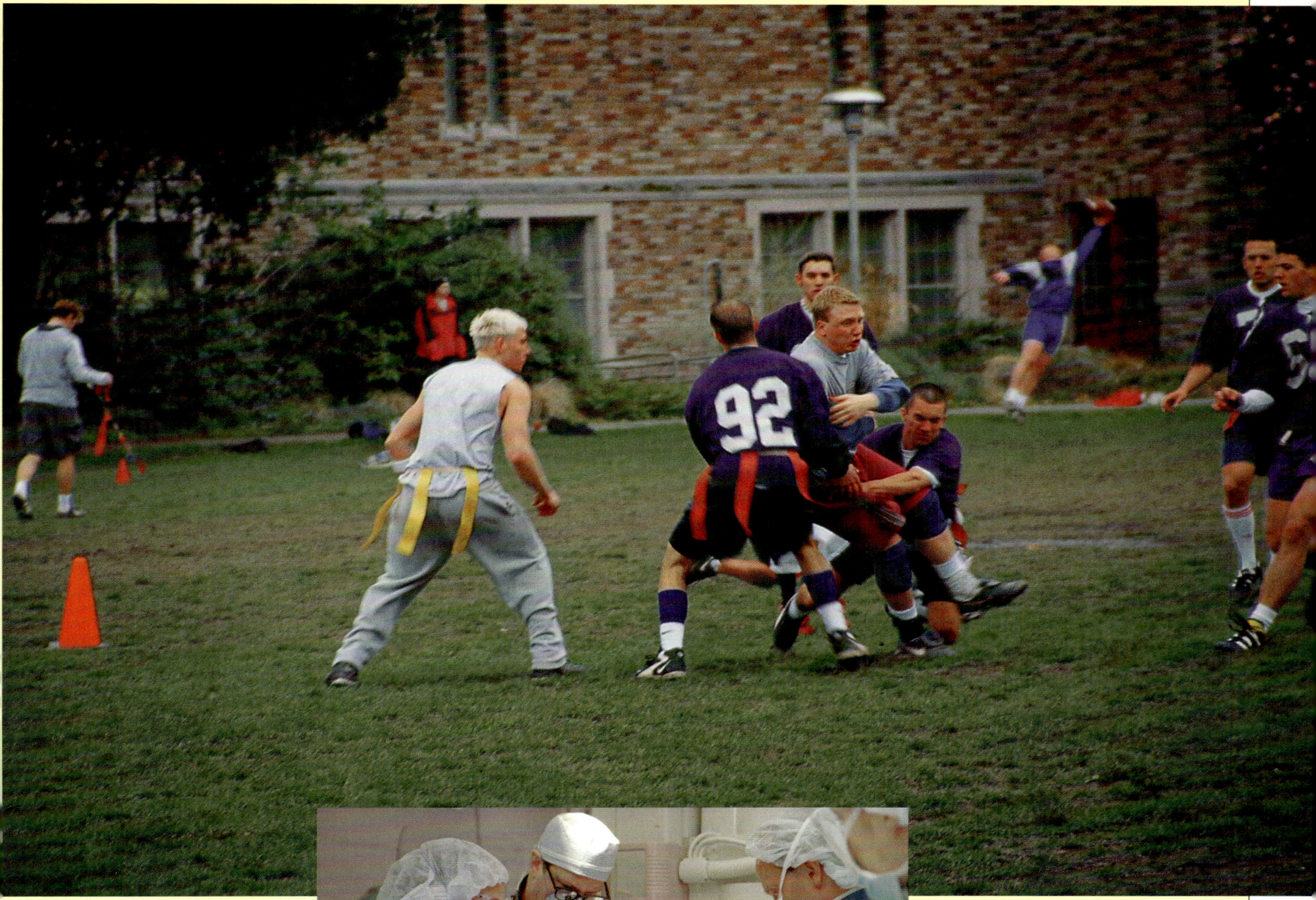

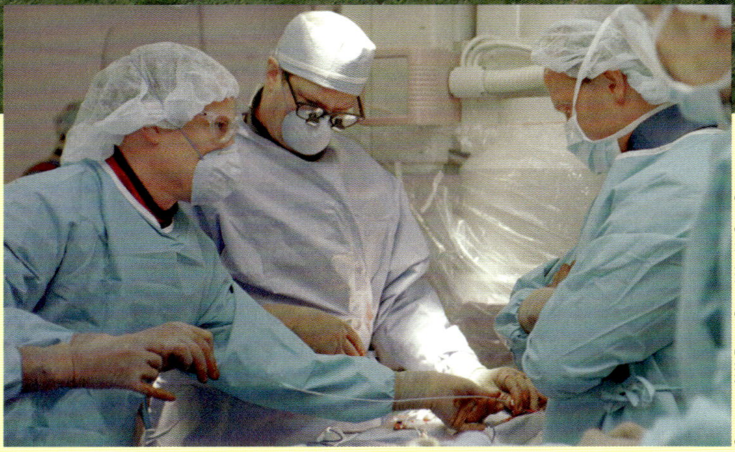

Courtesy of VA Puget Sound Health Care System

The VA Puget Sound Health Care System's complex mission incorporates a broad continuum of primary, specialty, and long-term care as well as mental health, addictions treatment, spinal cord injury treatment, comprehensive cancer care, dialysis, home health care, nursing home, hospice programs, outreach services, and sophisticated cardiovascular and surgical procedures.

King County International Airport is home to many of the area's emergency medical transport aircraft.

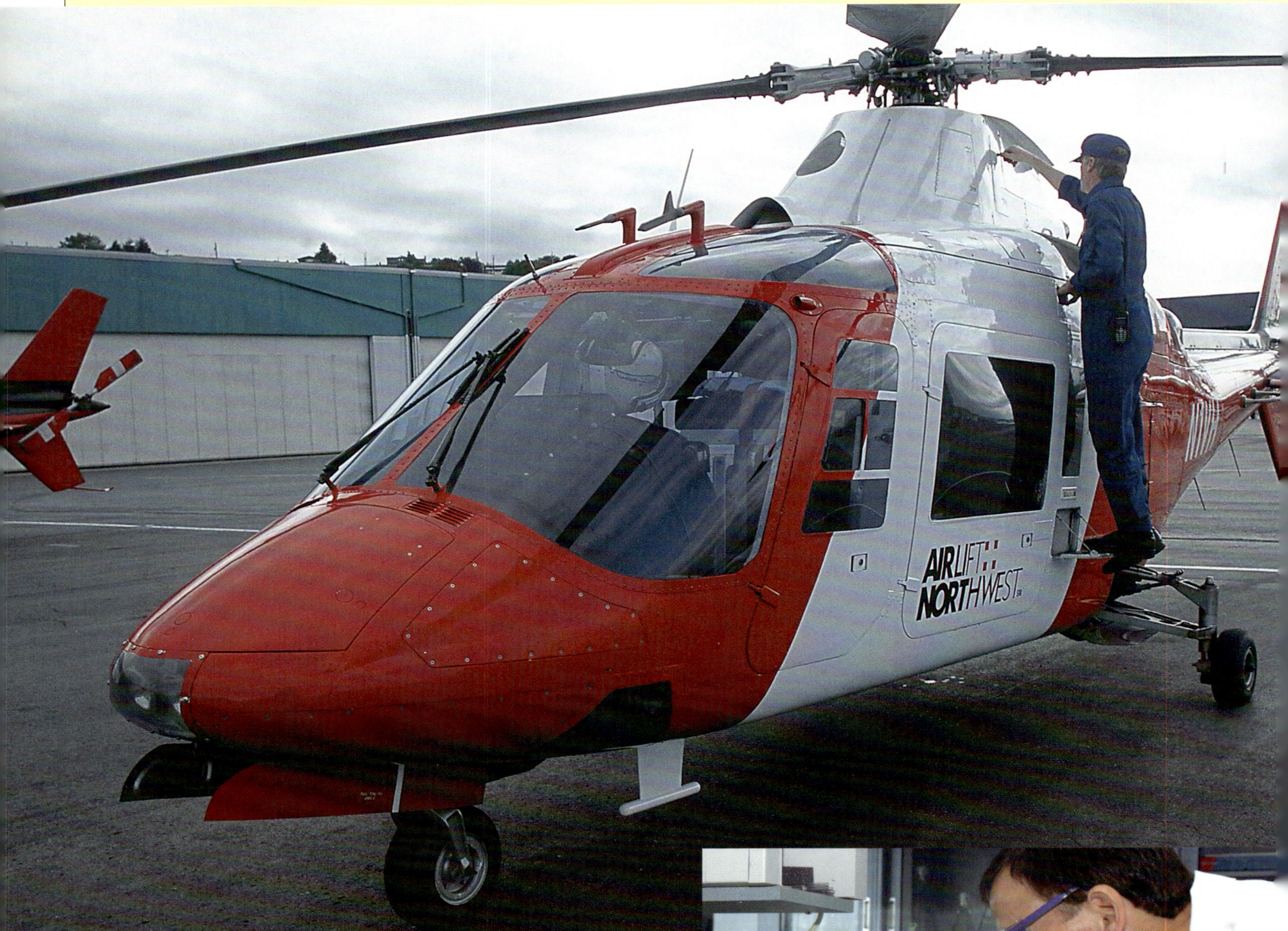

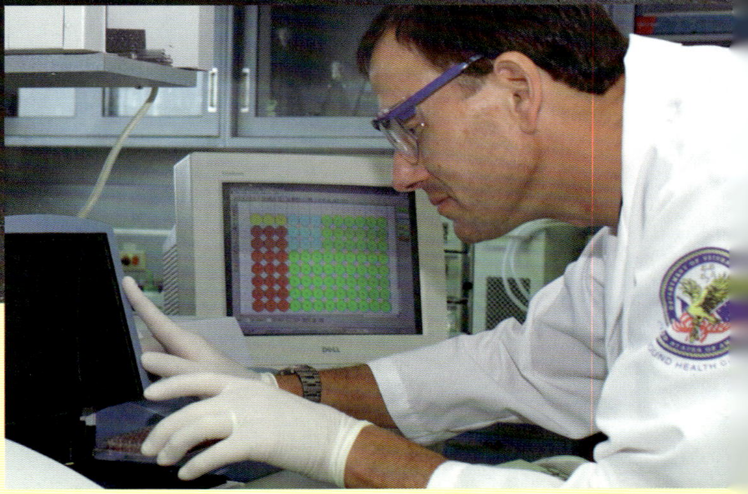

VA Puget Sound Health Care System is the largest facility in the VA's Northwest Network and is the major tertiary-care referral center for veterans from Alaska, Idaho, and Washington.

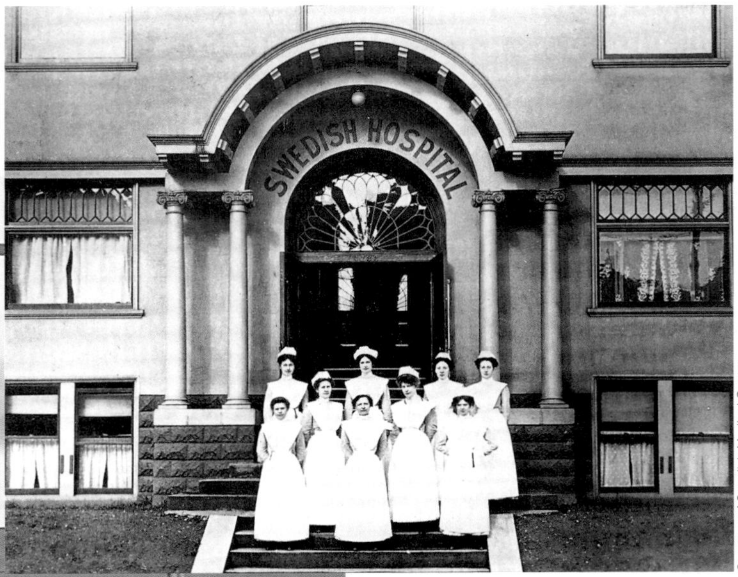

Courtesy of Swedish Medical Center

Swedish Hospital was founded in 1910 in a renovated apartment building with just 24 beds. Today, Swedish Medical Center has grown into the Northwest's largest, most comprehensive medical center.

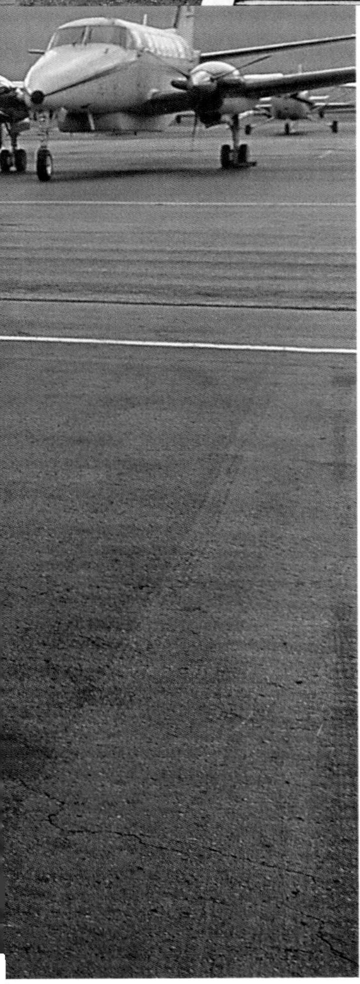

Courtesy of King County International Airport, Photo by Ed Ahrens

Harborview also boasts a nationally recognized burn center, as well as a top-notch neurological surgery unit. Other hospital services include Injury Prevention and Research, a paramedic training program, the Center for Sexual Assault and Traumatic Stress, and the Regional Epilepsy Center. Harborview is one of two primary teaching hospitals of the University of Washington School of Medicine.

Virginia Mason Medical Clinic, King County's largest hospital, has been serving this area since 1920. Modeled after the Mayo Clinic, Virginia Mason offers an acute care hospital as well as 16 neighborhood clinics located throughout the county.

In addition to routine medical care, Virginia Mason also operates the Bailey-Boushay House, a live-in nursing facility for AIDS patients. The first of its kind in Washington State, Bailey-Boushay House serves 17% of the King County residents living with AIDS. In addition to Bailey-Boushay House, Virginia Mason also operates a number of specialty centers, including centers for cancer, cardiology, diabetes, and women's health. Over 16,000 people receive treatment at Virginia Mason Medical Clinic each year.

The University of Washington Medical Center, located on the University of Washington campus, has received national recognition as one of the best hospitals in the country. Established in 1959, the Center is a state-of-the-art medical facility. In addition to routine medical care, the University of Washington Medical Center boasts a number of specialty centers, the Bone and Joint Center, cardiology and cardiac surgery, the Fertility and Endocrine Center, high-risk maternity and newborn intensive care, the Cancer Center, the Multidisciplinary Pain Center, and multi-organ transplantation services. The University of Washington Medical Center is one of two major teaching hospitals of the University of Washington School of Medicine

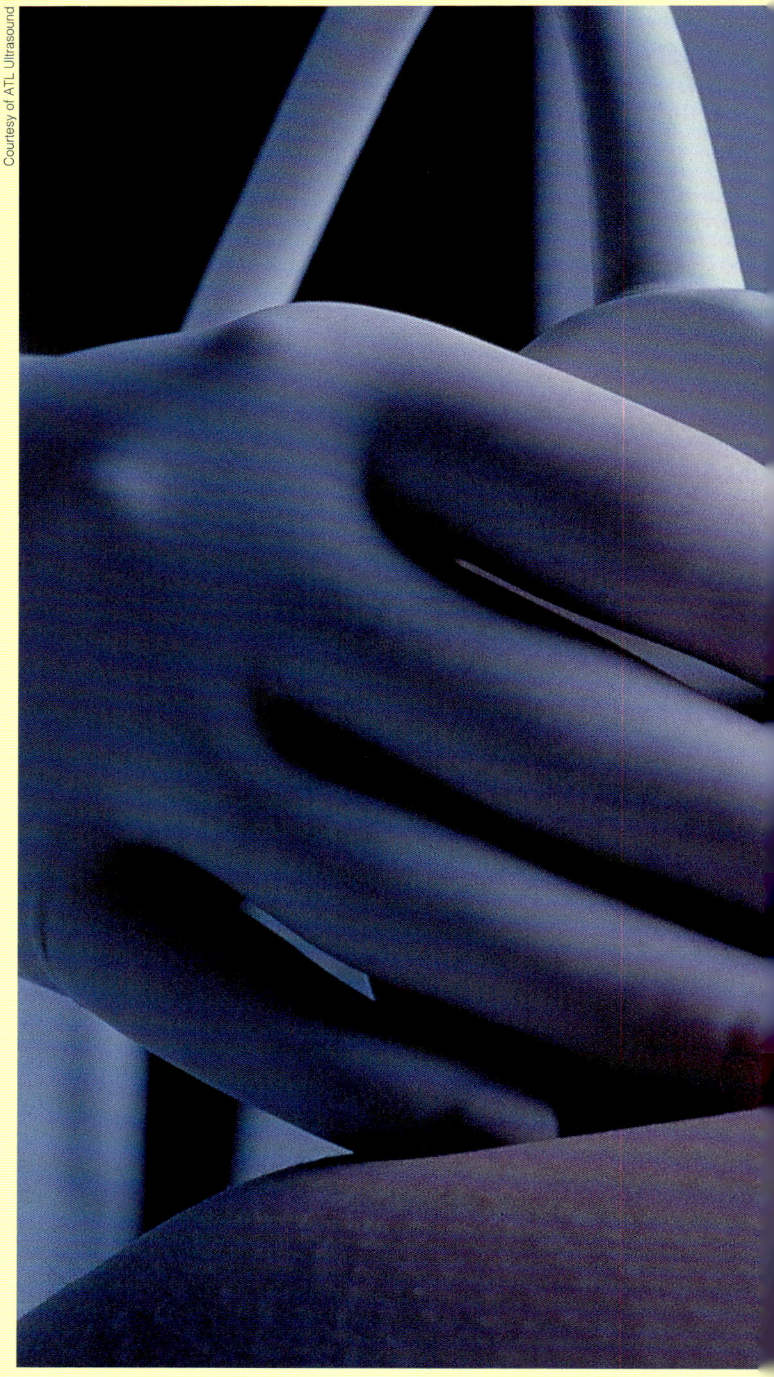

Not far from the University of Washington Medical Center is Children's Hospital and Regional Medical Center. Anna Clise founded children's Hospital in 1907 after her son died of inflammatory rheumatism. Then known as Children's Orthopedic Hospital, it was the first medical care facility of its kind on the West Coast.

Today, the hospital, which is affiliated with the University of Washington School of Medicine, is an exceptional medical and research facility specializing in medical and surgical treatment for young people aged birth to 21. Children come from Washington, Alaska, Montana, and Idaho to be treated at Children's Hospital and Regional Medical Center.

Children's Hospital also enjoys a national reputation as one of the country's finest pediatric research facilities. Research centers around pediatric health issues, with research focusing primarily on cystic fibrosis, infectious disease, virology, gastroenterology, and audiology.

Overlake Hospital Medical Center, located in Bellevue, is the premier health care facility in East King County. Established in 1960, Overlake offers a number of specialty programs, including a nationally recognized open-heart surgery program, a Spine Center, the Lang Oncology Unit the Multiple Sclerosis Center, and the Women's Hospital and Childbirth Center. Residents of east King County consistently rate Overlake as their hospital of choice.

Other hospitals are sprinkled throughout the county, including Swedish Hospital in Seattle, Evergreen Hospital in Kirkland, Providence Seattle Medical Center, Highline Community Hospital in Burien, Northwest Hospital in Seattle, St. Francis Hospital in Federal Way, and Auburn Regional Medical Center in Auburn.

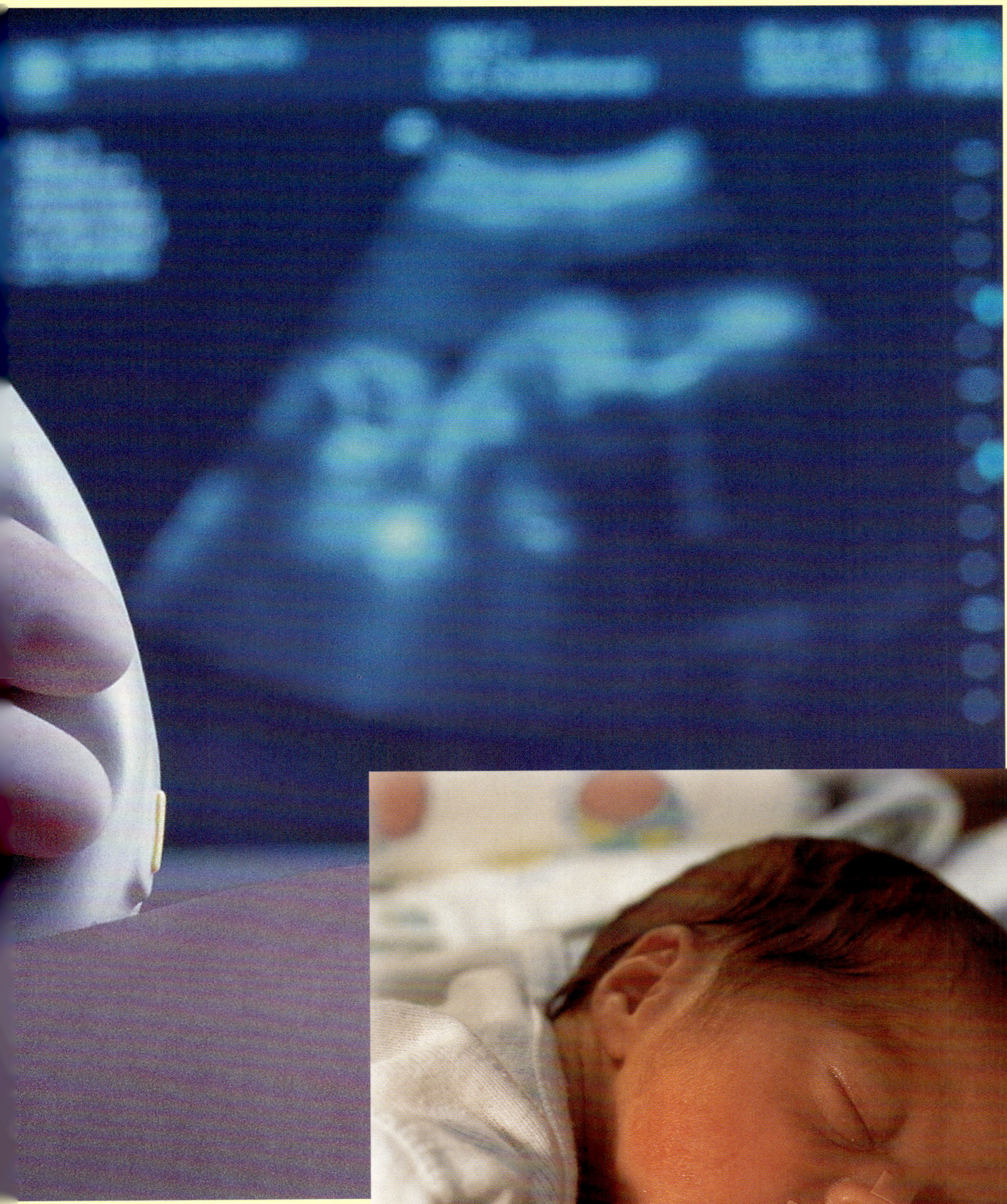

ATL's ultrasound systems are used for numerous applications, including OB/GYN, radiology, cardiology, vascular, and small-parts musculoskeletal imaging.

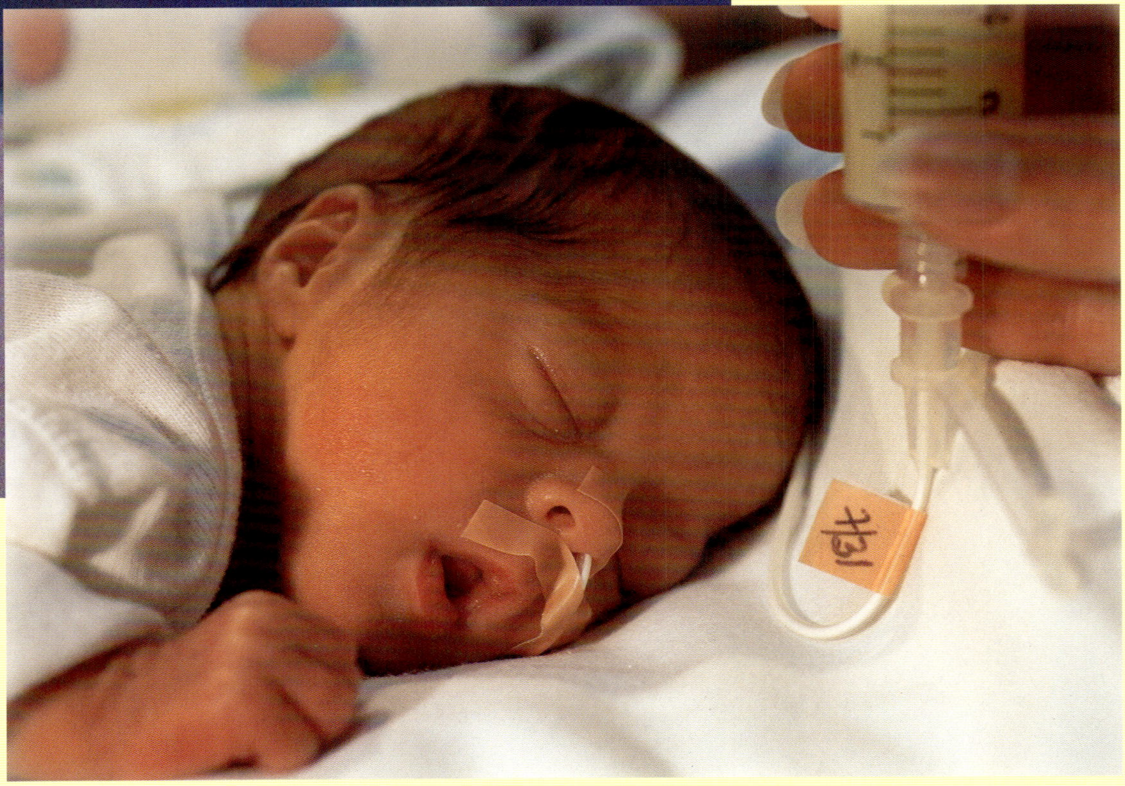

Courtesy of Swedish Medical Center

The Special Care Nursery at Swedish Medical Center is one of just a handful of intensive-care units in the Puget Sound prepared to care for premature and sick newborns. Each year, more than 500 infants "graduate" from the nursery.

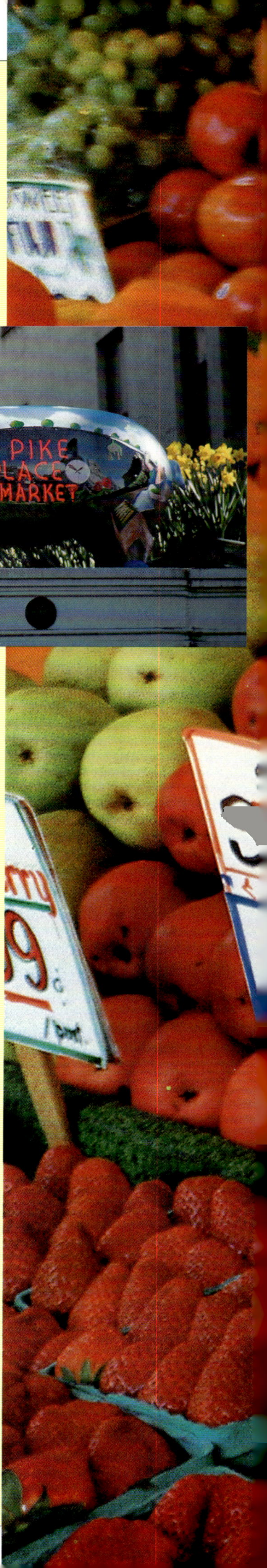

Courtesy of Wyndham Images

Natural Wonder, Metropolitan Flair

Natural beauty abounds in King County. There are towering trees, crystal waters, babbling brooks, and breathtaking vistas of the surrounding hills and mountains. The metropolitan character of city skylines serves as dramatic contrast to the region's natural endowments. For many who choose to live or visit King County, it is precisely these contrasting elements that make this region so attractive. Where else can one find first-class shopping centers, arts and cultural events, and nearly limitless economic opportunities just minutes from rural farmlands, lush green forests, glistening waters, and the pristine power of the Cascade and Olympic Mountain ranges?

The people who live and work in King County celebrate the region's natural and manufactured attributes by protecting open space and rural character while promoting economic development and tourism. It is a delicate balance to achieve, but nobody does it better. As a result, the people who live in King County enjoy a quality of life that is considered by many to be the best in the nation, and the entire region has become a major tourist destination.

Arguably the number one attraction for tourists, the Pike Place Market serves as a vibrant reflection of the region's strengths, from its thriving fishing and farming industries, to the creativity of its artists and musicians. What began as a 1907 experiment to cut out the "middleman" in transactions between farmers and consumers, the Pike Place Market has flourished. Today, the market houses 200 permanent businesses (including the original Starbucks coffee house), 200 registered artists and craftspeople, and as many as 125 farmers. With gourmet specialty stores, top-drawer bakeries, the freshest fish and meats available, and produce that is second-to-none, the Pike Place Market has earned a reputation for offering some of the best foods on earth. In fact, many local restaurants look to the market for inspiration and direction. The Pike Place Market is a bustling place, alive with sights and sounds that are unique to this Pacific Northwest landmark. From the fish handlers who juggle fish and call out orders with the flair of a circus act, to the street musicians and performers who entertain passersby, to Rachel, the great brass pig, the Pike Place Market has much to offer beyond the produce, foods, and wares that are sold there.

Courtesy of Wyndham Images

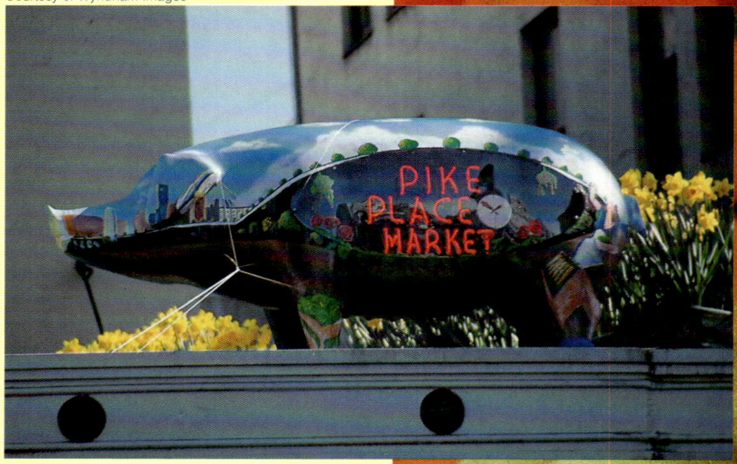

In many ways, Pike Place Market is more than just a place to buy fresh fish and fruit. For many, it is the heart of the city.

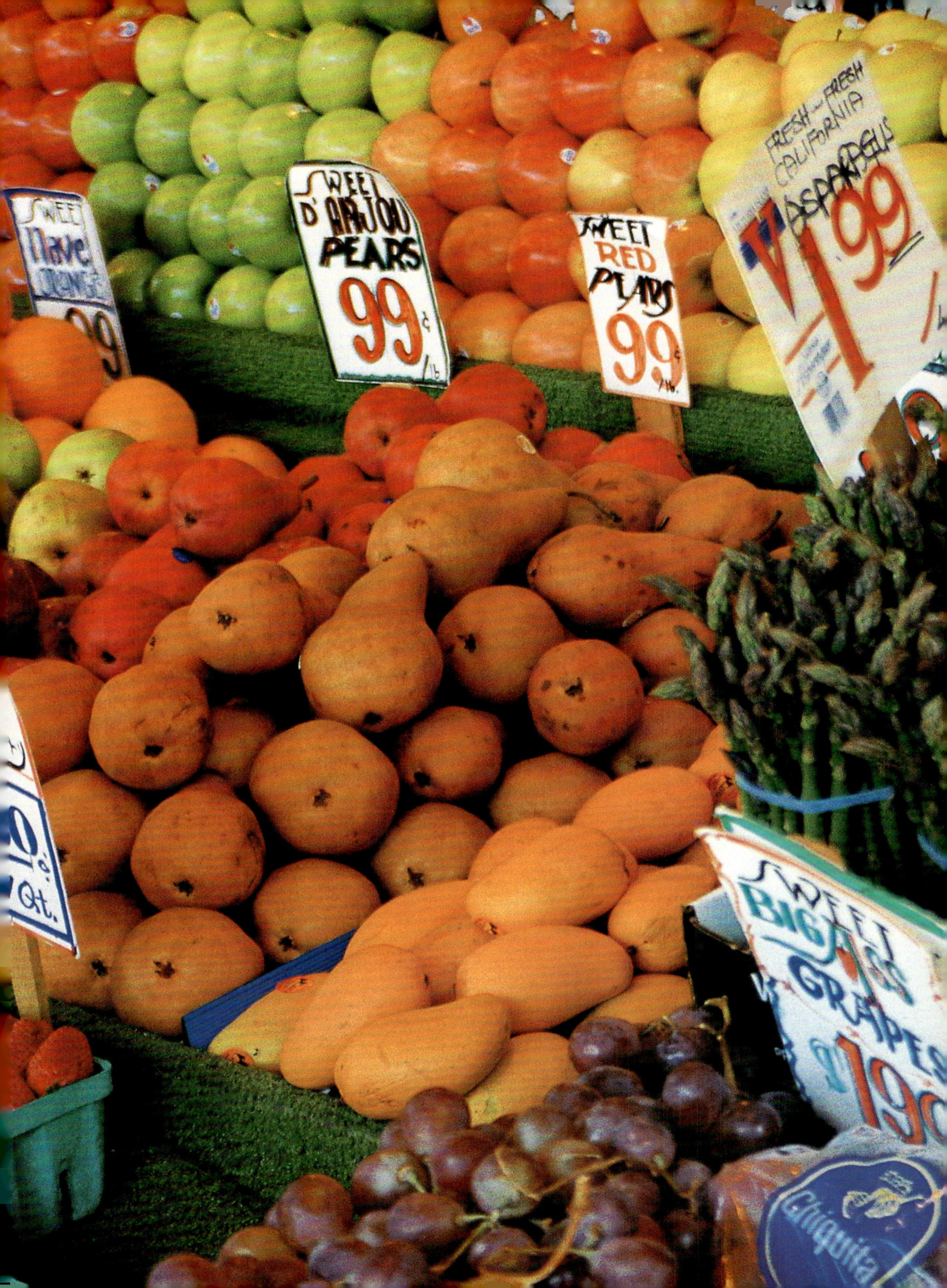
SWEET
D'ANJOU
PEARS
99¢
/lb.
SWEET
RED
PEARS
99¢
/lb.
FRESH — FRESH
CALIFORNIA
1.99
SWEET
GRAPES
Chiquita

The historic West Point Lighthouse on Elliott Bay was first lit in 1881 and is still operational today.

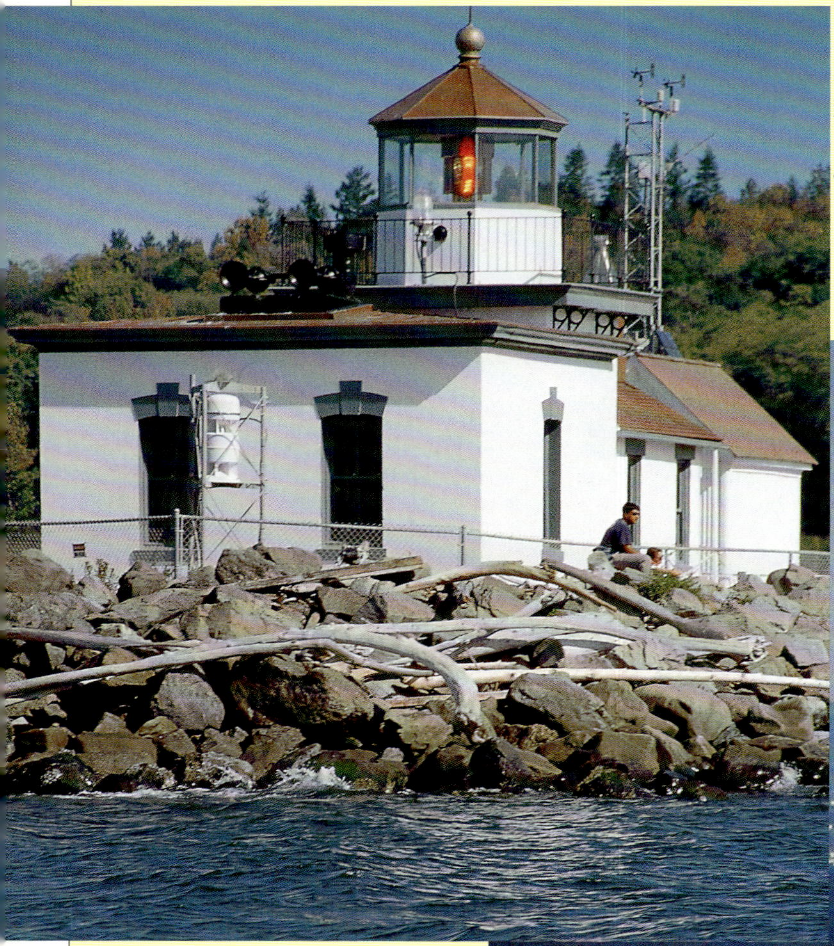

Courtesy of Wyndham Images

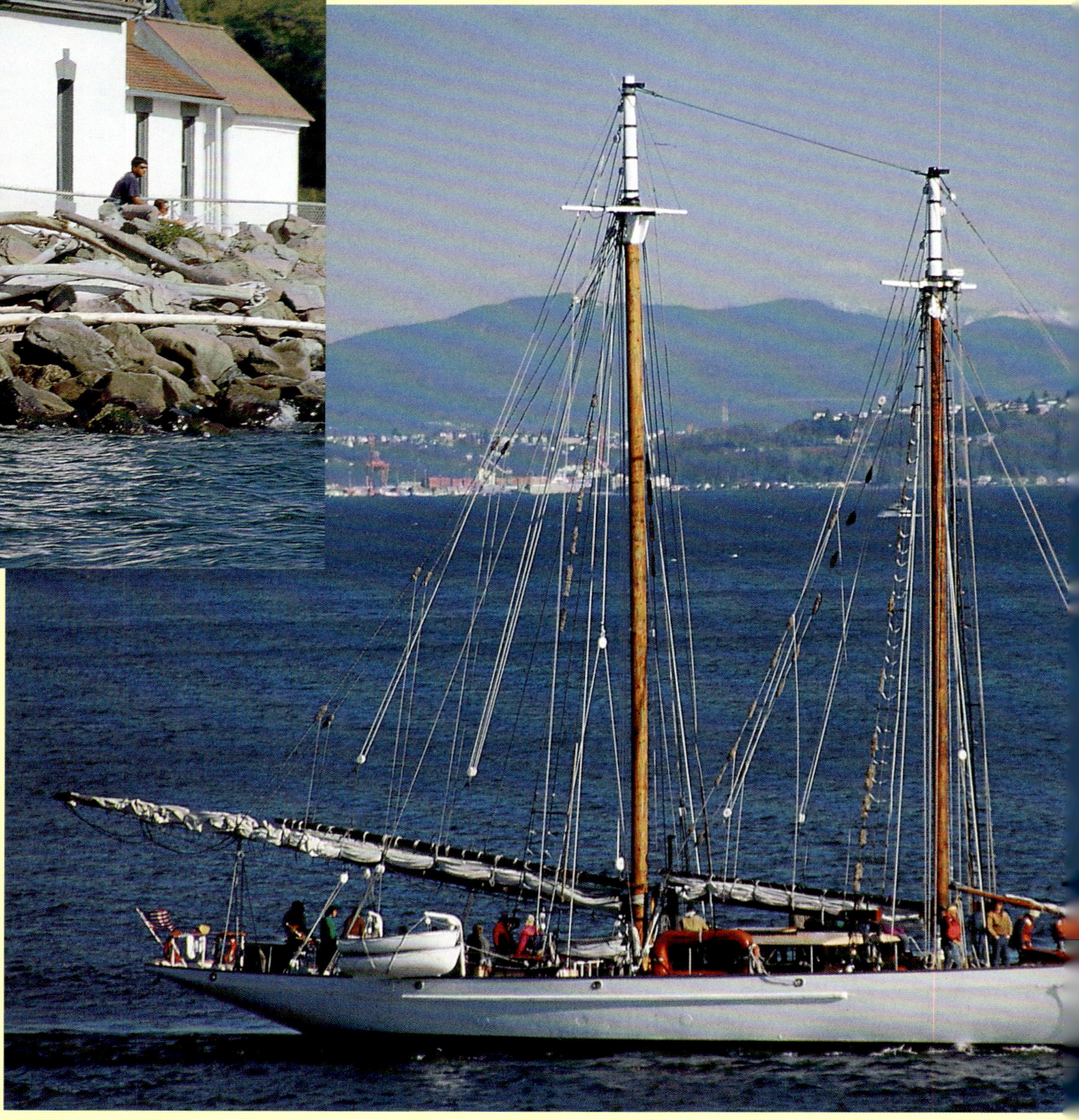

Built in 1924, this 127-foot schooner still plies the waters of Puget Sound.

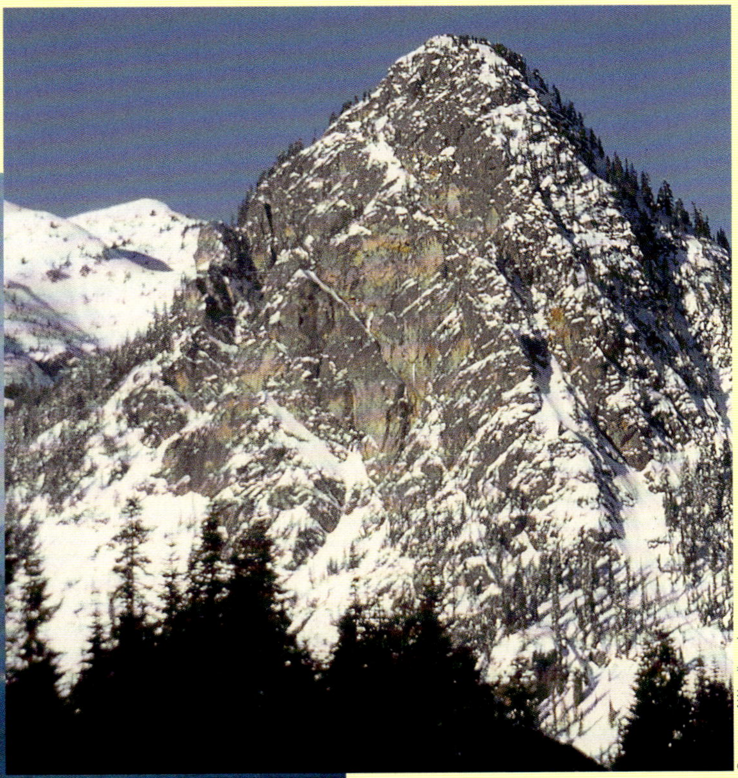

Courtesy of Wyndham Images

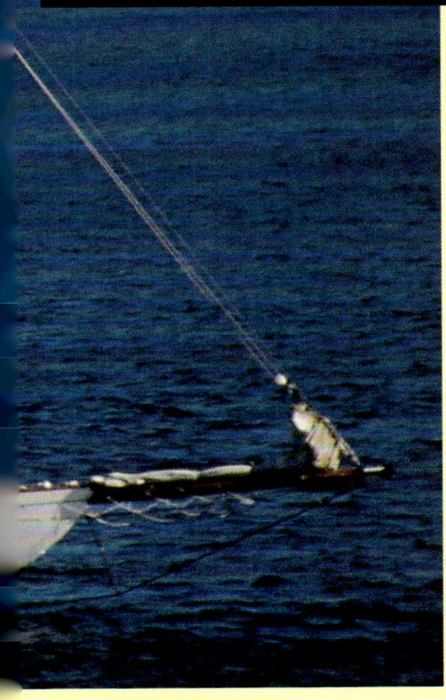

Courtesy of Wyndham Images

Nestled between glistening waters and soaring mountains, King County is blessed with a variety of opportunities for outdoor adventure. Skiing, snow-boarding, and other winter sports draw enthusiasts to Snoqualmie Pass.

Literally steps away from the Pike Place Market, the Seattle waterfront is also very popular with tourists and locals alike. Scattered along the waterfront are eclectic souvenir shops, tour-boat operations, ferry stations, grab-and-go eateries, and full-scale restaurants. As an alternative to walking the long distance from one end of the waterfront to the other, some folks prefer to catch a ride on the waterfront trolley or in one of the horse-drawn carriages that are evocative of a bygone era. More adventurous spirits can get a birds-eye view of waterfront activity by parasailing over the Sound. The piers that jut out over the edge of the Puget Sound offer uncompromised views of the Olympic Mountains, Mount Rainier, and neighboring islands. The Seattle waterfront is also home to the Seattle Aquarium—featuring 380 species of fish, sea mammals, and invertebrate creatures—and Odyssey, the Maritime Discovery Center, which is an interactive center that highlights the natural and commercial uses of Seattle's marine environment. During the summer months, One Reel Productions presents *Summer Nights at the Pier*, an open-air concert venue for twilight performances by popular musicians.

The Space Needle, built for the 1962 World's Fair, is easily the most recognizable landmark in King County. The 605-foot-tall futuristic structure towers above the 74-acre Seattle Center grounds, which are also home to the Pacific Science Center and IMAX theater; the Seattle Opera House; Bagley Wright, Intiman, and Children's theatres; the Fun Forest and arcade; Key Arena; and the new Experience Music Project (EMP). EMP was founded and funded by local billionaire Paul Allen, to pay homage to music legend Jimmy Hendrix and other innovative musical artists who have their roots in the Pacific Northwest. Throughout the year, there are a number of colorful and lively festivals, including Bumbershoot, the Folklife Festival, and numerous smaller but equally vibrant celebrations of culture and arts. With the constant activity and all-ages enjoyment available in numerous venues on the grounds, it is little wonder that the Seattle Center has remained a favorite of both visitors and locals for nearly 40 years.

A climber hones his skill at Marymoor Park's practice climbing facility.

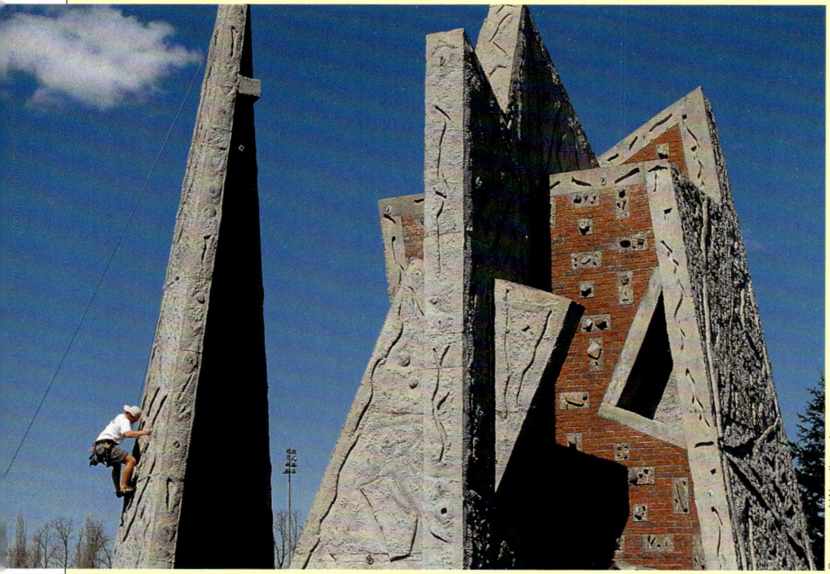

Courtesy of Wyndham Images

In a region that is blessed with the kind of natural beauty that is native to King County, parks are plentiful and well loved. Woodland Park, with its world-famous zoological gardens, is certainly one of the most popular parks in the county. The Woodland Park Zoo, which just celebrated its 100th anniversary in 1999, has been distinguished as one of the ten best zoological gardens in the country. For the past 20 years or so, zoo planners and staff have dedicated themselves to creating a zoo that honors its inhabitants by closely replicating their natural environments. They have succeeded with exhibits like the African Savanna—a vast open space where giraffes, zebras, monkeys, gazelles, lions and hippos cohabitate as they would in the wild—and Tropical Asia—featuring the 4.6-acre Elephant Forest and the 2.7-acre Trail of Vines, which is home to orangutans, lion-tailed macaques, siamang apes, and Malayan tapirs. Other popular exhibits include the Northern Trail inhabited by wolves, bald eagles, grizzly bears, elk, and mountain goats; the Lowland Gorilla Enclosures where a charming family of gorillas make their home; and the Tropical Rain Forest, which houses more than 50 species of exotic animals and as many as 20,000 plant species that are indigenous to tropical rainforests. While any zoo is a popular choice with children, the Woodland Park Zoo does an exceptional job of catering to youngsters; they offer pony rides, a Family Farm petting zoo, and numerous structures that are perfect for imaginative tykes who like to pretend to be a favorite zoo animal.

Other parks in the region range from tiny to enormous and provide a wide variety of things to do and see. The King County Park System alone operates more than 150 parks and an extensive trail system. The jewel of the Park System is Marymoor Park in Redmond. In addition to playfields for soccer, softball, and radio-controlled aircraft, the 638-acre park also features a climbing rock, a velodrome, tennis courts, a rowing club, and an exercise station course. The park is accessible by both the Burke-Gilman and the Sammamish River trails, and it is the site of a National Historic District that includes the Clise Mansion and the Marymoor Museum of Eastside History. A number of special events are held at the park throughout the year. The most popular of these include the annual Heritage Festival, WOMAD USA, the Evergreen Classic Horse Show, the All British Field Meet, and Northern Lights.

Some of the City of Seattle's parks are so well known that they have been featured in movies and visited by the President of the United States. Greenlake Park, which borders the lower half of Woodland Park, is a gathering place for locals who like to get their exercise lakeside. The path around the lake is always teeming with

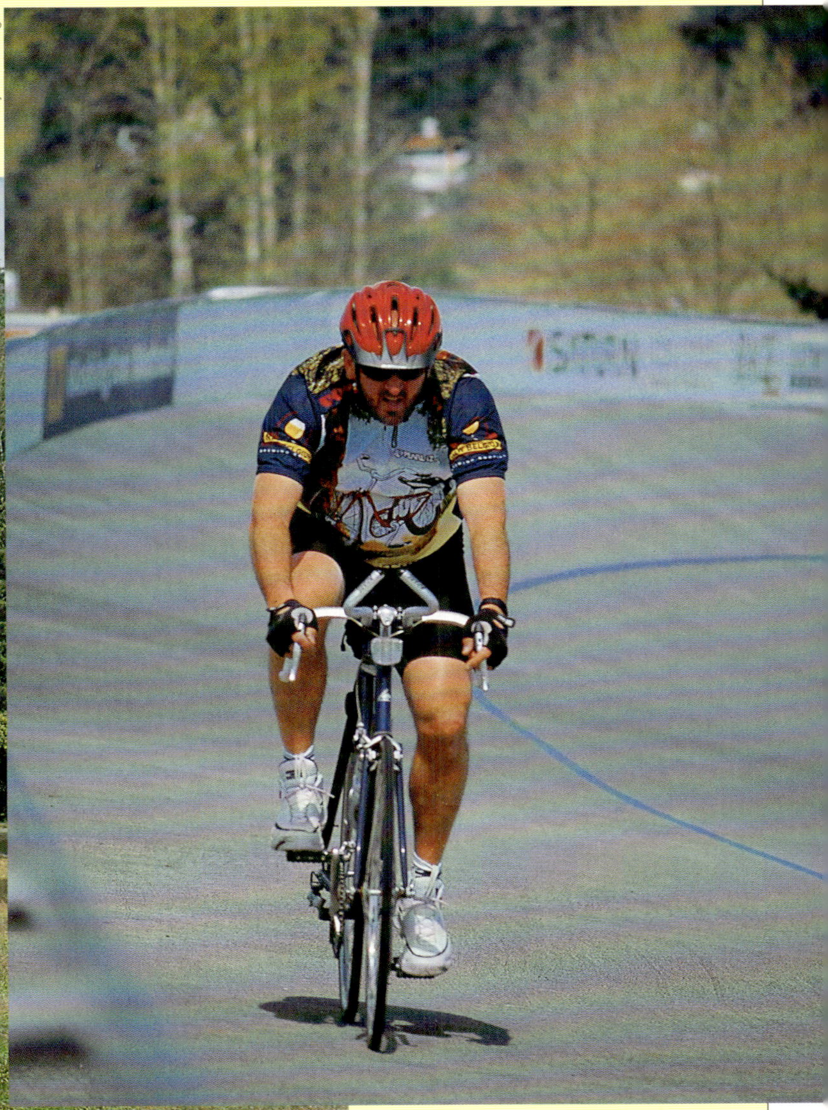

Courtesy of Wyndham Images

A cyclist works out at the Velodrome in Marymoor Park.

Kayakers glide up the Sammamish River.

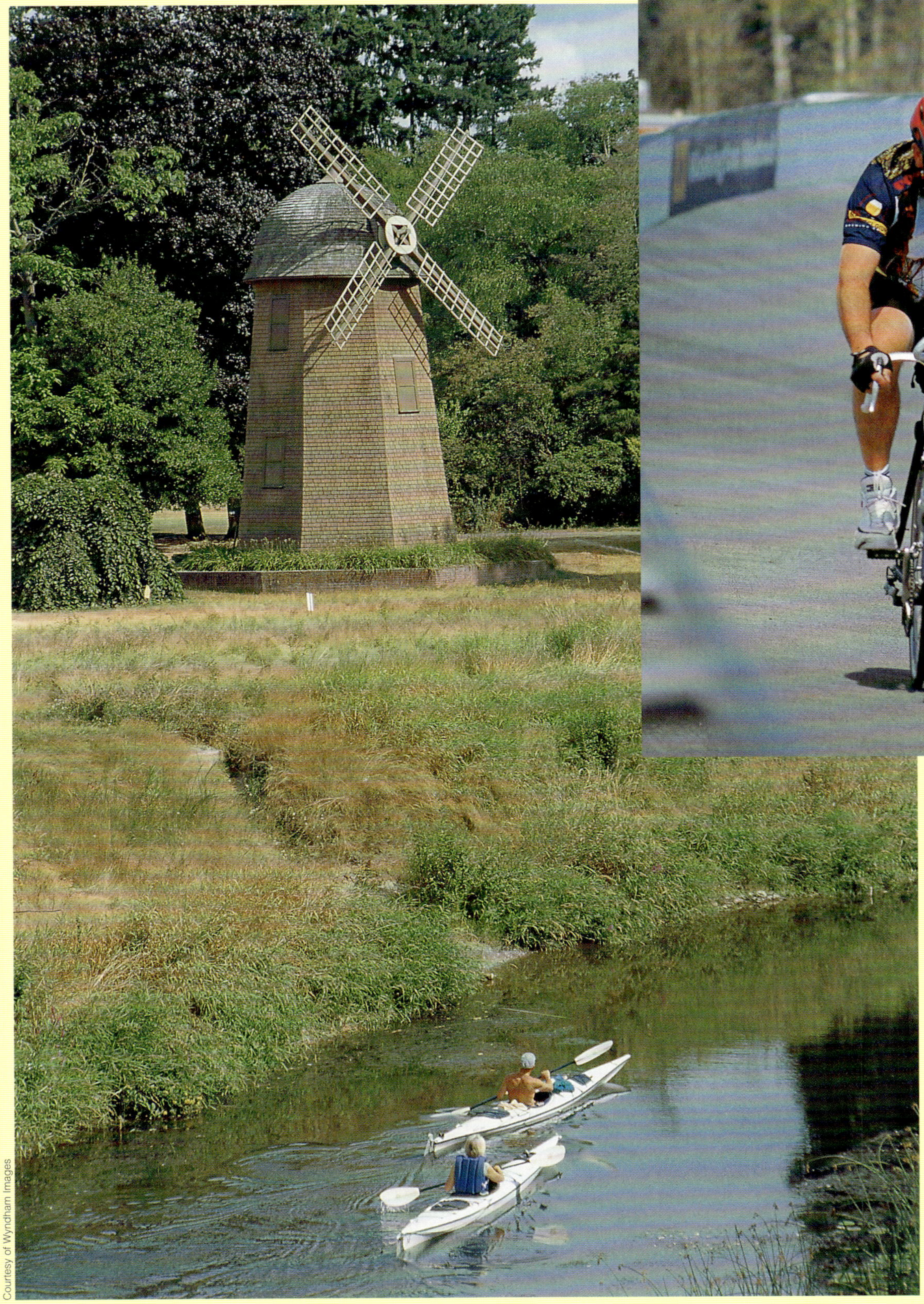

Courtesy of Wyndham Images

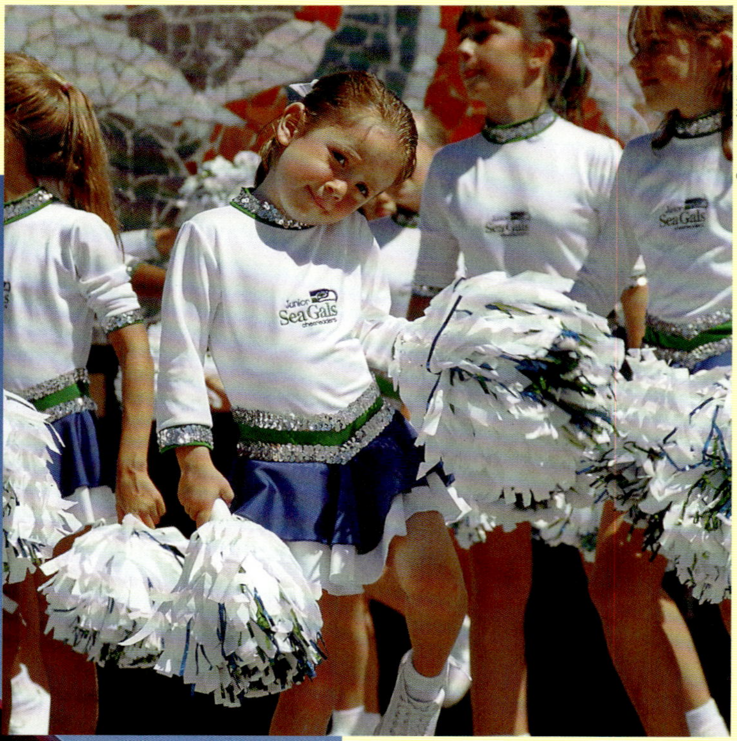

Courtesy of Wyndham Images

The Junior Seagals entertain the crowd in Seattle Center.

The Spirit of Washington dinner train pulls into its Renton station.

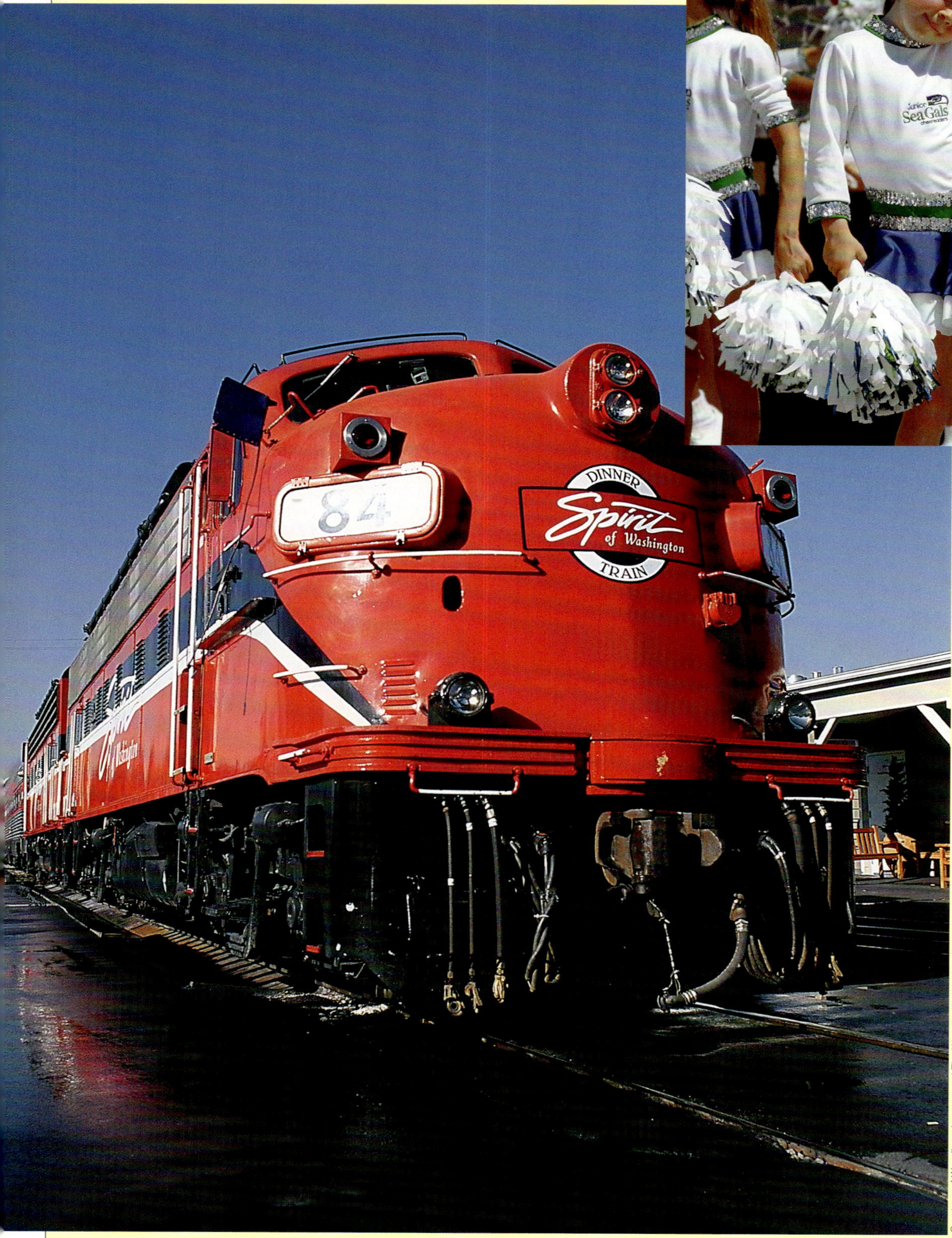

Courtesy of Wyndham Images and The Woodinville Weekly, Photo by Wade Williams joggers, walkers, skaters, and strollers. Swimming, rowing, and windsurfing are also available at Greenlake, as are golf and tennis. Seattle's Discovery Park is a favorite with nature lovers. This 513-acre densely foliated park serves as a welcome wilderness respite just minutes from the city. Discovery Park is also home to Daybreak Star Cultural Arts Center, the Pacific Northwest's largest arts and cultural center owned and managed by Native Americans. Gas Works Park, which sits along the shores of Lake Union near Fremont, the self-proclaimed "Center of the Universe," boasts the best view of the Seattle skyline. And on a clear day, the omnipresent grandeur of Mount Rainier and the shimmering blue waters of Lake Union make for a gorgeous snapshot of the quintessential contrasts that distinguish this region as one of the most beautiful places on earth. Many tourists make the trip to Gas Works Park just so they can capture such beauty on film. Gas Works Park is also the site of the AT&T Family Fourth fireworks extravaganza that takes place each Independence Day.

Tourism

As glorious as it is, the natural beauty of King County is not the only thing that draws visitors. The area is also a hot-bed of ingenuity, vision, and plentiful economic opportunities that attract countless conventions, trade shows, and business dealings each year. Ample accommodations, convention facilities, and service providers are available throughout King County to welcome business and pleasure travelers alike. Visitor and convention services are provided by the Washington State Convention and Trade Center, the Seattle-King County Convention and Visitors Bureau, the Bell Harbor International Trade Center, Meydenbauer Center in Bellevue, and numerous other facilities around the county.

This young man is a SEAFAIR Pirate-in-Training.

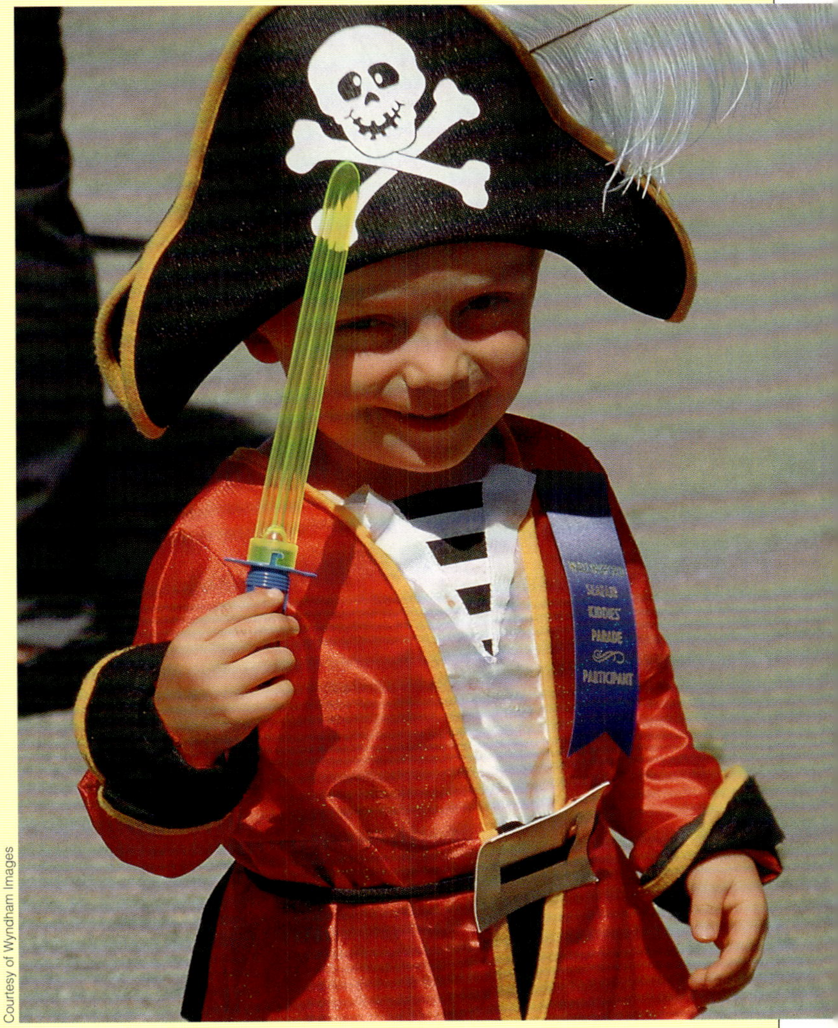

Courtesy of Wyndham Images

Accommodations are also plentiful throughout the county. They range in price and style from Spartan to opulent. There are bed-and-breakfast inns, motels, hotels, and even longer-term suites for people who are relocating or planning extended visits to the area. While the most popular hotels are in downtown Seattle, there are many excellent alternatives in Bellevue, Tukwila (near the Sea-Tac Airport), and in smaller cities.

With 891 guest rooms, the Westin Hotel in downtown Seattle is the region's largest hotel. Integrating top-notch business amenities with first-rate visitor services, the Westin has earned its stellar reputation. The Westin's twin towers and outer balconies offer most guests amazing views of the city and surrounding natural setting. Other renowned hotels in downtown Seattle include the Four Seasons Olympic Hotel, the Sorrento Hotel, the Alexis Hotel, and the Seattle Sheraton.

The Four Seasons Olympic Hotel exudes luxury and class. From the elegance of its guest rooms to the allure of fine dining in The Georgian Room, Four Seasons guests are treated to unforgettably good food and lodging. The nearby Sorrento Hotel is much smaller but offers its guests a similarly memorable experience. Fashioned after the architecture of the Italian Renaissance, designer Harlan Thomas named the hotel after his favorite Italian city. Today the décor of the guest rooms is evocative of Asian cultures, while the culinary delights served in the hotel's Hunt Club Restaurant take their inspiration from Mediterranean cuisine.

Regardless of where visitors choose to stay in King County, they are sure to find a friendly welcome and the services and amenities to suit every need and desire.

SEAFAIR is the largest community festival in the Pacific Northwest. The festival's grand finale is the hydroplane race on Lake Washington.

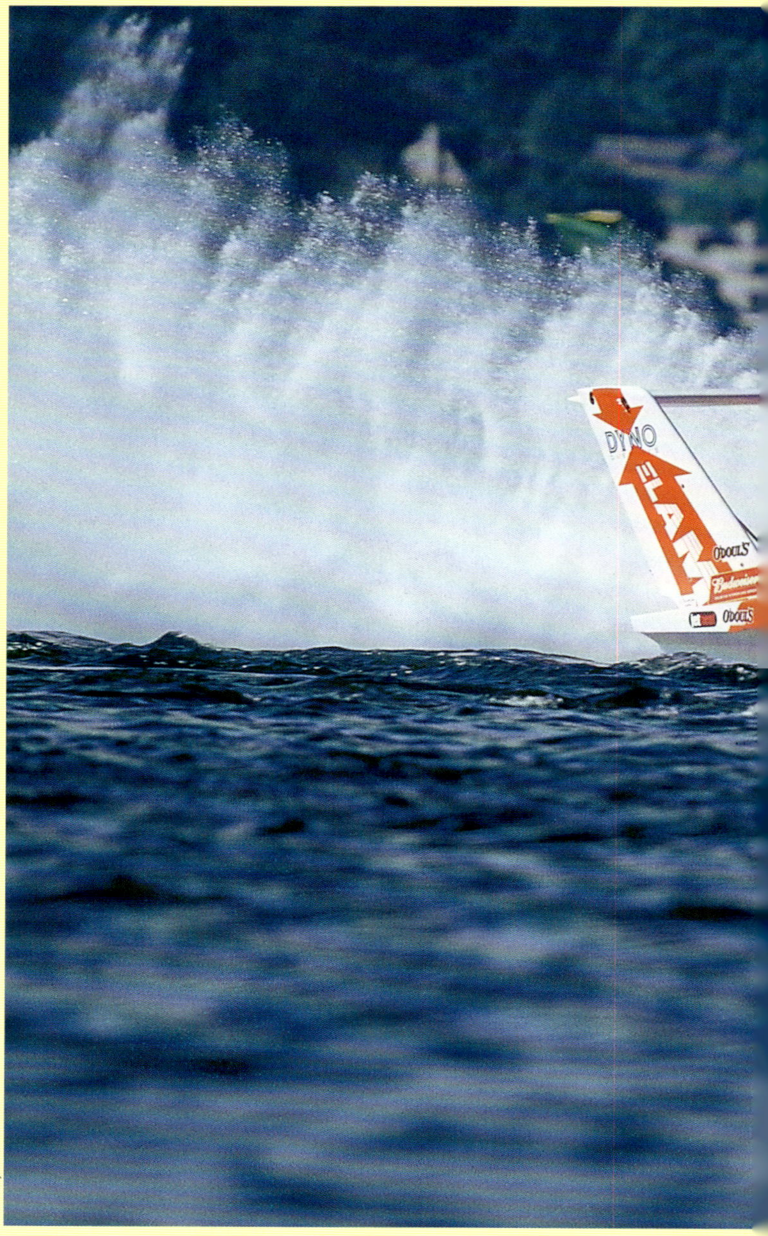

Courtesy of SEAFAIR

Courtesy of SEAFAIR

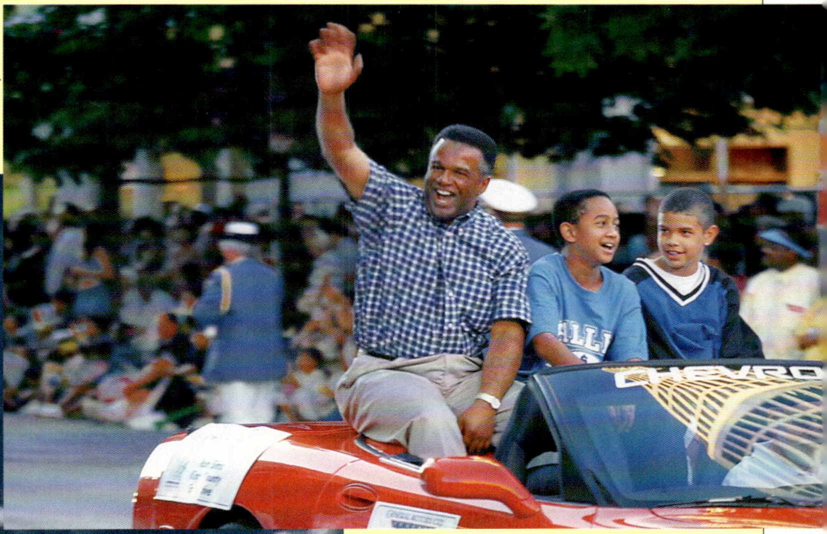

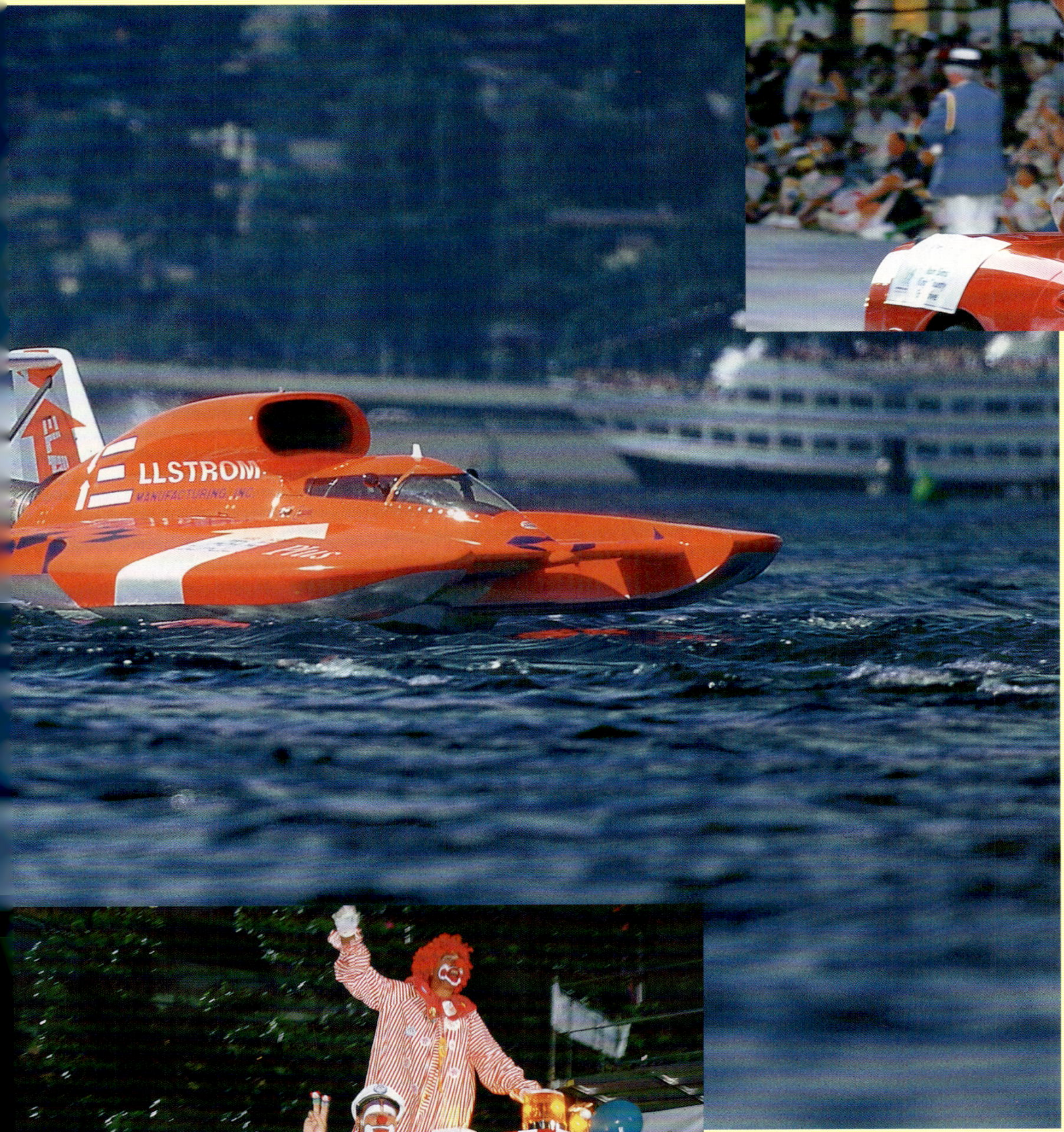

King County Executive Ron Sims waves to the crowd during SEAFAIR's Torchlight Parade. During the course of the festival, many parades, large and small, take place in neighborhoods throughout the area.

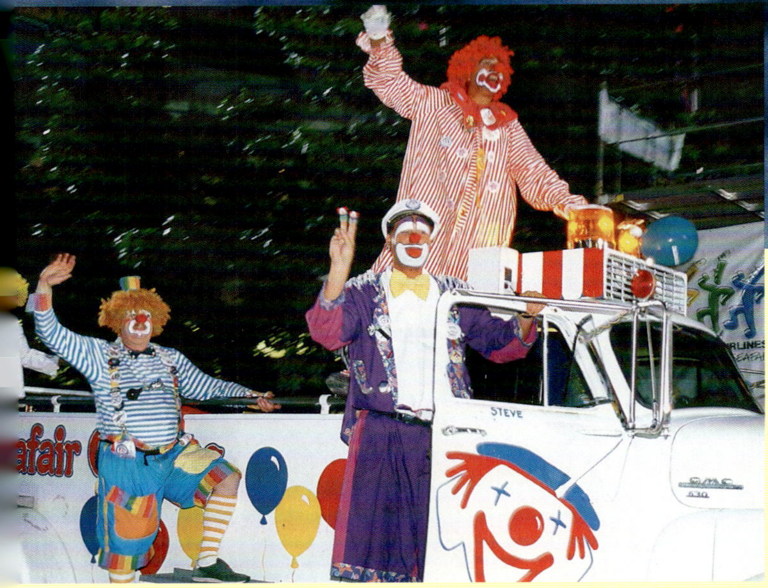

Courtesy of SEAFAIR

The SEAFAIR Clowns make their mark as a community-service organization year round with visits to community events, convalescent homes, and especially to children's hospitals. The Clowns, who now number 70, originated when SEAFAIR's founding fathers approached members of the Seattle University Graduates Club about forming a group. In keeping with tradition, each Clown must be an SU graduate.

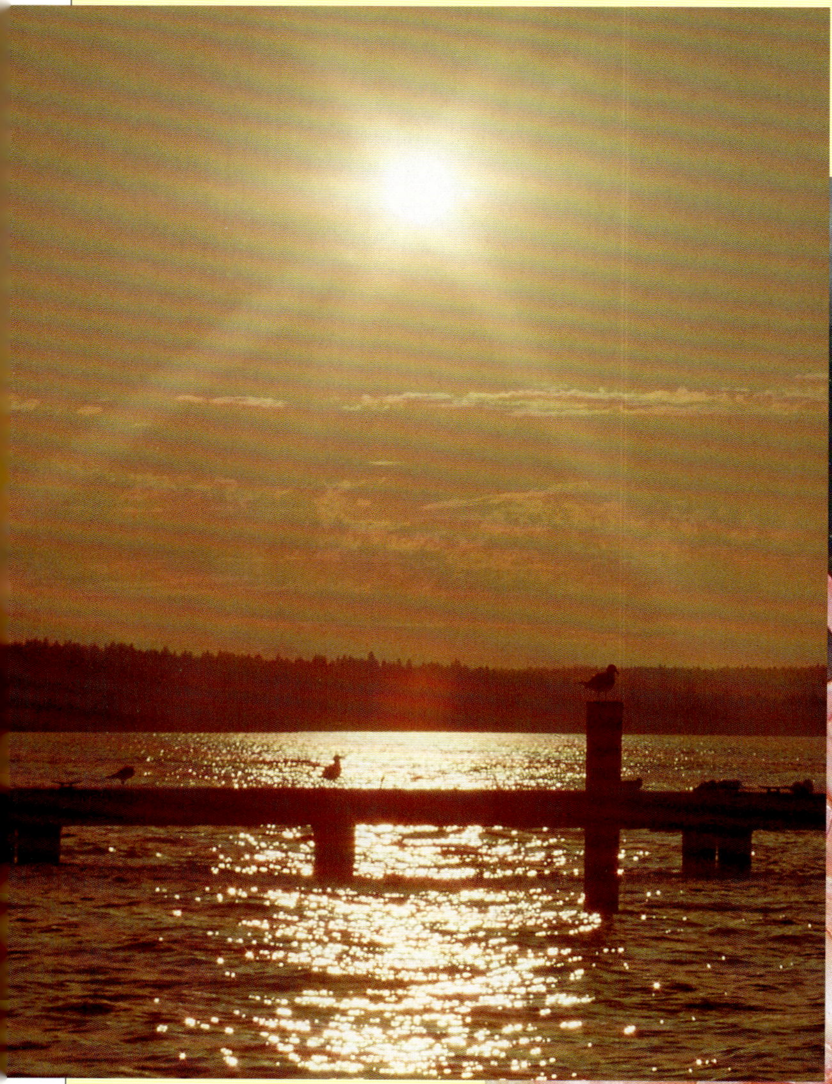

Courtesy of Wyndham Images

Sunset over Lake Washington.

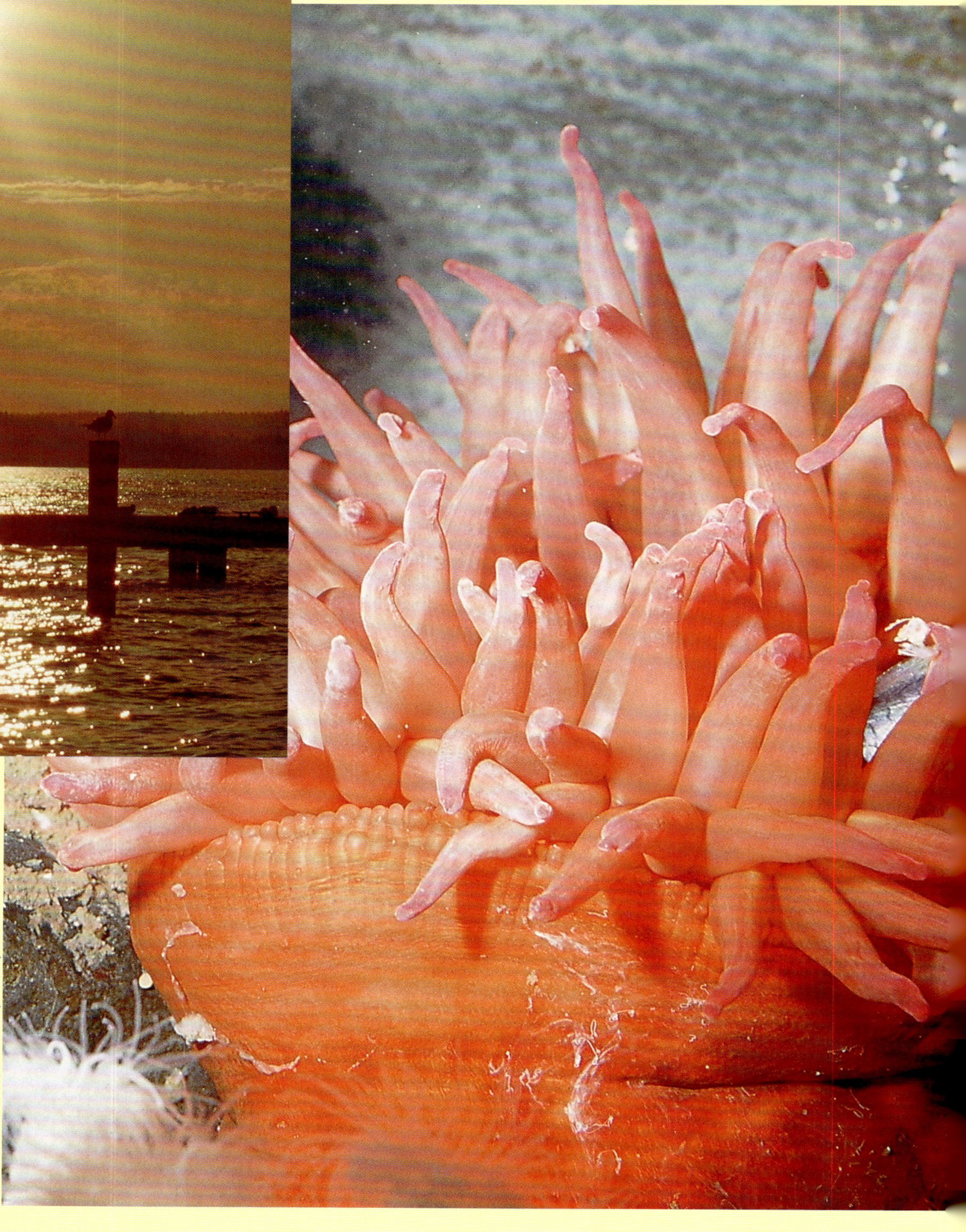

Courtesy of The Seattle Aquarium Society, Photo by Leo J. Shaw

Island Life in King County

Contrary to common misconception, King County's westernmost border does not end at the shoreline of Elliott Bay. Instead, it extends out across the Sound to Vashon-Maury Island. Vashon-Maury is a small, unincorporated island (just 37 square miles), with a rural character and a population of 10,500 that would not want the island any other way. The island is well known for its pristine natural environment where it is not uncommon to see eagles soaring overhead and Orca pods gliding through the crystal waters of the Puget Sound.

The residents are known for their love of nature and the arts, their respect for education, and their feisty resolve not to become another suburb of Seattle. Over the years, several proposals have been made to construct a bridge connecting Vashon-Maury Island with Seattle, but residents have repeatedly and soundly defeated such a plan. Instead, the only way to get on or off Vashon-Maury Island is via the Washington State Ferries. The Fauntleroy ferry dock in West Seattle will get travelers there by car. For those on foot, a ferry from downtown is the preferred method of travel. In either case, the trip is fast—15 minutes from Fauntleroy and 35 minutes from downtown Seattle.

Nestled amid the Olympic Mountains to the west and the Cascade Mountains to the east, and overlooking the waters of Puget Sound, the island of Vashon-Maury remains an unspoiled testament to the natural beauty of this region.

A sea anemone dines on a popular local dish at The Seattle Aquarium.

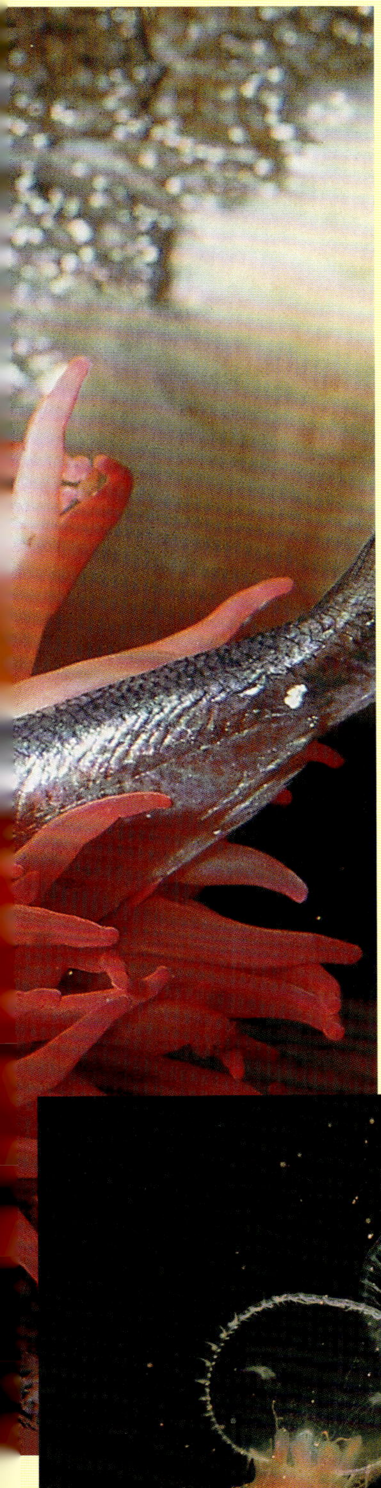

One of many fascinating tank displays at The Seattle Aquarium.

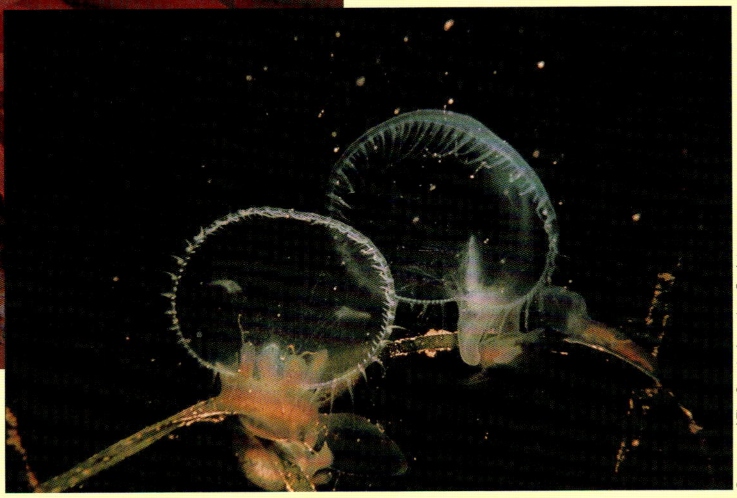

Courtesy of The Seattle Aquarium Society

The Sporting Life

A Natural Beauty

One of the greatest gifts bestowed upon King County is its abundance of natural beauty. On a clear day, one can look across the glimmering waters of the Puget Sound to see the Olympic Mountain range rising majestically in the distance. In the opposite direction, the Cascade Mountains define the horizon, setting a craggy contrast to the cool blue sky. And looking to the south on a clear day, the grandeur of Mount Rainier has the power to strike awe and inspire movement. The region's weather is mild year round, with an average temperature of 75 degrees in the warmest month, July, and fewer than 15 days per year (on average) when temperatures dip below freezing. Under these conditions is there any wonder that this region has become known as a recreational paradise?

Each day thousands of people answer the call of the wild and take to their bikes, boats, or feet. Featuring more than 200 miles of trails, the King County Regional Trail System is one of the largest trail networks in the United States. The county's most popular multi-use trail is the Burke-Gilman, which begins at Gas Works Park—on Seattle's Lake Union—and continues more than 12.5 miles to Kenmore's Logboom Park on the shores of Lake Washington. Whatever the season, the Burke-Gilman Trail is a lively and scenic route for bicyclists, rollerbladers, joggers, skateboarders, or people who are just out for a stroll. The Burke-Gilman, which is built along an old railway bed, is constantly being extended and improved. Beyond the trail's end at Kenmore, bicyclists can continue across Juanita Drive to the Sammamish River Trail, which meanders peacefully alongside the gently flowing river for 9.5 miles until it reaches the edges of Redmond's Marymoor Park. Other trails in the system include the Bridle Crest, Preston-Snoqualmie, Snoqualmie Valley, Green River, Coal Creek Parkway, Soos Creek, Cedar River, Tolt Pipeline, and Issaquah to Highpoint trails.

The region's hills and mountains provide ample inspiration to day hikers and mountain climbers who prefer the path less traveled. The Issaquah Alps, at the foothills of the Cascade Mountain range, offer a number of beautiful hiking trails that range from easy to strenuous. For those truly adventurous in spirit, the challenge of climbing Mount Rainier is ever present, and guided treks are offered through

Courtesy of Wyndham Images

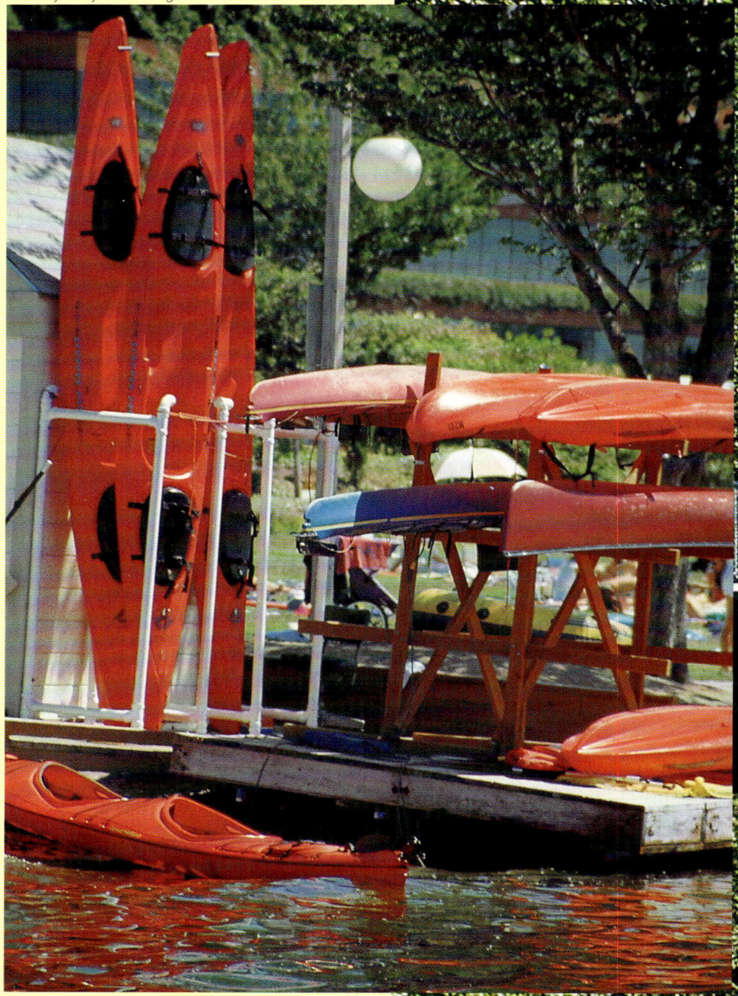

Kayaks ready for rent on Lake Washington.

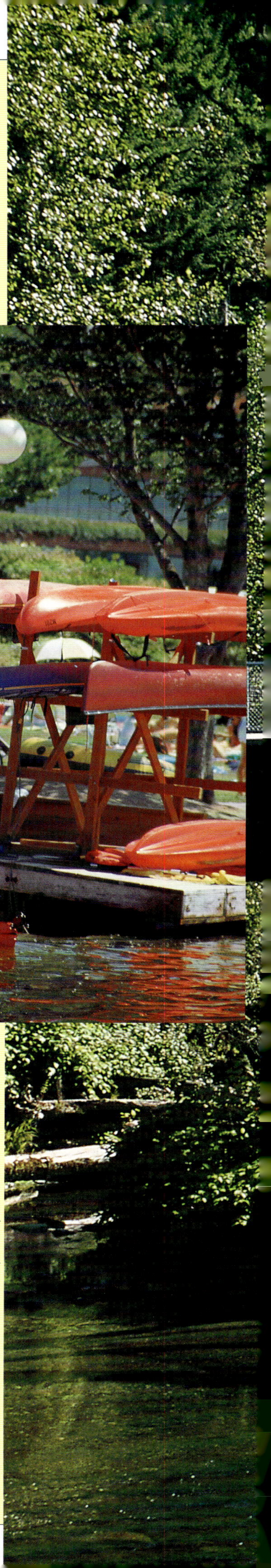

A bridge spans a river in Maple Valley.

Courtesy of Wyndham Images and The Woodinville Weekly. Photo by Wade Williams

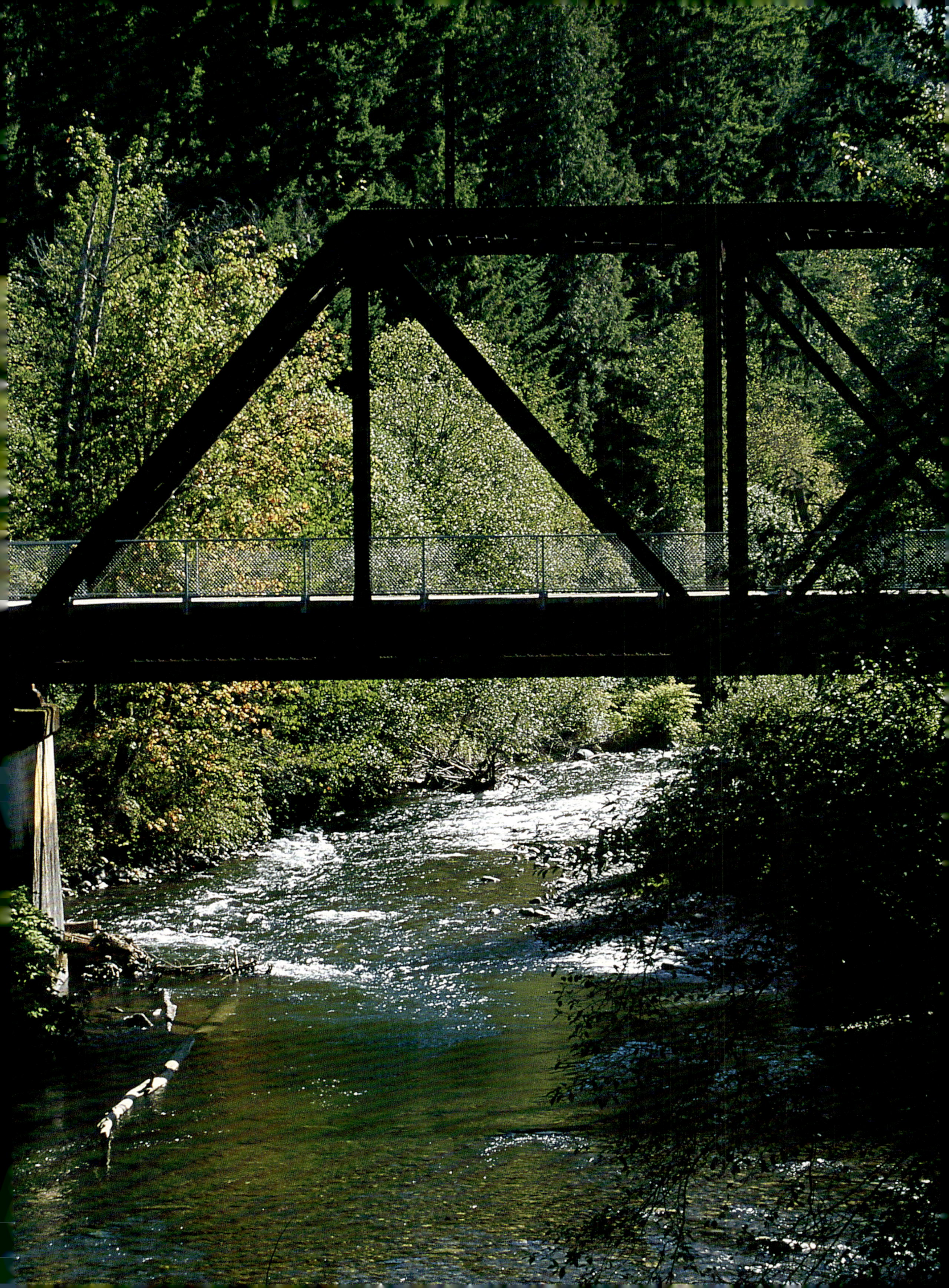

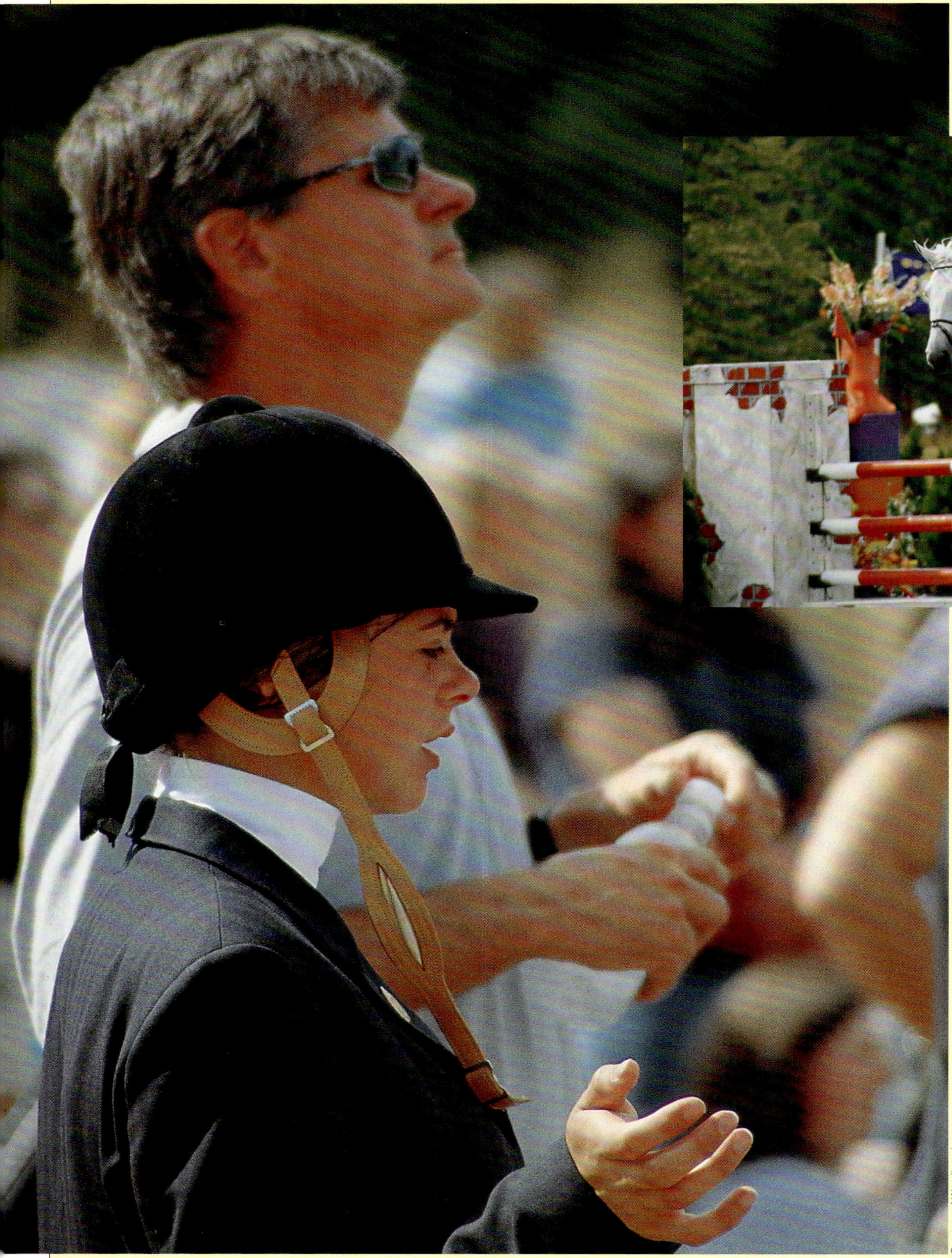

Courtesy of Wyndham Images

Courtesy of Wyndham Images

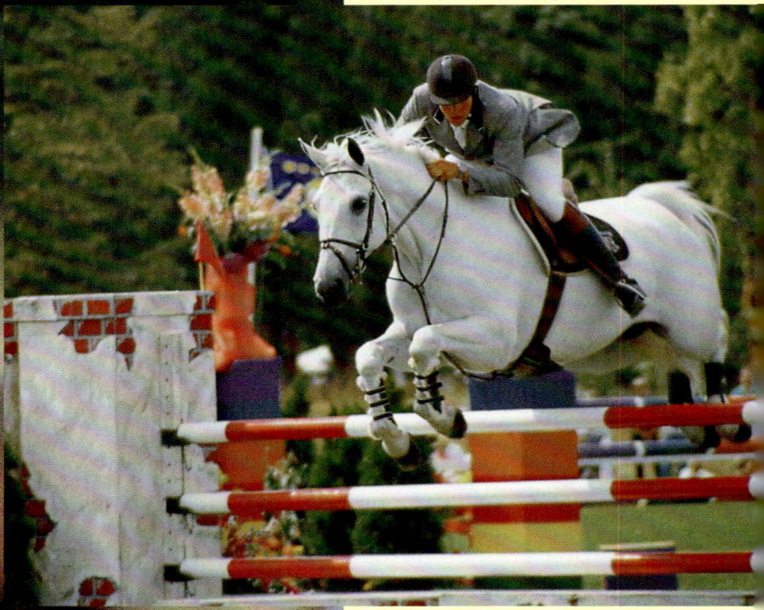

Marymoor Park was the site for the Evergreen Classic Benefit Horse Show.

the Mountaineer's Club. Climbers who want to hone their skills during inclement weather will find ample opportunity at indoor climbing walls such as the REI Pinnacle in REI's flagship store; the Big Pointy in Redmond's Marymoor Park; Stone Gardens in Ballard; and a choice of two Vertical World climbing structures in Ballard and Redmond.

The Cascade Foothills are also popular with folks who prefer to take to the trails on horseback. Tiger Mountain Outfitters in Issaquah offers three-hour guided trail rides through logging roads and forests to a lookout up the mountain. Kelly's Riding and Boarding Ranch, also in Issaquah, leads horse enthusiasts on shorter guided rides along the base of Squak Mountain. Other recreational activities that are popular with the equestrian crowd are available at Bridle Trails State Park, a 480-acre horse-lover's heaven that features groomed trails, wooded trails, and an exercise ring. One of the trails connects with Marymoor Park, which also features trails expressly for horseback riding.

When snow blankets the Cascade Mountain Range and its foothills, King County nature lovers gear up and head for the hills. Within King County itself there are ample opportunities for cross-country skiers and folks who prefer the leisurely pace of a snowshoe walk. Those seeking the greater intensity and adrenaline rush of downhill skiing or snowboarding can drive just minutes past the county line to the Summit at Snoqualmie, which features four neighboring ski areas that all honor the same lift ticket. Collectively, these four areas—Alpental, Summit West, Summit Central, and Summit East—feature runs to challenge skiers of every level of ability and offer instruction for downhill and cross-country skiers and snowboarders. Stevens Pass and Crystal Mountain ski areas are also within easy driving distance King County's metropolitan areas. Both cater to downhill and cross-country skiers, and both are distinguished by their incredible views of the beauty that surrounds them. The Nordic Center at Stevens Pass boasts 25 kilometers of groomed trails and is reputed to be the best cross-country skiing in the region.

Thanks to the mild climate and beautiful natural setting, King County's golf courses are some of the finest in the nation. There are countless private and public courses sprinkled throughout the county. In 1998, Redmond's Sahalee course was host to the PGA tournament. The golfers were so pleased with the course that the PGA plans to return for another tournament at Sahalee in 2002.

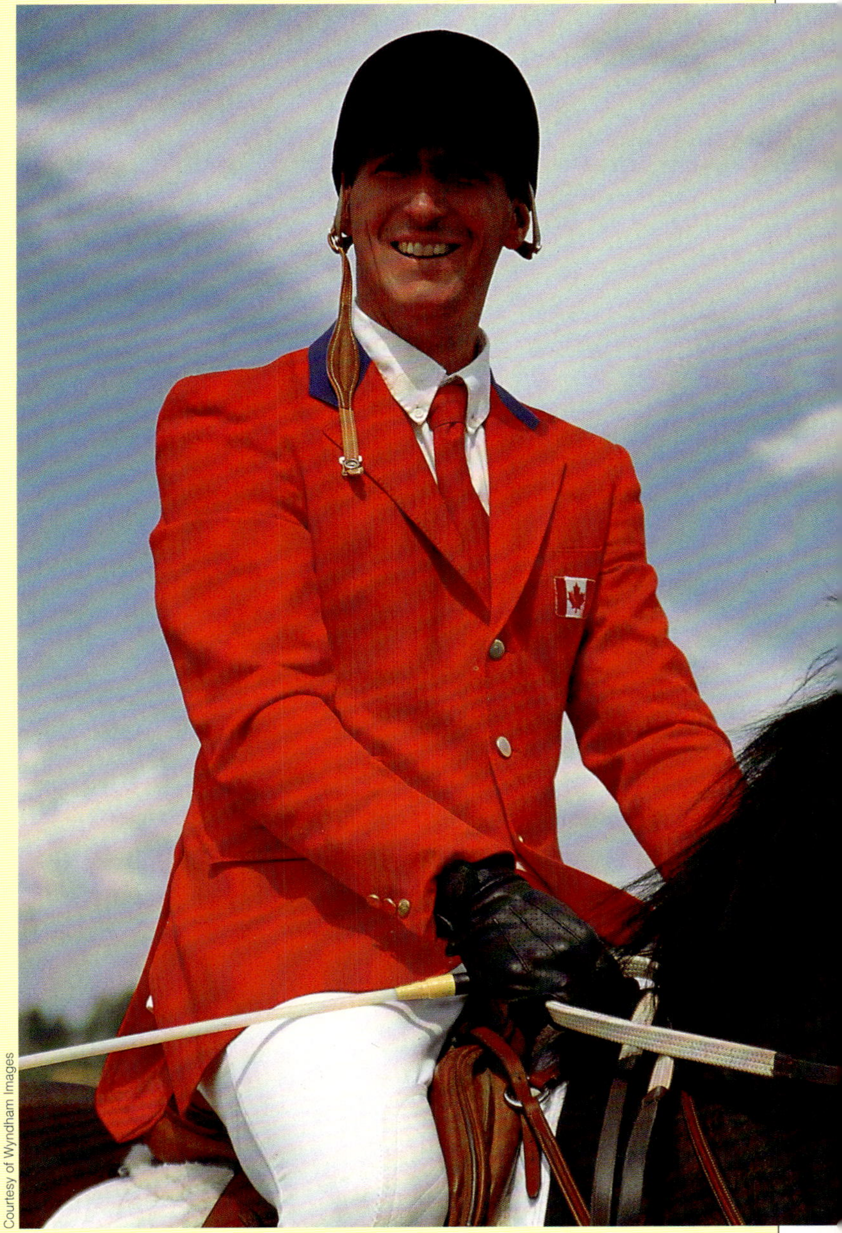

Courtesy of Wyndham Images

This Canadian competitor readies himself and his horse for a jumping competition at the Evergreen Classic.

Flanked by water on nearly all sides—from the rivers and streams that meander through woods and valleys, to the shimmering waters of Lake Washington, Lake Sammamish, and Lake Union, to the vast, deep waters of the Puget Sound—it is no surprise that water sports are king in King County. The mild climate is a boon to sailing enthusiasts who can enjoy their sport year round. Sunny days can draw so many people out onto the water that sailboats, yachts, and pleasure craft are scattered like low-lying clouds against the backdrop of the blue sky. Water lovers who prefer a greater degree of solitude and communion with the water will find it in kayaking, which has a history in this region that dates back some 6,000 years. Windsurfing is another popular water sport, especially with the younger crowd. Equipment rentals and instruction are available at Green Lake Park and at various parks along Lake Washington, Lake Union, and Puget Sound.

For folks who like to move through the water rather than atop it, there are a number of guarded and unguarded swimming beaches along the region's bodies of water. In addition, there are numerous public pools, including Colman Pool, an outdoor saltwater pool in West Seattle's Lincoln Park. This region is also home to the King County Aquatic Center, a state-of-the-art swimming and diving facility in Federal Way, which was built to host the 1990 Goodwill Games. In recent years, Olympic trials for diving and synchronized swimming have been held at the Aquatic Center.

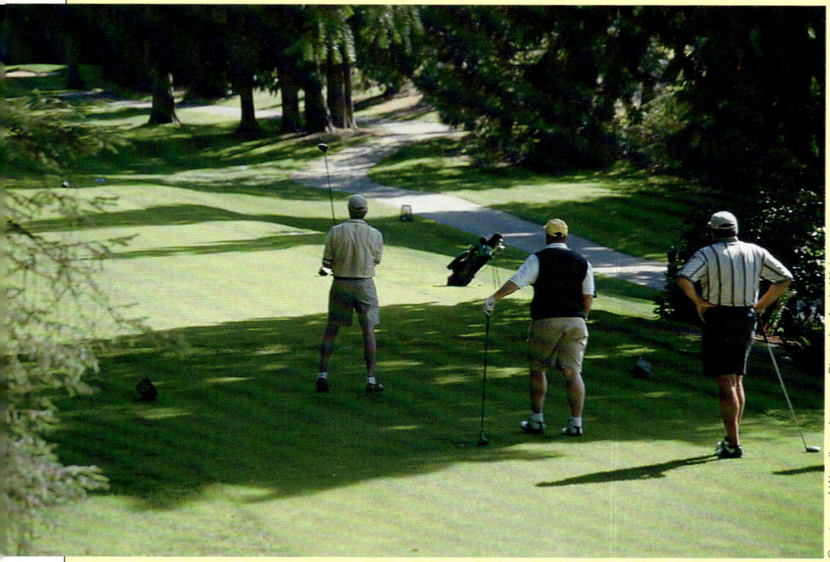

Courtesy of Wyndham Images. Photo by Andy Wolgamott

Golfers navigate the 27-hole course at the Sahalee Country Club.

Team Players

Spectator sports are also big in King County. Home to the Championship University of Washington Husky football team and professional football, baseball, basketball, hockey, and soccer teams, there is never a dull moment for sports fans.

The Seattle SuperSonics basketball franchise was the first prime-time professional sports team on the scene in King County, debuting in 1967 as an NBA expansion team. After nearly a decade of hits and misses, the SuperSonics reached a milestone with the 1974-75 season, as the team made it into the NBA playoffs for the first time. Fans relished the intense play and undeniable chemistry of stars like Slick Watts and "Downtown" Fred Brown. Building on the success of that season, the team again made it into the playoffs the following season and finally earned the NBA title in 1979, under the leadership of coach and former Sonics All-Star point guard, Lenny Wilkens. By the early 1990s, with Coach George Karl at the helm and Gary Payton tearing up the court, the Seattle SuperSonics began to regain some of the momentum of their earlier championship years. In the eight seasons between 1991 and 2000, the destiny-bound Sonics boasted winning records, gained a devoted fan base, won four Pacific Division Titles, set numerous records, and proved to be one of the most entertaining and talented ball teams in the NBA.

The Seattle Seahawks football team made its first real connection with sports fans in the region during the mid 1970s when the strength and precision of quarterback Jim Zorn found a perfect match in the speed and grace of receiver Steve Largent. Those golden days of record-setting crowds and adrenaline-punching noise have proven hard to follow, but loyal fans have kept the dream alive and joined forces with local billionaire Paul Allen in 1997 to save the team from an almost certain relocation. To prevent the loss of the local NFL franchise, Washington State voters struck a unique deal with Allen, agreeing to foot the bill for a new sports stadium and exhibition hall if Allen would purchase the team. As a result of this deal, 1999 was the Seahawk's last season in the Kingdome. The dome was demolished in the spring of 2000, and the new stadium is expected to open in the summer of 2002.

A short drive in any direction from King County will bring the adventurer to completely different vistas, from lonely mountain streams to crashing Pacific waves.

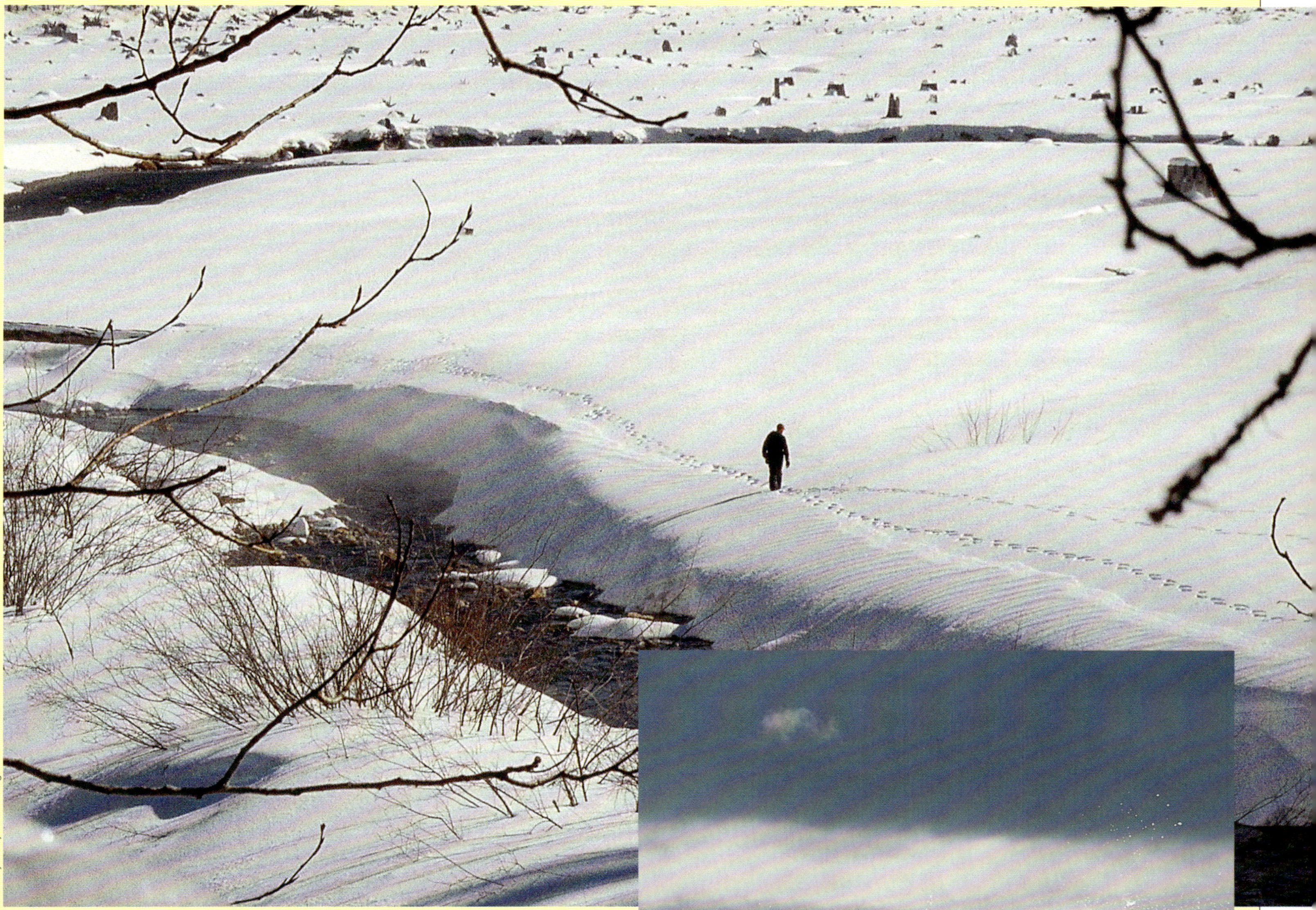

Courtesy of Wyndham Images

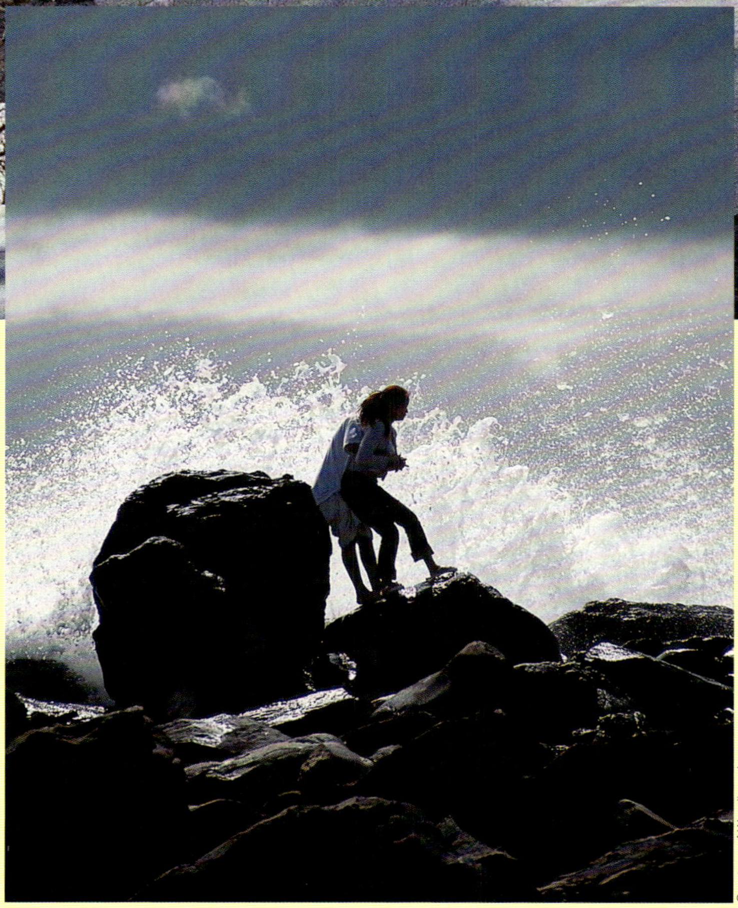

Courtesy of Wyndham Images

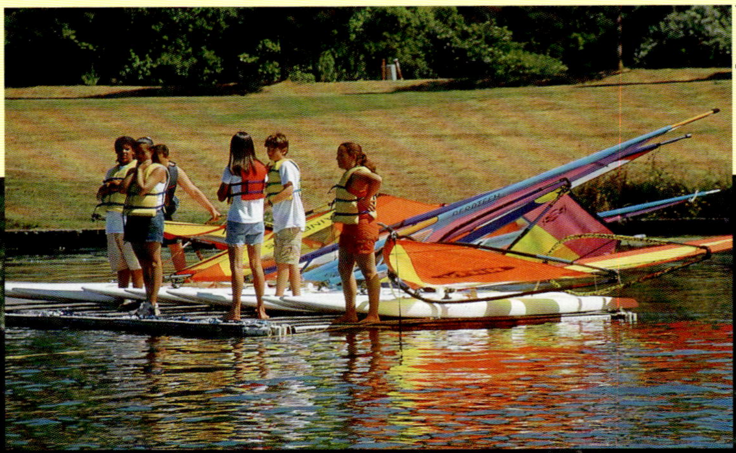

Courtesy of

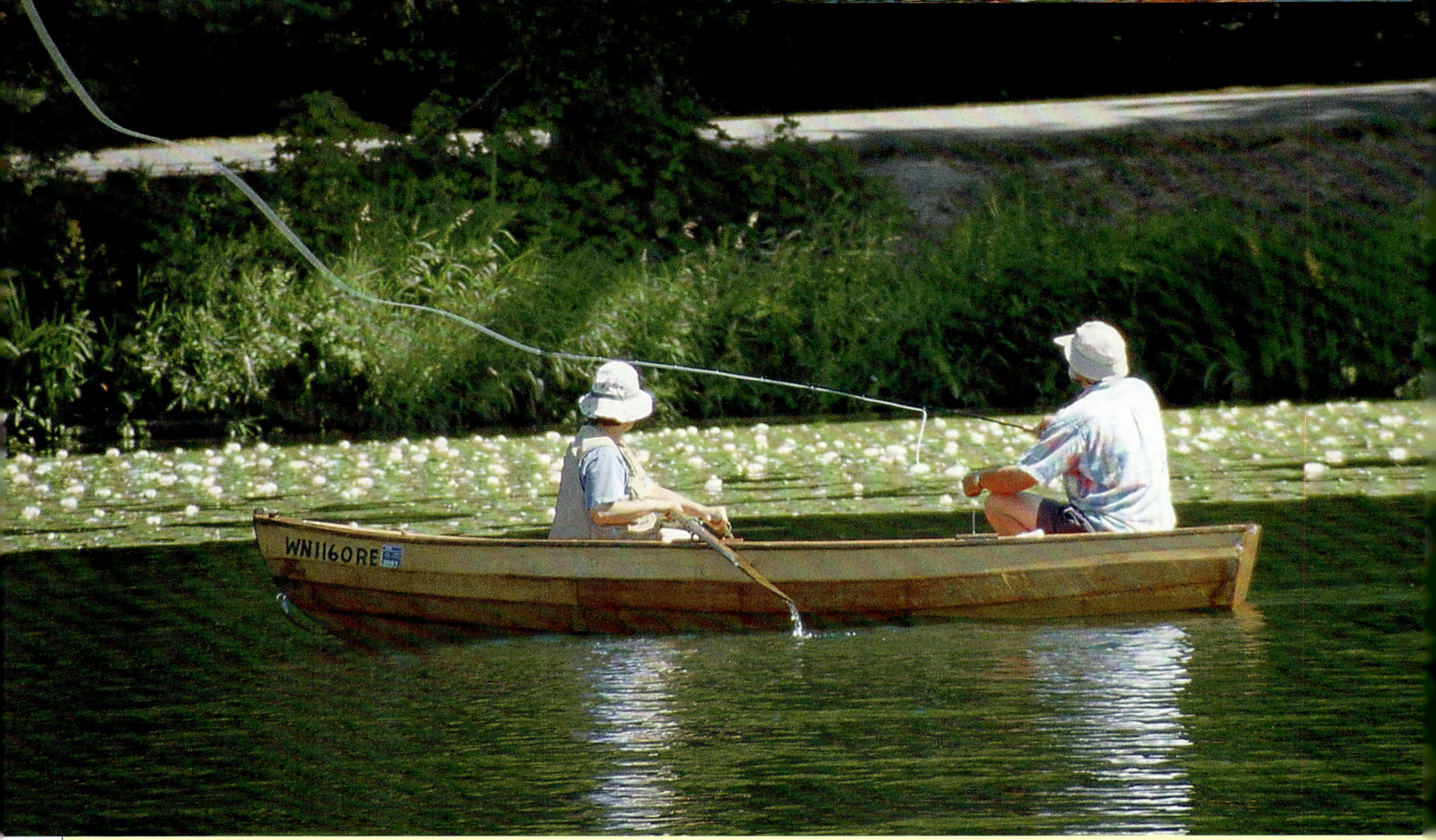

There is an outdoor activity to suit every level of sportsperson. For a relaxing outing, one might go fishing among the lily pads near Seward Park. For more excitement, one might take up windsailing on Lake Washington. However, for a real thrill, why not try parasailing over Elliott Bay?

Courtesy of Wyndham Images

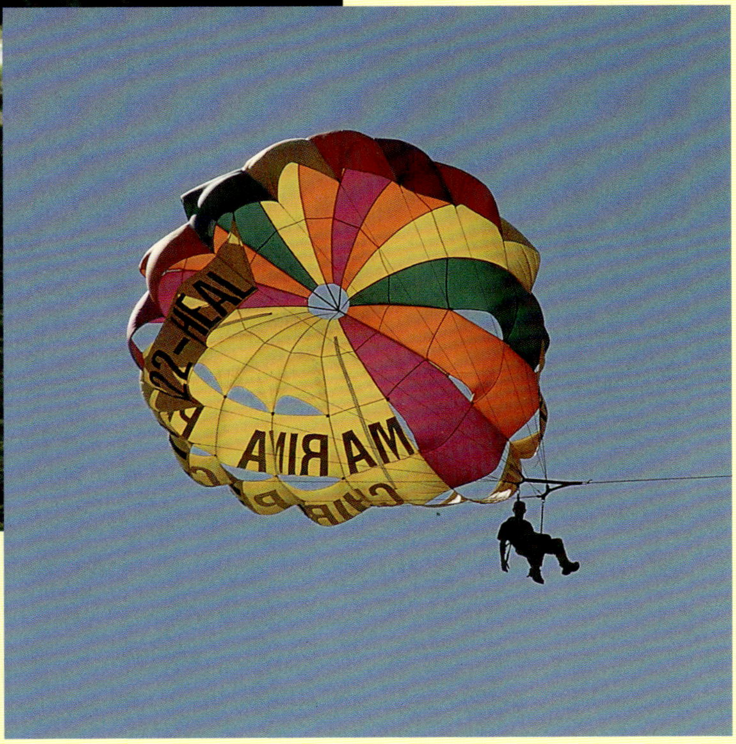
Courtesy of Wyndham Images

The Seattle Mariners baseball club made its major league debut in 1977 in an April 7 contest against the California Angels. Ken Griffey, Jr. joined the Mariners in 1989, and the team made history when Junior played two seasons with his dad, Ken Griffey, Sr., in 1990 and 1991. By 1991, the Mariners had the makings of a great team; the Griffeys took the field with Edgar Martinez, Jay Buhner, and ace pitcher, Randy Johnson. With powerful hitting, dramatic fielding, and strong pitching, the Mariners began to win games. In 1994, the team took third place in its division, but it was the 1995 season that would prove to be magical. In a wild card contest that seemed to be fated, the Mariners again faced the Angels (now Anaheim). In one of the most riveting games in baseball history, the Mariners prevailed, and soon everyone was a fan. The Mariners went on to win the American League West Championship that year, and dreams of the World Series were born. For the next two years, fans kept the dream alive, and in 1997 the Mariners delivered a second division championship. As a result of these victories and the growing popularity of the team's All-Star players, the team joined with taxpayers to build new open-air, retractable-roof baseball stadium. The team began enjoying its new stadium, SAFECO Field, in July of 1999. Although the 2000 season began with some uncertainty after superstar Ken Griffey, Jr. was traded away, it would prove to be the ballclub's best season to date. The Seattle Mariners led the American League West Division by a wide margin for most of the year, but faltered a bit toward the end of the regular season. After earning the Wild Card berth into the American League Championship Series, the Mariners went on to sweep the American League Central Champion Chicago White Sox, 3 games to 0, and the team was on to New York to face the defending World Series Champion Yankees. In a tough contest of will and skill, the Yankees prevailed in the sixth game of a best-of-seven series. Though the Mariners and their fans were surely disappointed, the season rekindled dreams of a World Series pennant.

Although the Seattle Sounders soccer team has been around since the mid-1970s, it has taken some time for Northwesterners to fully embrace the sport that is arguably the international favorite. While the team currently plays at the 10,000-seat Memorial Stadium, they will get to move into their new home, the stadium they will share with the Seattle Seahawks, in 2002.

The Seattle Seahawks' ever-present defense pounds the opponent to the turf.

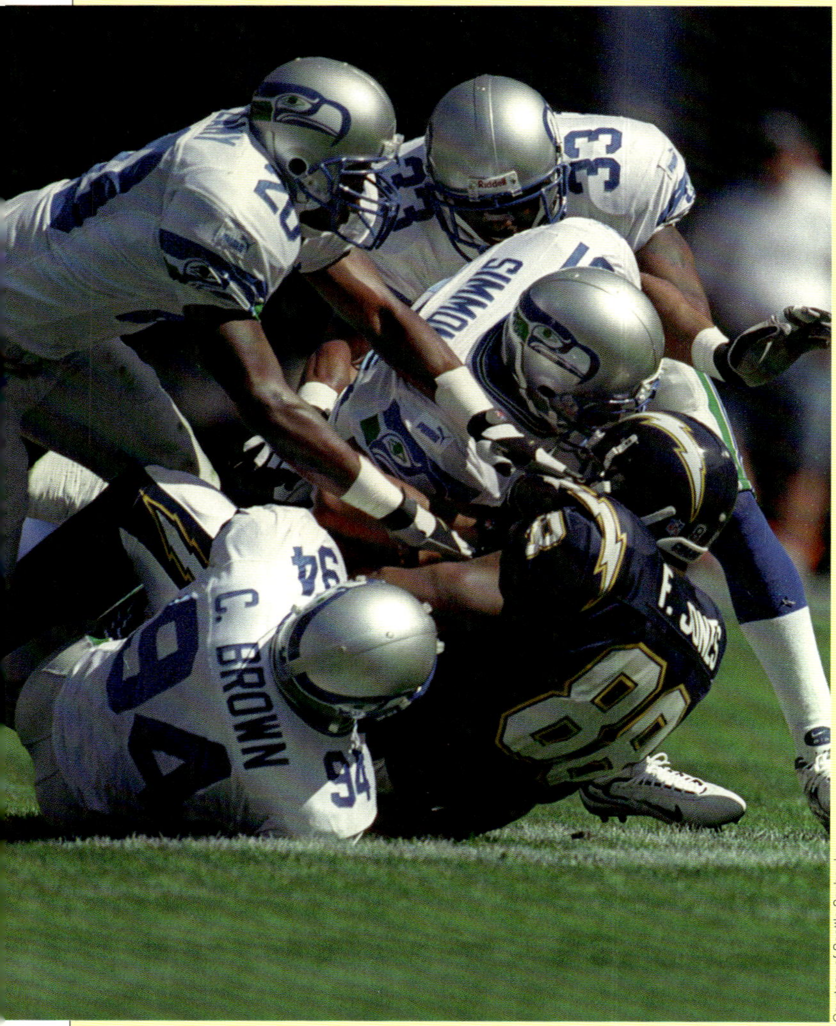

Courtesy of Seattle Seahawks

Sports fans who like the fast-paced action and intensity of professional hockey will not be disappointed with the Seattle Thunderbirds. Though the Thunderbirds are a young team, they won the 1996-97 Western Hockey League championship, and they have earned a devoted following.

Women's basketball fans were disappointed after the American Basketball League was forced to fold, seemingly ending the region's brief infatuation with the Seattle Reign. Good news came in 1999, when local sports fans learned that a WNBA (Women's National Basketball Association) team would be based in Seattle. Coach Lin Dunn was hired to lead the new team, even before it had a name. Coach Dunn brought with her an exuberant spirit and a contagious affection for women's basketball. She also brought along a distinguished reputation with numerous professional successes, including many winning seasons and three Big Ten championships during her tenure at Purdue University and leading the Portland Power to a Western Conference Championship in her first full season with the team. Under Dunn's leadership, the team began to sign top-ranked ballplayers like Sonja Henning and Charmin Smith, and in January 2000, the Seattle Storm team name and logo were revealed to an expectant fan base of more than 1,500 season ticket holders. It is clear that women's professional basketball now holds a significant fan base along with the other professional sports that are so popular in King County.

Coach Dunn brought with her an exuberant spirit and a contagious affection for women's basketball. She also brought along a distinguished reputation with numerous professional successes, including many winning seasons and three Big Ten championships during her tenure at Purdue University and leading the Portland Power to a Western Conference Championship in her first full season with the team. Under Dunn's leadership, the team began to sign top-ranked ballplayers like Sonja Henning and Charmin Smith, and in January 2000, the Seattle Storm team name and logo were revealed to an expectant fan base of more than 1,500 season ticket holders. It is clear that women's professional basketball now holds a significant fan base along with the other professional sports that are so popular in King County.

As one of the NBA's 50 Greatest Players, future hall-of-fame center Patrick Ewing gives the Sonics an inside presence with big-game experience.

Courtesy of Seattle Seahawks

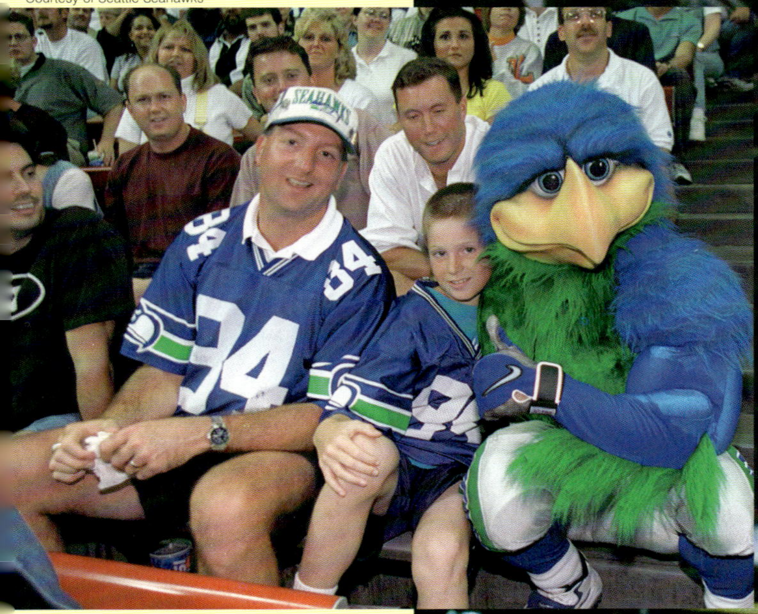

Fans, both young and old, enjoy posing for the camera with the Seahawks' mascot Blitz.

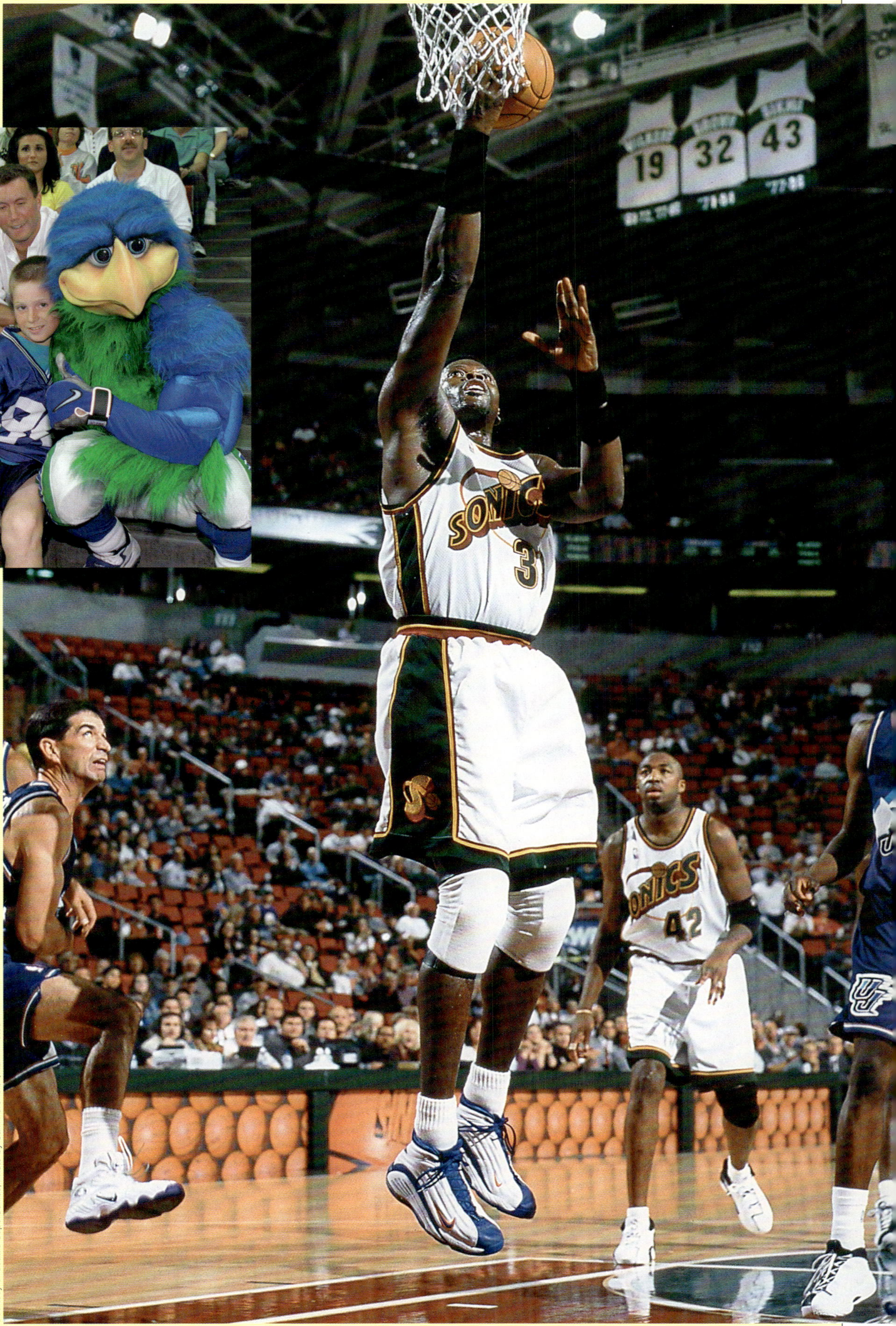

Courtesy of Seattle SuperSonics, Photo by Sam Forencich/NBA Photos

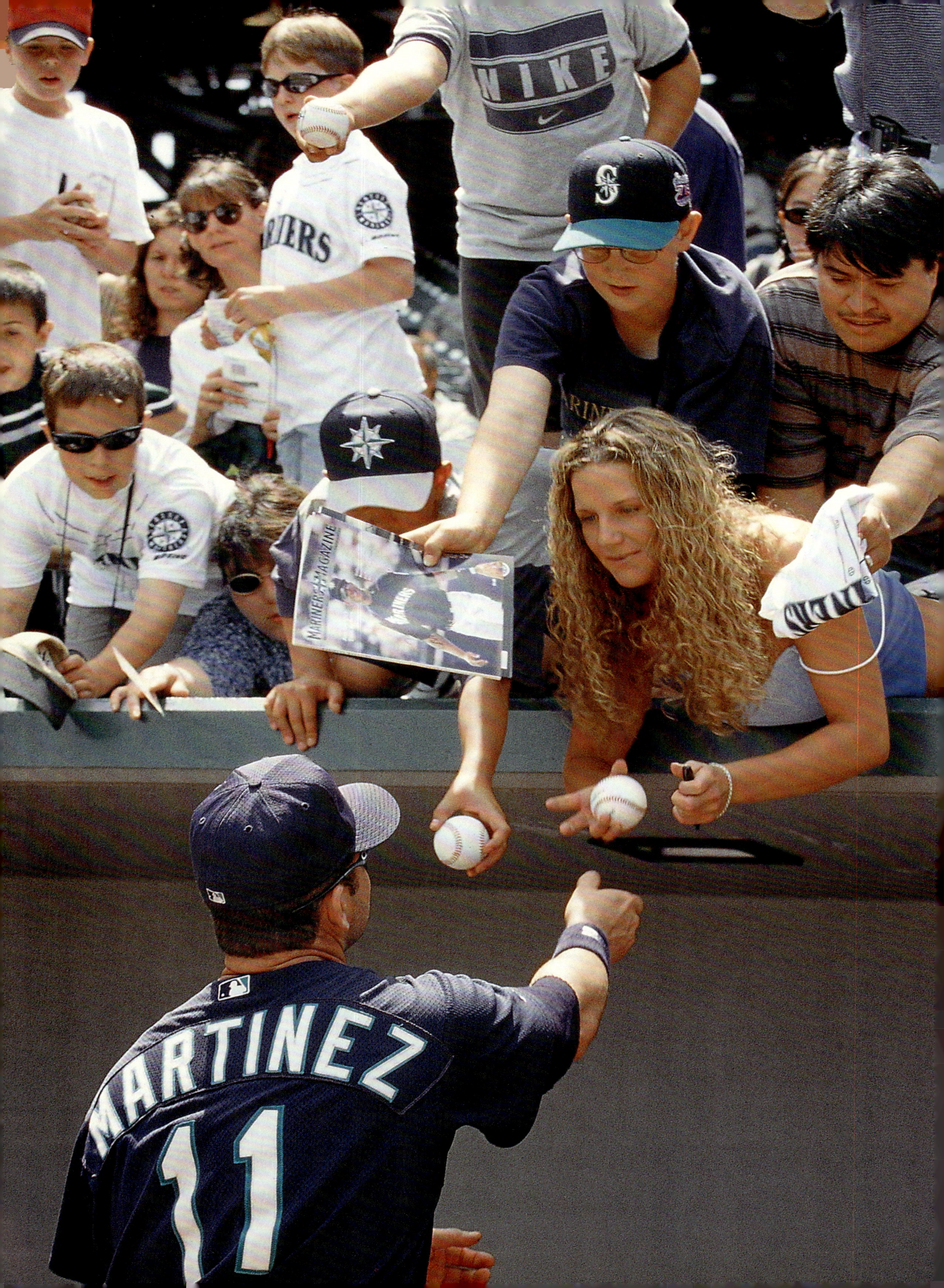
NIKE
MARINERS MAGAZINE
MARTINEZ
11

Fan favorite Edgar Martinez stops to sign autographs before a game.

A Brief History of Baseball in Seattle

While professional baseball has been headline news around King County for the past several years, few fans of America's favorite pastime are aware of the sport's inauspicious beginnings in the region.

Seattle's first professional sports team took to a baseball diamond at the end of Madison Street on May 24, 1890. In those days, they had no need for fancy names or logos, they were simply known as "the Seattles," and the team they played on that historical day was aptly called "the Spokanes." The Seattles won that game 11-8 and would go on to win the Pacific Northwest League Championship pennant in 1892. Not long after that, the league went bust.

After many fits and starts with minor-league teams that had colorful names such as "the Turks," "the Rainiers," "the Braves," and "the Siwashes," the city got its first Major League baseball team in 1969. Dubbed "the Seattle Pilots," the region's first big-league team brought with it big-league changes, including a stipulation from the American League that the existing ballpark, Sicks' Stadium, be improved and eventually replaced with a domed indoor stadium. It was upon this agreement (and approval of 63 percent of voters) that the Kingdome was built. Despite that the Pilots would leave town just a year after playing their opening game. It was not until April 6, 1977 that the Seattle Mariners played their first home game in the Kingdome, and they have been the city's team ever since.

With the recent success of the Seattle Mariners, Seattle now proudly calls itself a "baseball town." With one of the newest and best ballparks in all of Major League Baseball in SAFECO Field, a playoff-caliber team, and a date to host the 2001 All-Star game, it seems in fact that Seattle is destined to be one of the great baseball towns of all time.

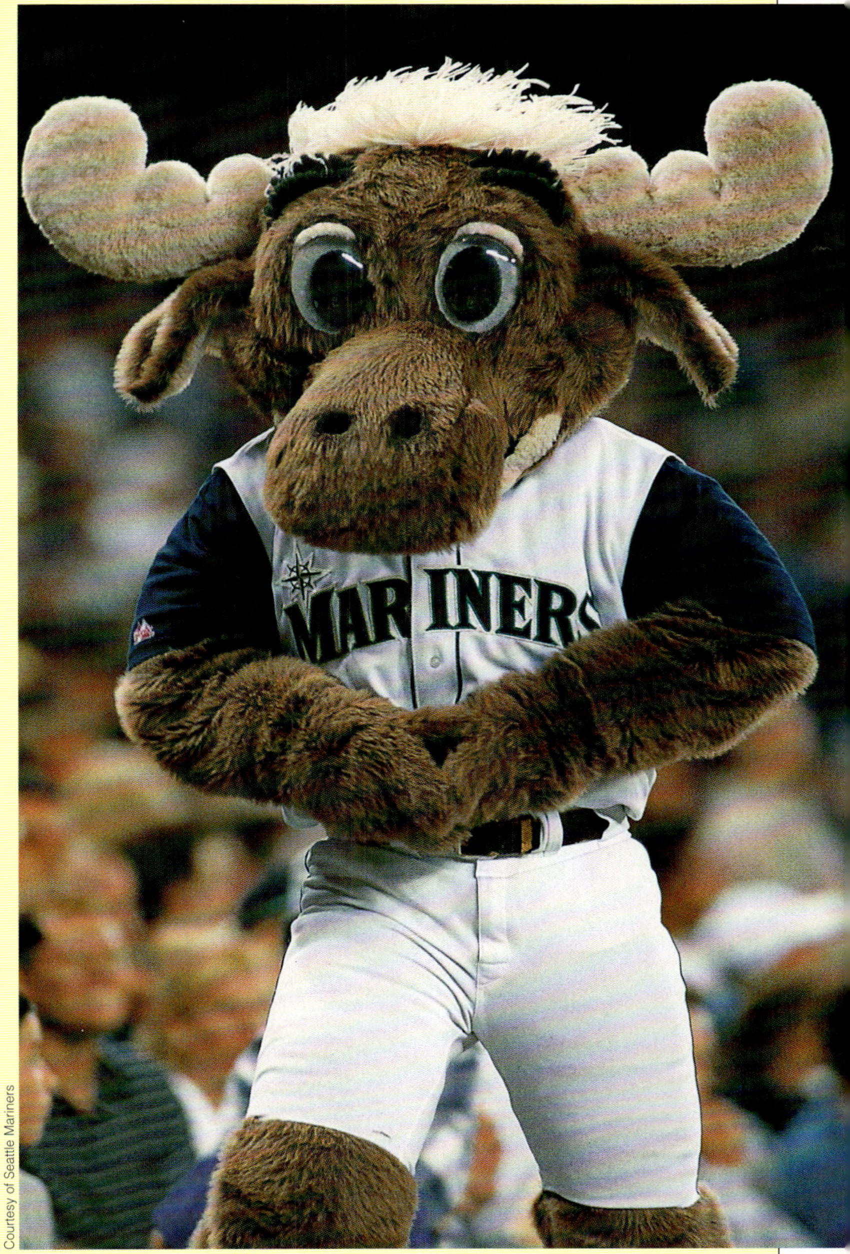

Courtesy of Seattle Mariners

Team mascot the Mariner Moose entertains fans from atop the first-base dugout.

The Lively Arts

King County enjoys a reputation for being strongly supportive of the arts. From art museums in Seattle and Bellevue, to small theatre groups in Issaquah and Kent, the visual and performing arts are an important part of life for the people of this area.

The arts in King County encompass the full spectrum of mediums, from mainstream theatre, opera, and symphony orchestras, to quirky theatre companies, sculpture, and dance. Intimate art galleries in Kirkland coexist with major Broadway shows in Seattle, and the residents would not want it any other way. The people of King County love their art. That much is clear.

Theatre

On any given weekend, theatre-goers can catch a major Broadway show in downtown Seattle or a small production in Kent. King County theatre offers a broad spectrum of entertainment options from big-budget plays and musicals, to little known performance pieces. Arguably, the theatre is at its most compelling and diverse in Seattle—Seattle has the highest live-theatre attendance per capita of any major city—although fine theatre can certainly be found outside the city. There are major theatres in the central downtown area and intimate playhouses in neighborhoods such as Capitol Hill and Greenwood.

The Fifth Avenue and Paramount Theatres in downtown Seattle are the forebears of many of the smaller theatres that have appeared over the last several decades. The Fifth Avenue Theatre, located on Fifth Avenue between Union and University streets, still inhabits its original location. Built in 1926 as a vaudeville house, the Fifth Avenue has gone through many incarnations. Several years after it opened, it was transformed into a movie house and remained as such for more than 50 years. Sadly, the popularity of multiplexes in the 1970s spelled disaster for the Fifth Avenue. It could not compete and closed its doors in 1978. The Fifth Avenue averted demolition when a group of concerned citizens raised $2.6 million to renovate the theatre. In 1980, the theatre re-opened with the musical *Annie*. In the years that followed, the non-profit theatre has played host to scores of top-flight musicals and plays and remains one of the best-loved theatres in the area.

Courtesy of Northwest Asian American Theatre, Photo by Lester Lee

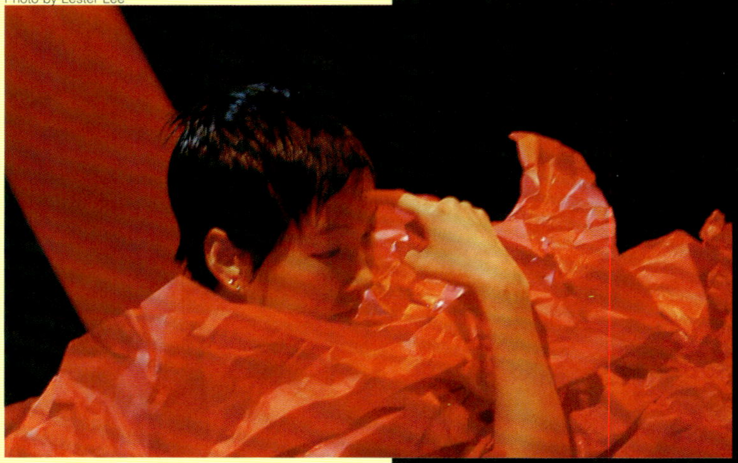

Northwest Asian American Theatre presented The Three Yells in Remember Me—Installment 6 *during A-Fest 2001.*

Courtesy of Pacific Northwest Ballet, Photo by Angela Sterling

Patricia Barker and Ariana Lallone in The Sleeping Beauty.

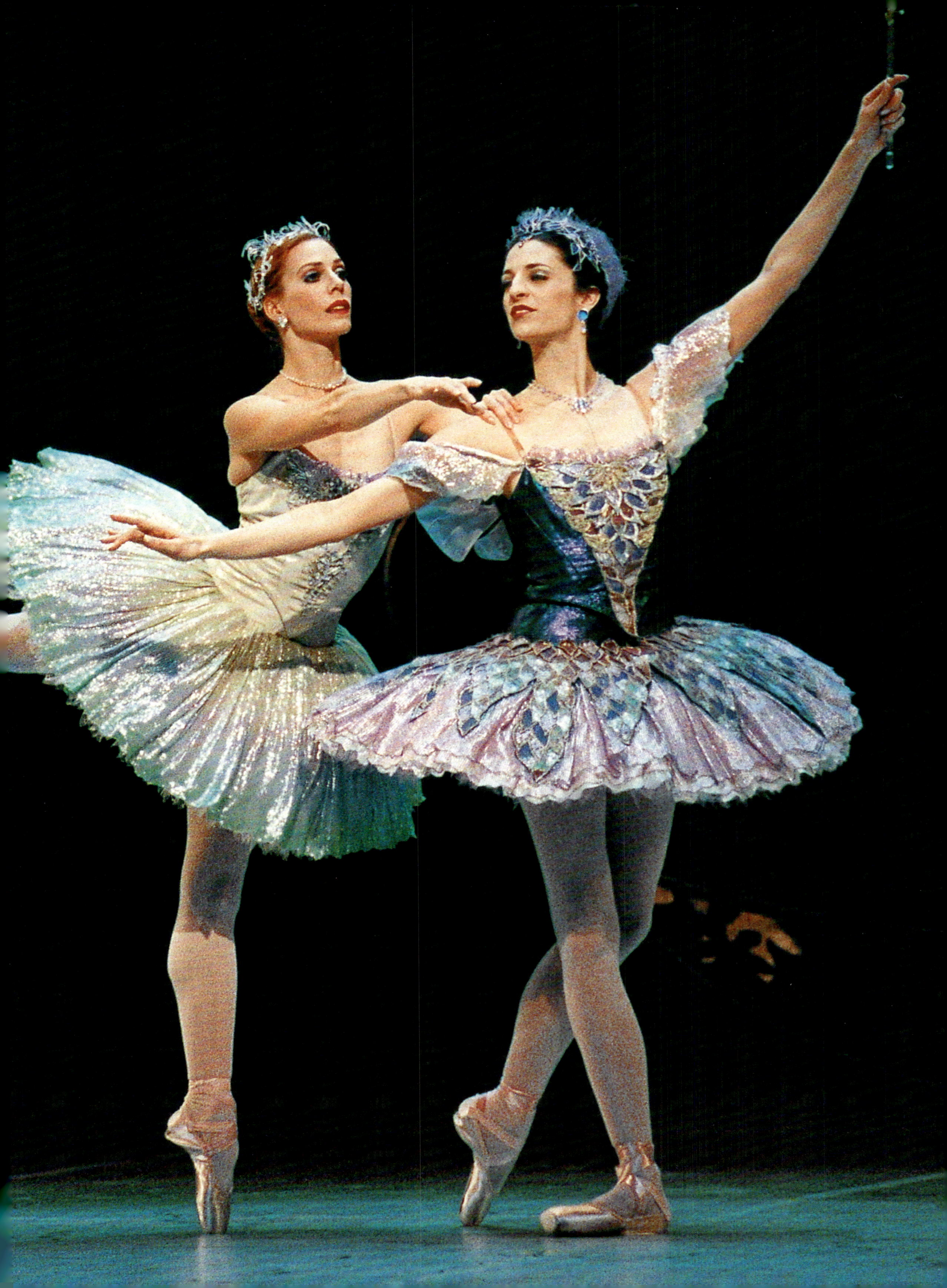

Opening Night at Benaroya Hall, September 12, 1998. A packed audience listens intently as Maestro Gerard Schwarz, Music Director, conducts the Seattle Symphony in the S. Mark Taper Foundation Auditorium.

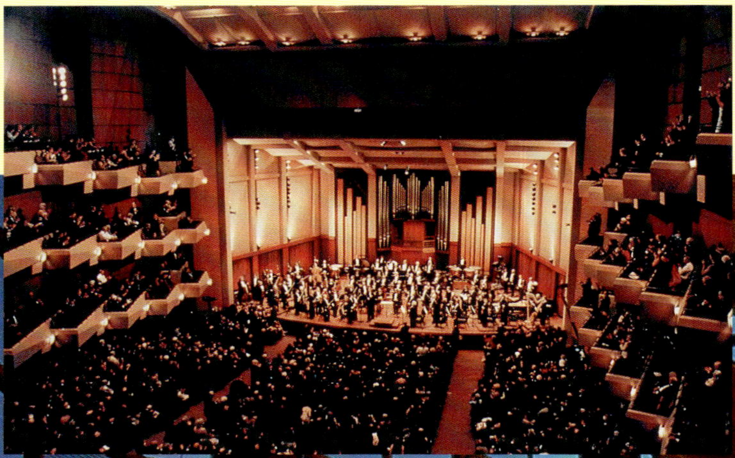

Courtesy of Seattle Symphony, © Dan Lamont Photo

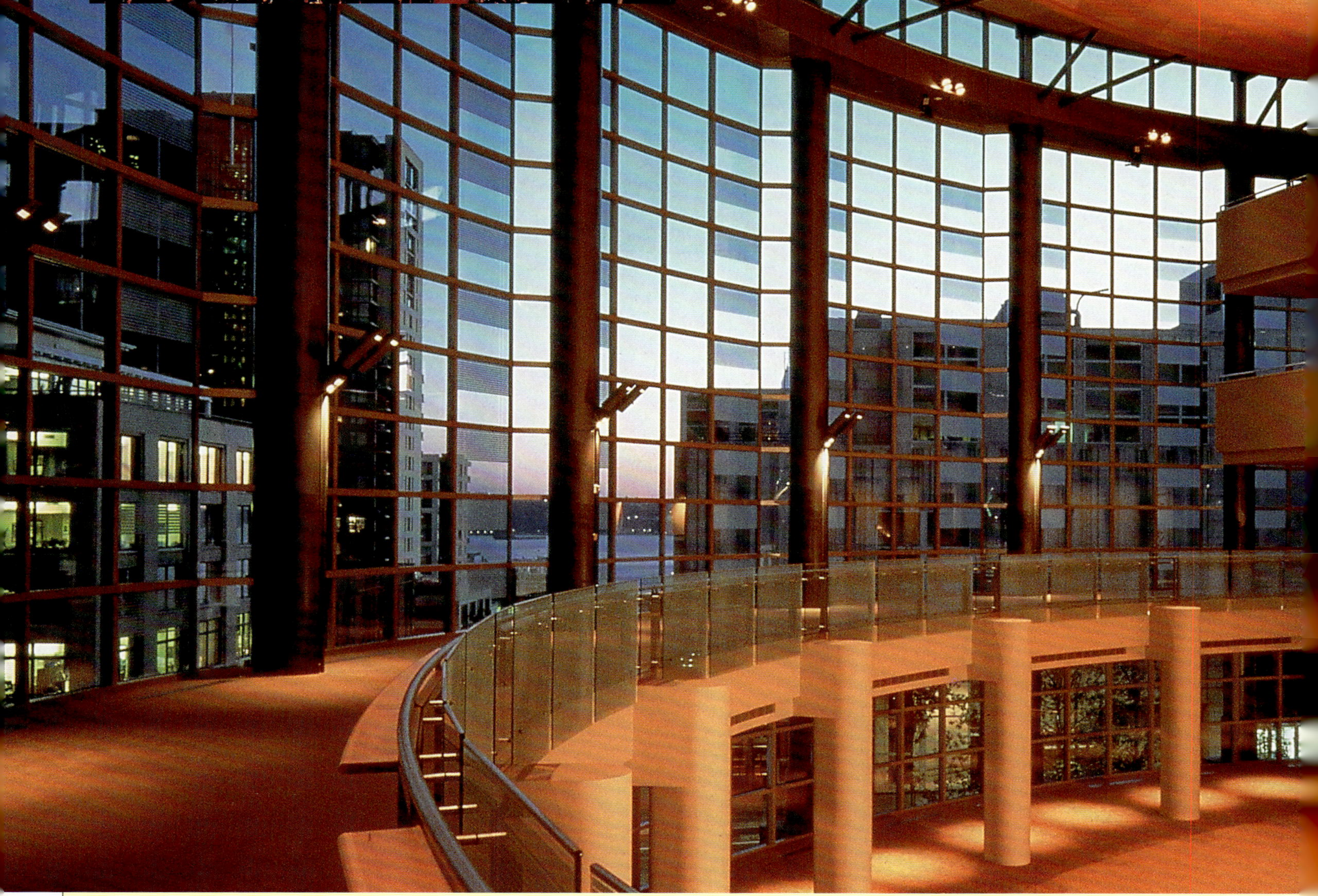

The Samuel and Althea Stroum Grand Lobby in Benaroya Hall, home of the Seattle Symphony, Gerard Schwarz, Music Director.

The Paramount Theatre, located at the corner of Pine Street and Ninth Avenue in downtown Seattle, is another long-timer in King County. When it was built in 1928, the Paramount was one of the largest theatres in the country. Like its cousin The Fifth Avenue, the Paramount served first as a vaudeville theatre and silent movie house. Up until a few years ago, the Paramount was in a state of disrepair. Worse yet, the small, cramped stage and shabby backstage area made it unattractive as a venue for major Broadway shows. The Paramount was badly in need of major renovations or demolition would certainly be its fate.

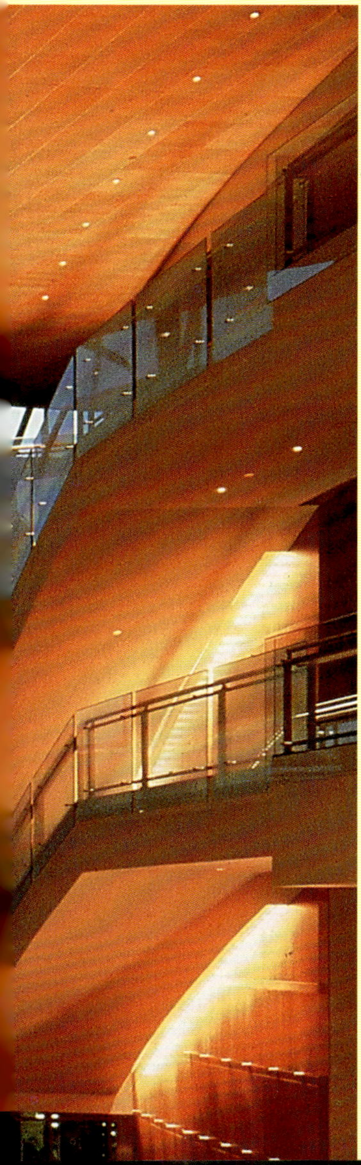

Courtesy of Seattle Symphony

Thankfully, renovation was its fate, not demolition. Several years ago, the Paramount underwent six months of intensive renovation and restoration. The result is a truly beautiful and awe-inspiring theatre. The Paramount is now one of the favorite stops for major Broadway shows, most notably *The Phantom of the Opera*, *Showboat*, and *Sunset Boulevard*, and is also becoming an increasingly popular venue for music concerts. The people of King County are grateful that the Paramount's cause was taken up—to lose such a treasured part of local history would have been a tragedy.

Several theatres are located on the Seattle Center grounds. One of the best known and highly respected is the Seattle Repertory Theatre. The Seattle Repertory Theatre, or the Seattle Rep as it is affectionately known, is the oldest theatre company in the area. The Seattle Rep performs in both the Bagley Wright and Leo K. Theatres on the Seattle Center grounds. The Seattle Rep is on the cutting edge of King County theatre; shows that premiere at the Rep often later make it to Broadway. Seattle Rep performances are quite popular and are often sold out weeks in advance of show time. In 1990, the Seattle Repertory Theatre was the recipient of a Tony Award for outstanding regional theatre.

Music Director Gerard Schwarz conducts the Seattle Symphony at the September 1998 opening of Benaroya Hall, the $118 million concert-dedicated hall, in downtown Seattle.

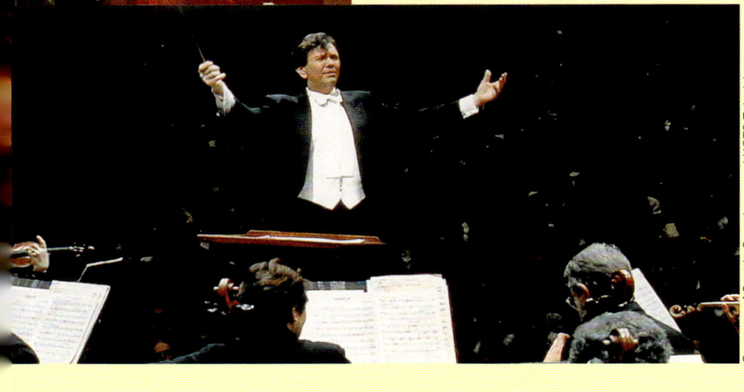

Courtesy of Seattle Symphony and KCTS Television

The Intiman is another venerable theatre in King County. The Intiman was established in Kirkland in 1972. It rapidly outgrew its Kirkland quarters, however, and moved to a new venue at the Seattle Center in 1974. The Intiman is well known for producing intense and controversial plays such as Tony Kushner's *Angels in America* but tempers this with more mainstream classics by Henrik Ibsen, Anton Chekhov, and Edward Albee.

The well-respected Seattle Children's Theatre has been entertaining audiences for 25 years. The Seattle Children's Theatre performs at the Charlotte Martin Theatre complex at Seattle Center.

Northwest Asian American Theatre (NWAAT) is committed to showcasing the talents of exceptional developing artists. The International Artists Program is one venue in which NWAAT accomplishes this. Shown here is a 1998 production photo from Home: Places Between Asia & America.

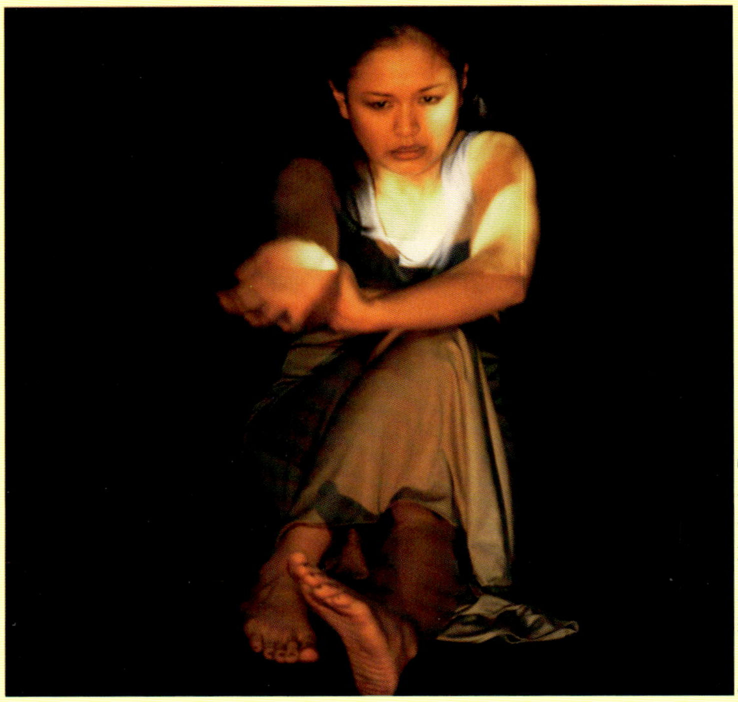

Courtesy of Northwest Asian American Theatre

A Contemporary Theatre, better known as ACT, is the area's second oldest theatre group. ACT performs in the Falls Thrust and Allen Arena Theatres at Kreielsheimer Place in downtown Seattle. The building, located at the corner of Seventh Avenue and Union Street, was at one time the Eagles Auditorium. ACT specializes in contemporary theatre and prides itself on the use of local actors.

In the center of quirky Fremont, self-professed "center of the universe," is the Empty Space Theatre. The Empty Space is well known as the place for nonconformist and at times irreverent theatre, but it manages to put on a few mainstream productions each year as well. The theatre itself is a bit on the shabby side, but that is the way they like it at the Empty Space. Inscribed in gold paint in the theatre's lobby are these words by theatre director Peter Brook: "I can take any empty space and call it a bare stage. A man walks across this empty space whilst someone else is watching, and this is all that is needed for an act of theatre to be engaged."

The performing arts in east King County are growing, thanks in large part to the newly opened Kirkland Performance Center. The center, which opened its doors in June 1998, is the result of ten years of hard work by hundreds of volunteers and nearly a thousand generous donors. This 402-seat theatre, located in the heart of Kirkland, offers professional music, theatre, and dance to the many residents of east King County.

Farther East in Issaquah is the well-respected Village Theatre. The Village Theatre performs in the Francis J. Gaudette Theatre on Front Street in downtown Issaquah and has been a mainstay in Issaquah for 20 years. The theatre boasts an admirable mission that includes training young people in theatre skills for career opportunities and enriched lives and promoting positive values through art. The Village Theatre is definitely worth a trip for theatre and art lovers.

Smaller theatre companies are sprinkled throughout the county. The Annex, located on Fourth Avenue, the Open Circle Theatre at South Lake Union, the Taproot on 85th Street in Greenwood, and Theater Schmeater on Capitol Hill are all respectable theatre companies with their own loyal followings.

Dance

The Pacific Northwest Ballet is one of the best-loved artistic groups in the area. Each holiday season, adults and children alike anxiously await the always-stunning performances of *The Nutcracker.* The Pacific Northwest Ballet, which performs in the Opera House, treats audiences to both contemporary and traditional ballets.

Other dance groups, such as the University of Washington World Dance Series, the Mark Morris Dance Group, and On the Boards (which is also a theatre group), also offer top-flight dance performances. Other smaller dance groups are located throughout the county.

Music

The venerable Seattle Symphony Orchestra is arguably one of the best-known musical groups in the area. The Symphony, which performs at its new home at Benaroya Hall at Second Avenue and University Street, boasts a diverse program that runs the gamut from classical to popular. The Symphony's annual *Basically Baroque* and *Mostly Mozart* series are always immensely popular, as is the annual holiday performance of Handel's *Messiah.* The Symphony does not shy away from the unusual, however. Each season's offerings are liberally sprinkled with other more uncommon programs.

Opera attendance in Seattle is one of the highest per capita in the nation, and consequently, Seattle Opera performances are frequently sold out. The Seattle Opera, founded in 1964, performs at the Opera House on the Seattle Center grounds.

Other popular musical offerings abound throughout the county, including the Bellevue Philharmonic, Seattle Pro Musica, the Seattle Choral Company, the Federal Way Philharmonic, the Seattle Baroque

Northwest Asian American Theatre offers a variety of programs for Northwest theatre patrons and participants.

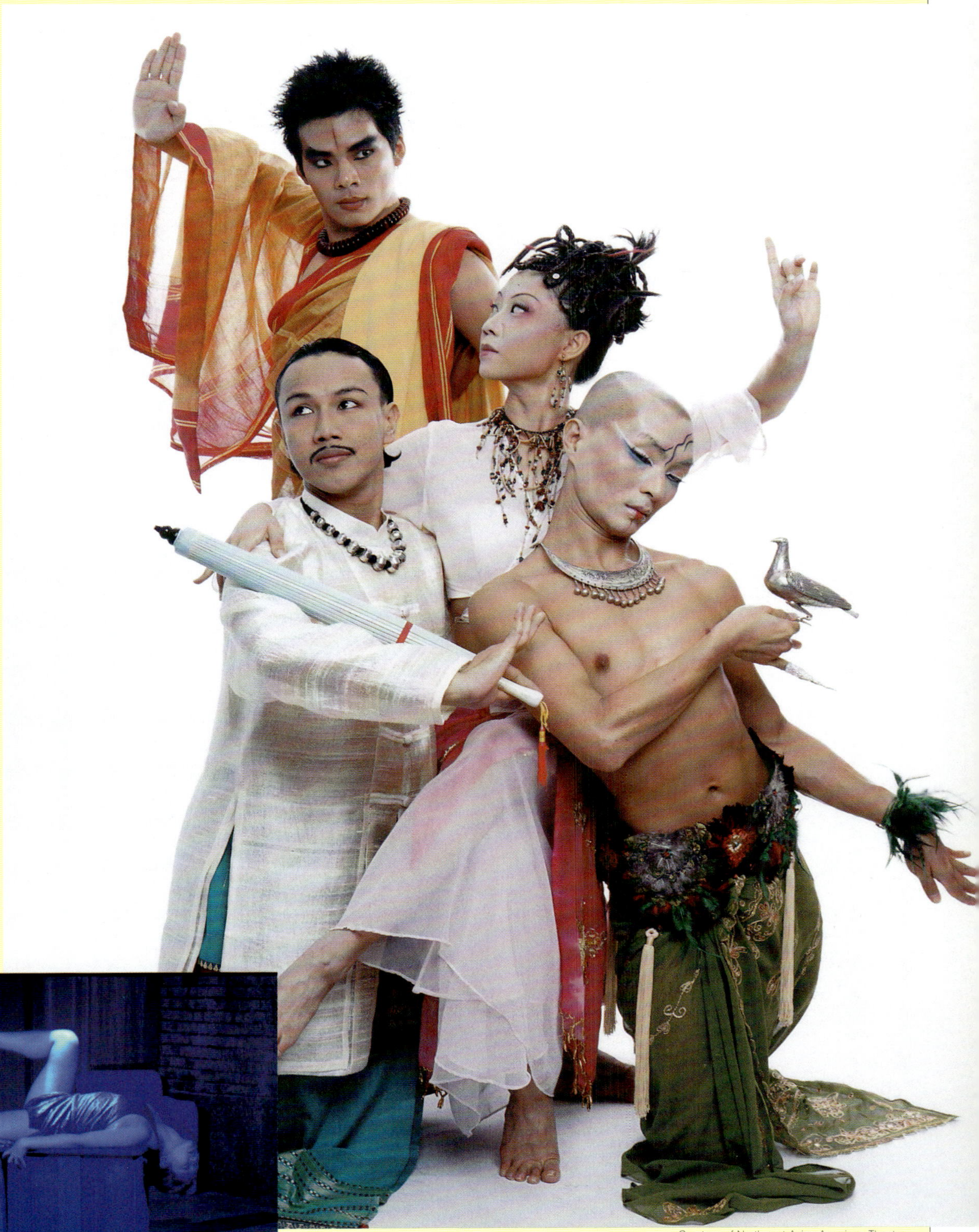

Courtesy of Northwest Asian American Theatre

NWAAT's International Artists Program production of Home: Places Between Asia & America.

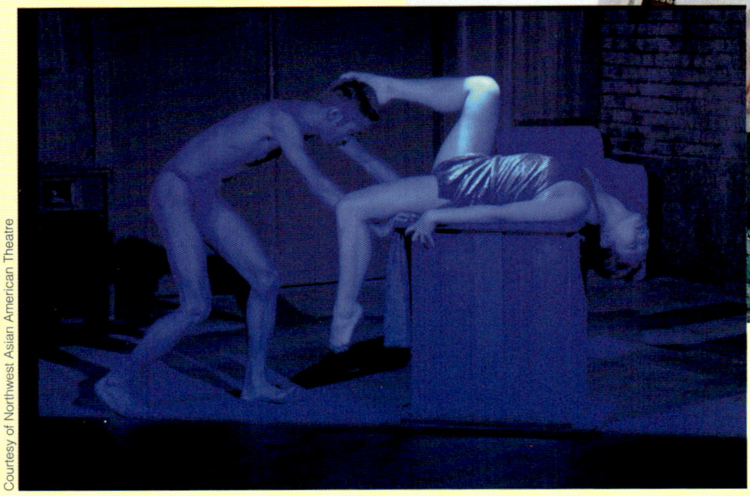

Courtesy of Northwest Asian American Theatre

Nadine Secunde (The Marschallin) in Seattle Opera's 1997 new production of Der Rosenkavalier *by Richard Strauss.*

Courtesy of Seattle Opera,
Photo by Gary Smith Photo

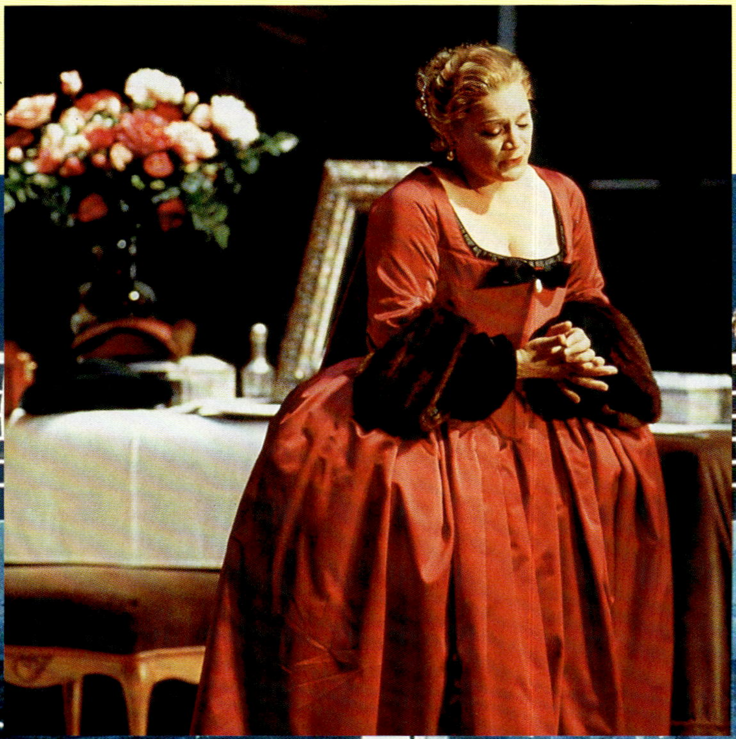

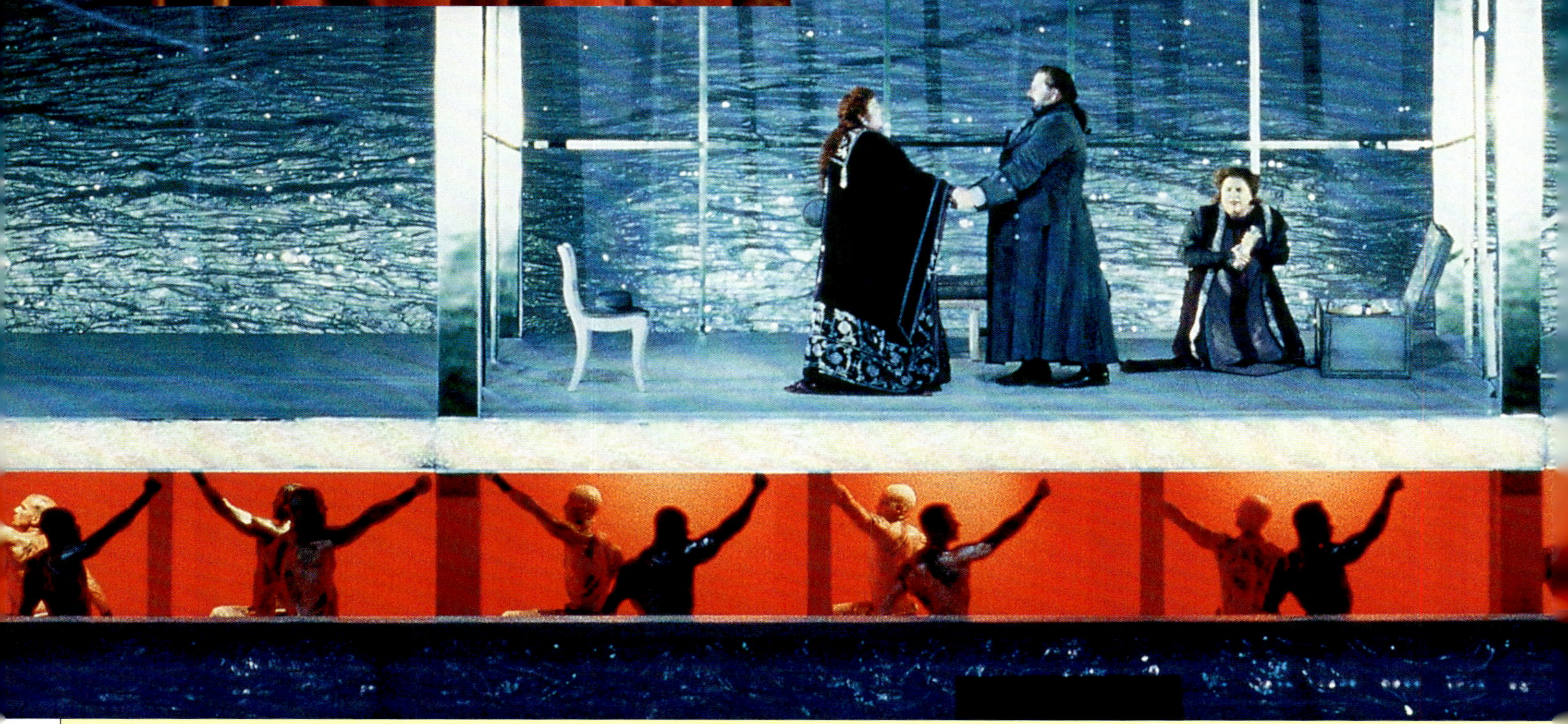

Act I finale of Seattle Opera's 1998 new production of Tristan und Isolde *by Richard Wagner.*

Orchestra, the Northwest Chamber Orchestra, the Seattle Men's Chorus, and the Early Music Guild. King County also is home to hundreds of large and small music venues for just about every taste. There are so many, in fact, that it would be impossible to begin to name them all.

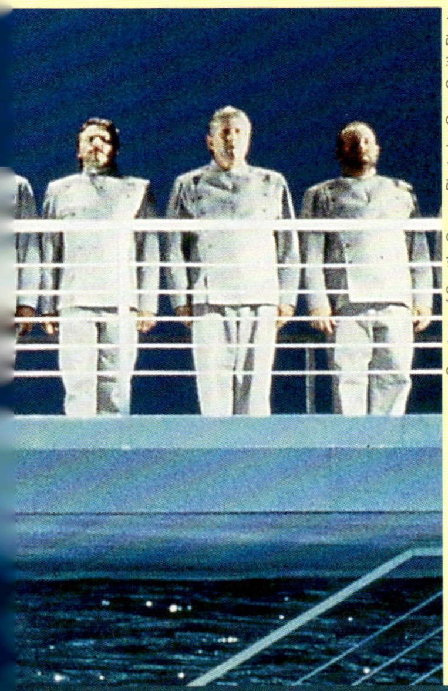

Courtesy of Seattle Opera, Photo by Gary Smith Photo

The Literary Arts

Books are well loved in King County. Bookstores abound, from the huge chains to the small neighborhood bookstores, and the area is home to several well-known writers. There is not a shortage of words here. Readings are popular, whether it is poetry or an excerpt from the latest *New York Times* bestseller. In fact, downtown Seattle's Elliott Bay Book Company has the distinction of being one of the busiest lecture and reading series of any similarly sized bookstore in the nation.

Several years ago, this collective love of the written word was given an outlet with the Northwest Bookfest. The annual autumn event has become immensely popular. Bookfest features readings, workshops, interviews, panels, and signings, and of course lots of books for sale. The event draws about 200 authors and thousands of attendees. Other literary events can be found on any given night at a variety of venues throughout the county.

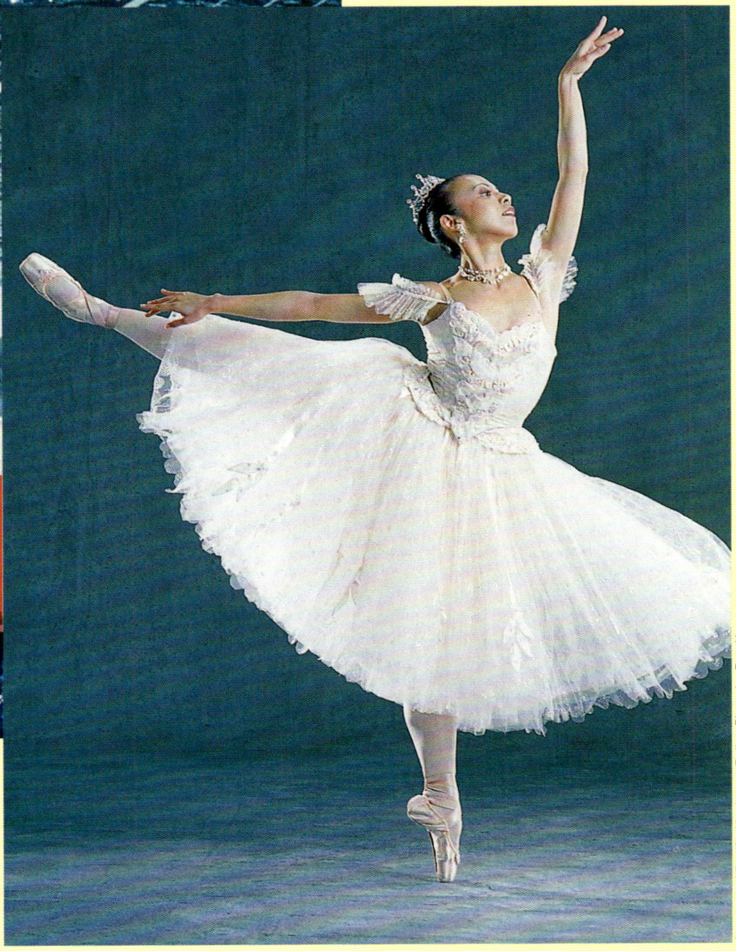

Kaori Nakamura in Pacific Northwest Ballet's Cinderella.

Courtesy of Pacific Northwest Ballet, Photo by Ben Kerns

Museums

The Seattle Art Museum and the Seattle Asian Art Museum are the two best-known art museums in the region. The Seattle Art Museum's collection is impressive and includes nearly 23,000 pieces. The museum particularly prides itself on its Asian, Northwest Coast Native American, African, and modern and decorative art objects. Asian art is on display primarily at the Asian Art Museum in Volunteer Park on Capitol Hill. Other art collections can be seen at the downtown museum at the corner of University Street and First Avenue.

The highly respected Burke Museum can be found on the University of Washington campus. The Young Naturalists Society founded the museum in 1885. Fourteen years later, the state legislature designated the museum as the Washington State Museum. It was not until 1969, however, that the museum was given its current name in honor of Judge Thomas Burke.

The Burke Museum promotes understanding and appreciation of the natural and cultural history of Washington, the Pacific Northwest, and the Pacific Rim. The museum's extensive collection includes Native American artifacts such as totem poles and hand carved canoes, a dinosaur skeleton, and numerous fossils.

Not far from the University of Washington is the Museum of History and Industry (known to locals as MOHI). The museum, which celebrates its fiftieth anniversary in 2002, owns an extensive collection of artifacts that tell the story of this area's rich and diverse history from 1780 to the present day. Thanks to Internet technology, MOHI's library and archives can now be accessed through their website (www.seattlehistory.org), bringing a large piece of Pacific Northwest history to the world.

Other smaller museums can be found throughout the county, such as the Frye Art Museum on First Hill in Seattle, the Bellevue Art Museum in Bellevue, the Wing Luke Asian Museum in Seattle's International District, and the Rosalie Whyel Museum of Doll Art located in Bellevue.

Children enjoy educational programs at the Burke Museum.

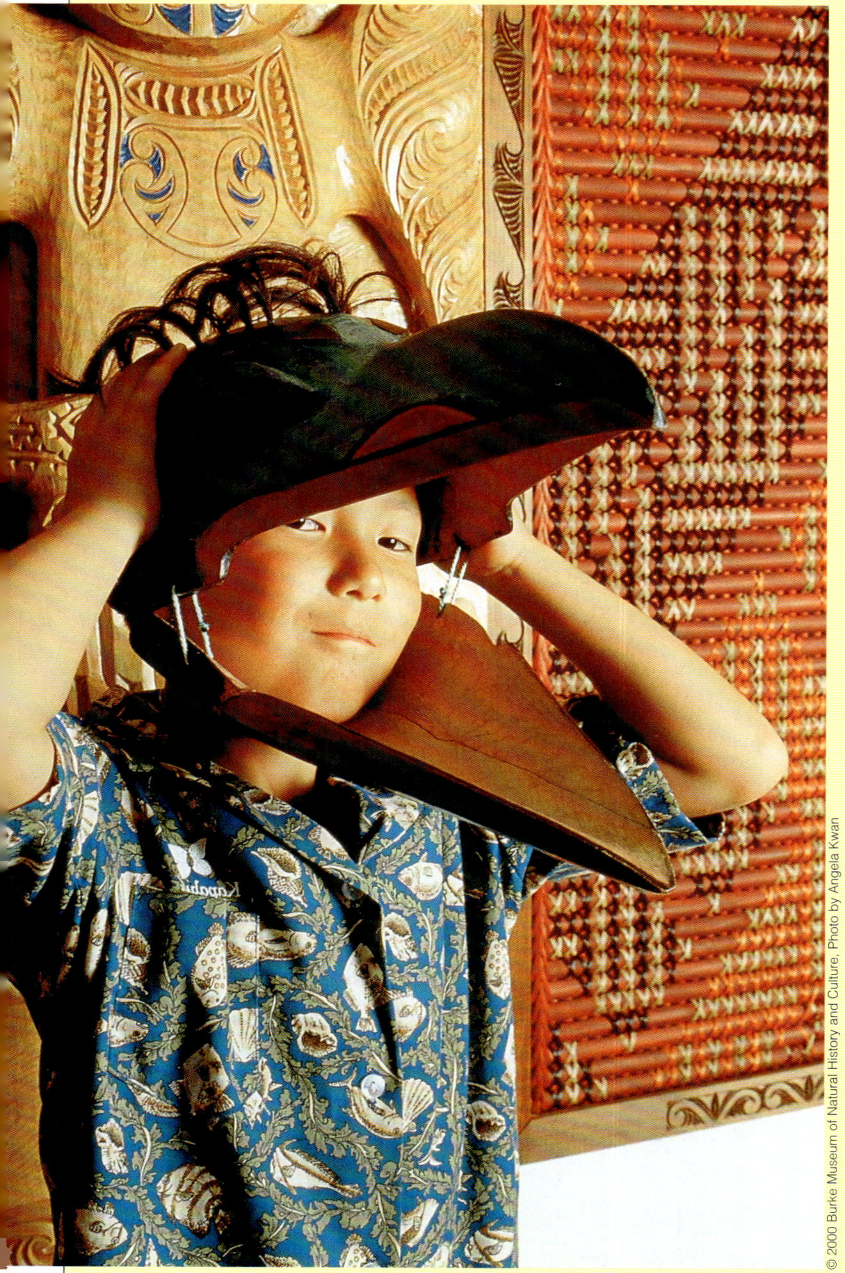

Arts Schools

Pilchuck Glass School: In 1971, Dale Chihuly founded the Pilchuck Glass School. In the 30 years that have passed since then, Dale Chihuly and his school have made this area a center for glass art. The Pilchuck Glass School, with campuses in Seattle and Stanwood (Washington), attracts students from around the globe who come here to learn the fine art of glass blowing, and also the beauty of glass as an artistic medium. The school is renowned for its creative and experimental spirit, and its founder Dale Chihuly for the artistic beauty his schools teach others.

Children wear rain slickers as they participate in "Salmon Stakes," a popular exhibit with hands-on activities at the Museum of History & Industry.

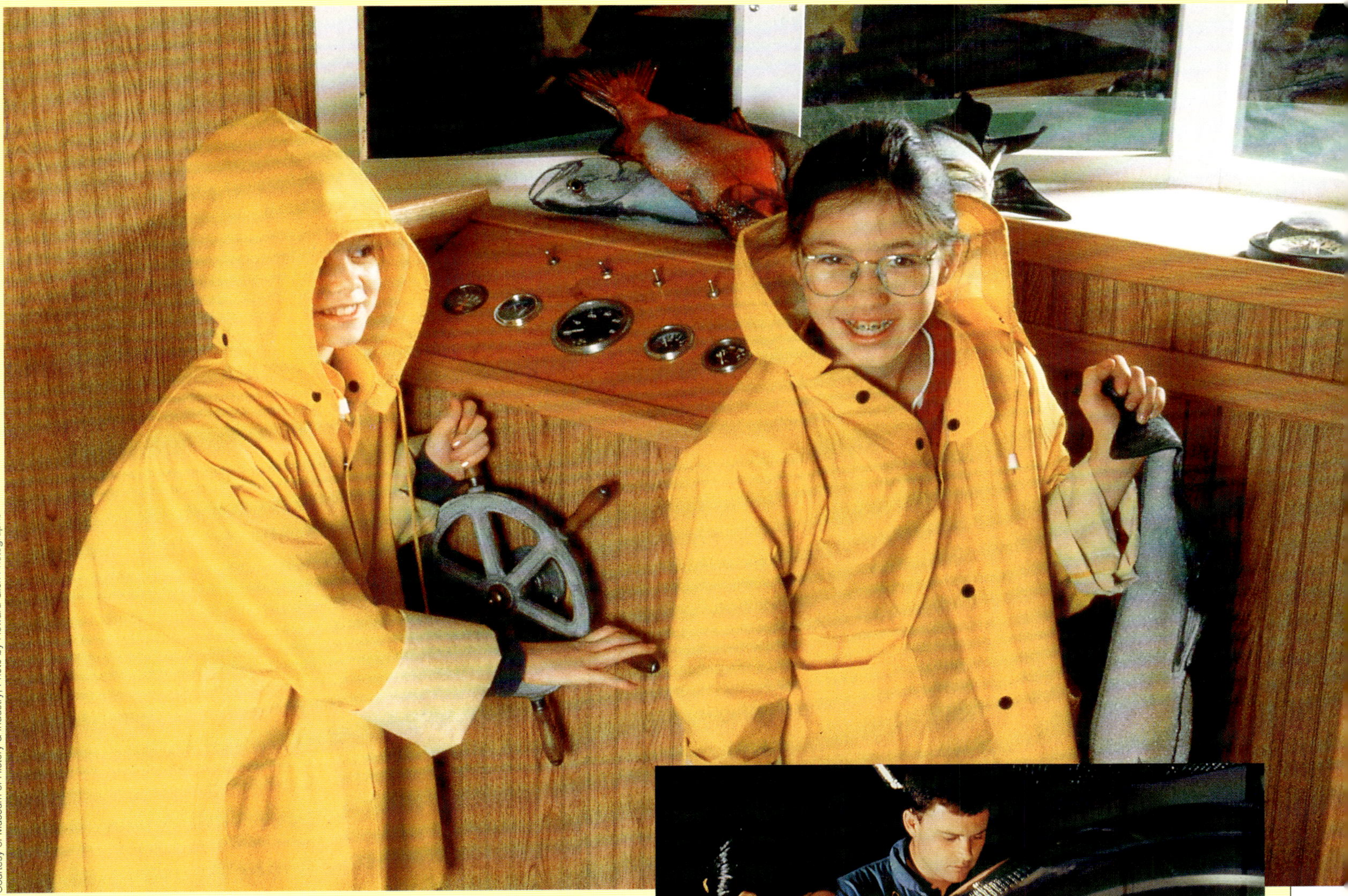

Courtesy of Museum of History & Industry, Photo by Howard Giske Photographs

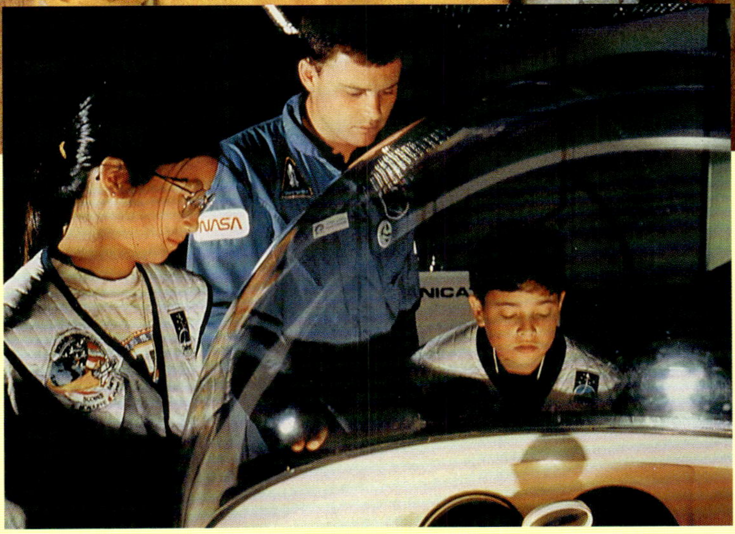

Courtesy of Museum of Flight

The astronaut bubble is part of the Challenger Learning Center, a simulated-space station environment at the Museum of Flight.

Festivals, parades, and celebrations of every type abound in King County, particularly in the summer months. Not all the fun takes place at the larger festivals such as Northwest Folklife and Bumbershoot. Many neighborhoods and communities have kiddie parades and civic festivals of their own!

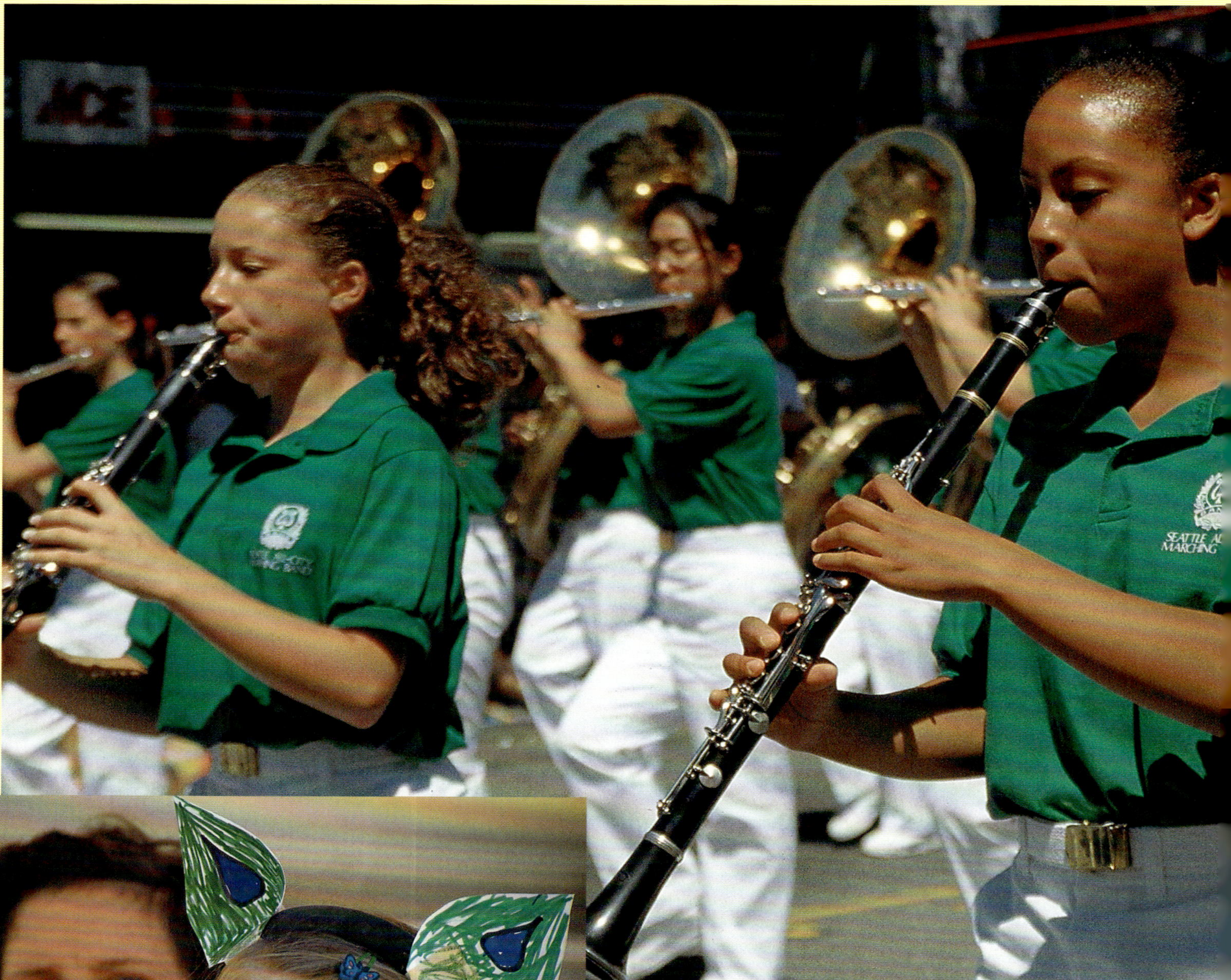

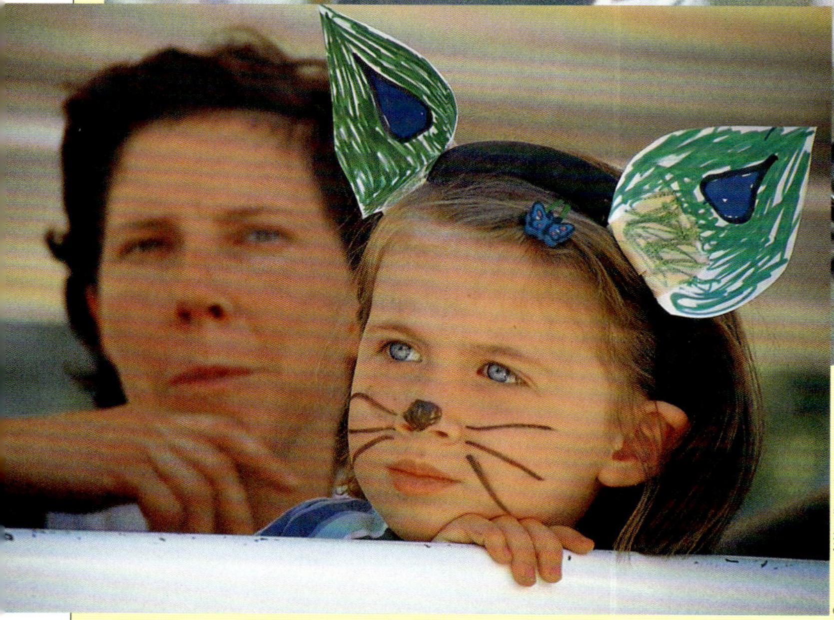

Courtesy of Wyndham Images

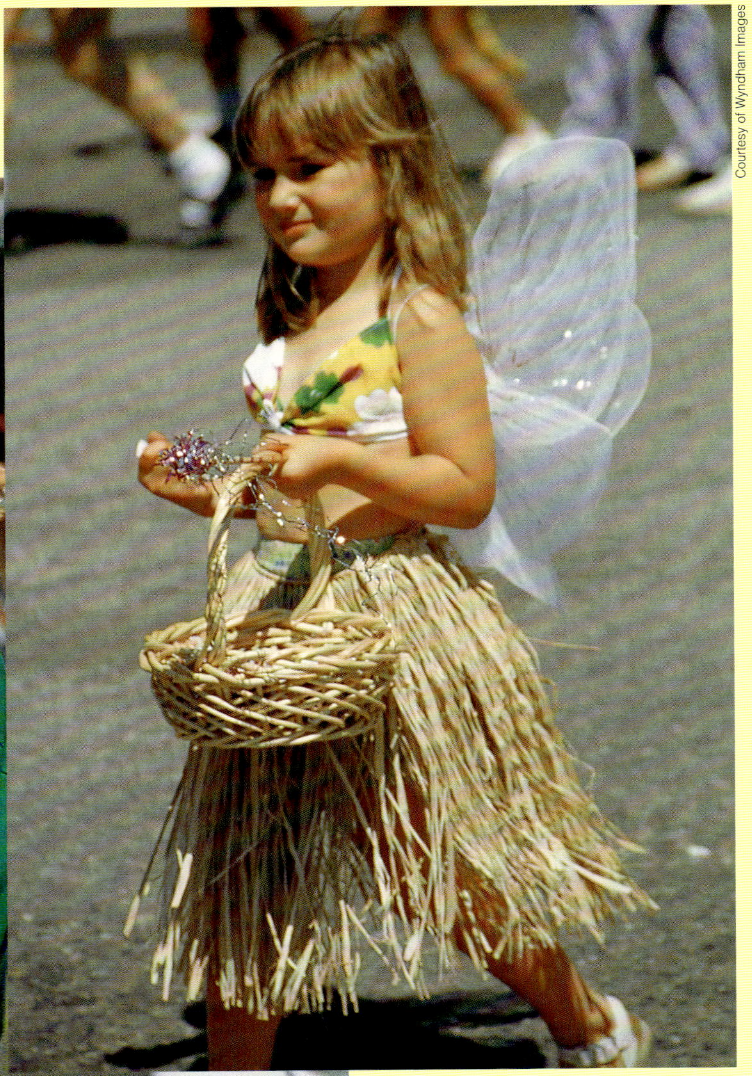
Courtesy of Wyndham Images

Courtesy of Wyndham Images

Art Institute of Seattle: The School, located on the Seattle waterfront, offers a diverse program of artistic degree programs including culinary arts, graphic design, commercial photography, interior design, and visual merchandising.

Cornish College of the Arts: On Seattle's Capitol Hill one will find the Cornish College of the Arts, a performing and visual arts school. Cornish, with an enrollment of about 700 students, offers programs in art, dance, design, humanities, music, performance, and production.

Arts Festivals

Thousands of Pacific Northwesterners anxiously await two of the area's premier annual arts festivals: Northwest Folklife and Bumbershoot.

The Northwest Folklife Festival marks the unofficial start of summer. Each Memorial Day weekend, multitudes of art lovers flock to the Seattle Center grounds to take part in this free arts festival that includes music, dance, exhibits, workshops, and lots of great food. In 2001, the Folklife Festival will celebrate its twenty-ninth year.

The Bumbershoot Festival, which gets its name from a synonym for umbrella (which is sometimes needed!), marks the unofficial end of summer. Bumbershoot takes place each Labor Day weekend and is a joyous celebration of all the arts have to offer. Bumbershoot presents a profusion of sights and sounds, from popular music and dance, to short films and literary readings. Bumbershoot features local artists, as well as nationally and internationally known performers.

Another up-and-coming arts festival is World of Music, Arts and Dance, or WOMAD. WOMAD, the brainchild of Peter Gabriel, takes place in mid-summer at Marymoor Park in Redmond. Its goal is to bring together the music, arts, and dance of cultures and countries of the world. King County is one of several sites around the world for WOMAD festivals.

A Unique Culture

Northwest Flair

Since the first settlers arrived in Seattle in the mid-nineteenth century, King County's culture has been inextricably linked to the region's climate, geography, and, most notably, its people.

The trends most often identified with Seattle and King County seem to be direct responses to the rainy climate and awe-inspiring natural beauty of the Pacific Northwest. Perhaps the coffee craze has caught on here because people like the soothing warmth of a good cup of java on a cool, cloudy day. And where else but in the shadow and light of majestic Mount Rainier would one expect to find the flagship stores of REI and Eddie Bauer, two of the best-loved outer-wear purveyors in the world. King County locals were wearing flannel long before flannel was cool. The people of King County are so in love with the grandeur and beauty of the natural world around them that they brave the damp and rain to be a part of it. When the weather gets to be too much, many locals curl up with a favorite book, take in a film, go shopping, or seek refuge in one of the areas innumerable coffeehouses.

When the sun comes out, so do the boats and the shades (in Seattle alone there is one boat for every twelve people and there are more sunglasses sold here than in any other place in the nation). Around the county, people of all ages enjoy hiking, bicycling, walking, horseback riding, or just soaking up the sunshine in the region's many beautiful forests, open spaces, parks and trails. Microbrews are the adult drink of choice for warm-weather days.

Whatever the weather, there are a few constants in the living culture of King County, two of the major ones being eateries and shopping. The restaurants of this area feature inspired foods that integrate the abundance of the surrounding lands and seas with the multitude of ethnic cultures represented by the region's people. Prime examples can be found in Seattle's International District, which is teeming with restaurants that feature delicious edibles created in the traditions of China, Japan, Thailand, Korea, Vietnam, and other Asian countries.

Courtesy of Wyndham Images

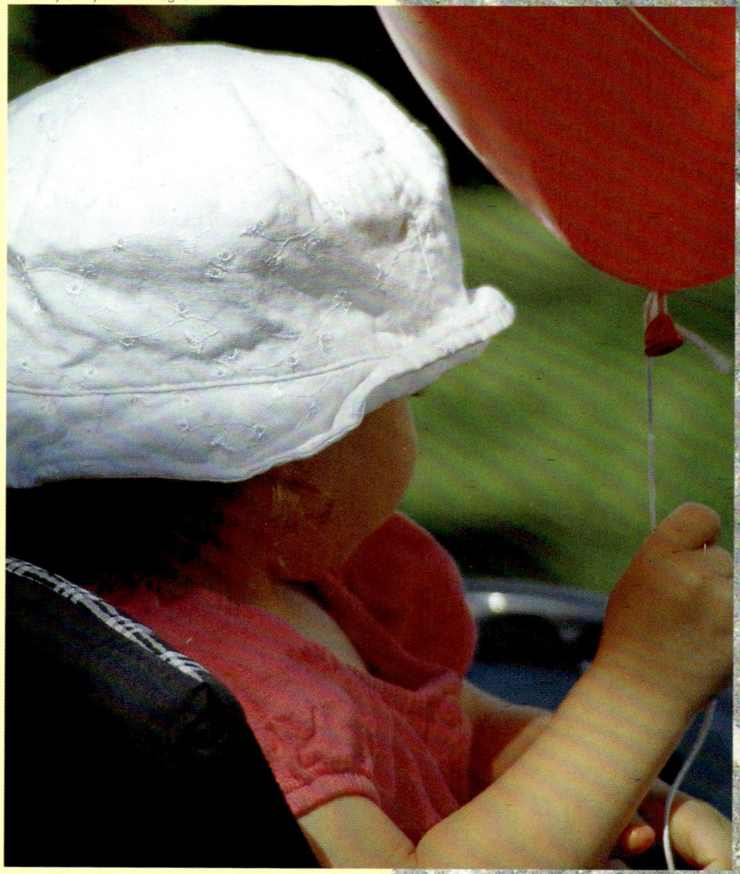

A youngster looks on (above) while others cool off at Seattle Center's International Fountain (right).

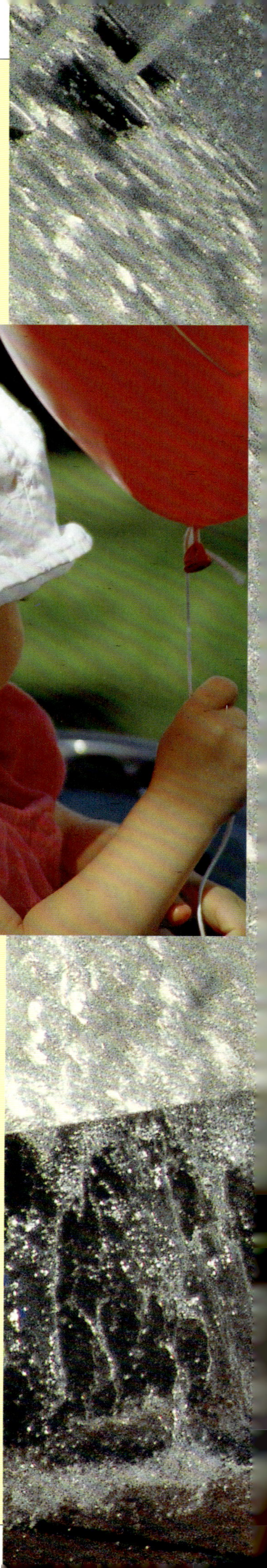

Courtesy of Wyndham Images

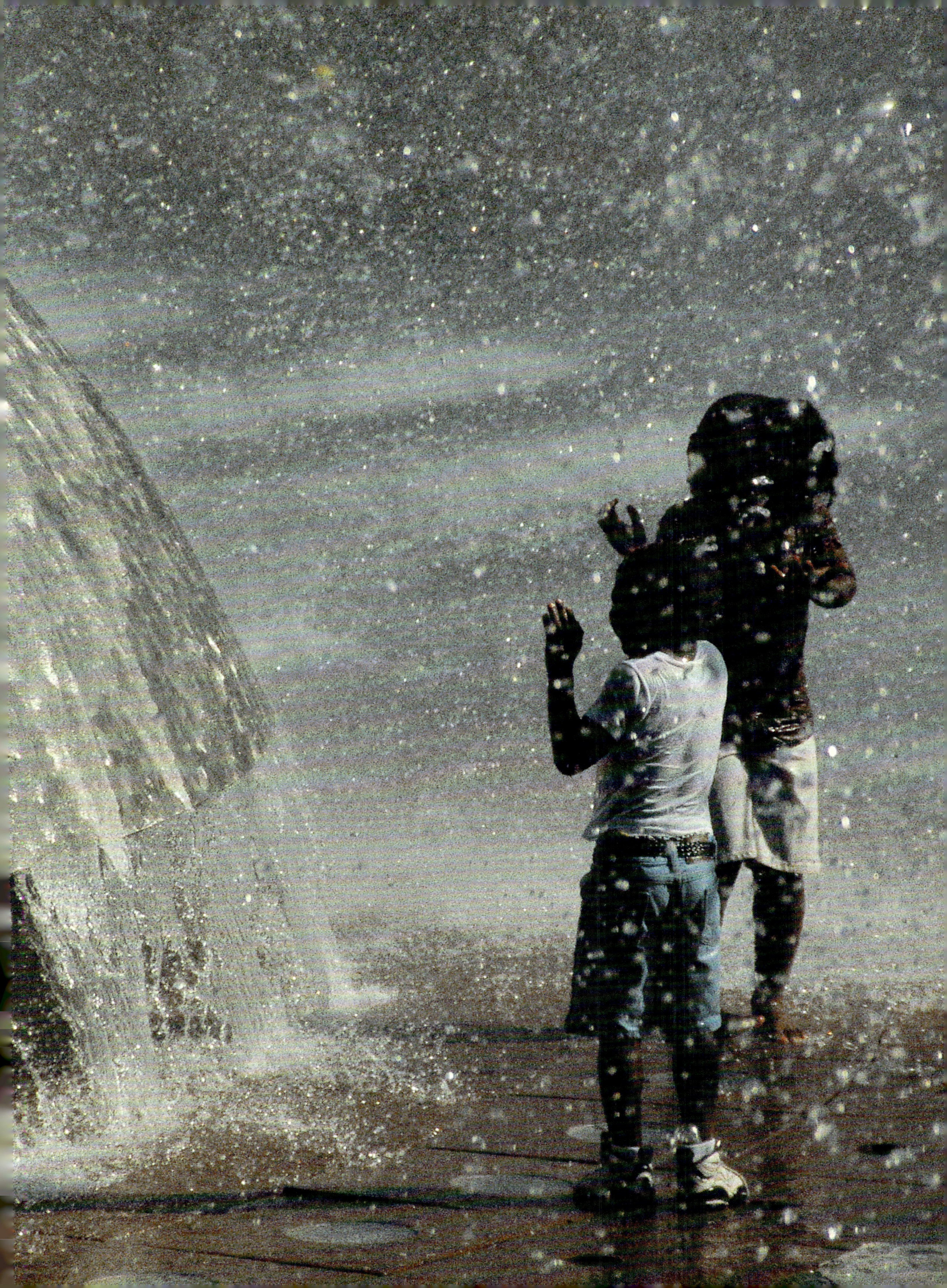

For those who prefer a decidedly urban lifestyle, King County has a great deal to offer, particularly in Seattle itself. The area is home to an exciting world of fine cuisine, compelling theater, world-class musical performances, provocative dance, avant-garde art, and lots of coffee and shopping!

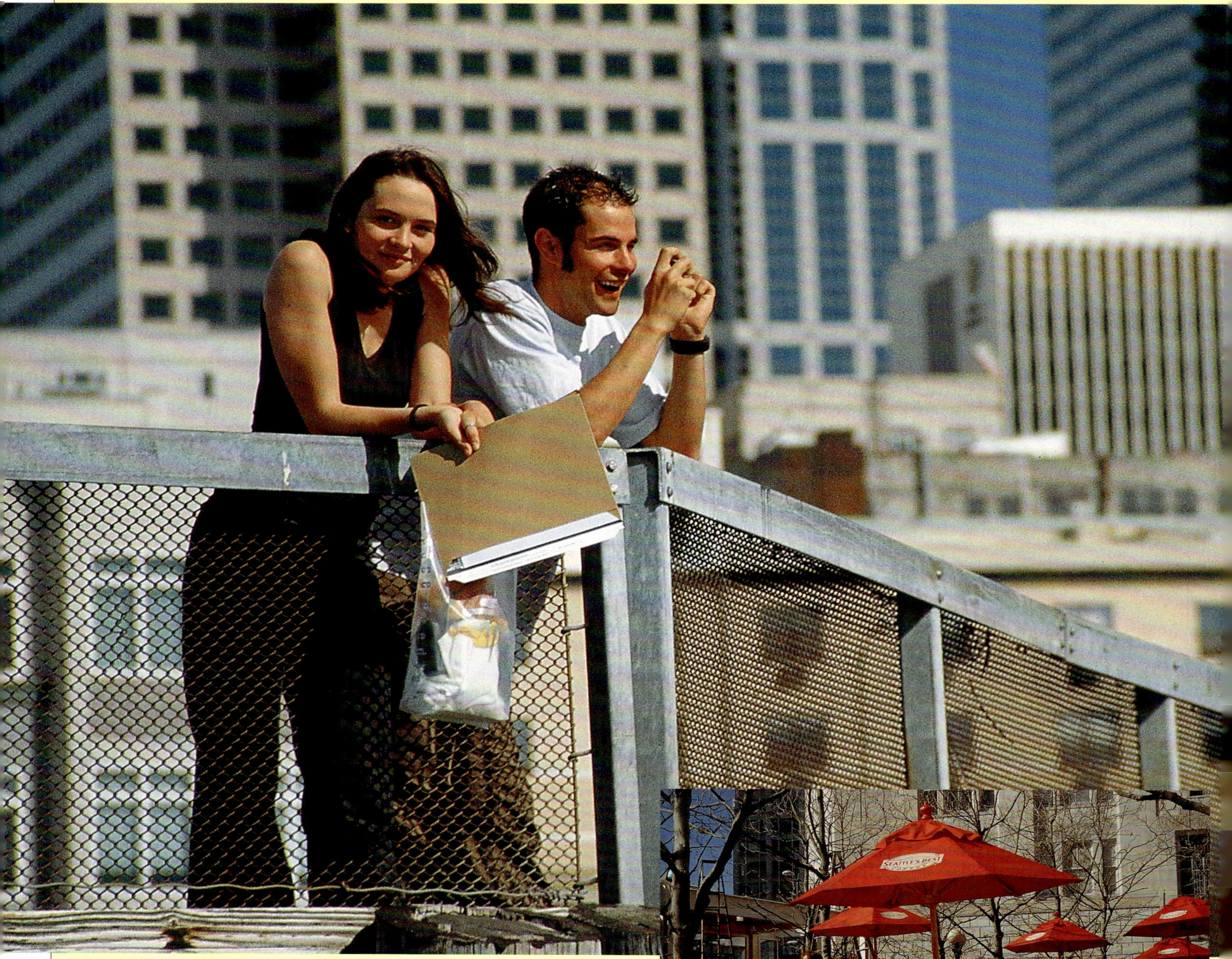

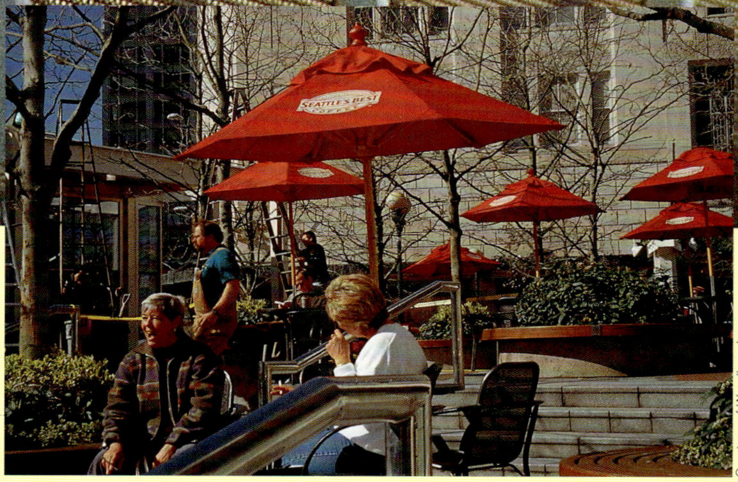

Courtesy of Wyndham Images

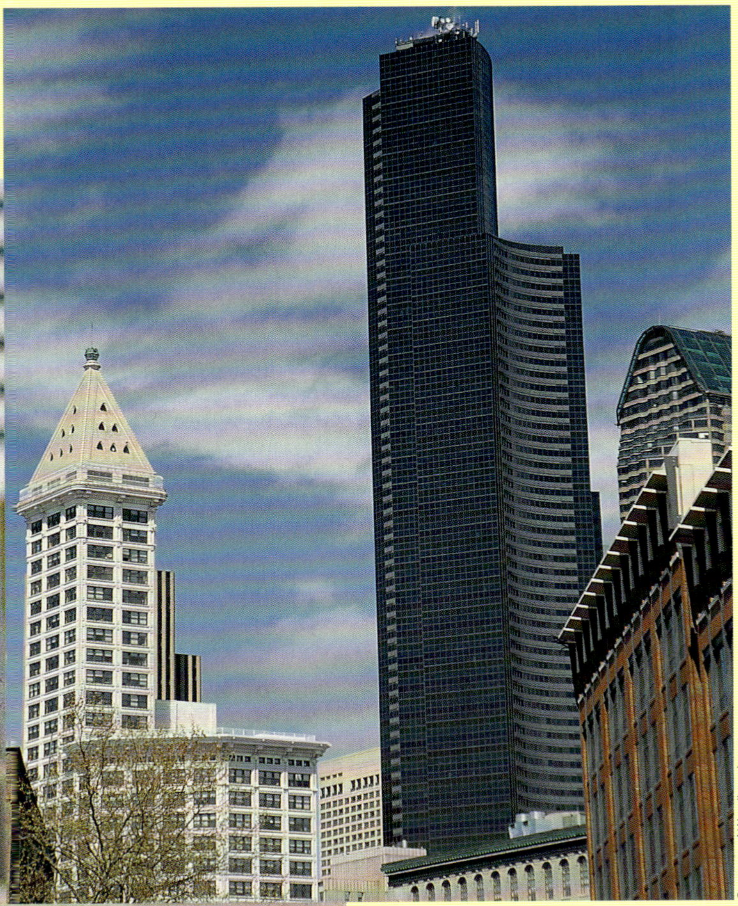

Courtesy of Wyndham Images

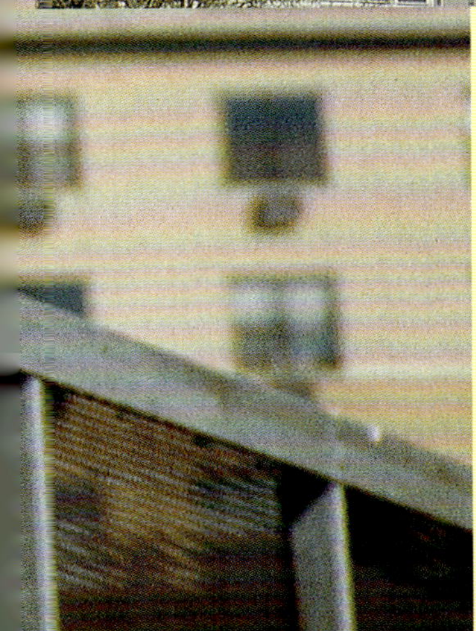

Courtesy of Wyndham Images

A trademark of Northwest Cuisine is known as "fusion", a technique that joins the strength of one culinary style with the subtleties of another. One resulting creative style, "Pan-Asian Cuisine," has gained international acclaim and recognition. One of Seattle's longtime favorite restaurants featuring Pan-Asian foods, The Wild Ginger, has been joined in recent years by a bevy of newer Pan-Asian restaurants including the trendy and upscale Blowfish Asian Café, located on the ground level of the Paramount Hotel; University Village's more casual, but equally creative Asia Grille; and numerous affordable noodle houses in neighborhoods from Belltown to Fremont. The technique of fusing culinary styles has helped to create healthy competition among the region's restaurateurs, giving rise to the number of four- and five-star restaurants in the Pacific Northwest.

Still, the most popular of all of King County's restaurants are the fish houses and seafood restaurants that dot the borders of nearly every body of water in the region. On Seattle's waterfront alone, choices include Ivars Seafood Restaurant (and outdoor fish and chips stand), Shuckers, Elliott's Oyster House, and Anthony's on Pier 66. A few blocks east of the waterfront one can savor the delicacies prepared by classic restaurants like McCormick and Schmicks, the Brooklyn, or the Dahlia Lounge. In the seaside neighborhoods of Ballard and West Seattle, there are countless seafood restaurants where the dining experience includes glorious views of Puget Sound glistening against the backdrop of the Olympic Mountain range. The expertly prepared foods—that range from delicate crab cakes to classic grilled salmon—become even more delicious in the glow of a Northwest sunset.

In recent years, there has been a boom of shopping centers and specialty boutiques in King County. Auburn, in south King County, is home to the Supermall of the Great Northwest, an enormous indoor outlet mall that features discount stores for Anne Klein, Liz Claiborne, Nordstrom, Eddie Bauer, Mikasa, and numerous other retail stores. Two-story Bellevue Square is the most popular shopping center in east King County. Issaquah's Gilman Village exudes the charm of a small-town retail center. Though North Bend's outlet mall is outdoors and has considerably fewer shops than the Supermall, it is very popular, especially during the holiday shopping season.

This landscape architect has a bit of work ahead of her! While the Puget Sound region is known for its year-round greenery, a lovely show is also put on each autumn as deciduous leaves turn red, orange, and gold.

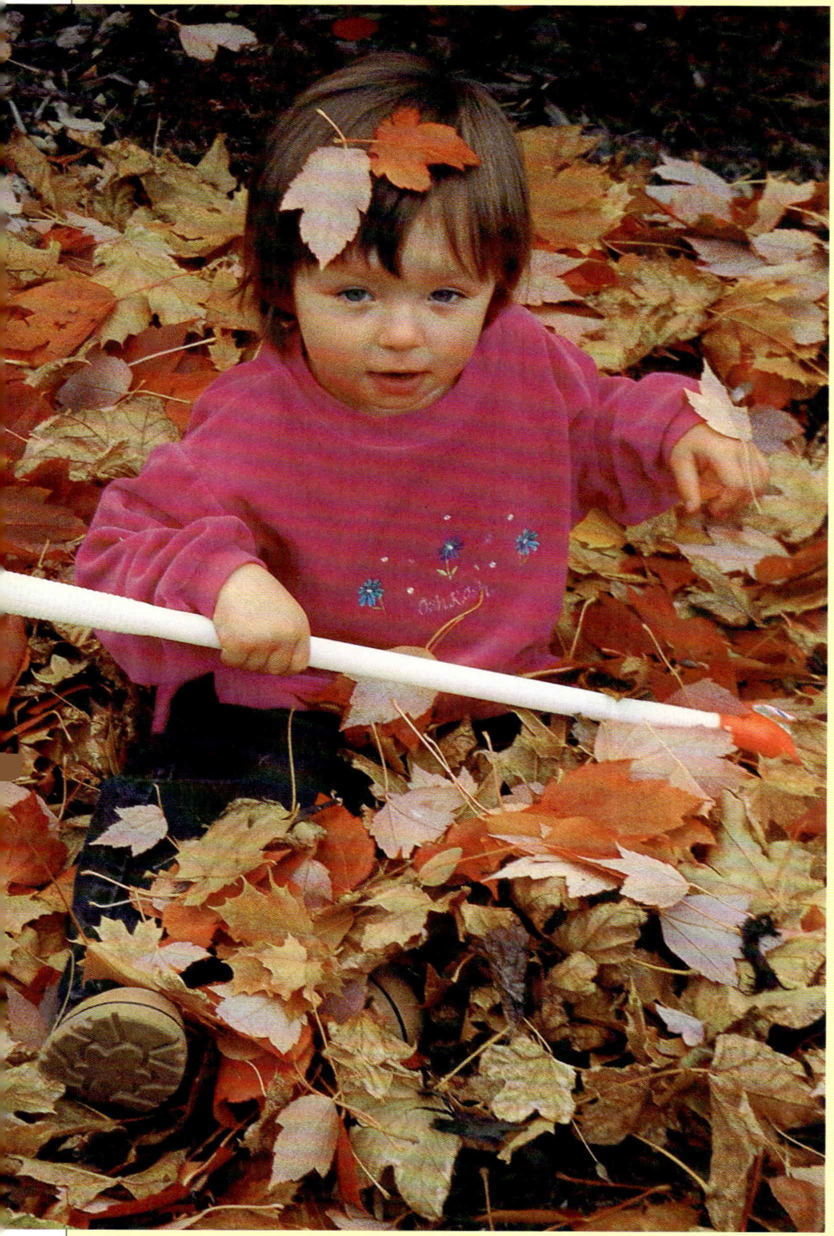

Courtesy of Wyndham Images

University Village, an outdoor mall in Seattle's University District, has redefined the shopping experience for many Northwesterners. Perhaps the greatest boon to shoppers has been the revitalization of downtown Seattle. Longtime favorites, the Bon Marché and Nordstrom, have been joined by Pacific Place, which is home to high-end retailers and a modern multiplex movie theater, Nike Town, GameWorks, Old Navy, FAO Schwarz, and the Original Levi's Store. Westlake Mall houses an eclectic collection of lively gift shops and trendy clothing stores. The improvements to downtown Seattle have been so dramatic that sidewalks and streets that were little traveled a few years ago are now bustling with activity.

While King County's opportunities for nightlife are not limited to Seattle, the city is definitely the heart of the action. Though grunge is no longer synonymous with the Seattle scene, music remains the primary draw for after-hours fun, and it can be found in a variety of venues to fit any taste. Those who prefer smaller, more intimate venues will find much to like in the numerous pubs that feature local and visiting artists who perform everything from rock and roll to bluegrass. Jazz lovers can find bliss in the more plush settings of Jazz Alley and the Baltic Room, and there are a number of music houses that continue to host musical groups on the cutting edge of alternative music.

Dance has made a big comeback in recent years, so for many, nightlife means salsa or swing. The New Century Ballroom in Seattle has become one of *the* places to be in the city, and its carefully crafted setting and live orchestral arrangements are evocative of a bygone era. The Orion Ballroom, in the nearby city of Kirkland, features a state-of-the-art suspended hardwood floor that is the delight of many local dancers.

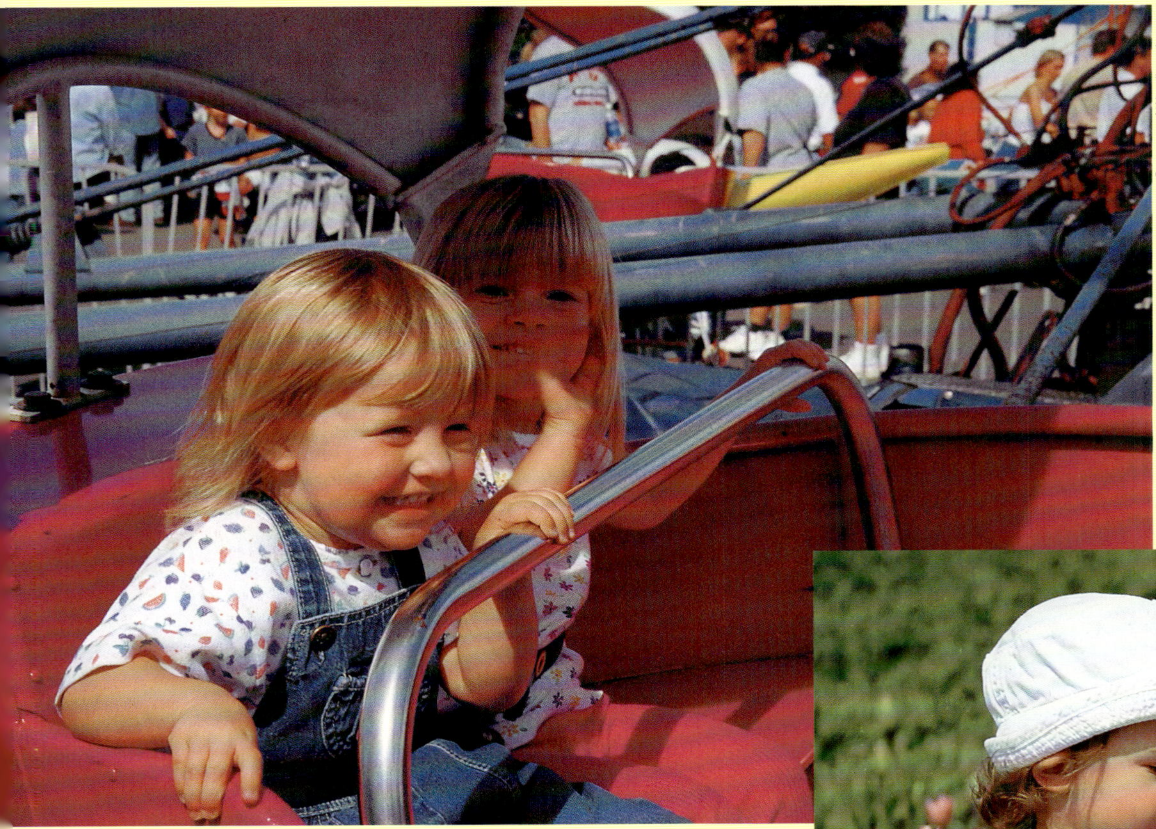

Courtesy of Wyndham Images

Thrill seekers need not go far to find their favorite amusement rides. Seattle Center, local fairs, and community festivals all provide breathtaking excitement for the family.

Many of the tulip fields in the region are visited by legions of admirers in early spring.

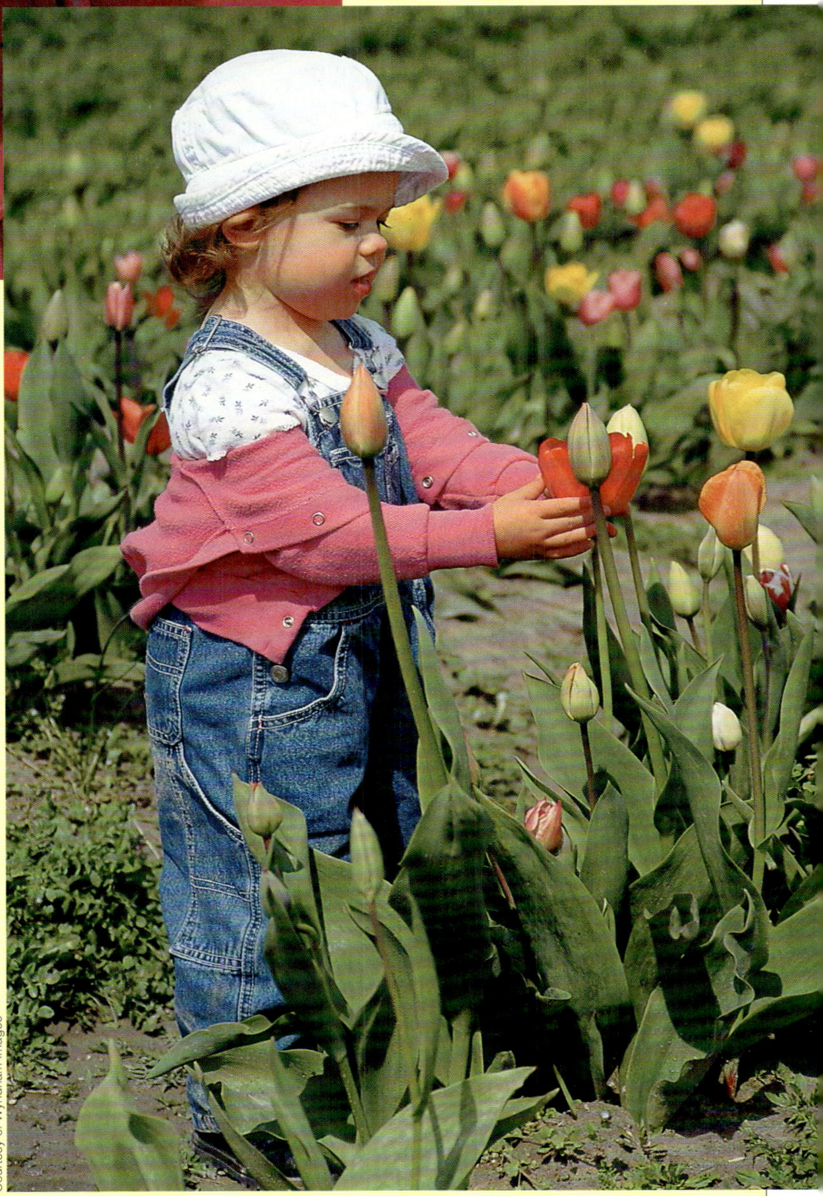

Courtesy of Wyndham Images

Families that live in King County know that there are good reasons why the area is repeatedly mentioned on lists that describe it as one of the most livable regions in the nation—there is a high quality of life that is conducive to raising children and enjoying "the good things in life."

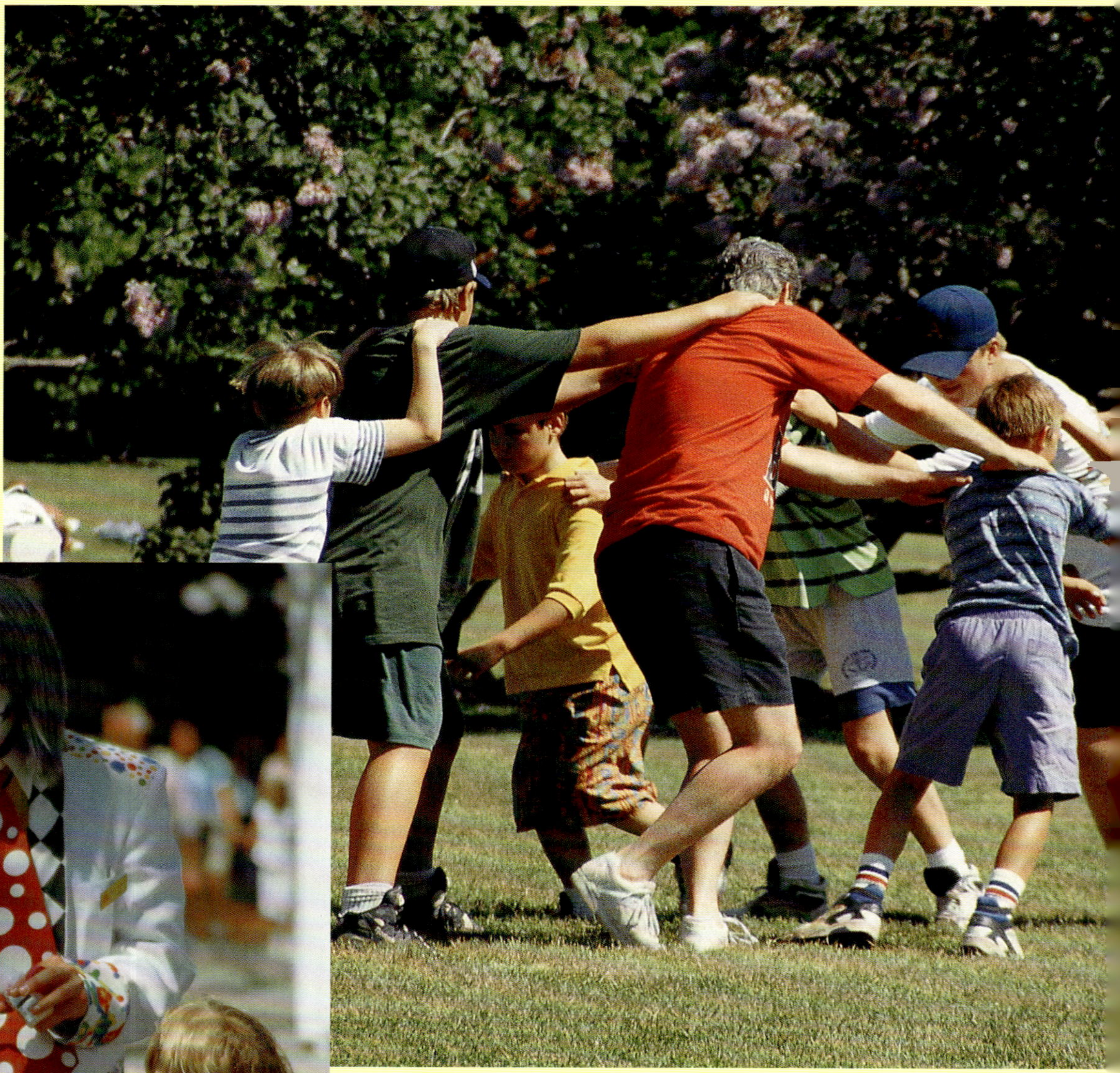

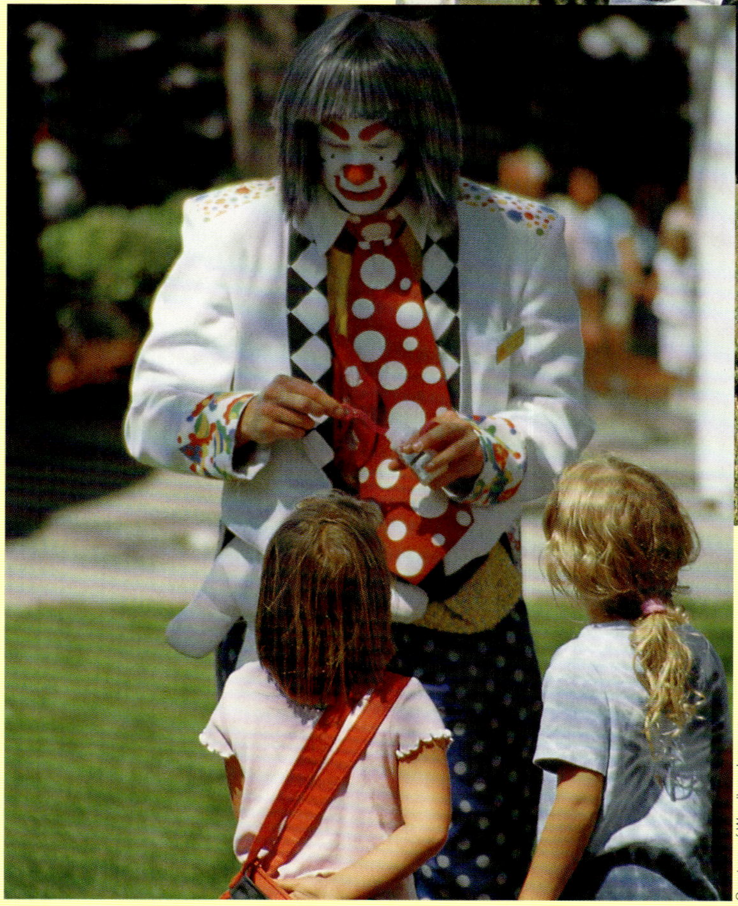

Courtesy of Wyndham Images

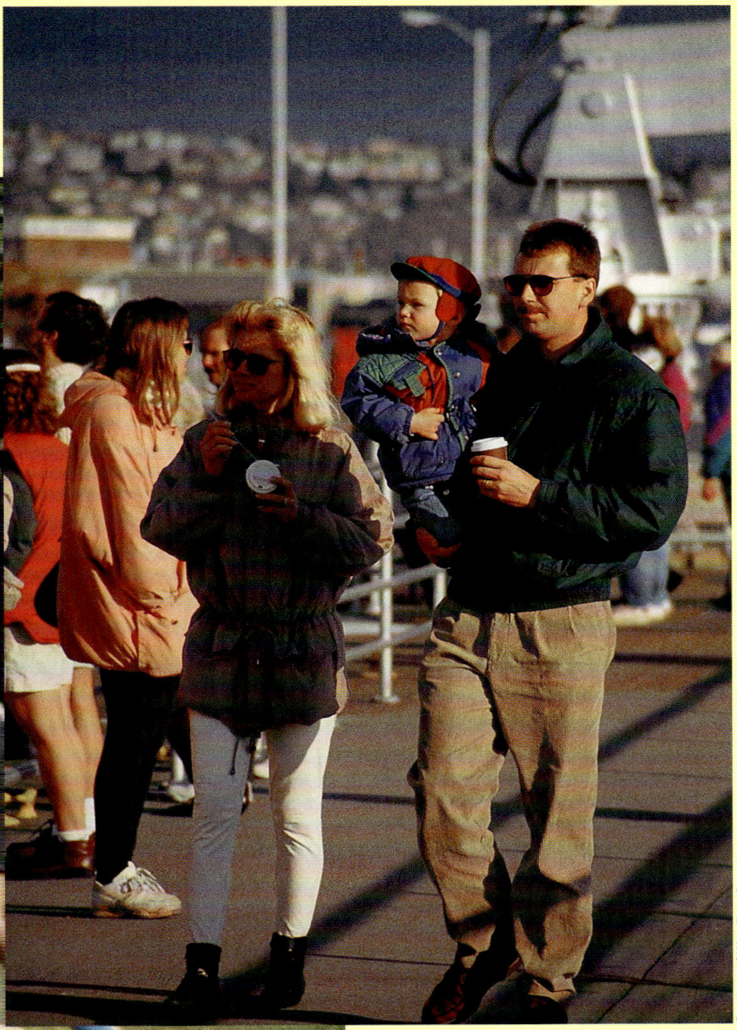

Courtesy of Wyndham Images

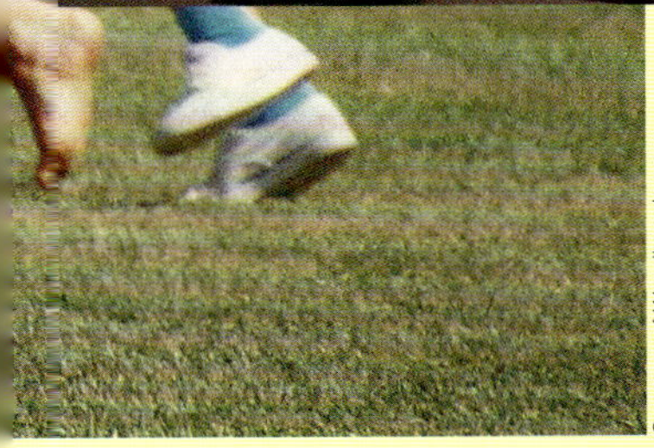

Courtesy of Wyndham Images

Celebrating Many Cultures

The people of King County celebrate the cultural diversity that beautifies and strengthens this region. In fact, not a month goes by in King County without some kind of cultural celebration. In late January, the streets of Seattle's International District come alive with colorful parades, lively music, and dancing dragons to celebrate the Chinese New Year. February brings with it Festival Sundiata, the Northwest's largest African-American Festival, as well as numerous other gatherings to honor Martin Luther King, Jr. and Black History month. In mid-March, locals celebrate Irish Week, parading through downtown Seattle in their finest green garb. The Cherry Blossom and Japanese Cultural Festival brings people together each April to experience the history, arts, foods, music, and traditions that have their origins in Japan.

May is a particularly significant month for cultural celebrations in King County. In May, Bellevue hosts its Annual Worldfest, an arts and crafts fair featuring the creative works of more than a hundred ethnic groups; descendents of Norway flock to Ballard to celebrate Syttende Mai, Norwegian Constitution Day; and hundreds of thousands of visitors and more than 6,000 participants gather on the Seattle Center grounds for Northwest Folklife, the premier ethnic and folk festival in the entire Pacific Northwest. There are many things to love about Folklife. It is a four-day multi-sensory extravaganza of music, dance, food, storytelling, and crafts that represent the arts and traditions of people from around the world. The International Children's Village is a great place for children to learn about different cultures and traditions; there are many artistic and musical activities and performances geared toward children. Northwest Folklife is also the only festival of its size and scope that charges no admission (though there is a suggested, and well-appreciated, donation).

In June, King County's gay, lesbian, bisexual, and transgender communities celebrate Pride Week, which begins with a weekend festival and culminates the next Sunday with a vibrant and colorful parade and Freedom Rally on Seattle's Capitol Hill. July kicks off the Seafair Festival, which celebrated its fiftieth anniversary in 1999. Seafair, a three-week celebration of the region's rich maritime history, begins with numerous neighborhood festivals, gains excitement with the Torchlight Parade, and reaches its peak with the arrival of the Blue Angels and hydroplane races on Lake Washington. The parade itself is a virtual sampler of the many cultures and traditions that distinguish King County as one of the most vital and culturally diverse regions in the country.

One of the region's newest and most exciting cross-cultural celebrations is the World of Music, Arts and Dance festival (WOMAD), which brings musicians and artists from around the globe to Redmond's Marymoor Park for three days at the end of July. WOMAD, which was founded in 1982 by musical vanguard Peter Gabriel, made its United States debut in King County and has been embraced with great enthusiasm and excitement by locals and visitors alike.

In mid-September, just before summer turns to fall, locals join together for Salmon Homecoming Celebration, a Native American tradition that honors the salmon through dance, pow wows, storytelling, and lectures. The fall and winter months drive King County's cultural celebrations indoors. In October, there are two film festivals celebrating diversity: the Asian American Film Festival and the Lesbian and Gay Film Festival. A December film festival features the work of Jewish filmmakers. Each year ends as it began, in celebration.

The culture of King County is embodied in its people and its places. It is a culture vibrant with the sights, sounds, foods, arts, and traditions that reflect all that the people of this region hold dear. It is a culture that is as abiding as its history and as expansive as its future. It is a culture unique in all the world.

On any warm sunny day, the shimmering lakes are dotted with white as sailboats glide with the wind. Flecks of color dash along the water as kayakers paddle through the waves. Spectators await the next waterfront event, be it a fireworks display, a regatta, or the compelling drama of a sunset.

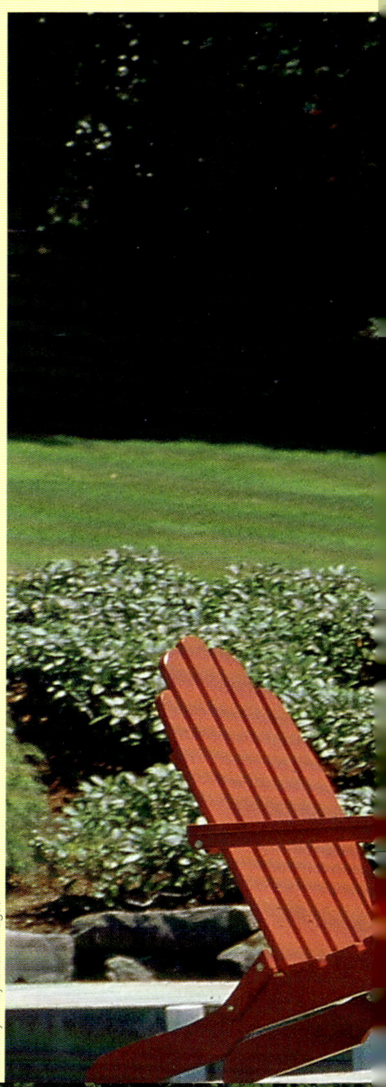

Courtesy of Wyndham Images

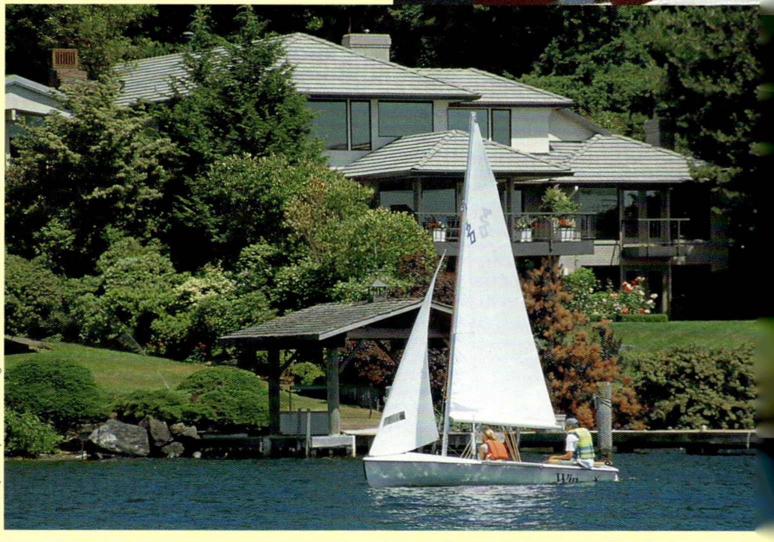

Courtesy of Wyndham Images

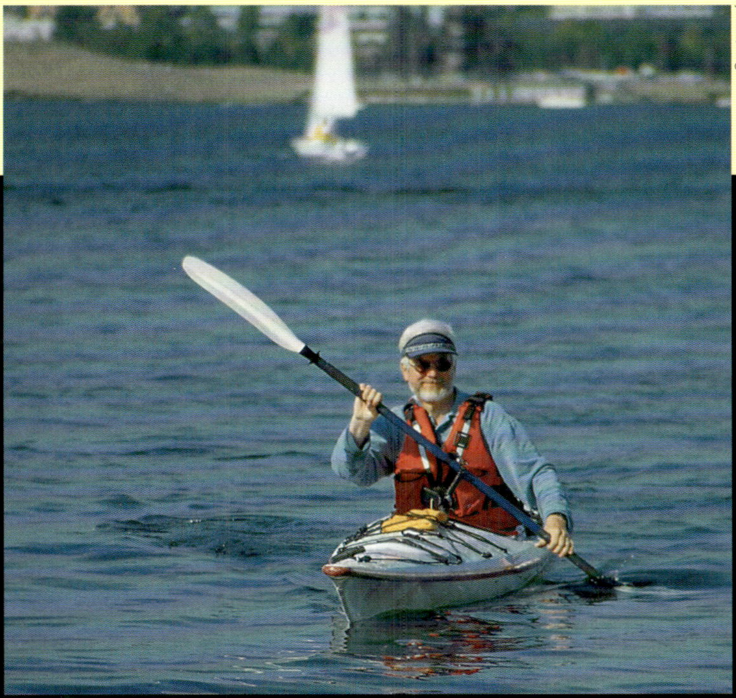

Courtesy of Wyndham Images

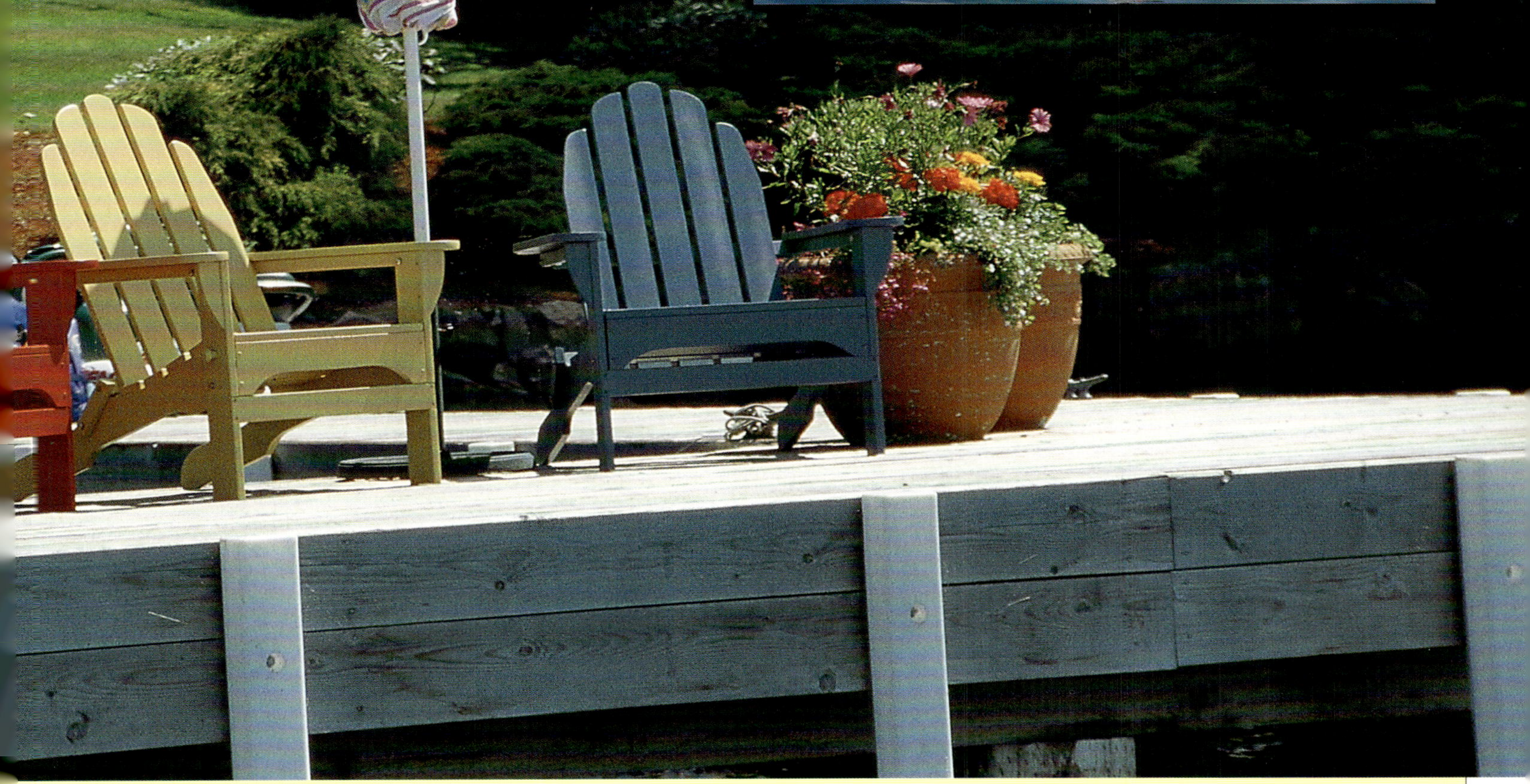

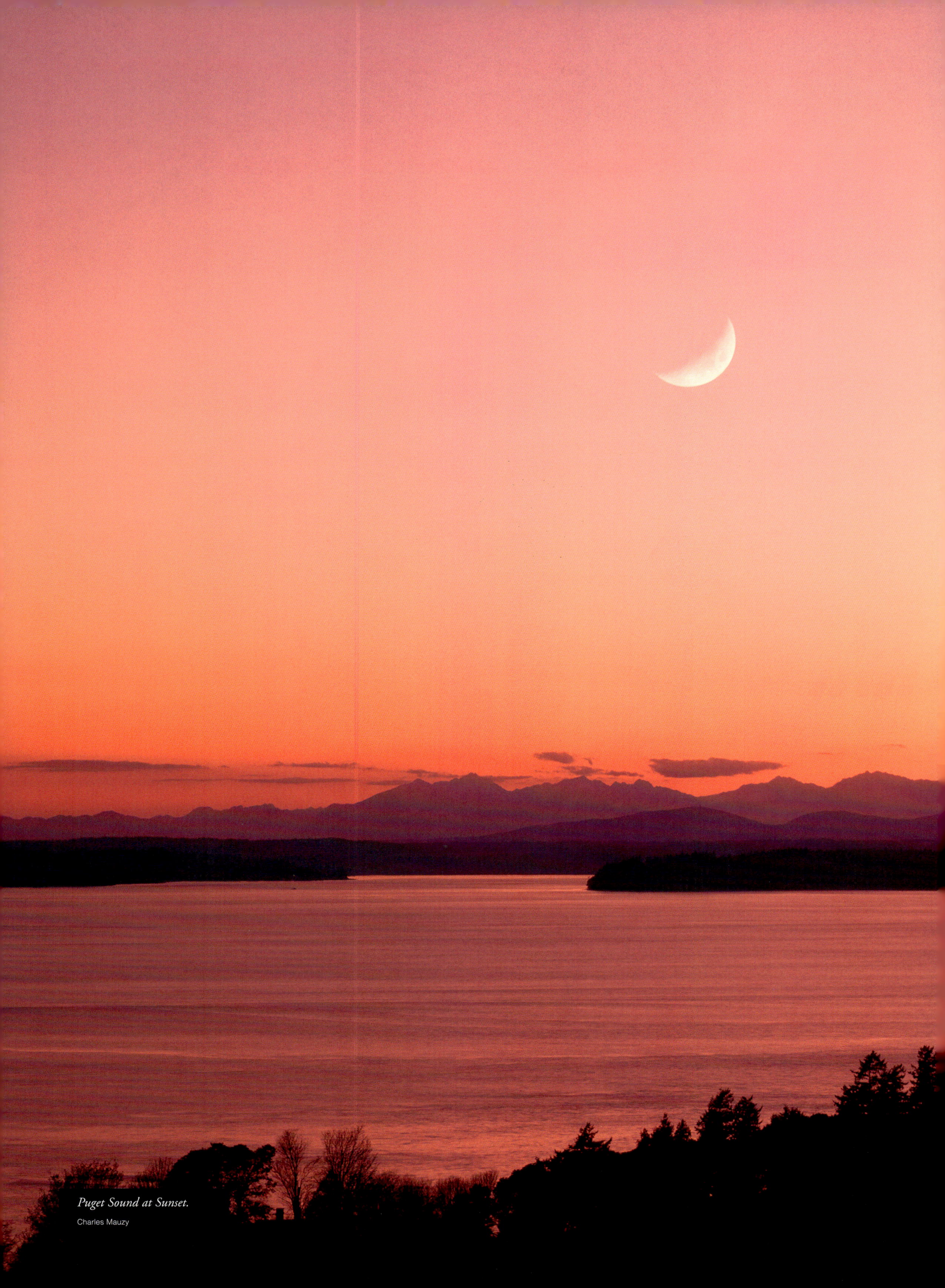

Puget Sound at Sunset.

Charles Mauzy

Part Two

Government and Community Organizations

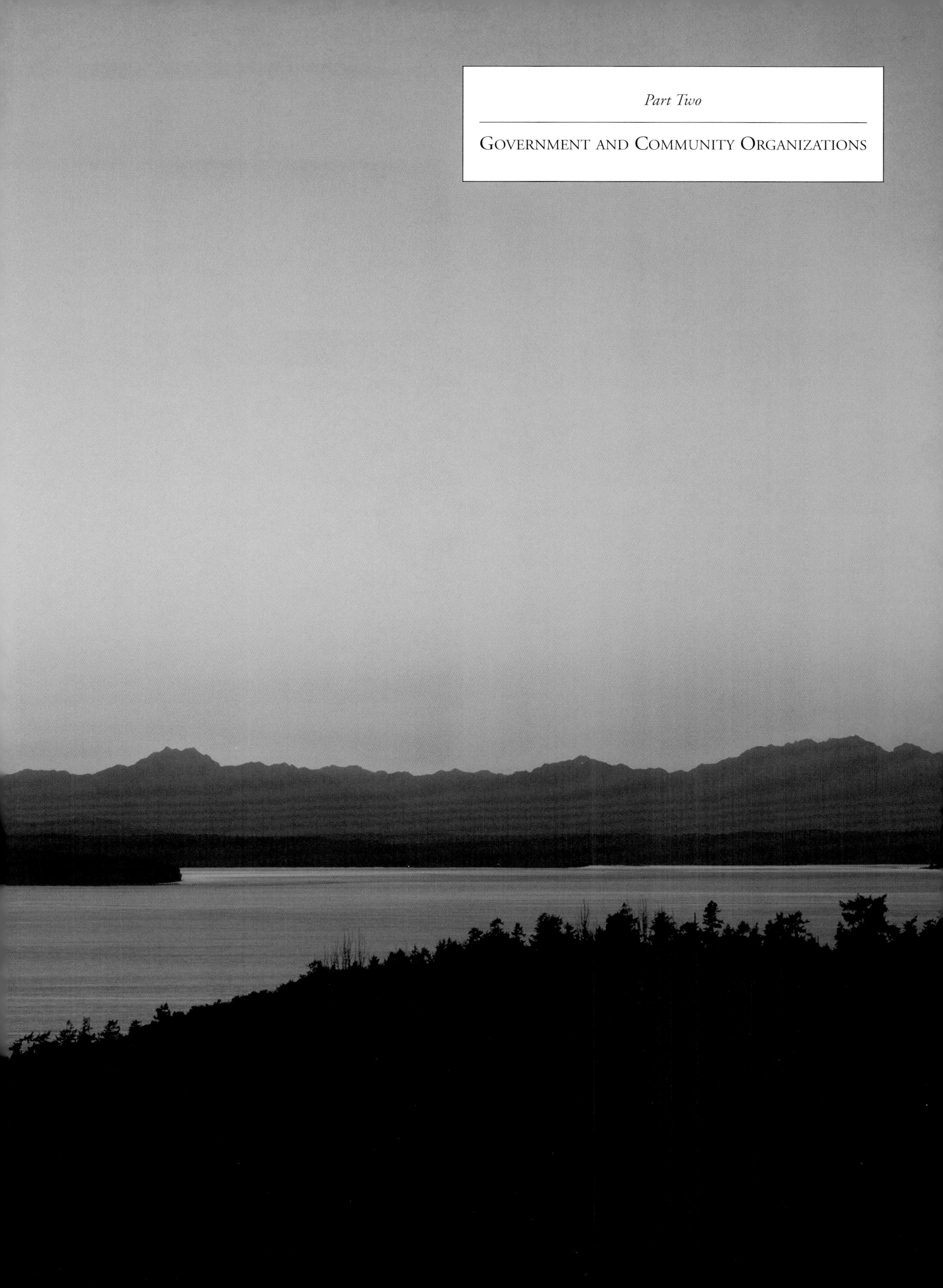

Greater Seattle Business Association (GSBA)

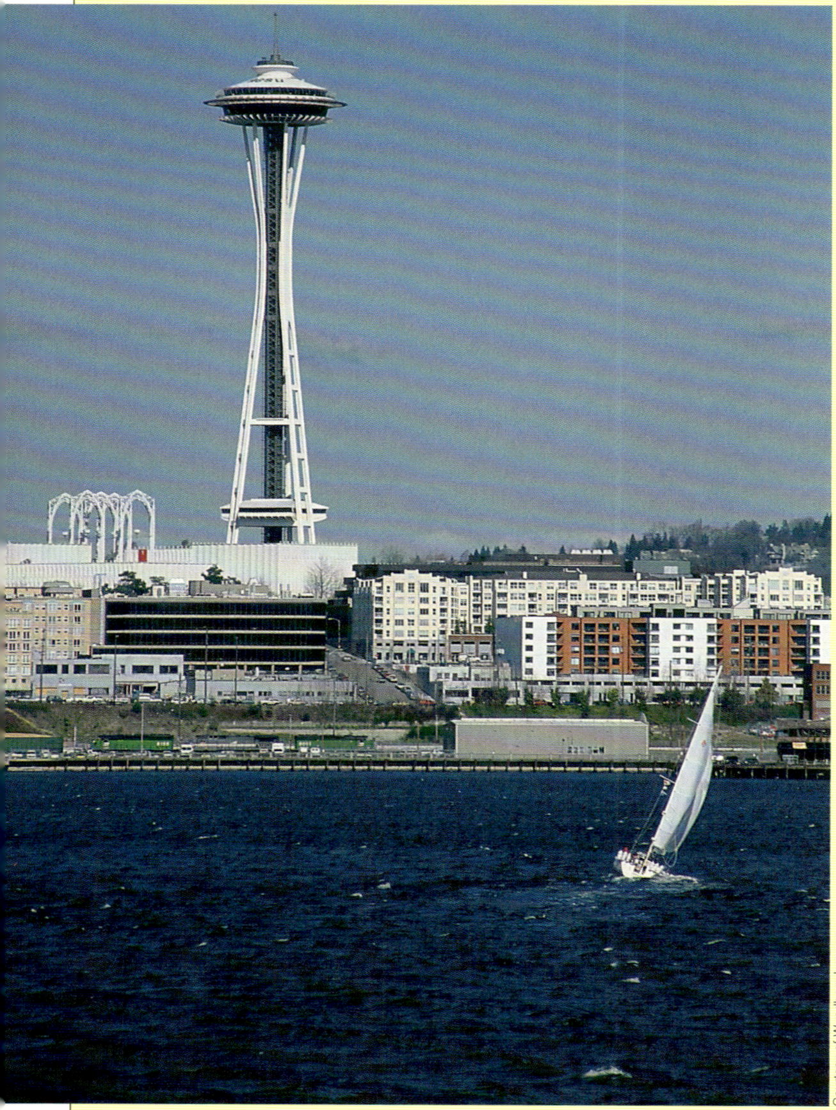

Courtesy of Wyndham Images

What is the GSBA?

The Greater Seattle Business Association (GSBA) is an association that includes business owners, professionals, working people, and retirees who have joined together for the purpose of networking. Members come from all sexual orientations, races, political affiliations, and professions. The primary goals of the GSBA are to strengthen and expand business and career opportunities for members and to aid in creating a strong advocate, both within and outside the sexual minority community.

Most members are located in the Greater Seattle area, although the organization has members in several other states and in British Columbia. The GSBA Web site helps connect members to one another and makes membership in GSBA even more valuable.

All members of GSBA agree to abide by the GSBA Code of Ethics. Membership is open to any business or individual who subscribes to the purposes of the association.

History of GSBA

In late 1980, a group of gay business owners met to form a coalition to work with Seattle police officers and fire department officials in an effort to reduce discriminatory actions by city agencies towards gay men and lesbians. They quickly realized that a new energy was developing—energy that could be valuable even after relationships with city government improved.

Like nearly every other gay and lesbian group in Seattle, the new committee members met in private homes, classrooms at Seattle Central Community College, and community restaurants. They brainstormed about the possibilities of what an organized, focused group could accomplish for business owners and for the community at large. They knew that along with the day-to-day challenges of business ownership, additional challenges existed for gay business owners. The group set out to create a formal organization that could be used to strengthen and grow businesses, and to strengthen and grow the gay and lesbian community's political impact.

Early suggestions for the name of the organization included "Gay Business Owners on Broadway" which even today reminds one of how important the Broadway neighborhood has been to the development of a gay and lesbian community identity. On a practical level, that name did little to include all of those that the founders hoped to attract to the association. With inclusiveness the goal, the name Greater Seattle Business Association was adopted. By September of 1981, approximately 30 founding members paid their dues and became the nucleus of today's GSBA.

The founding principles of GSBA continue to be the core of today's organization: building a strong business community, affording members opportunities to meet one another in educational, social, and recreational settings, and advocating on behalf of the entire community. Now over 800 members strong, GSBA includes gay, lesbian, bisexual, and transgender members from all walks of life. GSBA also has a large number of non-gay members who support GSBA goals, agree with the organization's Code of Ethics, and realize that doing business with the community is good business. The GSBA welcomes all who share the organization's goals and values to consider joining.

What does GSBA do for its Membership?

- Affiliation with one of the largest and strongest gay and lesbian chambers of commerce in the nation.

- Affiliation with the organization, which founded the Pride Foundation—the G/L/B/T community's version of the United Way. GSBA is honored to note that the Pride Foundation is recognized as an outstanding organization in the philanthropic/grant making community and by thousands of donors who support their incredible work.

- Affiliation with the largest scholarship program of any chamber of commerce in the USA. The GSBA Scholarship Program promotes cultural diversity and actively supports the work of students committed to building the G/L/B/T community.

- Opportunities to network with hundreds of other business owners and professionals committed to similar goals of business and community development as well as a monthly newsletter, *The Perspective.*

- Opportunities as a member to interact with other local chambers that the GSBA has affiliations with, such as the Greater Seattle Chamber and the Capitol Hill Chamber.

- Networking with more than 20 other G/L/B/T business associations, nationally and internationally through the Western Business Alliance.

- Participation in the Annual GSBA Community Awards Banquet, Scholarship Awards Event, The Taste Of GSBA, The Pride March and Festival, Oktoberfest, The New Years Eve Gala, monthly luncheon speakers, as well as monthly Prime Time Socials.

As the GSBA has worked to build the organization, the GSBA board and members have come to realize how fortunate it is to live in a community that rallies together in support of each other's growth and success. It is said that strength comes in numbers. This is certainly true when it comes to the members of the GSBA.

The organization is proud of the fact that many departments in the State of Washington have used services provided by GSBA members and the results have been exemplary. GSBA members are expected to conduct their businesses with honesty, fairness and integrity as it states in the organizations Standards of Ethics & Conduct. The GSBA stands by these standards and enforces them with all member businesses.

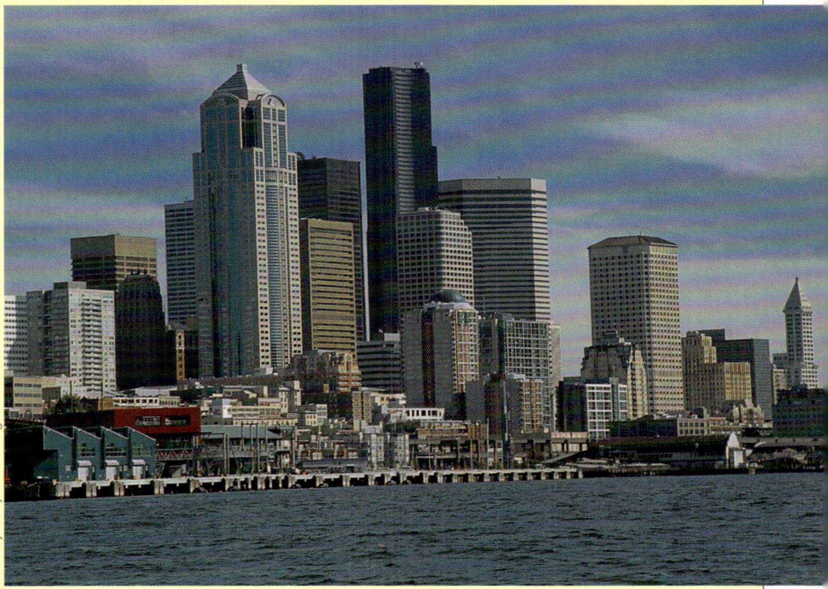
Courtesy of Wyndham Images

STANDARDS OF ETHICS & CONDUCT

We, as members of the Greater Seattle Business Association, strive to recognize, promote, and improve gay & lesbian business and the gay & lesbian business community and to that end, agree to be honor-bound by these Standards of Ethics & Conduct:

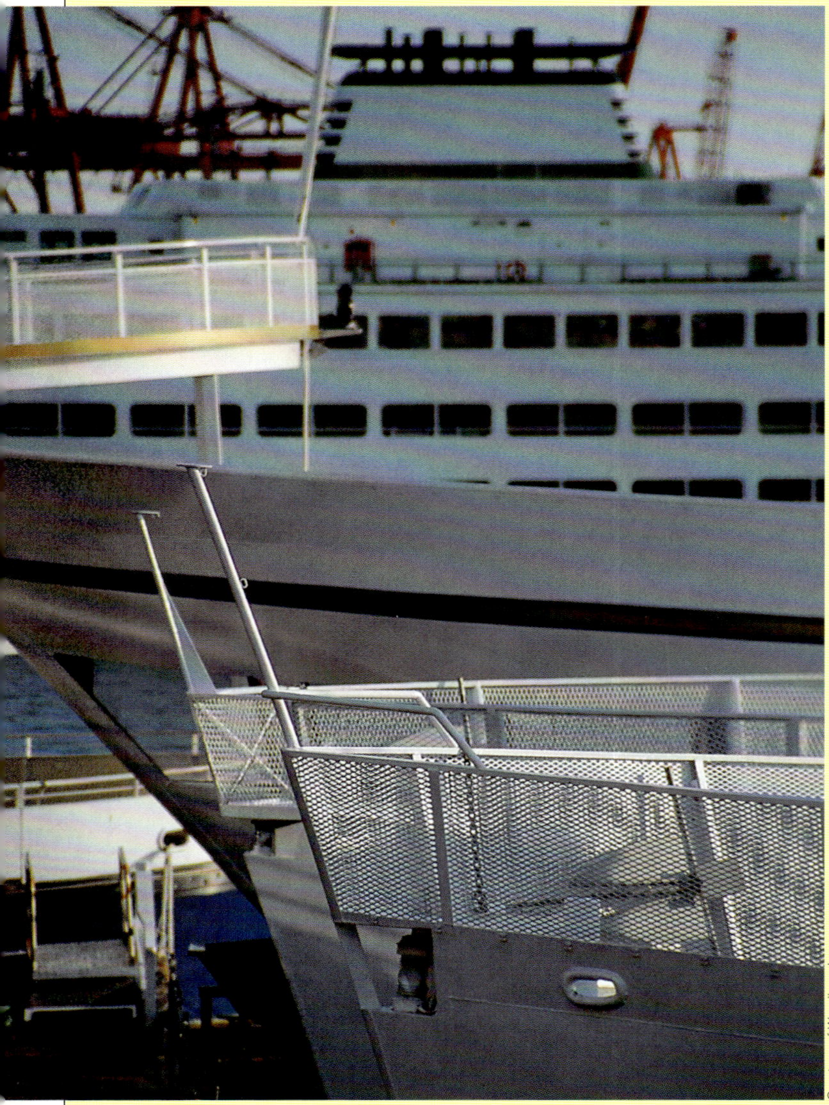

Courtesy of Wyndham Images

A member will conduct business with honesty, integrity, and fairness with respect to customers, clients, and employees alike.

A member will be accessible and accountable to customers or clients and make every reasonable effort to act for the customer's or client's best interest and benefit.

A member will not discriminate based upon race, color, creed, religion, national origin, age, disability, marital status, gender, or sexual orientation.

A member will be responsible at all times for truthful and non-deceptive advertising and promotion regarding their business and its products or services.

A member will not use or condone advertising which is untrue, misleading, deceptive, fraudulent, falsely disparaging of competitors or which contains insincere offers to sell, nor advertising which as a whole, may be misleading or result in misrepresentation by direct statement, inference, or omission.

A member will conduct business with strict adherence to the law of the state where located and to business or professional codes existent for the particular business or profession, and in accordance with generally accepted business practices.

A member will support the ideals and goals of this organization, a well as support the gay & lesbian community in general, in a constructive and positive manner.

GSBA MISSION STATEMENT

Amended Feb. 9, 1991 by unanimous vote of the GSBA Board of Directors

The Greater Seattle Business Association is a non-profit organization established to promote and support the gay & lesbian business and professional community. The association does this by working toward the following objectives:

- Promoting the association and its members to all segments of the community at large.
- Supporting current or future business or related issues on which the association wishes to promote a position.
- Providing educational opportunities and information assistance to the membership through education, training, research, and information.
- Providing a forum for members to enhance their business or organization.
- Providing a support system for all members to meet socially and professionally.

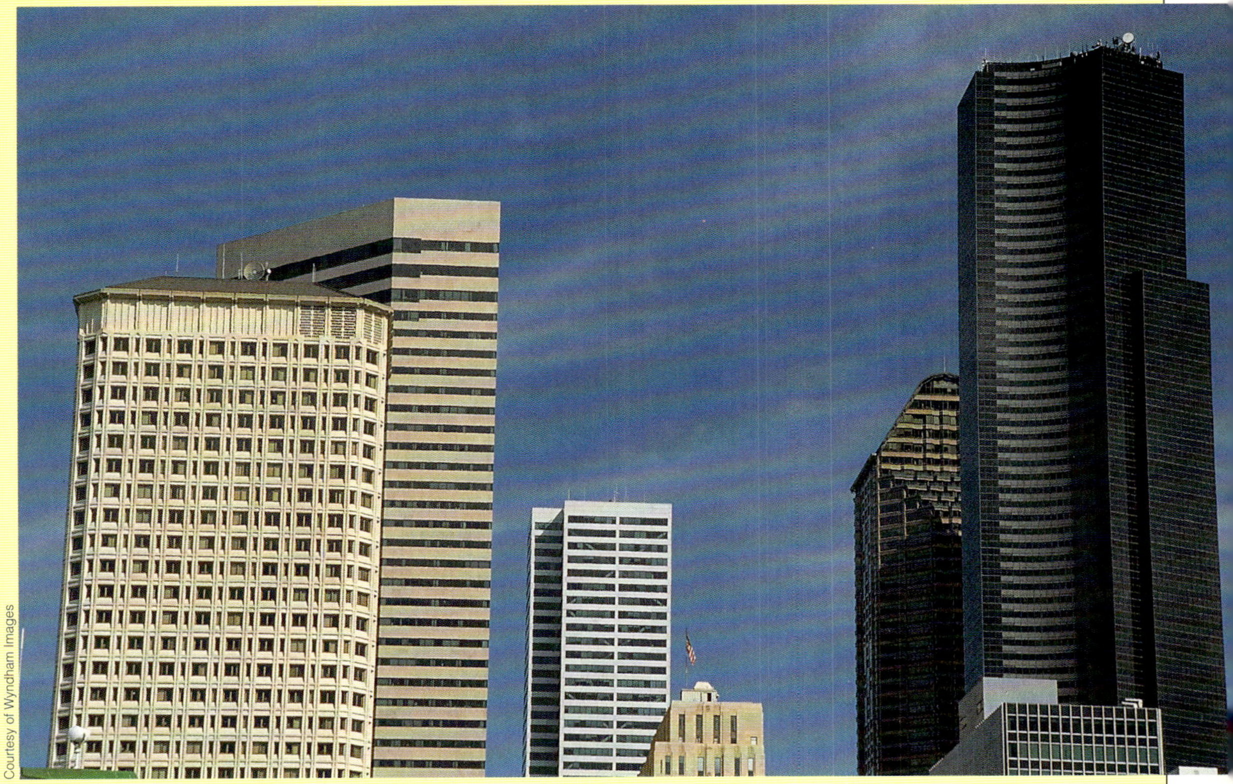

Courtesy of Wyndham Images

The GSBA Scholarship Program

The Greater Seattle Business Association Scholarship Program grants educational scholarships to promote diversity and leadership in the lesbian, gay, bisexual, and transgender community. Recipients are Washington State high school or post-high school undergraduate students who demonstrate need, potential, and commitment to human rights. Gay, lesbian, bisexual, and transgender students and children of sexual minority parents are particularly encouraged to apply.

The purpose of the GSBA Scholarship Program is to build diverse leadership in the sexual minority community and promote human rights in the larger society. The program promotes visibility, support, and role models for lesbian, gay, bisexual, and transgender students and families.

Since 1990, hundreds of supporters have built a self-sustaining endowment fund of over $200,000, which ensures an ongoing source for scholarships year after year. In addition, a generous bequest by Richard Rolfs, a committed community activist and civic leader, created a second $200,000 endowment in 1998.

Periodic updates on the activities of recipients are printed in the GSBA newsletter. GSBA members are encouraged to develop mentoring relationships with recipients who share business or community interests.

GSBA Guide & Directory

The *GSBA Guide & Directory* has grown greatly over the past 21 years. With over 275 advertisers and 320 pages of business and community services to work with, the GSBA Guide is one of the most valuable resources offered in the state of Washington. In the last few years, the GSBA has raised the number of guides distributed from 20,000 to 30,000 and plans another increase for the upcoming year. The GSBA Guide stands to be the largest G/L/B/T guide and directory of its kind in the nation. The GSBA has developed both publications and marketing committees to oversee the continued development of the GSBA and its programs in preparation for this expansion. The organization has also been fortunate enough to have the corporate support of such sponsors as Budweiser, Safeco, Argosy Cruises, Columbia Distributors, Miller Brewing Company, and Chivas Regal.

The GSBA continues to share its vision of a progressive, inclusive, open-market business environment that espouses fundamental ethical standards. Due to the dedication of GSBA members, it is a vision that is rapidly becoming a reality—to the great benefit of all.

King County Executive Office

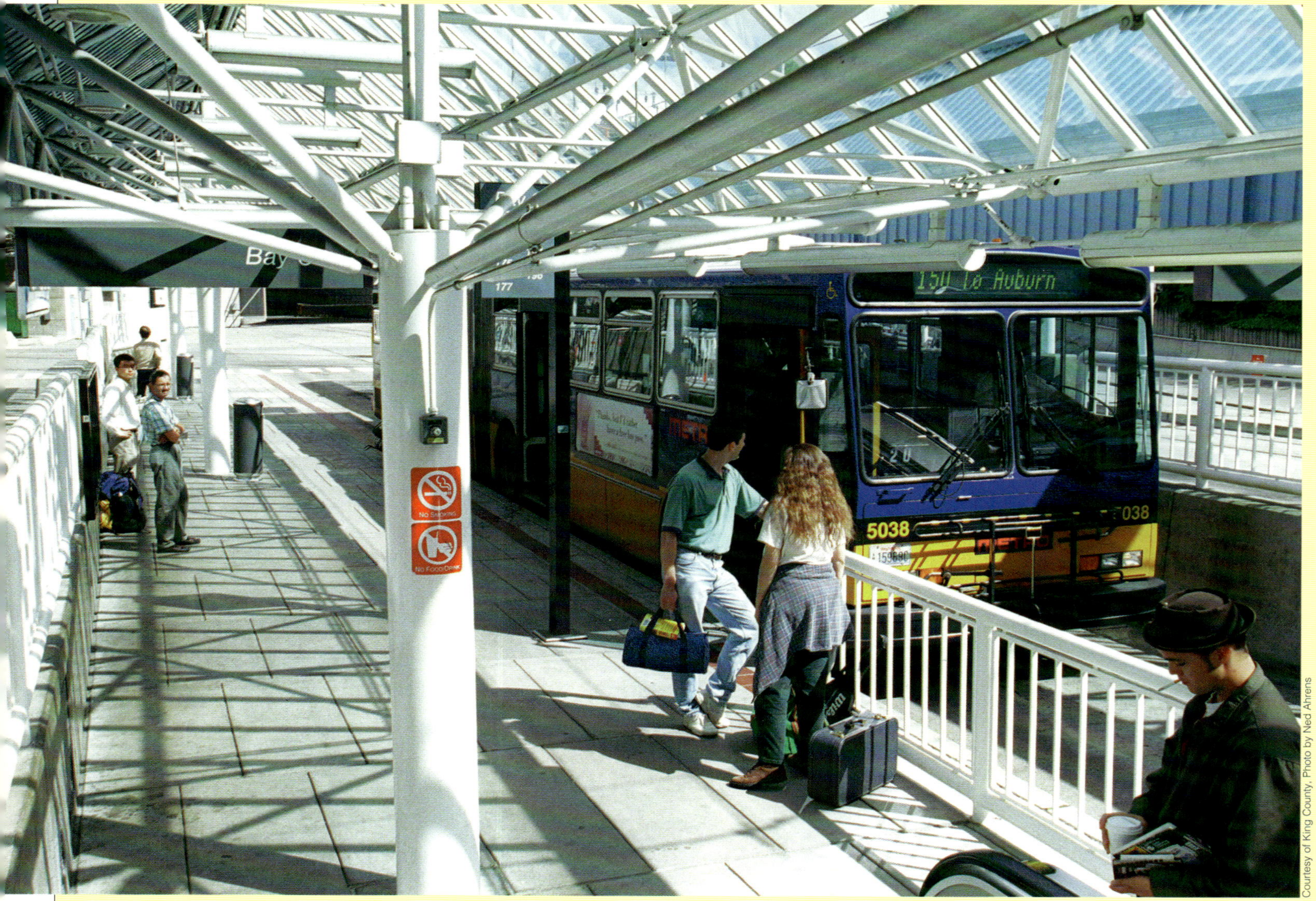

Courtesy of King County, Photo by Ned Ahrens

Convention Place Transit Station.

King County was founded in 1852 by act of the Oregon Territorial Legislature. In 1969, King County was the first county in the state of Washington to adopt a home charter rule establishing two branches of government—Executive and Council. This basic restructuring of county government has allowed the county to manage the increasingly complex range of services demanded by its residents.

Since the creation of the King County Executive Office, six individuals have held this position: John Spellman, Ron Dunlap, Randy Revelle, Tim Hill, Gary Locke, and the current Executive Ron Sims.

The job of the King County Executive has many facets. As a political leader of the second-largest government in

Washington State and the eleventh-largest county in the nation, the Executive oversees the delivery of such services as criminal justice, transportation, environmental protection, wastewater treatment, and public health. Like other metropolitan regions, while the area prospers, King County faces challenges such as threats to the environment, increasing traffic congestion due to explosive growth, and rising home prices. The Executive must address these issues while also striving to maintain and improve the quality of life for the citizens of the county. Providing essential, core services to the people of King County through sound financial planning and regional leadership is the way to maintain that quality of life for all the future generations of the region.

Through the leadership of the King County Executive, the county also works to ensure the safety and well being of its residents as well as to provide opportunities for those who need assistance.

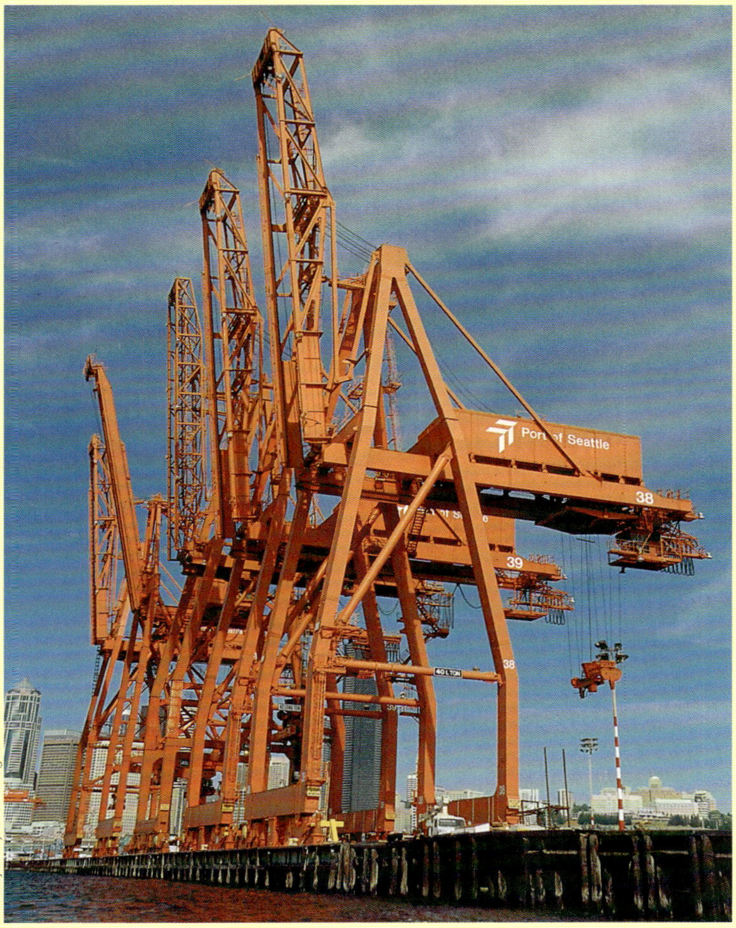

Courtesy of Wyndham Images

King County is an important Pacific Rim port. Goods flow through a large working waterfront, two major airports, rail lines, and two major interstates.

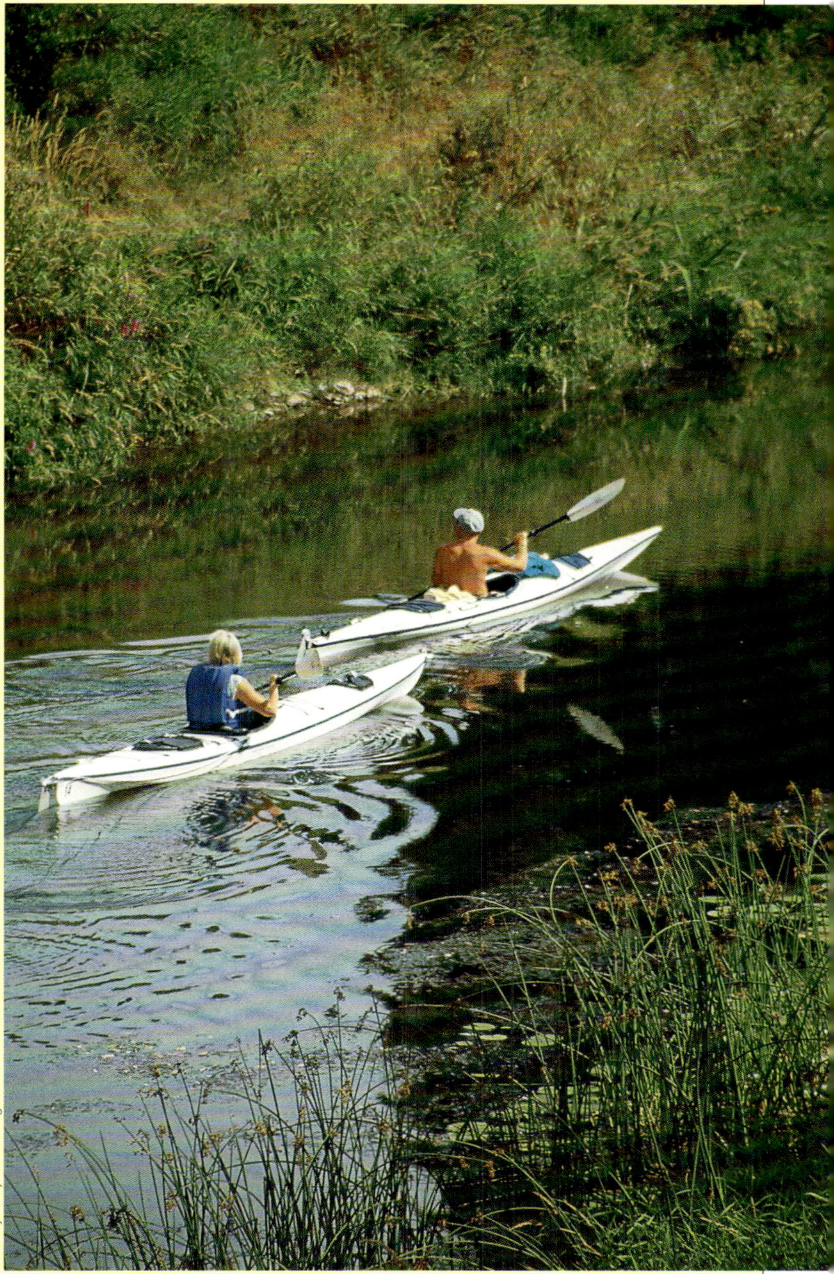

Courtesy of Wyndham Images

King County's regional parks offer a variety of recreational opportunities for outdoor enthusiasts.

Rhododendrons bloom in heavy abundance from March to June. King County residents are proud of the lush natural environment that the region's mild temperate climate fosters.

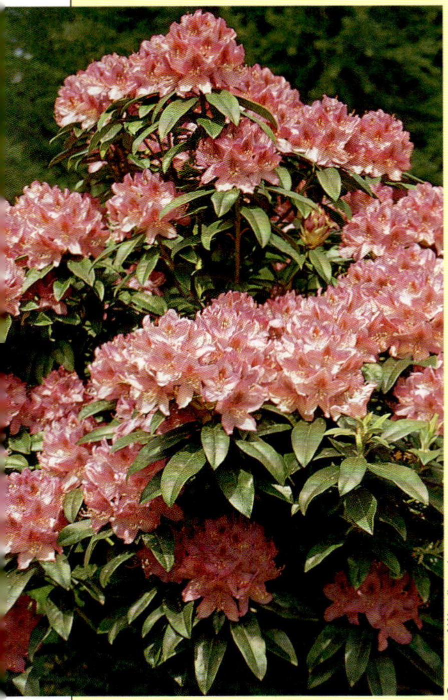

Courtesy of Wyndham Images

In this new century, county government must ask, "What will our legacy be? Are we prepared to do right by our children?" There is great potential among the residents of King County. The Executive Office must continue to work with its regional partners—schools, businesses, cities, and rural communities—to achieve long-term economic growth and maintain the area's exceptional quality of life. With effective and sound leadership, King County can continue on its path toward further progress and prosperity. Working together, the King County leadership can secure a future in which people will continue to earn a living wage, afford a home, and maintain a sense of community.

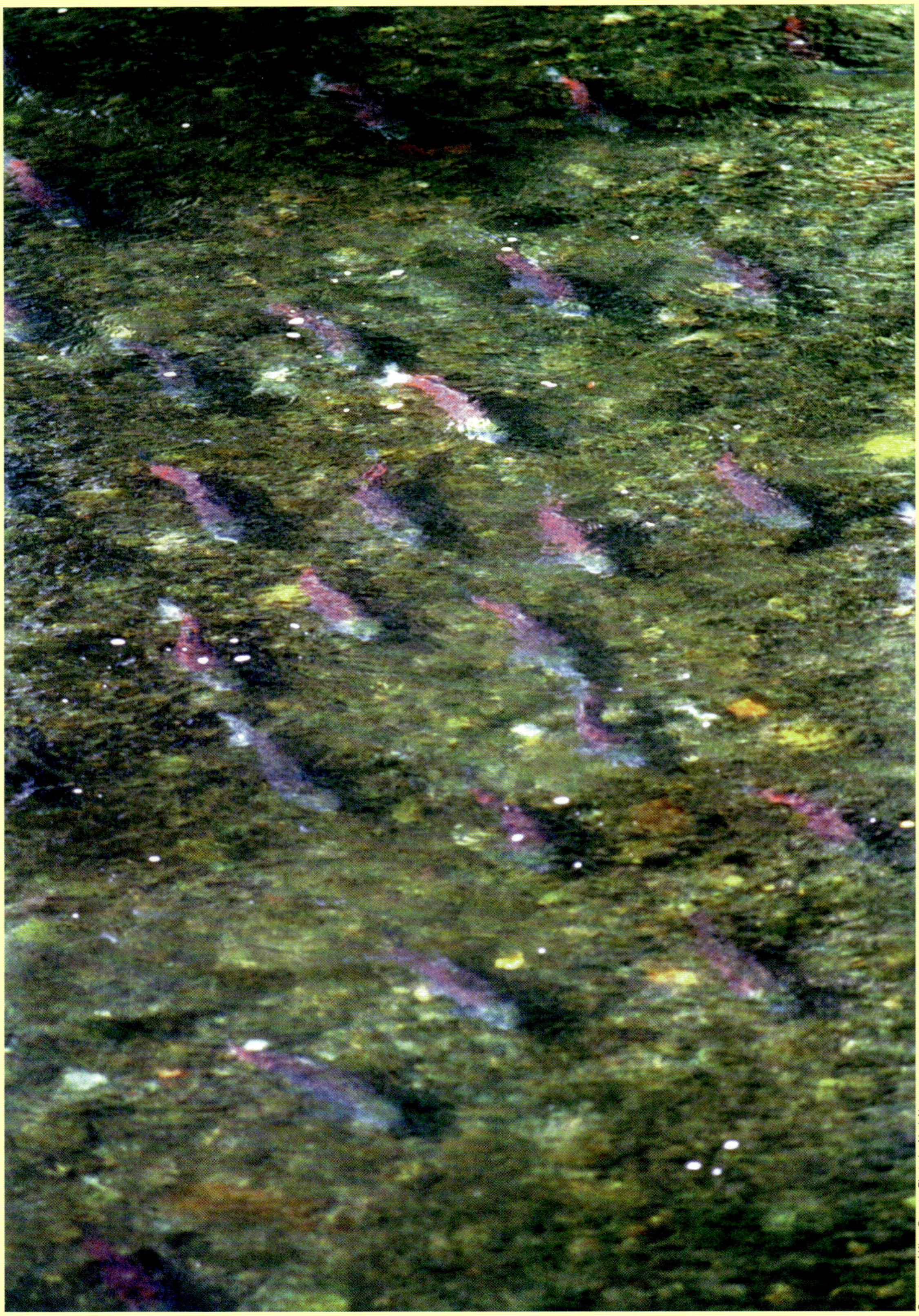

Courtesy of King County. Photo by Ned Ahrens

Threats to the environment are a major concern to the King County Executive Office. One challenge is the preservation of salmon habitat, such as the Cedar River, shown here brimming with Sockeye salmon on their way to the waters of their birth in order to deposit the eggs for the next generation.

The King County Sheriff's Office

Leadership, Integrity, Service, and Teamwork

From patrol to prevention, from canines to computer fraud, the King County Sheriff's Office (KCSO) provides comprehensive services that are distinctly tailored to serve individual communities. The KCSO is a major metropolitan law-enforcement agency that is committed to using innovative technology and policing techniques in its efforts to protect and serve.

The KCSO has served King County since 1852, and has continually changed to meet the county's needs. Today, the KCSO serves unincorporated areas, and provides contract law-enforcement services to 13 cities, King County Metro Transit, and the King County International Airport. Nine school districts participate in the KCSO's School Resource Officer program.

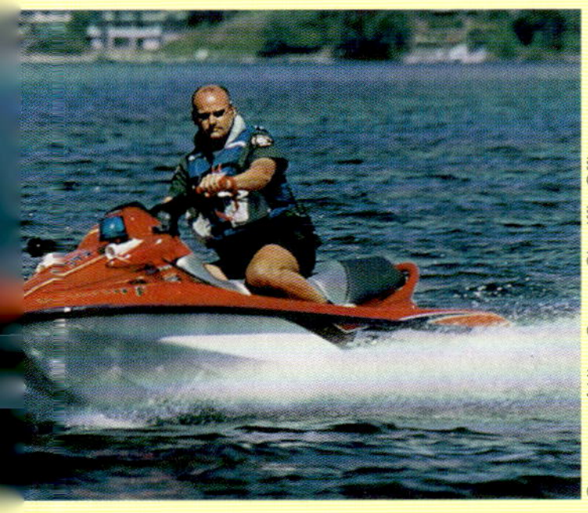

Courtesy of King County Sheriff's Office

The King County Sheriff's Office's Marine Unit patrols lakes and rivers in unincorporated areas and for some cities.

The KCSO emphasizes police work that focuses on community policing and crime prevention. Officers work closely with citizens and the private sector to identify concerns, develop solutions, and assess the results. The KCSO supports Block and Business Watches, conducts Crime Prevention Through Environmental Design reviews, and sponsors the very successful Crime Free Multi-Unit Housing landlord training program.

When crimes do occur, the KCSO's response is among the best. The office is nationally recognized for its expertise in homicide investigations and latent fingerprint identification; both are services provided to all King County jurisdictions. The KCSO has developed computer systems to compile and analyze crime information, and the office is leading efforts to share such information with other criminal justice agencies.

In short, the King County Sheriff's Office keeps its citizens safe through solid partnerships, effective intervention, and strong enforcement. That is the KCSO's foundation as well as its future.

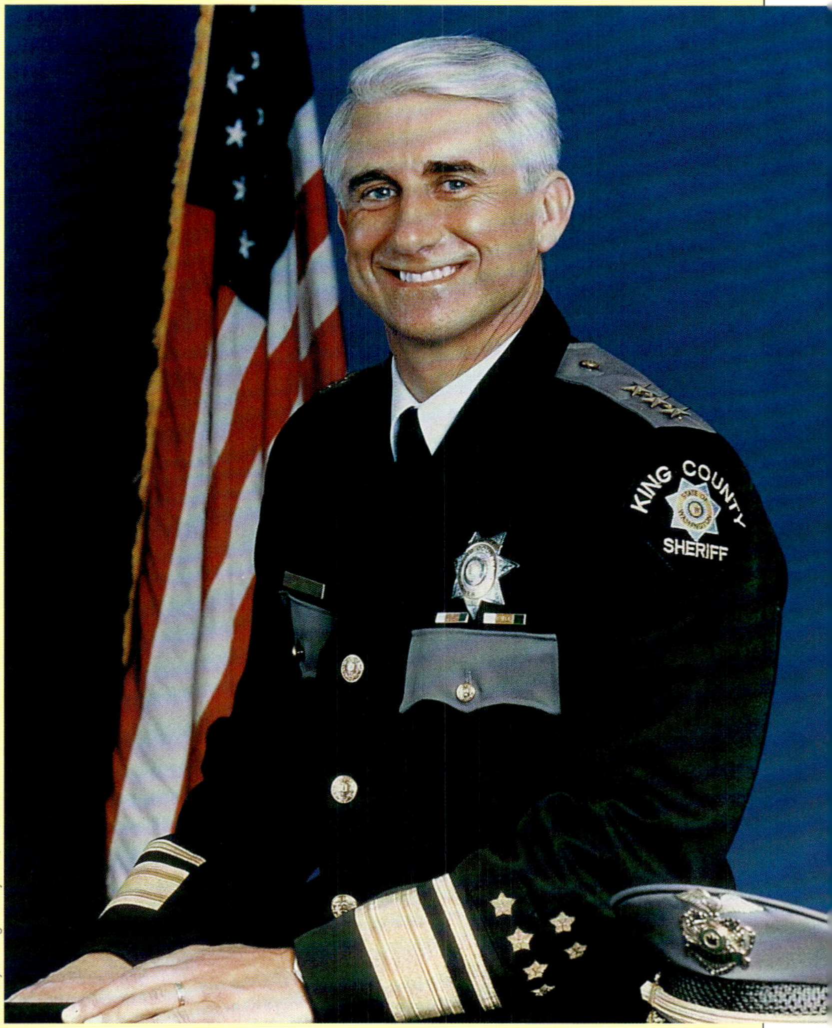

Courtesy of King County Sheriff's Office

David Reichert, King County Sheriff.

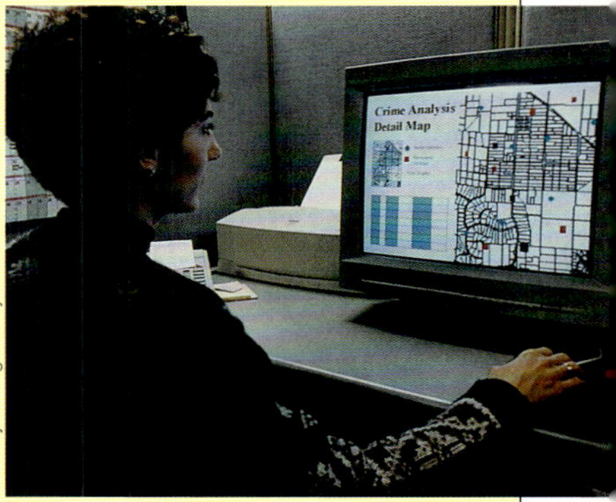

Courtesy of King County Sheriff's Office

Sophisticated computer software helps the King County Sheriff's Office to report, track, and analyze crime.

King County Council

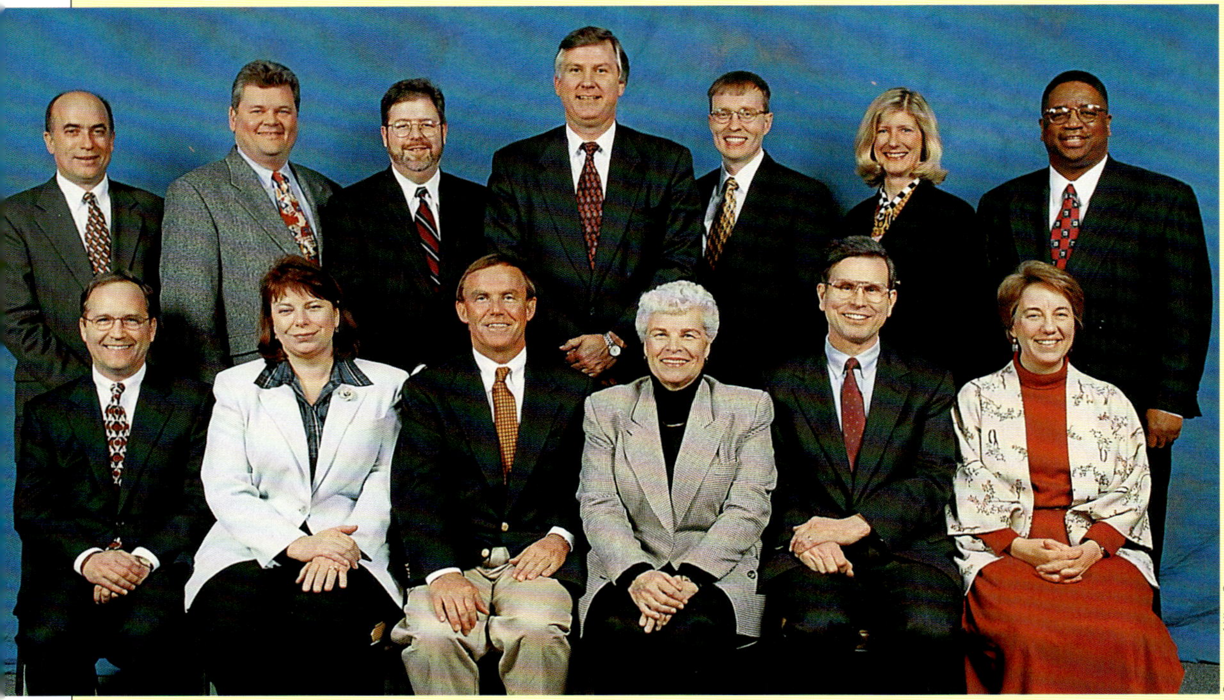

Courtesy of King County

The 2000 Metropolitan King County Council consisted of: (back row from left) Dwight Pelz, Greg Nickels, Chris Vance, Larry Phillips, Rob McKenna, Jane Hague, and Larry Gossett; (front row) David Irons, Cynthia Sullivan, Pete von Reichbauer, Louise Miller, Kent Pullen, and Maggi Fimia.

King County is one of the largest and most prosperous counties in the country. Local government plays an important role in ensuring the vitality of this region. The Metropolitan King County Council has a special charge as the regional governing body to provide solutions to a vast array of issues.

The structure of King County government follows the federal model. The 13 councilmembers lead the legislative branch, while a separately elected county executive heads up the county departments that make up the executive branch. Other independently elected officials include the sheriff, prosecutor, assessor, and the various district and superior court judges.

The council adopts ordinances that establish laws for the county, levy taxes, and appropriates revenues. The council also holds final approval over the county budget. Beyond taxes, the council actions that most often directly impact local citizens are ones dealing with the quality of life. Councilmembers take great pride in the wide variety of cultural and recreational opportunities provided by King County. The county maintains huge regional parks that offer everything from Little League baseball to wilderness hiking. The trail system is extensive, connecting city dwellers, suburbanites, and rural residents.

Protection of the natural environment is an ongoing goal for the council and is carried out through the preservation of open space, commitment to water quality, and visionary programs to protect native fish and wildlife.

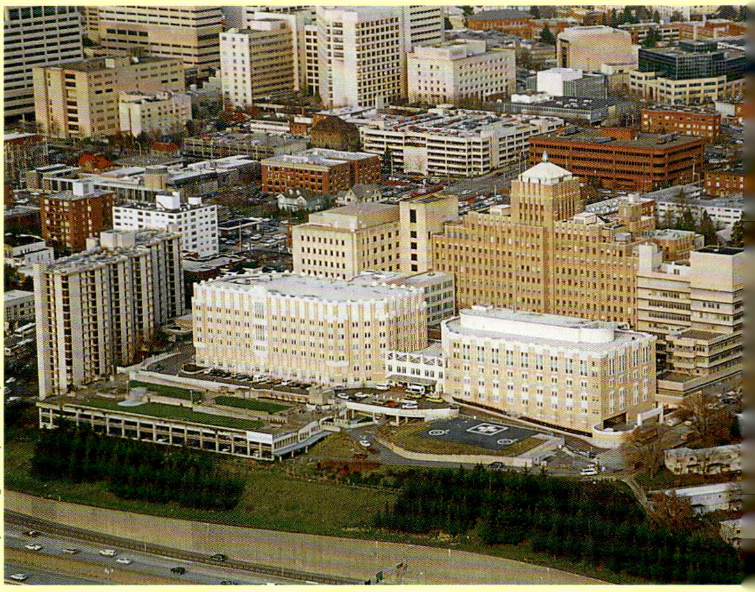

Courtesy of King County. Photo by Ned Ahrens

King County's Harborview Medical Center is the Level 1 trauma center for the entire Northwest Region. It is also one of the few public hospitals in the nation that operates in the black.

Maintaining the natural environment in a way that is best for people and wildlife is one of the biggest challenges facing county government.

Here, volunteers plant native vegetation to restore salmon habitat along the Sammamish River.

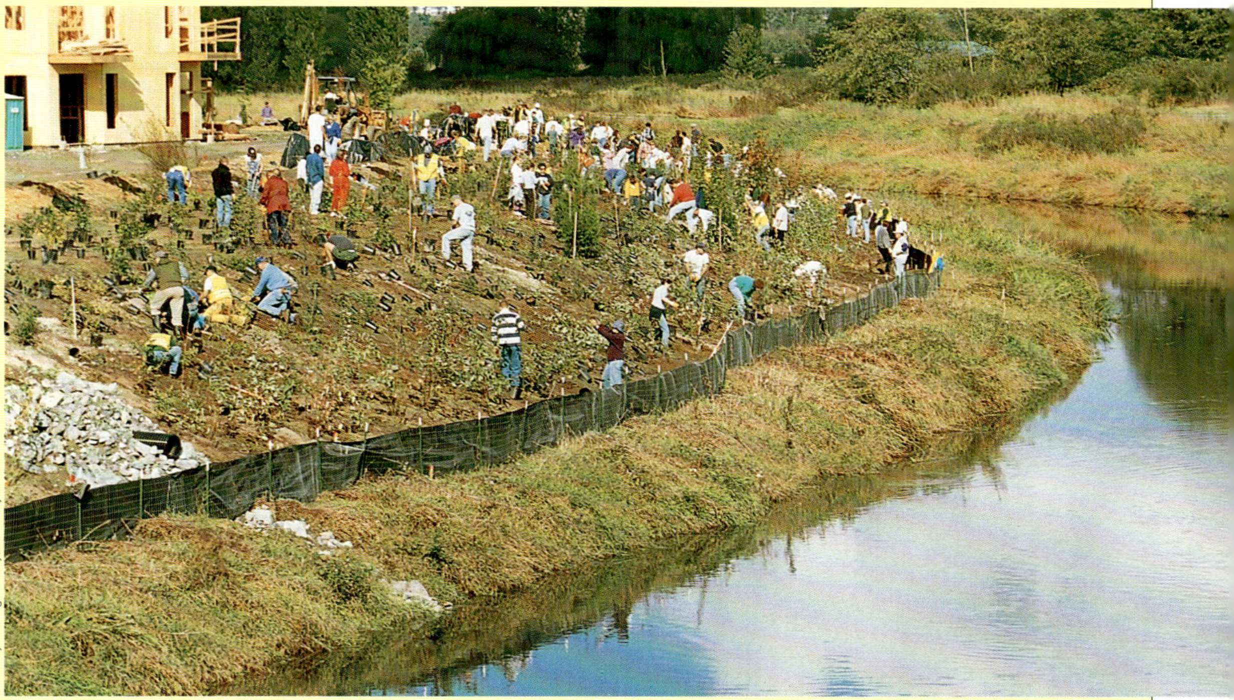

Courtesy of King County, Photo by Ned Ahrens

King County government has been in transition for the past ten years. The council has guided the switch from a government that provides only local municipal-style services in the unincorporated areas to one that directs regional decision-making with other agencies and governments.

King County provides a variety of regional services to all residents, no matter where they live in the county. With the completion of the merger of Metro and King County in 1996, these services now include Metro transit and water quality, as well as traditional county services such as courts and jails. Other regional services include elections, property tax appraisals, regional parks and open space, Harborview Hospital, and King County International Airport (Boeing Field). The county council also sets policy that influences countless land-use decisions.

Some of services are often provided as part of a contract with the 39 cities in the county. In addition, the county still is the local government for more than 350,000 citizens in unincorporated areas. Covering more than 2,200 square miles, King County is nearly twice as large as the average county in the United States. With more than 1.6 million people, it also ranks as the tenth most populous county in the nation. It is also a very economically diverse county. Established industrial giants, such as Boeing and Weyerhaeuser, have long called King County home. Consumer-popular companies, such as Starbucks and Costco, are headquartered here. And, thousands

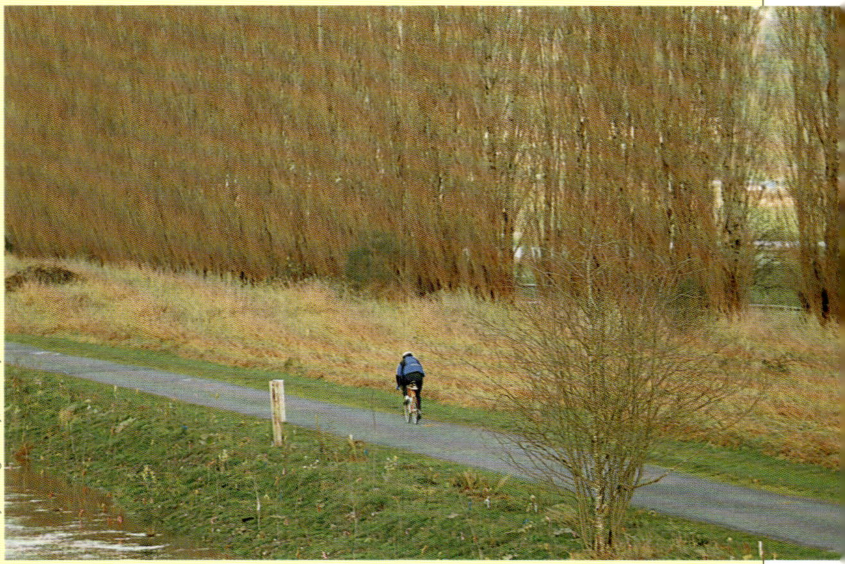

Courtesy of King County, Photo by Ned Ahrens

The King County recreational trail system is extensive. The Sammamish River Park Trail (see above) connects to the Burke-Gilman Trail, providing a route around the north end of Lake Washington.

of high-tech companies continue to flourish here alongside Microsoft. The county is also an important Pacific Rim port with a large working waterfront, two major airports, rail lines, and is bisected by two major interstates.

King County leaders carry out their duties through cooperation and caring. The elected leaders may make the tough decisions, but they are backed up by the local citizens. Government is only effective when its citizens take a vested interest in the legislative process. The council encourages citizen participation through membership on county boards and commissions, serving on special task forces, and providing public testimony—both at council meetings and via the Internet.

Since the 1850s, King County government has taken the lead in this region to improve the quality of life for all residents. Whether it was building the first roads in the 1800s, providing for the poor during the Great Depression, or creating a network of green space in the 1990s, King County has led the way.

King County maintains huge regional parks that offer everything from biking and hiking trails to children's play areas for the family to enjoy.

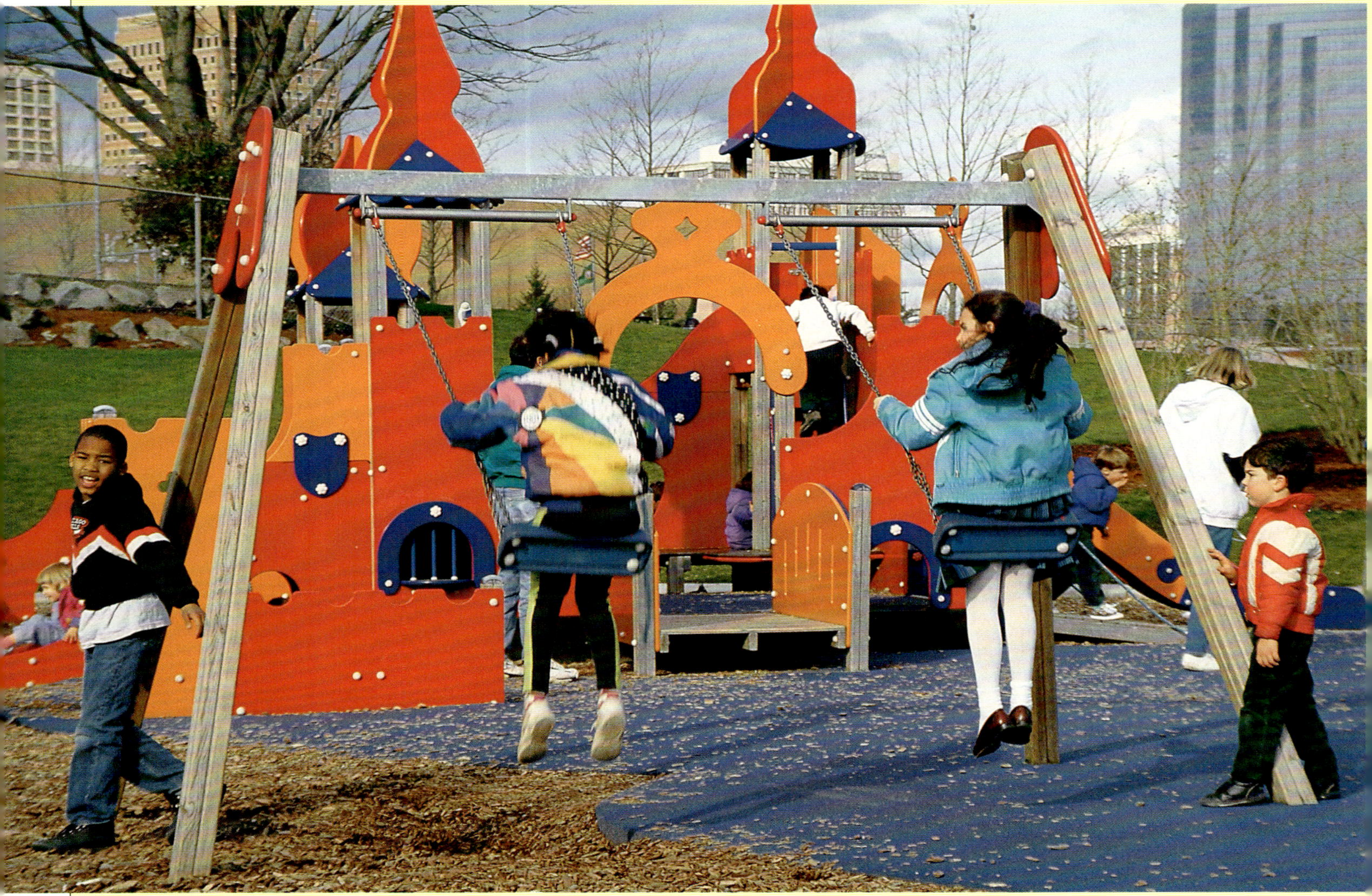

Economic Development Council of Seattle & King County (EDC)

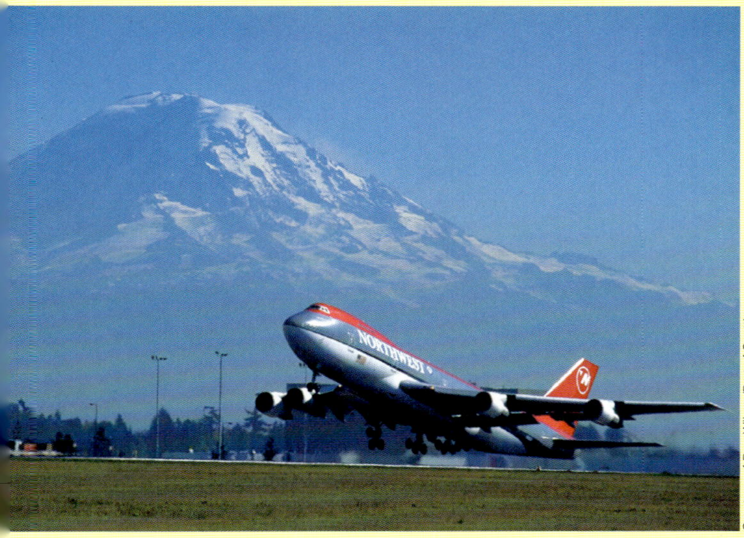

Northwest Airlines Boeing 747 taking off from SeaTac International Airport with Mt. Rainier in the background.

Washington State's Seattle-King County region offers a wide range of lifestyles, from the sophisticated urban environment of Seattle to the picturesque, small-town life offered by its many rural and suburban areas. In 1999, *Forbes Magazine* touted Seattle as one of the top ten regions in the nation to do business—first out of 162 metropolitan areas in terms of growth in jobs, income, and output in the area's high technology industries, including aerospace, computer software, biotechnology, telecommunications, Internet companies, and others. In 2000, *Fortune Magazine* ranked the Seattle area sixth out of the ten best U.S. cities for business.

King County is well known for its highly educated workforce. The region's emphasis on education, from primary school through the doctoral level, gives King County an abundant resource of skilled, stable, and productive personnel. Maintaining a high quality of life—affordable housing, transportation options, and a diverse mix of goods and services—is critical to the region's overall success. The Economic Development Council of Seattle & King County (EDC) works to preserve and promote this success.

The EDC is a nonprofit organization funded by a coalition of business, government, non-governmental organizations, education, and environmental interests. The EDC's vision is to marshal public and private resources to create and capture opportunities for attracting and retaining leading edge industries, including manufacturing and technology-based business and trade services. The EDC promotes the region as a premier location for business development through a flexible business development system that works directly with companies to address their concerns, including site selection, financing, permitting, and workforce issues. The EDC coordinates these efforts with cities, businesses, and chambers of commerce to help keep the region's economy viable and competitive, and ultimately, to recruit and retain family-wage jobs for King County. The EDC also manages three long-range economic development projects:

- Action Plan for Continued Prosperity in King County—a summary of work being done throughout the county to help maintain economic momentum with respect to infrastructure, workforce, regulatory balance, and economic development;
- Freight Mobility Roundtable—an industry/government coalition group that works to ensure freight mobility issues are addressed and funded in regional transportation plans; and
- Commuter Challenge—a program that increases highway capacity through promotion of high occupancy vehicle commuting and encouragement of work options such as compressed workweeks and teleworking.

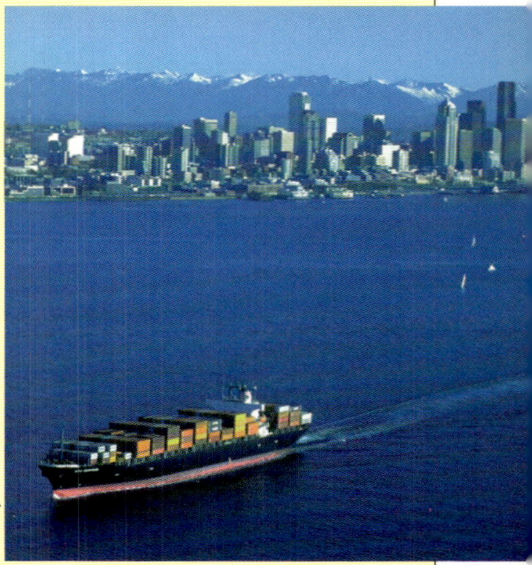

View of downtown Seattle as a container ship departs the Port of Seattle.

National Oceanic and Atmospheric Administration

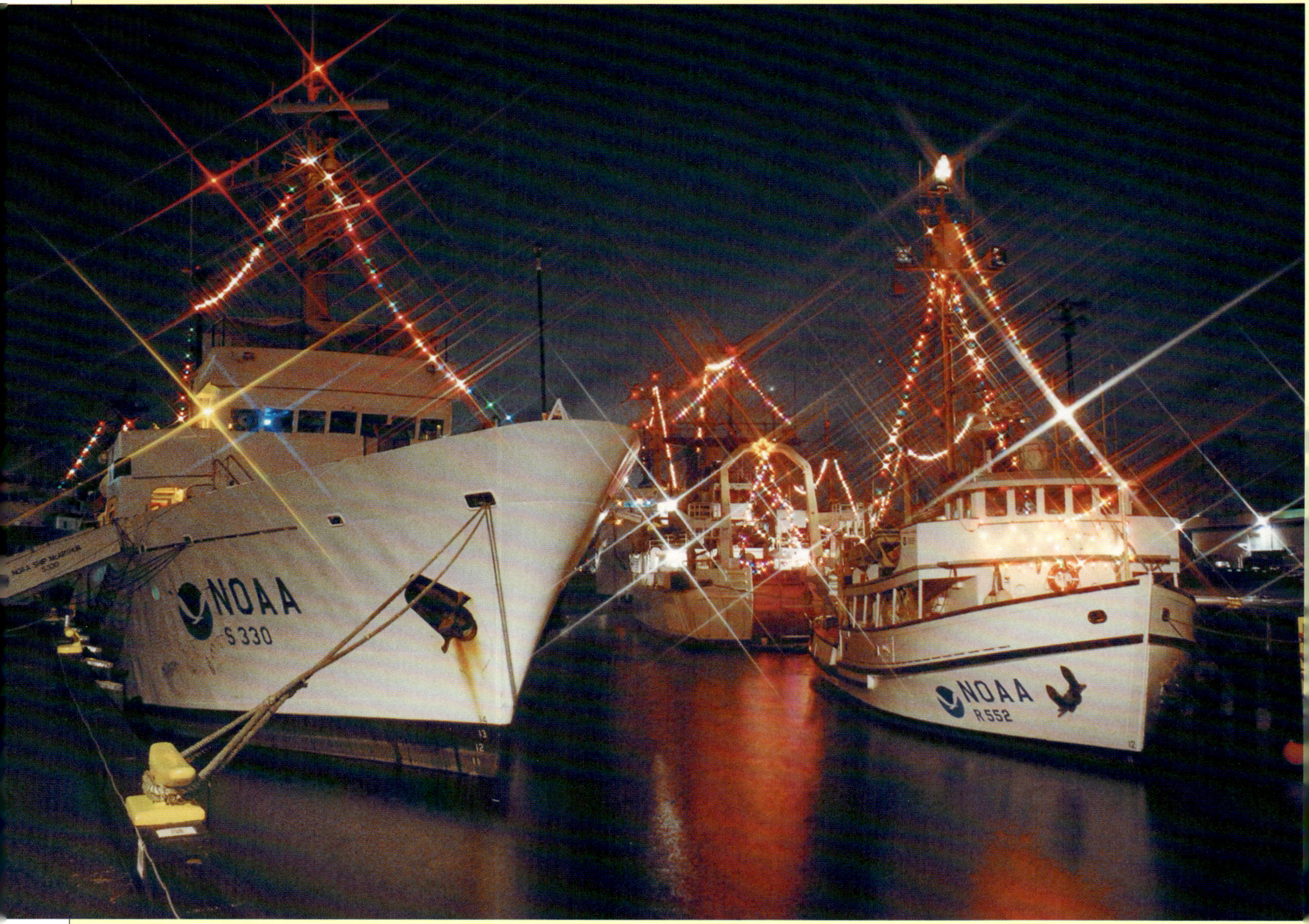

Holiday season at NOAA's Marine Operations Center on Lake Union.

NOAA in Seattle, Working With Others to Serve the Nation

Formed a third of a century ago in October of 1970, the National Oceanic and Atmospheric Administration's (NOAA's) charge for the twenty-first century is to provide the United States with environmental assessments, predictions, and stewardship which will ensure quality of life and healthy commerce for generations to come. Nearly 1,000 NOAA employees work in the Seattle area, the largest contingent of NOAA employees outside of metropolitan Washington, D.C.

In Seattle, the majority of NOAA employees work at the NOAA Western Regional Center, which is located on 114 acres at Sand Point along the western shoreline of Lake Washington. Other major facilities in Seattle include the Montlake Facility on

Portage Bay near the University of Washington and the NOAA Pacific Fleet Facility on the eastern shore of Lake Union. The facilities include offices, laboratories, auditoriums, equipment assembly and maintenance areas, warehousing, ship piers and staging areas, a cafeteria and health services building, and a day care center.

All major line elements of NOAA—the National Weather Service, the National Marine Fisheries Service, the National Ocean Service, the Office of Oceanic & Atmospheric Research, and the National Environmental Satellite, Data & Information Service—are represented in Seattle. NOAA's staff Office of Marine and Aviation Operations' Marine Operations Center provides ship services throughout the Pacific in support of NOAA's research, assessment and surveying missions. The Western Administrative Support Center provides administrative services in the western region to NOAA and the Department of Commerce, the parent organization of NOAA.

NOAA's Western Regional Center on Lake Washington.

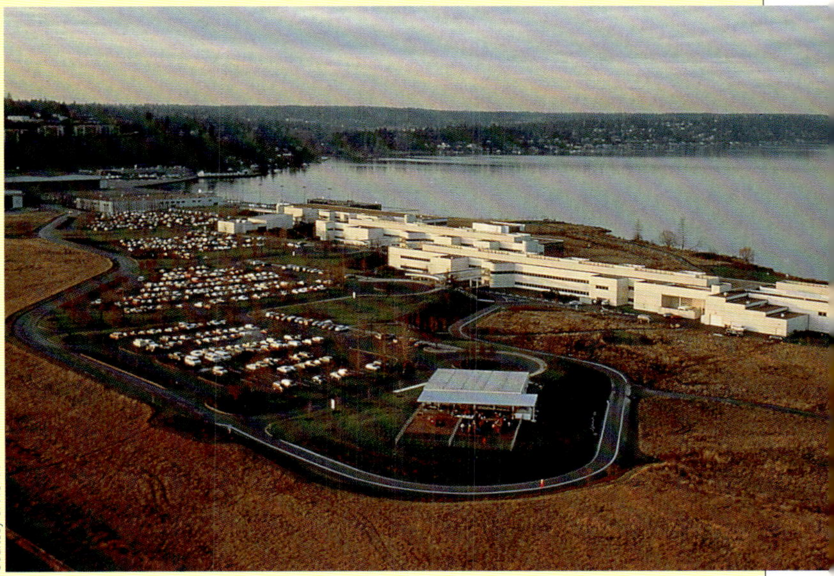

Courtesy of NOAA

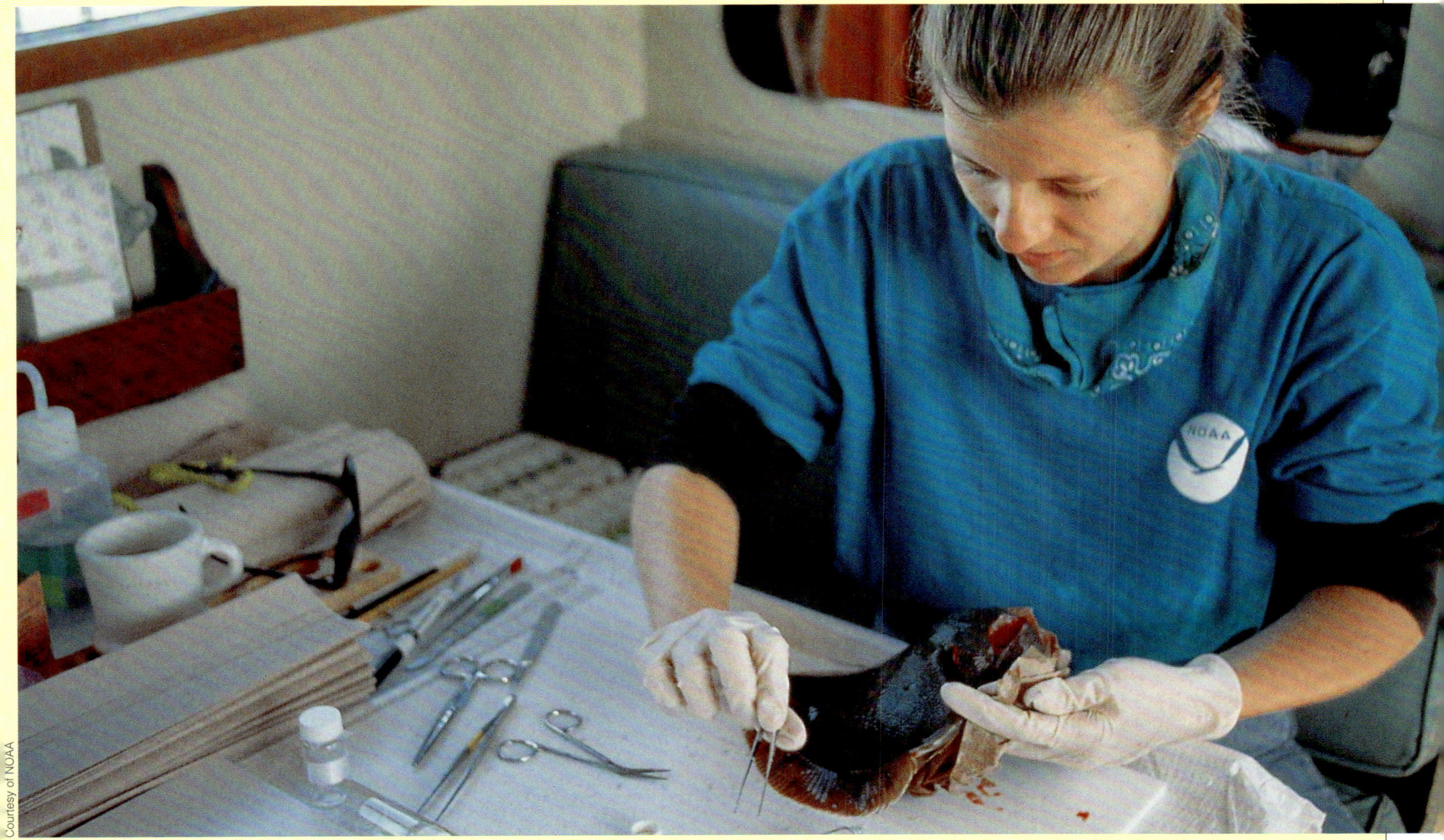

Courtesy of NOAA

NOAA Bottomfish Contaminants and Reproductive Success Research in Puget Sound.

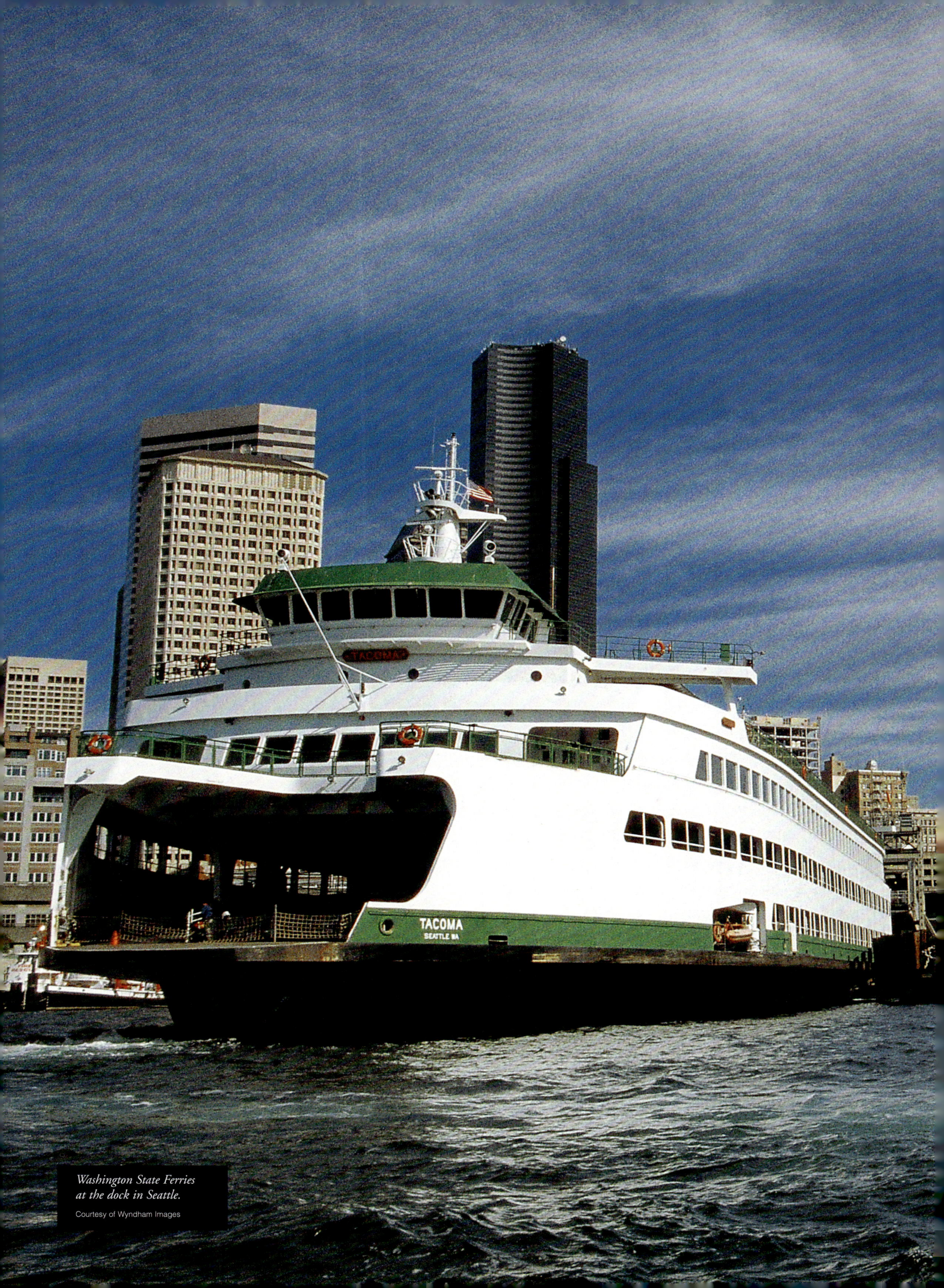

Washington State Ferries at the dock in Seattle.

Courtesy of Wyndham Images

Part Two

Networks

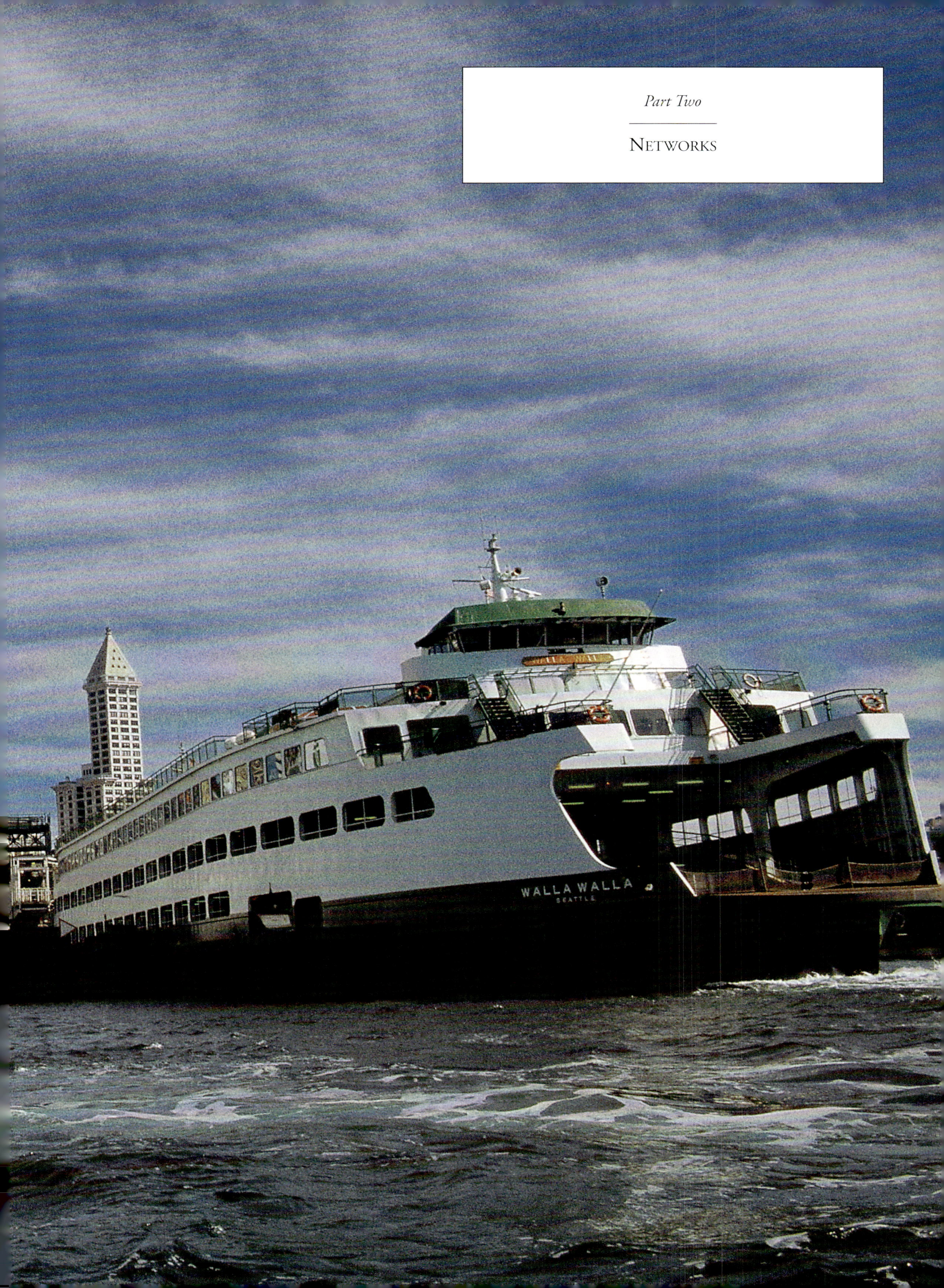

The Seattle Times

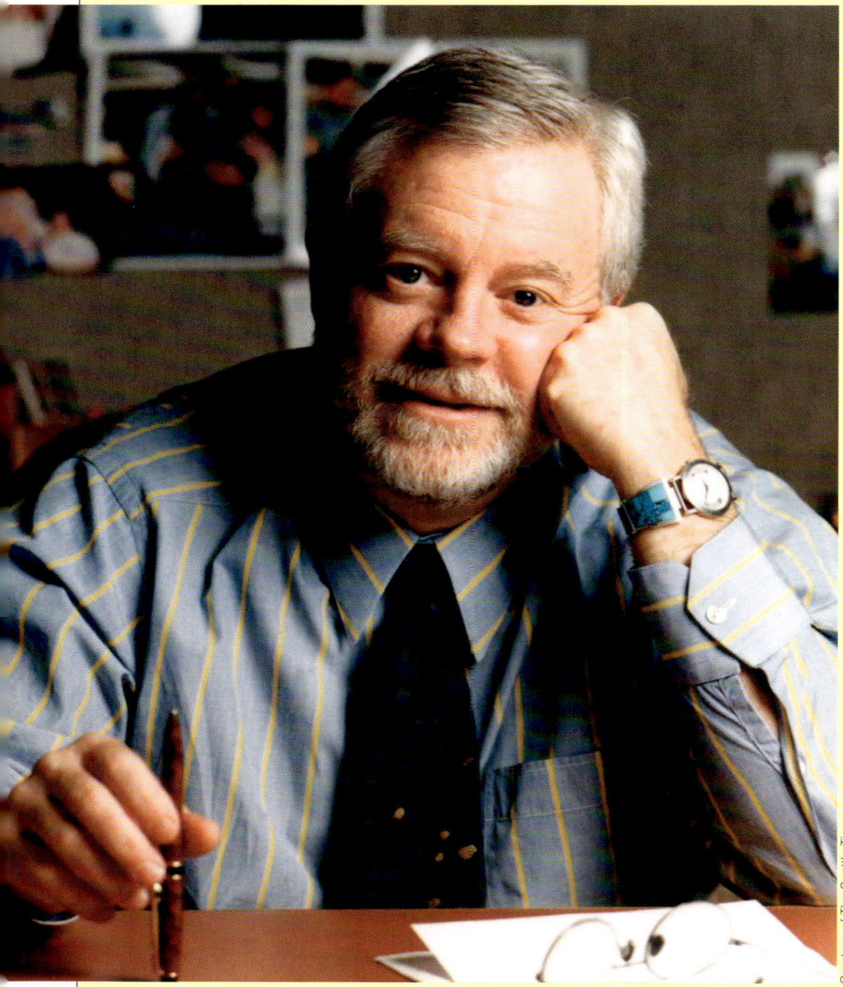

Courtesy of The Seattle Times

Frank A. Blethen, Publisher and CEO.

Family-Owned and Independent

The Seattle Times is the largest locally and family-owned and operated metropolitan newspaper in the United States. For over a century, the paper has been under the continuous ownership of the Blethen family.

Committed to Quality

The Seattle Times Company is dedicated to remaining independent and to serving the community through quality journalism. In 1997, *The Seattle Times* received two Pulitzer Prizes, for a total of seven won overall. It is the only Puget Sound-area newspaper to receive more than one.

Excellence is a hallmark of many aspects of *The Seattle Times*. For the second year running, the Society of American Business Editors and Writers named the Business section one of the four best among newspapers of its size. *The Times* also won top honors from the National Awards for Education Reporting, a topic given special emphasis at *The Seattle Times*.

Extensive Local Coverage

The Times provides focused, local coverage of topics like education, transportation, natural resources, and other defining issues of the region. Every weekday, *The Seattle Times* publishes and distributes four zoned editions to meet the needs of readers in distinctive geographic areas. The zones in and around Seattle are defined as Metro, Snohomish County, South King County, and the Eastside.

Seattle Times bureaus in Olympia, Washington and Washington, D. C. stay abreast of news from those two capital cities that may affect readers in *The Seattle Times* coverage area.

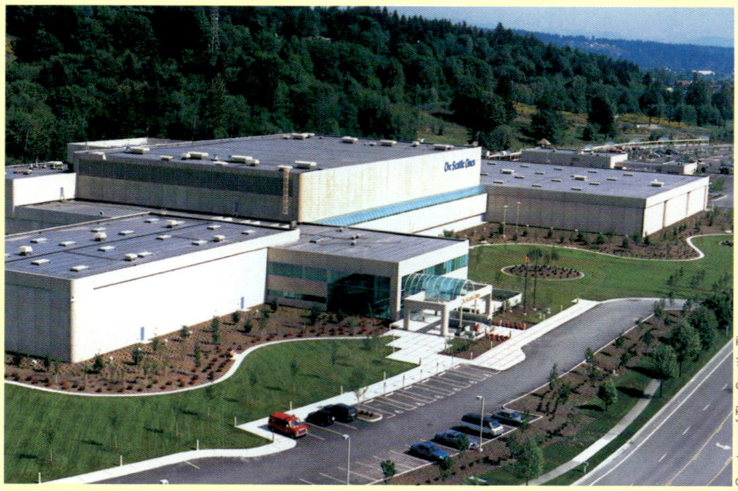

The Seattle Times North Creek printing plant.

The Seattle Times Pulitzer Prize winners, left to right: Deborah Nelson, Eric Nalder, Alex Tizon, Byron Acohido.

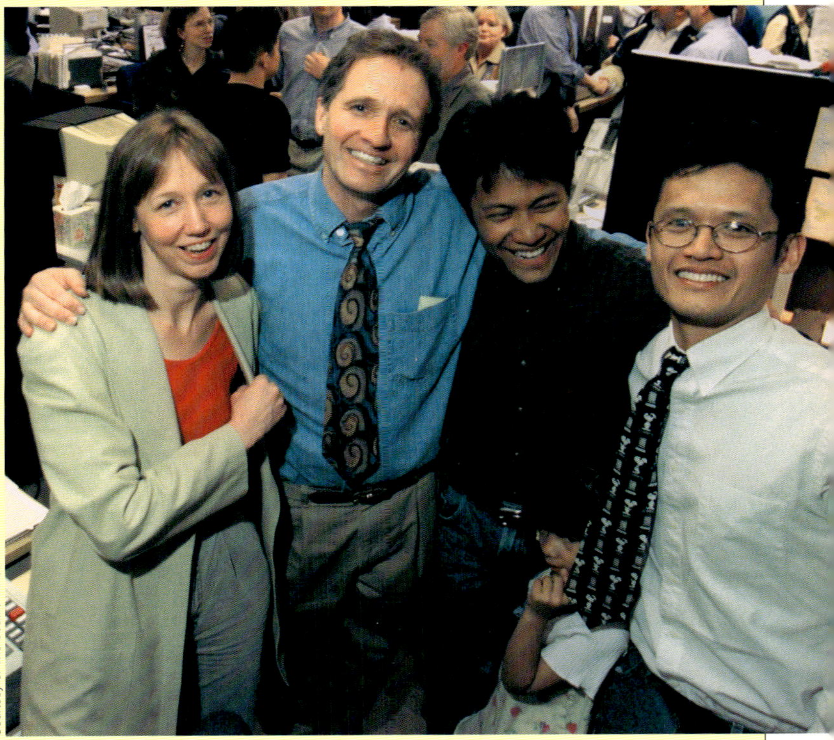

Courtesy of The Seattle Times

A Comprehensive Source

The Seattle Times daily and Sunday papers carry sections covering a wide variety of interests. Each day, *The Times* features: *Main News*; *Local News*; *Scene*, focusing on lifestyle issues; *Business*; *Sports*; and *Classified Advertising*.

Weekly sections include: *Ticket*, a guide to arts and entertainment; *Families*, focusing on family life and activities; *Job Market*; *Personal Technology*, to help readers stay on top of a rapidly changing computer industry; *Food*; *Arts*, covering people and trends behind Seattle's vibrant art scene; *Movie Times*; *Northwest Weekend*, devoted to outdoor recreation; *Travel Northwest*; and *Sunday Travel*, bringing the world a little closer. Other sections cover *Real Estate*, *Motoring*, and *Religion*. *Pacific Northwest*, a popular full-color Sunday magazine, profiles unique Northwest people and places.

Advertising Value

As Washington State's largest daily newspaper, *The Seattle Times* provides an excellent vehicle for both local and national advertisers. Reaching more than a million readers on Sunday, it is the leading source of timely consumer information in the marketplace.

The Company in the Community

The Seattle Times Company values its special relationship with the community. Company giving programs focusing on women, youth, education, health and human services, diversity, literacy, and the arts support many community organizations and activities.

Contributions made by *The Seattle Times* include: the annual Fund for the Needy drive, education scholarships, an Urban Newspaper workshop for minority students, a Newspapers in Education program, and a wide range of community partnerships benefiting local nonprofit organizations. In addition, *The Seattle Times* provides leadership and ongoing support to some of the most successful annual United Way campaigns in the country.

In 1990, *The Seattle Times* launched a unique cooperative public service media campaign to remind people of the reasons behind the Martin Luther King, Jr. holiday. *The Seattle Times* underwrites all expenses. The campaign currently includes 33 newspapers, 16 television

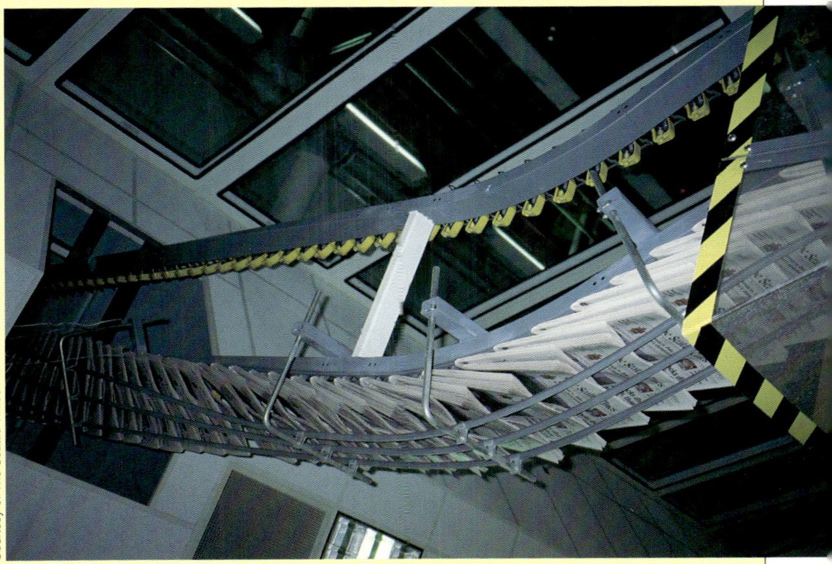

Courtesy of The Seattle Times

The Seattle Times newspapers coming off the press.

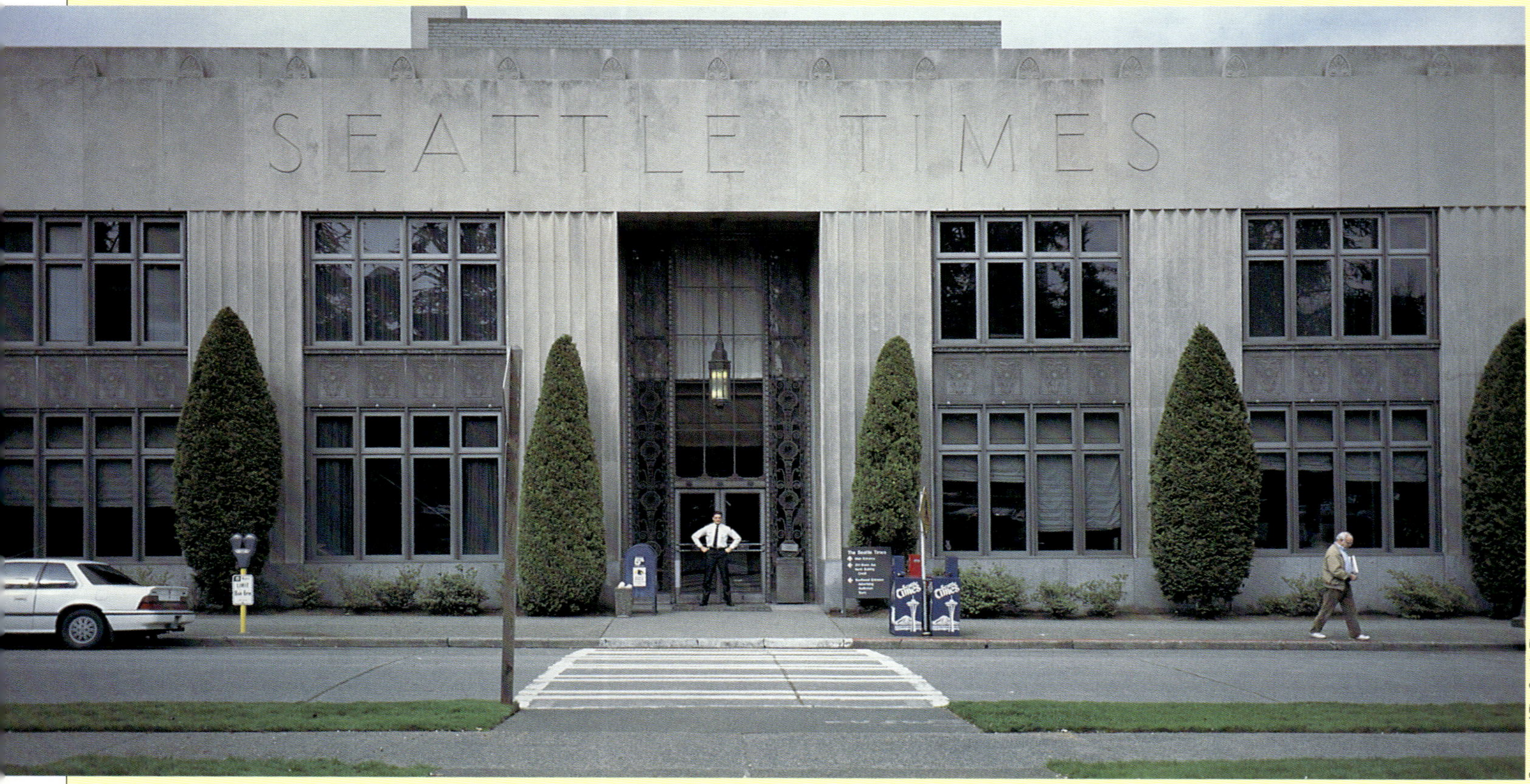

Courtesy of The Seattle Times

The Seattle Times Fairview Building.

outlets, 35 radio stations, and an outdoor advertising company, all promoting a singular message about the values Dr. King represented.

The Seattle Times takes an active role internally as well as outside the company in promoting diversity. *Seattle Times* publisher Frank A. Blethen has been honored as a national leader in advancing gender and racial equality in the workplace and in the community. In the newsroom, *The Seattle Times* ranks among the top metro dailies in the country with minority employment constituting about 24 percent, compared to a nationwide news average of 11.5 percent. The National Association for Women in Communications recently selected *The Seattle Times* to receive its first Ruth Weyand Award for outstanding contributions in advancing women in the workplace.

The Seattle Times is recognized for providing an excellent work environment for the more than 4,000 people employed in all departments of the company. For eight consecutive years, *Working Mother* magazine has named *The Seattle Times* newspaper one of the best 100 employers in the country.

In keeping with a philosophy of preserving and protecting the resources of the Northwest, The Seattle Times Company practices and promotes recycling. Currently, more than 80 percent of *Times'* newsprint contains recycled fibers. All newspaper waste is reused: ink, office paper, printing plates, silver film, and even oil from presses and delivery trucks are recycled.

These efforts have been recognized with environmental awards from The Washington State Department of Ecology, King County, and the Weyerhaeuser Company.

Newspapers in Education

Research shows that students who use newspapers as a learning resource have a better awareness of the world. The Seattle Times Newspapers in Education (NIE) program benefits both teachers and students by bringing newspapers and learning materials into classrooms throughout *The Times'* circulation areas.

Seattle Times Subsidiaries

The Seattle Times is part of a family of companies. Each is autonomously operated, but strategically aimed at bolstering the company's goal of being a leading information provider.

The Seattle Times Company publishes a number of other newspapers that function independently, each maintaining its own distinct editorial voice to serve its community. These publications include the *Walla Walla Union-Bulletin*, *Yakima Herald-Republic*, and *Issaquah Press*. The company also owns Blethen Maine Newspapers, which includes the *Portland Press Herald and Maine Sunday Telegraph*, *Kennebec Journal*, *Morning Sentinel*, *Coastal Journal*, and the web site *maintoday.com*.

Seattle Times Publications, Inc. produces the monthly *Mirror* and *Bar Bulletin/Trial News*, a publication for legal professionals. Other company holdings include Rotary Offset Press, Inc., Direct Marketing of Puget Sound Times Distribution, Inc., New Media Development Group, and Voice Information Services.

Robert C. Blethen, Vice President, Corporate Marketing.

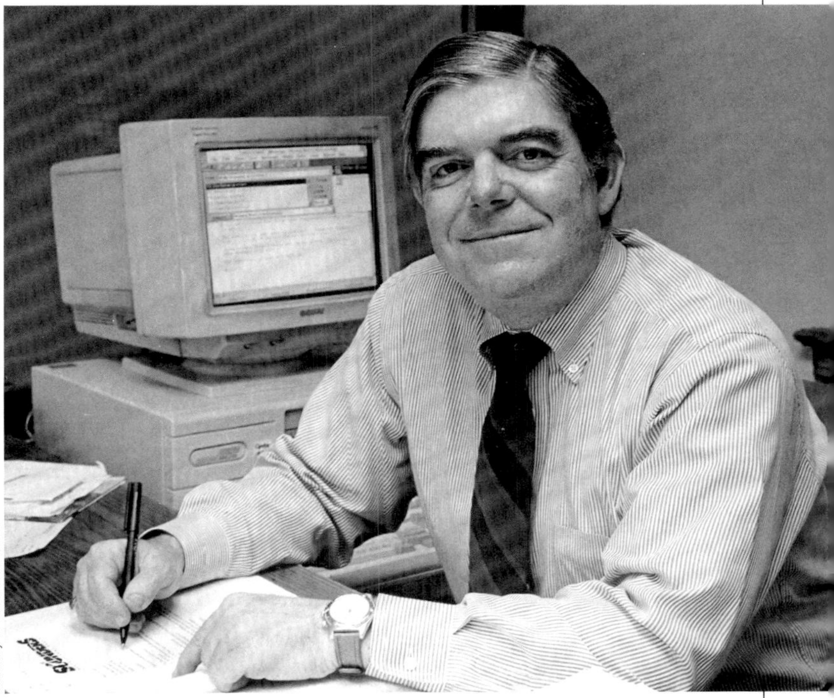

Courtesy of The Seattle Times

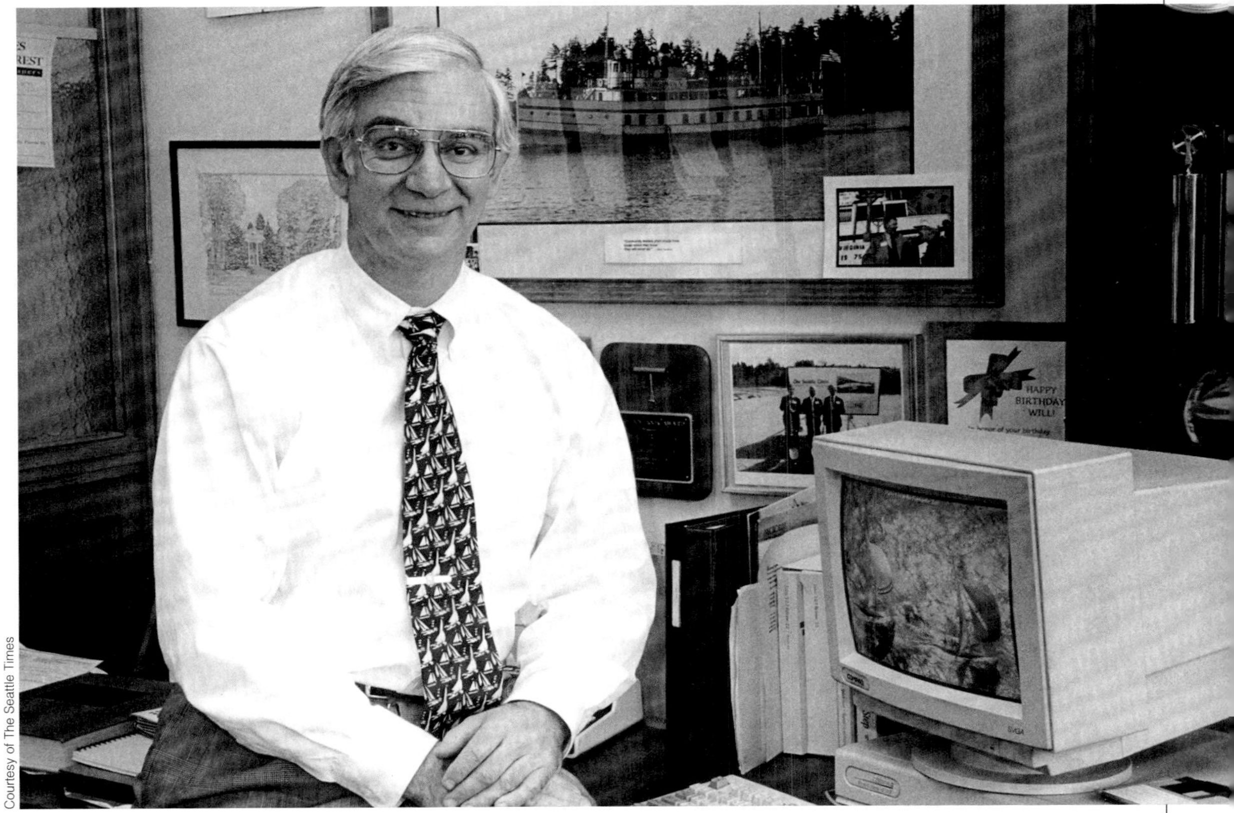

Courtesy of The Seattle Times

William K. Blethen, Treasurer.

Fisher Communications, Inc.

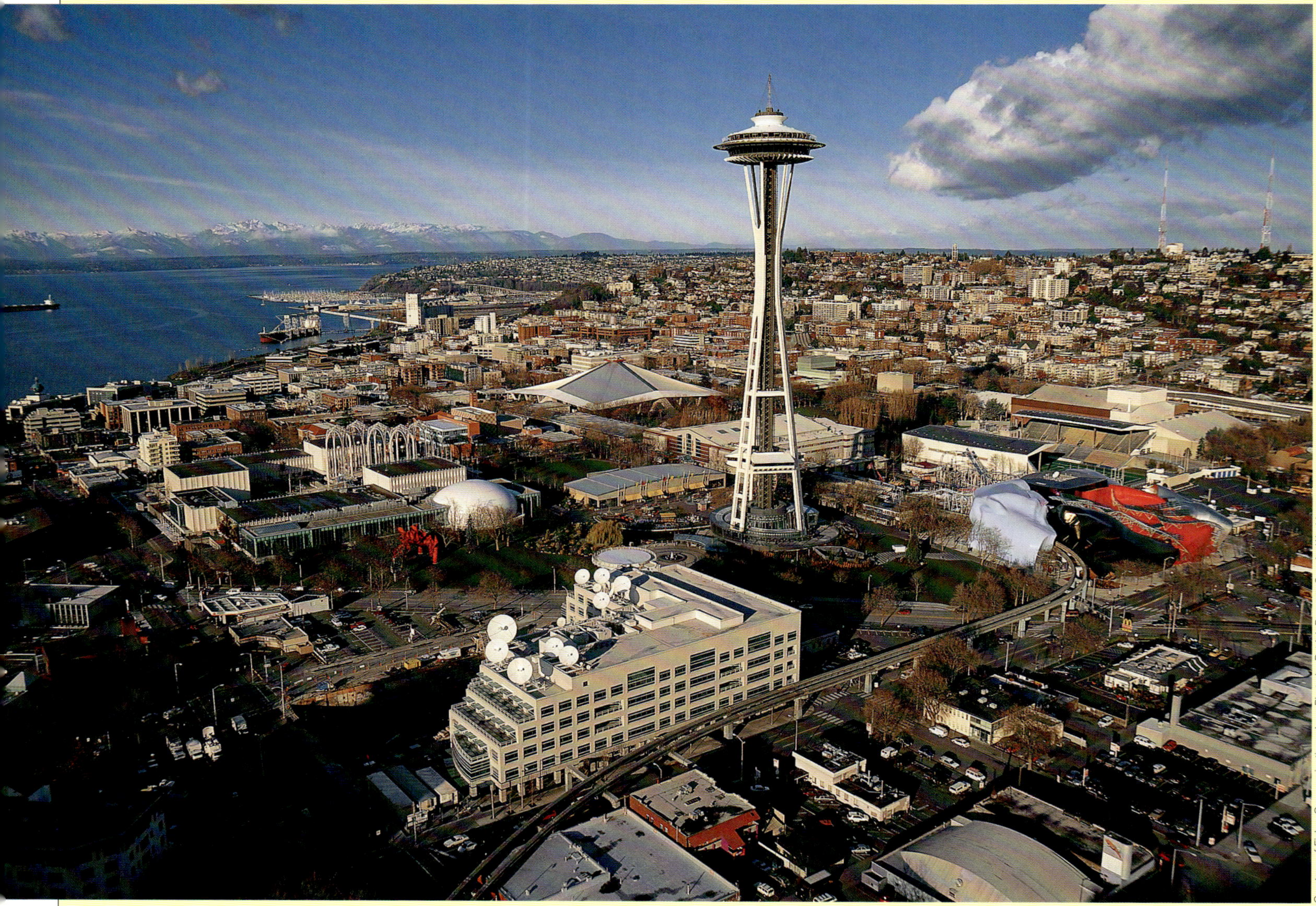

Fisher Plaza, a world-class communications and media hub, is the center of connectivity in Seattle, Washington. Pictured here in the foreground, Fisher Plaza is surrounded by some of Seattle's most exciting attractions including the Experience Music Project to the right, the Space Needle, Key Arena, and Pacific Science Center directly behind, and the breathtaking vista of Elliott Bay and the Olympic Mountains in the left background.

The glass façade of Fisher Plaza reflects the striking image of Seattle's Space Needle, located just across the street. It is a fitting visual metaphor. The Space Needle was the central symbol of the future for the 1962 Century 21 World's Fair; and today, as the twenty-first century unfolds, Fisher Plaza is the realization of technologies scarcely conceived of in 1962. A facility created to serve as a technology hub in a technology-driven region, in a technology-driven era, Fisher Plaza sets an international standard for communications infrastructure and services.

Fisher Plaza also represents an amazing Northwest business success story, known formally as Fisher Communications, Inc. With the opening of the Plaza in 2000, an enterprise that started by milling flour has now taken a bold step into the new millennium as a leader in innovative communications resources and business environments.

After establishing the flour milling business in 1911, O.W. Fisher and his sons looked for ways to reach larger markets for their flour products, and this need led them into the emerging commercial radio business. Eventually, their pioneering experience in broadcasting facilitated the company's utilization of yet another emerging medium: television. In the course of managing these two successful businesses, there arose opportunities for land and building acquisitions, and ultimately a third business element was added in commercial property development and management.

Today, Fisher is much more than a collection of diverse divisions. It is focused on leading the diverse and rapidly changing communications and media industry. In Fisher's media division, Fisher Broadcasting, current holdings include 26 radio stations, with audiences concentrated in the Northwest, and 12 television stations located in the 11 Western states and the Southeast that now reach over 4.2 million viewers. Komo 4 television's new high-tech operations within Fisher Plaza will help the station maintain its leadership position in digital communications.

The people behind both the radio and the television media for Fisher Broadcasting are focused on a single goal: that of connecting communities with the information they want, when they want it, and how they want it, in an increasingly complex world. In short, the goal is to win the hearts and minds of their audiences. The key to Fisher's success in doing so is the company's commitment to be a world-class, high performance communications and media company.

Fisher's broadcasting and properties business units work together in many ways. Fisher Properties, initiated as a property management by-product of the company, has emerged as a leader in the development and delivery of commercial office space that links facility to function and creates an environment

Historical photograph of Fisher Mills Milling and Distribution Center on Harbor Island in Seattle.

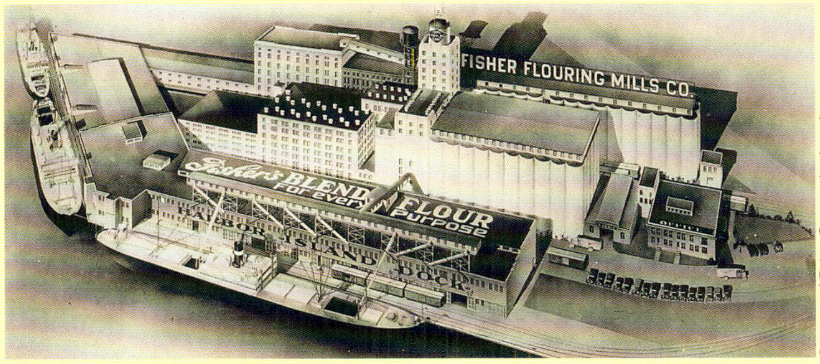

Courtesy of Fisher Communications, Inc.

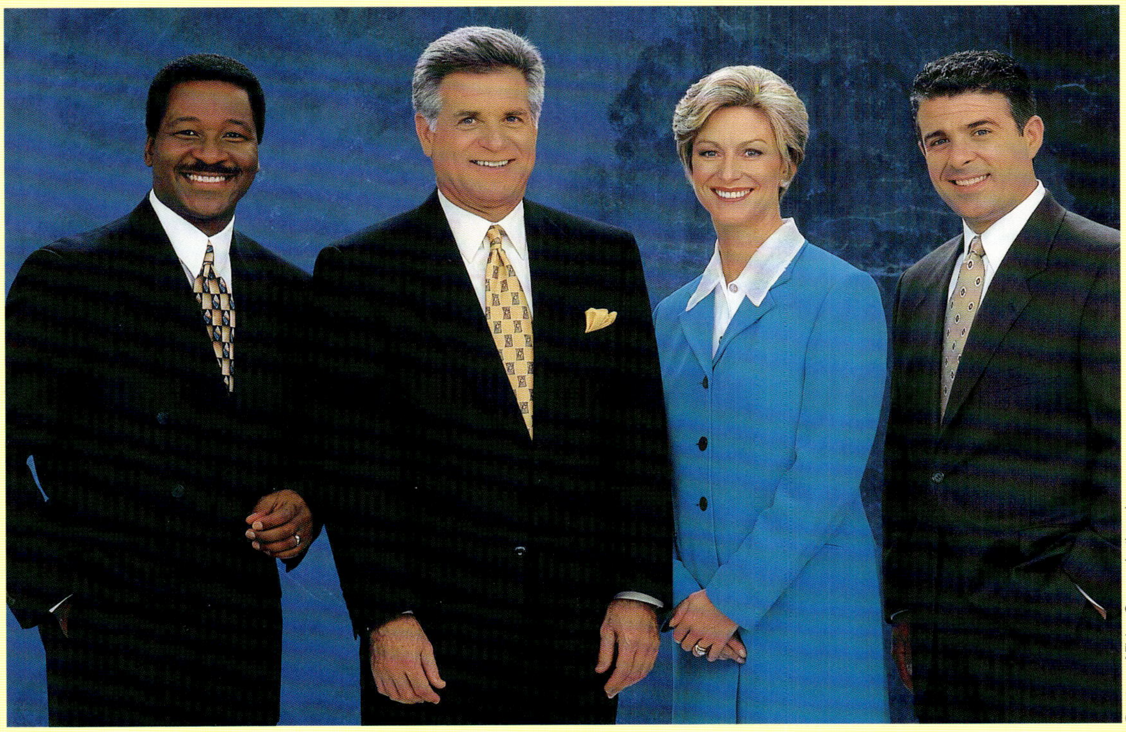

Courtesy of Fisher Communications, Inc.

KOMO 4 News Anchors Dan Lewis and Kathi Goertzen, Weather with Steve Pool, and Sports with Eric Johnson.

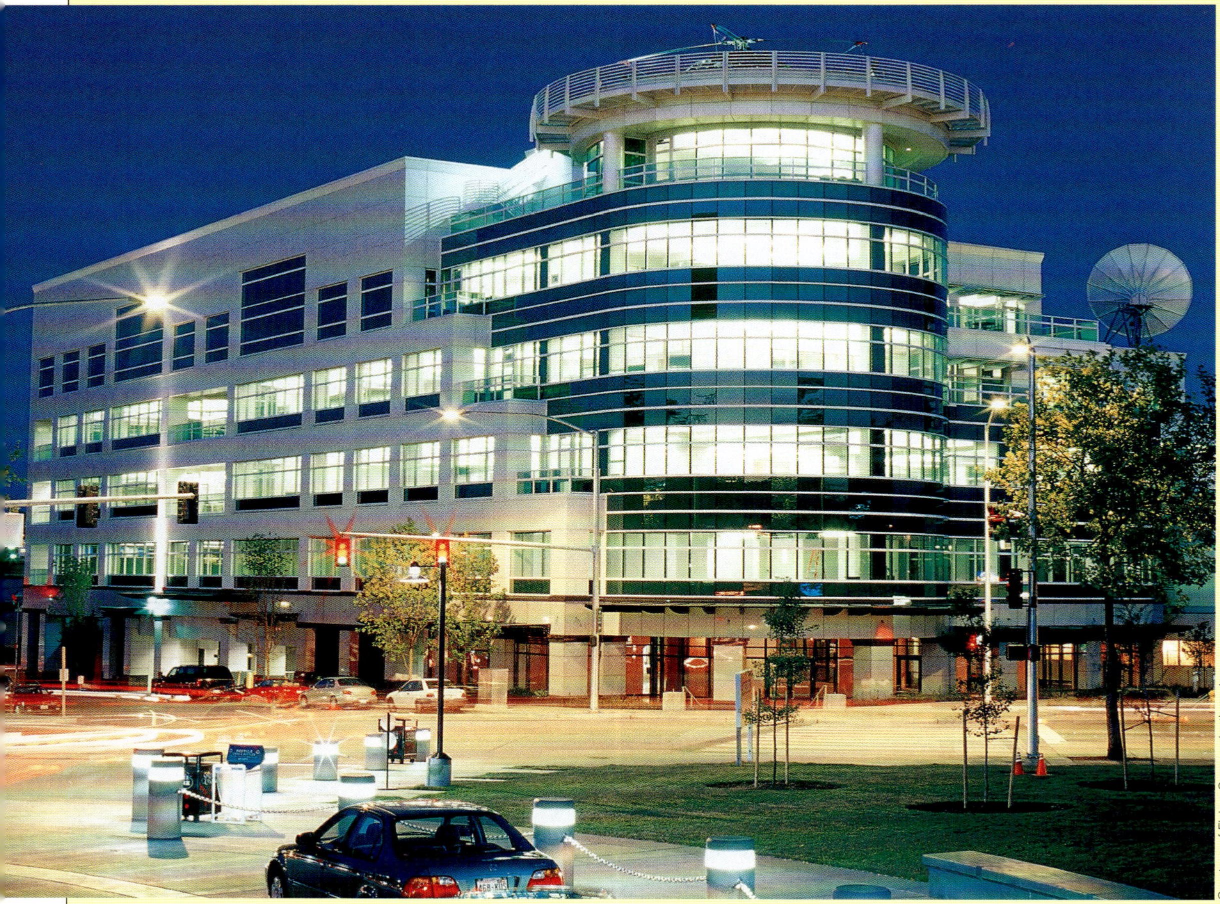

Courtesy of Fisher Communications, Inc.

Fisher Plaza provides state-of-the-art business environments and sets the standard for communications infrastructure and services.

attuned to the requirements of communications and integrated technology.

Fisher Plaza illustrates the future of business environments. Its 200,000 square feet of commercial space houses numerous business entities, each one sharing technological resources with partners, consumers, and the world. The unique building design features raised floors and enables easy access to communications systems and the potential for rapid reconfiguration of space as new demands emerge. Members of this "communications community" will keep ahead of changing technologies, while competitors in older buildings will be faced with the time-consuming and costly challenges of catch-up renovations.

Fisher Plaza is also home to other Fisher enterprises that add value to this unique array of communications and media services. In June 2000, for example, Fisher's satellite and fiber business provided transmission services to national and international press covering the Experience Music Project's grand opening at the Seattle Center. This monumental music event was covered from Fisher Plaza by VH1 and MTV, inviting the world to experience architect Frank Gehry's whimsical and exciting building in real time.

Fisher Entertainment, the Los Angeles- and Seattle-based development, production and program sales division of Fisher, produces content for major cable networks including Discovery Communications, Buena Vista Television, and specials distributed by Hearst-Argyle Television Productions and Eclipse TV. Fisher Entertainment's current development line-up features a variety of content, from reality-based programming such as game shows and talk shows to scripted animated comedy.

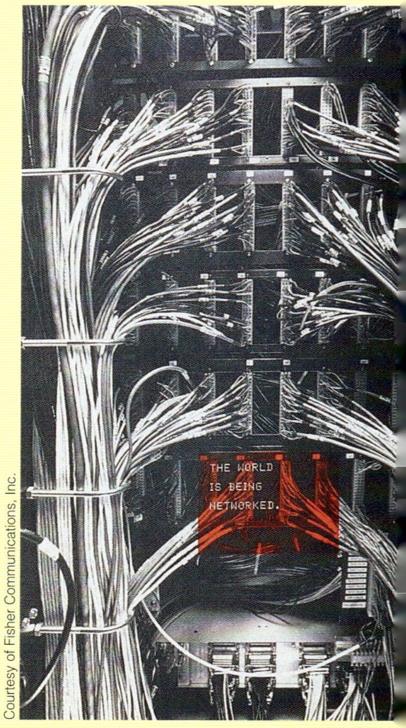

Courtesy of Fisher Communications, Inc.

"The world is being networked"— A page taken from Fisher's 1999 Annual Report.

The Space Needle was the central symbol of the future for the 1962 Century 21 World's Fair; and today, as the twenty-first century unfolds, Fisher Plaza is the realization of technologies scarcely conceived of in 1962. Fisher Plaza offers cutting-edge, technology-friendly environments for businesses at the forefront of this technology-driven era.

President and CEO William W. Krippaehne Jr. offered this perspective on the company's future in Fisher's Annual Report:

"By combining these skill sets and tools to create highly differentiated products and services, we occupy areas of competency that are difficult for competitors to enter, much less emulate. Moreover, development of these areas is helping us attract highly capable associates and leading-edge customers to leverage unique market positions."

As Fisher moves forward into the twenty-first century, the company will continue its focus on the area of communications and media, which it considers vital to its future success. And as it reaches across the country and around the world through its broadcast facilities and its Internet connections, Fisher will continue as a tribute to business innovation in the Pacific Northwest. Few companies share Fisher's history of developing local enterprises and its recognition as a global leader in the complex industry of communications.

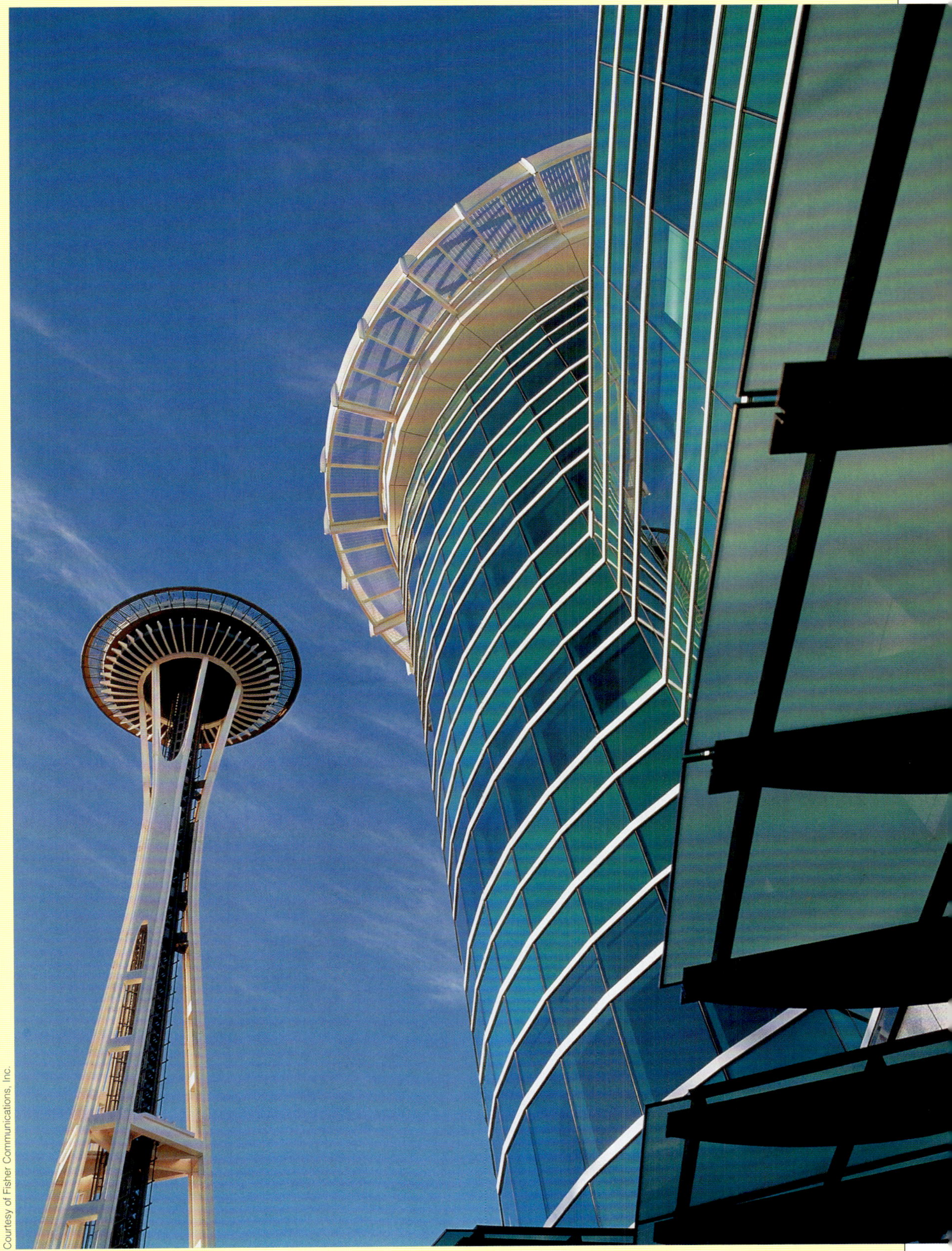
Courtesy of Fisher Communications, Inc.

King County International Airport/ Boeing Field

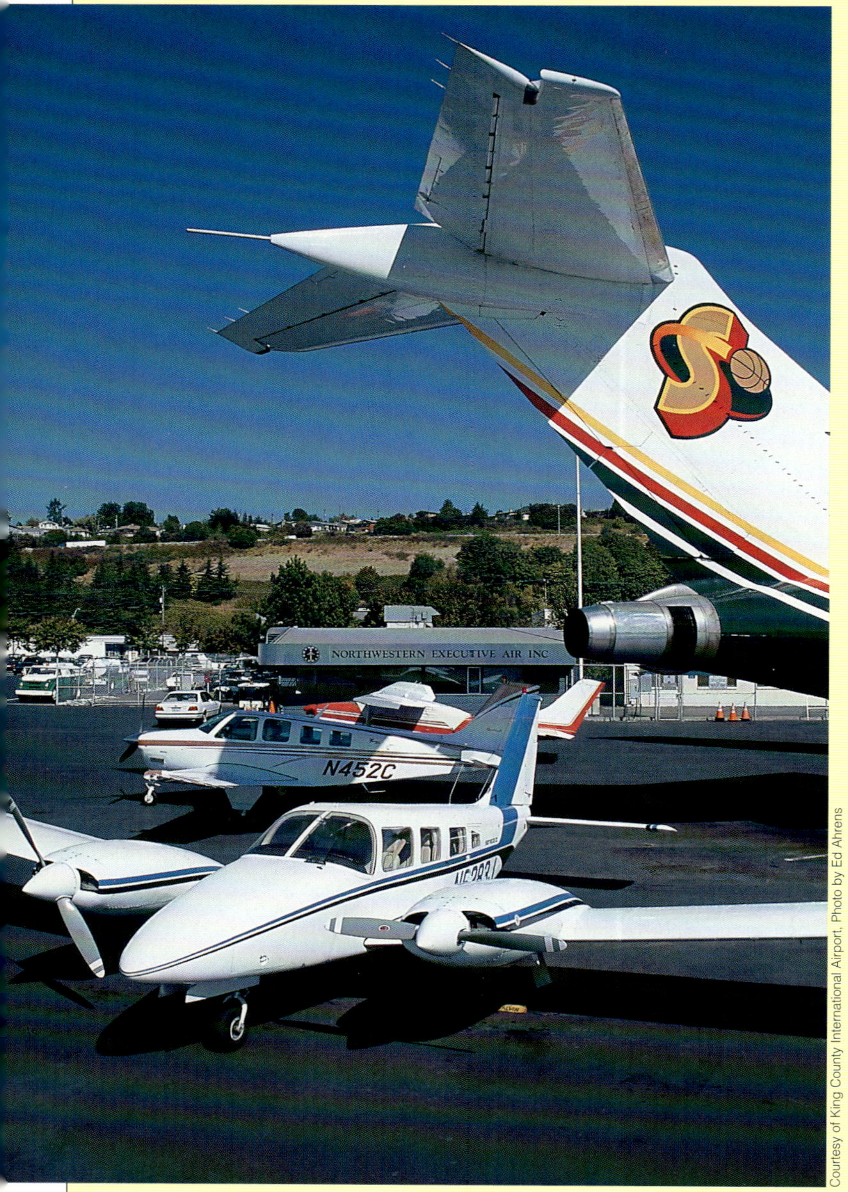

Courtesy of King County International Airport, Photo by Ed Ahrens

Unique in its class, KCIA handles a wide variety of aircraft operations, from the business jets of local high-tech companies, cargo, and professional sports teams to local flight school and emergency medical services.

In the reception area of the Administrative Offices at the King County International Airport there is a picture of Air Force One in flight. The picture has an inscription on it from the crew of Air Force One, expressing thanks to the staff of the airport for their courtesy and efficiency in hosting a recent visit by the President's plane. It is true that one of the most famous airplanes in the world is a periodic visitor to the King County International Airport (also known as Boeing Field); but this picture tells only one of the hundreds of stories that could be told by the staff about this busy facility.

The airport has evolved over the years and is today a bustling place that serves many specialized needs. On a daily basis, the latest models of private jet aircraft land and take off from the airport, carrying top corporate executives, entertainment and sports celebrities, and domestic or foreign government dignitaries. Each year, the tarmac is crowded with the jets of the world's top corporate CEOs when Microsoft's Bill Gates hosts his annual CEO Summit.

The airport has the honor of serving the first production aircraft of most new Boeing models. Also, with significant ceremony, new planes take off from the field for delivery to purchasing airlines.

Created in 1928 by the citizens of King County, the airport was originally built as a means of encouraging and assuring the continued location of The Boeing Company in the area. With this act, King County residents established what has since become "the birthplace of modern aviation." It is that reputation that manifests much of the pride in the minds of airport management and staff. Though operated by King County, the airport remains "Boeing Field" in the minds of

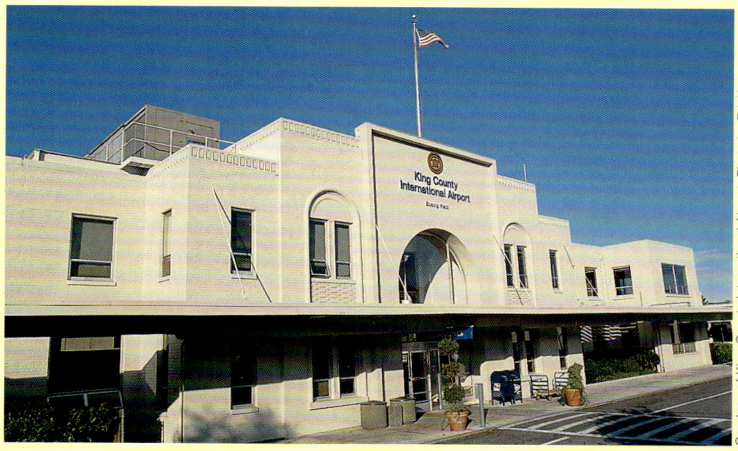

Courtesy of King County International Airport, Photo by Ed Ahrens

In 1928, residents of King County voted by an overwhelming 86 percent to develop an airport on what had originally been low-lying farmland with the Duwamish River meandering through it. A landmark since its dedication in April 1930, KCIA's Terminal building has stood proudly since the early days of aviation.

many county residents. As the first, and remaining, home of The Boeing Company, the King County International Airport boasts a history unparalleled in all of aviation.

In the early years, the airport was not only the birthplace of Boeing airplanes, but was also the primary passenger terminal for the Puget Sound region. In 1947, when the new Seattle-Tacoma (Sea-Tac) Airport took over the passenger business, the King County International Airport was left to develop new ways of contributing to the local economy. In subsequent years, the success of the airport has confirmed its place as a vital and growing part of Pacific Northwest, and indeed international, aviation.

Over the years, as airplanes have increased in size and number, runways have been extended and others added. As the airport entered the new millennium, county officials and airport management were in the midst of creating a major Master Plan that projected the airport's future over the next 15 years. The consistent conclusion in the development of this plan was that the airport's business will continue to grow and, although its location will not allow for significant physical expansion, its efficiency and technological capabilities will be dramatically enhanced and its economic contribution to the region will expand as well.

The airport currently records over 375,000 operations (take-offs and landings) annually, with projections from the Master Plan placing this number well above 500,000 by 2020. Of the current operations, approximately 80 percent are in the category of General Aviation (private or corporate planes or helicopters). The remaining operations are divided between Boeing Company business and the myriad of commercial aviation entities that call the King County Airport their home. The airport incorporates full international operations, including U.S. Customs Service functions, Immigration Services, Department of Agriculture and Federal Aviation Administration inspections.

While The Boeing Company has manufacturing operations in many other locations, Boeing Field remains the airport for final testing and delivery of most models of new jetliners, both commercial and military. The field is also the site of many of the test flights of new models as they are introduced and seek the certification of the Federal Aviation Administration. Boeing planes account for approximately 3,000 of the airport's annual flight operations. The United States Military also has a significant presence at the airport in its development and

Courtesy of King County International Airport

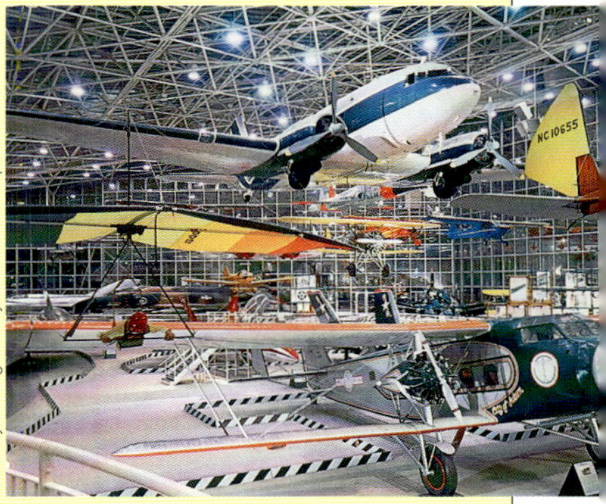

KCIA straddles both the past and future of aviation with the on-site Museum of Flight. The museum features 54 awe-inspiring, authentic, mint-condition airplanes. More than half a million visitors per year take advantage of the museum's tours and educational programs.

Courtesy of King County International Airport, Photo by Ed Ahrens

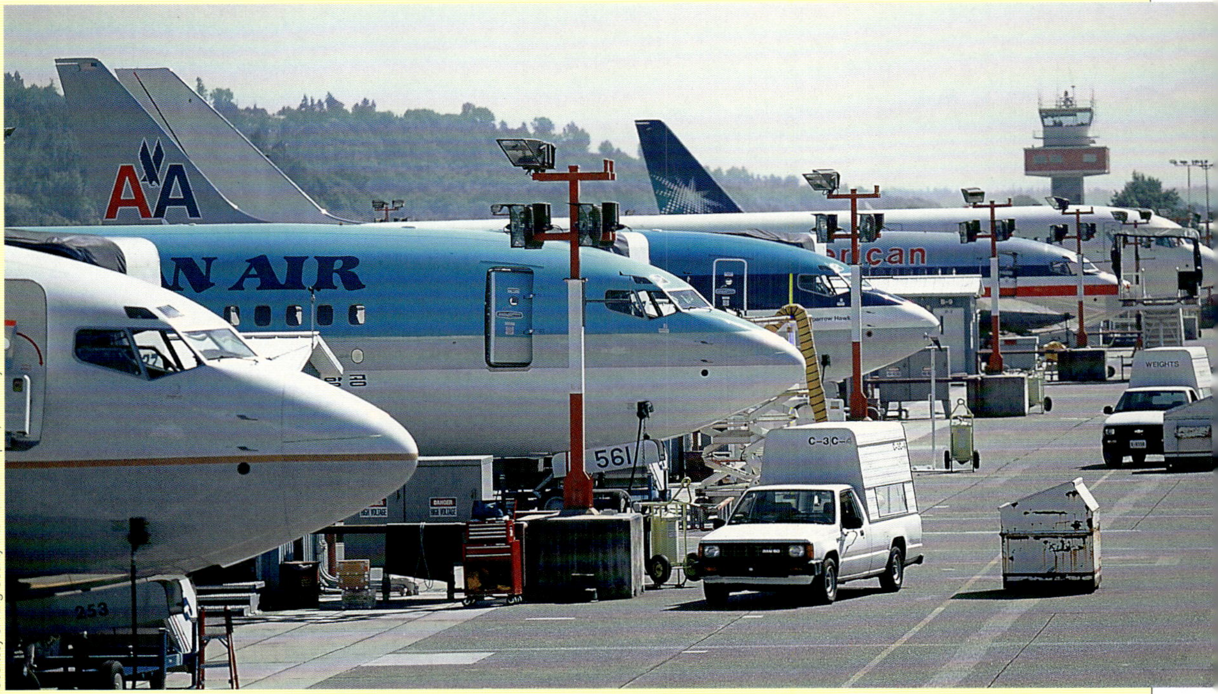

Home to the Boeing Company and "the birthplace of modern aviation," KCIA's facilities support the aviation industry worldwide and make air travel safe for the public. Boeing's Flight Test Center conducts flight and ground test flights of today's modern aircraft before shipping them to airlines in countries around the globe, from the United States to Azerbaijan.

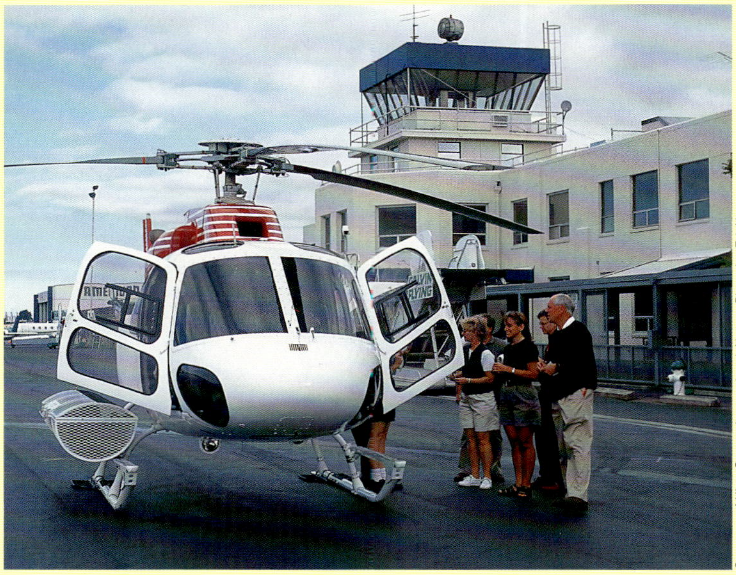

Courtesy of King County International Airport, Photo by Ed Ahrens

U.S. Customs, Immigration, Department of Agriculture, and the FAA provide the services necessary to support regularly scheduled and charter international flights from around the world.

testing of the Advanced Warning Airborne Command System (AWACS) planes being built and equipped by Boeing.

Located adjacent to the King County Airport on its western perimeter is the Museum of Flight. This world-renowned museum incorporates the Red Barn, which was the birthplace of the Boeing Company. The museum features amazing history, from the first Boeing plane to some of the current vehicles designed, in part by Boeing, for travel into outer space.

The other critical component of the recent Master Plan is the focus on the economic contribution of the King County International Airport to the local area. The economic impact of the airport is a source of pride for King County and airport officials. Although the airport itself employs only about 60 employees, the numerous businesses and services provided at the airport support over 4,000 jobs. An Economic Impact Study, conducted as a part of the Master Plan, suggests that the total economic impact of the airport on the local economy includes 4,078 direct jobs and over 6,500 indirect or induced jobs. These jobs produce a direct labor income of $187 million and an indirect labor income of another $175 million. The study includes a figure labeled "final demand," which reflects the total impact of input and output from the airport in 28 categories of business. In its conclusion, the study indicates that, coupling this figure with the labor income and the direct purchase of local goods and services, the total economic output of the King County International Airport is over $1.4 billion.

The airport currently is home to six flight schools, two air taxi services, the King County Sheriff's Guardian 1 Helicopter, and seven air cargo operators. The air cargo business makes a significant contribution to the number of operations at the airport with over 26,000 flight operations annually that involve cargo flown into or out of the facility.

In its Master Plan, the airport contemplates some restructuring of the various operations through clustering of like functions and new efficiencies in such operations as fueling and maintenance. Throughout all of

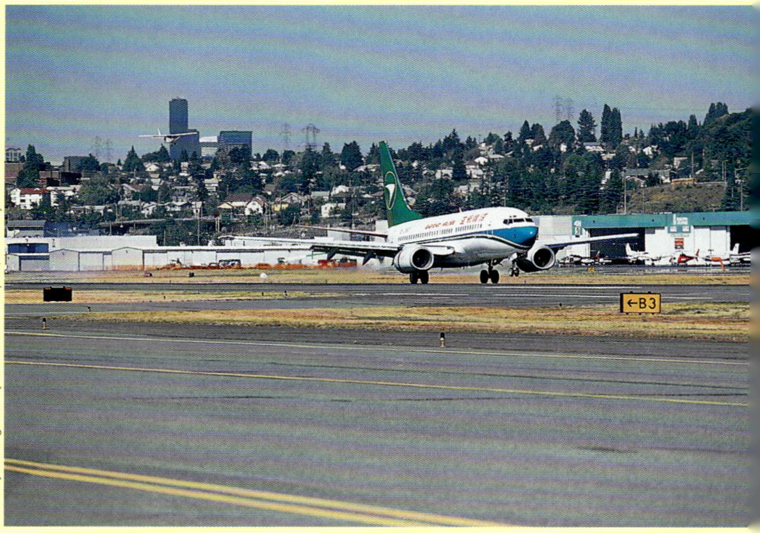

Courtesy of King County International Airport, Photo by Ed Ahrens

Major interstate highway and railway systems run parallel to King County International Airport, making it ideally located for cargo operations. A transportation backbone of the regional economy, KCIA generates $1.4 billion annually in economic output including labor income, direct purchase of local goods and services, and input and output in 28 business categories

Emergency medical flights transport thousands of patients each year to the world-famous medical facilities located in King County.

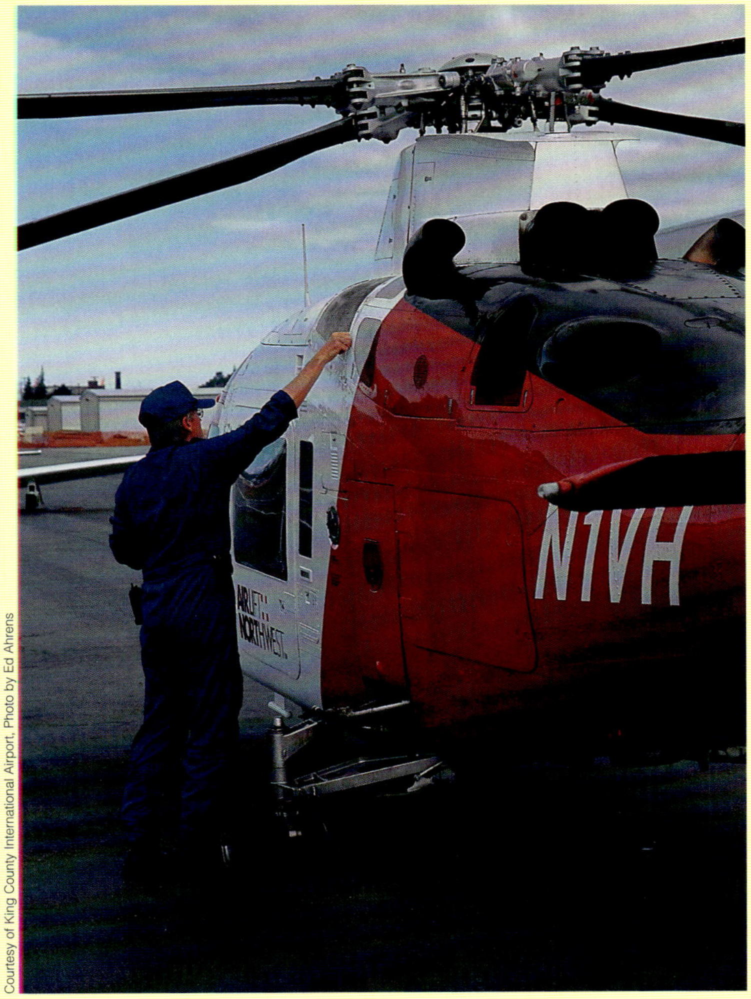

Courtesy of King County International Airport, Photo by Ed Ahrens

The amazing history of the King County Airport includes many fascinating time periods and events. One historic event took place on December 6, 1941, just one day before the attack on Pearl Harbor. On that day, the federal government took over the airport and closed it to the public because of its strategic location and the importance of Boeing in the production of warplanes. Throughout World War II, Boeing Field was devoted to the production of B-17 and B-29 bombers, both of which played key roles in the Allied war effort.

Following the war, the airport gave up its position as a passenger terminal and expanded into other operations. A key historical landmark was achieved in 1951 when the main runway was extended to 10,000 feet, with approximately 62,000 square yards of nine-inch paving added. In 1969, the small-plane runway was expanded to its current length of 3,710 feet.

Throughout its storied past, King County International Airport has maintained its proud position as "the birthplace of modern aviation" while continuing to build an even more impressive reputation as "a hallmark of aviation enterprise". But, with all the excitement, the management and staff of the King County International Airport just continue to do what they have done for nearly 80 years, serve the community well.

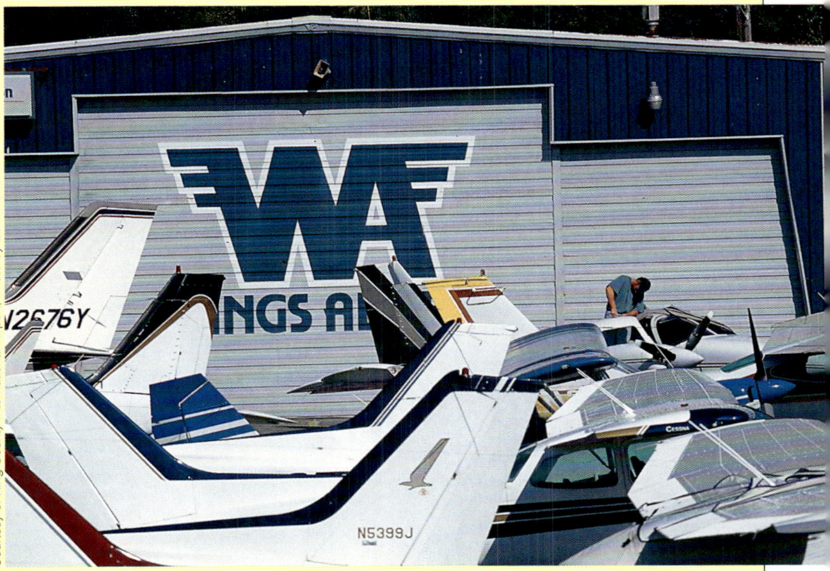

Courtesy of King County International Airport, Photo by Ed Ahrens

Eighty percent of the airport's operations are in the category of general aviation (private corporate planes and helicopters), making King County International Airport one of the busiest general aviation airports in the United States. Future planning is committed to maintaining that status with a wide variety of services for the recreational and private pilot.

its future planning, a clear focus continues to be the predominance of general aviation at the airport. The airport is currently one of the busiest general aviation sites in the United States. The proximity to downtown Seattle makes it an attractive arrival and departure site for local businesses with visiting partners and customers. The growing economy of the Puget Sound region and its draw for rapidly expanding e-commerce businesses suggests increased use of the King County Airport as the hub of business travel for private jets.

Sound Transit

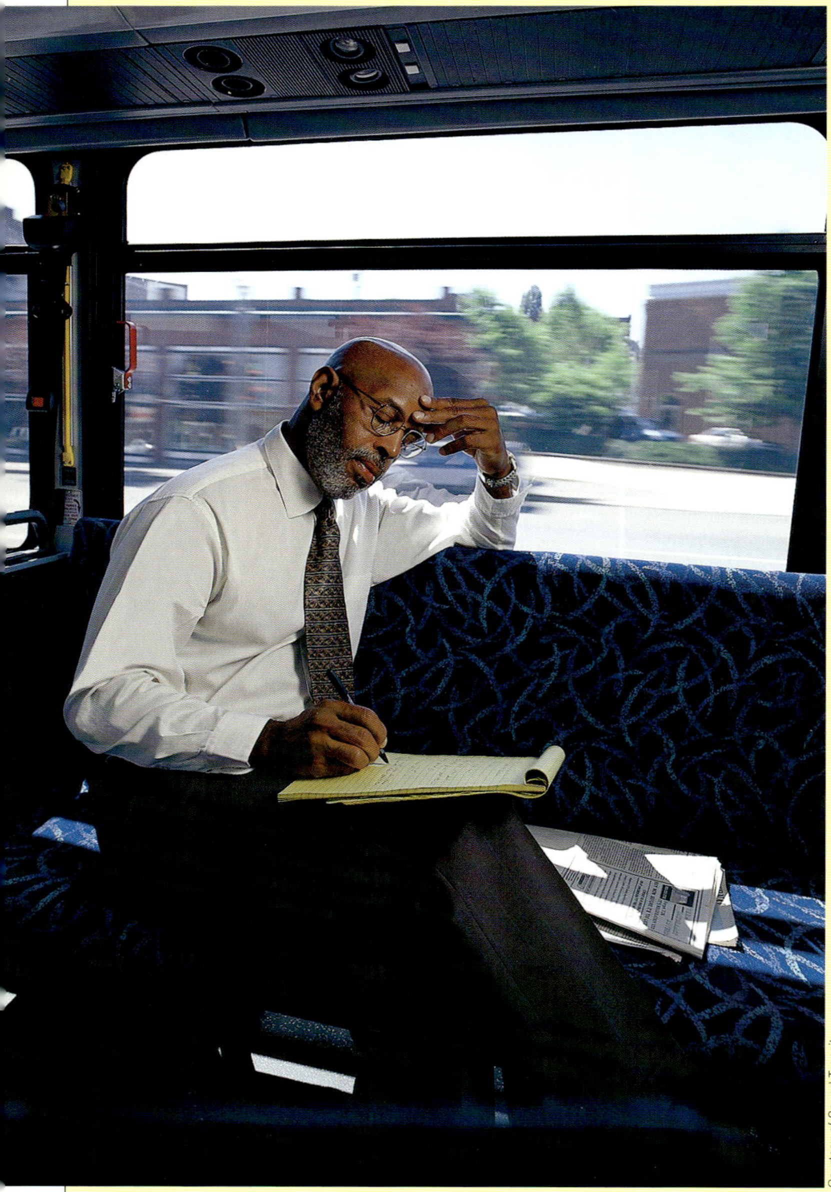

Courtesy of Sound Transit

Many of the ST Express buses have bike racks, high-back seats, reading lamps, and adjustable air vents.

If traffic in the Seattle area hummed along smoothly and everyone worked, shopped, and played near their homes, there would be little need for a regional mass transit system. But in the real world of Central Puget Sound, many people work or attend classes miles from where they live. People are simply traveling more miles to get to more places, and the area's traffic congestion is worse than just about anywhere else in the nation.

In the fall of 1996, voters in Central Puget Sound, increasingly weary of that congestion, approved a mass transit system stretching from Tacoma to Everett. Those voters agreed to raise their taxes to pay for express buses, commuter trains, light rail, and other improvements that would give them new options for getting around. Sound Transit is the agency responsible for that new system of buses and trains.

Now, a few years after the vote, Sound Transit's network of express buses and commuter trains is carrying thousands of riders every day. Work also continues on a light rail system in Tacoma and between Seattle and Seattle-Tacoma International Airport.

While other transit agencies focus on local service, Sound Transit's ST Express buses, Sounder commuter rail, and eventually, Link light rail connect major regional centers.

ST Express

In September of 1999, the first 40-foot low-floor and 60-foot articulated ST Express buses began service on 9 of the planned 18 new express routes in King, Snohomish, and Pierce counties. In that first year alone, the routes had more than four million passenger boardings. By the fall of 2000, ST Express was running 13 long-haul limited-

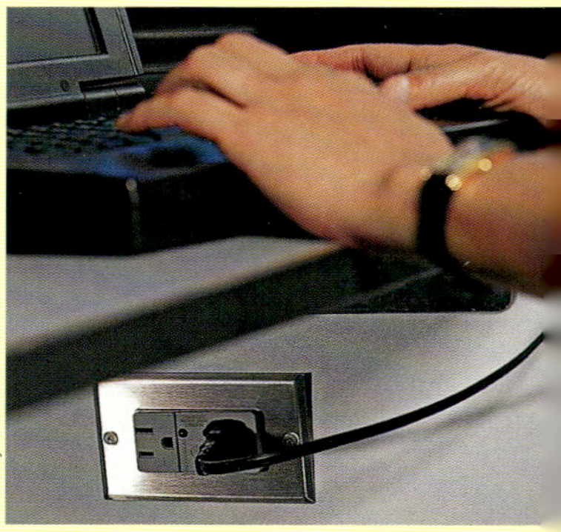

Courtesy of Sound Transit

All Sounder coaches include worktables and surge-protected outlets for laptop computers.

stop bus routes, including popular runs to Sea-Tac Airport and King County cities and job centers. Ridership continues to increase. All 18 ST Express routes will be operating by 2002.

The distinctive blue and white buses were built for passenger comfort. They are roomy, air-conditioned, and the newest coaches have custom-designed upholstery, reclining seats, extra-large overhead luggage racks, and reading lamps.

The ST Express bus fleet ranges from standard-length coaches to articulated diesel coaches and even compressed natural gas. By 2006, Sound Transit expects to run a fleet of about 203 buses.

The ST Express program is more than just buses, however. It includes High Occupancy Vehicle (HOV) ramps at certain freeway locations to improve transit speed and reliability. The projects also include an expanded and improved downtown Bellevue Transit Center, a new park-and-ride and transit center at the Northeast 40th Street Overlake Transit Center, a new Mercer Island transit station, and HOV improvements throughout King County.

Sounder

In the fall of 2000, the first commuter trains in more than 60 years began whisking passengers from Tacoma to Seattle with stops in Sumner and Auburn. From the start, ridership on the new weekday service grew steadily as commuters discovered a new, reliable rush-hour ride to work and back. The climate-controlled, two-level train cars have worktables, surge-protected outlets for laptop computers, and cupholders. The trains can reach speeds of up to 79 mph, making the trip from Tacoma to Seattle in about 54 minutes. The ride to Seattle takes about 37 minutes from Sumner, 28 minutes from Auburn, and 22 minutes from Kent. New stations in Puyallup, Kent, and Tukwila will be in service in early 2001. Sounder trains will eventually link Everett in the north with Seattle

Sounder trains provide plenty of room for everyone.

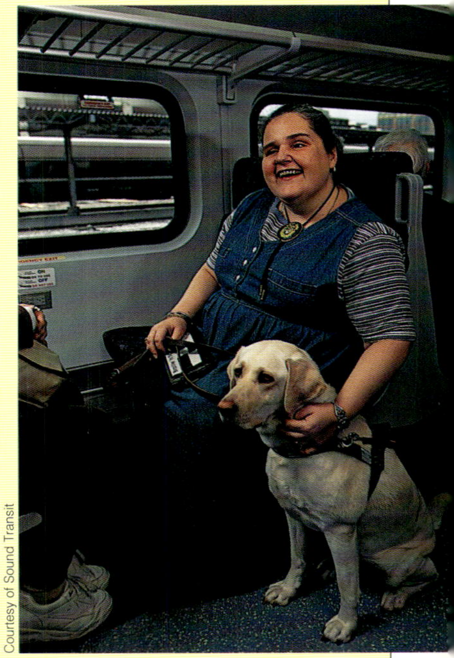

Courtesy of Sound Transit

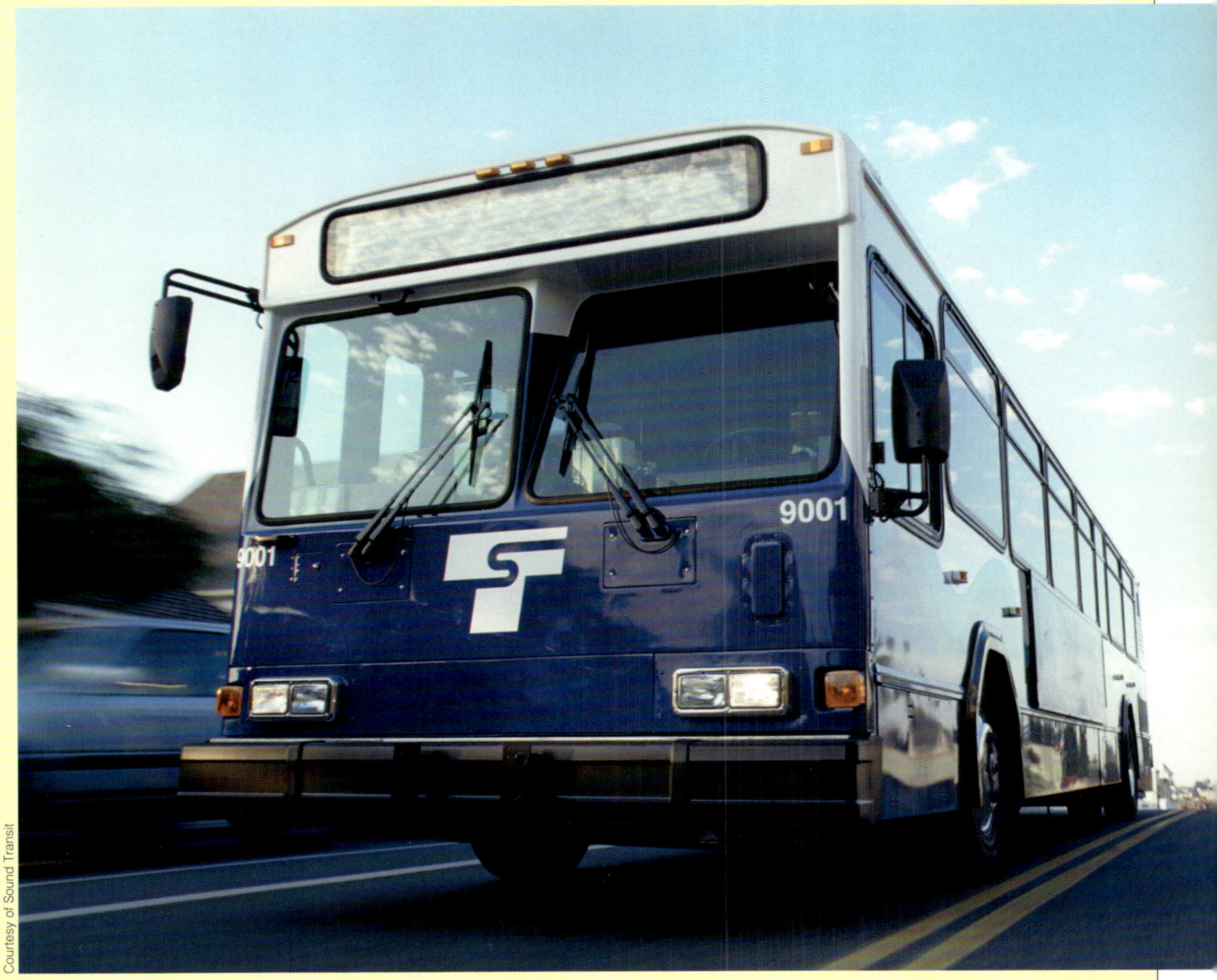

Courtesy of Sound Transit

ST Express buses, which began service in the fall of 1999, connect major destinations throughout Central Puget Sound.

to Tacoma and Lakewood in the south, a total of 82 miles through three counties. When the system is operating fully, 30 trains will run every half hour during peak commuting hours.

The Sounder program includes improving tracks and signals to ensure safe train operations and crossings. Sound Transit is working with community residents, businesses, school districts, the railroads, local police, and Operation Lifesaver to increase public awareness of safety rules around trains. The trains, operated by Burlington Northern Santa Fe and maintained by Amtrak, run on freight tracks owned by BNSF. Sound Transit owns the stations and provides security.

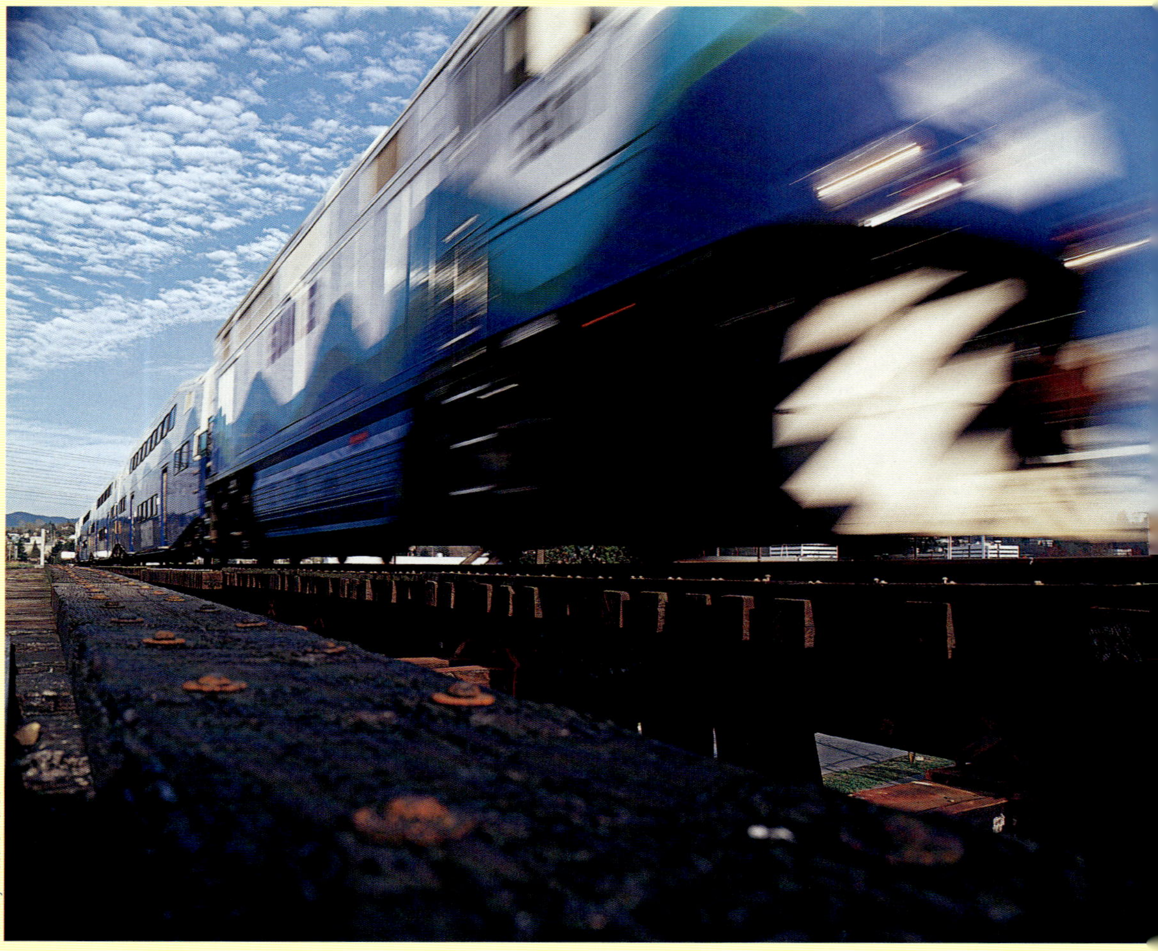

Courtesy of Sound Transit

New Sound Transit Sounder commuter trains began rush-hour service between Tacoma and Seattle in the fall of 2000.

Central Link

Seattle is the last major metropolitan region on the West Coast, and one of the last in the nation, to start building a light rail transit system. When they are up and operating, the trains will run on their own tracks, free from fender benders, rainy-day slowdowns, and other traffic tie-ups that currently slow commuters. Trains will come by every few minutes, giving

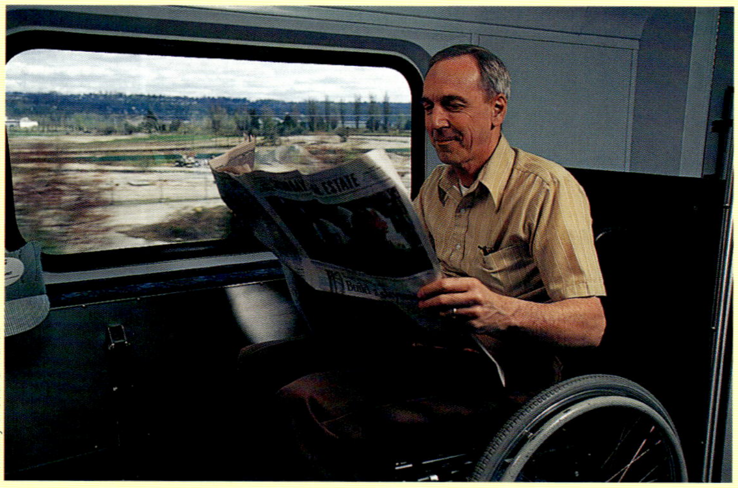

Courtesy of Sound Transit

Sounder trains run on existing freight tracks. The trip from Tacoma to Seattle takes about 54 minutes with stops in Sumner and Auburn. The trains will also stop in Puyallup, Kent, and Tukwila.

Puget Sound residents a dependable option for getting to work, school, shopping, or medical appointments. Because of Central Puget Sound's unique topography of hills and water, Link trains will run roughly a third in tunnels, a third on surface streets, and a third on elevated tracks.

Throughout the overall Sound Transit system, local taxes generated in different areas of the district are used for projects tailored to those areas. And the new park-and-ride stations, train stations, and transit centers are designed with public art that reflects the character of the communities and neighborhoods.

Sound Transit is governed by an 18-member board that sets policy and direction for the agency. The board is made up of local elected officials from within the Sound Transit District, which generally includes the urban areas of King, Pierce, and Snohomish counties. The board meets twice a month in open, public sessions. Committees comprised of board members meet regularly as well. The headquarters for Sound Transit are located in the beautifully renovated Union Station just across Fourth Avenue from where the Sounder trains stop at the King Street Station.

All Sounder train coaches are climate controlled and have worktables, upholstered seats, and overhead storage.

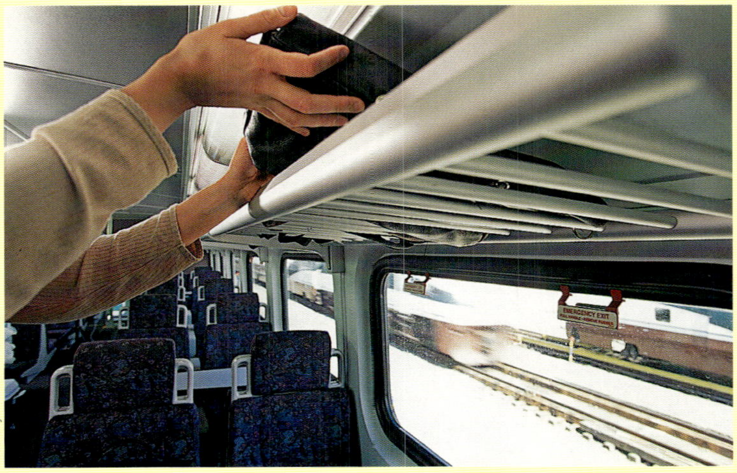

Courtesy of Sound Transit

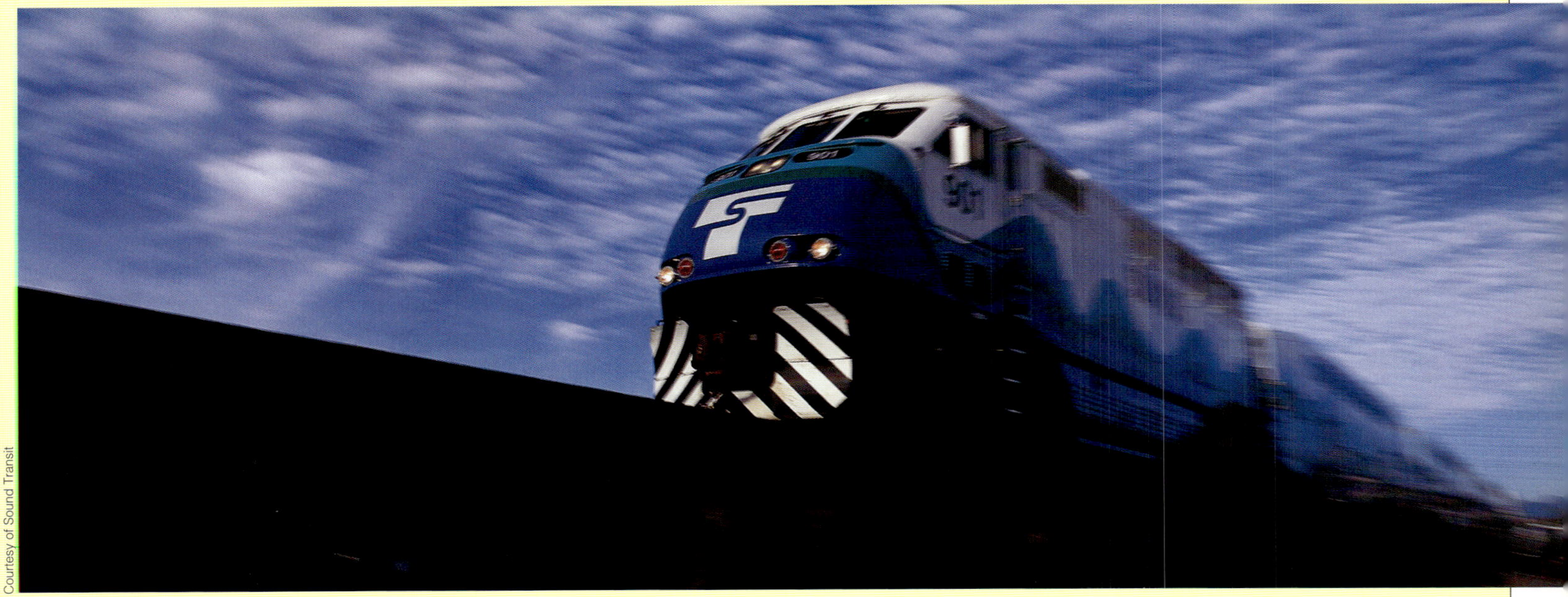

Courtesy of Sound Transit

The two-level Sounder trains can reach speeds of up to 79 miles per hour between Tacoma and Seattle.

Northwest Airlines

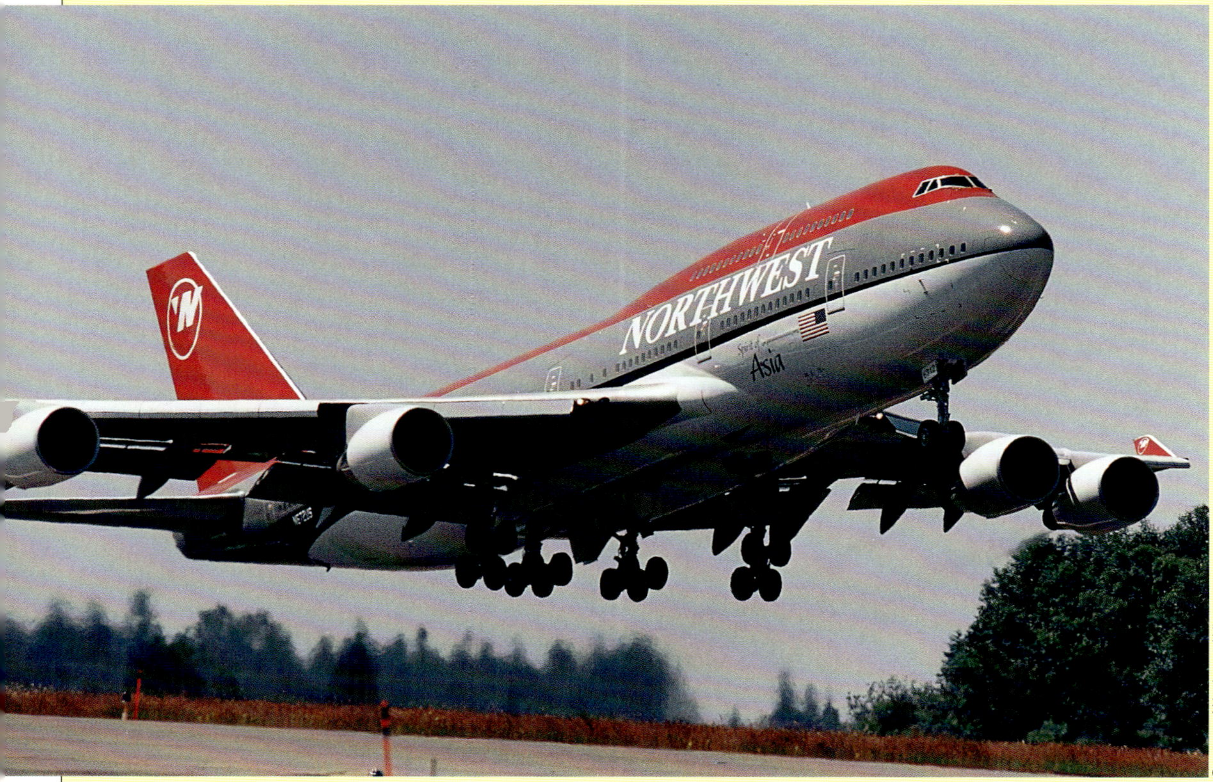

Courtesy of Northwest Airlines

Northwest was the original launch customer of the Boeing 747-400. The "Spirit of Asia" was one of four new 747-400s delivered by Boeing to Northwest in 1999. Seattle is a primary international gateway for Northwest, where it operates up to 14 weekly nonstop flights to Japan with connecting service throughout Asia.

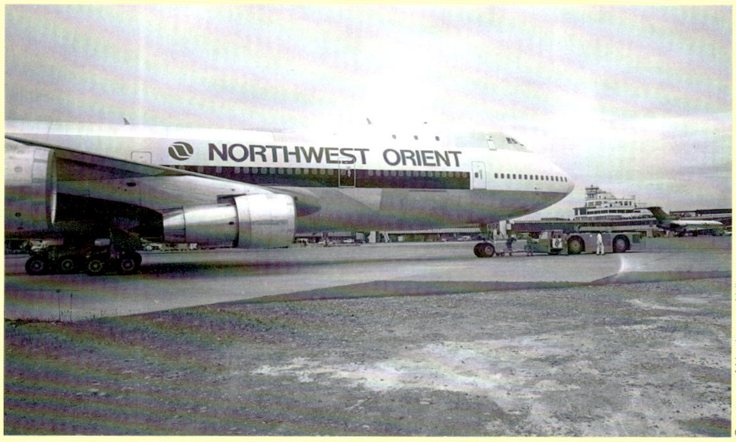

Courtesy of Northwest Airlines

One of the original Boeing 747s, painted in Northwest Orient livery, is shown pushing back from the gate at Sea-Tac Airport in this photograph from the mid-1970s. Northwest Orient became Northwest Airlines.

Northwest Airlines has played a vital role in providing Seattle and King County's transportation links to the world for more than five decades.

In 1947, Northwest began operating passenger service from Sea-Tac Airport to cities throughout the United States as well as Asia. Today, the King County region continues to be a primary gateway for Northwest Airlines, which is the largest international airline operating at Sea-Tac Airport. Each week, as many as 21 Northwest flights operate nonstop service from Seattle to key international markets such as Tokyo, Osaka, and Amsterdam.

Because of Northwest Airlines' extensive international route network and its alliances with global partners such as KLM Royal Dutch Airlines, Alitalia, and Continental Airlines, the King County region is one stop away from hundreds of destinations throughout Asia, Europe, the Middle East, Africa, and India.

In addition to its international network, Northwest operates as many as 20 daily flights to its U.S. hubs in Minneapolis-St. Paul, Detroit, and Memphis—carrying more than 2,500 passengers in a single day.

Northwest's presence in Seattle and King County goes far beyond simply operating flights at Sea-Tac. Due to the region's strategic importance as an international gateway, a number of important jobs must be based in the area to support Northwest's daily operations. To that end, more than 2,500 Northwest Airlines professionals live in the Puget Sound region. The area is home to both a pilot and flight attendant base, as well as a key international reservations center, which alone employs more than 500 customer reservation agents.

No list of highlights of the Northwest Airlines-King County relationship would be complete without mentioning The Boeing Company. Today, Northwest's fleet of 415 planes includes more than 350 Boeing aircraft—33 of which are the all-important Boeing 747s. Northwest is proud to have been the launch customer of both the original 747-100 and the state-of-the-art 747-400. The Boeing 747 serves as the backbone of Northwest's extensive Asia-Pacific operations.

Air freight is a growing business both worldwide and in the Pacific Northwest. Because Washington is the most trade-dependent state in the nation, the Seattle-King County region plays a vital role as an air freight gateway. Northwest Airlines is the second-largest cargo carrier at Sea-Tac Airport, handling as much as 700 tons of cargo each week on all-cargo Boeing 747 aircraft. From transporting fresh cherries and asparagus to high-tech components and seafood, Northwest Airlines Cargo provides a critical link between regional shippers and producers with their markets around the world.

Northwest is committed to remaining Seattle-King County's transportation leader in the twenty-first century.

Northwest Airlines and KLM Royal Dutch Airlines are recognized as leaders in developing the first and most successful global alliance among major air carriers. This Boeing DC-10 aircraft's special livery was commissioned in 1998 to celebrate the Northwest-KLM alliance. Northwest operates daily nonstop service between Seattle and Amsterdam.

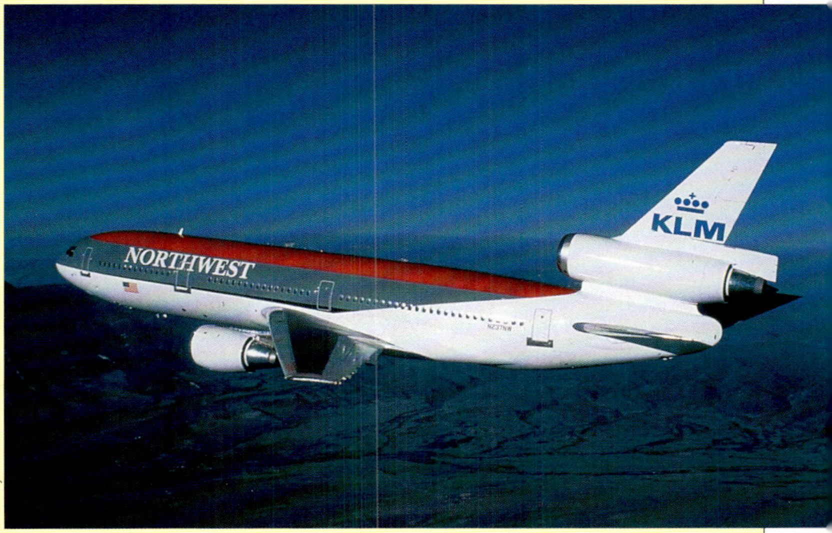

Courtesy of Northwest Airlines

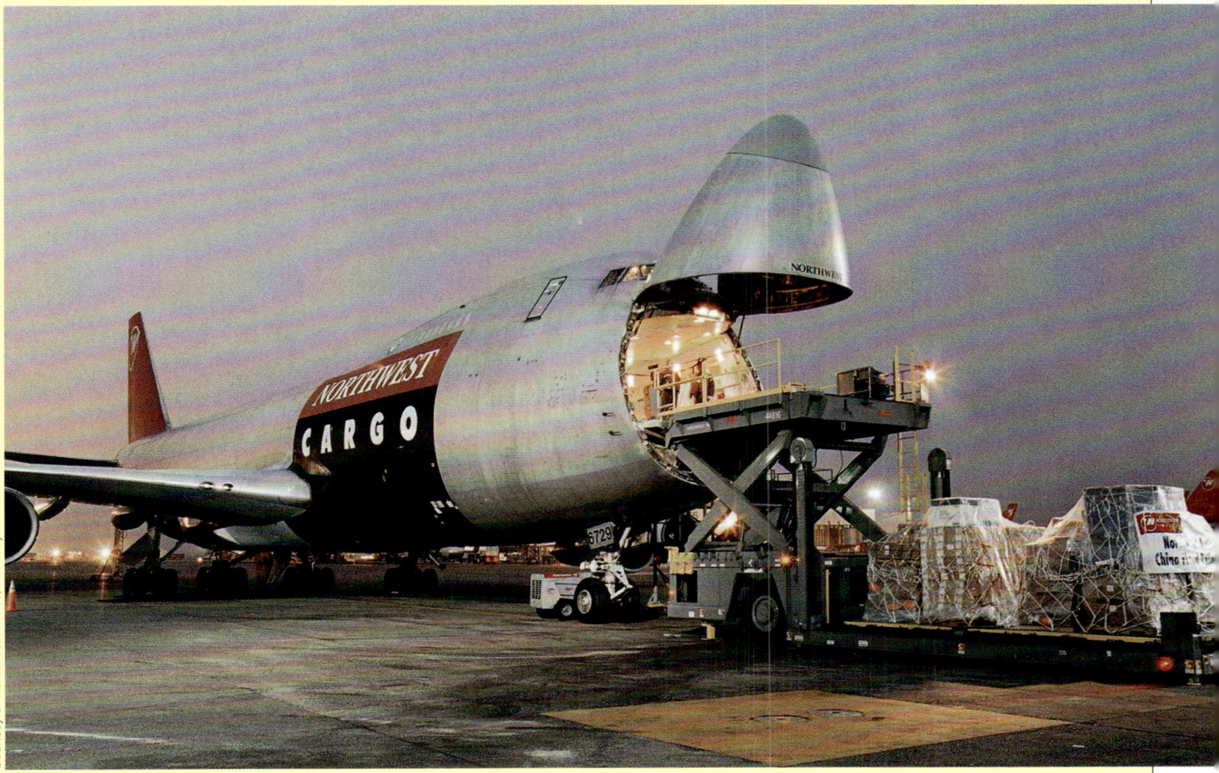

Courtesy of Northwest Airlines. Photo by Richard Brown

Northwest Airlines Cargo operates up to four flights each week from Seattle to Tokyo, Japan, utilizing a fleet of ten Boeing 747 freighters. Northwest is the second largest cargo carrier operating at Seattle-Tacoma International Airport.

Lynden Air Freight

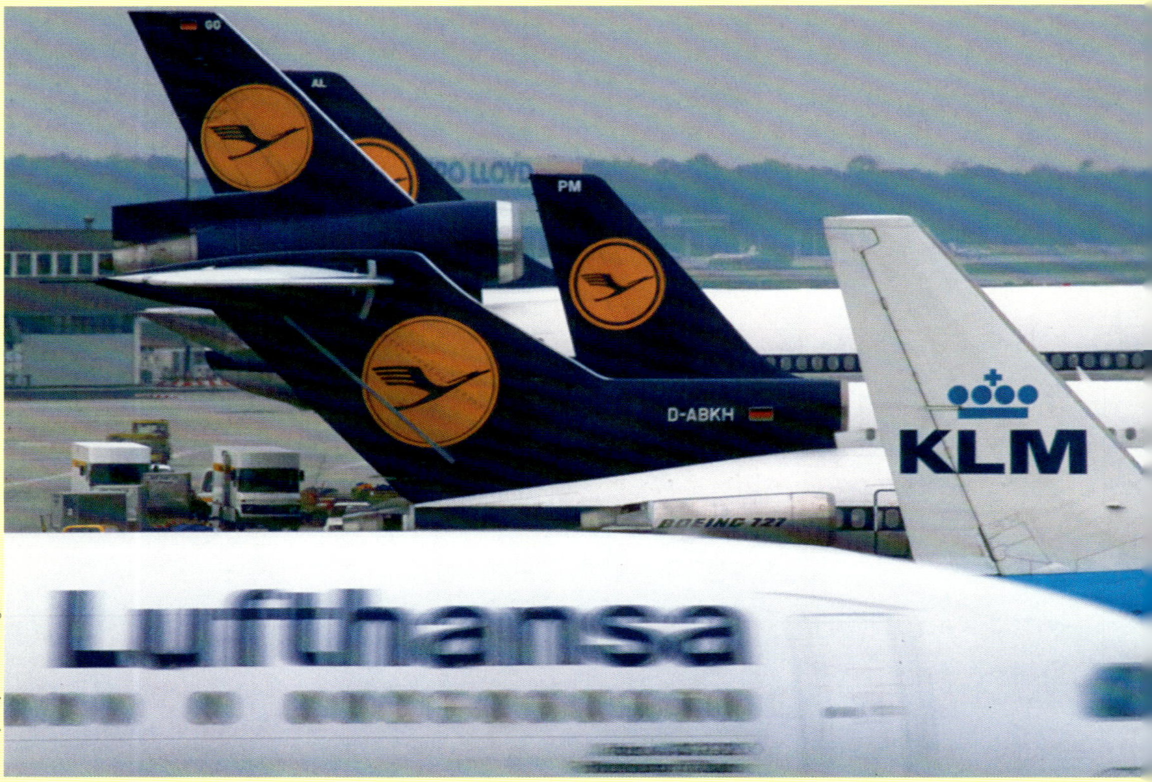

Courtesy of Lynden Air Freight

Lynden Air Freight is a full-service domestic and international ocean and air freight forwarder.

While the Internet has made the world seem smaller and given rise to a global economy, the reality is that the world is still the same physical size it has always been. Part of making this new economy work is the ability to transport products, and the equipment to manufacture those products, by land, sea, or air from one point on the globe to another. A Pacific Northwest company has made its name and reputation by providing the resources necessary to make global business more than just a digital connection. Lynden Air Freight, and its several partners within the broader Lynden Family of Companies, has provided the link between digital communication and the real movement of product and product-producing equipment.

The parent company in the Lynden family got its start in the early 1900s by transporting milk for the dairy farmers of northwestern Washington State. Later, Lynden Transfer became the first scheduled shipper of goods across the newly opened Alcan Highway. These early beginnings are still evidenced in the larger family of companies of which Lynden Air Freight is an integral part. Lynden Air Freight is a full-service domestic and international ocean and air freight forwarder. Its specialization is in the transportation of heavyweight cargo, and its well-supported boast is *"Our people deliver the world."*

When the oil companies operating on the North Slope of Alaska need a replacement generator in an emergency, there is no question as to who they will call. Lynden Air Freight is not only equipped to deliver the needed equipment, but is skilled at arranging such delivery in the most difficult of circumstances. If normal shipping resources are unavailable because of harsh winter conditions, the company simply collaborates with its sister company, Lynden Air Cargo, which can transport

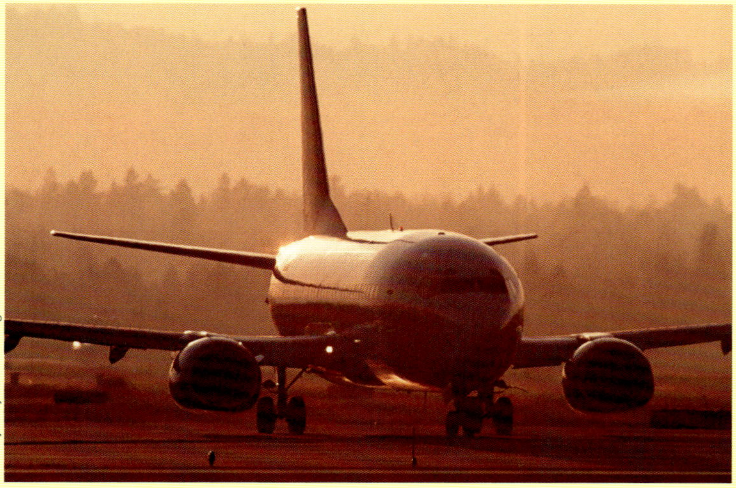

Courtesy of Lynden Air Freight

Lynden Air Freight provides fast, on-time service between any locations with offices throughout North America and around the world.

almost anything on its Hercules aircraft and deliver it to remote sites with nothing but a gravel or ice runway.

At the same time, Lynden Air Freight will provide its customer with total assurance of scheduling through sophisticated communications and tracking software to monitor every step from pickup to delivery. This same high-tech capability is utilized by a division of Lynden Air Freight which specializes in the global forwarding of time-sensitive exhibition materials. Lynden Expo Air provides a vital service to trade-show participants and planners by offering complete show-circuit transportation, assuring exhibitors of timely delivery of their show materials at every stop on the circuit.

Another division of Lynden Air Freight is Lynden International, which specializes in providing customers with everything from logistical support for construction projects in foreign countries to resources for dealing with the import, export, and customs regulations. Companies doing business with several foreign countries face complex and ever-changing regulations related to tariffs and customs. Lynden Air Freight is uniquely prepared to handle these complexities for its customers, assuring timely delivery and cost-saving efficiencies.

Key to Lynden Air Freight's success in the business of freight forwarding is its network of over 50 offices worldwide. Each of these offices provides expertise unique to that region of the globe, both in terms of customs and in terms of the geography and the unique challenges of delivery because of weather or remote-site access. This local expertise is invaluable to the customer a half a world away.

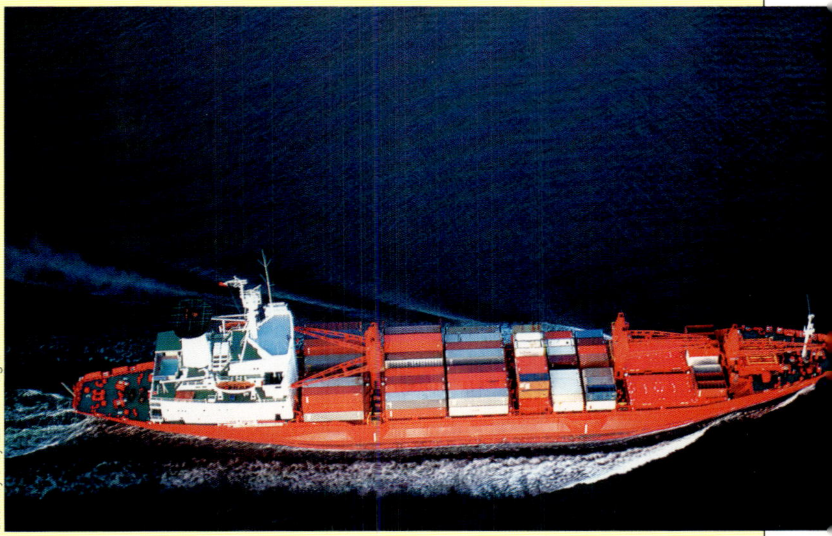

Courtesy of Lynden Air Freight

Lynden utilizes virtually every commercial transportation system, including aircraft, ocean-going vessels, and expedited motor carriers, to meet the needs of customers in the international marketplace.

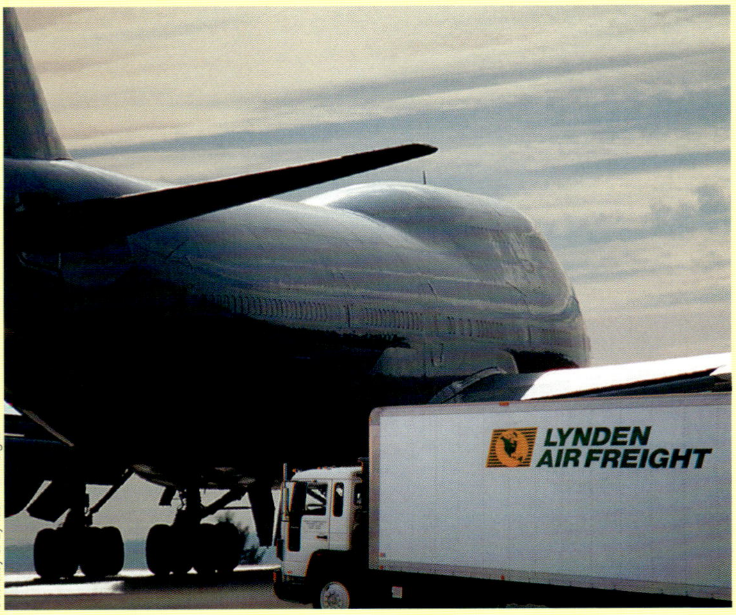

Courtesy of Lynden Air Freight

Lynden matches the service level of larger multinational companies, while preserving the personal attention and care that only a smaller company can offer.

In addition to its strong commitment to customer service and its continuing commitment to be available to deliver almost anything to almost anywhere in the world, Lynden Air Freight is also very proud of its place in helping meet the emergency needs of the world's less fortunate. The company is always ready and willing to divert some of its resources to meet an emerging need. Relief flights to war-torn regions or to sites of natural disasters are commonplace diversions for the employees of Lynden Air Freight. If there is no international crisis to respond to, one can always find Lynden Air Freight employees doing their part to support such local programs as United Way or the Run For the Cure.

Among the operating companies under the Lynden name, Lynden Air Freight is proud to be a central force in the continuing expansion of this industry "family." Lynden Air Freight is a local success story, always ready to meet a need and overcome a challenge, be it for a customer or in a crisis.

The Woodinville Weekly

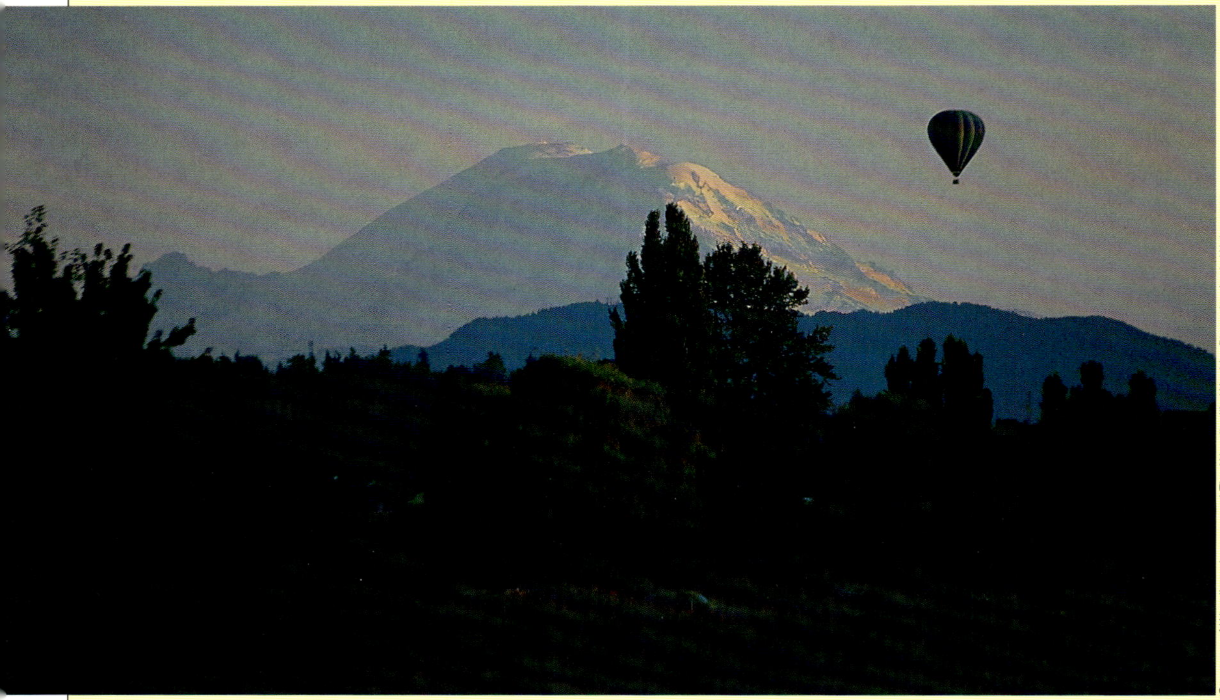

Courtesy of Wyndham Images and The Woodinville Weekly, Photo by Andy Wolgamott

Celebrating 25 Years of Community Service

The Woodinville Weekly, independently owned and operated, has proudly served Woodinville for 25 years. The first edition of *The Woodinville Weekly* was printed in publisher/owner Carol Ann Edwards' garage on a tabletop press on November 1, 1976. As the community has grown, so has the newspaper. After Edwards started *The Woodinville Weekly* she began five other newspapers in King County. She now runs three of the papers from her Woodinville office. *The Woodinville Weekly*, *The Northlake News*, and *The Valley View* have a combined circulation of 31,700 with direct mail to Woodinville, Duvall, Carnation, and Fall City, and the papers are counter-topped in various establishments throughout Bothell and Kenmore. Serving Northshore and the Lower Snoqualmie Valley, just 25 minutes outside of Seattle, the papers have chronicled the changes in the area from its original rural character to the upscale suburban area it is today, with large commercial and retail developments. As Washington state's first newspapers on the Internet, the three papers are known for pioneering a new medium for community news.

Edwards and her staff were instrumental in the creation of what are now established community activities such as the Woodinville All Fools' Day Parade and Basset Bash, the Woodinville Community Band, and The Woodinville Wine Festival and Art Walk.

Edwards, believing in the importance of participating in the community, has served as president of the Woodinville Chamber of Commerce, and as a board member of the Northshore YMCA, Shoreline Community College foundation, and other local organizations. She was a founder of Teen Northshore, a non-profit organization.

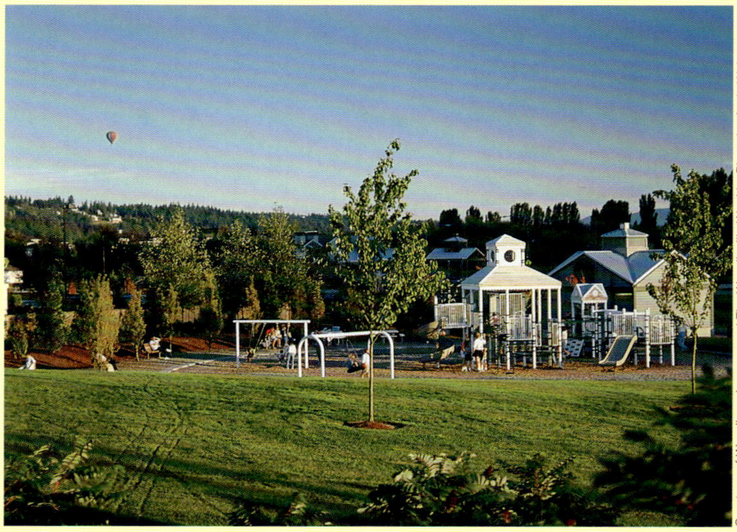

Courtesy of Wyndham Images and The Woodinville Weekly, Photo by Andy Wolgamott

King County Department of Transportation

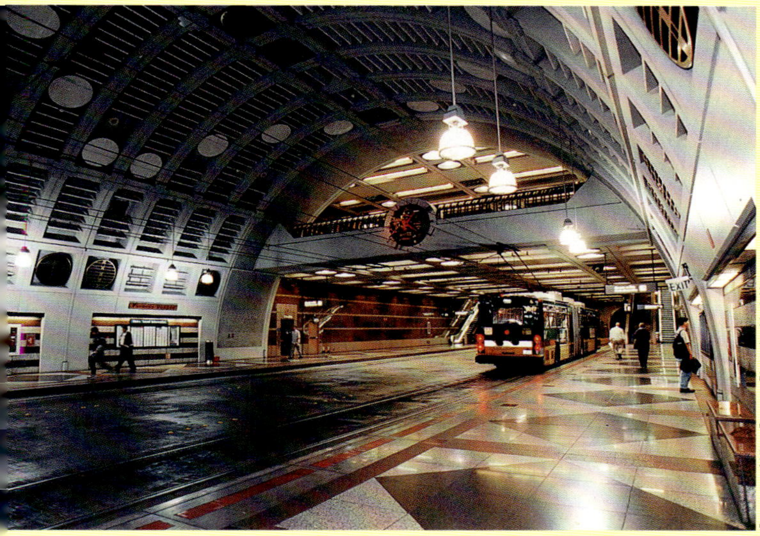

Courtesy of King County, Photo by Ned Ahrens

A dual-powered electric and diesel bus in the Pioneer Square Station of the 1.3-mile-long downtown Seattle transit tunnel. Like the other four tunnel stations, this station is designed to reflect the historic downtown neighborhood it serves.

"Mobility for the Region" is the transportation system motto for providing public transit and safe roadways in the Seattle/King County area. There are two divisions of the King County Department of Transportation that are responsible for coordinating efforts to help move people, vehicles, and freight—Metro Transit and Road Services.

To reduce congestion, pollution, and lengthy commutes, Metro plans, builds, and operates a reliable, affordable, safe, and convenient public transit system. It follows the highest environmental standards in selecting, designing, and maintaining its vehicles and facilities.

Metro has been honored twice as the best-run large public transportation system in North America. It services an annual ridership of more than 80 million, operating more than 1,300 buses that are fully accessible to people with disabilities. More than 225 bus routes serve Seattle, Bellevue, suburban cities, and rural areas.

But the division is more than buses. Metro also runs the largest publicly operated vanpool program in the nation, putting more than 680 vans on the road each year. It also operates a regional ridematch system that sets up carpools and vanpools for commuters in seven counties.

Many of those vehicles run on roads, bridges, and pathways built and maintained by Road Services. The division strives to make the county's transportation system safe and efficient for all uses and modes of travel. It practices environmentally friendly project design, maintenance, and operation.

Road Services is responsible for more than 1,784 miles of roadway, more than 210 bridges, 86 miles of unpaved roads, and many pathways in unincorporated areas. It maintains more than 480 traffic signals and nearly 85,000 traffic signs. With 12,000 Adopt-a-Road volunteers, Road Services is also committed to keeping county roads litter free.

All county roads get 24-hour emergency assistance, as do roads in some cities under contract with King County for selected services. Extensive safety improvements have paid off. Total traffic accidents on unincorporated county roads have decreased steadily since 1992.

Not all roads lead to the Seattle/King County area, but those that do are served by a department committed to moving people, vehicles, and products as safely, reliably, and efficiently as possible.

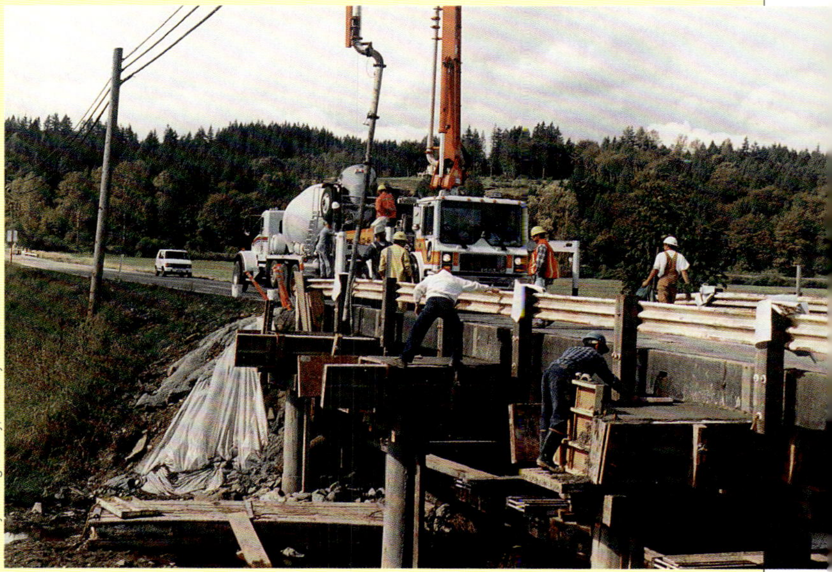

Courtesy of King County, Photo by Herb Griffith

King County Road Services crews retrofit one of 117 county bridges to withstand earthquakes far into the twenty-first century. The Bridge Seismic Retrofit Program earned an Achievement Award from the National Association of Counties in 1999.

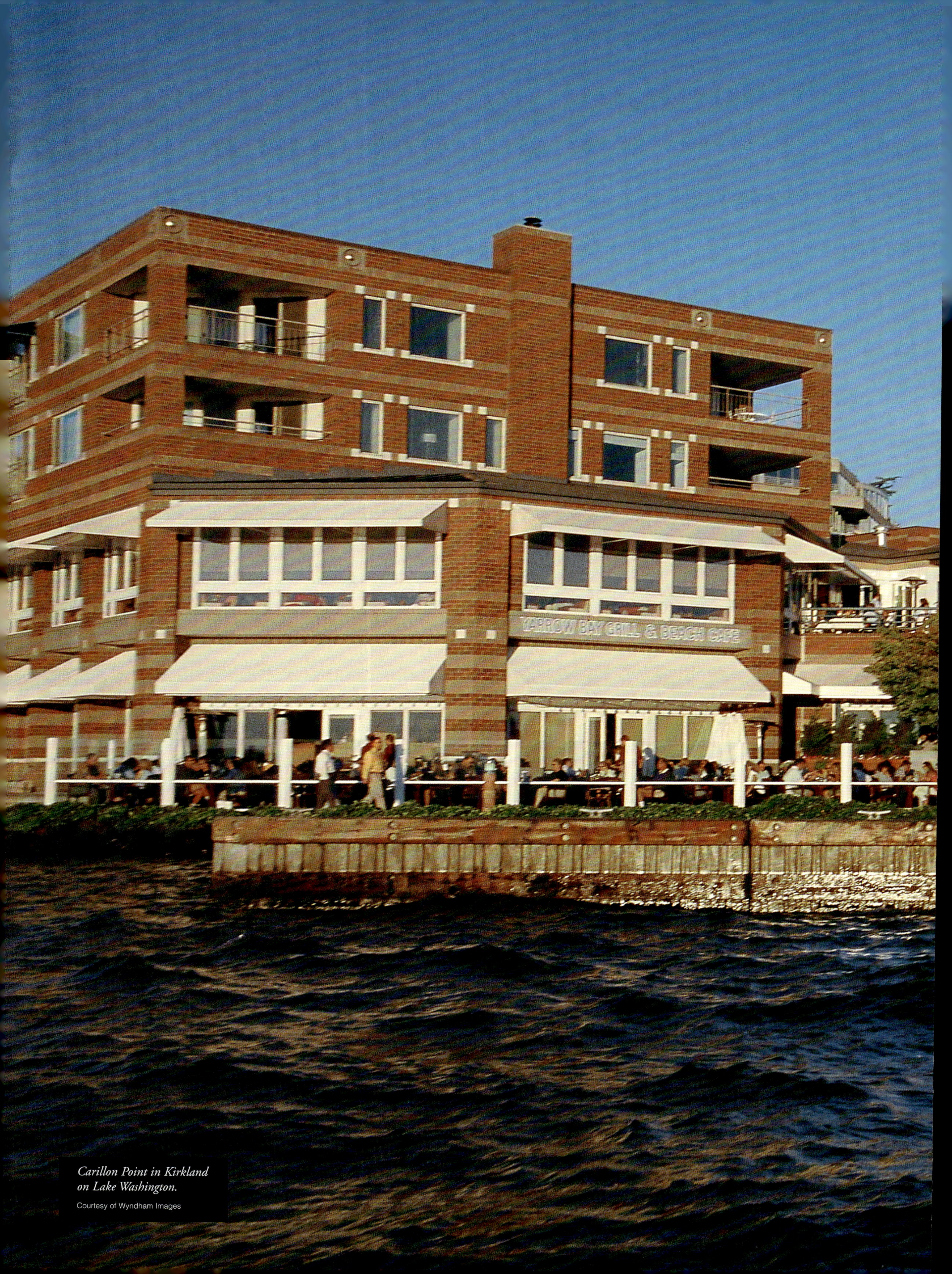

Carillon Point in Kirkland on Lake Washington.

Courtesy of Wyndham Images

Part Two

Business and Professional Services

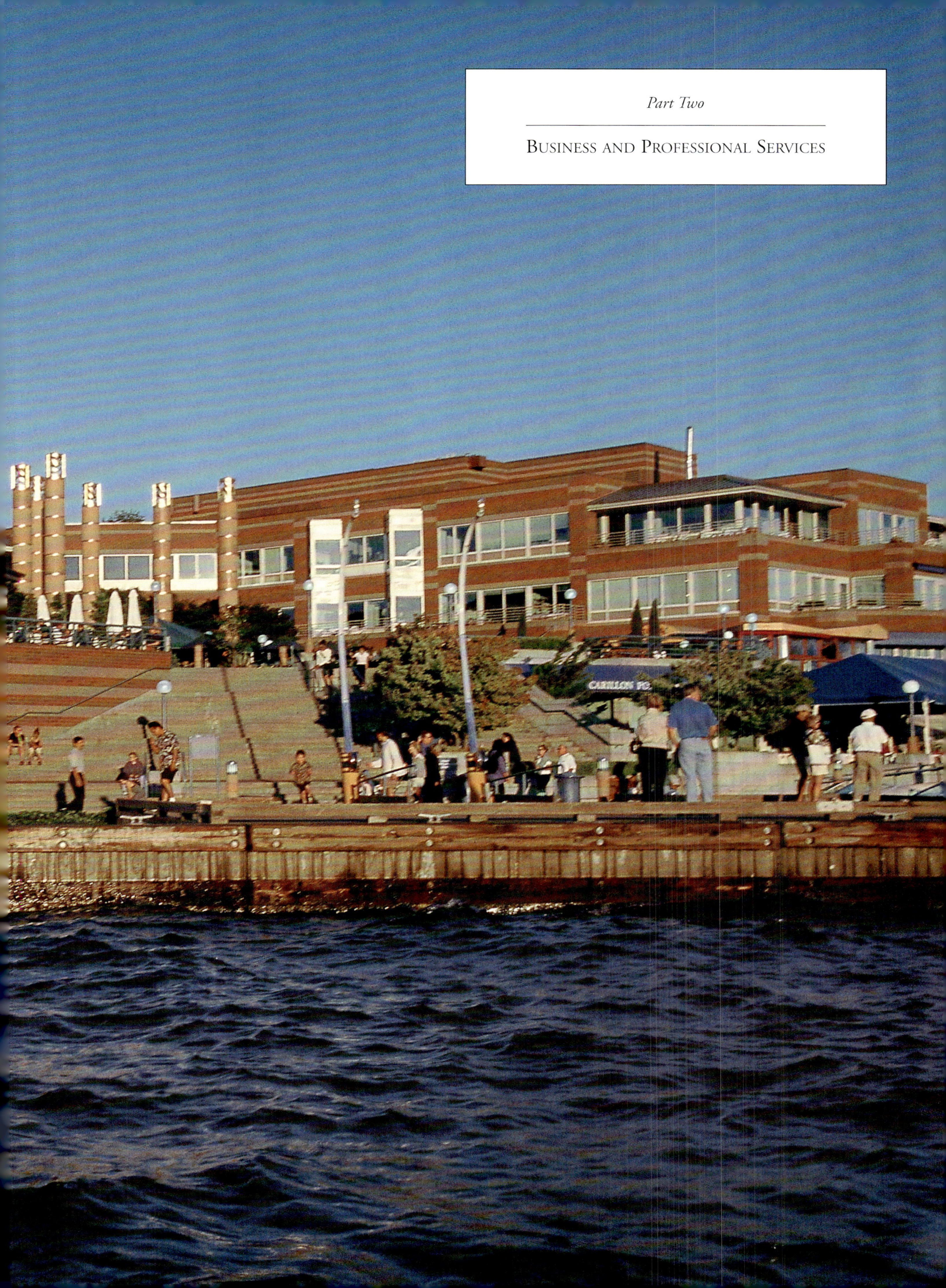

Bank of America

The 76-story Bank of America Tower in Seattle is the tallest building west of Houston and Chicago. Rising 943 feet, the building has helped define the skyline and the economy of the region. Today it serves as headquarters for the region's largest bank.

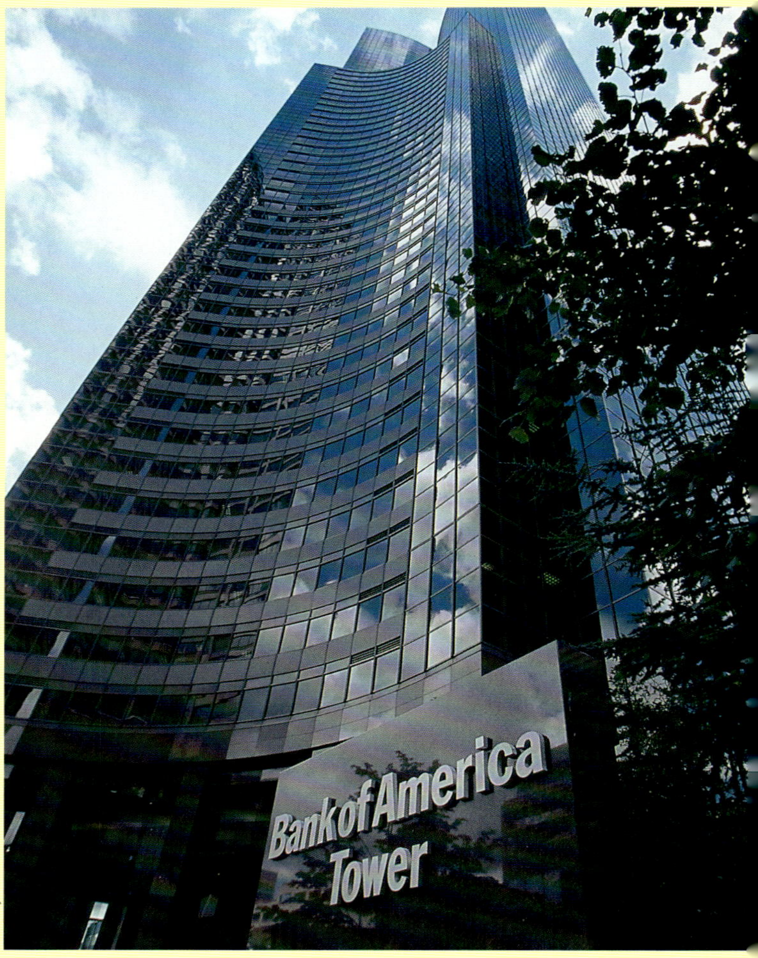

Courtesy of Bank of America

Today, financial customers expect more than ever from their bank. They want convenience and financial solutions that fit their individual needs.

Bank of America understands this and delivers every day on the promise to make banking work for customers in ways it never has before. It serves customers 24 hours a day — helping them pay for education, manage personal and business assets, meet payrolls, raise capital, start businesses, purchase homes and autos, and save for retirement.

"Our associates have created a bank of unparalleled convenience and capacity, with both a strong local presence and global reach," says John Rindlaub, president of the Northwest Region, Bank of America. "What's more, customers expect us to do all this and have the heart to serve the communities in which we do business. It is a responsibility we take seriously."

The bank's community involvement is renowned. Bank of America has one of the largest corporate foundations in the nation, with the Bank of America Foundation providing more than $80 million to charitable causes in 2000. In recognition of its community involvement, Bank of America was awarded the prestigious 13th annual Spirit of America Award, the highest national honor given by United Way of America.

In King County alone, the foundation provides millions of dollars in charitable donations each year to nonprofit organizations — focusing its support on education, health and human services, community development and the arts. Likewise, Bank of America generously supports civic projects, economic development groups and others.

Past examples of local donations include $75,000 to the Seattle Public Schools, $40,000 to the Bellevue Community College's new child learning center and $100,000 to the Success By 6® initiative supporting early childhood development in King County.

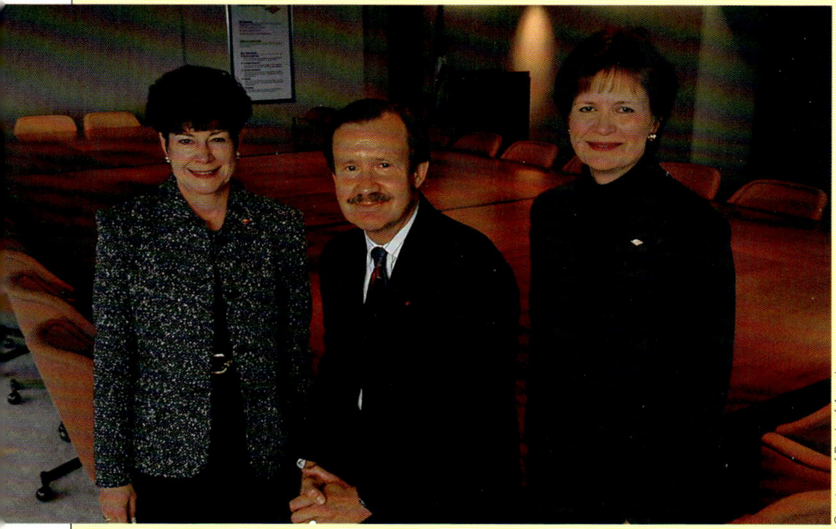

Courtesy of Bank of America

(From left) Marie Gunn, president of Bank of America Washington, John Rindlaub, president of the Northwest Region of Bank of America, and Joan Enticknap, executive vice president of Northwest Commercial Banking, lead the region's largest financial institution.

The Most Extensive Banking Network in the State

Customers never have far to go for their banking needs. Nationwide, Bank of America provides comprehensive financial services for 30 million households through approximately 4,500 banking centers and 13,000 automated teller machines located throughout the company's coast-to-coast franchise in 21 states and the District of Columbia.

In King County, Bank of America operates 96 banking centers and more than 424 ATMs. Statewide, the bank

Ardie Warren sells local merchandise at his news and gift stand inside SeaTac Airport. His small business venture was made possible with financing from Bank of America.

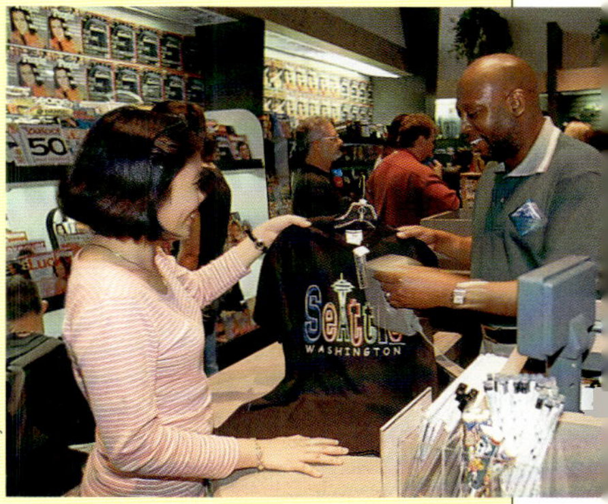

Courtesy of Bank of America

ɔperates approximately 239 ɔanking centers and more than 360 ATMs, making the Bank of America network the most extensive and convenient in the state.

Closer still, Bank of America s at its customers' fingertips with online banking and 24-hour, automated telephone ɔanking. Bank of America is committed to providing a variety of delivery channels to make t convenient for customers to do their banking — a pattern started in the 1970s when Bank of America installed the first ATMs in the region. Since then the bank was the first provider of 24-hour telephone banking in the 1980s and embraced the nternet, online banking and check-cards in the 1990s.

Customers say they want the option of banking on the nternet, but with the advantages and responsiveness of a full-service bank. Bank of America listened. And the bank's commitment to developing new and innovative ways to bank is as firm as ever as it heads into the 21st century.

SMALL BUSINESS BANKING

At Bank of America, small business is big business. The bank serves approximately 1.7 million small businesses (companies with annual sales up to $10 million) nationwide and has a history of helping businesses start and grow through loans guaranteed by the Small Business Administration. In Washington state, Bank of America has consistently been ranked the No. 1 producer of SBA loans for the past six years. It is a ranking in which Bank of America takes pride.

In the Northwest, the bank's team of 120 small business bankers realizes business and personal finances often overlap for the entrepreneur. As a result, Bank of America has developed enhanced services and better pricing for customers who ask the bank to manage more of their finances.

One product of importance to small businesses is the business lease. The typical small business leases more than it purchases, including office equipment, vehicles and computer equipment. To meet this need, Bank of America introduced new equipment and vehicle leasing products to its small business customers across the franchise, exemplifying the many ways the bank strives to make banking better for its customers.

Likewise, Bank of America is expanding its offering of cash management services to small business customers and provides retirement plan solutions for small business clients through its retail brokerage affiliate, Banc of America Investment Services, Inc.

PROFESSIONAL SERVICE CLIENTS

In today's world, a one-size-fits-all approach to banking no longer works. One area where this is particularly true is in meeting the banking needs of professionals, including doctors, dentists, attorneys, certified public accountants, business managers and executives. Bank of America has developed a specialized team called Premier Banking to serve the professional services client. The goal is

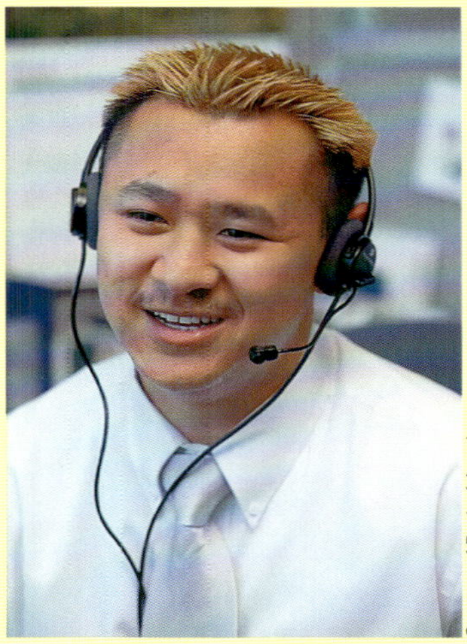

Courtesy of Bank of America

Jeff Lau, customer service representative in the Telephone Banking Group, is intent on responding to a client—just as he and his colleagues do for 22,000 callers in Washington and Idaho every day.

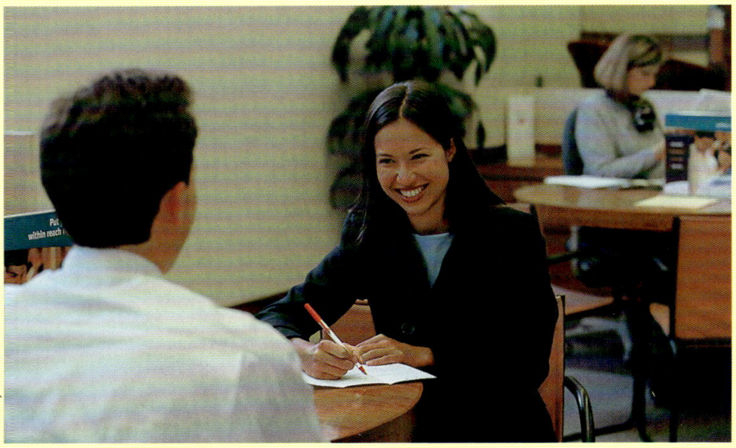

Courtesy of Bank of America

Kamila Hruby, personal banker, enjoys helping a customer open an account at the Main Office Banking Center.

Matt Lynch, (standing) senior vice president, Private Bank, collaborates with Ray Ifert, market executive Private Bank, as they keep abreast of current market performance for the bank's clients.

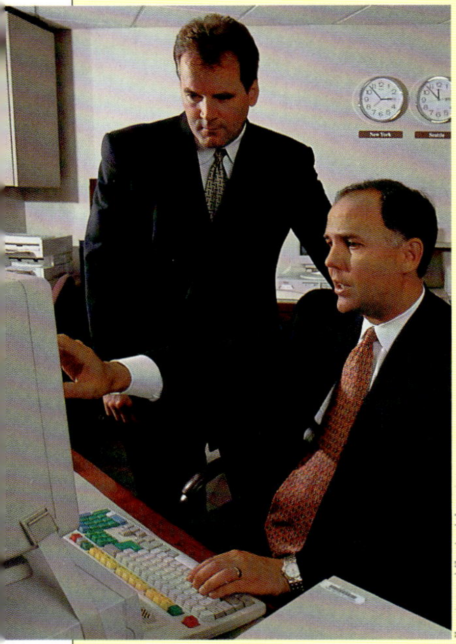

Courtesy of Bank of America

to redefine banking by providing a level of service beyond what clients expect from a bank.

With Premier Banking, clients with a combined relationship of $100,000 or more in deposits, loans, mortgages and investments with Bank of America and its affiliates are matched with an experienced client manager. The client manager, supported by a team of professionals, is a single point of access to the bank's array of financial services and is there to help the client build wealth both personally and professionally.

Because Premier Banking clients bring more of their financial business to the bank, Bank of America rewards them with preferred pricing on its products and services. Premier Banking client managers are also registered representatives of Banc of America Investment Services, Inc., and can assist their affluent clients in making their money work harder for them through the power of investing.

The High-Net-Worth Client

At Bank of America, the Private Bank is rewriting the rules on what a bank's financial relationship should be with its wealthy clients — whether they are individuals or families with a net worth greater than $1 million (excluding their primary residence) or investable assets greater than $1 million.

Clients say time is their most valuable commodity. Yet, Private Bank clients often have complex financial needs. At Bank of America, clients are matched with a relationship manager, who draws upon the resources of the bank to deliver the financial solutions needed. The result is personal attention and the resources to get the job done.

The goal of the Private Bank is straightforward: build and preserve the wealth of its clients. Private bankers provide investment management, asset allocation, specialized asset management including real estate, wealth transfer and personal trust services, tax and estate planning, customized lending, mutual funds and brokerage.

The Private Bank of Bank of America is the largest private bank in North America and the third largest in the world, with more than $130.5 billion in assets. In the Northwest, the Private Bank invests more than $7 billion in assets under management for local clients, serving them through 10 dedicated local offices. In the Seattle area, the Private Bank has offices in Bellevue, Seattle, Everett and Tacoma.

In the highly competitive financial-services market found in the Puget Sound area, investment expertise helps set the Private Bank apart. Bank of America customers appreciate the emphasis on the importance of after-tax returns and the consistent returns that have outperformed the Standard and Poors benchmarks for more than five years. In fact, the Private Bank is ranked the No. 1 money manager for high-net-worth clients by Private Asset Management, a publication of Institutional Investor, for 1999.

One of today's growth markets is the entrepreneurial segment — individuals, company owners and executives whose fortunes have been made in high technology, pharmaceuticals and other high-growth markets. To serve this sector, the Private Bank has rolled out its Option Plus program, which allows entrepreneurs to obtain liquidity without exercising their stock options.

Commercial Clients

Commercial clients describe the financial solutions offered by Bank of America as comprehensive in scope and global in reach, while decision-making

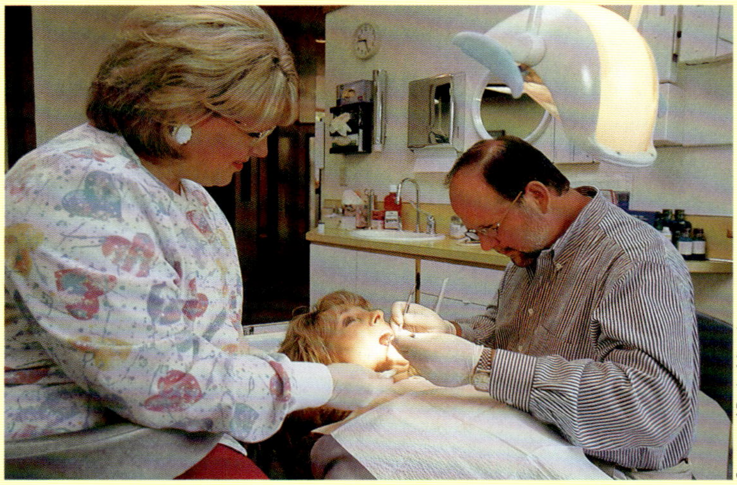

Courtesy of Bank of America

Above: Dr. Rob Walker, DDS, performs a routine operation with the help of state-of-the-art equipment financed by Bank of America through the Premier Banking group.

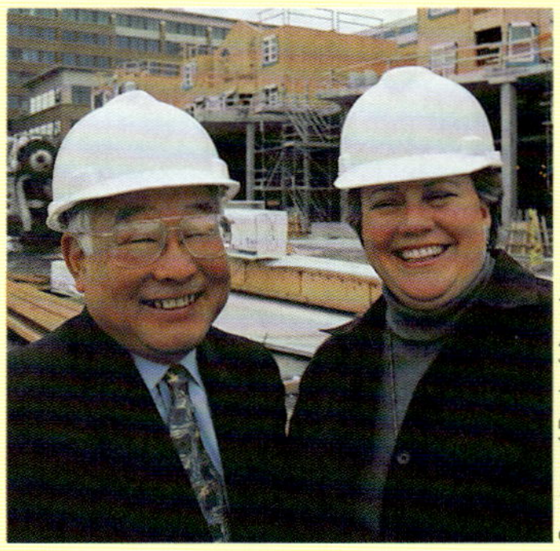

Courtesy of Bank of America

Right: Tomio Moriguchi, chairman of Uwajimaya, and Jan Morris, from the Bank of America Real Estate Group, check on progress at the construction site of Uwajimaya Village, a project being funded by Bank of America.

Khalilah Jones thanks a customer at the Main Office Banking Center, where she works as a part-time teller after school. Khalilah has been gaining work experience and opening doors of opportunity for herself as a participant in the Bank of America Youth Job Program.

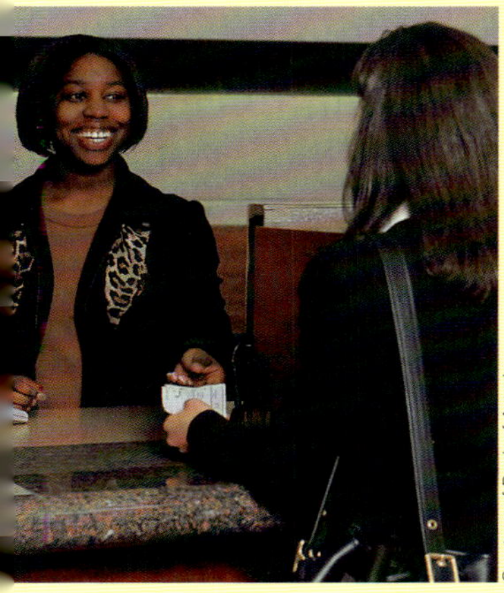
Courtesy of Bank of America

and service remain local and responsive. More than half of the 32,000 businesses served by the Commercial Banking unit have operations in more than one state, giving the coast-to-coast franchise of Bank of America a strong competitive advantage in this market.

In nearly every category of commercial banking, Bank of America leads the nation — the No. 1 provider in the United States of commercial and industrial loans and No. 1 in loan syndications, cash management, traditional private placements, foreign exchange and derivatives.

Bank of America provides services for 80 percent of the Fortune 500 companies and 80 percent of the Fortune 1000. In the Northwest, Bank of America serves more than 40 percent of companies with annual sales from $10 million to $75 million and 75 percent of companies with annual sales from $75 million to $250 million.

From 10 commercial banking offices throughout the region, Bank of America is readily available to its 2,100 commercial clients in Washington and Idaho. The bank's commercial team integrates financial solutions to clients through a client manager who serves as a single, local point of contact for all of the resources of the bank, which include credit products, treasury management, investment banking, personal wealth management, institutional investing and group banking. As a result, commercial banking client managers are able to develop customized solutions from a wide range of resources that help their clients meet specific growth objectives.

Additionally, commercial banking has a dedicated capital markets team for mid-sized companies, offering direct access to the entire spectrum of capital markets from traditional senior bank debt to private and public equity.

The Bank's Commitment to Community Lending

Bank of America is committed to serving all members of the community. One area, in particular, where this commitment is demonstrated is in the bank's community development efforts. The bank has pledged a record $350 billion over 10 years to community development lending and investment, including small businesses, affordable housing, consumer loans and economic development.

In its annual review of achievements, Bank of America in 1999 reported that lending for community development exceeded $39 billion at the national level — which equates to $14 million in loans and investments every business hour.

Of that amount, nearly $1 billion was earmarked for the Seattle area, including more than $500 million in local affordable housing, $200 million for small business lending and nearly that much for home and auto loans for borrowers below the median income. It also involved $76 million in loans and investments to community-based nonprofit institutions, businesses, financial institutions and venture funds specifically involved in economic development of local communities.

Improving the Lives of People and Communities

Corporate citizenship is more than a slogan at Bank of America. It is woven into the fabric of the bank's involvement in the community and the tremendous spirit of volunteerism demonstrated by its associates.

Throughout the year, Team Bank of America volunteers participate in a variety of worthwhile programs, such as the March of Dimes' WalkAmerica, the American Cancer Society's Daffodil Days, Christmas in April, United Way Day of Caring and the Angeline's Day Center for Women, as well as clothing and food drives sponsored by many other non-profit organizations.

In 1992, Bank of America launched a one-of-a-kind Youth Job Program in the Northwest, encouraging high school students from low-income families to stay in school. The students are offered part-time jobs, mentoring and a $10,000 college scholarship after they graduate from high school. Since the program's inception, more than 300 students have participated, and 28 have already graduated from college.

Whether it's financial solutions or community service, Bank of America uses its tremendous resources to do what's right. The bank and its associates look forward to serving King County — and the Northwest — in the years to come.

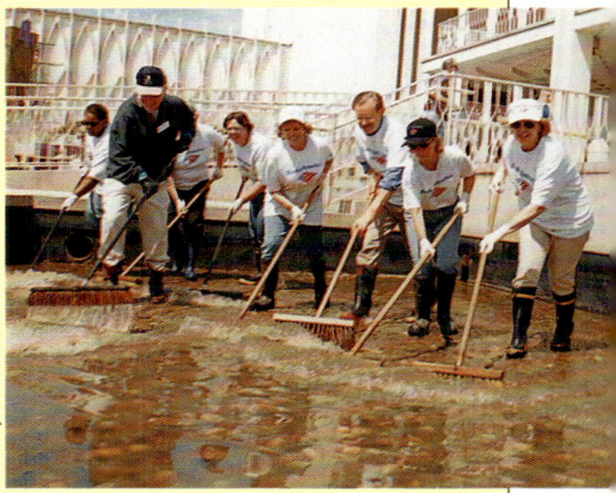
Courtesy of Bank of America

Team Bank of America volunteers put their money-handling skills to work as they join John Rindlaub (center), president of the Northwest Region of Bank of America, and George Moynihan, Pacific Science Center executive director, in collecting coins and scrubbing the center's ponds.

Bullivant Houser Bailey PC

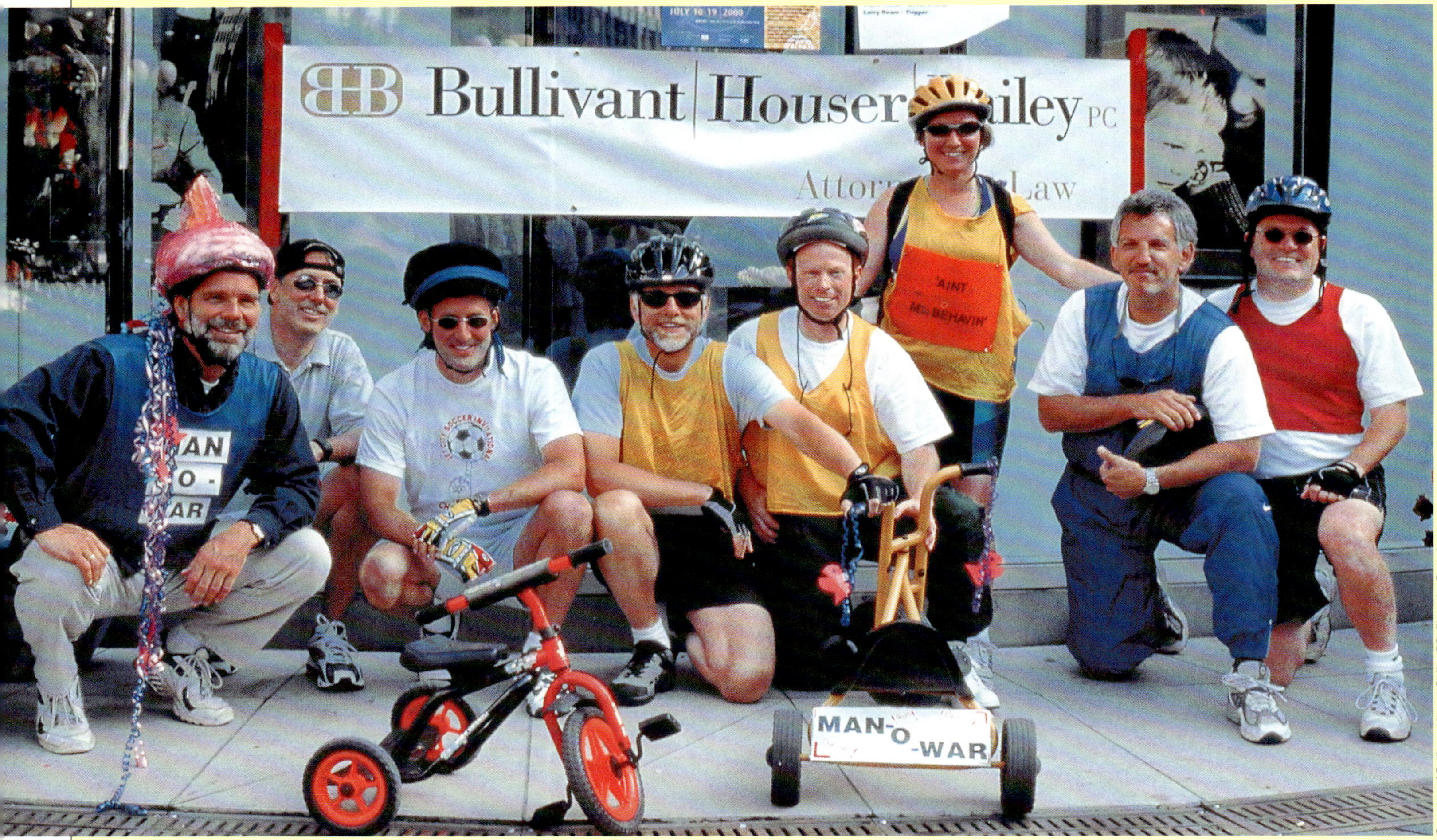

Shareholders' show their support for Food Lifeline by volunteering to participate in a fundraising tricycle race.

At the law firm of Bullivant Houser Bailey PC, it is quite common to hear the words, "the Bullivant Way" in everyday conversation. The Bullivant Way is more of a mindset than a motto. The reference could concern the servicing of clients, or perhaps the manner in which business is conducted, or even the positive work environment and constructive interaction among the staff members and attorneys. The Bullivant Way pertains to the unique quality of character and pride exhibited by all those who work in the 150-attorney law firm—from the Managing Partner to the newest support-staff member. The firm takes pride in the talent of its attorneys and staff, the depth of their expertise, and the collaborative teamwork effort in responding to clients' needs. The firm has a history of developing innovative and lasting alliances with its clients.

Bullivant Houser Bailey PC is one of the oldest West Coast law firms. It has offices in six locations covering Washington, Oregon, and California. Approximately 100 of the firm's 350 employees are in its Seattle office. Founded in 1938, the firm originally built its distinguished reputation by specializing in representing financial institutions. Today, Bullivant Houser Bailey PC has attorneys concentrating in over 35 practice areas, from complex litigation to transactional matters. The firm represents clients locally, nationally, and internationally.

View of the Puget Sound from the offices of Bullivant Houser Bailey PC, Seattle.

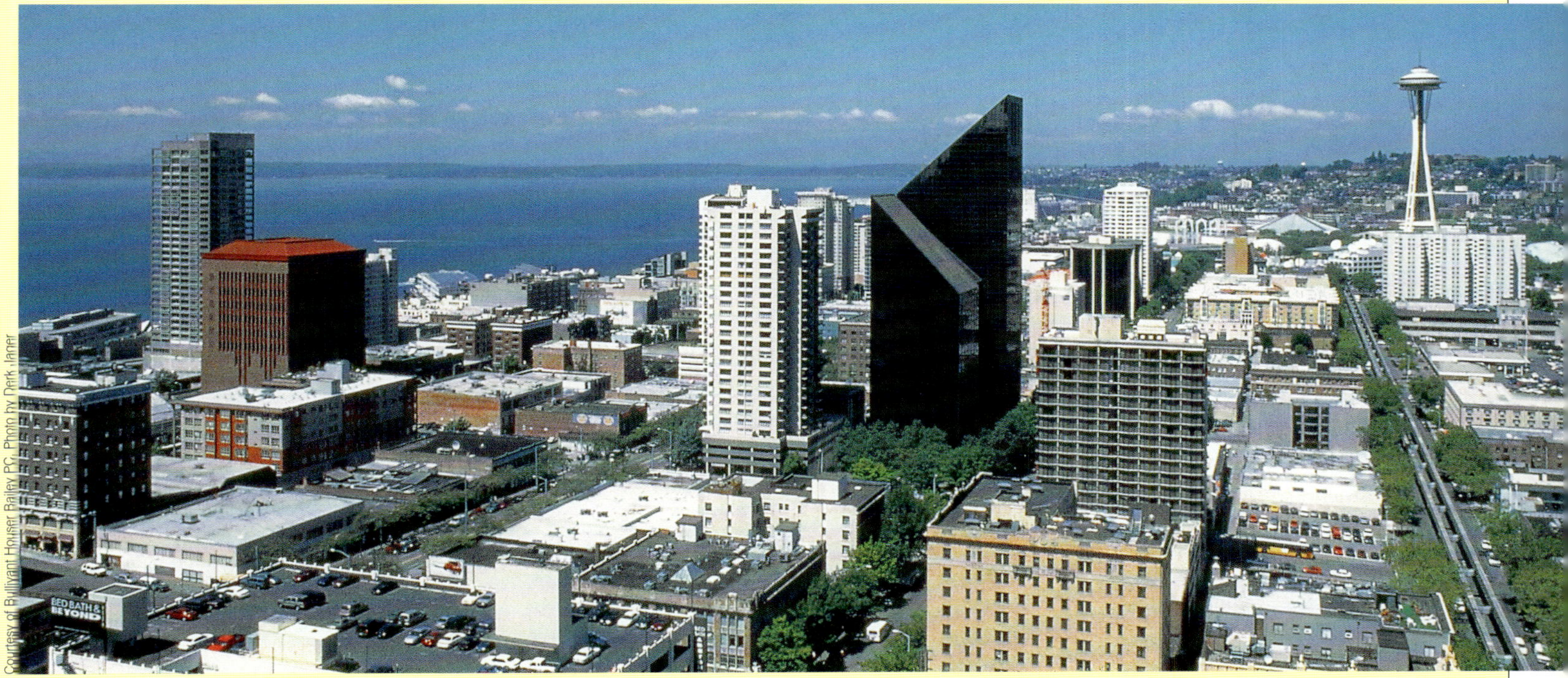

Courtesy of Bullivant Houser Bailey PC. Photo by Derk Jager

Bullivant Houser Bailey PC embraces a commitment to three basic principles: service to its clients and community, commitment to the highest standards of ethics and excellence in legal work, and personal attention to each client. Perhaps it is the last of these that most often prompts the reference to the Bullivant Way. At Bullivant Houser Bailey PC, individual clients are treated with the same level of attention and respect as multinational corporate clients.

The firm's sophisticated Wide Area Network, which provides both voice and data to all six West Coast offices, serves as the framework from which the firm shares and disseminates information. In addition to sharing resources throughout the firm, these systems and network infrastructure have streamlined every aspect of the firm's internal and external communications. Its Extranet client access is an example of the firm's ongoing efforts to create innovative ways to involve clients directly in the management of their cases. This is an Internet-based tool that provides a secure platform for online communication and data-sharing between the firm and its clients. Through its sophisticated technology systems and the use of Extranets, the firm has realized a decline in traditional communication expenses, yet has accelerated the delivery of information while at the same time establishing a high level of attorney-client collaboration.

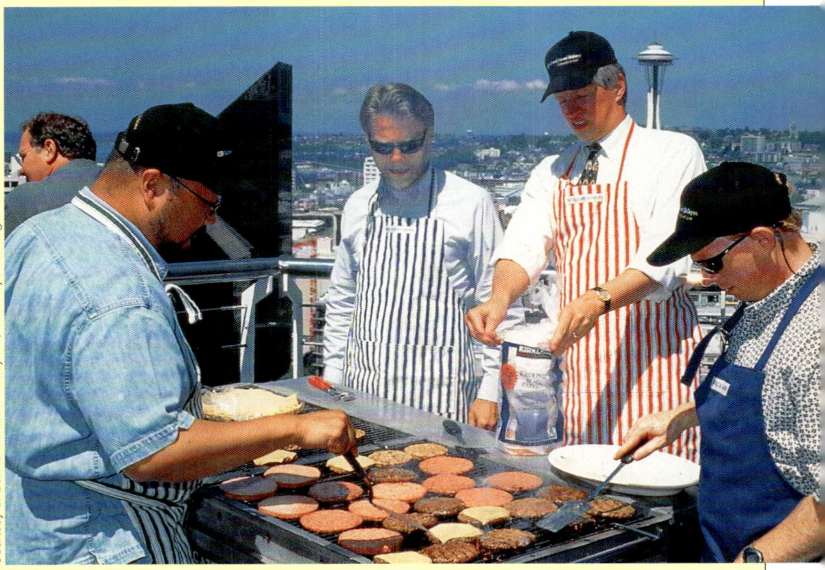

Courtesy of Bullivant Houser Bailey PC. Photo by Derk Jager

Annual fundraising barbecue that benefits Food Lifeline and the 250 food banks and meal programs it supports throughout Western Washington.

Bullivant Houser Bailey PC is committed in its resolution to maintain a positive work environment, to create unity among its attorneys and staff, and to preserve that unique quality of character and pride that is "the Bullivant Way."

Hugh G. Goldsmith & Associates

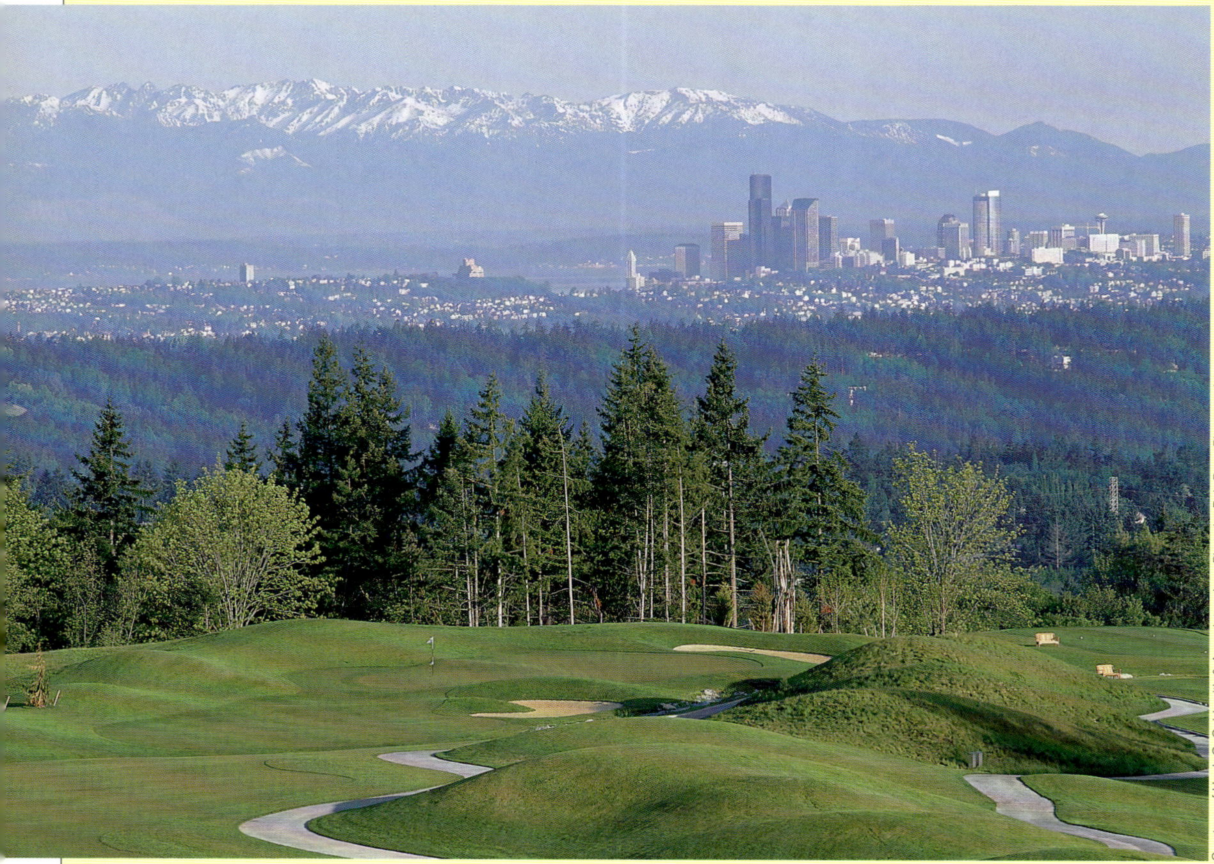

Courtesy of Hugh G. Goldsmith & Associates, Inc.; Photo by Rob Perry Photography

The Golf Club at Newcastle provides sweeping panoramic views of the Seattle skyline and Olympic Mountains. Site conditions and challenging terrain were overcome to produce this unique, one-of-a-kind experience in golf in the Northwest.

Hugh G. Goldsmith and Associates, Inc. has contributed to the Northwest in very significant ways for over 40 years. Founded in 1958, when Hugh G. Goldsmith purchased a small civil engineering company, the firm grew from its original 5 employees to over 50 today. A civil engineering, land surveying, and land development consulting firm, Goldsmith and Associates, through their designs, has had a hand in literally changing the landscape of the Puget Sound region and areas beyond.

Originally located in the historic Pioneer Square area of Seattle, the firm relocated to the nearby city of Bellevue in 1988. Goldsmith and Associates has developed a reputation for expertise in land-use consultation and permitting services. The firm serves clients throughout the Pacific Northwest, including Washington, Oregon, Idaho, and Alaska as consultants for the development of residential and commercial lands. The firm has become one of the premier land-use-engineering consultants in the area and continues to serve its clients as lead planner, civil engineer, and land surveyor for a variety of residential developments, master-planned communities, and golf course projects. While its primary specialization has been small residential land developments, large projects such as the Redmond Ridge Master Planned Community and Klahanie Master Planned Community in King County, and McCormick Woods in Kitsap County are a few of the company's most notable award winning designs. Goldsmith and Associates sets itself apart through its focus on project success, attention to the economics of land development, and sensitivity to the preservation

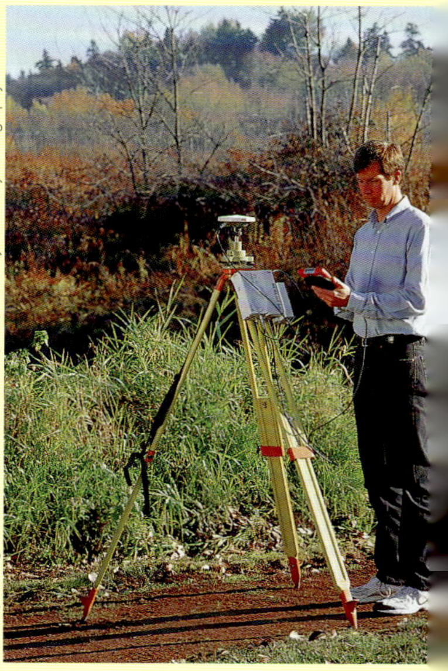

Courtesy of Hugh G. Goldsmith & Associates, Inc.; Photo by Rob Perry Photography

Working from undeveloped ground to completed site development, Goldsmith and Associates is a full-service land-development consulting company.

This suburban streetscape illustrates Goldsmith and Associates' primary specialization, the planning and engineering of residential-land subdivision.

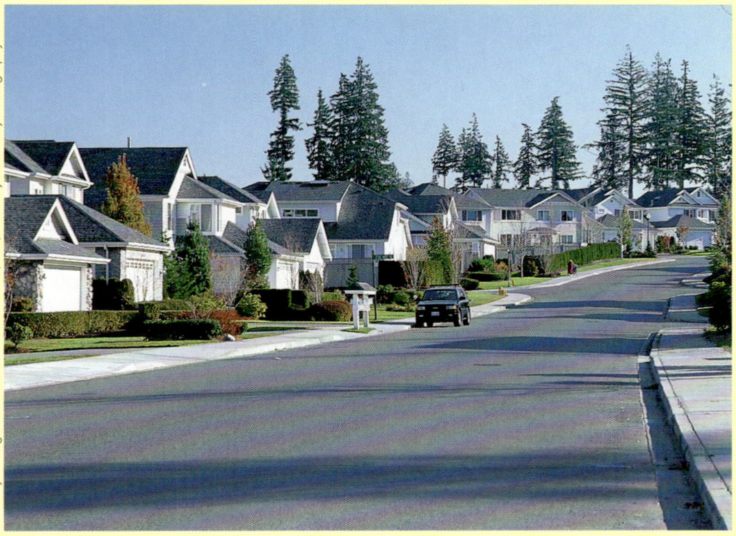

of the natural environment. The company strikes a balance between these goals, which ultimately results in the highest quality living environment for a residential community.

Goldsmith and Associates has also developed a unique expertise in permit consultation and engineering for golf courses. The company has provided lead design-engineering services to such renowned golf courses as Sahalee Country Club (host to the PGA Championship in recent years), Bear Creek Country Club, and Fairwood Golf Club. These well-known and beautifully designed projects are some of the older, more established residential and golf course communities. The firm has also participated in similar golf-course developments outside of King County, such as McCormick Woods in Kitsap County and Horn Rapids in the Tri-Cities area of Eastern Washington. More recent accomplishments are the Golf Club at Newcastle, the Plateau Golf and Country Club, and the Members Club at Aldarra. These projects feature unique environmental planning with surrounding upscale residential communities.

Members of the firm possess a vast knowledge of the development history of downtown Seattle, which stems from their early years in Pioneer Square. This contributes to their ability to participate in projects within the downtown urban core. Examples include site boundary surveying for several downtown business, hotel, and civic buildings; the original Nordstrom Building; Harborview Medical Center; Seattle School District facilities; the Kingdome site; the University of Washington Husky Stadium; Coleman Dock Ferry Terminal; Port of Seattle facilities; and portions of the I-5 and I-90 corridors.

Goldsmith and Associates has been helping to shape the landscape of the Pacific Northwest for over 40 years. The new generation and current management team will continue to provide surveying and land development engineering services well into the twenty-first century.

Courtesy of Hugh G. Goldsmith & Associates, Inc.; Photo by Rob Perry Photography

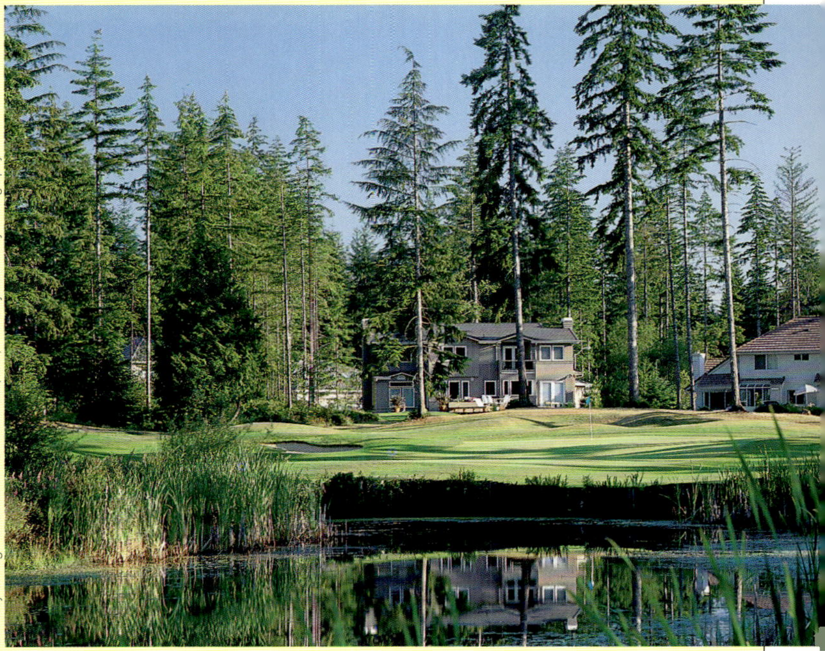

The McCormick Woods Golf Course required innovative planning and engineering in concert with forest, wetland bogs, and lakes to create one of the premier golf-course communities in the state.

Christensen O'Connor Johnson Kindness PLLC

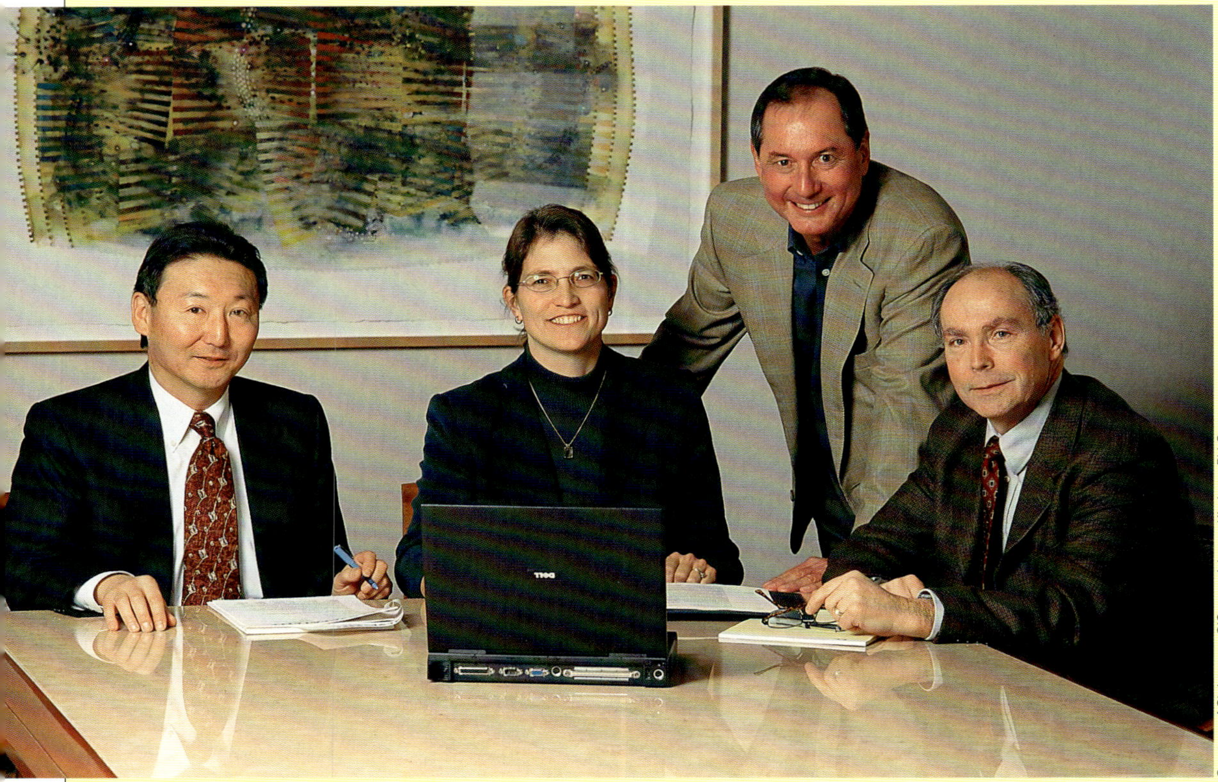

Courtesy of Christensen O'Connor Johnson Kindness PLLC

COJK's 2000 Management Committee members. From left to right, Jerald E. Nagae, Marcia S. Kelbon, Lee E. Johnson, and Executive Director Gary L. Tomlinson.

The client list of Christensen O'Connor Johnson Kindness PLLC (COJK) reads like the *Who's Who* of the Pacific Northwest. It represents every possible field from higher education to manufacturing, from medical research to art. Established in 1929, this Seattle law firm has emphasized a single aspect of legal practice, that of intellectual property, over its entire history. While the terminology has changed over the years, the firm's focus is still on patents, trademarks, copyrights, trade secrets, unfair competition, and related litigation.

The firm has grown along with the community it serves and with the increasing reach of its clients. What was once primarily a Pacific Northwest law practice has, with the rise of the information age, become a widely known and respected global practice. Much of the firm's current work involves assuring the protection of patents, trademarks, and copyrights in global trade. As a result, COJK currently does business in over 100 countries.

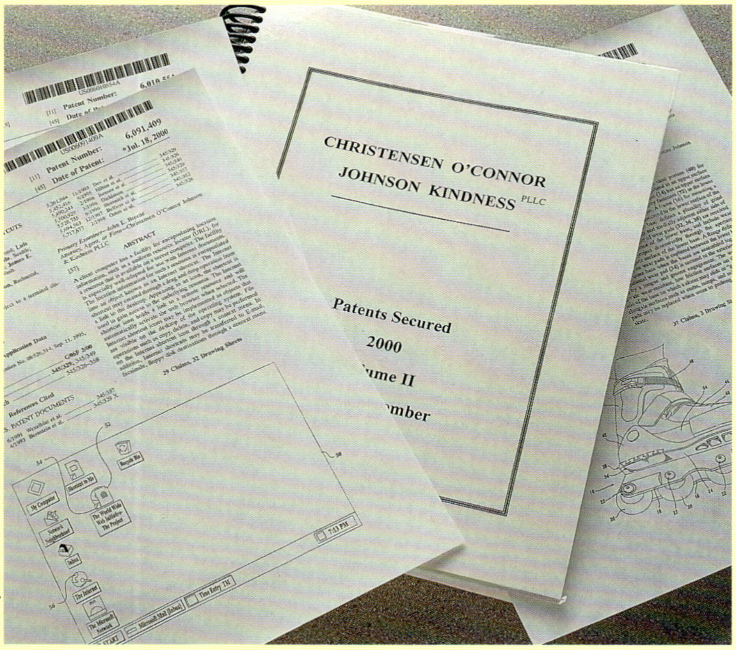

Courtesy of Christensen O'Connor Johnson Kindness PLLC

COJK is a law firm emphasizing intellectual property law. Patent prosecution is one of the many legal services provided to clients. Shown above are COJK's Year 2000 Patent Secured book and samples of recently awarded patents.

An article published in the *Washington State Bar Association Magazine* once described COJK as providing "an environment, an ambiance, of cooperation and teamwork among staff and attorneys that nearly all firms claim to want." In this article,

Standing in the lobby of their downtown Seattle office, two senior COJK attorneys, Gary S. Kindness (left) and Bruce E. O'Connor.

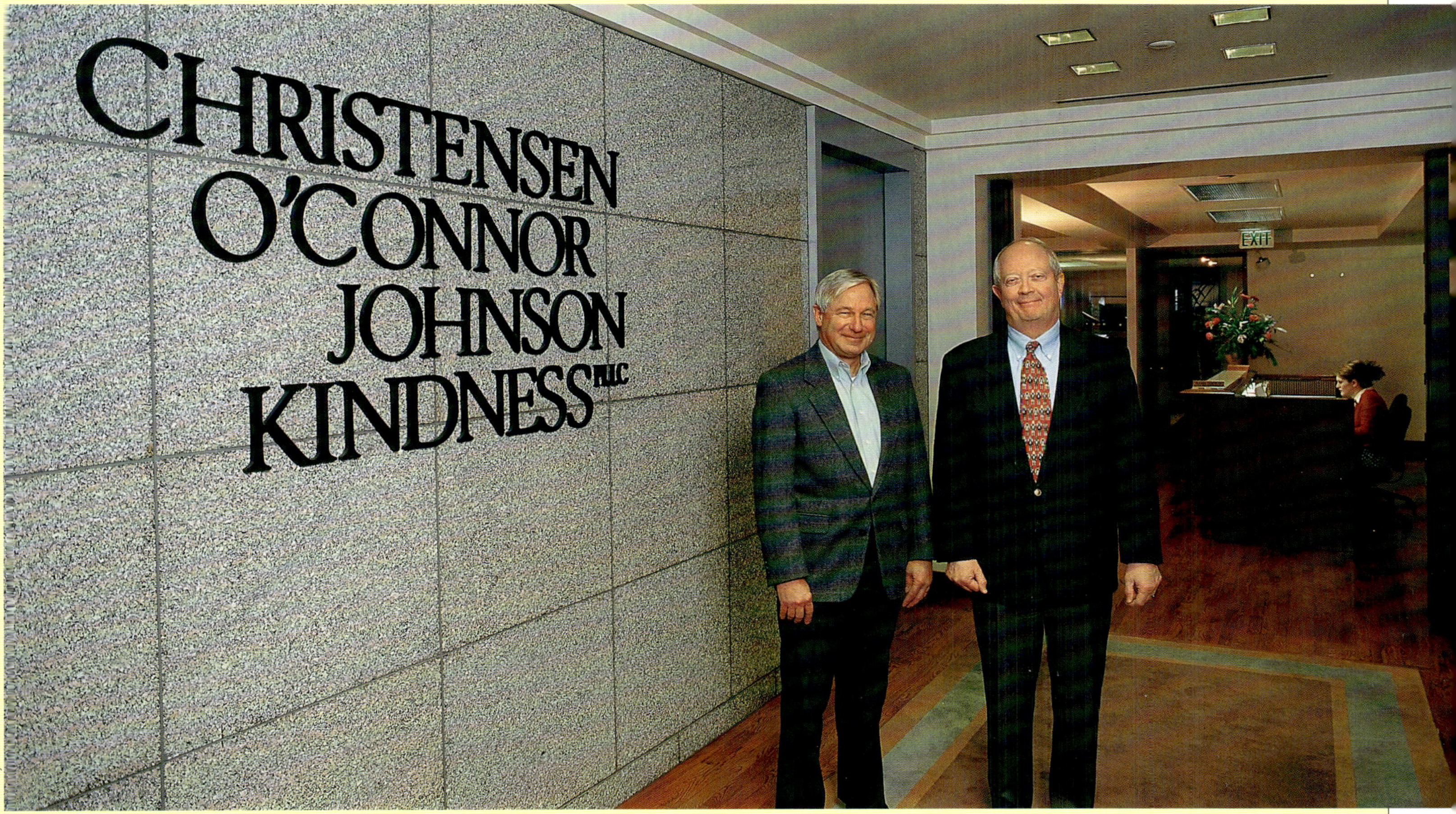

Courtesy of Christensen O'Connor Johnson Kindness PLLC

the firm was judged on its strategic planning, communication, training, firm management, partner compensation, and firm-wide marketing. The conclusion was that COJK represented a model for all law firms of similar size, anywhere.

The firm has been able to maintain such a respected reputation, in large part, because of the high level of training and expertise of its attorneys and staff. Due to the highly technical nature of much of their work, many of the firm's attorneys also hold advanced degrees in other fields. Represented within the firm are attorneys with degrees in Electrical, Chemical, Mechanical and Computer Engineering; Organic Chemistry; Physics; and Biology.

The future of Christensen O'Connor Johnson Kindness PLLC is one of dynamic growth as demand for the firm's particular expertise increases worldwide. One certainty is that the firm will continue to focus its attention on intellectual property and on serving the unique needs of its local, national, and multinational clients.

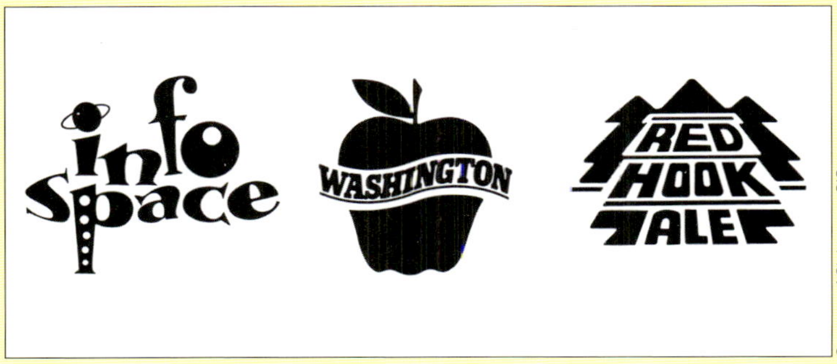

Courtesy of Christensen O'Connor Johnson Kindness PLLC

Trademark law is another practice area in which COJK provides legal expertise to clients. Shown above are representative trademarks for InfoSpace, Inc., Washington Apple Commission, and Redhook Ale Brewery, Inc.

URS

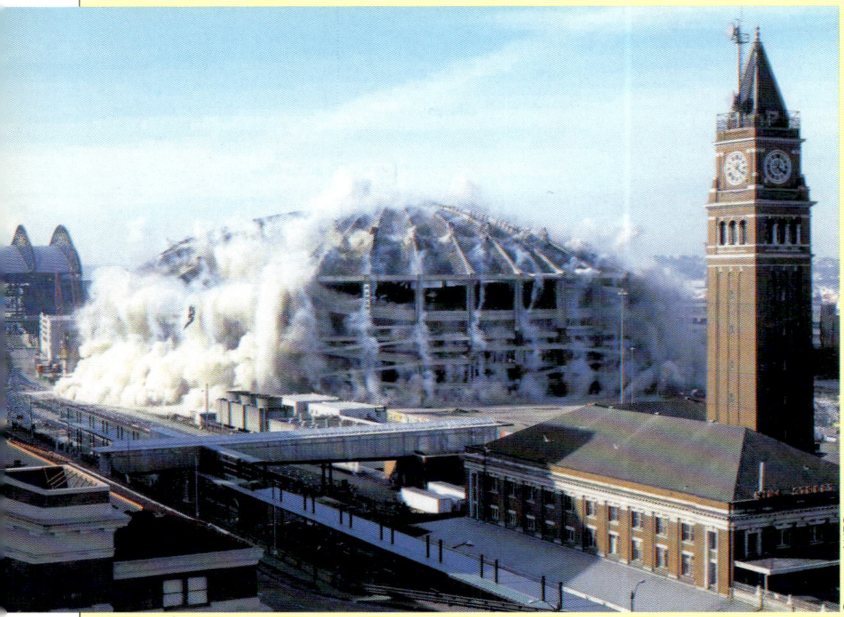

Courtesy of URS

URS demolished the Seattle Kingdome via implosion. The resulting 60,000 cubic yards of rubble were recycled for construction of a new stadium.

In 1999, URS was ranked as one of the 100 fastest growing companies by *Fortune Magazine.* In one decade, this San Francisco-based global engineering and construction services company has increased the number of its employees from 1,000 to more than 16,000. Through foresight, growth, and strategic acquisitions, URS is now one of the world's leading engineering, environmental, and construction management companies, operating in 38 countries.

The URS Seattle office got its start in 1891. In the early 1900s, it was instrumental in some of the earliest land surveys of both the University of Washington campus and the Seattle Tide Lands. URS has a long history in the development of systems for wastewater treatment and has contributed to the design of much of the infrastructure that has supported the Puget Sound Region's growth. However, its historical project experience is only part of the extensive involvement of today's URS in the economic development of the Pacific Northwest.

URS has met the challenge of assisting clients in improving their bottom-line effectiveness by diversification. Locally, the firm has expanded its capabilities in infrastructure engineering and has added and increased its expertise in air and surface transportation, facilities architecture, and construction. One of URS' key roles was serving as the general contractor for one of the Pacific Northwest's most memorable events—the demolition of the Seattle Kingdome.

URS has also been in the forefront of web-application development of technical and geographic information systems (GIS), as well as cutting-edge technologies, such as advanced telecommunications systems, high-speed communications infrastructures, and electronic systems. URS is currently assisting the Port of Seattle in the planning and design of communications and security systems upgrades in connection with Seattle-Tacoma International Airport's rigorous expansion program.

URS takes pride in its continuing contributions to the regional economy and especially to the preservation and protection of the environment. URS is committed to environmental issues and is a recognized leader in environmental permitting, waste management, contaminated site clean-up, and habitat restoration. URS' vision for the 21st century is to provide engineering infrastructure for the private sector and the community based on environmental stewardship.

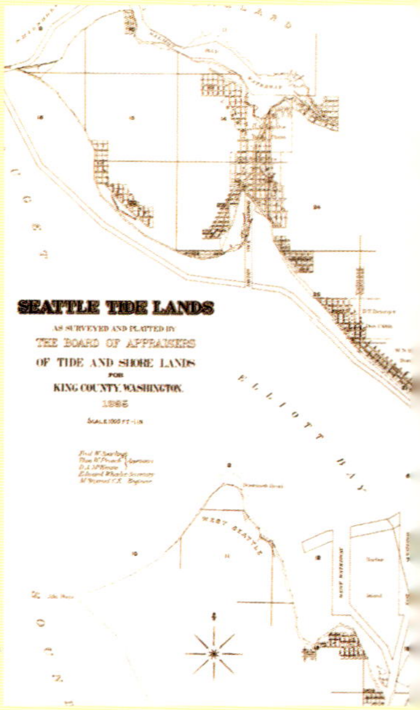

Courtesy of URS

URS was founded in 1891 as Stixtrud & Naston and surveyed such noteworthy projects as the Seattle Tide Lands.

Penhallegon Associates Consulting Engineers, Inc.

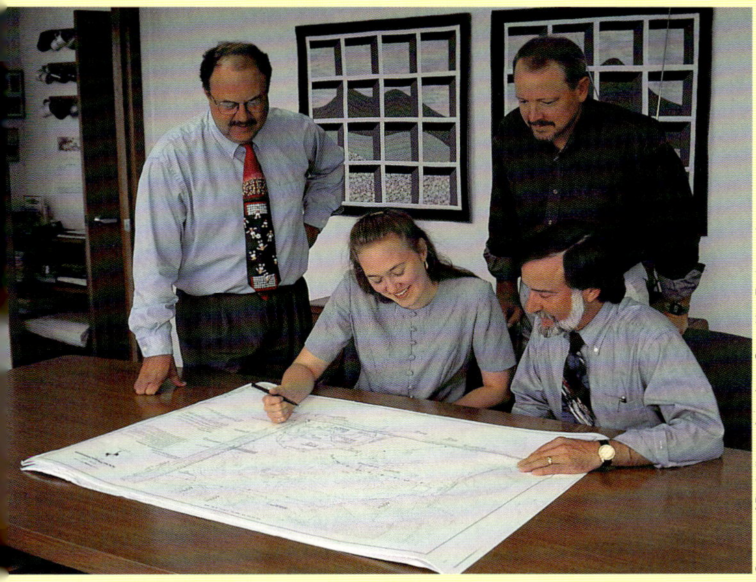

Courtesy of Penhallegon Associates Consulting Engineers, Inc.

PACE's staff works as a multi-disciplinary team that is capable of offering a broad spectrum of services to clients in both the public and private sectors.

Whether people live, work, or are just visiting in the Puget Sound Region, they benefit daily from work done by Penhallegon Associates Consulting Engineers, Inc. (PACE). While PACE is a relatively young company, its accomplishments cover a broad range of projects in several fields of expertise.

Founded in 1992 by Marty Penhallegon, PACE began with a staff that had many years of engineering experience in the Pacific Northwest. The company has broadened the expertise of its staff over the years to create a multi-disciplinary team, capable of offering its customers a complete package of services to both the private and public sector.

Providing high-quality professional engineering, planning and surveying services, PACE brings the latest knowledge and technology to a project. The company's survey teams use GPS (Global Positioning Systems) and robotics to assist in producing the most accurate drawings for engineers, planners, and construction personnel. Both the survey and engineering teams use the latest technology with CADD (Computer Aided Drafting & Design). Whether the project is a commercial site development, a municipal water system, or a complex utility grid, the PACE team provides a "one-stop-shopping" option for the customer.

PACE's customers include many development companies, architects, government entities, and numerous special-purpose districts, such as water and sewer districts. The company's projects include contracts for water supply systems, sewer systems, utility installations, and street and road design and engineering. With its broad experience in planning and project development, PACE also offers its customers valuable financial analysis and funding administration services to assure the most efficient use of customer resources.

Acknowledged as one of the top 100 fastest growing businesses in the Pacific Northwest, PACE continues to contribute significantly to the Puget Sound economy and infrastructure. In speaking about the company's accomplishments with underground utilities such as water and sewer systems, employees often quip that "we bury some of our best work." However, in addition to the water that residents drink and the lights that they turn on, one could be looking at a school, a residential neighborhood, commercial/industrial complex, or a redevelopment that was the result of PACE expertise. Key in the development success is PACE's intimate knowledge of local codes, standards, and environmental constraints such as Endangered Species Act issues.

As proud as the company is of its project accomplishments, it is equally proud of the "family" feel that PACE provides its employees and the fact that, over the years, this "family" has never lost a contract.

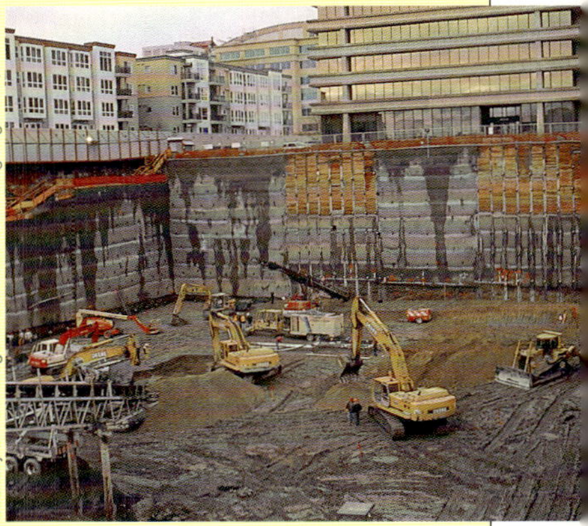

Courtesy of Penhallegon Associates Consulting Engineers, Inc.

The versatile team of experts at PACE is able to accommodate the demands of a wide range of clients, whether the project involved is a commercial site development, a municipal water system, or a complex utility grid.

Sverdrup Civil, Inc., A Jacobs Company

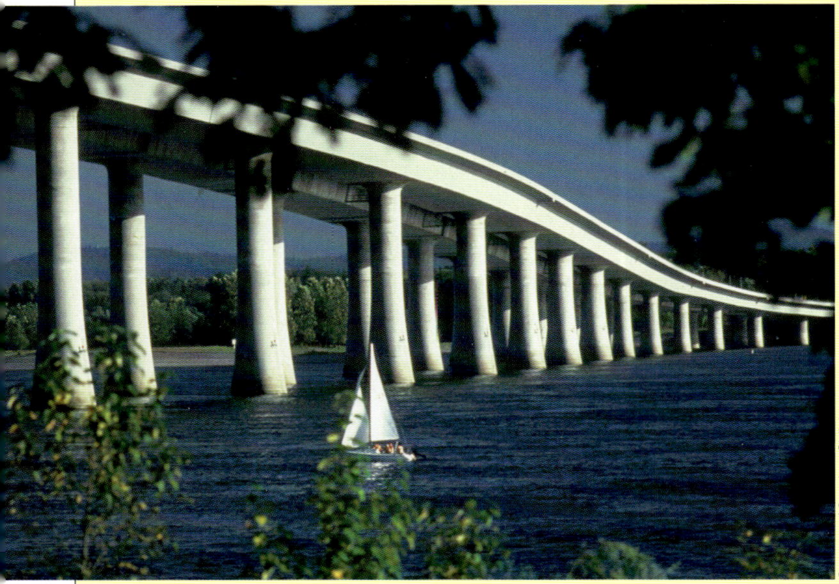

Courtesy of Sverdrup Civil, Inc.

The design of the I-205 Columbia River Bridge, near Portland, Oregon, was honored with the Grand Conceptor Award for Engineering Excellence by the American Consulting Engineers Council (ACEC).

When General Douglas MacArthur needed a construction project completed at the time of his assault on the Japanese military during World War II, he turned to his construction General – General Leif Sverdrup. The abilities of this businessman-turned-soldier helped turn the tide toward victory in the Pacific; in the post-war era, Sverdrup proved himself to be a powerful industry leader.

Originally founded in 1929, the construction firm of Sverdrup-Parcel combined Leif Sverdrup's management skills with the technical expertise of Dr. John Parcel, a Professor of Engineering at the University of Minnesota. Seeing an opportunity to contribute to the growth of the Pacific Northwest, Sverdrup established an office in 1965. In January 1999, Sverdrup Civil, Inc. joined the *Jacobs Engineering Group, Inc.* family of companies. Jacobs is one of the largest engineering and construction (E&C) firms in the world.

The Bellevue, Washington, office is responsible for projects in Washington, Idaho, Montana, Oregon, Nevada, Utah, and Alaska. As a major contractor on bridge design, transportation corridors, and waterway management in the Pacific Northwest, the projects that are easily recognizable to residents and visitors alike include the widening of Highway 520, the development of the Elliott Bay Marina, the new First Avenue South Bridge, and many others.

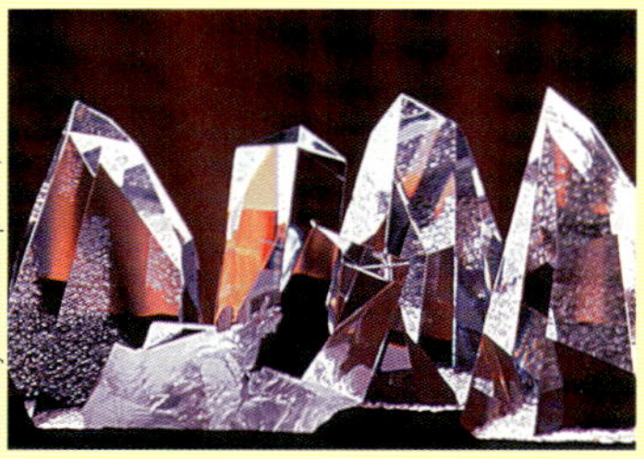

Courtesy of Sverdrup Civil, Inc.

Sverdrup is the first four-time recipient of the Grand Conceptor Award for Engineering Excellence.

Current focus on future projects includes such challenges as the protection and enhancement of fish habitat, and solutions for problems involving intermodal transportation in the busy ports of Seattle and Tacoma. Projects that facilitate the movement of goods from inbound ships to the markets of the Pacific Northwest and beyond, and from the industries and farms of the area to the docks for export are critical to the future success of the regional economy. As these projects move from the design stage to full implementation, special consideration will ensure minimal impact on the movement of travelers and commuters in the Puget Sound region.

Sverdrup Civil, Inc., a Jacobs Company, is proud of its past, present, and future contributions to the economy and livability of the Pacific Northwest and stands ready to continue its commitment to the Pacific Northwest for many years to come.

Documentary Book Publishers

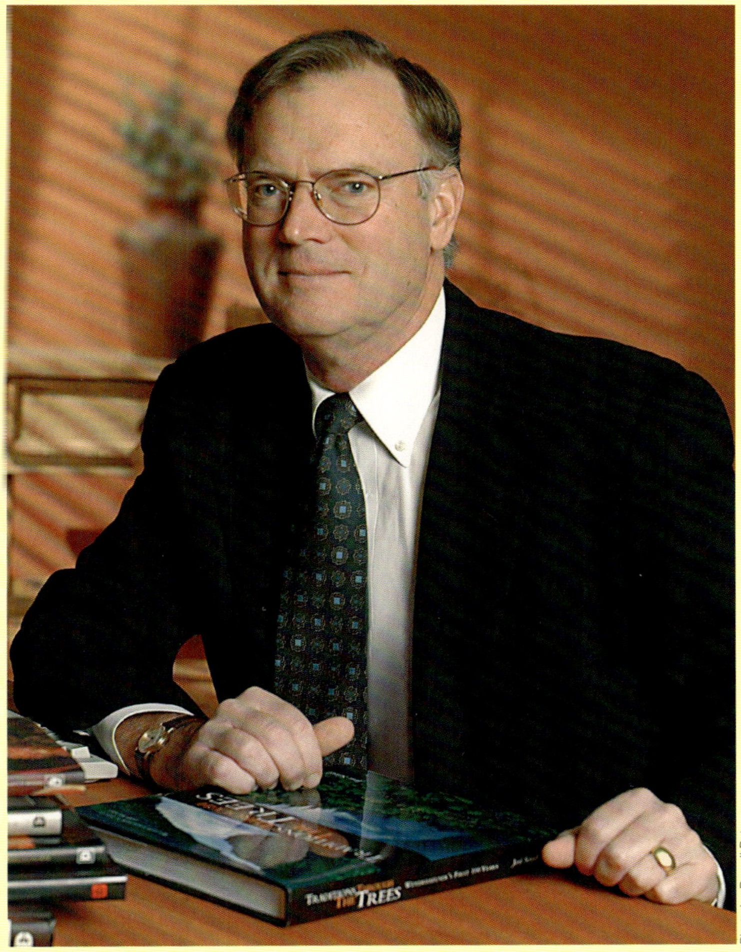

Photo by Darrell Peterson

Barry Provorse, Founder.

Documentary Book Publishers was founded in 1980 by corporate documentarian Barry Provorse. That year its first book, *PACCAR The Pursuit of Quality* was produced. Since then, the company has pursued the specialized business of documenting and publishing business and institutional history.

The company is driven by its core belief that the value of corporate and institutional history is immeasurable, and its application wide-ranging. One need only consider how a description of the origin of Weyerhaeuser's principal values helped to unify its employees' understanding of the company, how chronicling the social and legal history of the King County Bar Association enriched its members and community, and how preserving the stories of the principal western financial institutions added to the rich history of the regions they served.

Unsurpassed in integrity, credibility, and permanence, a book can be a powerful communication tool. Documentary Books has assisted companies in producing books that contribute to stockholder relations, build brand awareness, and document their origins, values, and philosophies. Its publications assist institutions such as the University of Washington in educating and motivating decision-makers, alumni, and contributors. The work of Documentary Books creates lasting impressions and preserves important legacies that might otherwise be lost to time.

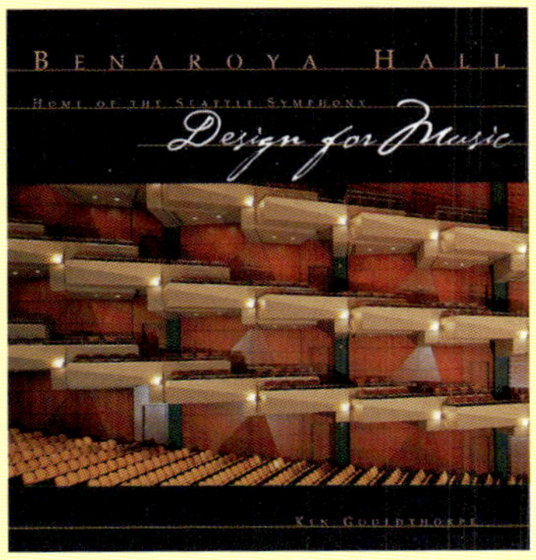

In 1999, Documentary Books produced Design for Music *for the Seattle Symphony Orchestra. Above right: The John Sarich series of cookbooks was created by Documentary Books in 1993 for Chateau Ste. Michelle.*

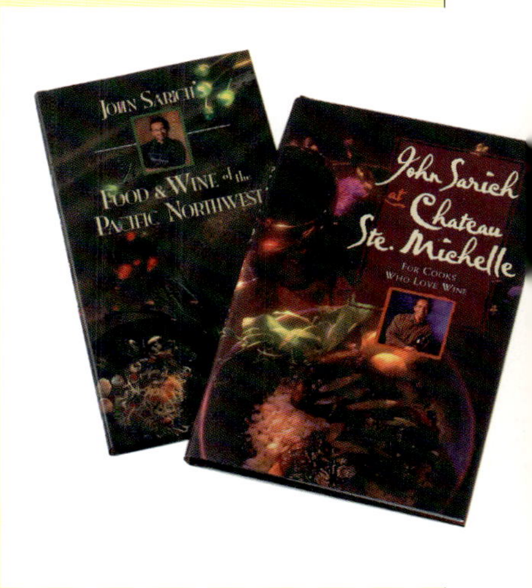

Documentary Book's client list includes Chevron, Dow Jones, The Principal, Chateau Ste. Michelle, PACCAR Inc (and its Kenworth and Peterbilt truck companies), The University of Washington, Pacific University, Pacific Northwest Ballet, Seattle Symphony Orchestra, Weyerhaeuser Company, The McCaw Foundation, and many others who believe in the power of a good story.

In 1996, Seattle-based Documentary Books merged with travel guide and regional non-fiction publisher Sasquatch Books, and together the companies publish books of lasting value to the West.

Part Two

HIGH TECHNOLOGY

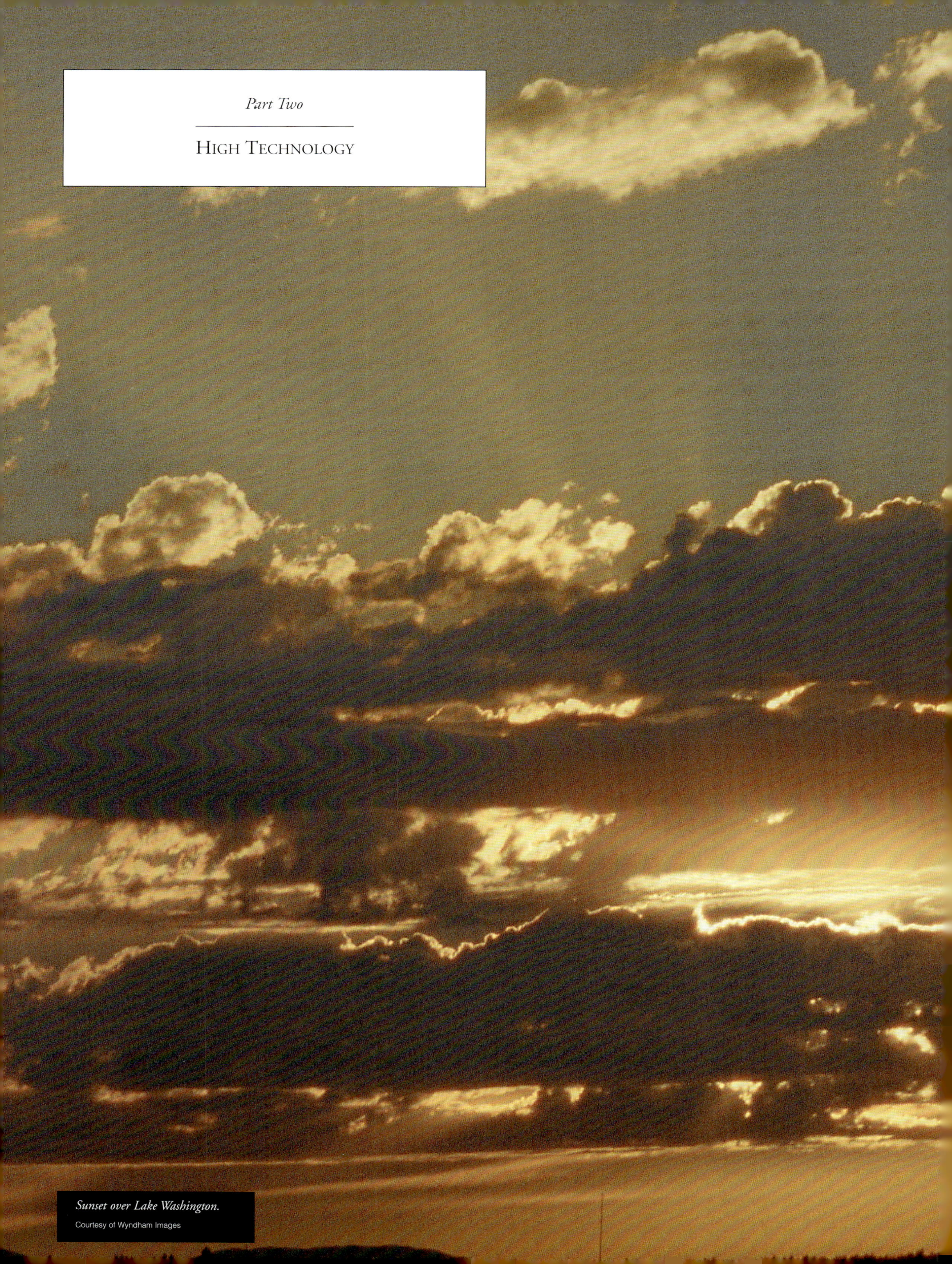

Sunset over Lake Washington.

Courtesy of Wyndham Images

Pro2Net

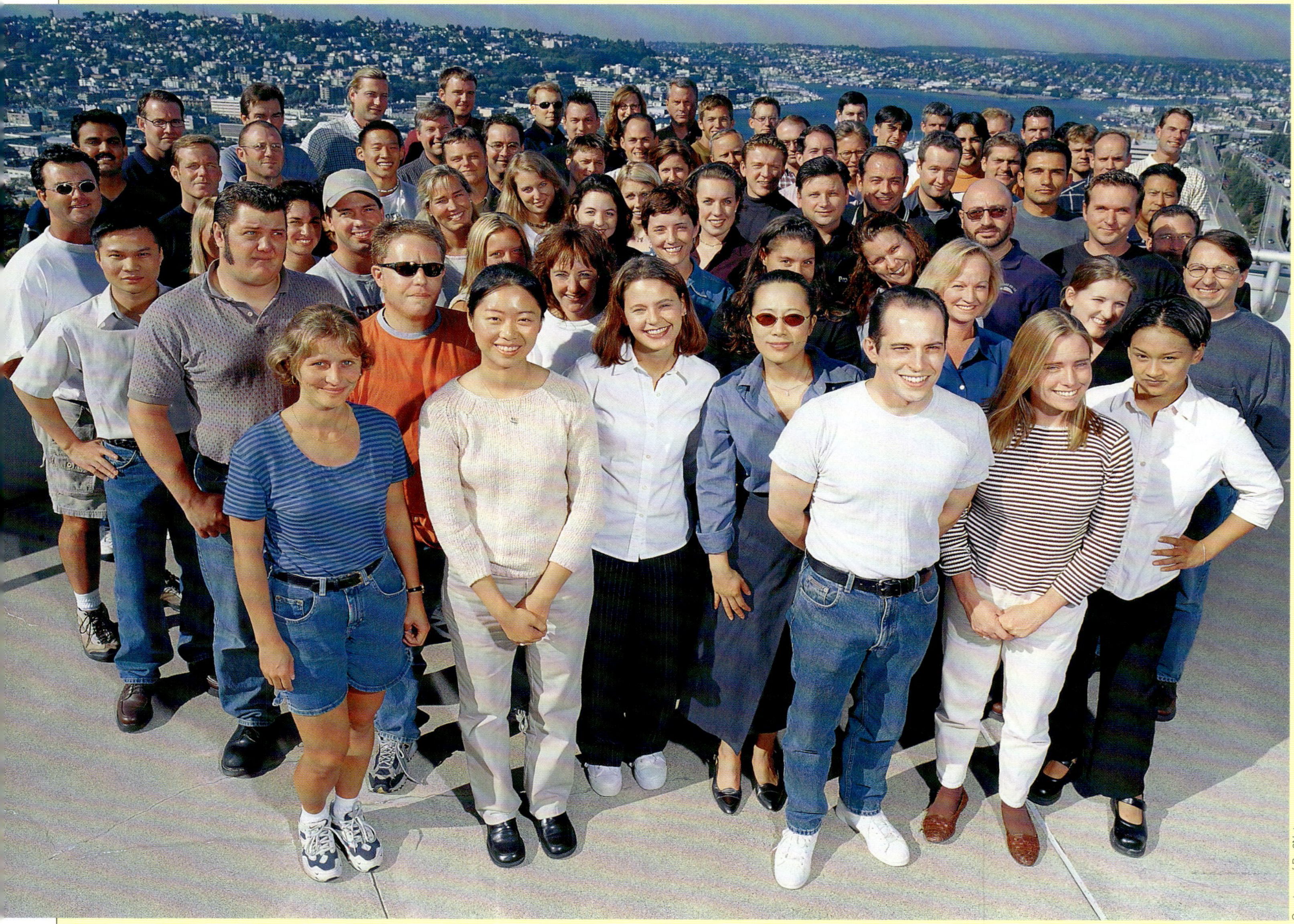

Courtesy of Pro2Net

Today, business is conducted in the blink of an eye—or the click of a mouse. Changes in the world of business happen just as quickly. Business professionals either move with the new speed of business or find themselves left behind. One company has proven itself to be quick enough to match the speed of this change—Pro2Net. The reason behind the company's ability to stay on the forefront of the business world is that the cutting edge of business *is* Pro2Net's business. Pro2Net is the most comprehensive online resource for business professionals, providing them the tools and information they need to stay ahead of the game.

In 1995, the company was established as AccountingNet, an online resource for accounting professionals. As the company grew, it changed its name to reflect the broadened scope of business services it offered. The new company, Pro2Net, had evolved from a single-focus Web site to one that encompassed five synergistic business professions: accounting, financial services, human resources, insurance, and law.

The goal of Pro2Net is to connect business professionals to the Internet. In so doing, the company can save its customers time and money, help them better serve their own clients, and enhance their careers.

Pro2Net's Web sites are the ideal place to employ the natural interrelationships that exist between the five professions. For example, the Web sites are focused on delivering unparalleled depth of business-sector-specific content in each of the five fields. This content is created, organized, and served based on relevance to each discipline. For instance, tax accounting information that is relevant to taxation law is delivered to lawyers, labor law information is delivered to human resources professionals, and financial information is delivered to insurance professionals. Intelligent content delivery across the five synergistic Web sites fulfills the new demands from today's multidiscipline professionals and their clients.

Pro2Net offers professionals news, commentary, research, and online educational products through its Web sites. Not only can professionals gather information, they can establish contacts within their own field, as well as utilize this unique forum to form relationships with professionals in other fields. The Web site itself is a meeting place for professionals across the boundaries of the five fields.

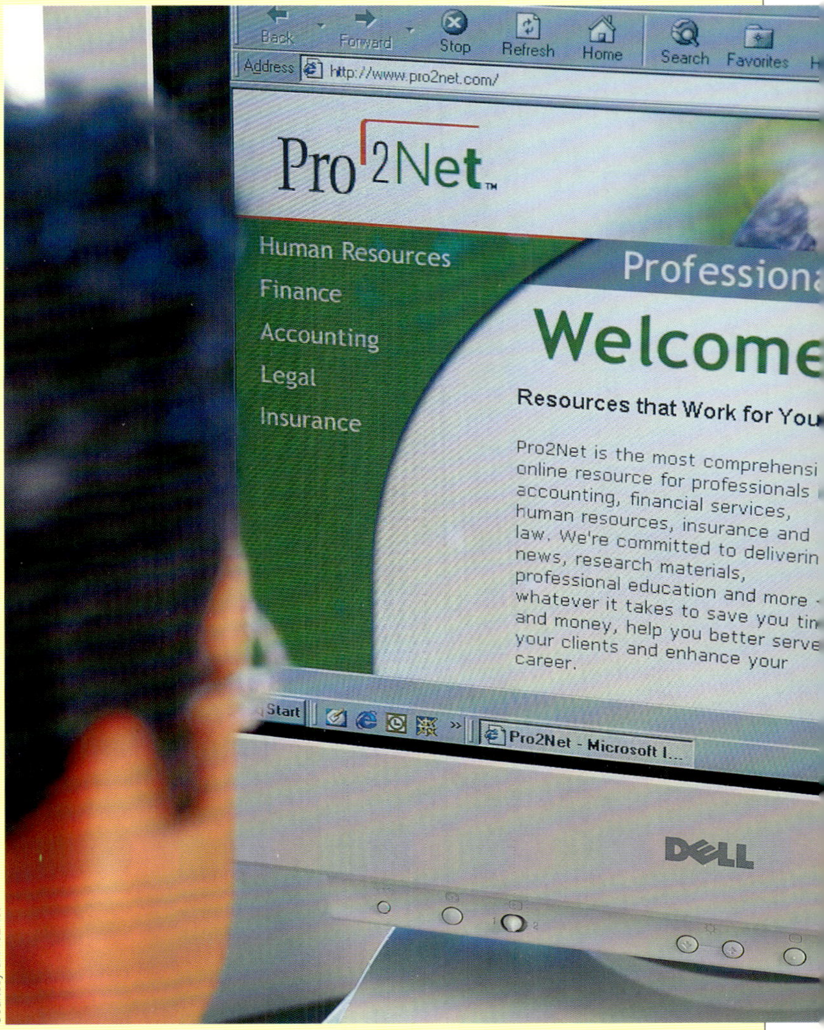

Courtesy of Pro2Net

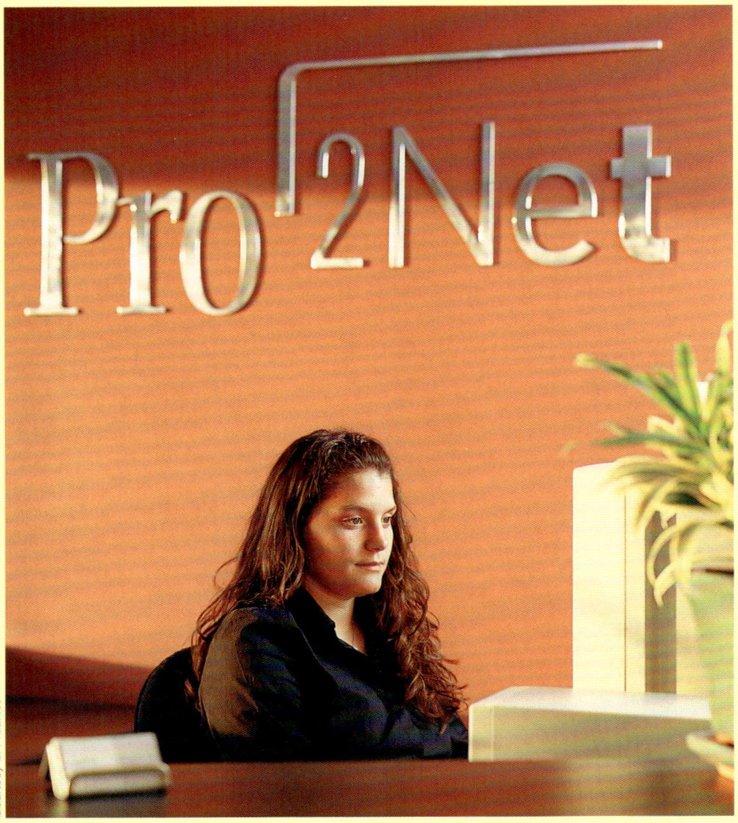

Courtesy of Pro2Net

Pro2Net is a timely and critical resource for news and trends in each of the areas. And, as much of this news focuses on issues that reflect the interrelationships between the fields, this resource is all the more valuable. Few professionals have the time to read all the information found in journals or other publications in their own field. And fewer yet would have the time for, or the access to, news about related fields. But, with Pro2Net, these limitations are overcome and valuable time and money can be saved.

The Resource Library for each type of professional includes research materials, directories, government and statistical information, forms, and more tools professionals use on a daily basis. Likewise, the Pro2Net Web site provides an important resource in the area of career management where professionals in any of the fields can monitor employment opportunities, track salary trends, and advance their careers.

Another valuable tool for the busy professional is the online marketplace created by Pro2Net. This marketplace is a source for books, software, tax guides, subscriptions to online research tools, and many other items tailored to the needs of the professional business audience. By serving professionals in the fields of accounting, financial services, human resources, insurance, and law with these critical tools, Pro2Net is making a major contribution to not only the Pacific Northwest economy, but to the global economy.

Perhaps the company's greatest competition is the "status quo"—that ingrained reluctance to change and the fear of the unknown. But the professionals that use the Pro2Net Web sites recognize that in today's fast-moving economy, the "status quo" will not advance them into the new economy. At Pro2Net, the focus is on change; the company's business thrives on change. Pro2Net inspires its professional clients to change with the evolving world of business. Also, most importantly, Pro2Net provides the tools for change.

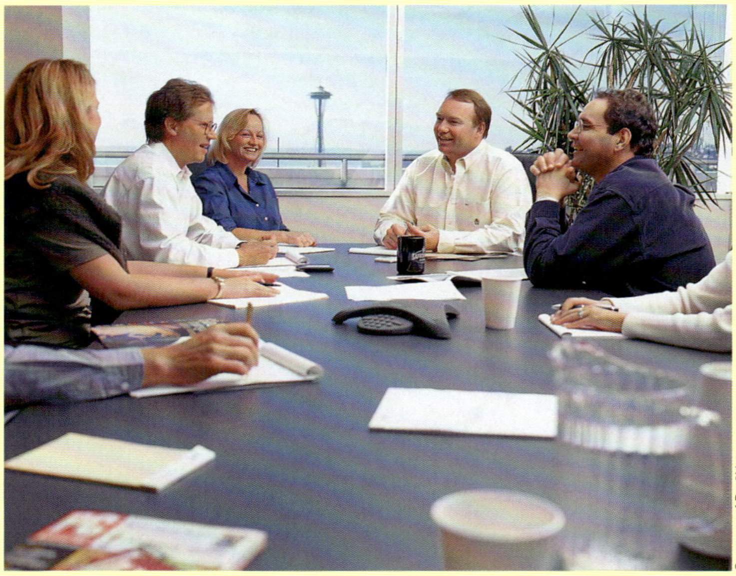

Courtesy of Pro2Net

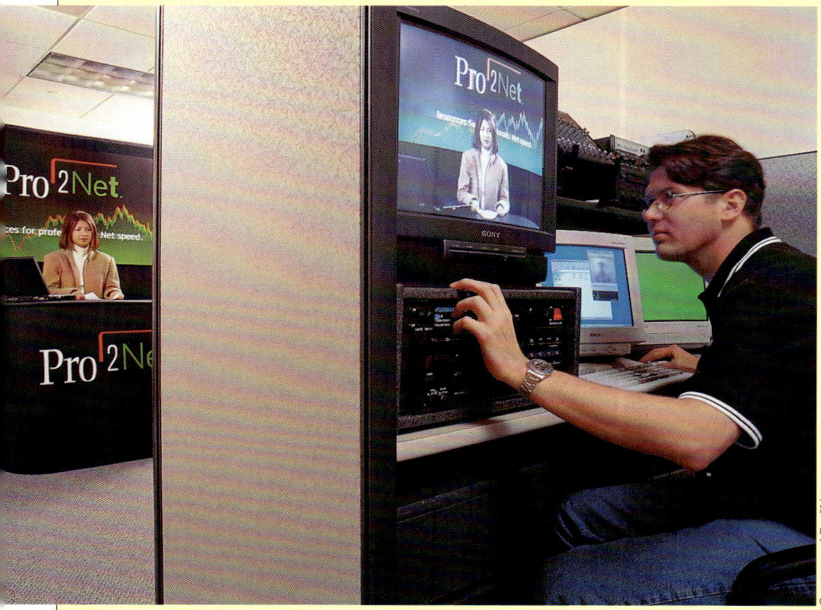

Courtesy of Pro2Net

Based on the early success of Pro2Net and the vision and expertise of its management and staff, the future of the company is not only assured, but is also beyond imagination. Perhaps the visionaries who created this powerful business tool have an idea of where it may lead in the next generation. Wherever the business community is in 2020, it will have arrived there in large part because of the resources provided by Pro2Net, and it will move from that point forward directed by the same kind of innovative and inspired business sense evident in Pro2Net today.

Onvia, Inc.

The Internet has truly leveled the playing field for small businesses that are competing in the new economy, and Onvia is on the cutting edge of helping those businesses succeed. Onvia has established its leadership position by creating the largest and most efficient online channel through which small businesses can increase their profitability. Onvia started as an online resource center for small business where they could buy and sell products and services but has evolved into much more—an exchange for small, medium, and large business as well as government entities looking for small business vendors.

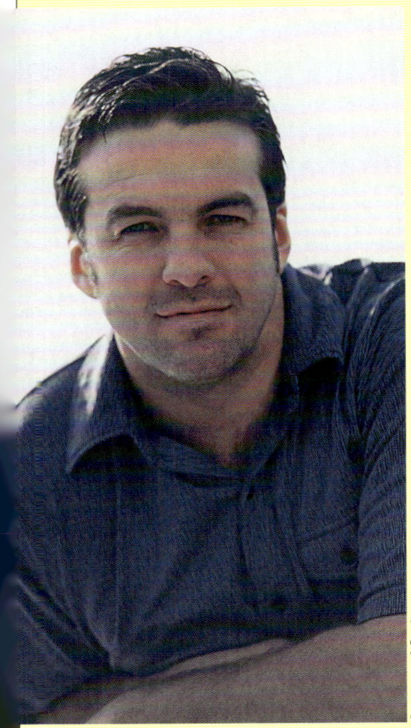
Courtesy of Onvia.com

Glenn Ballman, Chairman and Chief Executive Officer.

Onvia offers an online exchange where products and services can be bought and sold. The company's supply network of sellers increases sales effectiveness, and its demand network of buyers increases purchasing efficiency. Onvia specializes in serving the needs of small and historically under-utilized businesses in the U.S. by matching their products and services with government agencies and corporate buyers. The Onvia system automatically gathers, matches, and delivers buyer contracting opportunities to small businesses based on their unique profiles.

Onvia has also added Web hosting services to its small-business offerings, providing businesses with fast, easy, and affordable e-commerce Website solutions that can enable them to generate revenue. Onvia's Website Solutions is customized and scalable—growing as businesses grow.

In the fall of 2000, Onvia launched a strategic business alliance with VisaBusiness.com, a division of Visa U.S.A., the world's leading payment partner. Powered by Onvia, VisaBusiness.com has been designed specifically to help

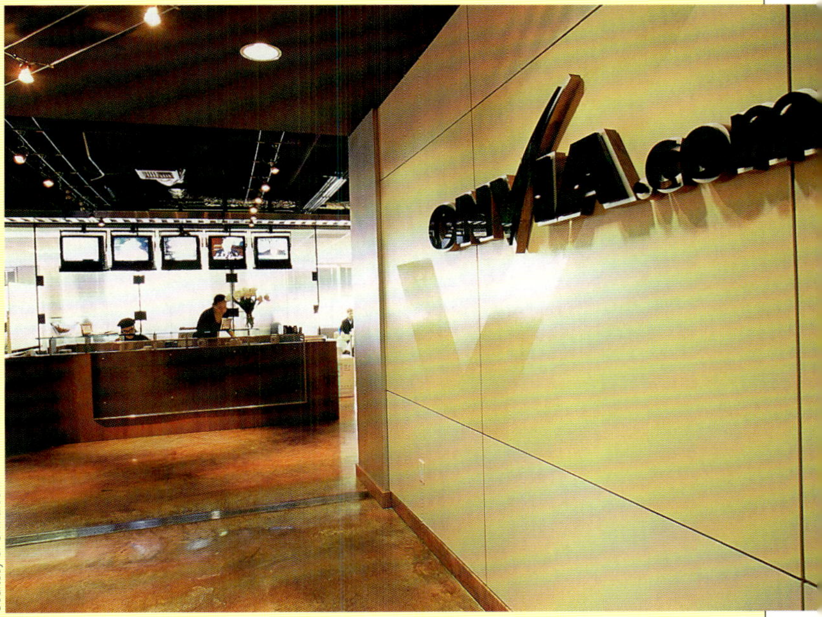

Courtesy of Onvia.com

small businesses use the Web more effectively for buying and selling products and services. Visa and Onvia build and deliver additional value-added online offers exclusively for VisaBusiness cardholders.

Onvia has partnered with the most prestigious small-business associations in the U.S. including the U.S. Small Business Administration, National Small Business United, American Management Association, Networking and Systems Professionals Association, and the American Business Women's Association. Onvia has also partnered with many Chambers of Commerce including Seattle, Detroit, Philadelphia, Chicagoland, Buffalo, Providence, Austin, and Orlando, among others, making Onvia the leading exchange helping small businesses succeed.

ATL Ultrasound

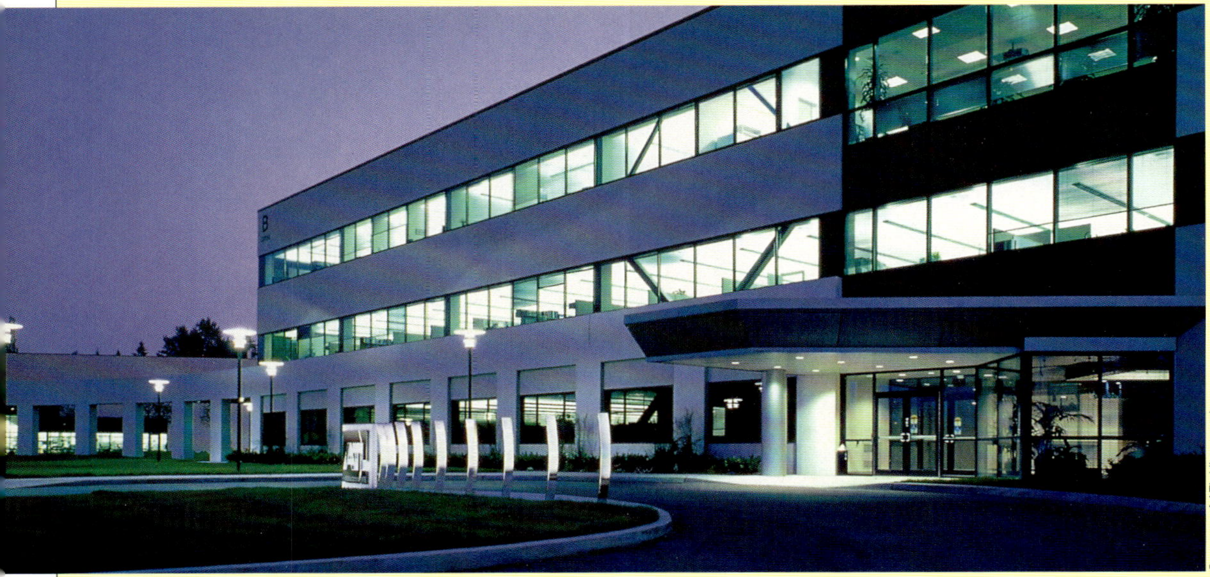

ATL Ultrasound is headquartered in Bothell, Washington.

ATL Ultrasound, a Philips Medical Systems company, is a worldwide leader in the development, manufacture, distribution, and service of diagnostic medical ultrasound systems. ATL systems are used in radiology, cardiology, obstetrics and gynecology, vascular, musculoskeletal, and intraoperative applications at more than 33,000 medical centers around the world.

Leader in Innovation

Over the years, ATL has accumulated an impressive list of breakthroughs in innovation, starting in 1977 with the first pulsed Doppler device. ATL was also the first to use all-digital HDI broadband technology and is at the forefront of recent advances in contrast and harmonic imaging on the HDI® 3000 and HDI 5000 systems.

The company is also the world's largest supplier of ultrasound scanheads, employing the latest in technology and manufacturing advances. ATL manufactures over 30,000 scanheads yearly for ATL systems and other ultrasound providers. This technology provides unprecedented views during surgical procedures. ATL's uniquely designed scanheads render a vital, dynamic anatomical depiction during abdominal and vascular surgery.

The company's success is due in large part to its growing family of HDI all-digital ultrasound systems. "ATL pioneered all-digital ultrasound a good decade before others in the industry, and now our expertise and product development advantages are taking ultrasound to places it has never been before," says Timothy C. Mickelson, president and CEO of ATL Ultrasound.

Digital Expertise: The Foundation for Continuing Innovations

In what is being described by leading radiologists as the most important development in ultrasound in more than a decade, ATL recently unveiled a sophisticated new ultrasound technology which will significantly improve the modality's effectiveness as a diagnostic tool. The new technology, called SonoCT™ Real-time Compound Imaging, uses advanced computer capabilities to compile up to nine times the information provided by conventional ultrasound, delivering clear, crisp ultrasound images for significantly improved diagnostic information. The ability to visualize pathologies such as breast lesions has taken a

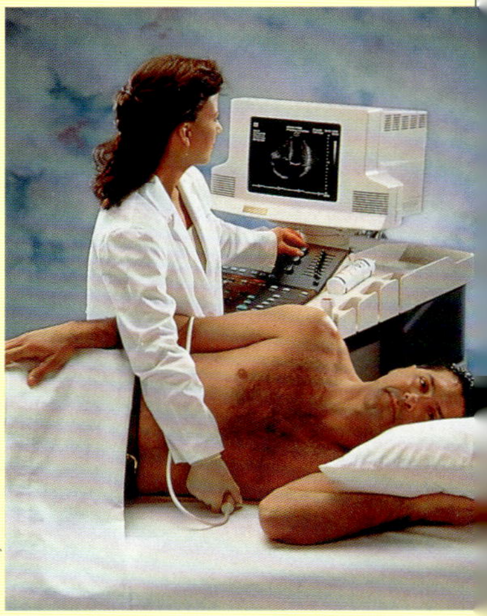

ATL is a worldwide leader in all-digital ultrasound systems.

Linking technologies on HDI ultrasound systems facilitate electronic data management and remote consultation.

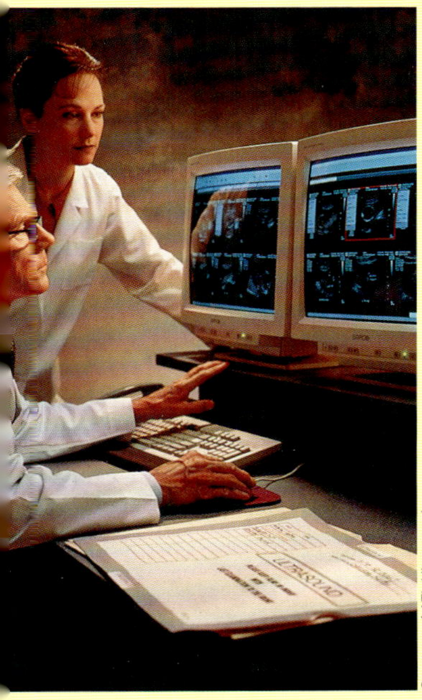
Courtesy of ATL Ultrasound

great leap forward, adding a vital ability to identify smaller lesions sooner.

"What has impressed me the most about SonoCT Real-time Compound Imaging is the amount of information we are seeing. We now realize what we were not seeing with conventional ultrasound, and it is quite significant," reports Dr. Christopher Merritt, M.D., Professor of Radiology and Director of Special Projects, Thomas Jefferson University, and one of the world's most renowned radiologists.

A Commitment to Education

The company is dedicated to the innovation and development of ultrasound technology that improves the quality and productivity of health care worldwide. This dedication includes a commitment to comprehensive education, training, and service programs that raise diagnostic confidence and productivity for clinicians and labs around the world.

Annually, ATL holds over 200 clinical educational events, reaching well over 10,000 professionals worldwide. "Our roots are in education," says Mickelson. "The company was founded on a technology agreement with the University of Washington, and we continue to be a technology partner with the university."

Pioneering New Frontiers

After extensive evaluation of a number of ultrasound systems, NASA has chosen ATL's HDI 5000 system to be onboard the International Space Station, which will be launched in the year 2000. Astronauts will use the system to conduct tests that evaluate the effects of zero gravity on blood flow, the heart and other organs, joints, and ligaments. The HDI 5000's sophisticated digital platform and connectivity capabilities plus ATL's reputation for maintaining the highest quality standards were important factors for the selection. The system's digital architecture is imperative for connecting Earth and the space station for study transmissions and diagnostics.

A Vital Part of the Northwest

Although ATL is now a worldwide company that is part of Philips Medical Systems (which is in turn a part of Royal Philips Electronics, one of the world's largest electronics companies), ATL's roots remain solidly in the Pacific Northwest, with headquarters located in Bothell, Washington. The company's momentum has been astonishing, with annual revenues topping $465 million. "A lot of our growth comes from being based in the Seattle area," says Mickelson. "We are at the pulse point of technology innovations, and our relationship with the University of Washington continues to be a foundation in our success."

With such a solid foundation and sound fundamentals, ATL Ultrasound's vitality and success are secured, as is their determined drive to maintain a leadership role in the cutting-edge technology of diagnostic medical ultrasound systems.

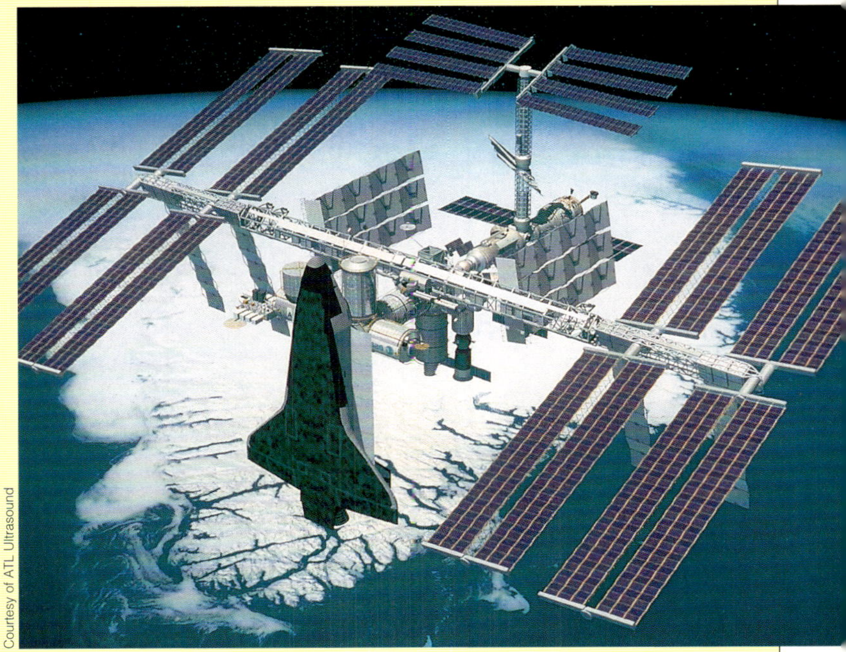
Courtesy of ATL Ultrasound

The HDI® 5000 system was selected for the international space station. It will be used to conduct tests on the effects of zero gravity on blood flow, the heart, and other organs.

RealNetworks, Inc.

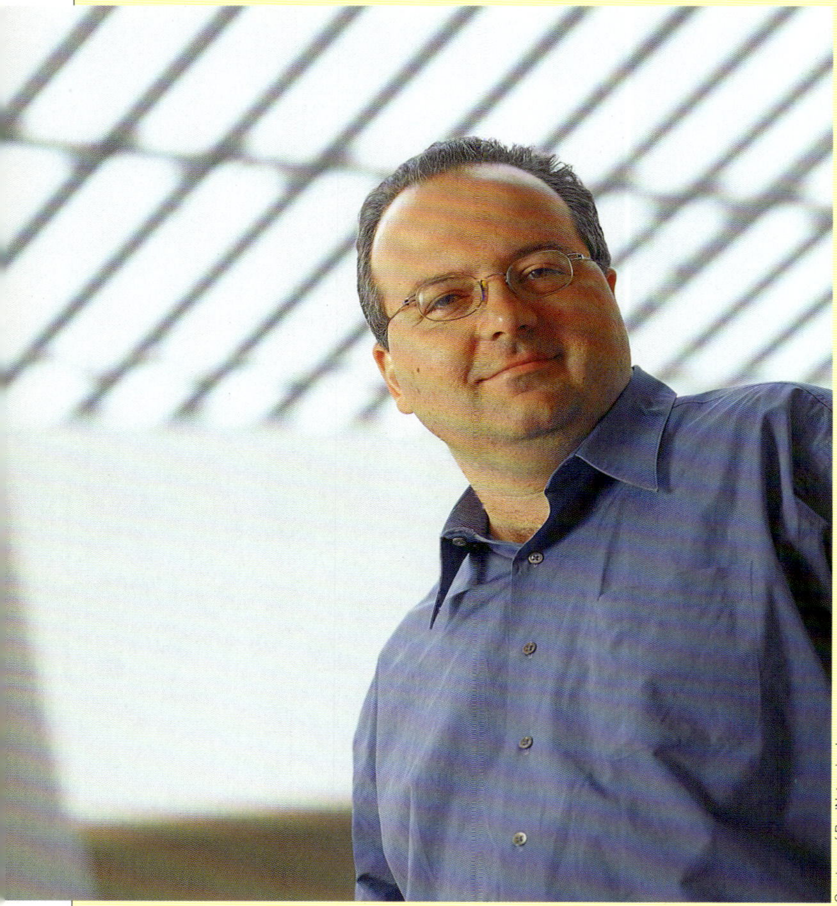

RealNetworks founder and CEO, Rob Glaser.

In the ever-expanding world of technology and communications, few companies have grown faster than RealNetworks, Inc. RealNetworks is among the vanguard of companies that are developing new concepts and expanding horizons for Internet users.

Originally named Progressive Networks, the company was founded in 1994 by Rob Glaser. A former Microsoft employee who managed Microsoft Word, Glaser then became Vice President of Multimedia and Consumer Systems. Upon leaving Microsoft in 1994, Glaser began work on a new business, focusing on the concept that there was an emerging connection between the worlds of media, computing, and communications. Rob Glaser's vision was not to create that connection, but to be there, with a viable product, when the connection took place.

Launching its first products in 1995, the company began what has been a phenomenal growth curve that shows no signs of leveling off. With the introduction of RealAudio and RealPlayer, the process of "streaming" media over the Internet captured the interest of consumers and potential partners alike. The new systems were offered as free "downloads" on the Internet and their popularity produced immediate records in the computer and software industry. Within less than five years, RealPlayer moved from zero users to over 115,000,000 users, with download rates as high as 175,000 per day, or more than two downloads per second.

The company name was changed to RealNetworks, Inc. in 1997, but the capacity to deliver streaming audio and music across the Internet was only a beginning for RealNetworks. In keeping with its founder's vision, the company has remained at the leading edge of new technologies with its introductions of RealVideo and updated versions of its earlier products which allow for the transmission and storage of MP3 and MPEG formats. With these products, the company has provided consumers the capacity to download CD quality music and with another tool, RealJukebox, the potential to create an extensive collection of music from every possible genre.

Rob Glaser once told an interviewer that if he had never created RealNetworks, his alternate dream would be to throw 95-mile-an-hour fastballs and to win the Cy Young Award in Major League Baseball. The fact is that in the software industry of the early twenty-first century, Glaser and RealNetworks are still throwing 95-mile-an-hour fastballs, and an occasional curve. In a highly competitive industry, RealNetworks has been able to stay ahead of the heavy hitters and has consistently maintained as much as an 85 percent share of the market in their area of specialty.

With all of its successes, RealNetworks has maintained a high level of commitment to the community in which it operates. Although the company operates in a global marketplace and has offices in numerous markets around the world, the company has grown roots in the downtown Seattle area where it has established its headquarters. As members of the Downtown Association, RealNetworks works closely with other area businesses to maintain and enhance the environment of downtown for its employees and the community's citizens. In addition, the company has made a significant commitment to social issues through a promise of five percent of all profits being directed to charities. As a part of this social commitment, RealNetworks has launched WebActive.com, an online source giving voice to progressive political and social opinion, news, and activism. WebActive.com also provides numerous resources to support non-profit organizations in the communication and promotion of their causes.

As a business still in its infancy, RealNetworks realizes annual revenues between $200-250 million. The most common question asked of Rob Glaser and his managers is, "How do you make money, if you give your product away?" The answers are quite simple, if not immediately obvious. With a user base in the hundreds of millions, few businesses can come close to the advertising potential of RealNetworks and advertisers clamor for the opportunity to get their message before audiences of this size. In addition, the free downloads of RealNetworks products is only the first level of sophistication and capability and the "Plus" versions (or upgrades) are purchased in equally astonishing numbers. Finally, the software technology developed by RealNetworks has created the potential for full-spectrum broadcasting over the Internet and has brought in customers like ABC, NBC, CBS, ESPNet, FOX, Warner Bros., MGM, MCI, Amazon.com...the list goes on.

And so does RealNetworks.

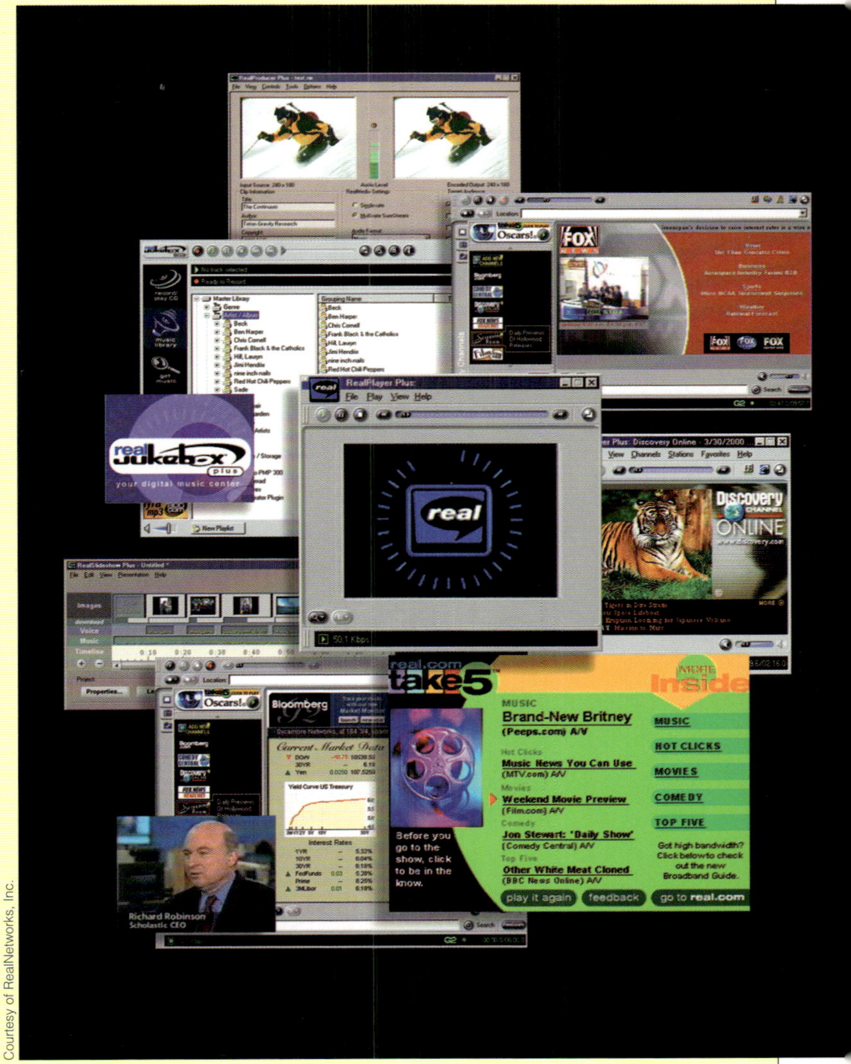

Courtesy of RealNetworks, Inc.

Nintendo of America, Inc.

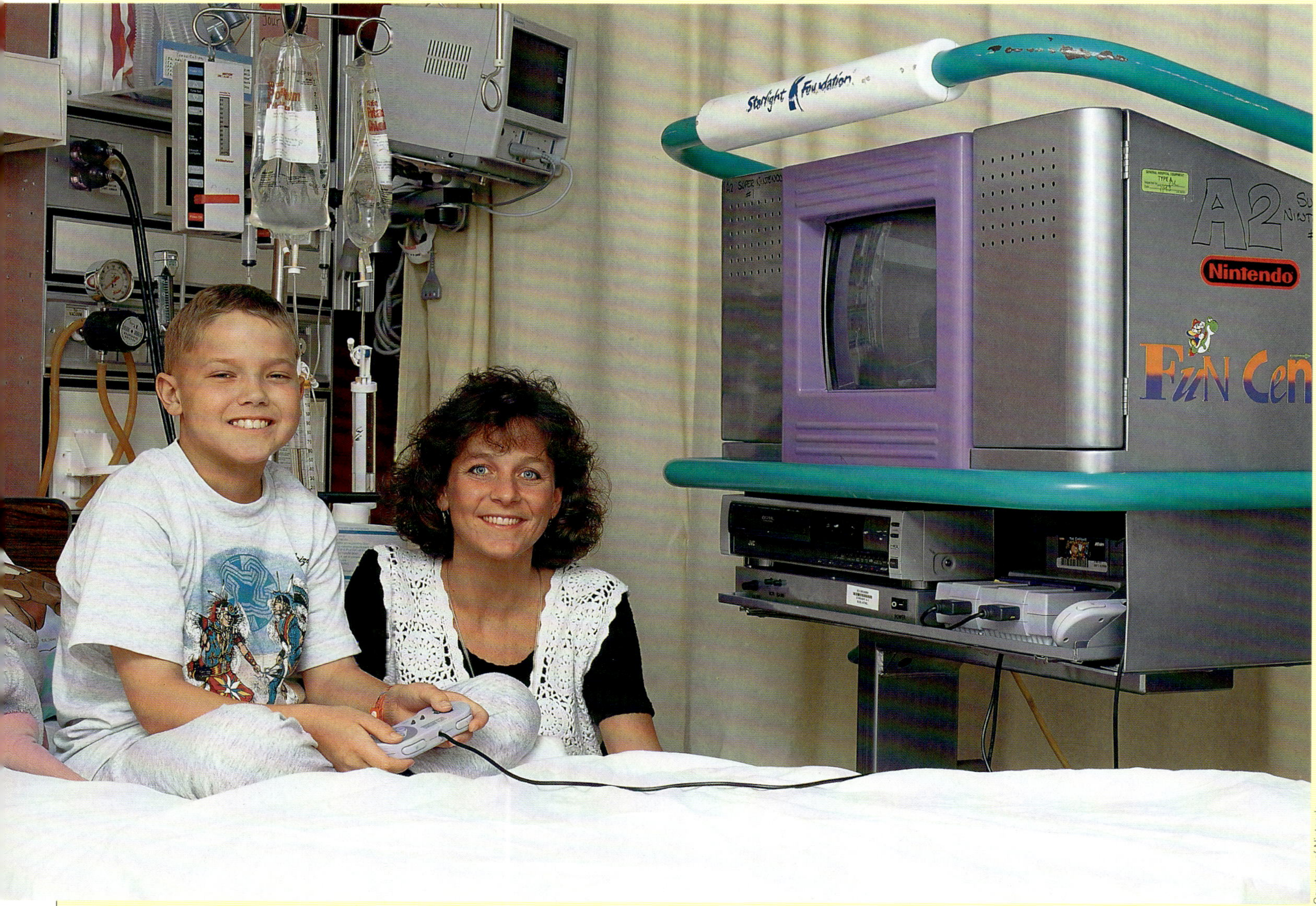

Courtesy of Nintendo

Nintendo Fun Centers provide hours of pleasure to sick children across the United States.

To describe a business as being "the leading interactive entertainment company" might have had little meaning a few years ago. But in today's intensely competitive environment, it is a hard-won, billion-dollar title that belongs to Nintendo. According to one description of the Nintendo phenomenon, "It's the only popular entertainment art where story telling is a shared responsibility with the end user." Nintendo has maintained its cutting-edge, state-of-the-art position in the forefront of this exciting arena where art and technology converge to create a new entertainment experience.

Video game super heroes like Mario, Donkey Kong, Pikachu, and Link have engaged new generations of devotees, and

Nintendo's sports-related games offer thrilling, lifelike involvement for the competitive spirit. Demand for Nintendo products has been intense. When Pokemon Yellow was released in 2000, it became the fastest selling video game in history. Over one million copies were sold in two weeks, at a rate of nearly one game per second. That record is only one of many industry-leading milestones for Nintendo.

Nintendo of America's offices in Redmond represent the Japanese parent company as operational headquarters for the Western Hemisphere. This King County presence contributes significantly to the Pacific Northwest economy.

The Redmond campus also includes a unique educational institution called the DigiPen Institute of Technology, the world's first four-year program awarding a Bachelor of Science Degree in Real-Time Interactive Simulation.

Nintendo and its employees are heavily involved in the community in which they work. In addition to the many contributions to local charities, Nintendo has a strong commitment to, and active participation in, The Starlight Foundation. The Foundation is a national organization established to grant the wishes of critically ill children and to provide some lighthearted fun in their lives. Through The Starlight Foundation, Nintendo donates interactive games to children's hospitals. A mobile Nintendo Fun Center can roll to a child's bedside and offer hours of relief from the suffering and boredom of a long hospital stay. One estimate suggested that these Fun Centers reach over 57,000 children every month.

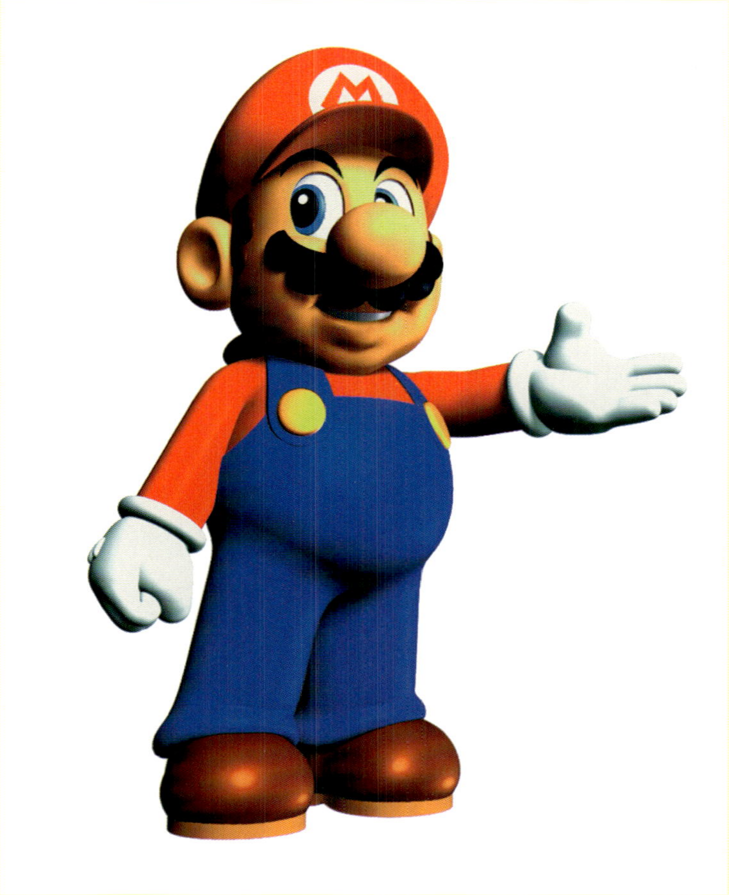

Courtesy of Nintendo

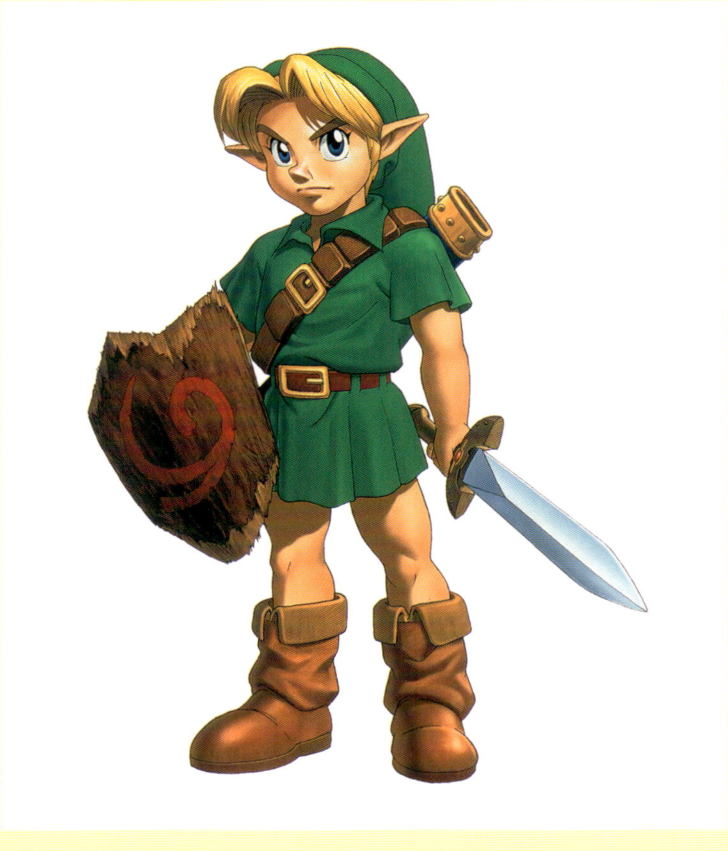

Courtesy of Nintendo

Company officials at Nintendo refer to their corporation as "playful" and in touch with its consumers. Perhaps this is the industry leader's key to its success and its ability to bring great joy to gamesters around the world.

ConneXt

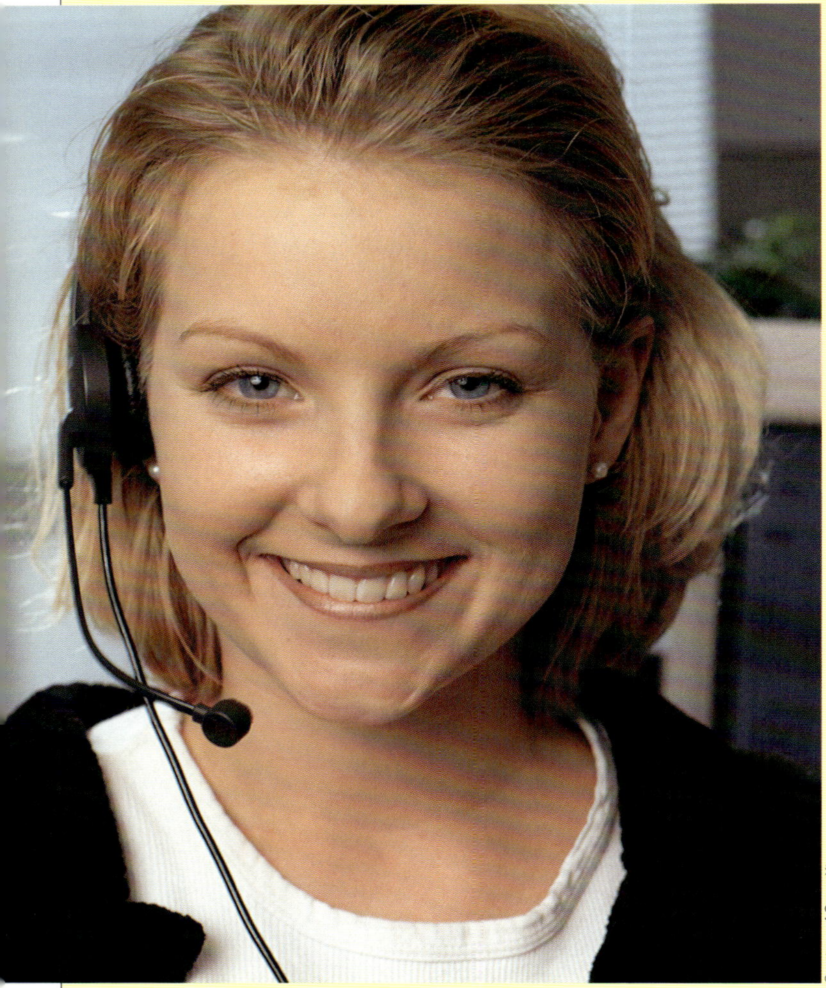

ConneXt develops billing and customer-care software specifically designed for the unique needs of the utilities industry.

In the world of business, one plan for success is to find a need and fulfill it. An even better plan is to anticipate a need and be the first, and the best, to fulfill it. ConneXt, one of the Pacific Northwest's newest cutting-edge businesses, used the later approach.

As the 1990s progressed, the Internet undoubtedly transformed the business landscape. Customer expectations grew more sophisticated, most notably when it came to dealing with energy providers.

Fortunately, advances in technology were also making it possible for utilities to meet the growing demands of their customers. ConneXt was formed in 1996 as a developer of billing and customer-care software that enabled utilities to thrive in today's complex, customer-centric energy marketplace.

ConneXt's primary product is ConsumerLinX™, a customer information system (CIS) for utilities. On April 10, 2000, ConsumerLinX™ was fully implemented at Puget Sound Energy, and ConneXt began marketing its system throughout North America.

A key advantage of the new technology is its flexibility and readiness to adapt to changes in the energy marketplace. For the energy consumer, primary benefits include the system's ability to provide market-based pricing for energy as well as real-time communications between customers and the energy provider regarding usage and billing.

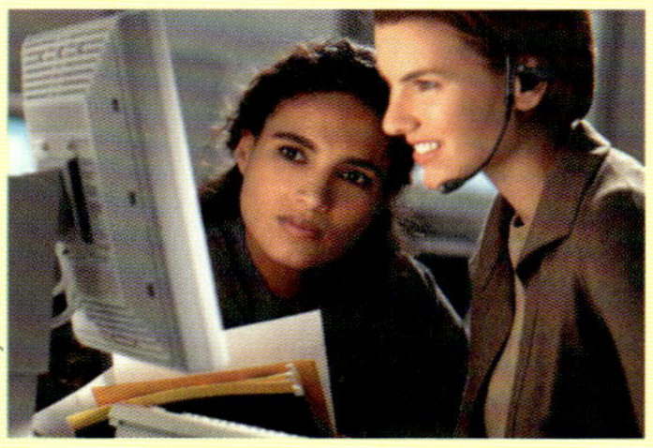

ConsumerLinX™ is ConneXt's primary product. It is a customer information system (CIS) for utilities.

For high-usage industrial customers, the system's versatility provides major cost-saving advantages. These high-value customers demand and receive more complex energy pricing arrangements based on summarized usage across multiple sites or incorporating flexible time-of-use pricing—often more complex than legacy utility systems can accommodate. This means that the bills for these customers are calculated by hand, creating a potential source of errors. ConsumerLinX™ offers unprecedented complex billing power with incomparable accuracy that allows utilities to rapidly develop and offer such arrangements to keep their industrial customers happy.

Benefits of the new system include private customer access to account information over the Internet, e-mail, fax, or telephone to monitor energy usage; customer choices about time of the month for bill payment; and customer options for bill payment through electronic transfer or even over the Internet.

After a few short years, the new and promising company has grown to over 200 employees, and its product serves over one million customers. ConneXt has certainly made a major contribution to the utilities industry and has established itself as an influential component of the King County economy.

LapLink Inc.

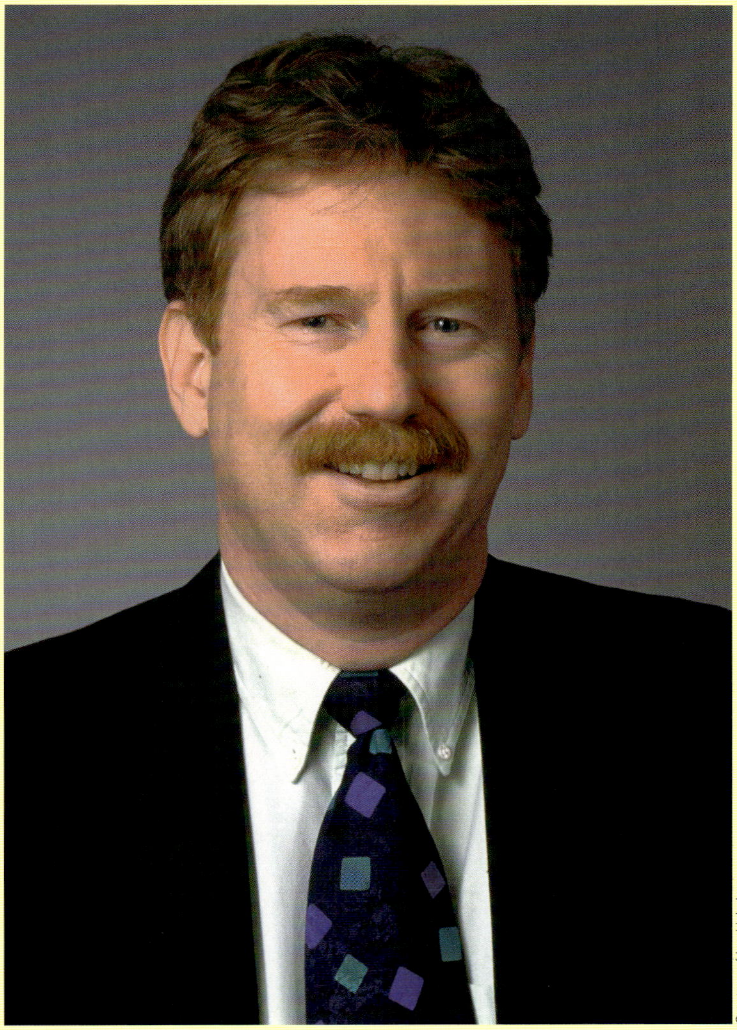

Courtesy of LapLink, Inc.

Mark Eppley, Founder and Chief Executive Officer of LapLink, Inc.

LapLink Inc. is a company that, just a few years ago, would have defied description. At the turn of the millennium, there were 80 employees and yet the company stretched worldwide. In the context of e-commerce, LapLink cannot be labeled a "small" company. As a specialist in document transfer software, LapLink estimates that in the first 13 years of its existence more than 2.5 trillion computer files have been transferred using its technology. Today, more than 2 billion file transfers take place every week using LapLink technology.

Founded by Mark Eppley in 1983, the company, originally known as Traveling Software, offered its first product to the market in 1986. The company's name change coincided with the release of LapLink 2000 in September 1999. The new product, carrying a name now very familiar to business users, had more copies downloaded in the first 25 days of its release than were sold in the first year of the original LapLink product. Today, LapLink has two new products that were released in October 2000, PCSync and LapLink Gold, which replaced LapLink 2000.

Designed to provide easier and faster connections and transfer of files for remote or traveling workers, LapLink technology now reaches into every aspect of the Internet market. With its patented SpeedSyncâ technology, LapLink can reduce file transfer time by transferring only the changes in the file rather than the entire document. The results are savings in both time and money. Industry estimates suggest that users can save as much as 86 cents on every dollar of connect time using this technology.

Mark Eppley, who stepped away from the company for a period of time and has returned to be its CEO, has vowed to maintain LapLink's position as the leader in file transfer technology. What started as a small company that produced a cable that connected a laptop and a desktop computer, has now become a world leader through that global cable called the Internet.

LapLink, though comparatively new in the greater Seattle area's "Silicon Forest," has established itself as a community partner, helping local businesses reach out to their global markets in a much more efficient manner and allowing those businesses' employees to maintain contact with their home offices from anywhere on the globe.

Aventail

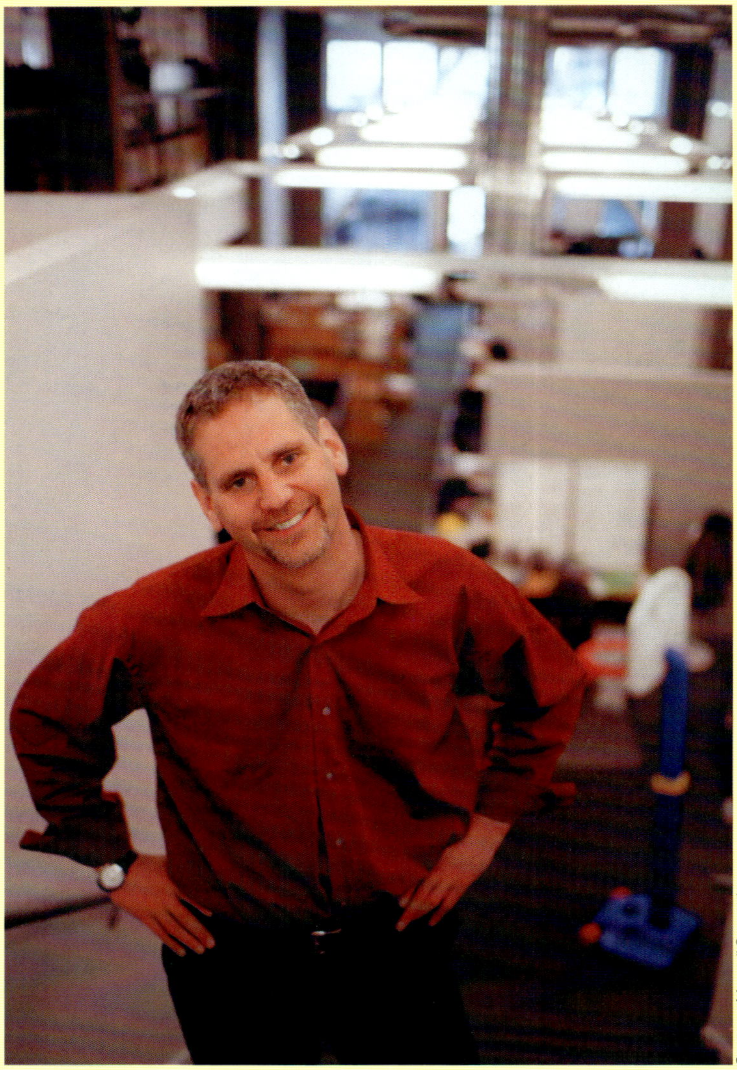

Aventail's President and Chief Executive Officer, Evan Kaplan.

When the name Aventail was suggested for a startup software company intended to develop security technology for business Internet users, it seemed a little strange, and perhaps ironic, to the company's founder. The reason was that he knew the word as a cheat code that allowed computer-game players to bypass certain levels. This notion was the very opposite of the purpose of the software technology being developed. But when it was discovered that Aventail was also the name of a piece of fourteenth-century French armor that protected the throat, the new company owners knew they had found the ideal company identification.

The software product being produced by Aventail was designed precisely to protect the throat, and other vital organs, of any business. Originally, it was a software program offering greater security to businesses that were embracing the Internet and creating links with other business entities. This key Aventail product soon became a full-service plan through which Aventail provided companies with a secure environment for electronic business. It required a set-up time of only ten weeks instead of the ten months that were needed when businesses installed the system themselves.

For many businesses, the growth of the Internet has necessitated greater acceptance of electronic business with customers, vendors, and business partners. With its product, Aventail helps businesses improve production, cut costs, increase sales, and eliminate fears of inappropriate access to critical company information. The infrastructure used is called a Business Partner Network, also known as an extranet. Aventail is an extranet service provider (ESP).

A Business Partner Network allows companies to securely extend their applications to clients, customers, employees, contractors, suppliers, and other authorized partners over the Internet. Authorized users can access it anytime, anywhere, while the company's information and resources remain secure.

Using Aventail's service, a company's vendor can monitor parts inventory and order a new shipment before production workers realize a shortage. Likewise, financial partners can monitor cash-flow needs and transfer funds to maintain fiscal stability. In each case, any user can go only as far as allowed by confidential passwords, and only into those realms of the company's business as is appropriate to the individual's function.

Aventail is at the forefront of the surge of high technology, meeting needs that were never considered only a decade ago. With the ever-increasing challenges raised in the ever-expanding virtual world of the Internet, Aventail offers businesses a much-needed layer of protection—and thereby living up to its fourteenth-century namesake.

Microsoft Corporation

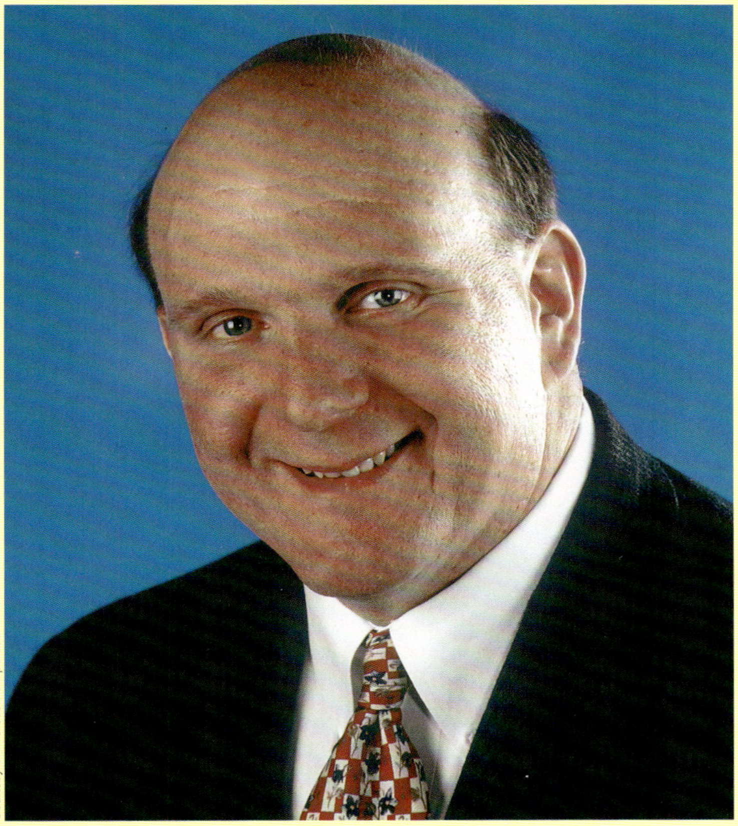

Steve Ballmer, Microsoft Chief Executive Officer.

History and Background

When Bill Gates and Paul Allen founded Microsoft 25 years ago, they had a vision: Every desk in every home across America would have a personal computer. A revolutionary idea at the time, that mission has since transformed computing technology into a powerful tool that consumers and businesses around the world use every day.

Products

As a global leader in software for personal and business computing, Microsoft today strives to produce innovative products and services that empower people, any time, any place, and on any device. The company's products include PC and network operating systems, productivity applications, interactive media, and online services. Most of them are available in over 30 languages in more than 50 countries.

But Microsoft also understands that success is about more than making great products. In addition to fostering a cutting-edge vision of technology, the company also nurtures corporate values such as integrity, diversity, and community, which are the cornerstones of the company's success and capture its spirit and day-to-day business practices.

Community Outreach

Microsoft's philosophy—if you provide the resources people need, they will accomplish great things—is the foundation of the company's business and its community affairs efforts. Microsoft makes grants of cash, software, and technical support to nonprofit organizations worldwide to help communities realize the benefits of information technology. It also supports Microsoft employees who take an active role in their community through volunteer and matching gift programs. As an example of the success of such a program, Microsoft employees donated more than $12.6 million in cash, $12.7 million in software, and countless volunteer hours in 1999 alone.

The Shape of the Future

Microsoft knows it is *people*—both consumers and developers—who shape the face of technology today and tomorrow. The company's commitment to innovation and its reliance on customer feedback are sure indicators that the best is yet to come.

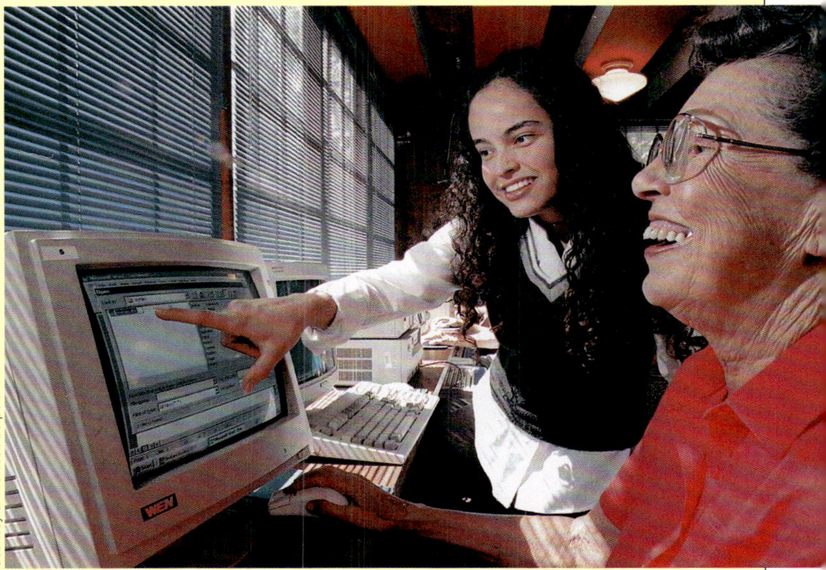

Microsoft strives to empower people with innovative products and services.

Part Two

MANUFACTURING

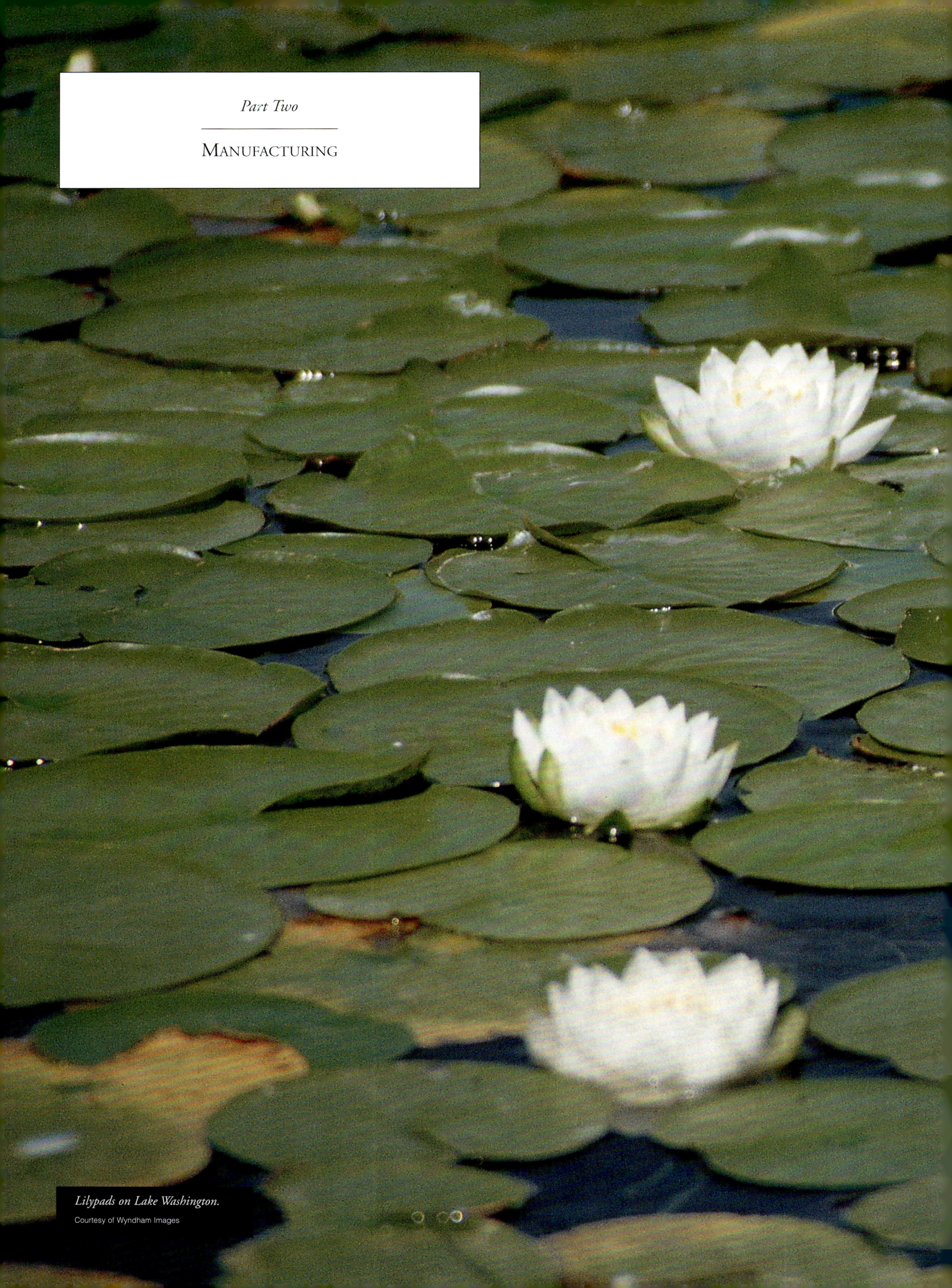

Lilypads on Lake Washington.

Courtesy of Wyndham Images

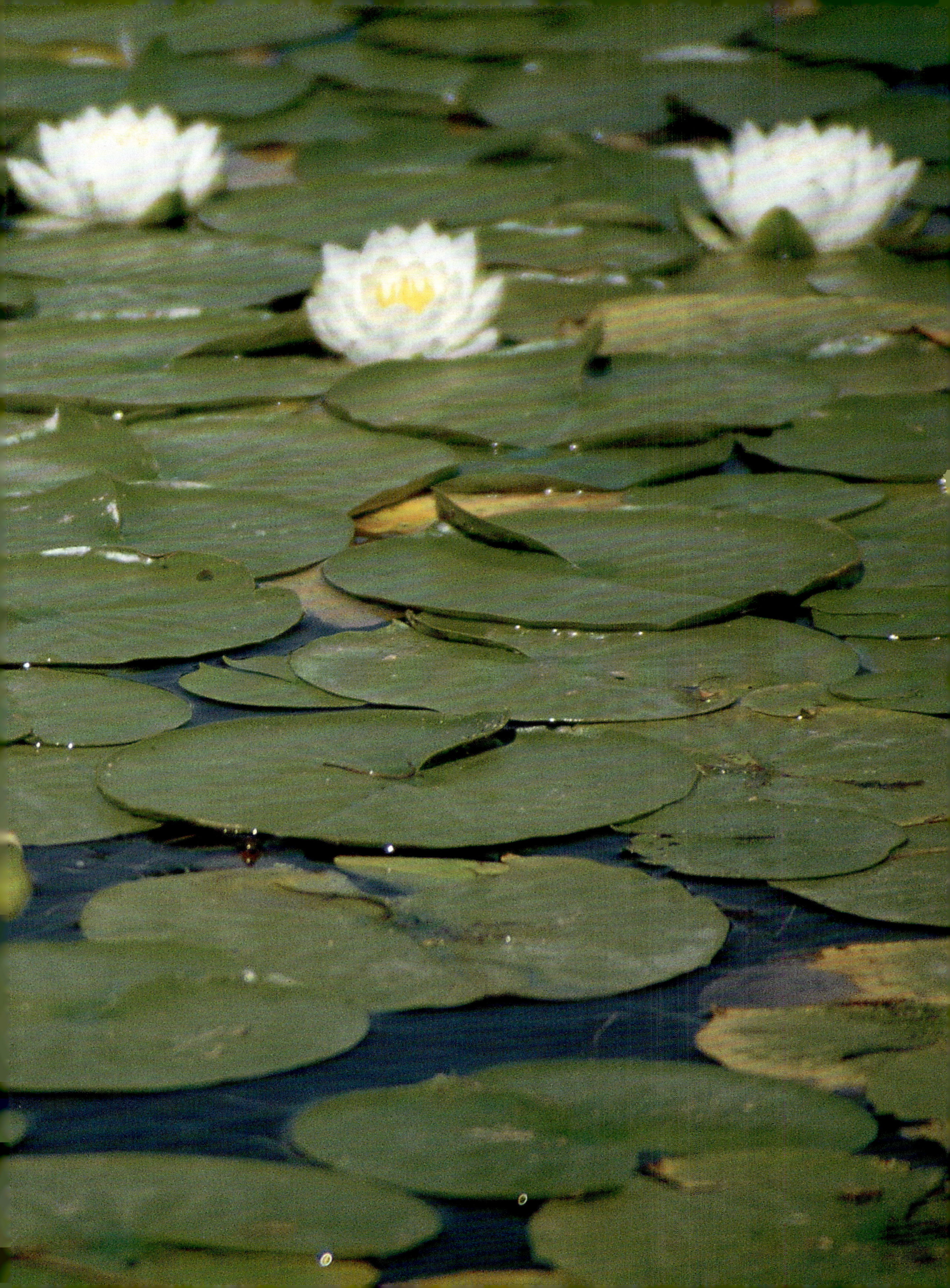

The Boeing Company

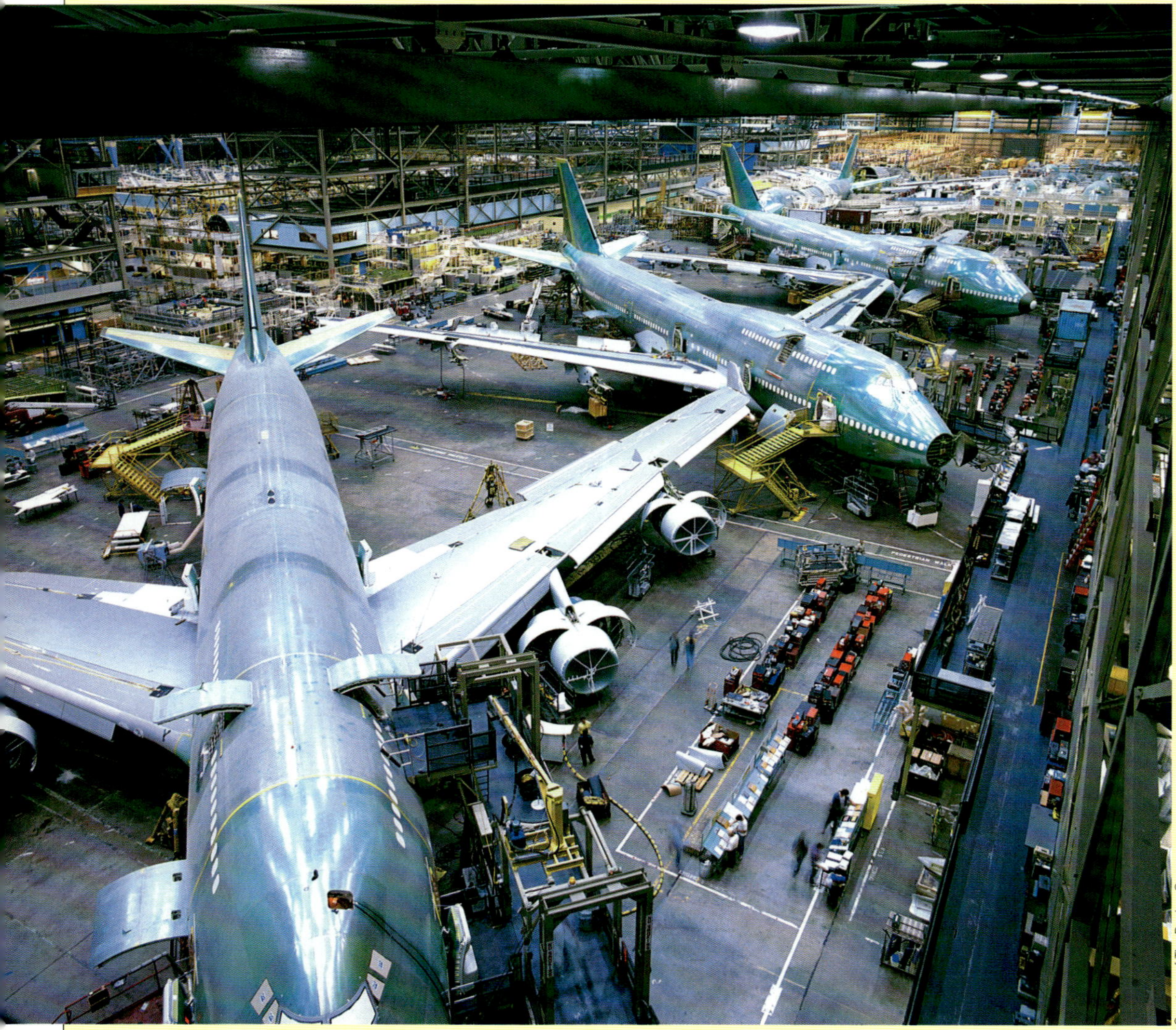
Courtesy of The Boeing Company

Known as the "Queen of the Skies," the Boeing 747 is the world's most recognized airplane—and appropriately is built in the world's largest building.

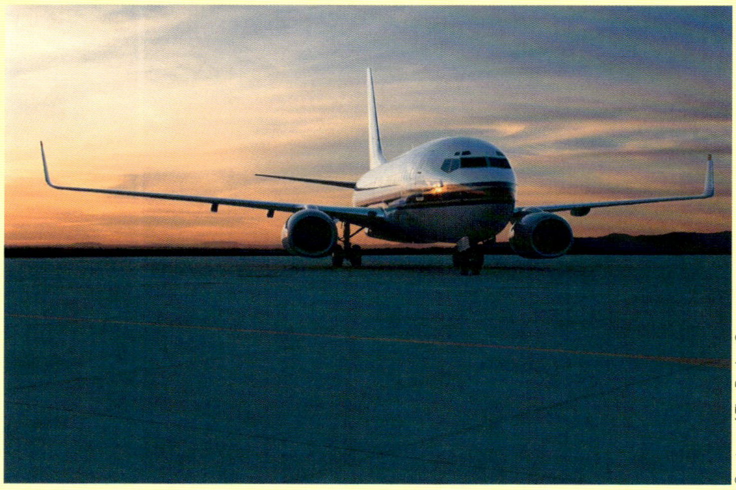
Courtesy of The Boeing Company

Launched in 1996, The Boeing Business Jet is a member of the 737 family—the most successful jet airplane in aviation history.

To lead, from one era to the next, is a great challenge. Over the last 84 years, Boeing has met that challenge repeatedly.

Boeing led in the transition from wood-and-canvas airplanes to metal airplanes. The company led in the transition from the piston era to the jet age. It pioneered in space exploration. And now, as an integrated provider of an expanding range of aerospace products and services, Boeing is pushing not just the envelope of flight, but the entire envelope of value for customers and partners around the globe.

William E. Boeing, the company's founder and a Yale-trained engineer, operated on a simple philosophy: Always insist upon the best, even if that means having to do it yourself. As a young-man-about-town in Seattle, he became interested in sailing. Finding he did not particularly like any of the sailing yachts that were for sale, he bought a shipyard in order to build one himself. When he became hooked on a new hobby, flying, he converted the shipyard into what would become the greatest airplane design and manufacturing operation that the world has ever known.

The first Boeing plane, a seaplane christened the *Bluebill*, completed its first flight on June 16, 1916, and the company was incorporated a month later. Boeing's first advertising slogan, "Built Where the Spruce

This Airborne Warning and Control System (AWACS) aircraft is one of 18 built for NATO to strengthen air defense systems in Europe.

Grows," reflected the advantages of the company's location in Seattle. Not only was there an abundance of the right kind of timber for making airplanes, but there were also plenty of skilled woodworkers in the Seattle area.

Through the decades that have followed, Boeing has gone on from wood, to metal, to an increasing use of composites; and from seaplanes, to airplanes, to jet planes, to space-faring vehicles, to exceedingly complex space-based systems. Today, more than 11,000 of the world's fleet of approximately 13,000 jetliners are Boeing airplanes. In the next 24 hours, three million passengers will board 42,300 flights on Boeing jetliners that carry them to nearly every country on earth.

Boeing is also the world's biggest builder of military aircraft and is NASA's largest contractor. For example, in the next 24 hours, 335 satellites put into orbit by Boeing launch vehicles will pass overhead and 6,000

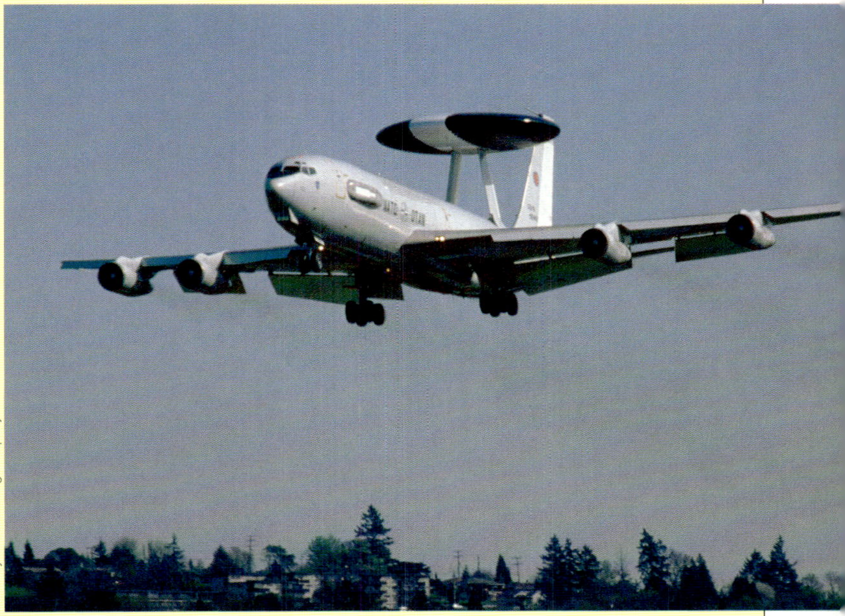

Courtesy of The Boeing Company

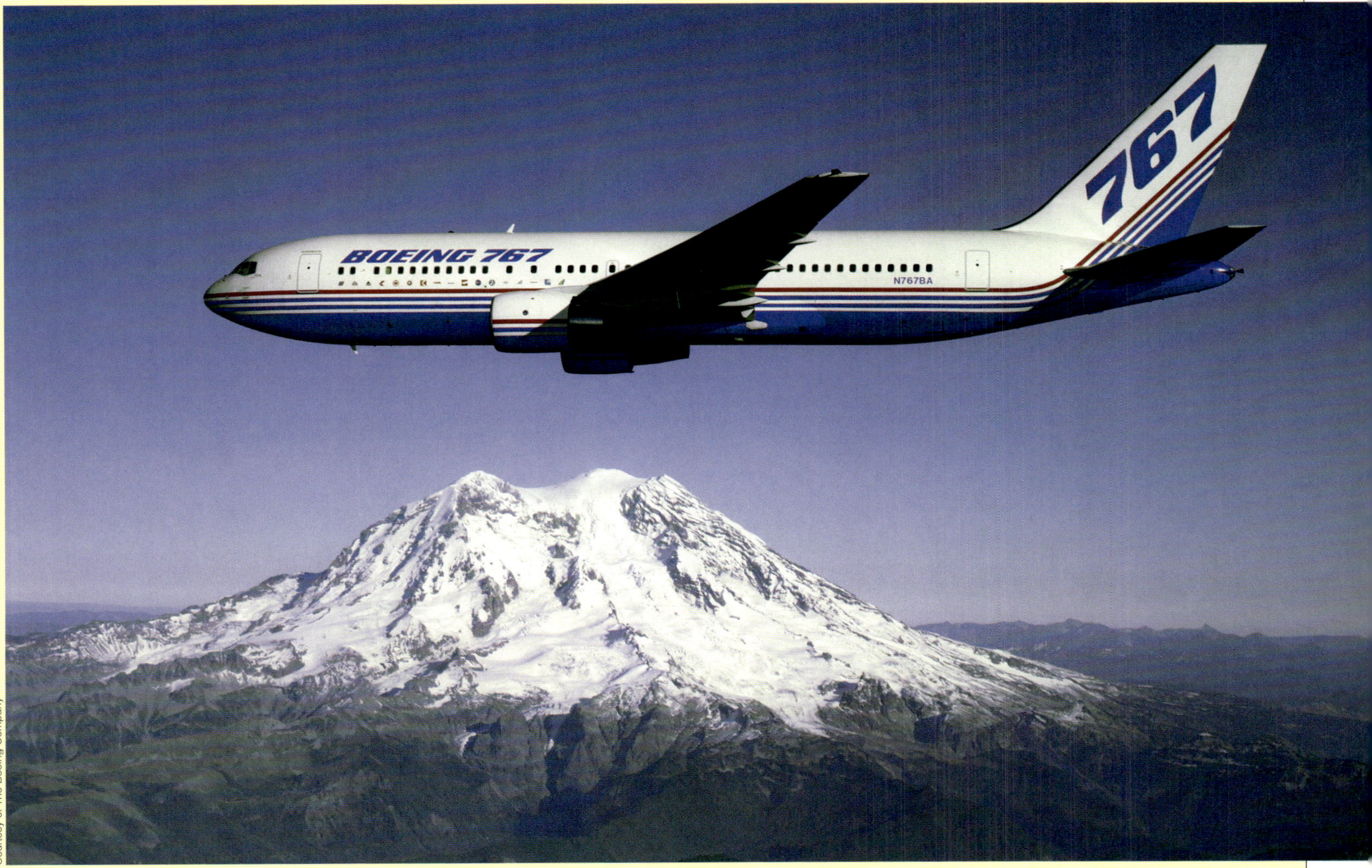

Courtesy of The Boeing Company

The Boeing 767 family, seating 181 to 304 passengers, provides maximum market versatility and is the most widely used airplane across the Atlantic.

The F-22 Raptor is being developed to counter threats posed by advanced surface-to-air missile systems and next generation fighters equipped with launch-and-leave missiles.

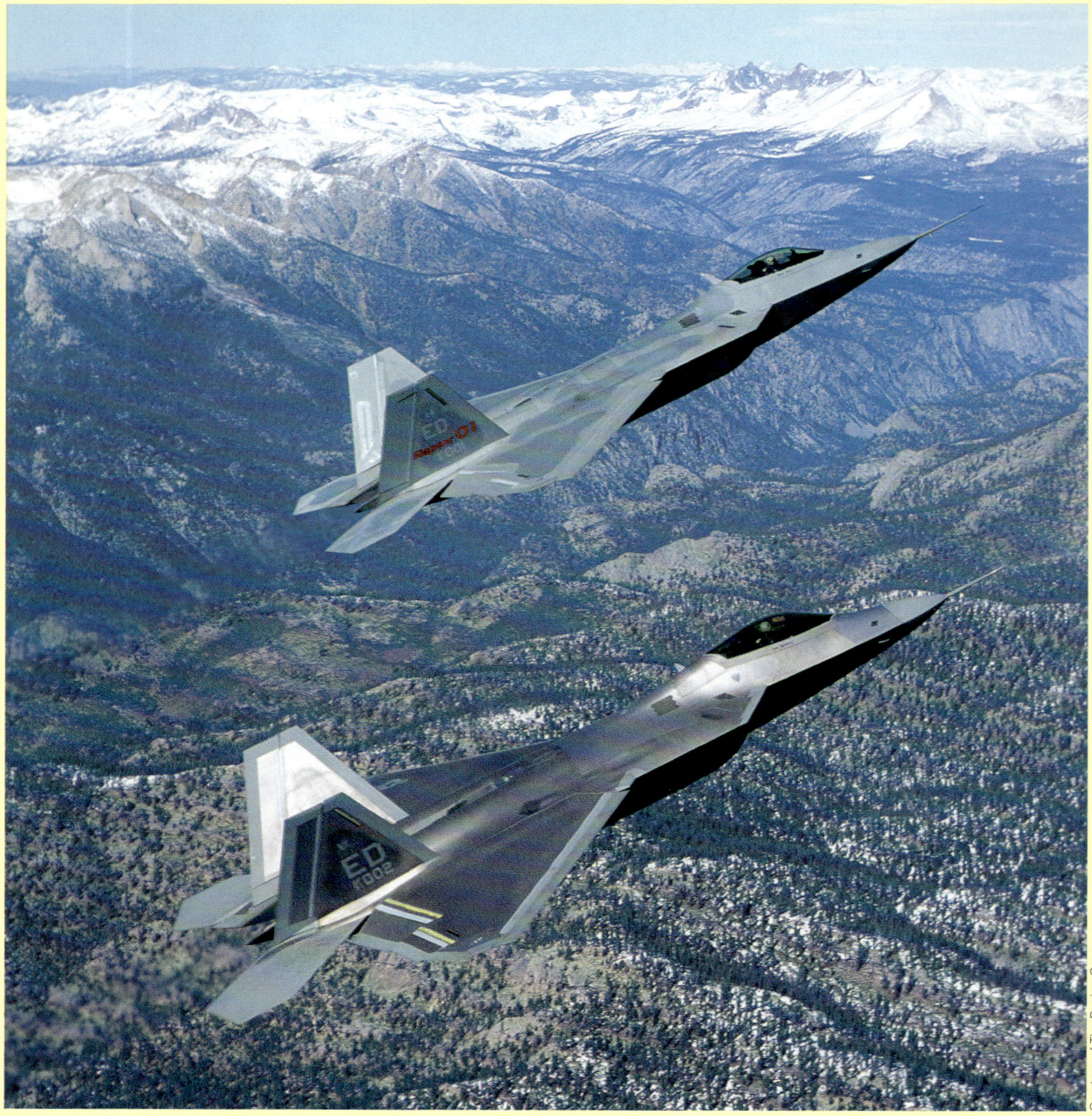

Boeing military aircraft will be on guard with the air forces of 27 countries and with every branch of the U.S. military. The company's capabilities and related services also include helicopters, electronic and defense systems, missiles, rocket engines, launch systems, and advanced information and communication systems.

Today's Boeing is a true global company. Its customers, suppliers, and partners span the globe. Boeing enjoys a unique capability of providing globally integrated aerospace solutions for complex customer requirements. For example, Boeing can provide the highest level of technical support to an airline for its airplanes that may be located in dozens of countries around the world. To an allied nation, Boeing can also offer an advanced airborne early-warning and control system that draws upon the company's combined expertise in space, defense, and aviation. In the next 24 hours, Boeing will export $72 million of goods and services to customers worldwide, send 4,650 shipments of spare parts to airline customers worldwide, and sell more than $1 million over the Internet at Boeing.com, putting the company in the top five of all web commerce sites.

In a fast-moving and increasingly interconnected global business environment, Boeing

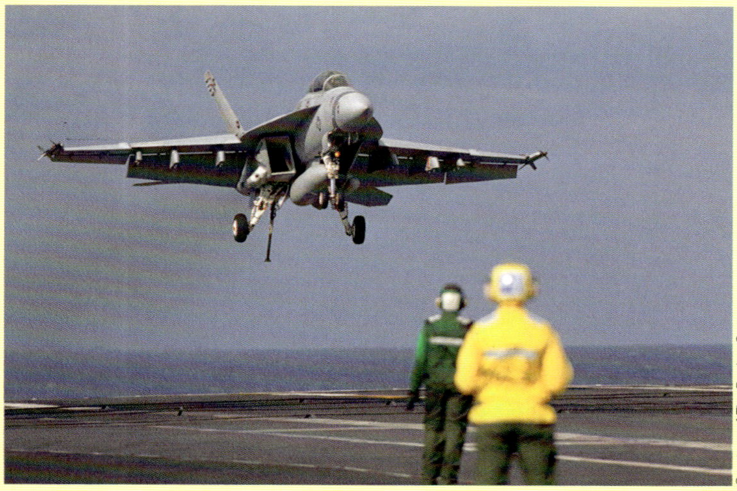

Courtesy of The Boeing Company

The F/A-18F Super Hornet comes in for a final landing aboard the USS Harry S. Truman *after completing carrier suitability tests.*

continues to be well served by having Puget Sound as its world headquarters and the center of its commercial airplane operations. While access to inexpensive and plentiful supplies of timber is no longer a factor, Boeing benefits from Seattle's position as one of the world's great hubs in the movement of goods by land, sea, and air. Of course, there are also great quality-of-life benefits to having a home base in the majestic Pacific Northwest.

In Seattle, as well as in other places where the company has large numbers of people, Boeing and its people are extremely active in the community. Boeing is the largest grant maker in the Pacific Northwest. In 1999, The Boeing Company and employee contributions of cash and in-kind services exceeded $96.6 million, supporting education, health and human services, arts and culture, and civic and environmental programs around the United States, with about 44 percent of those monies going to recipients in Washington state. Through a volunteer group called the Bluebills, named after the first Boeing plane, Boeing employees, retirees, and families donate their time and expertise to hundreds of nonprofit organizations in the Puget Sound area. Boeing volunteers serve on boards of directors, as chairs of funding-raising for capital campaigns, and as one-on-one volunteers.

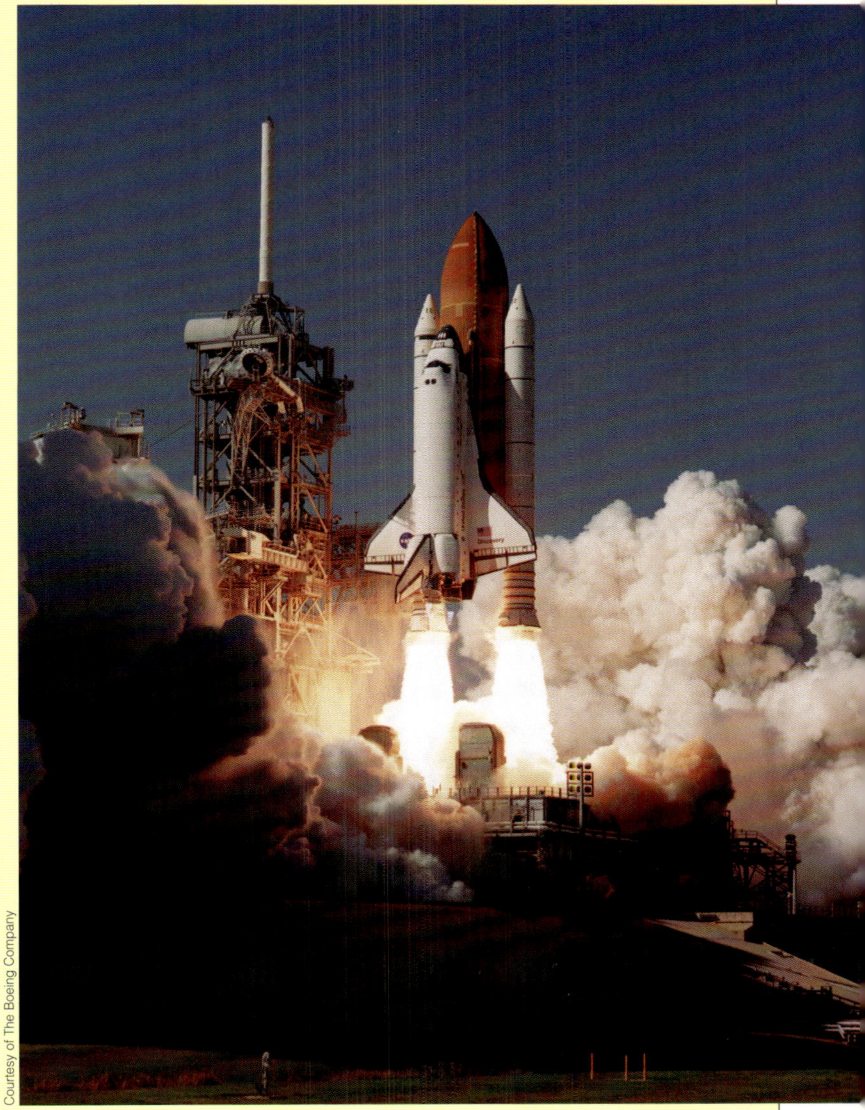
Courtesy of The Boeing Company

With upgrades by Boeing and the United Space Alliance, the four Space Shuttles for NASA will be flying to 2020 and beyond.

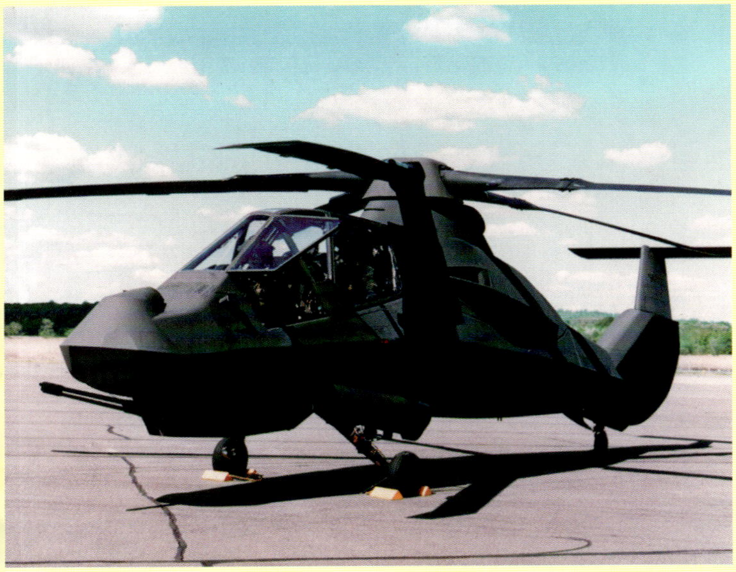

The Boeing Sikorsky RAH-66 Comanche armed reconnaissance helicopter, now in development for the U.S. Army, is the world's most advanced combat rotorcraft.

Boeing has an enduring set of values. These include a commitment to the highest standards of quality and safety, to design and engineering excellence, to the highest level of customer knowledge and support, and to community involvement and improvement. The future is bright. "We hope you will be along for the ride," Phil Condit, Boeing Chairman and CEO, said in the 1999 annual report. "There is no limit to this flight."

Aiphone Corporation

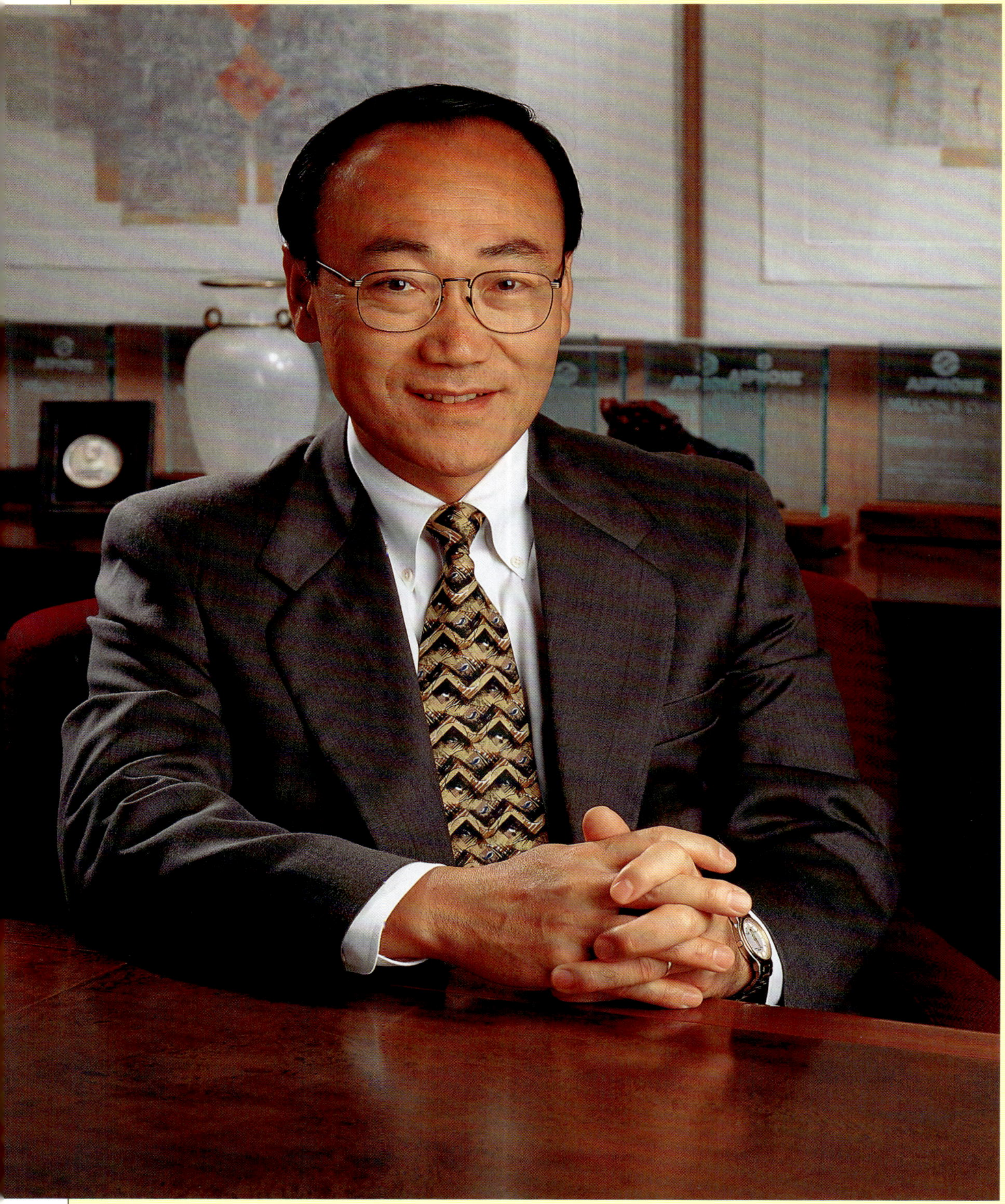
Courtesy of Aiphone Corporation

Jun Matsumoto, President and CEO, has spent more than 30 years developing internal communication systems for the international market, and currently holds patents in both the United States and Japan.

Wherever there is a need for security to enhance the safety and convenience of residents, workers, or customers, Aiphone products are available to fill that need. Aiphone, the largest manufacturer of intercom systems, offers everything from the most basic household intercom to sophisticated commercial security entry systems.

Aiphone Company Ltd. was formed in Japan in 1948 and is the primary manufacturing site for Aiphone products. Aiphone Corporation, located in Bellevue, was established in 1970 and serves all of the United States, Canada, and Puerto Rico.

Aiphone's systems reach into almost every possible aspect of business and personal life. Residential systems provide both audio and visual monitoring, which offers everyone inside a secured home, including seniors,

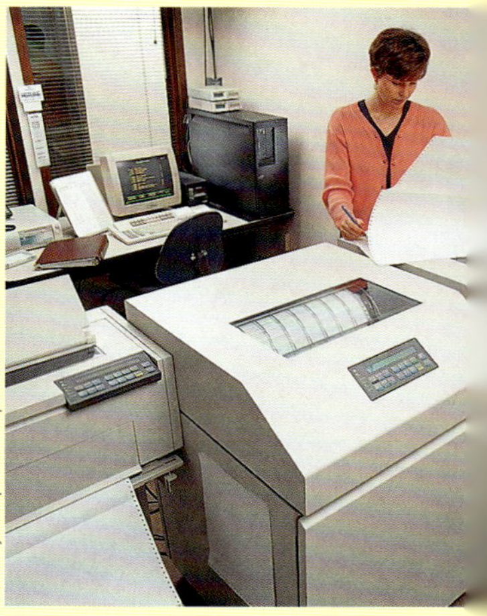
Courtesy of Aiphone Corporation

Aiphone's IBM AS-400 allows the company to immediately issue picking and shipping orders, create customer-specific reports, and maintain customer profiles, transaction histories and a constant inventory.

Customer Care enters the customer's order immediately into the company's IBM AS–400 to initiate picking orders, shipping, and invoicing. These representatives can answer questions about orders, product, and Aiphone in general.

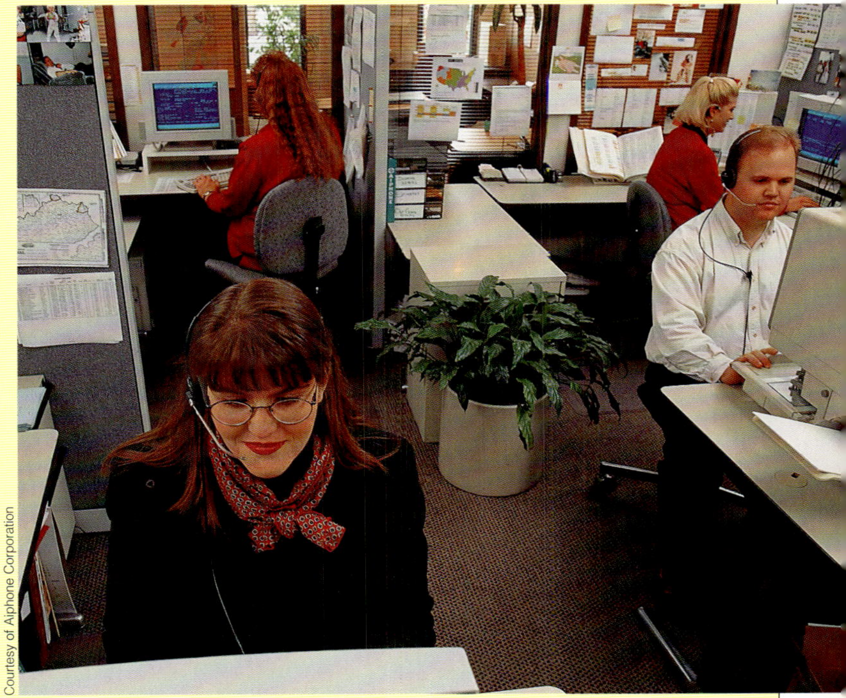

Courtesy of Aiphone Corporation

the handicapped, or children home alone, the ability to view a visitor at the door before deciding whether or not to grant admittance. More complex systems control access to large apartment complexes and condominiums. Specially designed systems serve nurses' stations in nursing homes and hospitals, providing the ability to monitor patients from a central location. Other Aiphone systems monitor access to businesses, while still others provide monitoring in jails and prisons. Sophisticated systems serve as the primary hailing function on U.S. Navy aircraft carriers and nuclear submarines. In fact, Aiphone systems provide security for the Federal Bureau of Investigation (FBI).

One of the most important roles that Aiphone's Bellevue office plays involves the design and production of accessories and modifications to the primary Aiphone products. With the engineering and technical skills available through this office, Aiphone Corporation can accommodate special customer needs and provide unique solutions to complex security issues. Jun Matsumoto, President and Chief Executive Officer of the North American Operation, has been with Aiphone since 1968 and has been in the United States since 1979. Among his prior positions, he served as Chief Engineer for the company and holds patents in both Japan and the United States.

Aiphone Co. Ltd. is one of the few companies in the world to be honored with the Deming Prize in recognition of its approach to Total Quality Control (TQC). The company

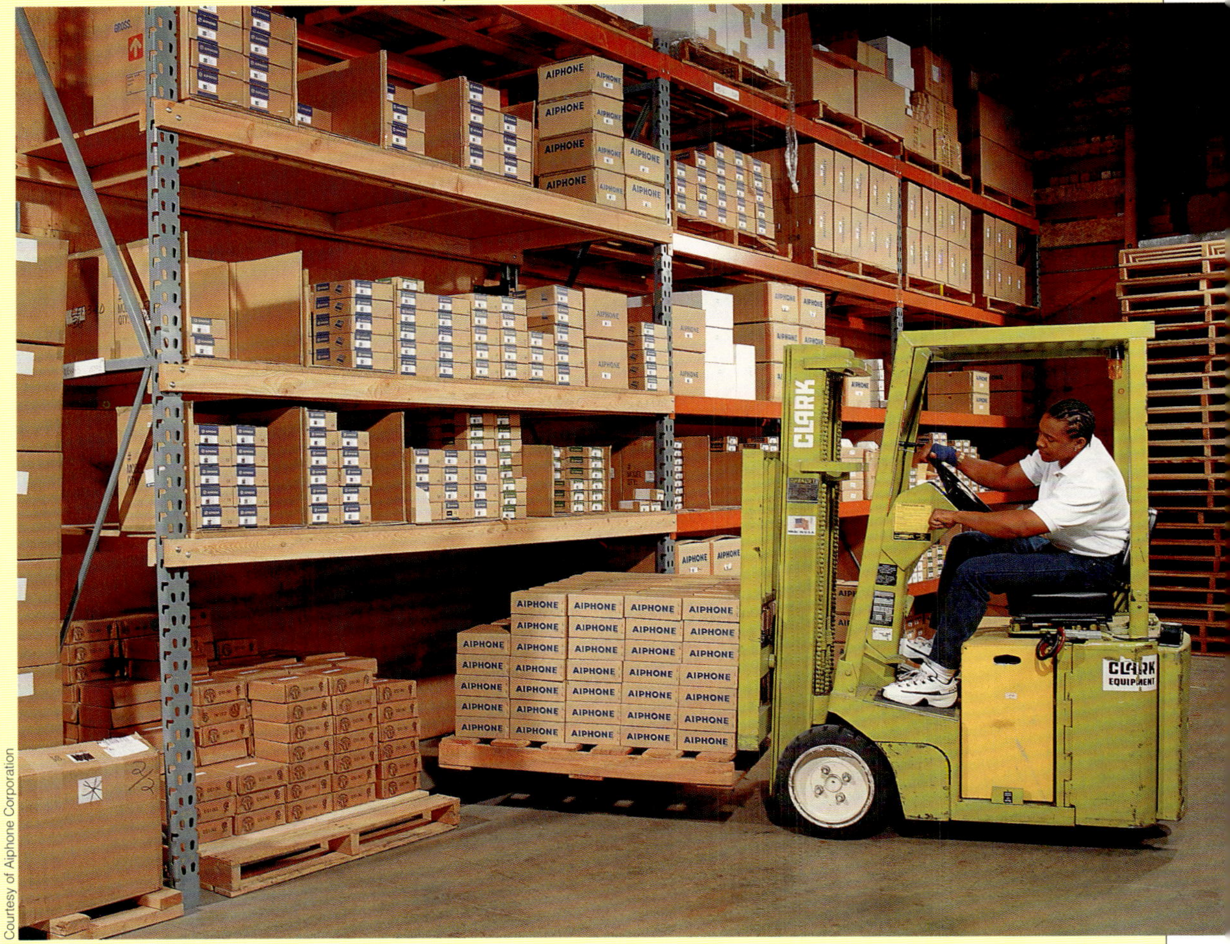

Courtesy of Aiphone Corporation

Orders received by 1 p.m. are usually shipped the same day. Aiphone's 10,000-square-foot warehouse holds over $3 million in inventory.

Aiphone's sales and marketing staff develop a variety of programs to help support the company's large sales force. *These efforts include advertising and sales aids, brochures, specification sheets, newsletters, and sales leads.*

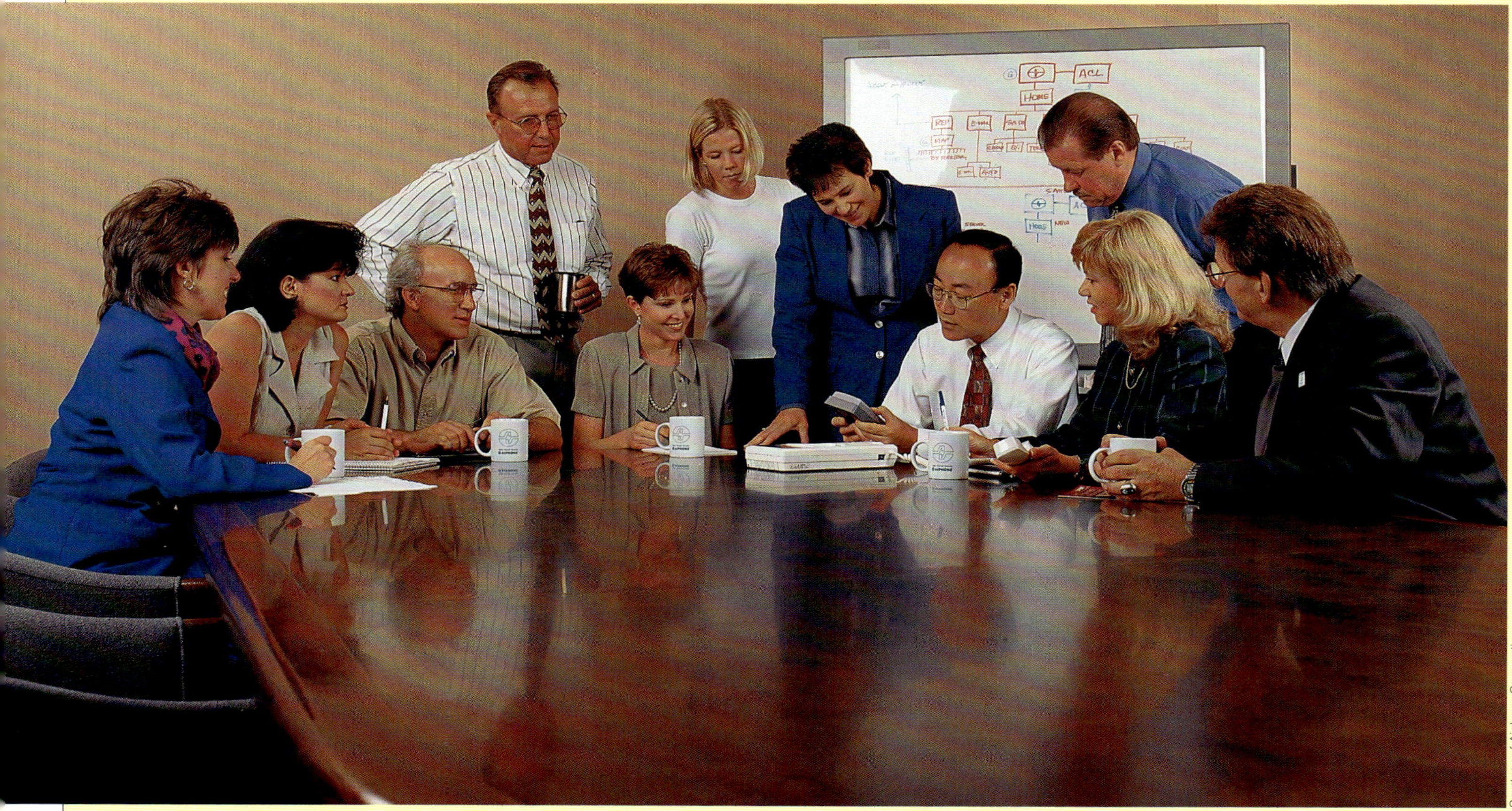

Courtesy of Aiphone Corporation

has also received ISO (International Organization for Standardization) 9001 certification for quality as well as ISO 14001 Certification for Environmental Excellence. Aiphone Corporation is proud to maintain this commitment to quality products and services by receiving its own ISO-9002 certification.

In a world that at times feels uncertain, Aiphone provides for all its customers, from the suburban family to the multinational corporation, a valuable sense of security. For the multinational corporation, that sense of security translates into dollars and cents; and for the family, that sense of security translates into something infinitely more valuable—a feeling of well being and peace of mind.

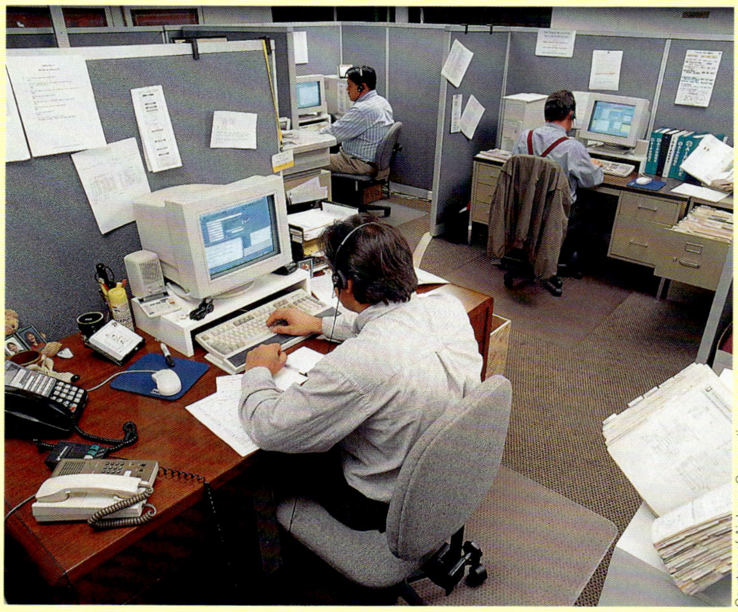

Courtesy of Aiphone Corporation

Technical Service representatives answer a wide range of questions on Aiphone products including system design, compatibility, wiring, installation, and trouble-shooting. With Aiphone's toll-free number, fax-back capability, and e-mail, technical staff can usually respond to questions the same day they are contacted.

Agilent Technologies

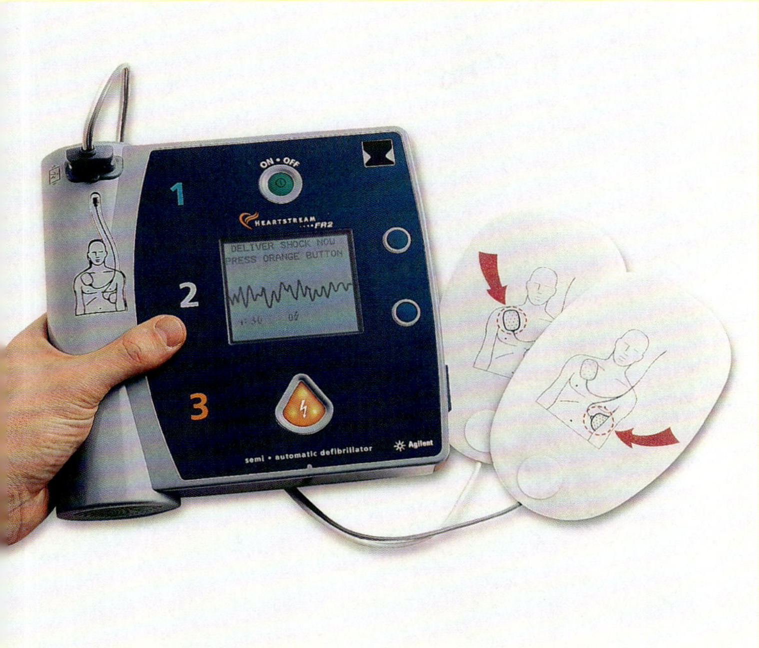

Courtesy of Agilent Technologies Heartstream

The Agilent Technologies Heartstream FR2 is a portable, lightweight automatic external defibrillator (AED) that requires minimal device training to use and is an essential part of administering first aid immediately to a victim of sudden cardiac arrest. Due to its easy-to-use design, superior technology, and affordability, Heartstream FR2 AEDs are now being placed in a wide range of settings such as hospitals and clinics, offices and industrial locations, airports and airplanes, health clubs and golf courses.

With over 350,000 cases of sudden cardiac arrest every year in the United States, and considering that the survival rate in such instances is less than five percent, immediate medical attention is imperative. Due to these startling statistics, compact units called automatic external defibrillators (AEDs) are being placed in office buildings, airports, sports stadiums, schools, malls, and other public locations. AEDs only weigh about four-and-one-half pounds and several major airlines now carry them on regular flights. The American Heart Association, a strong supporter of the use of these devices, states that if AEDs were readily available, more than 100,000 lives would be saved each year. Agilent Technologies is the manufacturer of the Heartstream AED, a device that will help to revolutionize emergency cardiac care.

With recent advances in technology, much of it pioneered by the Seattle-based Heartstream operation, the latest AED units pack much more than an electrical shock to stimulate and restart the heart of a victim of sudden cardiac arrest. The Heartstream AED becomes the "first-line medical expert" in such an emergency by analyzing the victim's heart condition, providing a voice command to shock or not to shock, and then analyzing the result. Along with appropriate CPR, the tiny unit can provide the difference between life and death while emergency medical units are in route to the scene.

While current regulations do require a prescription by a physician for the purchase of an AED in order to assure knowledge and understanding of its proper utilization, the advantage of the AED is its overall ease of use. Its proper operation only requires device training, and the AED can be used by trained lay responders and non-emergency responders. Personnel in the area of the unit's deployment are trained in its use in courses offered by the American Red Cross and the American Heart Association. In these courses, CPR and AED training are simultaneous and the combination can easily save lives.

The employees of Agilent Technologies' Heartstream Operation take great pride in what they produce. On the main wall of the lobby area is a large world map with pins and ribbons identifying "saves" made by a Heartstream AED. Ask any employee what they do at Agilent and they will tell you, "we save lives!"

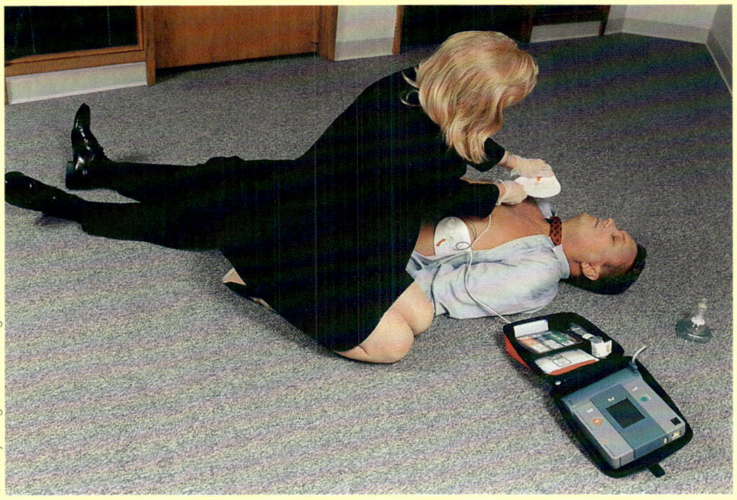

Courtesy of Agilent Technologies Heartstream

Timely defibrillation is essential to saving victims of sudden cardiac arrest (SCA). With each minute lost, the likelihood of someone surviving from SCA decreases seven to ten percent. Factors such as EMS delays to an office building, a shopping center, a stadium, or a golf course make it critical for organizations to be prepared with an automatic external defibrillator like this one, from Agilent Technologies.

GM Nameplate

In 1954, two local businessmen devised an ingenious process for manufacturing aluminum foil nameplates, and as a result, a small upstart company called GM Nameplate was born. In every modern home and office, one will find equipment with GM Nameplate products used to identify the product or as a key operating component. Few individuals in a modern economy, anywhere in the world, will go through a day without being in contact with several articles created by this amazing Seattle company.

As new technologies created fresh opportunities, the company added a wider range of products to not only stay ahead of the competition, but to further expand its vertically integrated manufacturing processes. When major strides were required to stay on top of the market, GM Nameplate acquired other companies and used their combined expertise to meet its goal of providing "one stop" custom manufacturing.

This corporate vision is driven by the company's Chairman, Don Root. In 1961, before his graduation from the University of Washington, Mr. Root was invited by one of the founders of the company to accept a management training position at GM Nameplate.

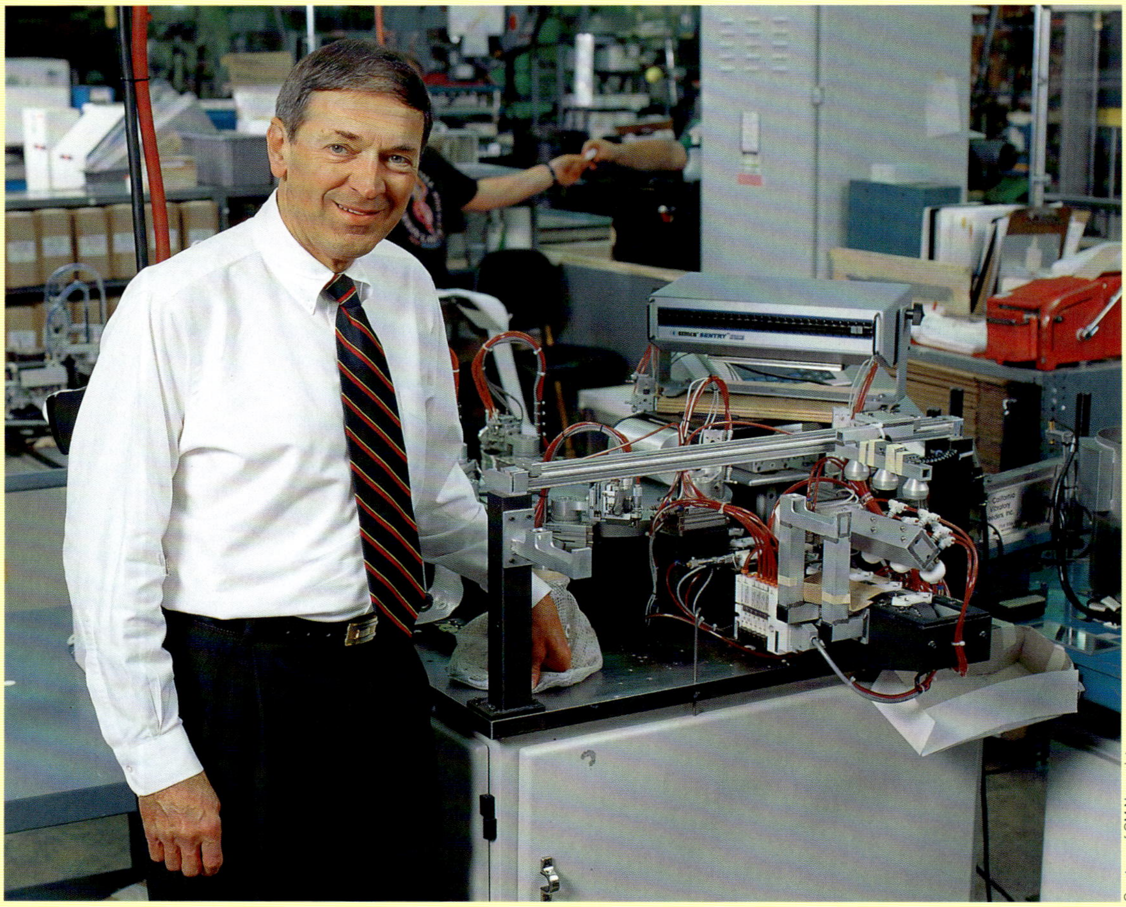

Courtesy of GM Nameplate

Don Root, Chairman and Chief Executive Officer.

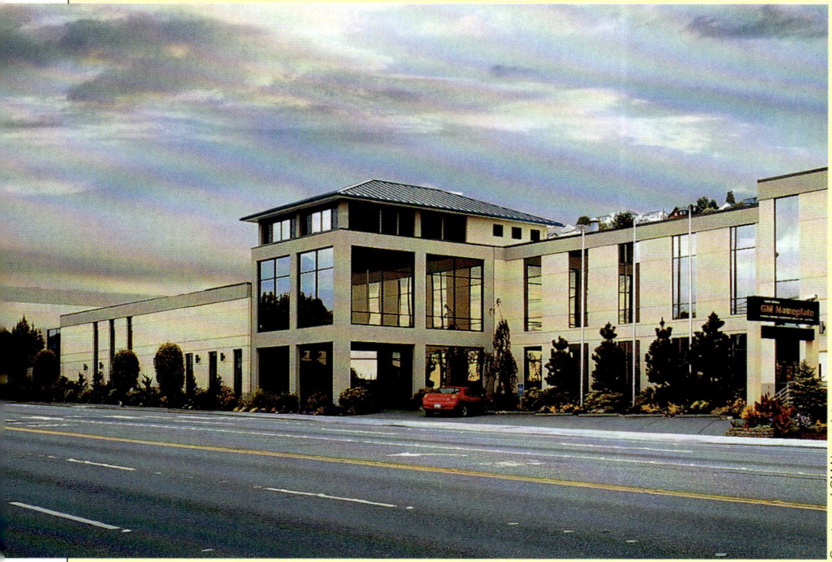

Courtesy of GM Nameplate

GM Nameplate Corporate Headquarters, Washington Division.

At that time, the company had 12 employees and annual sales of $120,000 at its only facility in Seattle. Today, Don Root is CEO of GM Nameplate, which has annual sales of over $83 million, has over 800 employees, and operates out of plants located in Seattle; Beaverton, Oregon; San Jose, California; Charlotte, North Carolina; Singapore; and Mexico.

GM Nameplate is much more than just nameplates today. Among its many products, it manufactures cutting-edge touch-screen and keypad controls for the computer, aerospace, medical, automotive, and appliance markets as well as a host of other electronic components. One of the more recent acquisitions by the company has placed it on the forefront of large-scale graphic imaging. GM Nameplate's XL images produces large-format digital imagery for cars, buses, airplanes, and building walls. XL images occupies a 25,000-square-foot building of its own just across the street from GM Nameplate's corporate headquarters. The headquarters building itself is further evidence of how much the company has grown. The original building was a single-level structure that occupied about 5,000 square feet. Today, GM Nameplate's headquarters in Seattle occupies more than 180,000 square feet. Combined, its plants total more than 400,000 square feet.

Courtesy of GM Nameplate

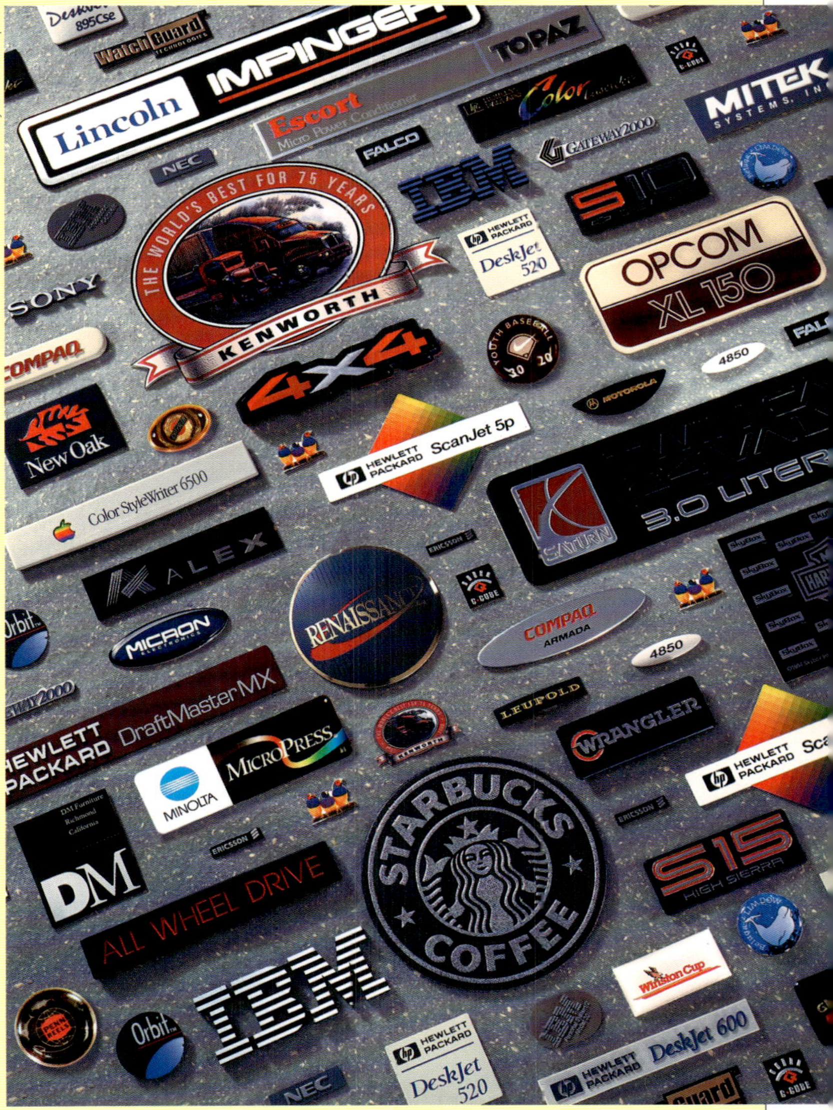

GM Nameplate specializes in the fabrication of product identification components. The nameplate processes include polycarbonate, embossed foil aluminum, domed, diamond-carved, and electroformed.

Courtesy of GM Nameplate

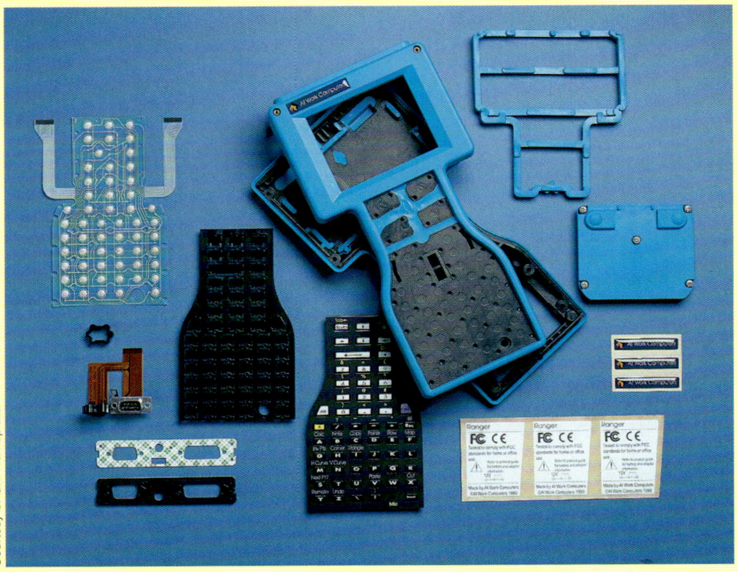

GM Nameplate's five plants produced components for the Ranger Series. This unique self-sealed housing, single-sheet tactile-domed polyester switch panel and molded hinged hard-key face with pad-printed graphics creates a waterproof keyboard and shell that meets Mil-Spec submersion and drop requirements.

GM Nameplate is a family and community-oriented, employee-owned business with its roots firmly in the soil of King County, the place that fostered its growth. This quality, along with a sharp eye on future technology and market advances, will ensure GM Nameplate's future as an innovative industrial resource for the Pacific Northwest—and for the world.

PRECOR

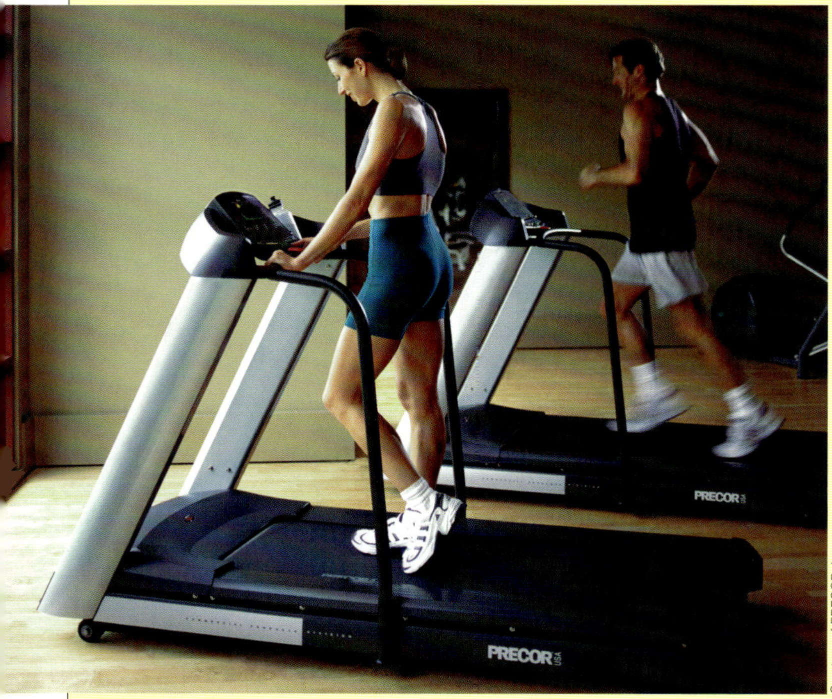

Courtesy of PRECOR, Inc.

"PRECOR has an amazing reputation in the commercial and home exercise equipment industry. Durability, safety, and state-of-the-art biomechanical technology has made PRECOR the preferred cardiovascular equipment."
—Josh Yonushonis, Fitness & Wellness Director.

As Americans devote more and more time and energy on health and fitness, one company, founded in King County, has become the undisputed leader in the production of high-end fitness equipment for both commercial and home applications. That company is PRECOR Inc., and it has made a definite impact on the fitness industry.

In 1980, PRECOR began with a single product, a rowing machine with an innovative design and quality craftsmanship that quickly captured the attention of a population interested in physical fitness. Building on the success of its original rower, PRECOR moved to the development and production of its first treadmill. As in all of its product development, PRECOR utilized input from outside research, the experience of professional trainers, and the response of consumers to create a treadmill that allowed the user to "Work Out Smarter." This term soon became the motto of the company.

With a product line that now includes climbers, bikes, treadmills, Elliptical Fitness Crosstrainers, Stretch Trainer™ flexibility products, and strength equipment, PRECOR has entered the world market. PRECOR's most recent product development, the Elliptical Fitness Crosstrainer™ (EFX®), is so innovative that it has created a new fitness-industry category. The EFX is a no-impact cardiovascular machine that has become the most popular piece of equipment in health clubs and is a highly sought-after addition to the home fitness market. The no-impact design of the EFX makes it a valuable tool for athletes, people new to exercise, or individuals recovering from injuries.

PRECOR and its employees are enthusiastic patrons of various charitable organizations and community programs. Both management and employees are huge supporters of the United Way, earning the company the prestigious "Spirit of Caring" award on more than one occasion. PRECOR is also the proud recipient of the "Distinguished Business in the Green" award from Green Works, a Department of King County. In a company-wide effort, PRECOR was recognized for programs that included recycling at least 60 percent of its waste.

Throughout its success, PRECOR has maintained a spirit that company insiders call "the PRECOR feel." At PRECOR, designers and product developers think of the consumer before they think of "the bottom line." The PRECOR feel has led the company to numerous, well-deserved awards for excellence in PRECOR products. PRECOR sets itself apart as a company that is committed to both the maintenance of individual health and the overall well being of the communities it serves.

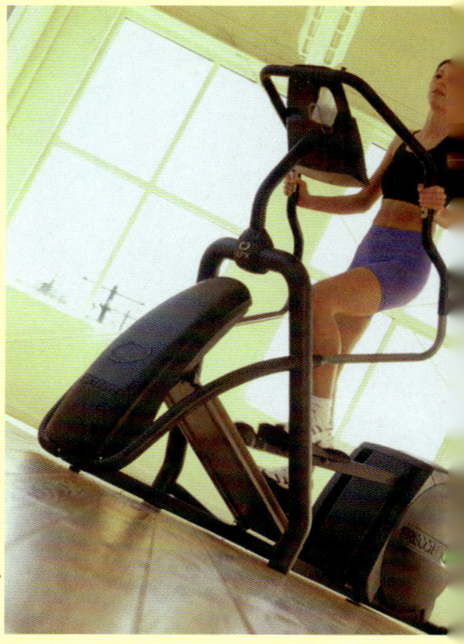

Courtesy of PRECOR, Inc.

The PRECOR EFX is acknowledged worldwide as the "gold standard" in today's leading fitness facilities. Its no-impact forward or reverse elliptical stride lessens joint stress and increases crosstraining benefits.

Data-Linc Group

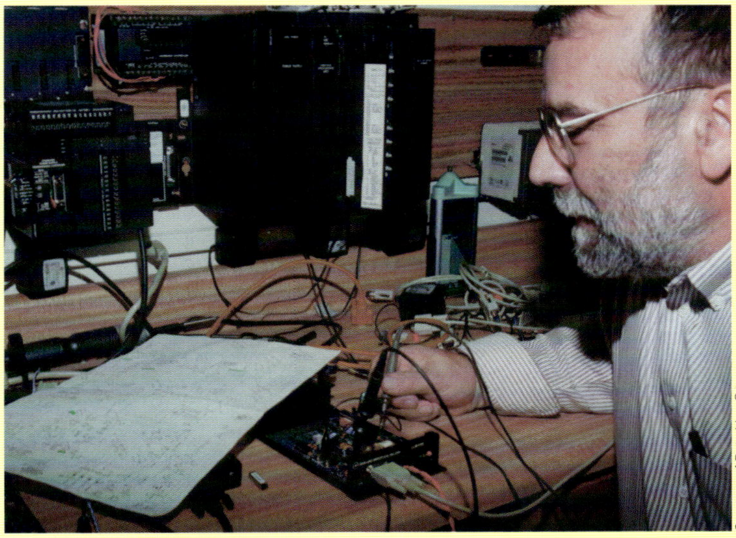
Courtesy of Data-Linc Group

Data-Linc performs in-depth laboratory and field testing on all products.

Data-Linc Group occupies a unique position among advanced-technology companies. It is one of the few firms worldwide that offers a complete line of modems specifically designed for industrial applications. Data-Linc has close affiliations and partnerships with all the top manufacturers of industrial automation equipment. The company has several branch offices in North America and is currently expanding into South America and Asia.

Industrial modems differ in many ways from the typical PC modem used in homes and businesses. Usually called upon to operate and survive in harsh and unpredictable environments, they are designed for robustness and versatility. Data-Linc makes all types of modems: radio; dial-up; private wire, leased line and power line; and fiber optic. They are built to function at extreme temperatures and designed to always get the data through, even under severe interference. Data-Linc also provides an exceptionally high degree of engineering and technical support to customers, including delivering modems factory pre-configured.

Data-Linc has deployed its modems in many unusual and interesting applications. They monitor and control industrial processes in thousands of places from wastewater facilities to oil refineries, large mines to railroads and river barges, factory robots to hydroplanes and racing cars. Among the more unique installations are:

- Continuous data communications on ferry boats from ship to shore,
- Traffic light controller programming,
- Amusement park rides monitoring,
- Railroad trackside signal monitoring,
- Oil refinery air quality diagnostics.

As the world becomes increasingly automated, Data-Linc's modems will be making ever-greater contributions to all phases of industrial progress.

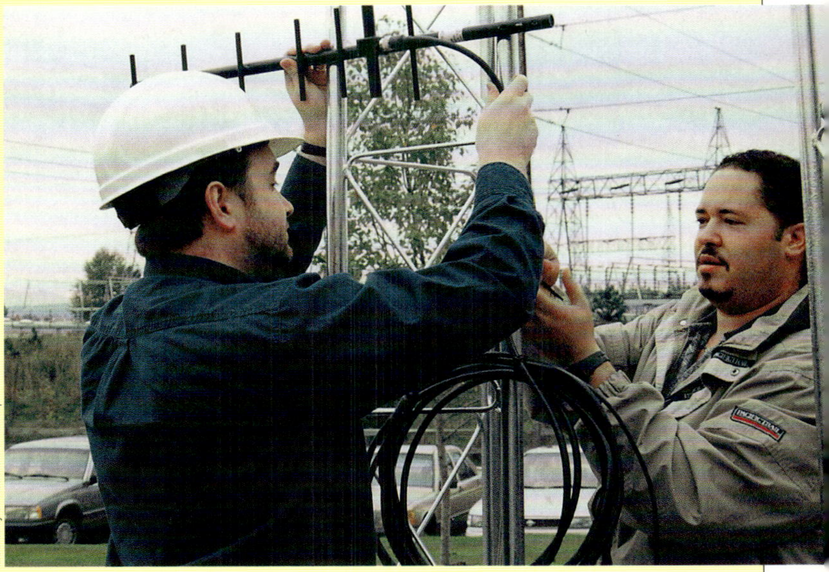
Courtesy of Data-Linc Group

Across the globe, Data-Linc radio modems serve a wide variety of industries and markets.

Part Two

Building

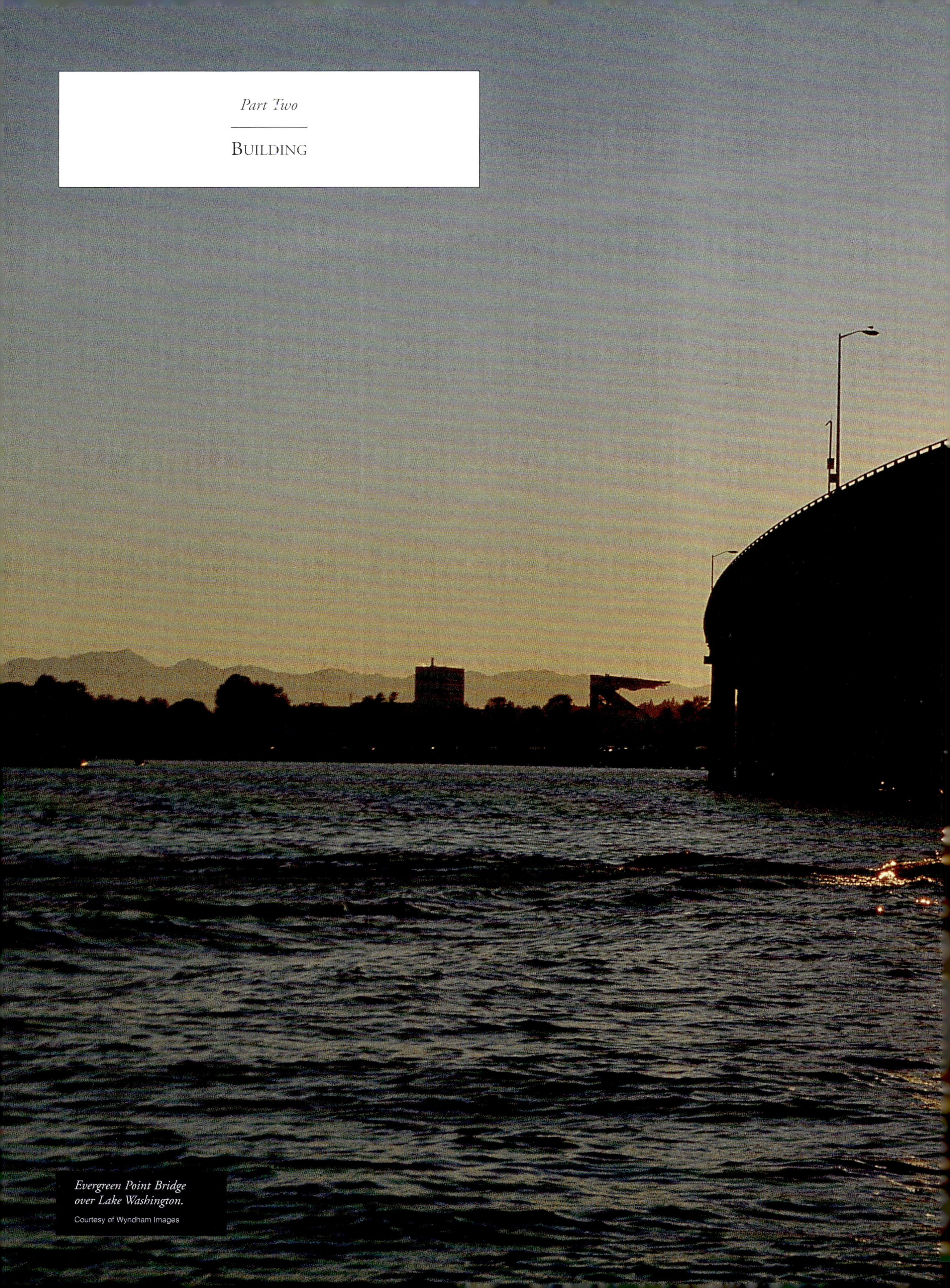

Evergreen Point Bridge over Lake Washington.

Courtesy of Wyndham Images

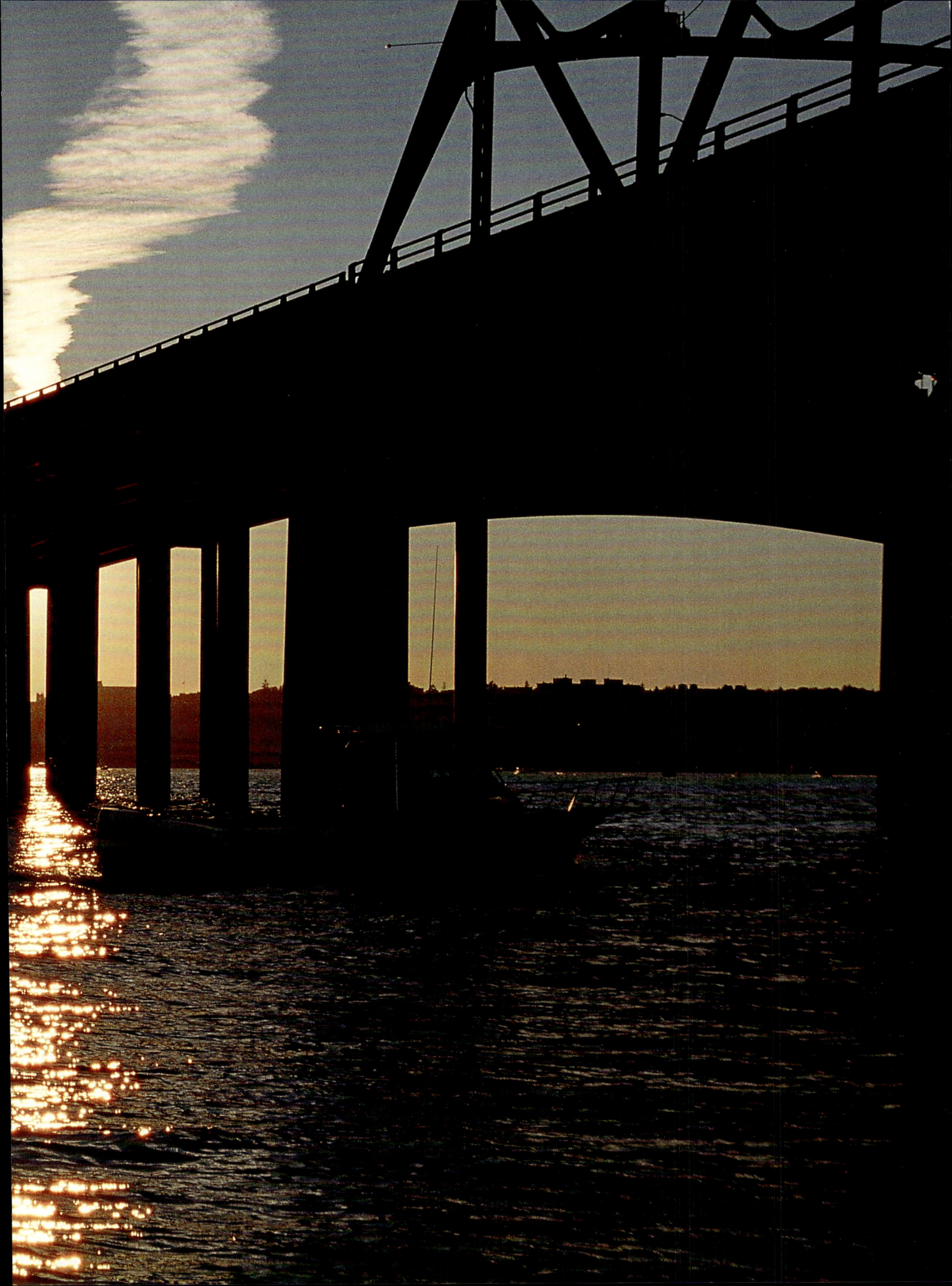

PCL Construction Services, Inc.

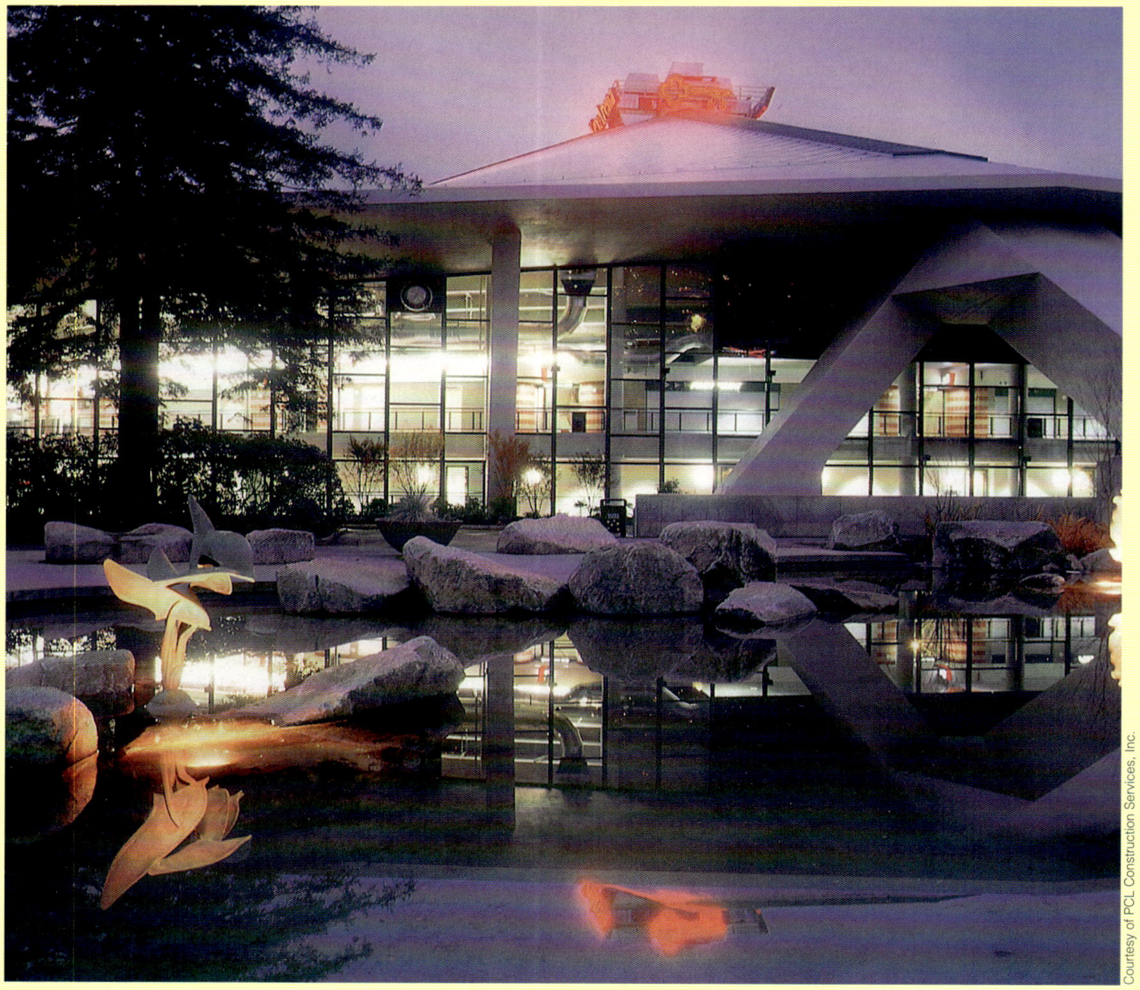
Courtesy of PCL Construction Services, Inc.

KeyArena in Seattle Center, home of the Seattle SuperSonics.

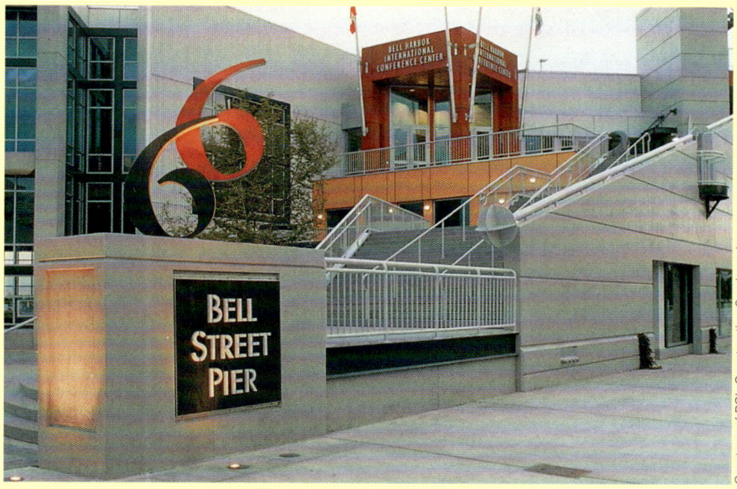

Courtesy of PCL Construction Services, Inc.

Bell Harbor International Conference Center, Pier 66, Seattle.

The skyline of Seattle and King County has dramatically evolved in recent years and PCL Construction Services, Inc. has had a major role in this evolution. Established nearly a century ago, PCL has grown to be one of the largest construction companies in North America. In 1976, the second-generation family that owned the business sold it to the employees, making PCL one of the largest and most successful employee-owned companies of its kind in North America. Employee ownership is what sets this company apart from the rest.

With an abundant staff of experienced builders, PCL continues to grow its construction presence in the Pacific Northwest. As owners of the firm, PCL employees take great pride in their work and in the projects they construct. From a complex, multi-building project on a college campus; to a massive $197 million, four-year Chesapeake Bay Bridge and Tunnel Parallel Crossing project; to reshaping the urban landscape of Seattle's Belltown area with high-rise condominiums; PCL executes each with the strictest attention to detail, workmanship, and contractual

Bell Street Pier Cruise Ship Terminal, Pier 66, Seattle.

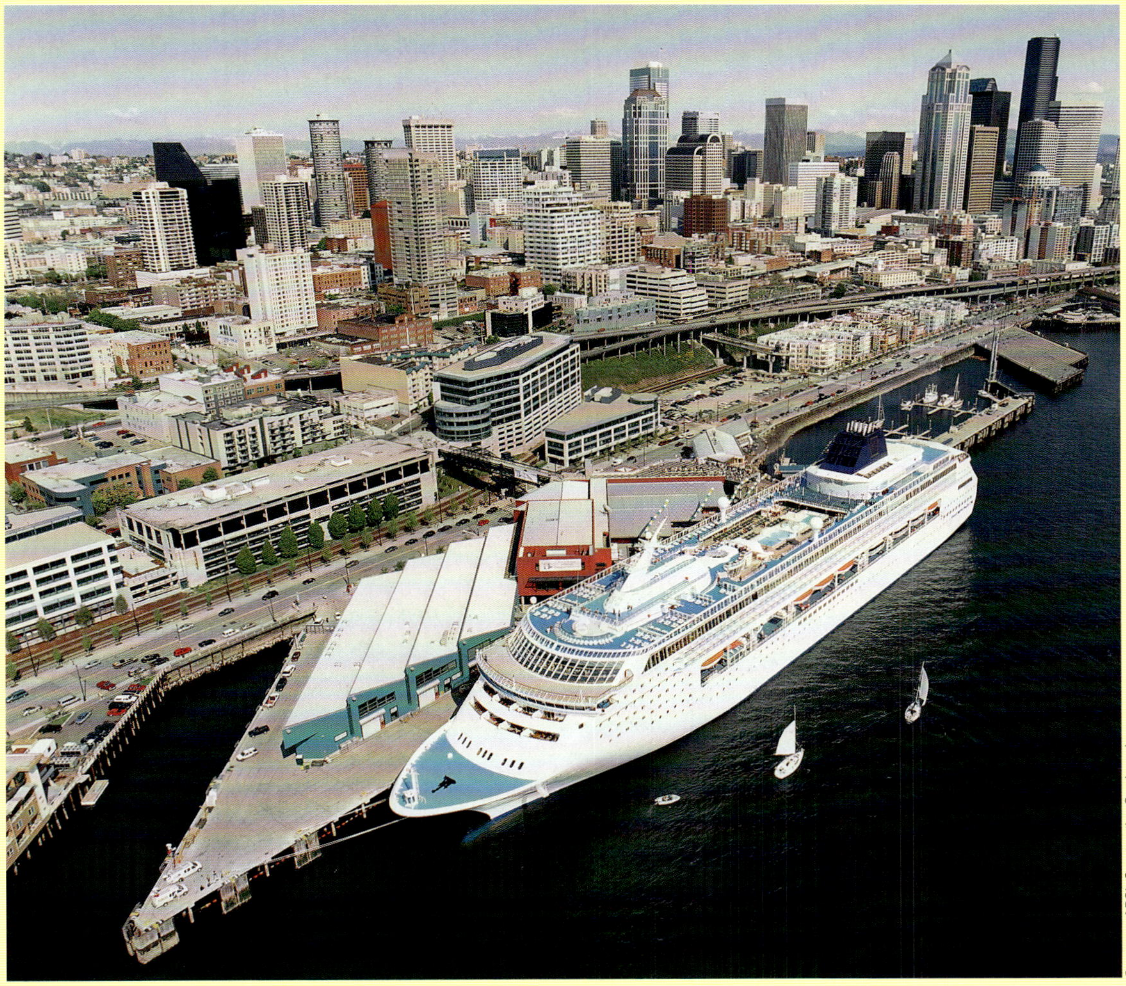

Courtesy of PCL Construction Services, Inc.

performance periods while maintaining a firm grip on the project budget.

The Hawaii Convention Center in Honolulu showcases PCL's expertise. In a design/build competition, PCL's concept won over state voters as well as the design commission against three other competitors. The investment of several months of painstaking research and design development paid off when the $201 million project was secured. In 1998, the Hawaii Convention Center was completed, receiving "world class" status and architectural acclaim.

PCL has provided numerous contributions to the skyline and cityscapes of King County. One of the most notable contributions is the Seattle Coliseum renovation into the KeyArena at Seattle Center—the home of the Seattle SuperSonics. At the Seattle waterfront, PCL constructed the Bell Street Pier Conference Center and Cruise Ship Terminal. In the financial district, the PCL-built IDX Tower at Fourth and Madison stands 40 stories above the busy streets. In Belltown, high-rise residential condominium dwellers are likely to be living in a PCL-built urban home, including One Pacific Towers, the Ellington, the Vine Building or Concord luxury towers. Across Lake Washington in Bellevue, the PCL-built twin-tower Lincoln Square mixed-use project is a one-of-a-kind "connected" community including an office tower, hotel tower, condominiums, and retail space.

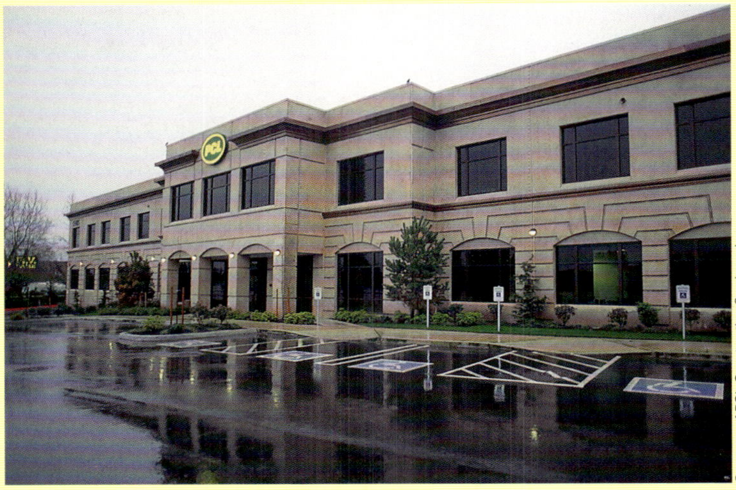

Courtesy of PCL Construction Services, Inc.

PCL's regional office in Bellevue.

The One Twelfth @ Twelfth campus-style office complex provides class-A office space in an urban setting. Other contributions throughout the area are equally impressive, such as the Paramount Hotel, Kirkland Performance Center, and new Sea-Tac Air Traffic Control Tower.

In order to keep the company a "construction leader," PCL invests heavily in its employees. Training is provided through PCL's College of Construction. Seminars are continually provided to make sure the employees' knowledge and skills are technically sound. The employees are exposed to cutting-edge technology in order to provide the best value for PCL's clients. In addition, PCL is committed to quality workmanship and puts customer satisfaction as its highest priority.

Safety is a main concern at PCL. Accident prevention is a line responsibility, beginning with the president of the operation to the district managers, job superintendents, individual supervisors, and tradesmen.

One Pacific Tower, Seattle.

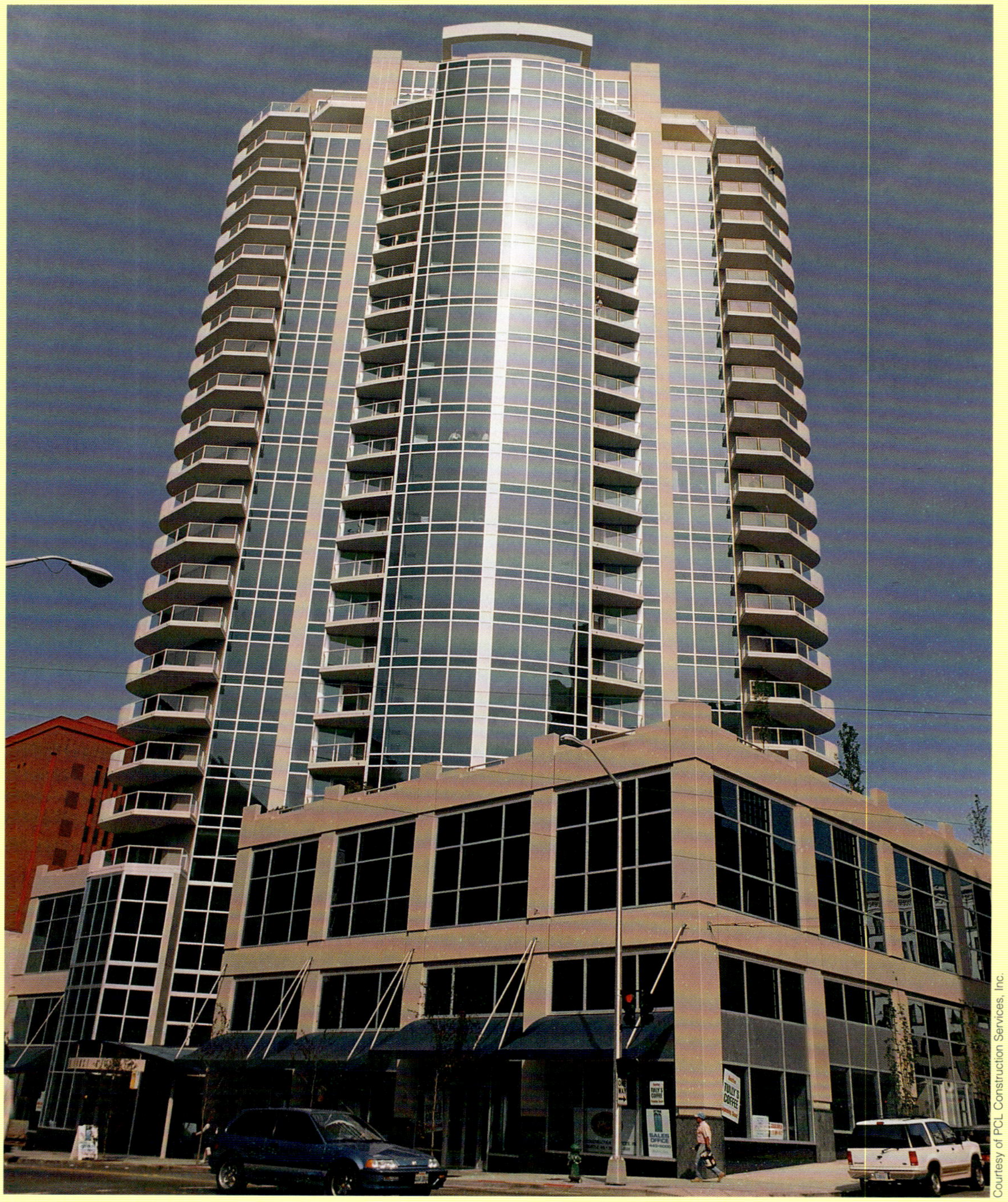

Courtesy of PCL Construction Services, Inc.

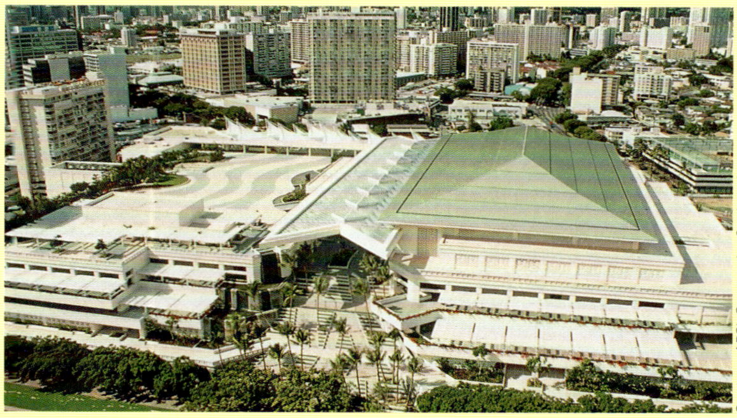

Hawaii Convention Center, Honolulu.

Courtesy of PCL Construction Services, Inc.

PCL cranes at work in downtown Seattle.

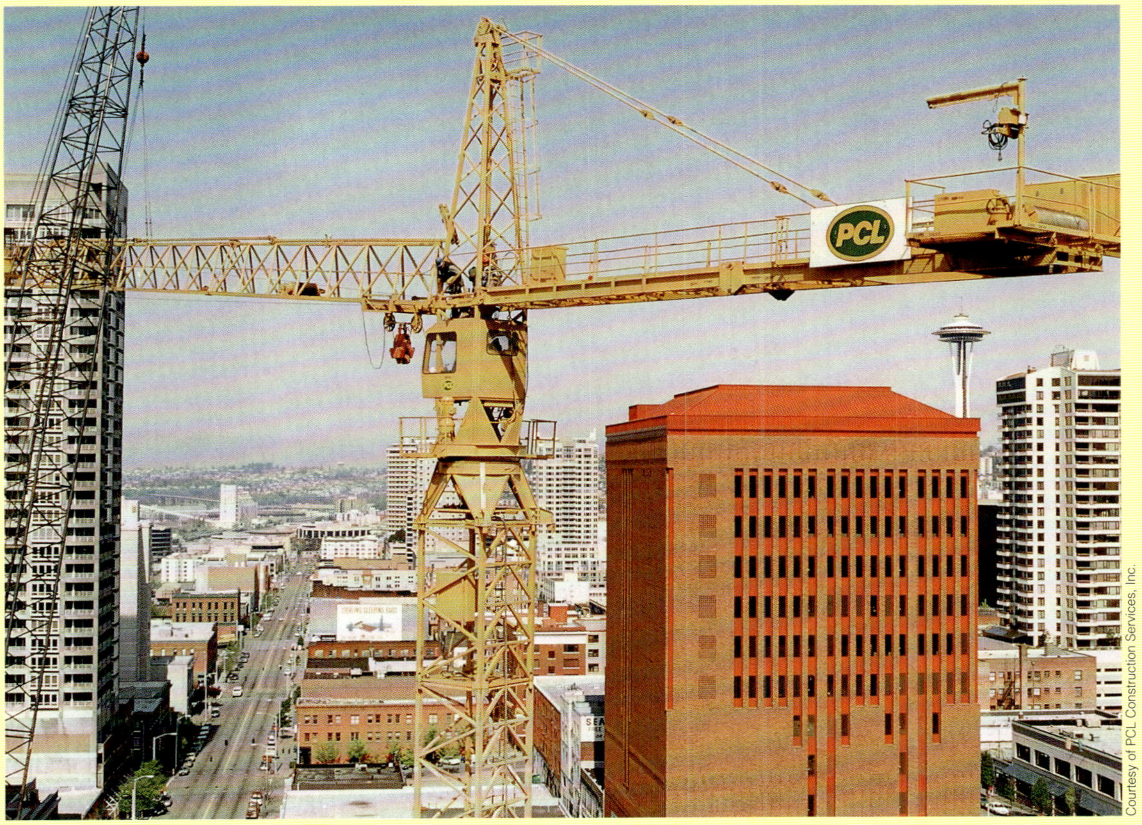

If an accident happens, the company's board of directors knows about it within the week—and the company never fails to investigate. PCL employees know that accidents can adversely affect productivity, costs, and employee relations—something that can affect them financially.

PCL and its employee-owners are deeply involved in the local community. As volunteers, employees assist in such programs as school renovations and park clean-ups. Employees have become solid supporters of the local United Way effort and sponsor families in need during the holiday season. PCL takes its responsibility of being a contributing Northwest citizen seriously.

PCL is in the Northwest to stay and its contributions, in terms of construction projects and community service, will continue to grow with each passing year.

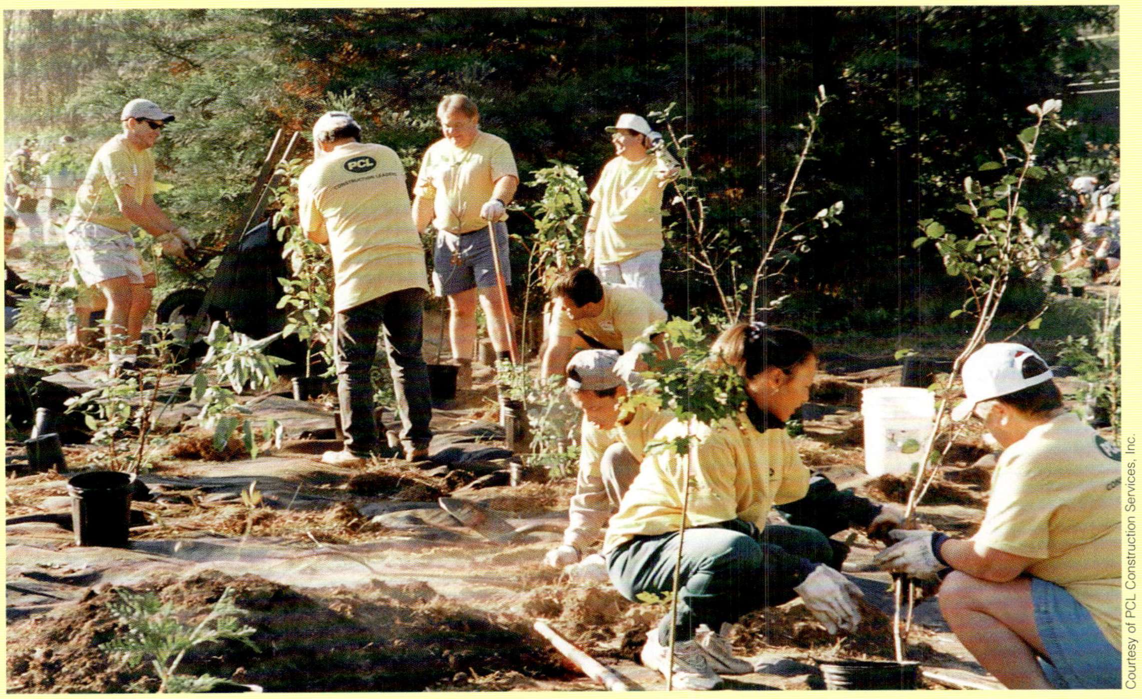

PCL employees support NAIOP's annual community enhancement projects.

Cadman, Inc.

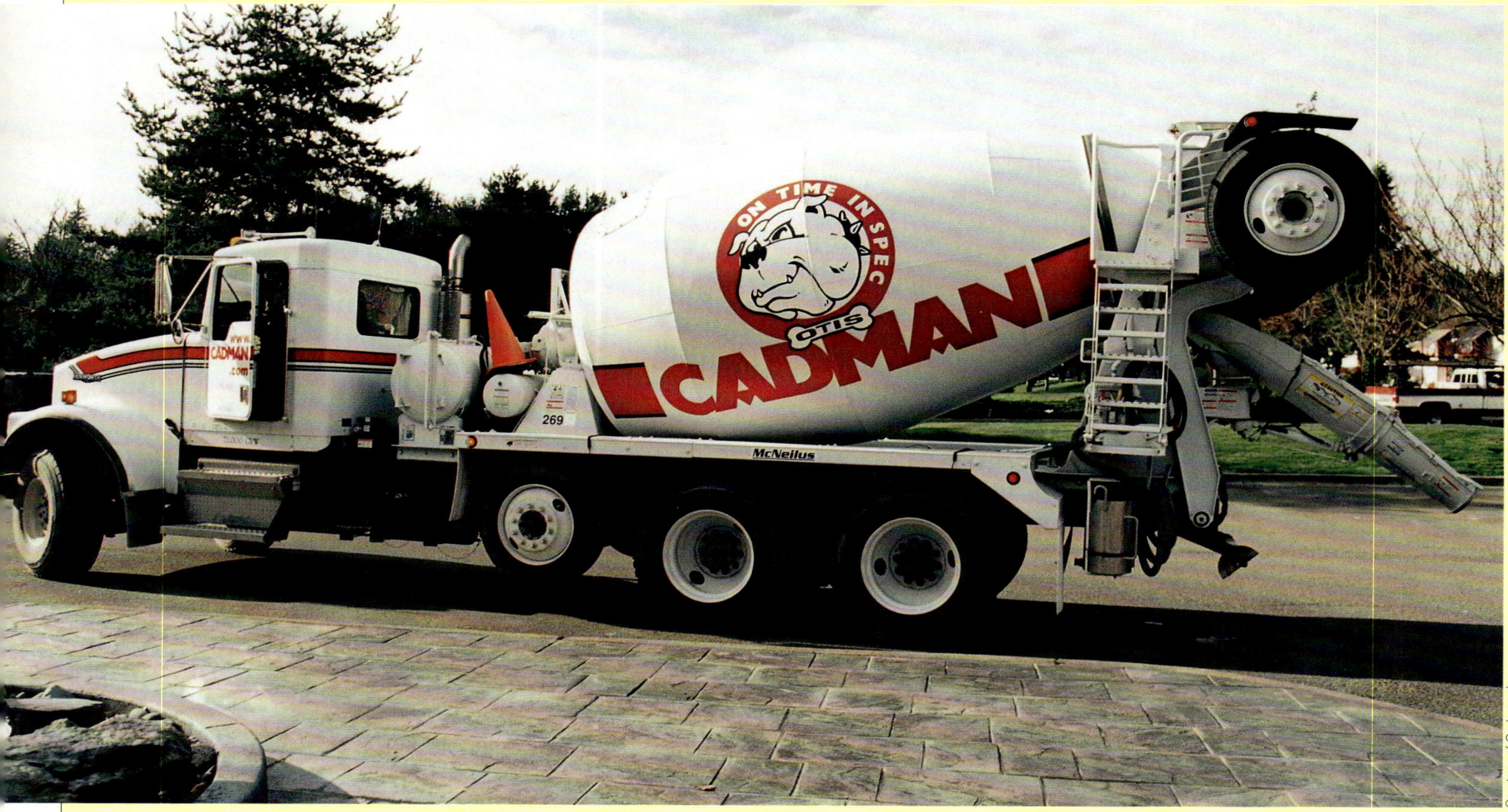

Courtesy of Cadman, Inc.

One of Cadman's ready-mix concrete trucks is ready to return for another load after pouring a decorative concrete walkway in Redmond.

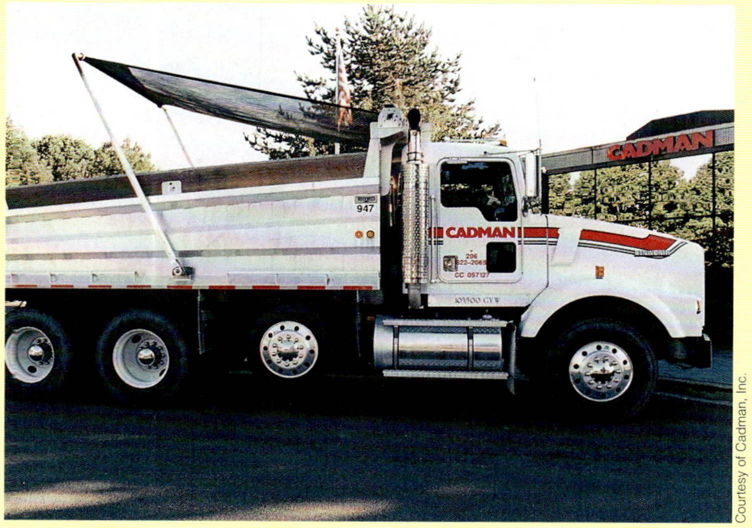

Courtesy of Cadman, Inc.

All dump trucks in Cadman's fleet are equipped with tarp covers to prevent rocks from spilling onto local roadways.

Anyone traveling the roadways of the King County area is, perhaps unknowingly, benefiting from products supplied by Cadman, Inc. The traveler may be further unaware of what Cadman is or what it produces. Headquartered in Redmond, the company lists itself as Western Washington's leading supplier of sand, gravel, and ready-mix concrete. From the roads that span the area, to the office buildings that are etched into the skyline, to the foundations of suburban homes, Cadman products have an unseen impact on everyday life.

The decorative concrete wall and entrance improvements exemplify Cadman's commitment to be part of the community.

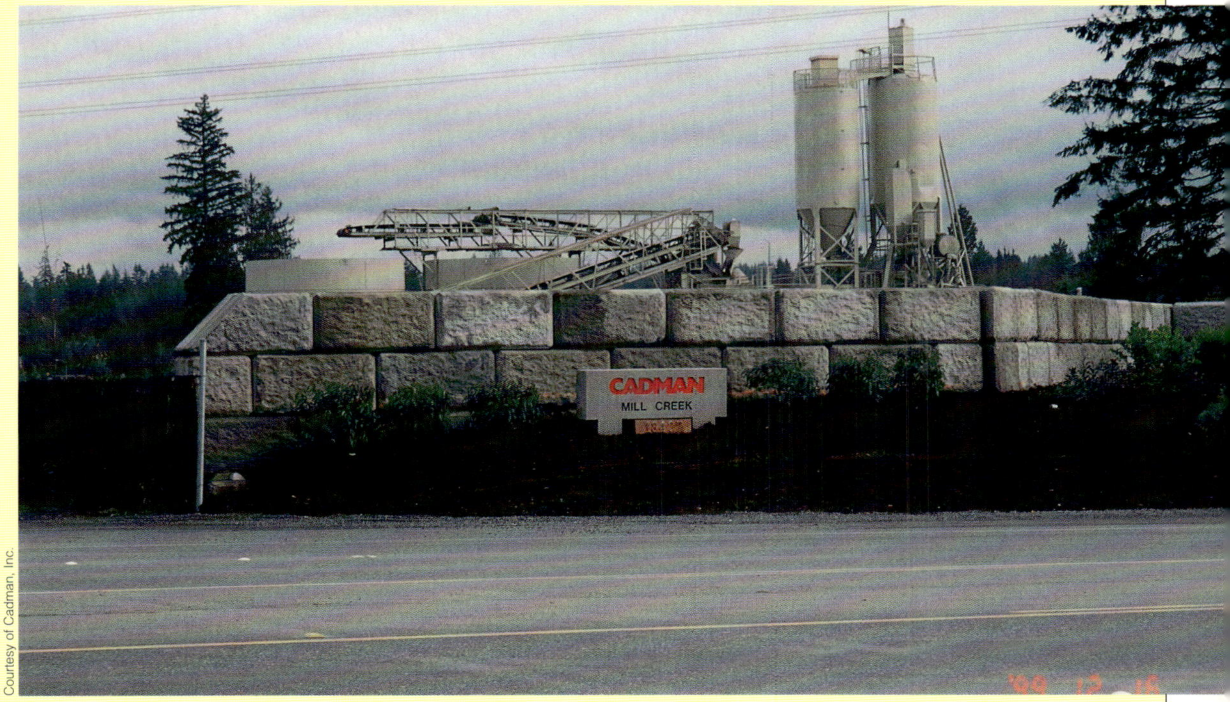

Operating from eight sites throughout the Puget Sound region, Cadman provides vital building materials for individuals, contractors, and government agencies. However, the company's focus is not solely on producing and selling materials. Its focus is on safety, quality, training, community outreach, environmental impact and employees. Cadman's efforts have resulted in numerous industry safety awards, government and industry environmental awards, a dedicated and committed workforce and broad community acceptance for its responsible approach to community needs.

"The Green Team Program" demonstrates Cadman's commitment to environmental issues. This environmental initiative involves every employee of the company and a Green Team employee action committee at each company site. The Green Team is responsible for the maintenance of practices and standards that protect the environment and provides ongoing training and education to employees, as well as to the public, on environmental issues.

OTIS demonstrates Cadman's commitment to its customers. An internally developed customer-service approach that stands for "On Time In Spec," OTIS promises on-time deliveries, made to individual specifications.

Cadman's products reliably serve the public, while respecting the environment and the communities and its employees without the negative impact of undue inconvenience and disruption, or environmental disregard. Roadways are smooth, buildings stand tall, firm foundations support homes, and life is just that much easier because Cadman is *"Working Together to Build our Communities."*

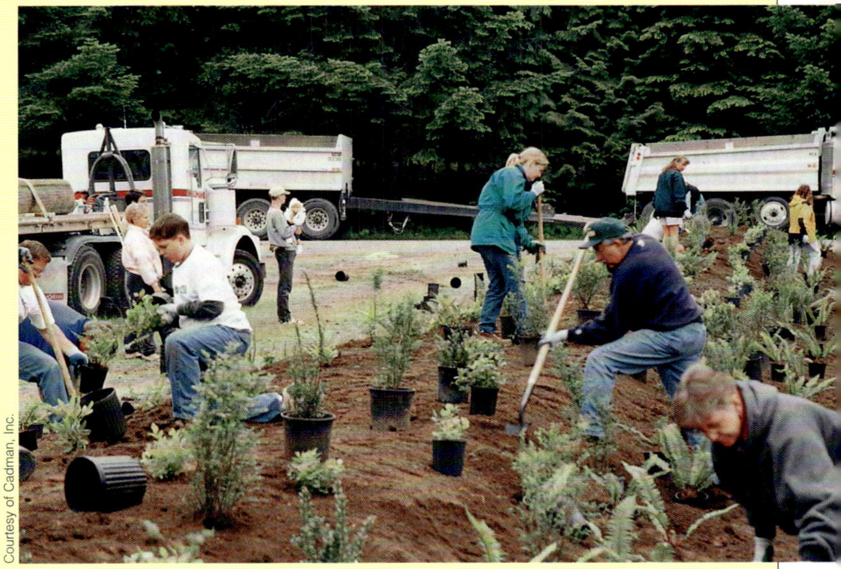

The Green Team organized this park restoration project to improve and enhance the experience of park visitors.

The Highridge Corporation

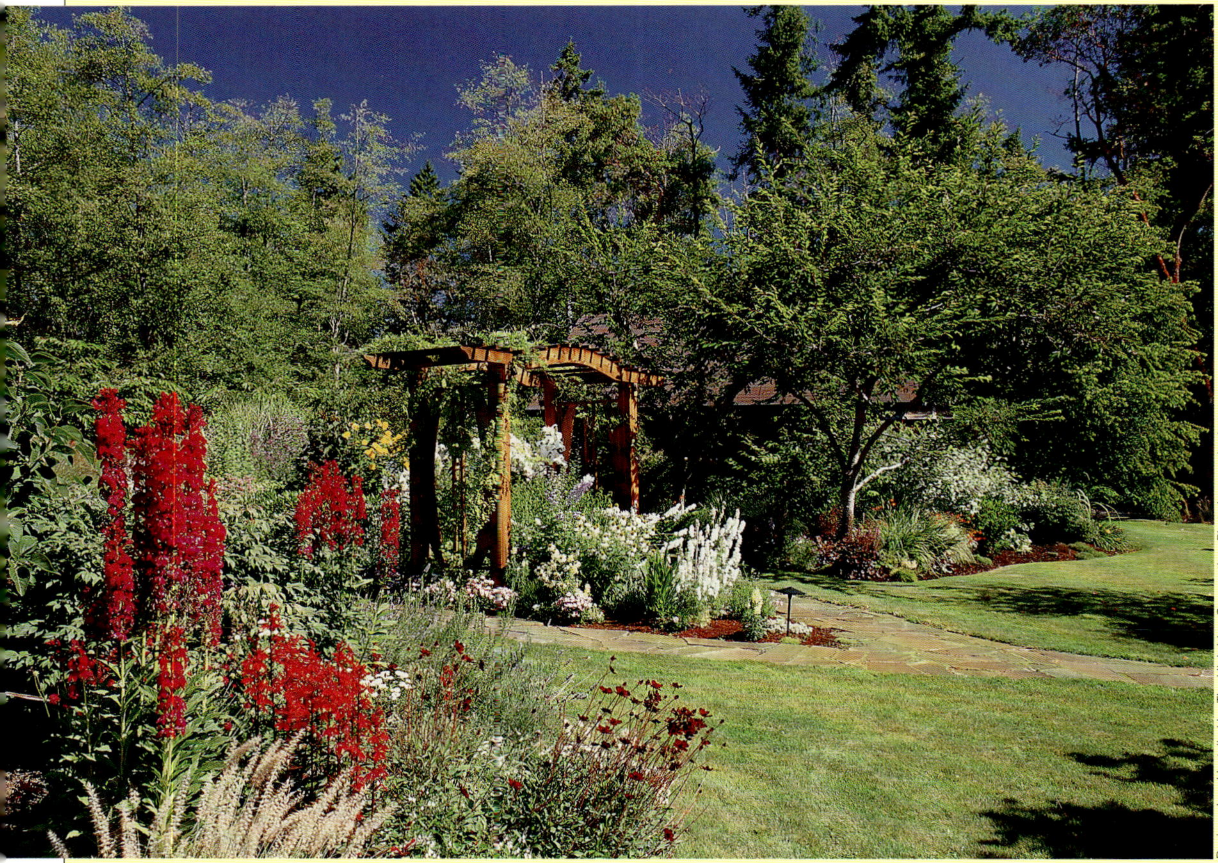

Designed and installed by The Highridge Corporation, Photo by www.jwphoto.com

This country estate garden was designed for a sunny afternoon stroll and closer contact with nature.

Washington State is known as the "Evergreen State" for good reason. Combine that lush native greenery with the rich color of blossoms and other flowers, set it in an arrangement of Northwest rocks, and the result is an extension of that wonderful feeling of nature right to the core of the city or the middle of an industrial development. That is the business of The Highridge Corporation.

Formed in 1985, Highridge has become one of the largest full-service landscape construction and design/build firms in the Pacific Northwest. Having started as a design and installation business, Highridge has developed into a multi-division operation which covers all aspects of landscape design, estimation, installation, and maintenance.

The company's design business ranges from single residential sites to the planning and design of landscaping for developments that include thousands of homes. In addition, a significant portion of Highridge's business involves the use of natural materials in attractive landscape designs that offset the stark appearances of large warehouses and industrial buildings.

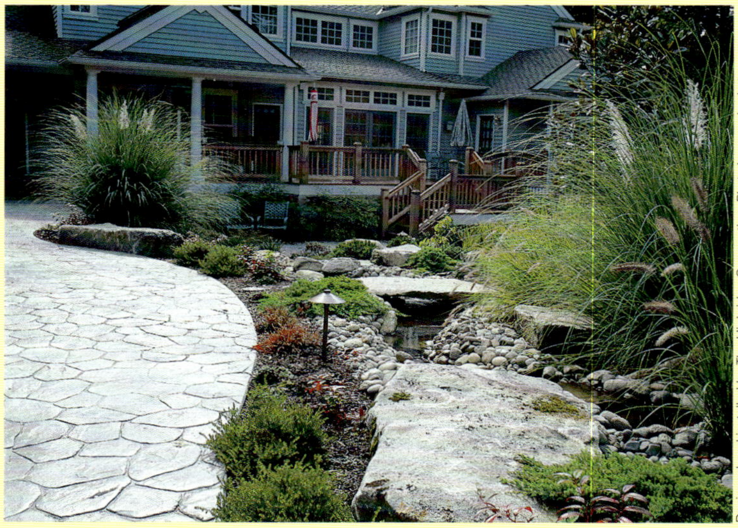

Designed and installed by The Highridge Corporation, Photo by www.jwphoto.com

This suburban garden retreat was carefully planned to integrate with the lifestyle of its King County resident.

A broad diversity of lifestyles is represented in Seattle and King County. The Highridge Corporation can install gardens planned to complement many different lifestyles.

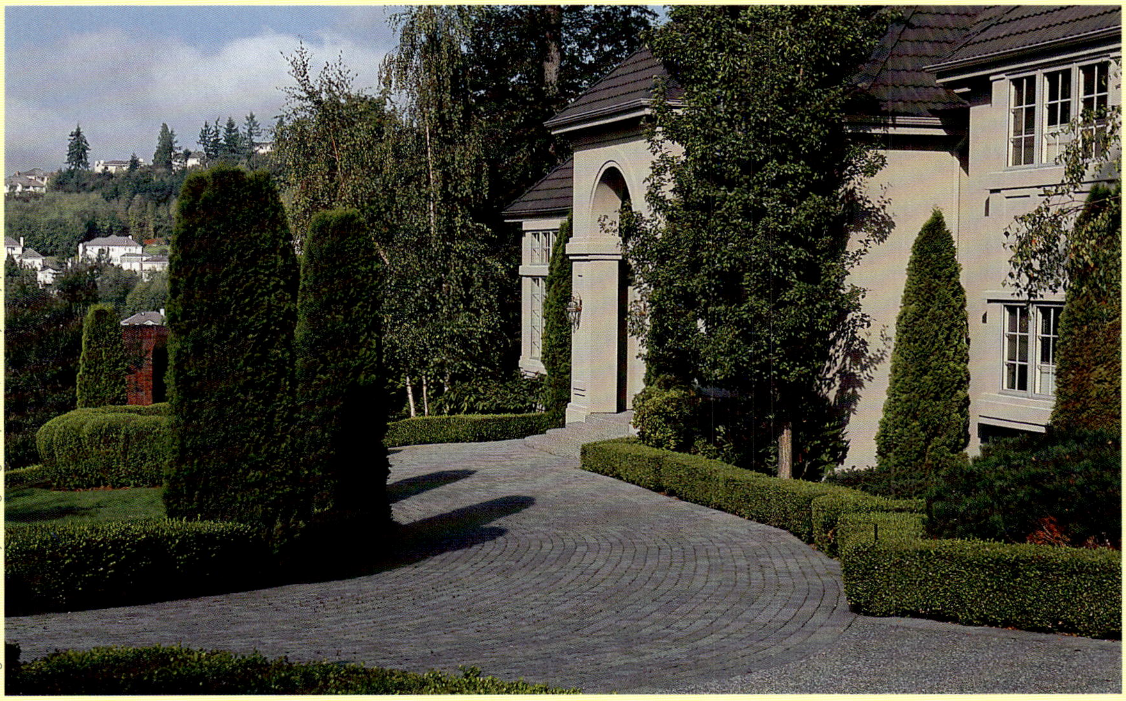

The maintenance division of Highridge has grown to over 18 trucks that operate full time maintaining lawns, shrubs, and trees. A color division handles nothing but flowers, keeping sites colorful year-round. The irrigation division includes registered technicians who specialize in efficient water useage. Altogether, The Highridge Corporation has over 100 trucks on the road and represents a major force in the horticultural industry.

The owners of Highridge are committed to the protection of the Pacific Northwest environment, and one of the owners has played a key role in Northwest Water Resource Management efforts, in cooperation with government agencies and other industry leaders. Highridge has been involved in a number of efforts to restore salmon habitat through the control of erosion and sedimentation.

Today, the company has grown to over 250 employees and boasts a branch office in the Portland area. Highridge points with pride to the many awards the company has received for excellence in design and for the major contributions the company has made to the Puget Sound area's reputation for natural beauty that extends even to the heart of the inner city.

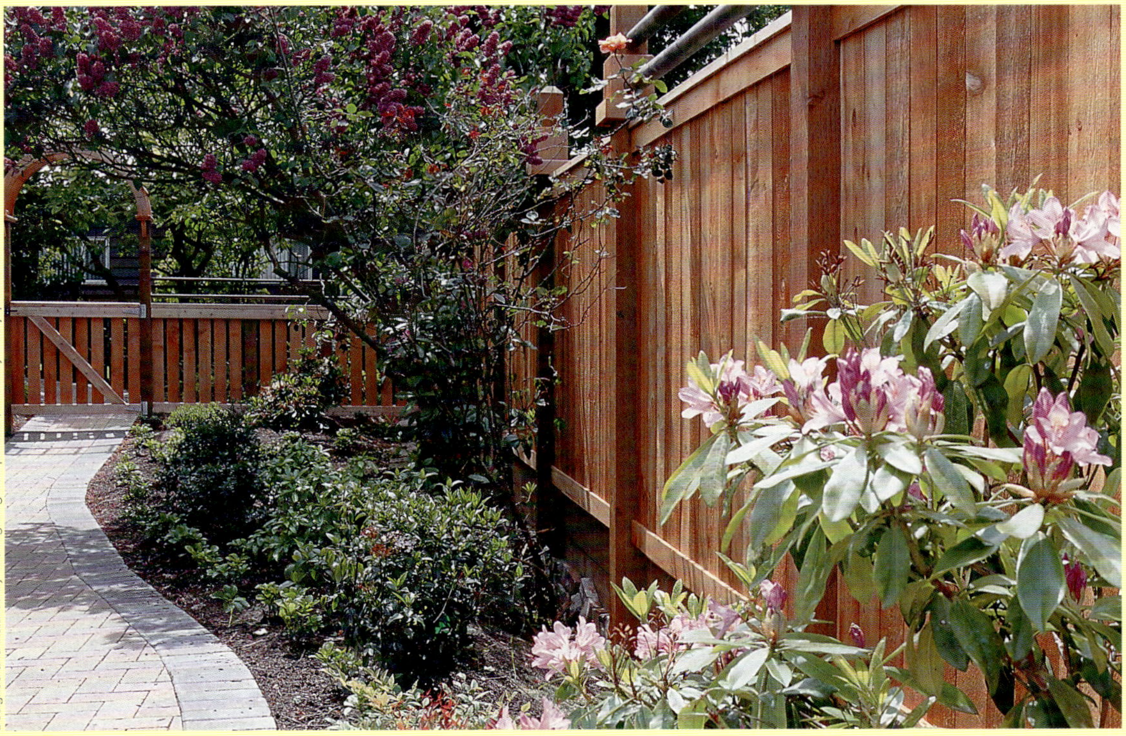

A well-crafted courtyard garden provides a restful haven from a busy day in the city.

Kiewit Construction Company

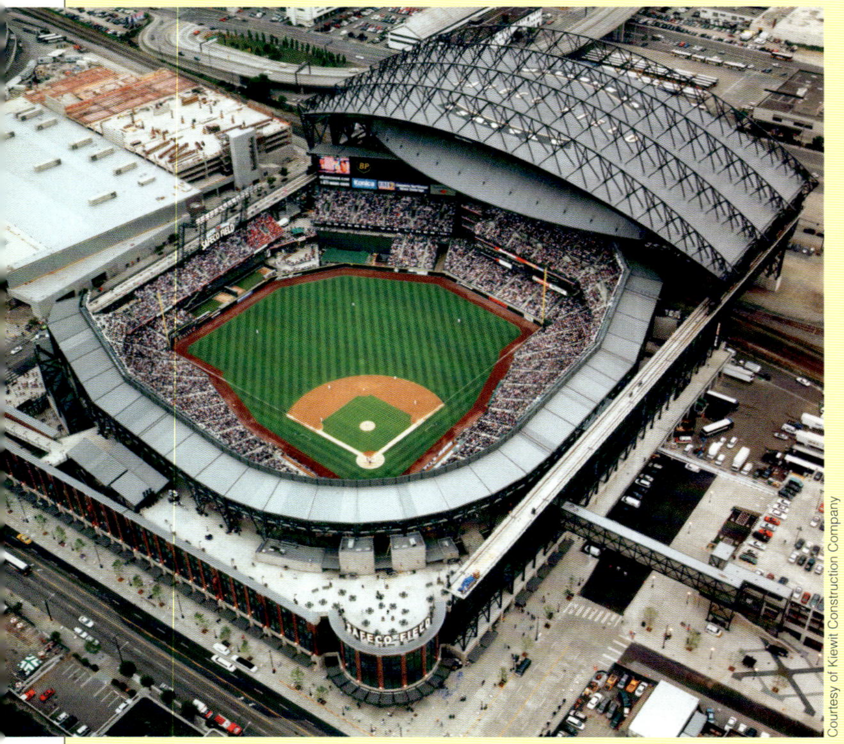

Safeco Field, completed in July 1999, includes 47,600 seats, Mariners' administrative offices, the Stadium Club, restaurants, state-of-the-art clubhouses, and retail and concession operations. The most notable feature is the unique 20,000-ton retractable roof.

No matter where people go in the Puget Sound region, chances are they will see a Kiewit-built building, or drive on Kiewit-built roads to get there. Kiewit Construction Company's Pacific Building District is responsible for airports, hotels, sports stadiums, schools, theaters, offices, and roads all over Seattle and the Greater Puget Sound region. And Kiewit's reputation for quality work done on time and within budget is as rock-solid as the structures the company builds.

Andrew and Peter Kiewit founded their company in 1884 in Omaha, Nebraska. From constructing buildings, the company quickly expanded and began building roadways, bridges, and tunnels. The company expanded geographically as well, and Peter Kiewit broke into the Pacific Northwest market rather dramatically in 1939.

In the winter of 1939, the United States was preparing for involvement in World War II. Young men were being drafted, and Fort Lewis needed barracks to house its inductees. Kiewit was awarded a contract to build 760 barracks, each designed to hold 64 men. Fort Lewis also needed roads, utilities, and support facilities. Kiewit agreed to build all of these—in 90 days. The project was made even more challenging when the Army doubled the order to 1,540 buildings without increasing the time frame. Equipment, managers, engineers, and skilled workers began pouring in from across the nation. Road equipment, idle for the winter, was transported by train or truck to Fort Lewis. Despite cold, wet, foggy weather, the project was completed on time and within budget and helped establish Kiewit as a presence in the Northwest.

Kiewit Construction Company went on to build many structures that are well known to Seattle residents. Among them are the Sears, Roebuck & Company building, finished in 1945 (now Starbucks' headquarters); the original Sea-Tac Airport parking garage; the VA Hospital; and numerous University of Washington buildings. Kiewit also built major sections of Interstates 5 and 90. Large, high-profile projects are a Kiewit specialty. The company's ability to operate under considerable pressure and within time and budget restraints guarantees that Kiewit will always have plenty of work in the Puget Sound region.

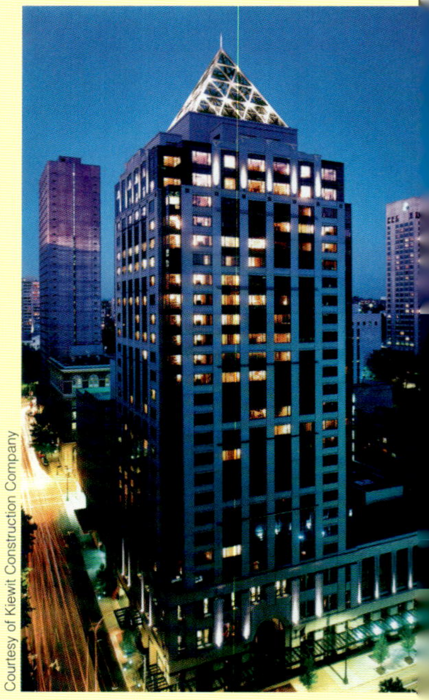

The 27-story, "four star" Starwood W Hotel includes 417 guestrooms, a fine-dining restaurant, meeting and ballrooms, and four levels of below-grade parking. It was completed in September 1999.

The new 244,000-square-foot Ballard High School, completed in August 1999, replaced the original building built in 1914. The new school has state-of-the-art features such as an in-house television studio, fiber-optic cabling, and closed-circuit television.

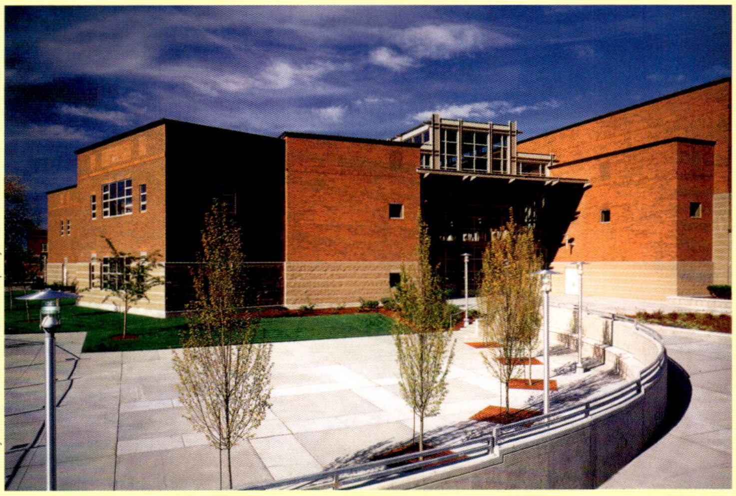

Courtesy of Kiewit Construction Company

One notable example of Kiewit Construction's gift for shining under pressure was the Kingdome stadium. When the original contractor walked off the project, Kiewit was called in to complete the half-finished building. Engineering mistakes complicated the job—the forms for the concrete roof ribs had become wedged in place. Kiewit workers engineered a way to release the forms and move them into position for the remaining pours of concrete and completed the dome in time for the Seattle Seahawks' 1976 inaugural season.

Kiewit also won the contract for the new Seattle Mariners' stadium. SAFECO Field was completed in just 27 months. The stadium's most notable feature, the unique retractable roof, weighs in at 12,000 tons and has become such a Seattle landmark that local residents joke that Seattle has only two kinds of weather: "roof open" and "roof closed."

Kiewit built the original buildings at the Pacific Science Center for the 1962 World's Fair, and since 1995, has completed six more projects for the facility. In 1995, Building 3 was renovated, and a generous donation from the Kiewit Foundation led to the naming of Building 3, "Kiewit Pavilion." Additionally, Kiewit built the Boeing 3-D IMAX Theater, the Ackerly Exhibit Gallery, the Butterfly Pavilion, and the James A. Claypool Memorial Parking Garage.

Kiewit constructed the new state-of-the-art Ballard High School, and in downtown Seattle, the 27-story Starwood 'W' Hotel, and the Washington State Convention and Trade Center Expansion. Challenging and unique building projects such as these have always attracted Kiewit's interest and given the company the opportunity to shine.

Kiewit's presence in the Pacific Northwest is part of a larger family of 20 decentralized regional offices throughout North America. The employee-owned company has more than 4,300 salaried employees and a workforce of nearly 20,000 people. The individual district offices often join together on projects, enabling Kiewit to cover every aspect of the project: materials, equipment, and expertise.

In 1939, Kiewit built barracks – lots and lots of barracks. Since then it has built nearly every kind of building imaginable. Any Puget Sound area resident or visitor has enjoyed the fruits of Kiewit's labor. With its hard-earned reputation for quality construction, Kiewit Construction Company will continue to play a major role in the building of the Northwest for a long time to come.

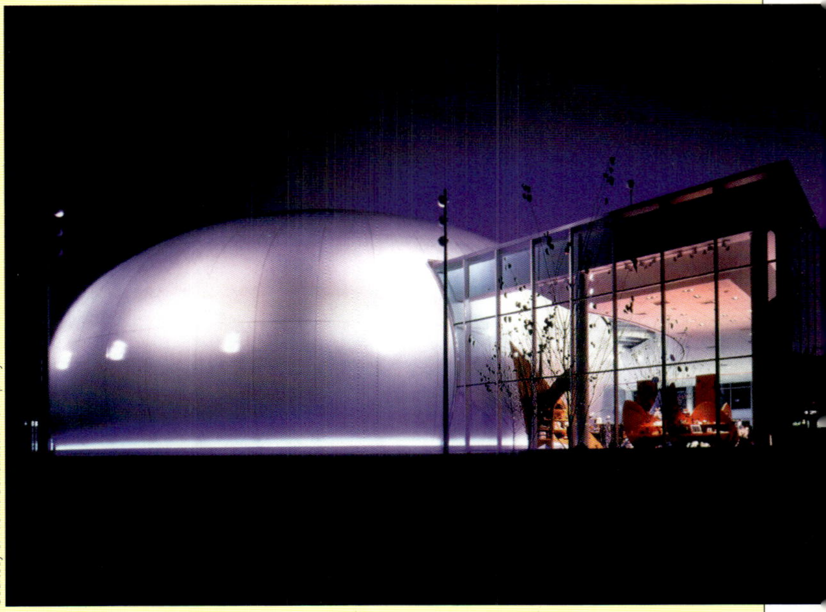

Courtesy of Kiewit Construction Company

The Pacific Science Center 3D/IMAX Theater is equipped with the latest 3D technology, a digital sound system, and over 400 seats. It was completed in October 1998.

Part Two

Quality of Life

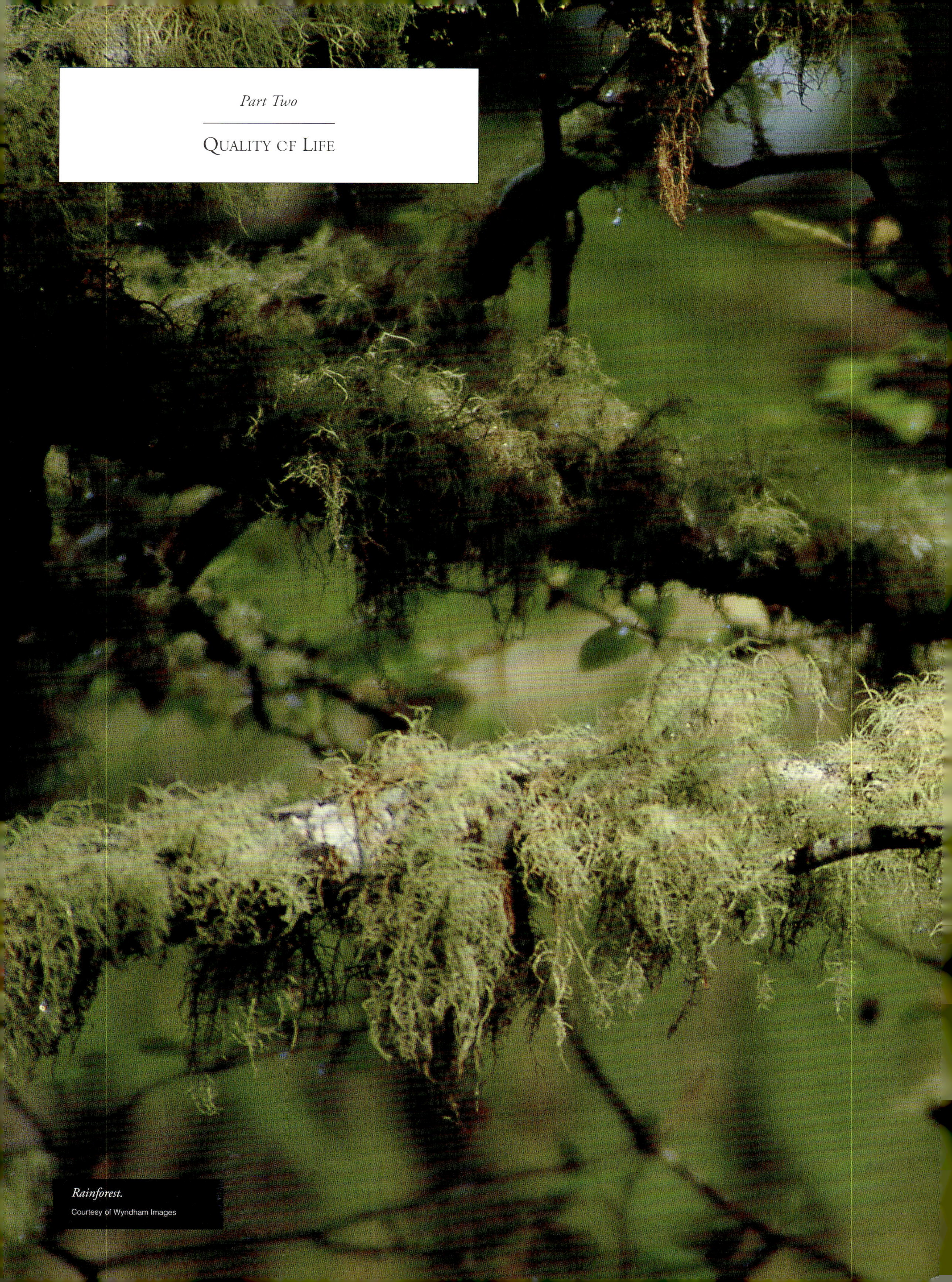

Rainforest.
Courtesy of Wyndham Images

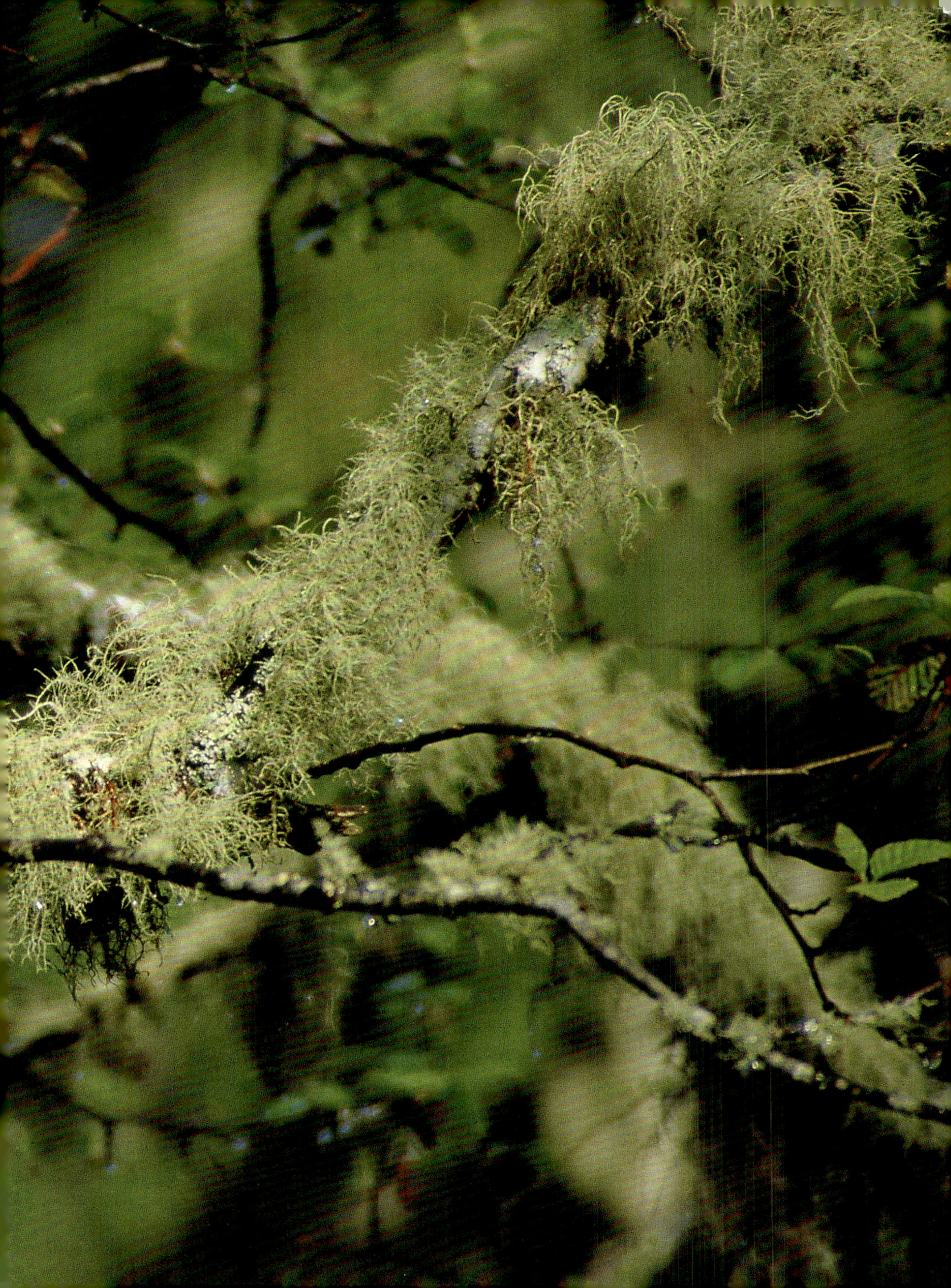

Children's Hospital and Regional Medical Center

"No one knows children like Children's" is a commonly heard phrase around Children's Hospital and Regional Medical Center. It is also quite commonly uttered throughout the Pacific Northwest. Since 1907, Children's (as it is most commonly called) has earned a special reputation built upon a unique knowledge, understanding, and commitment to the health and well being of children.

Originally Children's Orthopedic Hospital, this now legendary Pacific Northwest institution became so well known that a simple reference to the letters COH was enough to identify the place where children in need could get the very best treatment for the most critical health problems. From its beginnings, Children's has focused on its commitment to provide services to children with health care needs, without consideration for the families' ability to pay.

In the ensuing 90-plus years, the hospital has grown into much more than a place for sick children to receive treatment and serves children from Washington, Alaska, Montana, and Idaho. Today, the 208-bed Hospital is home to over 200 physicians and dentists, over 40

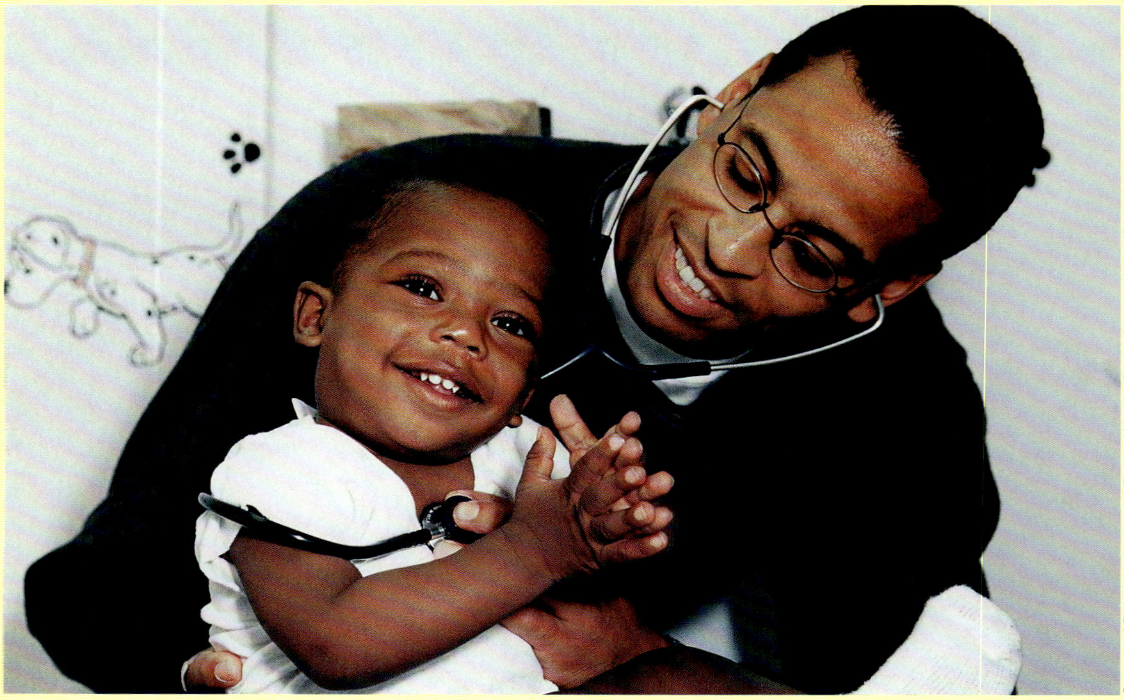

Courtesy of Children's Hospital and Regional Medical Center, Photo by William Stickney

Dr. Ben Danielson with a one-year-old patient at Odessa Brown Children's Clinic.

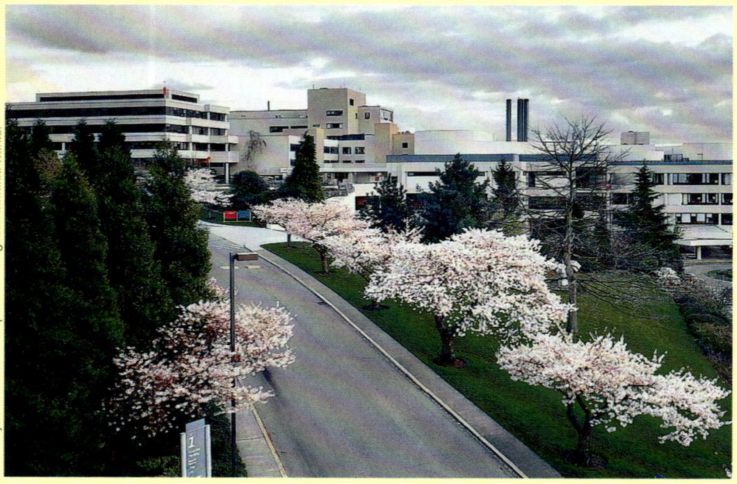

Courtesy of Children's Hospital and Regional Medical Center

Children's Hospital and Regional Medical Center's main campus during cherry blossom season.

outpatient clinics, a growing research mission, and is a most valuable training and educational setting for young physicians interested in the special needs of children. The main hospital campus occupies a 25-acre site, which was donated in 1953 and is located in the Laurelhurst neighborhood of Seattle.

Partnerships with other leading medical and research facilities and a number of regional specialty clinics provide a broader range of specialty-care services to children throughout the region. In 1907, one of the first patients treated at Children's was a young girl from Alaska. Nearly a century later, the hospital continues to serve children from a wide area. Many patients find their way to Children's based on referrals from physicians in their own communities who respect the high level of expertise and skill of the hospital's staff. Children's is the pediatric teaching hospital for the University of Washington School of Medicine, with the Department of Pediatrics based at Children's. A number of these physicians received a part of their own training at Children's and are fully familiar with, and confident of, the quality of care provided by Children's.

The hospital's mission continues to focus in four areas. Patient care is first and foremost; it includes the provision of over 170,000 patient visits annually (both inpatient and outpatient). The second area of focus is education, with over 150 medical students doing rotations through the hospital each year and nearly 500 residents and fellows receiving pediatric training in a variety of specializations.

Endocrinologist Gad Kletter with a Children's patient at the Endo clinic in Wenatchee.

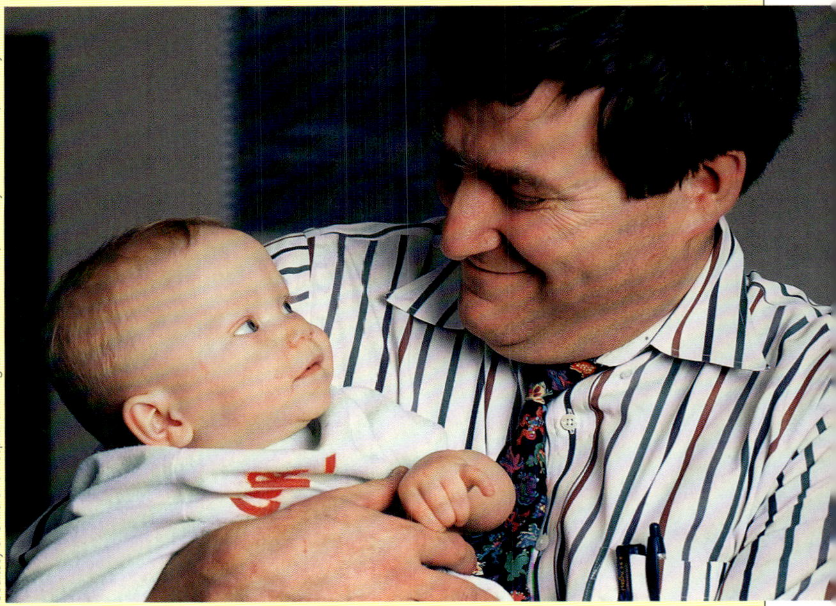

Courtesy of Children's Hospital and Regional Medical Center. Photo by Rich Villacres, Red Sky Photo

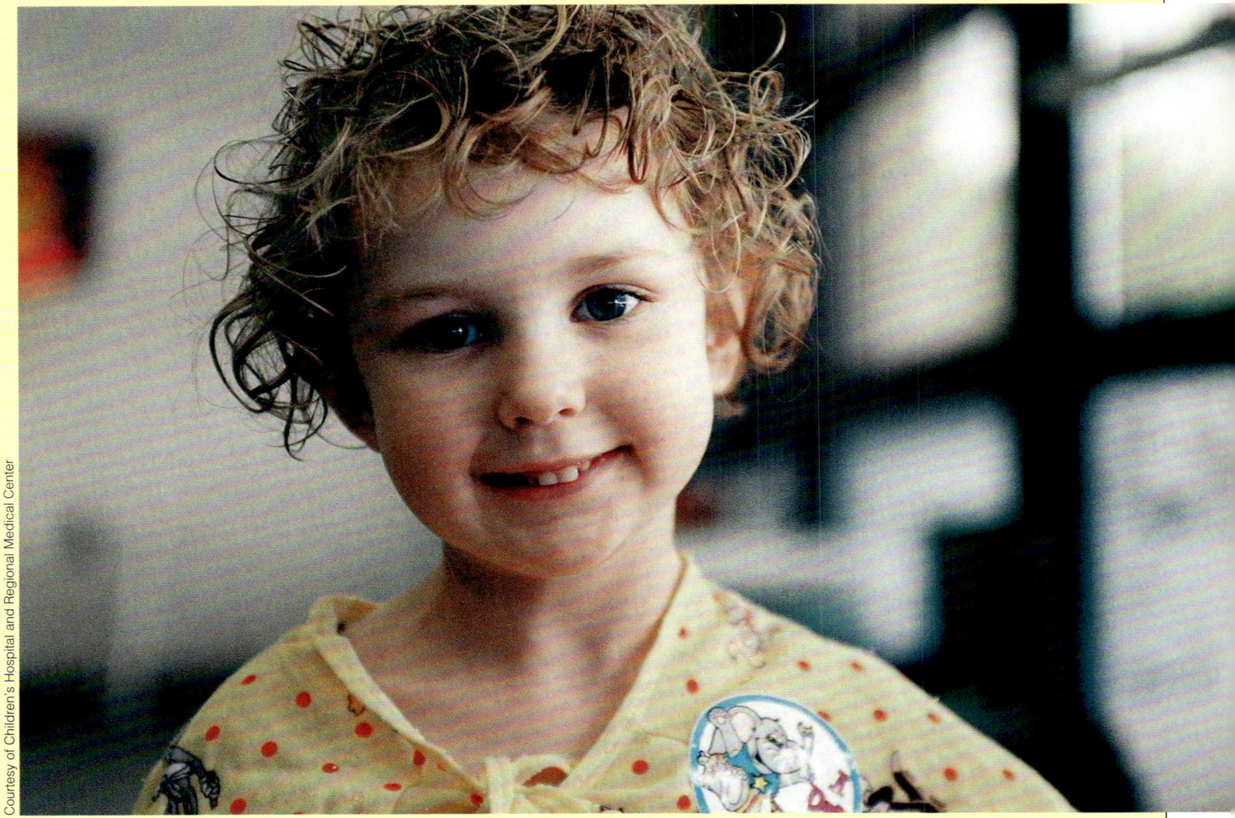

Courtesy of Children's Hospital and Regional Medical Center

Five-year-old patient from Skagway, Alaska.

A patient is pleased with the giraffes at the entrance of Children's.

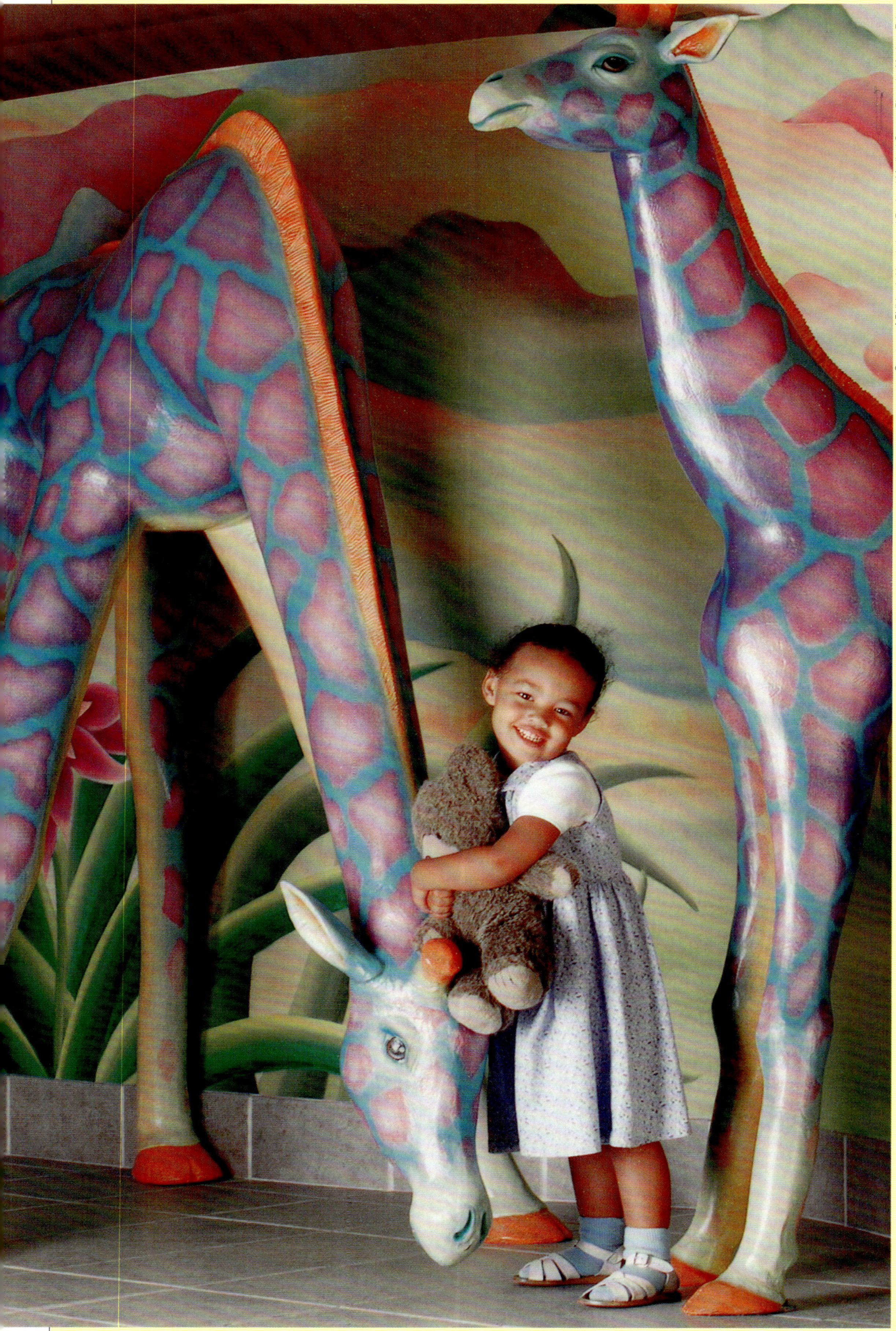

Courtesy of Children's Hospital and Regional Medical Center. Photo by Matthew Felton

The third area is research. Children's involvement in research has been increasing rapidly. Over the past 10 years, external funding for at Children's has more than tripled, and the number of research projects has grown by more than 100 percent. Immunology and infectious diseases, genetic and development conditions, and cancer are the research themes that will serve as the focus of Children's expanded research program. The commitment to research is, of course, always tied closely to patient care. An excellent example is the formation, with the University of Washington and the world-renowned Fred Hutchinson

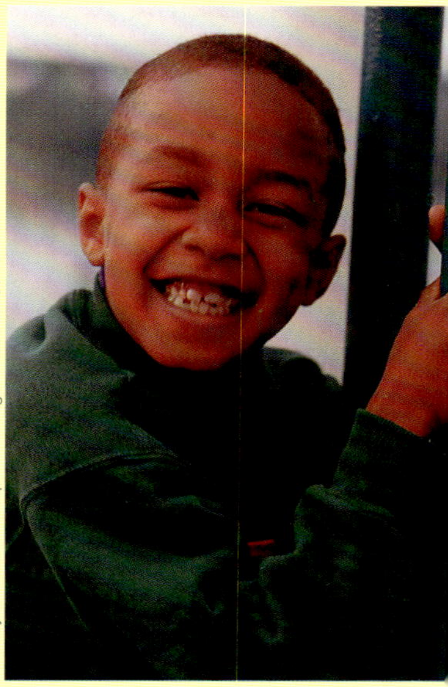

Courtesy of Children's Hospital and Regional Medical Center

Children's patient Jeremiah Latham.

A Children's volunteer is holding an infant patient at Children's Hospital.

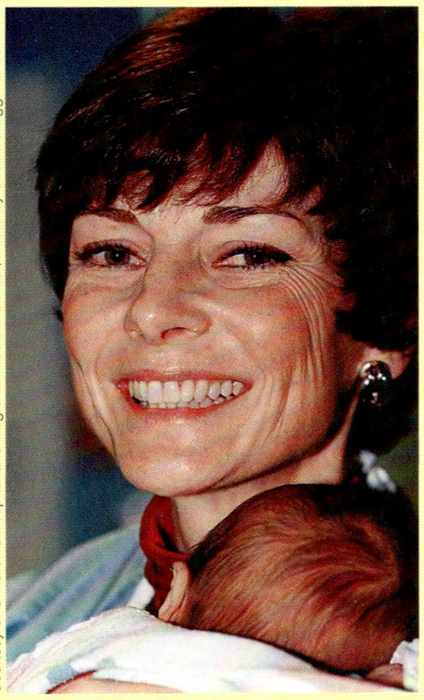

Courtesy of Children's Hospital and Regional Medical Center. Photo by Susan Gregg-Hanson

Cancer Research Center, of the Seattle Cancer Care Alliance (SCCA). This joint effort will speed the development of new treatments for various cancers and will provide integrated cancer care for both children and adults.

Finally, the fourth focus of the hospital's mission is advocacy for children in all aspects of their lives. This commitment has led the hospital to join campaigns for safety initiatives on such things as drowning prevention and bicycle helmets. Children's has also taken great strides in understanding the causes and helping to prevent Sudden Infant Death Syndrome and Shaken Baby Syndrome.

One other striking element stands out concerning Children's and its contributions to the Pacific Northwest. Perhaps it is due to the special, heart-felt appeal of issues concerning children and the compulsion of the parental instinct that burns strongly within so many; but whatever the reason, the reality is that Children's enjoys one of the strongest, most devoted volunteer support systems of any medical community anywhere. Children's' dedicated army of volunteers contributes thousands of hours of service to the hospital every year. Nearly 500 volunteer guilds, with 8,500 members, assist in fundraising and promotion for the medical center. Junior Orthopedic Guilds reach into high schools and build a tradition of volunteer followers, generation after generation. Contributions from individual and corporate donors also help ensure that no children are denied medical care, regardless of the families' ability to pay.

In this place of healing there exists a very special knowledge of children and their health care needs. For nearly a century, this institution has exhibited a particular dedication to using the latest innovations and technologies for the service and treatment of those needs and the highest level of commitment to finding answers where there seem to be none. In the end, the comforting fact remains, *"No one knows children like Children's."*

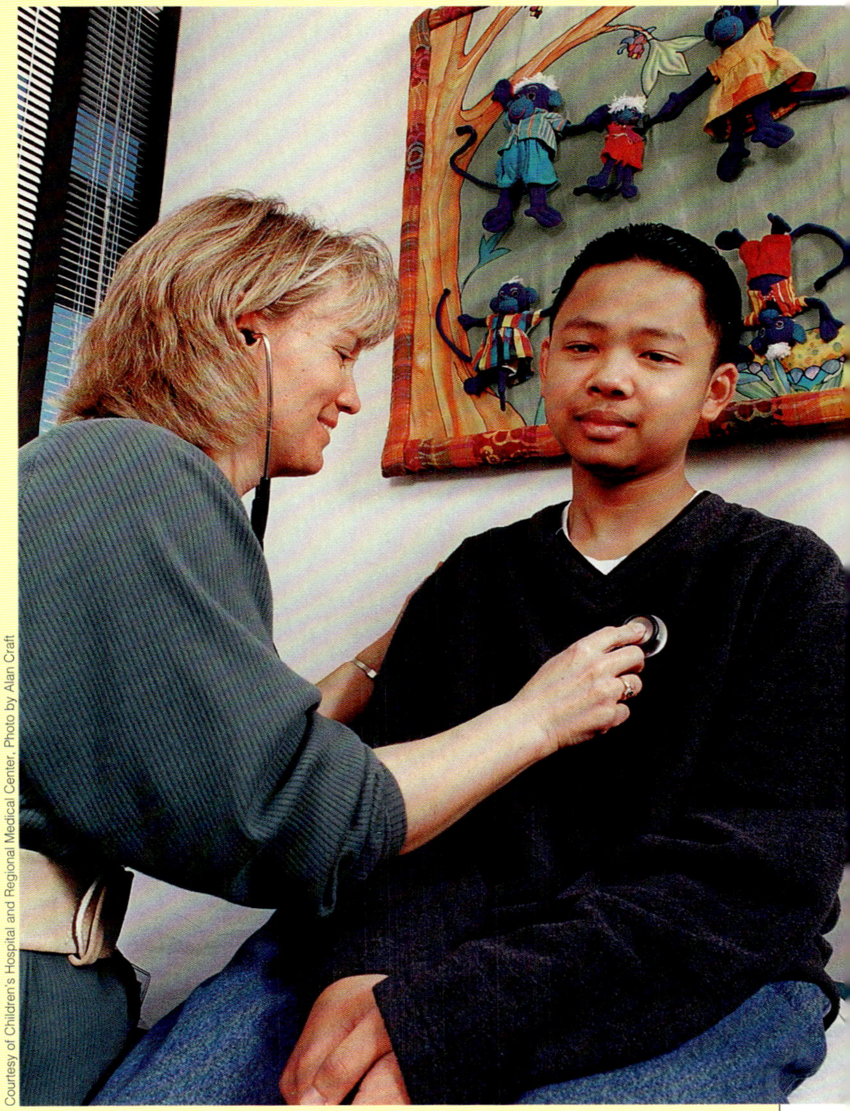

Courtesy of Children's Hospital and Regional Medical Center. Photo by Alan Craft

Nancy Nelson, pediatric nurse practitioner, examines a 15-year-old gastroenterology patient during a recent visit to Children's Olympia.

VA Puget Sound Health Care System—Seattle Division

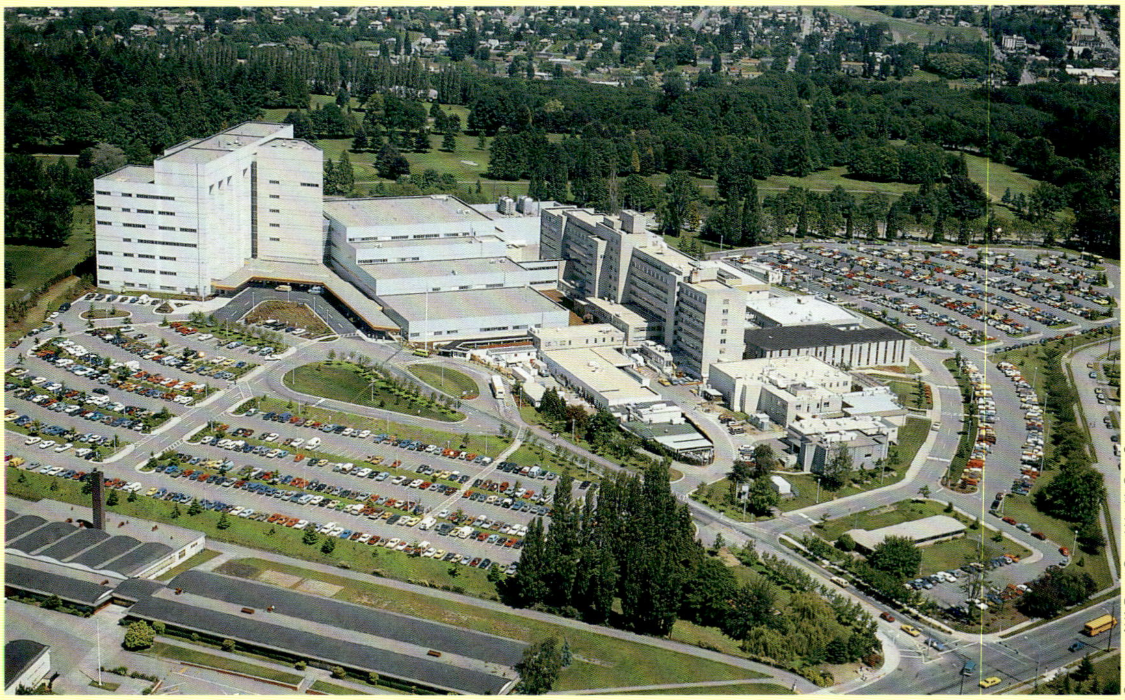
Courtesy of VA Puget Sound Health Care System

Aerial view of VA Puget Sound—Seattle.

The Puget Sound region is well known for its spectacular views of Mount Rainier, the historic Pioneer Square district, its burgeoning high-tech industries, and excellence in health care. VA Puget Sound Health Care System's two campuses, at American Lake in Tacoma and on Beacon Hill in Seattle, combine to be the largest provider of health care for veterans in the Pacific Northwest. With over 500,000 outpatient visits and more than 10,000 inpatient visits annually, VA Puget Sound Health Care System is the largest facility in the VA's Northwest Network and is the major tertiary-care referral center for veterans from Alaska, Idaho, and Washington. Its complex mission incorporates a broad continuum of primary, specialty, and long-term care as well as mental health, addictions treatment, spinal cord injury treatment, comprehensive cancer care, dialysis, home health care, nursing home, hospice programs, sophisticated cardiovascular and surgical procedures, and outreach services.

Both campuses have rich histories, delivering the highest quality of medical care and services supported by nationally prominent centers of excellence that incorporate teaching, research, and patient care initiatives. This is evident by the numerous national and state awards for leadership innovations and technology. With world-class leaders in fields ranging from geriatrics and aging to cardiovascular surgery, to mental health and rehabilitation medicine, VA Puget Sound is proud of its collaborative, integrated approach to health care.

This pride extends to the many achievements over the years, including the discovery of two major genes related to

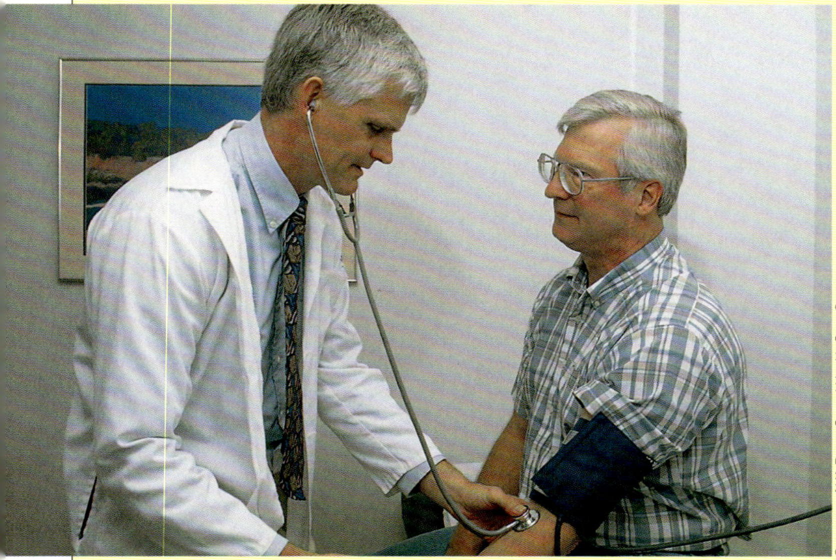
Courtesy of VA Puget Sound Health Care System

VA Puget Sound Health Care System offers a variety of specialized health-care programs providing veterans with individualized treatments.

Alzheimer's Disease and dementia, oncology radiation therapy participation in a national Shingles Vaccine Study, designation as the first medical center performing abdominal aortic stent grafting in the Northwest, and development of the world-famous Seattle Foot. Internationally known investigators working to unravel the mysteries of aging and dementia are also working to identify genetic markers for Multiple Sclerosis, Huntington's Disease, and other genetically based diseases. In collaboration with the Fred Hutchinson Cancer Research Program, VA Puget Sound is a national referral center for stem-cell transplantation for leukemia and lymphoma. VA Puget Sound Health Care System is also a leader in radioactive "seed" treatment for prostate cancer through its radiation therapy center.

VA Puget Sound hosts one of the largest research programs in the VA system; some of the nation's most prominent researchers reside at the medical center's two campuses. VA investigators routinely compete successfully for grant money against the best in the private industry. Cooperative studies involve the University of Washington, Fred Hutchinson Cancer Research Center, National Institutes of Health, and the private sector. Breakthrough advances range from the innovative design of footwear for diabetics being done in collaboration with the NIKE Corporation, to new computerized technologies designed to aid the mobility of those facing amputation and limb loss, to new therapeutic strategies for dealing with Post Traumatic Stress, mental illness, and severe depression.

External review and accreditation is a key measurement of VA Puget Sound's success and includes: the Joint Commission on Accreditation of Health Care Organizations; College of American pathologists;

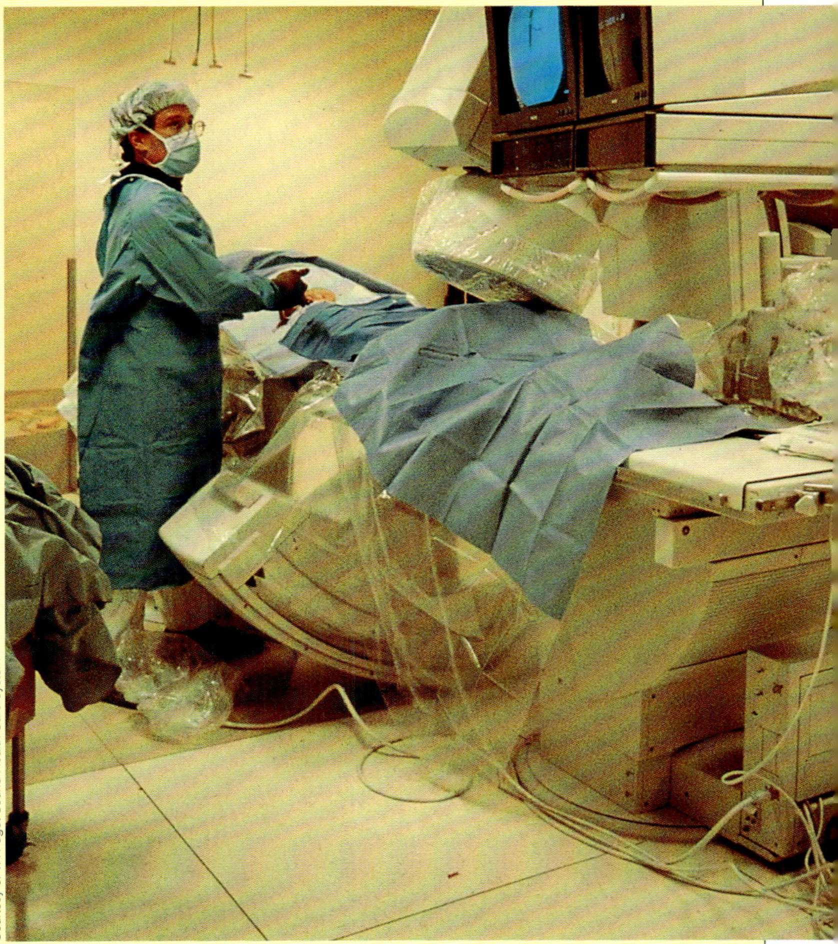

Courtesy of VA Puget Sound Health Care System

New imaging technologies, computers, and telemedicine all support the newest innovations that improve health-care options for veterans.

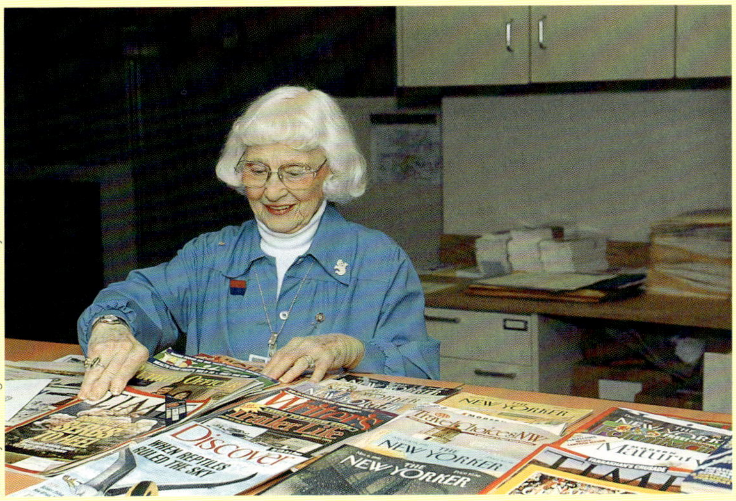

Courtesy of VA Puget Sound Health Care System

Volunteers play a major role in veterans' health care. Over 1,300 volunteers routinely donate more than 200,000 hours annually in support of veterans.

Using the latest advancements in surgical applications, patients are often able to return to normal activity more quickly after surgery.

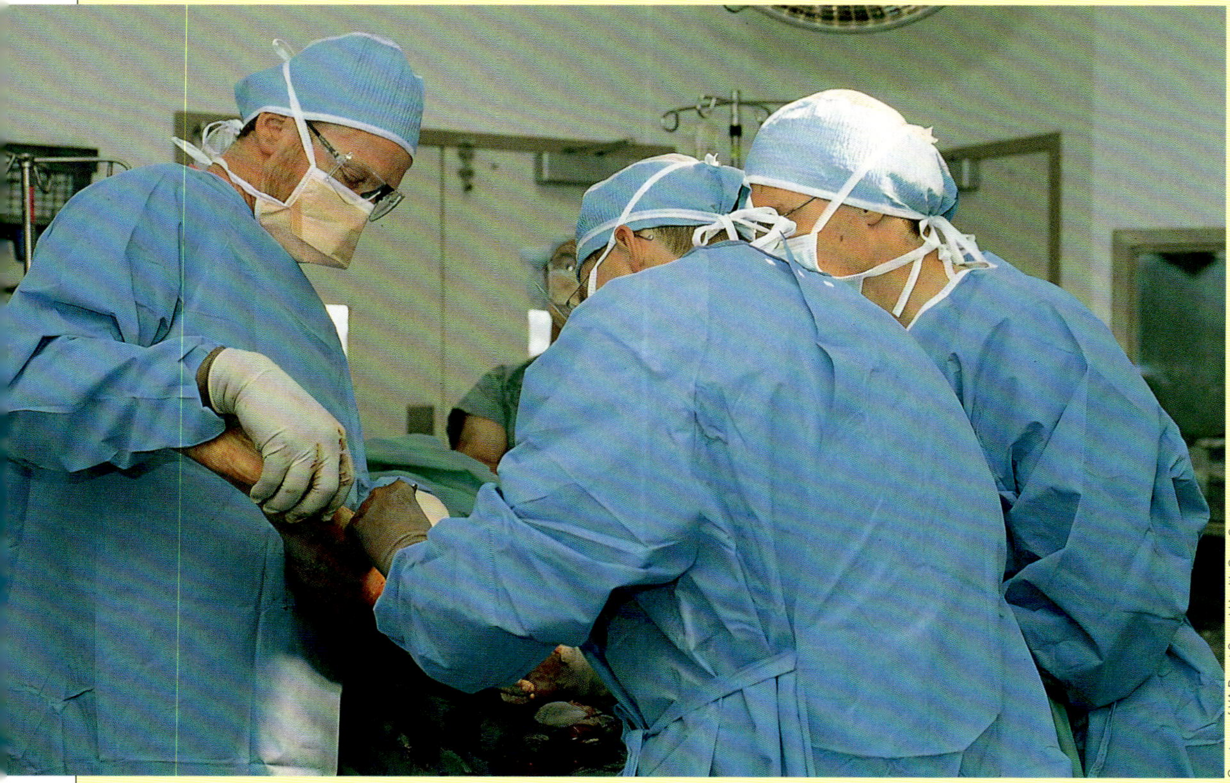

Courtesy of VA Puget Sound Health Care System

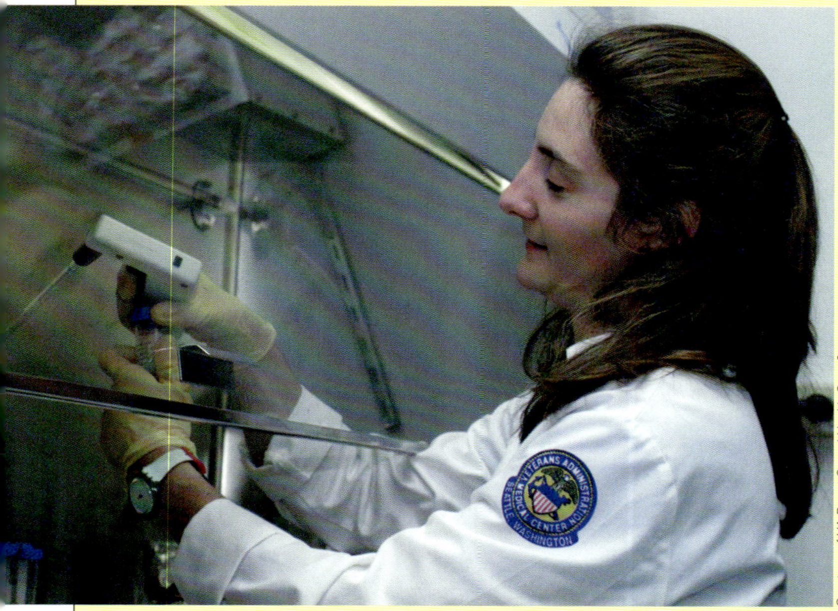

Courtesy of VA Puget Sound Health Care System

Research is an important component of health care, resulting in improved clinical outcomes through advanced treatment options.

American Association of Health System Pharmacists; Accreditation Council for Graduate Medical Education, State of Washington; Council of Accredited Rehabilitation Facilities; and the Commission on Cancer of the American College of Surgeons.

Clinical informatics is integral to daily business at VA Puget Sound's two campuses, bringing health care closer to patients by utilizing interactive computer technology. VA Puget Sound is a national leader in implementing a comprehensive, paperless computerized system for patient records, receiving the Nicholas E. Davies Award for Health Care Clinical Informatics. This highly specialized electronic tool enhances the exchange of medical information and provides immediate and seamless access to medical records, diagnostic tests, and clinical information. This advanced system is but one example of how VA Puget Sound uses sophisticated technologies to advance patient care.

VA is also leading the way in new technologies to enhance prescription medication safety. A new barcode medication administration system virtually eliminates medication errors in hospital dispensing of drugs. Telemedicine clinics have been developed in cardiology, the regional tumor board, dermatology, pre-surgical work-up, and home spinal cord injury care, bringing patient and provider together electronically over huge distances. These new technologies create a more seamless system of information sharing, but also contribute to greater patient safety, improve the quality and delivery of care, and provide new tools to prepare the next generation of health care providers.

University of Washington

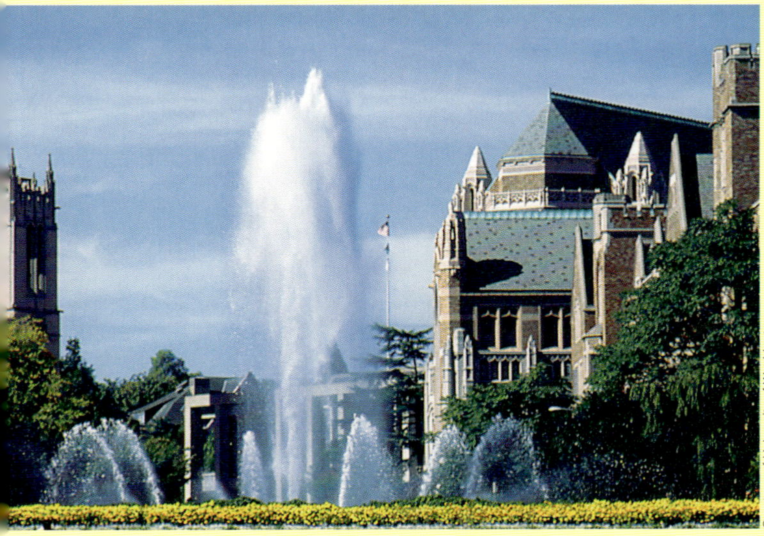

Drumheller fountain, a 1961 centennial gift from Regent Joseph Drumheller, is a cool and inviting place on a spring day.

Founded in 1961, the University of Washington (UW) has long been a leading institution of higher learning in the Pacific Northwest. With 16 schools and colleges located on its main campus in Seattle and new campuses in Bothell and Tacoma, the University of Washington has many programs that are among the best in the country—from aeronautics and drama to medicine, computer science, and zoology. In programs that stress broad-based education, students enjoy the benefits of a major research university: faculty at the forefront of their fields, a dynamic curriculum, opportunities for direct research experience, and extensive library collections. The university operates such state-of-the-art research centers as Friday Harbor Laboratories, widely acknowledged as the world's leading center for teaching and research on invertebrate animals.

Each year since 1974, the university has received more federal research funds than any other public university in the country, and it now ranks second among all universities, including private, in federal funding. The distinction reflects the quality and stature of the university's faculty.

The University of Washington has earned an international reputation for the quality of its graduate programs, which places it among a handful of elite institutions. The chance to work on the cutting edge of scientific and scholarly research draws almost 8,000 graduate students to UW programs, which include more than 90 special research centers and 25 field sites.

The university helps shape the identity of the Pacific Northwest. UW faculty and graduates helped launch Seattle's now thriving theater scene, and the university continues to enrich local culture and to support the arts with its two museums, three theaters and more than 450 performances each year. Plays, concerts, exhibits, and lectures draw thousands for visitors to the main campus annually. For sports fans, there are football games in Husky Stadium and events in 22 additional Husky sports.

The university bolsters the region's economy. It contributes high-quality workers to the labor force. Each year, 70 percent of its 9,000 graduates remain in the state and add their skills to the economy. The university also generates some 35,000 jobs in the state beyond the 20,000 people it employs directly.

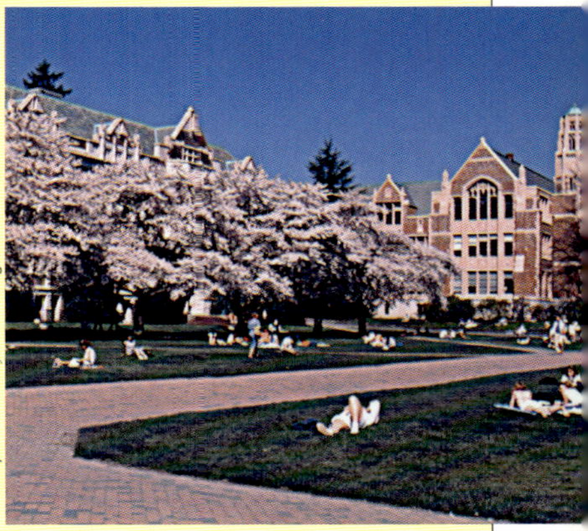

The Liberal Arts Quadrangle, framed with cherry trees, provides beauty and a convenient study spot for many undergraduate students.

Swedish Medical Center

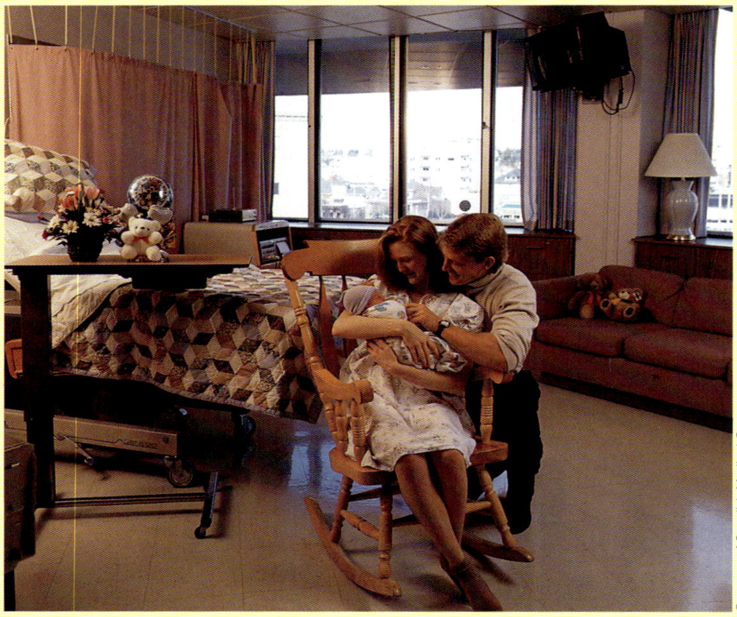

Courtesy of Swedish Medical Center

Birthing suites at Swedish offer parents-to-be the comforts of home and the most advanced obstetrics care in the region.

In 1910, Dr. Nils Johanson convinced each of 10 fellow Swedish immigrants to buy $1,000 bonds in order to fund a dream. With this modest stake, Dr. Johanson founded Swedish Hospital in a remodeled apartment building on Seattle's First Hill. The hospital had just 24 beds, but Dr. Johanson's vision of establishing a not-for-profit, state-of-the-art hospital drove the once-small facility to unimagined levels of success.

Today, Swedish is Washington state's largest, most comprehensive medical center. It encompasses three hospitals spanning 25 city blocks: a 697-bed tertiary-care facility on the First Hill campus; a 163-bed community hospital in Seattle's Ballard neighborhood (Swedish Medical Center/Ballard campus); and the 334-bed Swedish/Providence campus, which became part of Swedish after Swedish merged with Providence Seattle Medical Center. At its First Hill and Ballard campuses alone, Swedish records more than 30,500 inpatient admissions and 480,000 outpatient visits each year.

Beyond the inpatient facilities are numerous outpatient clinics, day-surgery centers, a research center, and a home-health and hospice program. In short, Swedish Medical Center provides expert care in almost every medical and surgical specialty, assuring patients of a thorough diagnosis and treatment.

Along with the comprehensive nature of care at Swedish, there is another defining element of the medical center's service: excellence. Swedish President and CEO Richard Peterson makes clear the vision that he and the Board of Trustees share. "Excellence," he says, "is not an end result. It is a process."

The staff and physicians at Swedish share that commitment to excellence. In independent research by National Research Corporation, Swedish is consistently named the area's best hospital, with the best doctors, the best nurses, and the best overall care.

More surgeries are performed at Swedish than at any other hospital in the region—more than 36,000 each year. Surgeons at Swedish have access to 58 state-of-the-art operating suites supported by highly trained surgical teams. Surgeons who practice at Swedish have earned worldwide recognition for pioneering new procedures. From delicate orthopedic surgery to sophisticated minimally invasive heart surgery to complex

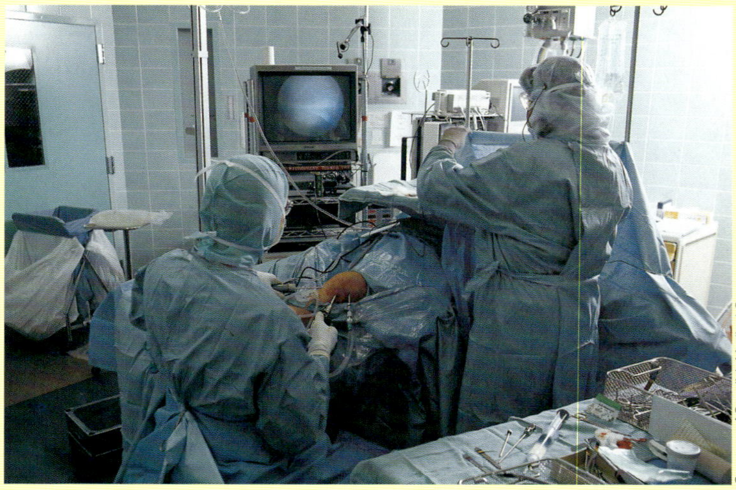

Courtesy of Swedish Medical Center

More than 36,000 surgeries are performed at Swedish per year. Surgeons at Swedish have access to state-of-the-art operating suites and highly skilled surgical teams.

More than 1,400 physicians practice at Swedish, representing nearly every medical and surgical specialty and subspecialty. Many are at the forefront of their fields.

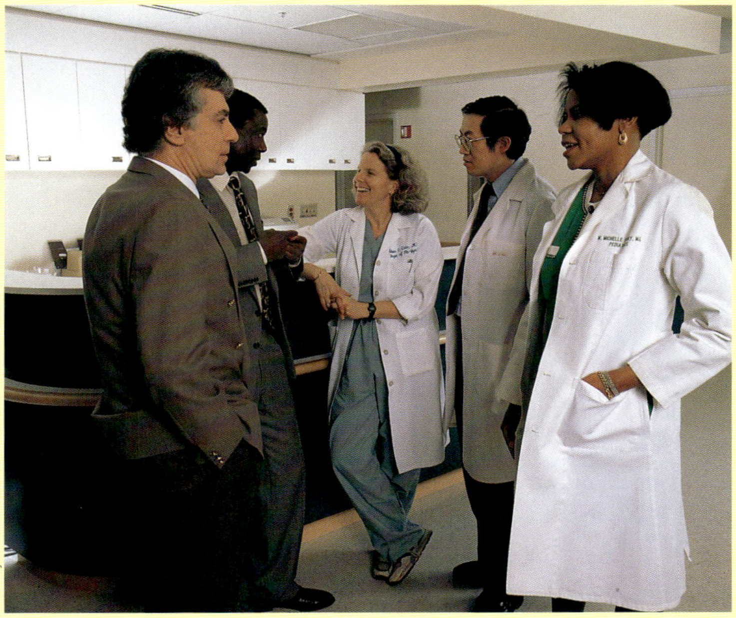

Courtesy of Swedish Medical Center

neurosurgery, Swedish surgeons practice cutting-edge medicine that transforms people's lives.

Swedish's obstetrics program is the largest in the region. More than 6,500 babies are born at Swedish Medical Center each year. Swedish offers beautiful birthing suites and the assurance of the area's most advanced care for mother and baby—just in case. Each year, more than 500 babies "graduate" from Swedish's Special Care Nursery, which is just one of a handful of Level III neonatal intensive-care units in the state.

The Swedish Cancer Institute is the Pacific Northwest's largest cancer-treatment program. In nearly 100,000 patient visits each year, Swedish treats more people for more types of cancer than any other facility in the Northwest. The Swedish Heart Institute is the largest, most comprehensive program for advanced cardiac care in the region and performs more than 2,000 open-heart surgeries and intervention cases annually. Swedish's orthopedic surgery program is the area's most active and performs more total-joint-replacement surgeries than any other medical center on the West Coast.

The medical center also includes a comprehensive Neuroscience Institute with a specialized epilepsy center, a dedicated pediatric program, a specialized program for sleep disorders, and many more specialized programs. Swedish is unique in that it houses the only hospital-based drug- and alcohol-treatment program in Seattle. Swedish was also the West Coast's first affiliate of the nationally known Joslin Center for Diabetes.

Swedish Medical Center was founded as a not-for-profit institution. As such, the medical center annually reinvests any income over expenses back into facilities upgrades and new equipment to ensure people of the Northwest access to the best quality health care. Swedish also invests in research, with more than 400 research projects in progress at any given time.

As part of its nonprofit commitment, Swedish is dedicated to serving all members of the community, regardless of their ability to pay. Each year, Swedish provides more than five million dollars in charity care—more than any other non-tax-payer-supported health-care facility in the state. The medical center also provides millions of dollars annually to support community benefit programs. These include everything from providing free flu vaccinations and community health education classes to funding residents who are part of an extensive training program caring for the underserved populations in the region.

"Redefining Excellence One Life At A Time" is Swedish Medical Center's compelling slogan. It describes the commitment and dedication of the more than 1,400 physicians and more than 6,800 employees and countless volunteers who have made Swedish what it is today. There is no doubt that Swedish Medical Center will be redefining excellence well into its second century of service in the Pacific Northwest.

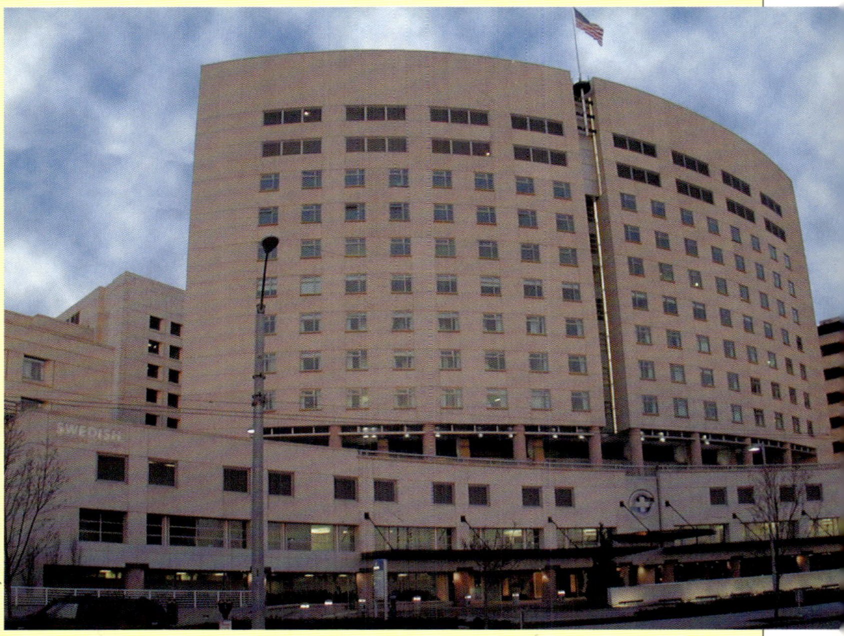

Courtesy of Swedish Medical Center

The East Tower is the newest addition to the Swedish/First Hill campus. Since its beginnings in 1910 as a 24-bed hospital, Swedish has grown into a 1,194-bed medical center comprised of three campuses—First Hill, Ballard, and Providence—and occupying 25 city blocks.

Virginia Mason Medical Center

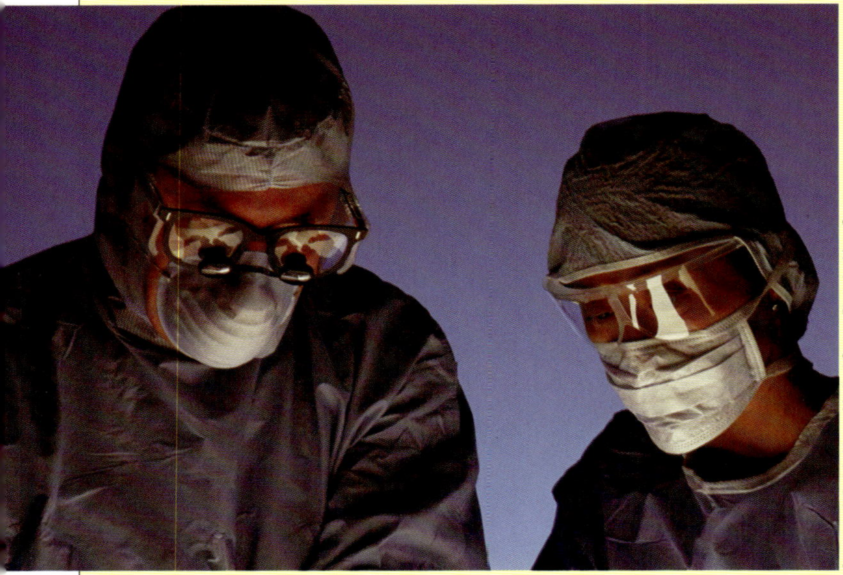

Most of Virginia Mason's specialists have regional, and sometimes national, reputations in their areas of expertise.

Virginia Mason Medical Center (VM) is large enough to provide innovative, one-stop health care, yet small enough that people experience the friendliness of an old-fashioned, patient-centered hospital and associated clinics. VM staff work together very closely in a "Team Medicine℠" approach that makes Virginia Mason unique in the Northwest. "Team Medicine℠" is a vital part of VM's ability to deliver integrated health care that results in superior outcomes.

This philosophy of exceptional, patient-centered care goes back to Virginia Mason's opening in 1920. Its founders had a then-radical idea: offer patients a single place to receive comprehensive medical care for virtually any medical need—all from providers employed by one organization.

Today, Virginia Mason boasts almost 400 doctors and more than 5,000 staff, with primary and specialty care in 45 different medical, surgical and diagnostic fields. VM's nursing staff consistently rates "exceptional" in *The Best Hospitals in America* and many VM doctors are listed in *The Best Doctors in America*. Virginia Mason is a place where specialists and primary-care physicians work as a team to offer high-quality service, care and patient outcomes.

Each year, VM has more than one million outpatient visits and about 16,000 hospital patients. In addition to a 336-bed hospital, Virginia Mason features a network of satellite clinics and occupational medical facilities, a philanthropic foundation, Bailey-Boushay House (a nursing residence and day health center for people living with AIDS), and the internationally recognized Benaroya Research Institute at Virginia Mason.

Patients benefit from VM's pioneering research, with more than 200 clinical trials and patient-based research projects taking place annually. The center offers dedicated clinical research units for cancer, arthritis and diabetes.

VM's Benaroya Diabetes Center is the oldest and largest diabetes care program in the Pacific Northwest. The Heart Institute, the Cancer Institute, and The Cosmetic Services Group at Virginia Mason also are among VM's areas of excellence.

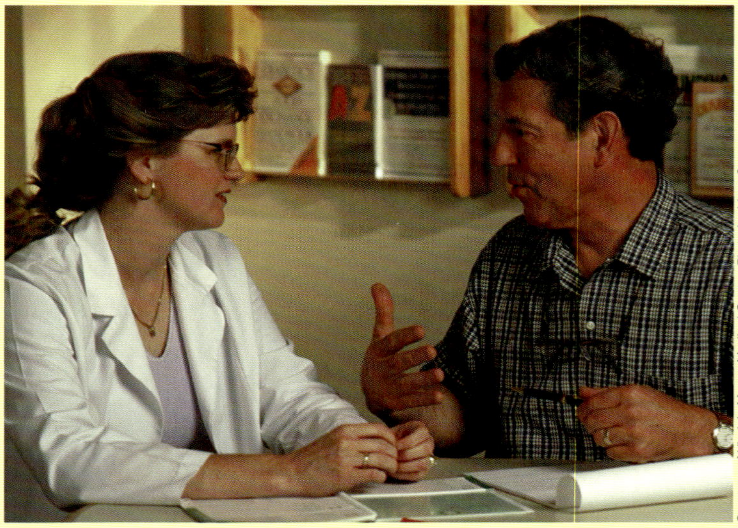

The patient is the focus of Virginia Mason's Team Medicine℠.

With the Benaroya Research Institute at Virginia Mason, patients benefit from clinical trials and the very latest research breakthroughs.

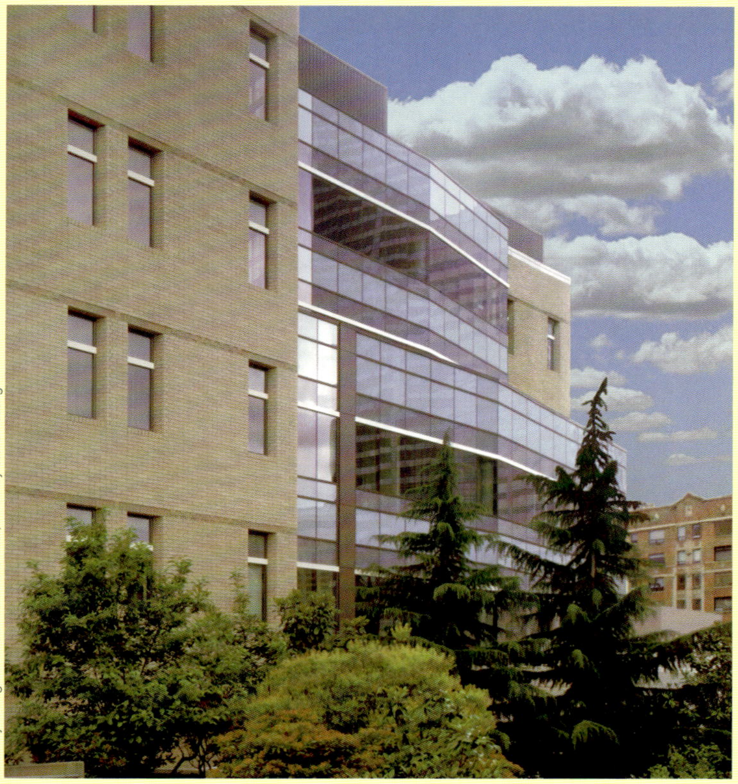

Courtesy of Virginia Mason Medical Center, Photo by Steve Keating

In VM's Heart Institute, patients receive comprehensive, integrated services, from diagnostic examinations and treatment to rehabilitation. The Heart Institute is a major referral source for Pacific Northwest hospitals and boasts a catheterization lab that is a training center for physicians nationwide. While patients receive leading-edge treatment in all types of cardiac care, the areas of electrophysiology and cardiac surgery are particularly noteworthy.

The Cancer Institute offers more than 18,000 patient treatments each year. VM focuses on a patient-centered, team approach to combating this terrible disease. Ongoing research provides patients with the latest cancer-fighting techniques and drugs and provides patients an entry into prevention studies conducted with the National Cancer Institute and the Fred Hutchinson Cancer Research Center.

The Cosmetic Services Group at Virginia Mason is unique in the region. The group is comprised of physicians from different medical and surgical departments, including dermatology, ophthalmology, otolaryngology/facial plastic surgery, and plastic and reconstructive surgery. The doctors work as a dedicated team to enhance the physical appearance of patients, whether the desired procedure is due to an accident, illness, birth defect or personal preference.

These services represent only a few of the reasons that Virginia Mason receives regional recognition as a pioneer in innovative practices. Its history exudes many firsts, including being the first to use insulin to treat diabetes and being the first hospital west of the Mississippi River to do an electrocardiogram. It was first in the region to provide short-stay surgery, establish a nurse-midwifery program, use an insulin pump for diabetes, and establish a bilingual, multi-Asian clinic within a full health care system.

For more than 80 years, patients have received exceptional care at Virginia Mason Medical Center. The center has experienced tremendous growth, yet maintains its warmth and team focus, which translates into extraordinary service and care.

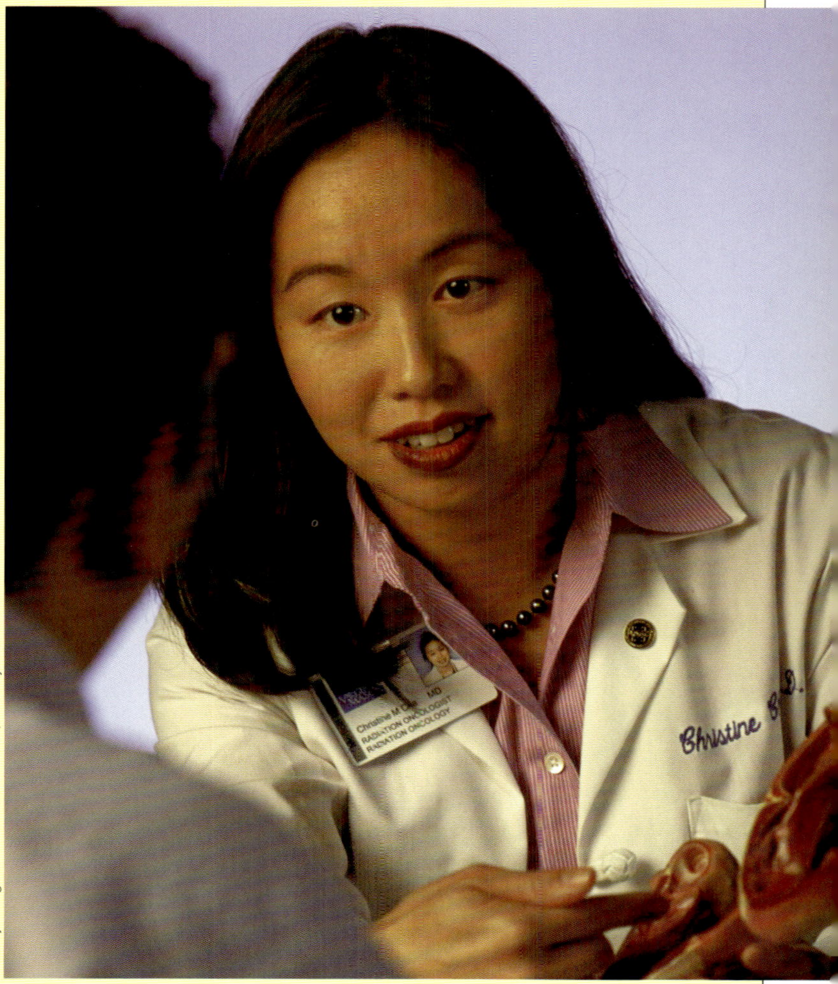

Courtesy of Virginia Mason Medical Center, Photo by Marc Carter

Virginia Mason has comprehensive, innovative services in many areas, including cancer (shown here), general and vascular surgery, cosmetic services, heart care, and diabetes.

University of Washington Medical Center

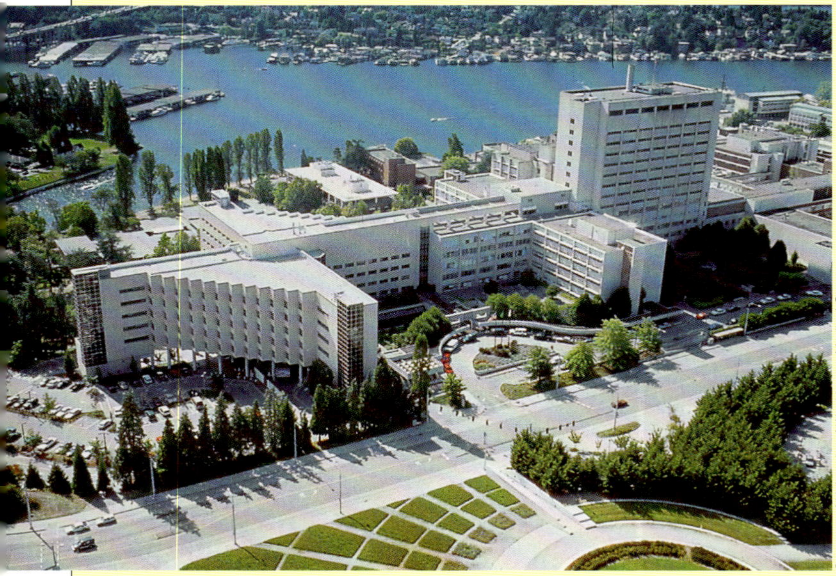
Courtesy of University of Washington Medical Center

An aerial view of University of Washington Medical Center.

University of Washington Medical Center (UWMC) has been committed to quality patient care for over 40 years, bringing hope and healing to thousands of people in the Pacific Northwest and beyond. A referral center for nearly 9 million residents of Washington, Wyoming, Alaska, Montana, and Idaho, UWMC provides outstanding, compassionate, appropriate care, and is regularly ranked among the very top hospitals in the nation.

UWMC has been nationally recognized twice as a magnet hospital for nurses, setting the standard for their profession. Many physicians who practice at UWMC—all UW School of Medicine faculty—are regularly identified among the "Best Doctors in America" by their peers. Scientific papers and books written by physicians at UWMC set the standards for medical care today and tomorrow.

Since the Medical Center opened its doors, its core missions have been to provide the highest quality patient care; to pioneer demanding new medical procedures that improve people's lives with research-based, state-of-the-art medical treatment; and to teach these procedures to other physicians throughout the region. UW faculty physicians regularly add to the body of knowledge and have developed new approaches to treat and cure certain medical conditions.

Looking toward the future, UWMC will continue its commitment to providing the very best in patient care through research-based medical advances. UWMC is a member of the Seattle Cancer Care Alliance, which unites efforts between the UW, Fred Hutchinson Cancer Research Center, and Children's Hospital and Regional Medical Center in oncology-related research and patient care services.

The development of the UW Physicians Neighborhood Clinics has expanded access to UW faculty physicians who also practice at UWMC and Harborview Medical Center. By coupling increased access and the art of compassionate healing with the boundless potential of medical science, University of Washington Medical Center will continue to provide the finest health care in the Pacific Northwest and carry out its primary mission to care for its patients.

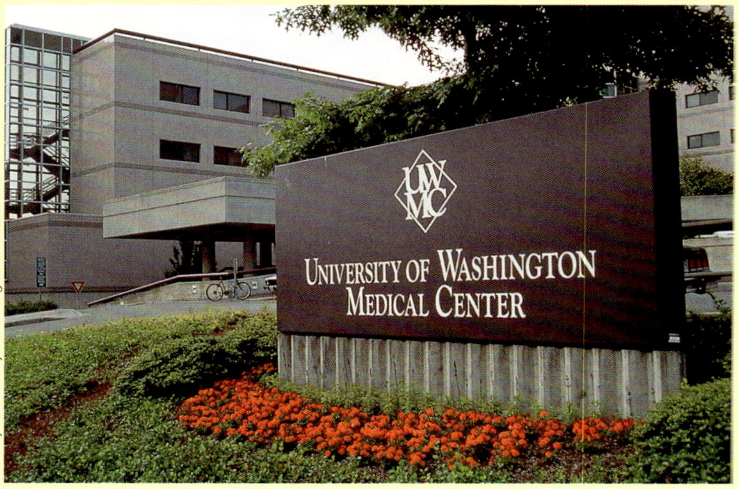

Courtesy of University of Washington Medical Center

For over 40 years, University of Washington Medical Center has provided dedicated, caring, quality service to the residents of the Pacific Northwest.

Harborview Medical Center

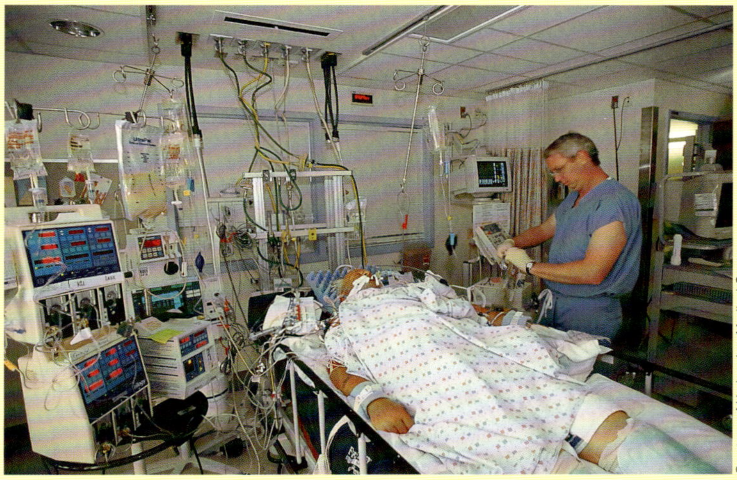

Courtesy of Harborview Medical Center

Harborview has 66 critical-care beds for care for the most seriously ill and injured from a four-state region. Critical-care beds housed in the new West Hospital Wing are considered to be state-of-the-art.

Since its beginning as a six-bed hospital in 1877, Harborview Medical Center has grown to a renowned patient care, teaching, and research facility owned by King County and managed by the University of Washington. Describing Harborview simply as a large, inner-city hospital would be understating its role in the Pacific Northwest today.

For many years the large, imposing building on the hill above downtown Seattle was simply known as "The County Hospital," presenting a somewhat stern appearance and image in the community. In sharp contrast to that image is today's conception of Harborview as a leading medical resource for the states of Washington, Alaska, Montana, and Idaho.

Best known for its Emergency/Trauma Center, Harborview has broadened its scope of service over the years to become a prominent teaching and research institution affiliated with the University of Washington (UW), with special programs based on the changing medical needs of the community.

The UW Burn Center at Harborview is one of the largest facilities of its kind in the United States and has served over 9,000 patients since opening in 1974. Harborview's Neurological Surgery program treats over 2,000 patients annually for disorders of the brain, spinal cord, and peripheral nerves.

The Harborview Injury Prevention and Research Center works to develop, apply, and evaluate methods of preventing and treating injuries. The positive impact of this center's work is seen in a wide range of applications, from the promotion of bicycle helmets to a better understanding of the causes and circumstances of domestic violence.

Seattle's Medic 1 program, a model replicated throughout the nation, was developed by UW faculty based at Harborview in cooperation with the Seattle Fire Department. The paramedic training program at Harborview serves as a training site for paramedics located throughout the Pacific Northwest.

Harborview has always had a tradition of reaching out to disenfranchised populations—the non-English-speaking poor, people with AIDS or STDs, victims of sexual assault, and the mentally ill homeless. Many of the medical center's programs strive to comprehensively care for these individuals.

With over 120 years of history and a tradition of dedicated service to quality health care, Harborview Medical Center's management and Board see a future which holds only greater opportunities to contribute to the health and well being of the people of the Pacific Northwest.

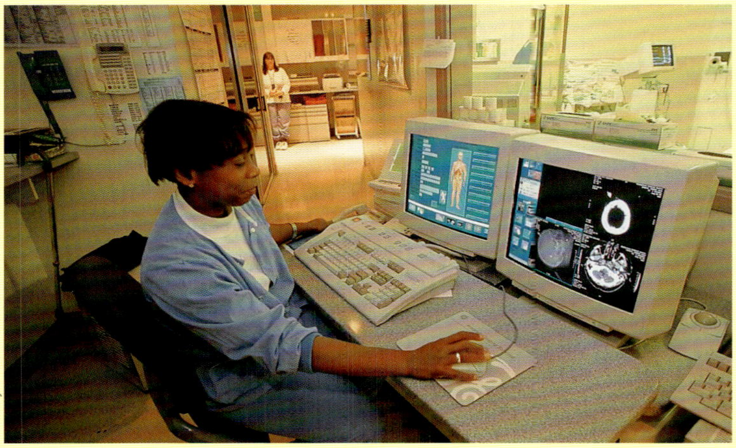

Courtesy of Harborview Medical Center

Radiology is a key diagnostic tool for critically ill and injured patients who come through the Harborview Emergency Department.

Minor & James Medical, PLLC

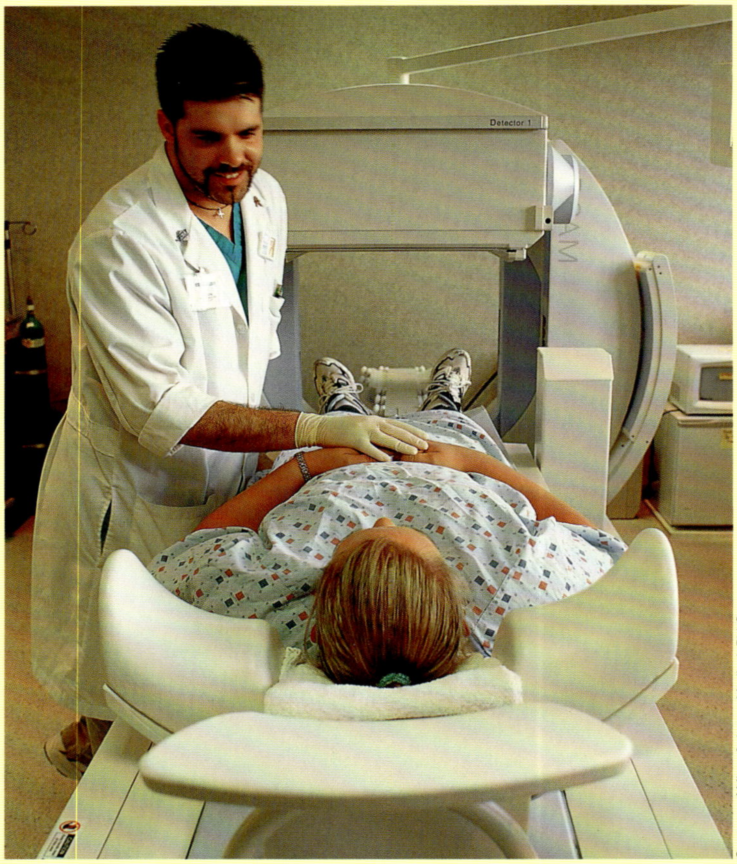

Courtesy of Minor & James Medical, PLLC

This technician prepares a patient for a nuclear scan. Minor & James specializes in state-of-the-art diagnostic technology.

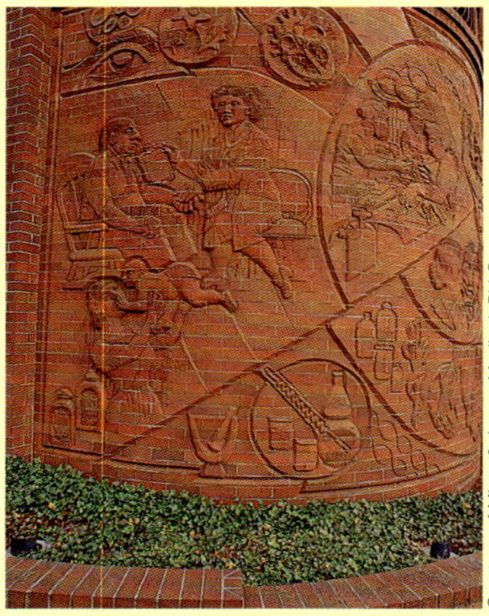

Courtesy of Minor & James Medical, PLLC

The distinctive brick relief on the corner of the Boren & James Medical Building, in which Minor & James Medical is housed, is a suitable visual metaphor for the "art of medicine."

Minor & James Medical, PLLC, is a Seattle-based, multi-specialty medical clinic with a 50-year history as a referral center, providing the best and most sophisticated care to the people of the Pacific Northwest. The specialties represented by the 70 physicians at Minor & James Medical include internal medicine, cardiology, pulmonology, infectious disease, nephrology, rheumatology, neurology, oncology, endocrinology, dermatology, gastroenterology, colon and rectal surgery, geriatrics, and obstetrics and gynecology. Supported by excellent laboratory and radiology services, the physicians at Minor & James Medical are skilled in managing the most challenging medical cases.

Located on First Hill, immediately south of Swedish Medical Center, Minor & James Medical physicians have ready access to one of the finest hospitals in the region. The close relationship and easy communication with Swedish Medical Center allow for a smooth transition between outpatient and inpatient care and provide ready access to those medical and surgical services not intrinsic to Minor & James Medical.

Most of the Minor & James Medical physicians hold clinical appointments at the University of Washington School of Medicine. Hospital-based teaching of interns and residents as well as office-based clinical tutoring of nursing and medical students are important components of a long-standing commitment to the future of the medical community.

Clinical research is an important aspect of the Minor & James Medical commitment to continuing excellence in medical care. By participating in the development of new medications, Minor & James Medical helps to assure that newer and better treatments will continue to be developed for safer, more effective, and less costly treatment of disease.

Minor & James Medical, PLLC, has committed itself to remain continuously in the forefront of excellence in medical care in the Pacific Northwest. At Minor & James Medical, the intent to maintain a devotion to excellence in medicine is exemplary and the enthusiasm for the quality of life in the Pacific Northwest is contagious.

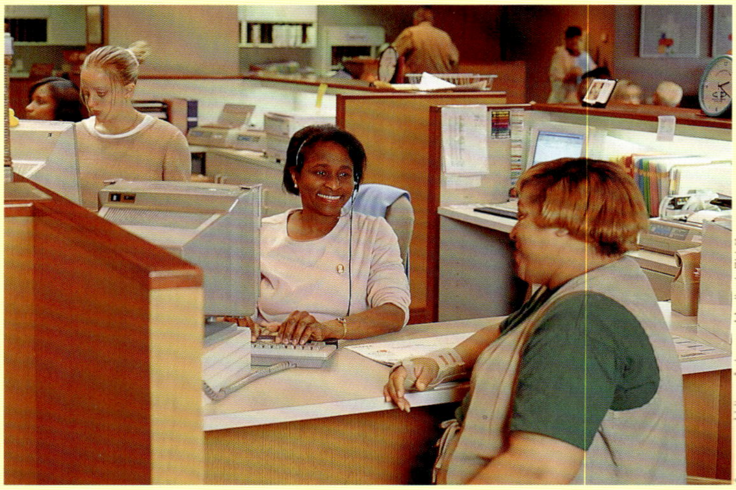

Courtesy of Minor & James Medical, PLLC

At Minor & James, medicine is about people.

Valley Medical Center

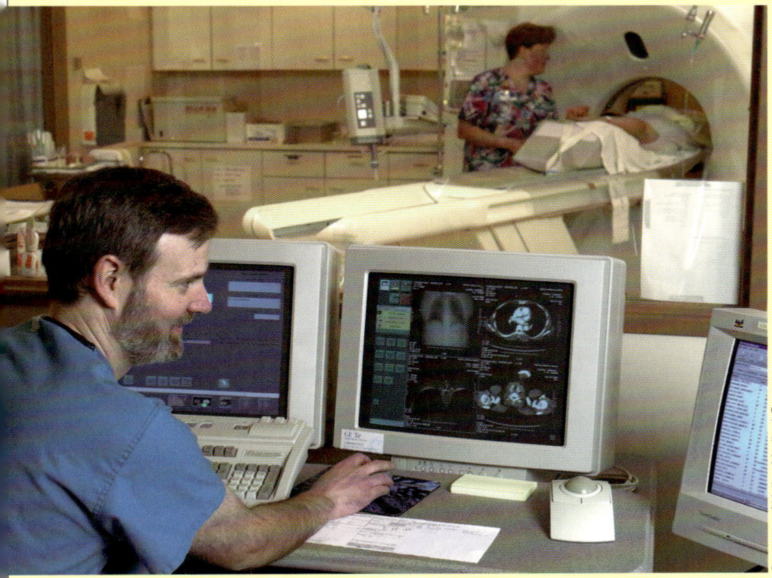

Courtesy of Valley Medical Center

Valley Medical Center's new CAT s canner reduces the time and increases the comfort for patients while they have this valuable diagnostic procedure. Technicians and board-certified radiologists work together with the latest technology for positive patient outcomes.

Valley Medical Center, located just south of Seattle, is committed to *"downtown medical care right in your own back yard."* That promise is confirmed by the institution's comprehensive health care services. Originally opened in 1947 as Renton Hospital, the facility was the first public hospital district in the state. In 1969, it was renamed Valley General Hospital, and in 1984, once again the name changed to Valley Medical Center in order to reflect the more comprehensive services that were provided. The growth and expansion of the medical center has not slowed since that time and shows no evidence of doing so in the near future.

Valley's busy obstetrics program handles the delivery of almost 3,000 babies each year and provides the highest quality pre-natal and post-natal care for expectant mothers. The Valley Medical Center ER, a Level III Trauma Center, provides specially trained trauma physicians, patient-care staff, and crisis counselors 24 hours a day, 7 days a week. Inpatient care services range from high-tech surgical units to on-site laboratory resources and numerous therapy options.

The clinic network created by Valley is reflective of its commitment to community. Seven primary care clinics, a specialty care clinic, a behavioral health clinic, and two occupational health clinics provide a vital resource for basic health care for residents living and working between Seattle and Tacoma. Many of the physicians practicing in these clinics are graduates of Valley's own Family Practice Residency Program.

Valley's community outreach programs include numerous health-related courses, a GoldenCare Program that reaches over 13,000 seniors with a broad range of services, and an on-site fitness center. The fitness center is open to the community and boasts of over 2,000 members, providing fitness training, injury or illness recuperation support, and weight-control assistance.

Valley Medical Center offers the expertise of approximately 500 physicians in more than 36 specialties and sub-specialties, and it is still growing. The recent addition of The Center for Joint Replacement, the initiation of a Breast Health Center, and collaborative efforts with other hospitals to bring expanded services for heart and cancer care are among the many signs of commitment on the part of the Board of Directors, Administration, and staff of Valley. That commitment will continue to meet the expanding health care needs of the community well into the new millennium.

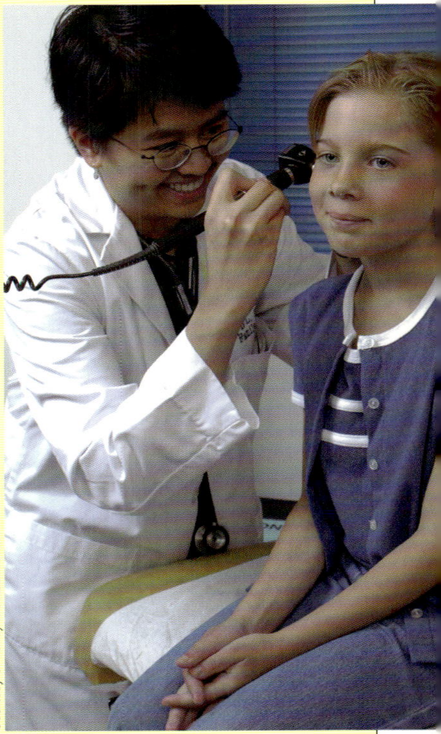

Courtesy of Valley Medical Center

Regular checkups can make the difference for children. Valley Medical Center's seven primary-care clinics make these checkups convenient for parents. The clinics are located in the Kent, Renton, and Tukwila areas of south King County.

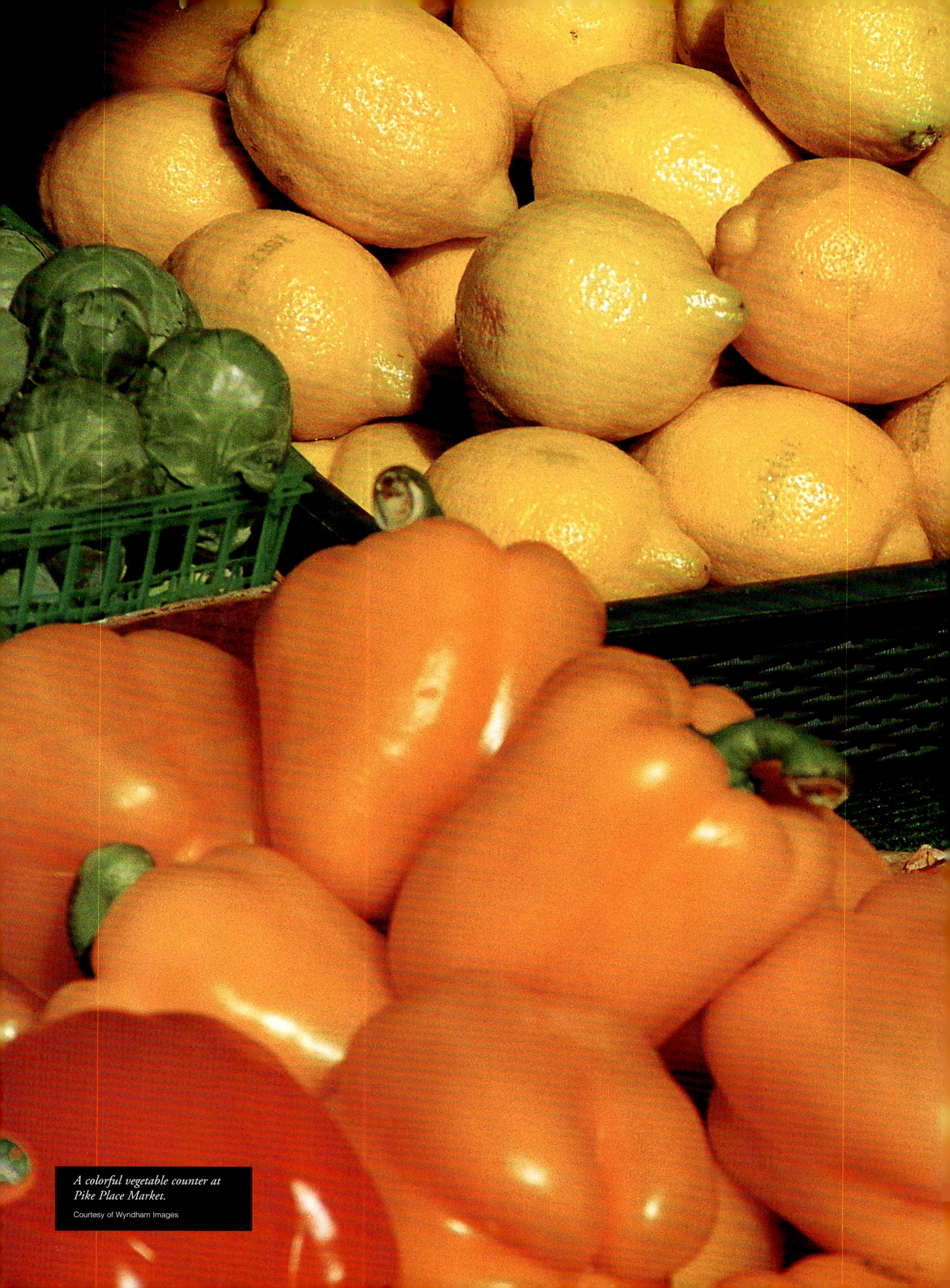

A colorful vegetable counter at Pike Place Market.
Courtesy of Wyndham Images

Part Two

MARKETPLACE

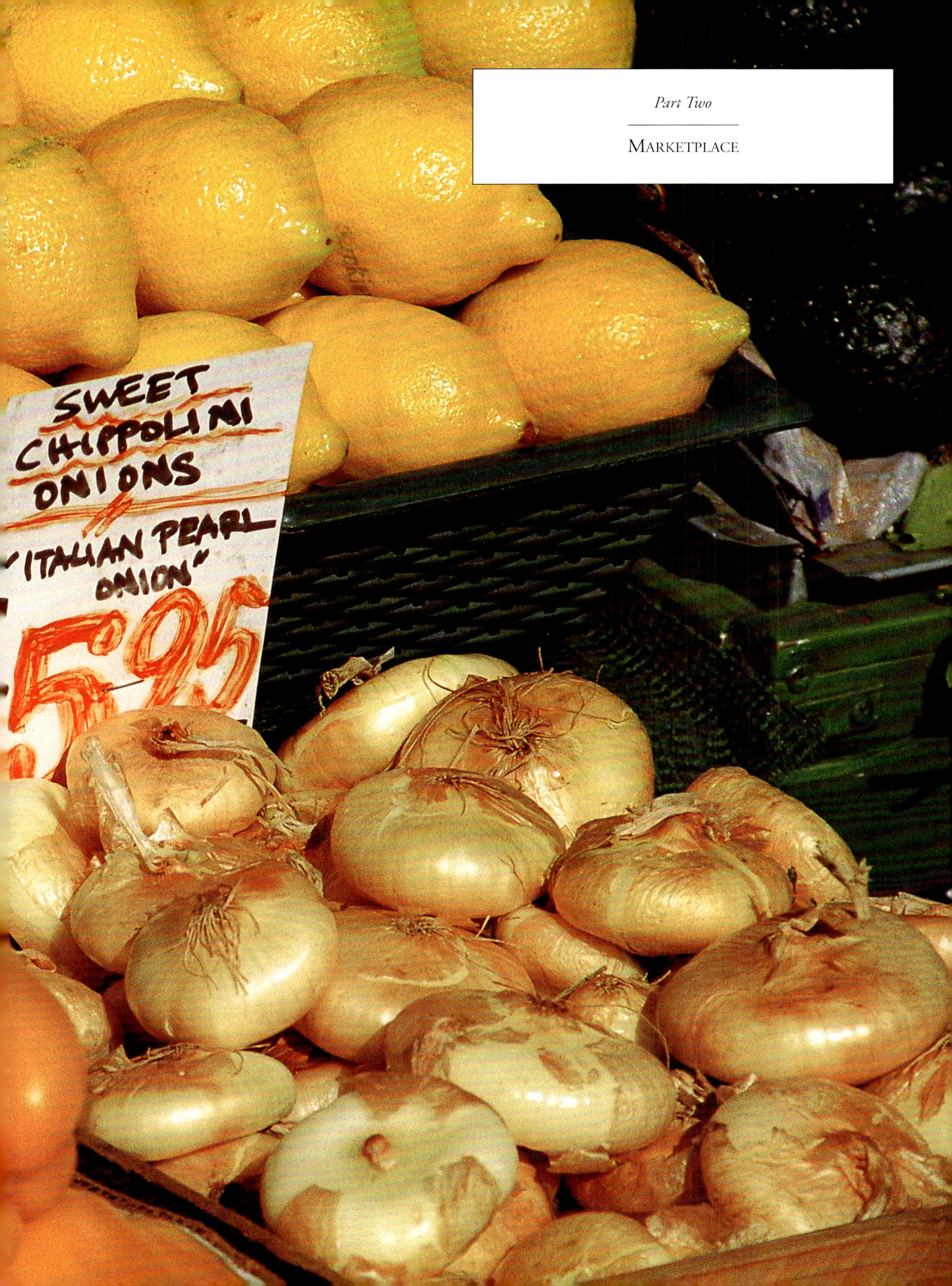

The Bon Marché

When a native Northwest resident thinks about Downtown Seattle, one of the first things that comes to mind is The Bon Marché. It is little wonder, when one considers that the department store has been in Seattle since 1890 and at the same location since 1929. Perhaps that is why a local business leader defined "The Bon" with a simple phrase. He said, "It's an institution!"

This gentleman was not the first to describe The Bon Marché as an institution. Knowingly or unknowingly, he had borrowed a line from a history of The Bon Marché written in 1929. The following excerpt tells the story:

Cable cars jangled as they slued round the curve from Pike Street to begin their ascent of the Second Avenue hill. Pedestrians jumped off the track for their lives. Passengers grabbed frantically for their hats. Plodding horses became suddenly skittish as the clanging vehicles moved by. Now and then a vagrant cow stopped in the middle of the tracks to nibble a tuft of grass, placidly unaware that it was obstructing traffic.

On the corner, ladies in long skirts swept the threshold of the newly built store building as they moved in and out. This was Seattle in 1900. The store was the new Bon Marché, just moved from its old location in Bell Town to what was the margin of Seattle's business district.

Now, twenty-nine years later, The Bon Marché has moved again, this time to its fine new home at Pine, Third, Fourth, and Olive. Its history parallels a community history startling even for the West. Sometimes you will find a store which people of a city have chosen for special favor, which they have molded according to their own desires and which they have raised to the level of a civic institution. Such a store is The Bon Marché. In the short space of thirty-nine years the people of Seattle have transformed it from a tiny dry goods store to one of the great retail establishments of the West.

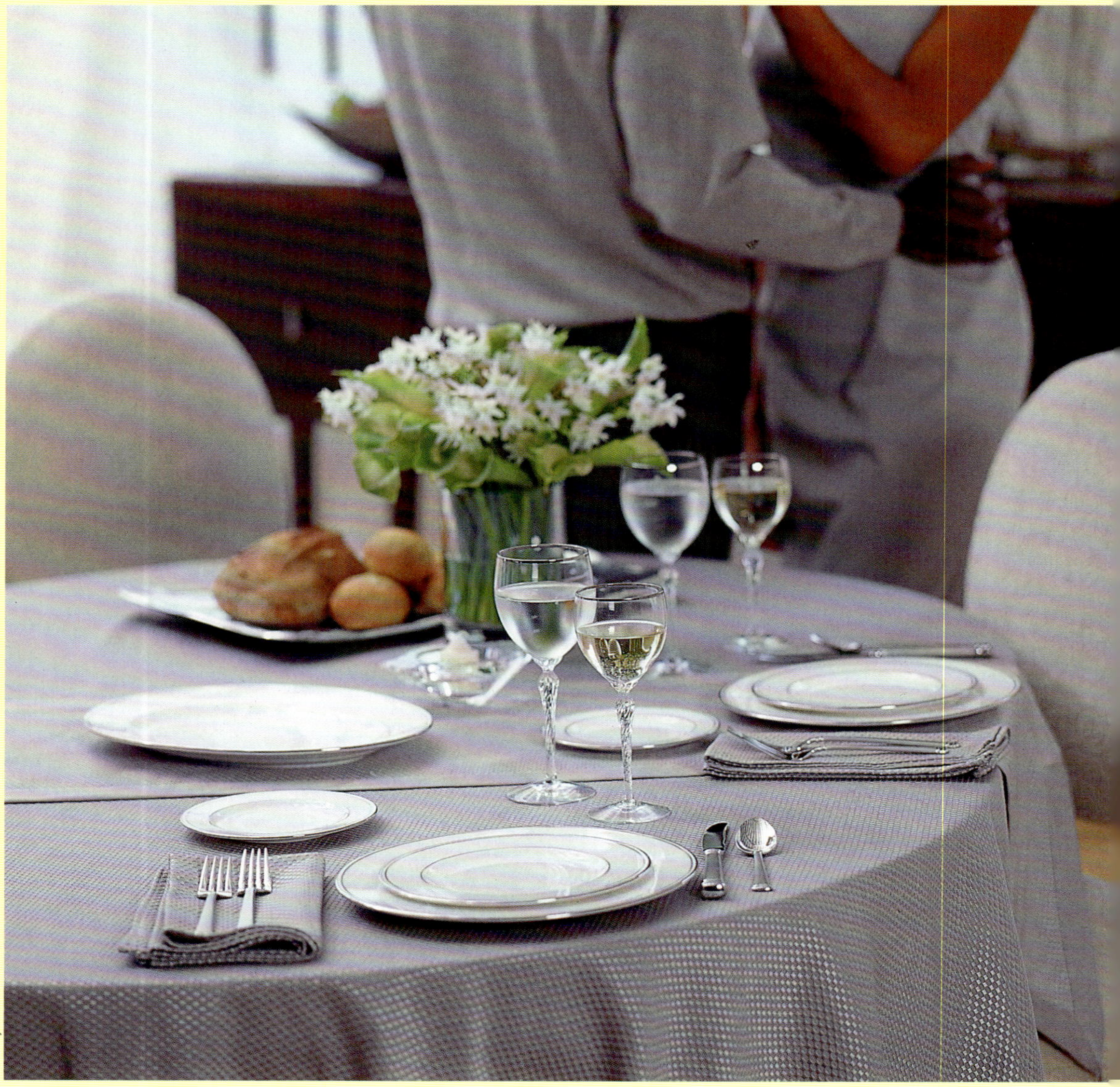
Courtesy of The Bon Marché

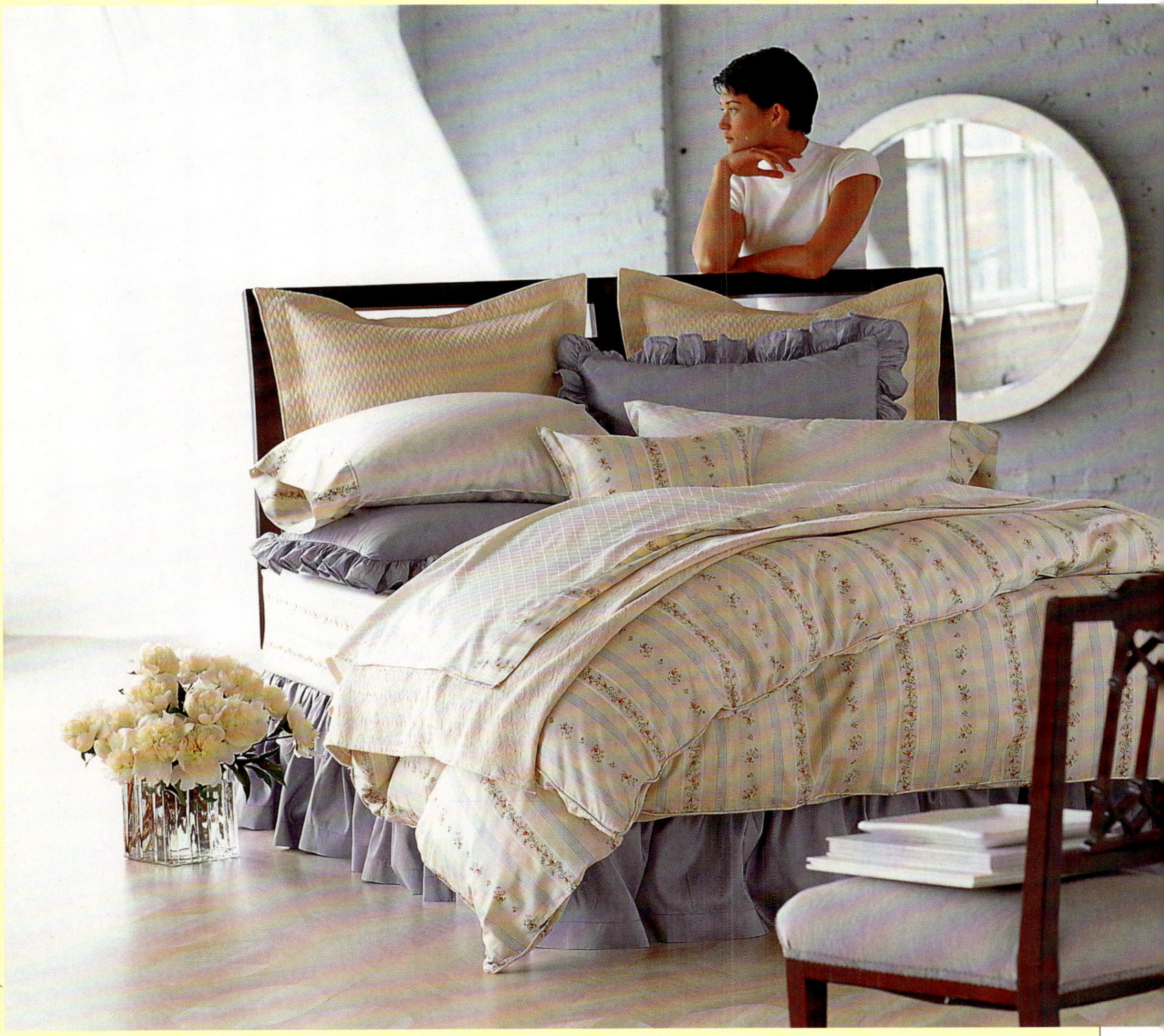

Courtesy of The Bon Marché

Every praise bestowed upon The Bon Marché by the author of that historical piece could be accurately repeated today, along with the addition of numerous comments applauding the twenty-first century features of Seattle's cornerstone retail establishment.

The flagship store in downtown Seattle remains the central focus for the entire Bon Marché operation. An extensive renovation, which was completed by the turn of the millennium, maintains the elements of The Bon Marché's impressive history as a retail leader in the Northwest. The building itself remains high on the list of Seattle's most impressive historical landmarks, praised for its architecture and firmly holding its dignity among the multitude of modern skyscrapers that surround it.

Within every Bon Marché, customers will see evidence of the Bon's commitment to serve the diverse needs of Pacific Northwest customers with a great variety of exciting personal fashions and home furnishings.

A significant factor of The Bon Marché's history as an outstanding retail establishment is its genuine commitment to community outreach opportunities. Building upon its strong historical ties to the region, the management and staff of The Bon Marché have earned a well-deserved reputation for giving back to the community that helped to build the company. A publication available from the store's management describes The Bon Marché Community Service Mission. For every cause to which the company provides monetary support, its staff members contribute time, energy, and expertise to several more worthy charities. Few Northwest charities have not felt the benefits of community service from The Bon Marché or its employees. A recent annual report estimates that a total of 6,000 Bon Marché employees provided over 15,000 hours of community service.

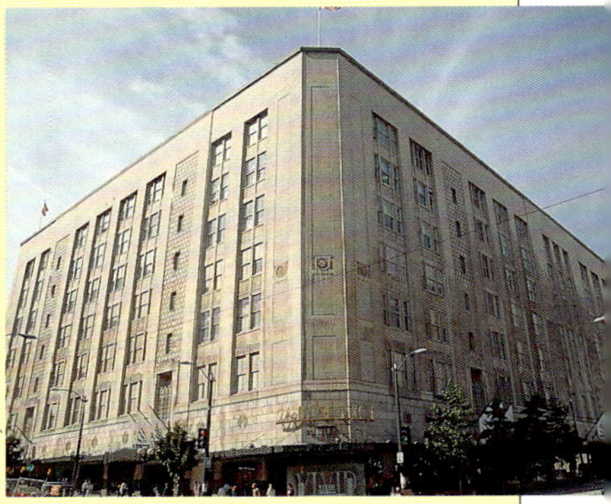

Courtesy of The Bon Marché

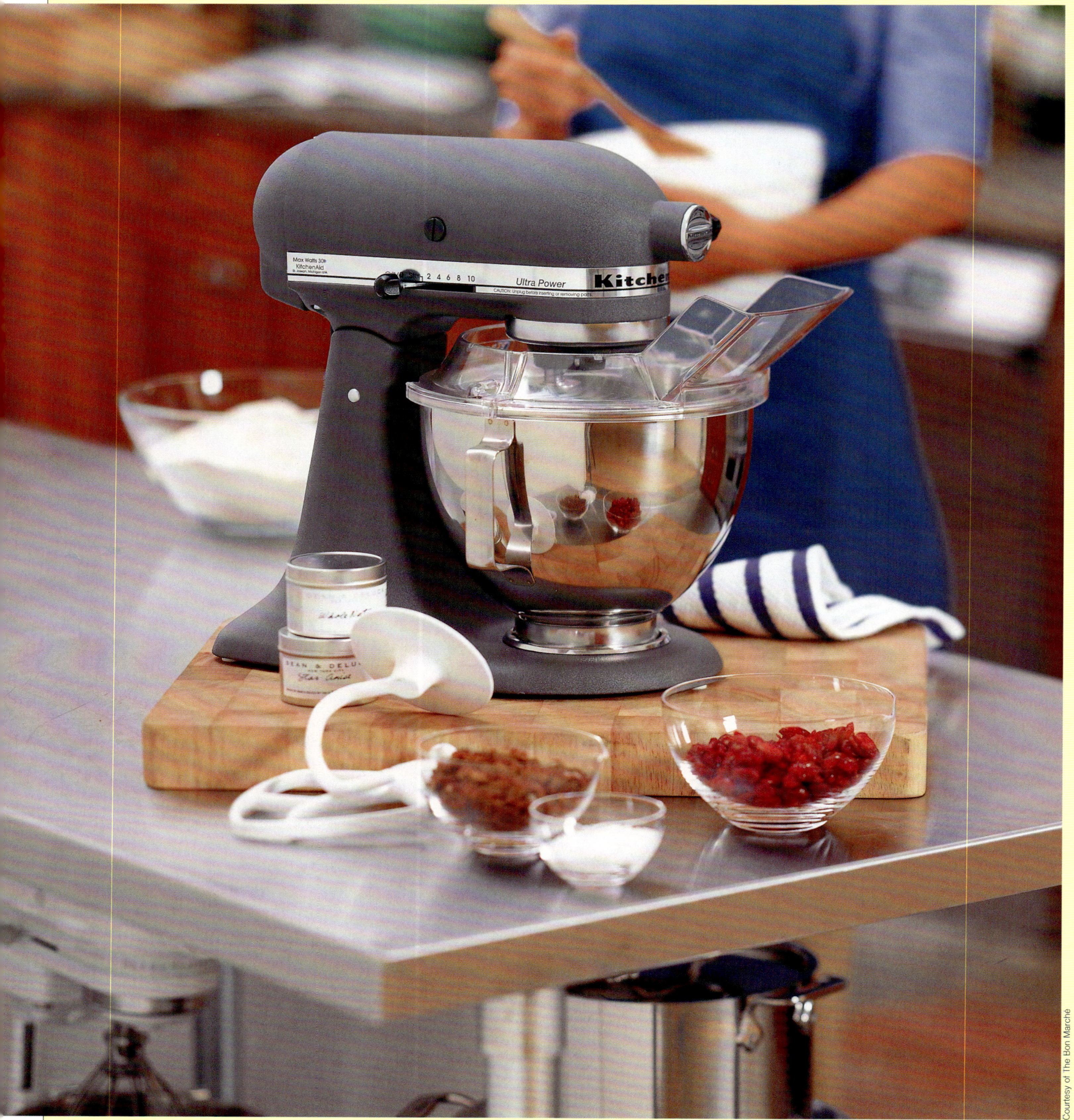

Courtesy of The Bon Marché

One of the more innovative programs established by the management of The Bon Marché has been its Follow The Leader program created in the mid-1990s. In this program, local students submit essays explaining why they would like to "follow the leader" for a day. These essays can refer to specific local business executives or particular career fields. The students with the winning essays are given an opportunity to observe the business process in "the real world" and spend a full day trailing their chosen executives. Winning students earn a $1,000 savings bond for themselves, and the top essayist also wins a $5,000 gift for his or her school. Each year, 25 students are selected, and The Bon Marché, along with their primary co-sponsors, KING5-TV and *The Seattle Times*, provide the financial support, which to date totals well over $150,000.

One key feature of the community outreach programs supported by The Bon Marché is the focus on cultural diversity. The Bon Marché sponsored a major tribute entitled *Black Pioneers in Northwest History*, as well as several other events that have highlighted the contributions of Chinese, Japanese, and Native American cultures to the growth and development of the Pacific Northwest economy and society.

Another important aspect of The Bon Marché's interest in community involvement is seen in the company's participation in several partnerships with public education programs. Employees volunteer time and expertise to act as tutors. Others initiate "pen pal" relationships with students, offering encouragement and support for educational efforts. In all of these efforts, the commitment of the Bon Marché management, and its employees, is to continually improve the communities where they work and live.

With a history of over a century of service to the community, The Bon Marché continues to adapt to the changing realities of the retail marketplace in the new millennium. Management and staff pride themselves on knowing how people live, what they want, and how they want to get it. In marketing a broad array of products in the face of a growing e-commerce environment, The Bon Marché continues to reinvent the tradition of retail shopping, offering customers the sensory perceptions unavailable on the World Wide Web. They acknowledge the reality of shopping as a social event and seek to offer the customer the opportunity to experience that event in an atmosphere of trust and dependability.

An appreciation of the spirit of The Bon Marché can be seen in the career longevity of many of its associates. Numerous employees boast 10, 15, and 25 years of service to the company, and one has reached the amazing milestone of 50 years of service with The Bon Marché. That kind of commitment is communicated to customers, bringing them back, again and again, for countless years.

Upon entering the recently renovated cornerstone store in downtown Seattle, one is greeted by a particularly interesting work of art. It is a series of historic-reproduction panels that pay tribute to the major industries that formed the foundation of the economy of the Pacific Northwest. In the center of the striking two-story opening, just inside the main entrance, five-foot square panels each represent a different industry, including aviation, mining, logging, and others. These artworks serve as a reminder of this store's historical ties to the region and its determination to maintain its own significant influence in the economy of the area for years to come.

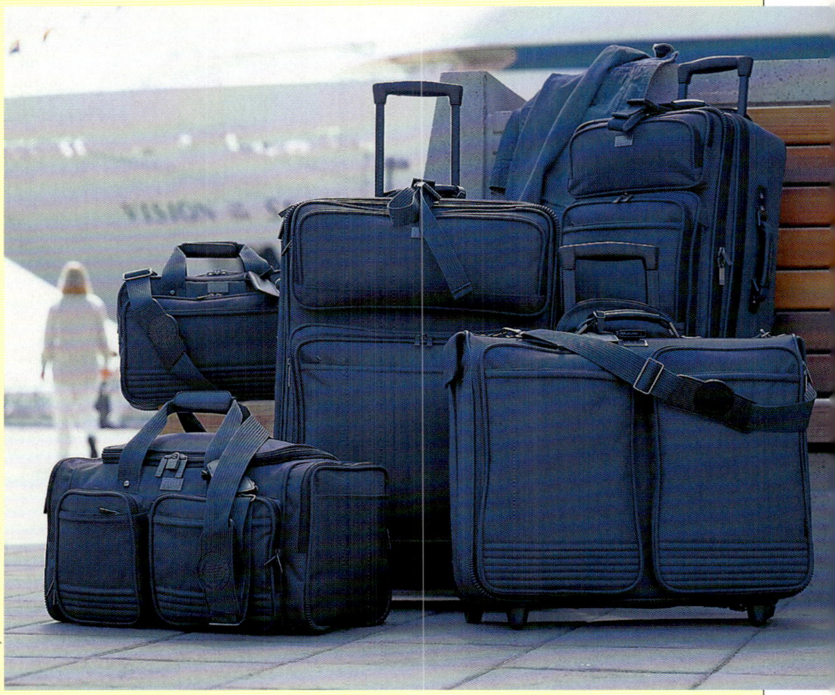

Courtesy of The Bon Marché

The Seattle Aquarium

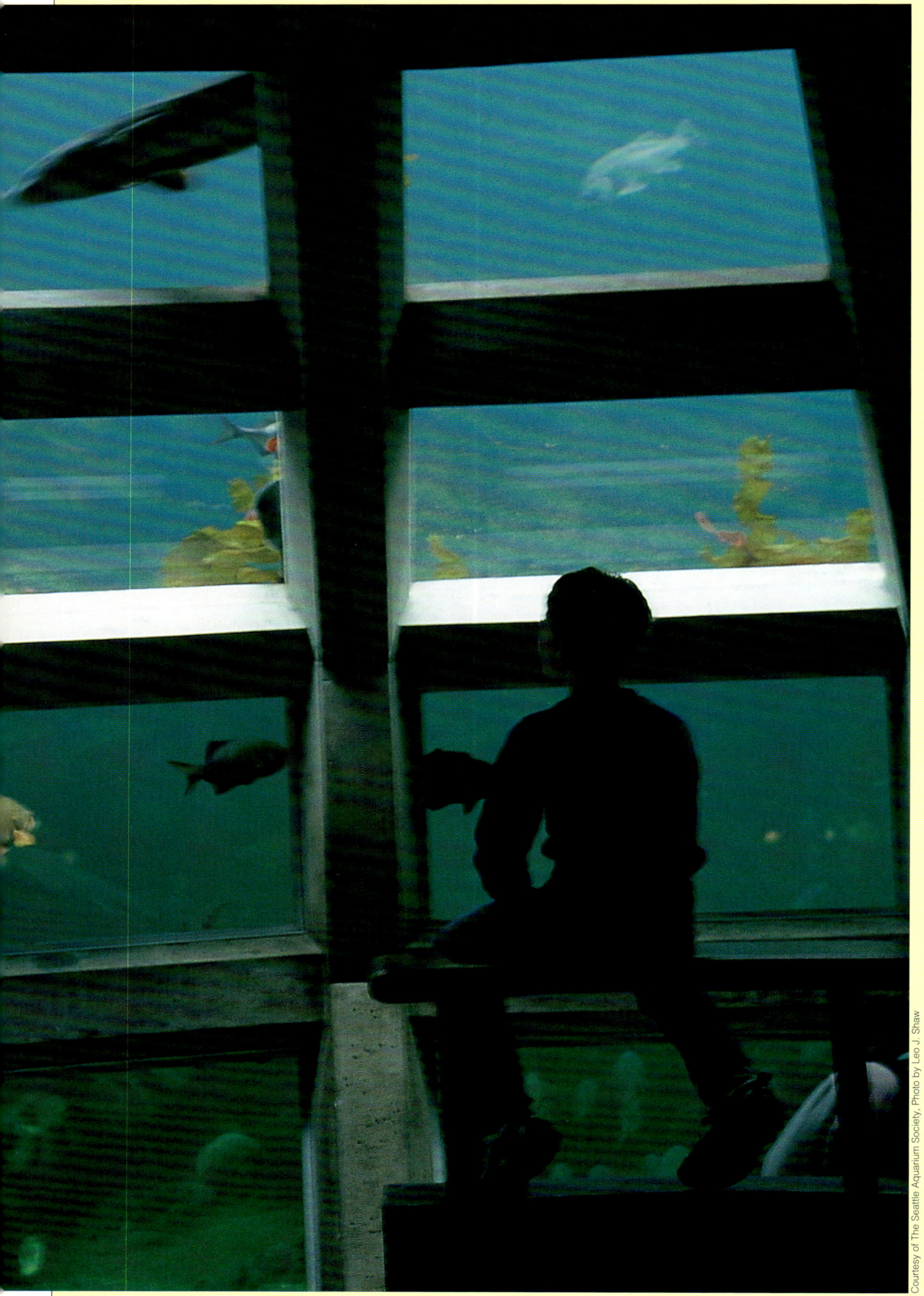

Courtesy of The Seattle Aquarium Society, Photo by Leo J. Shaw

The Underwater Dome offers a unique perspective from which to observe sea creatures.

Since its opening in 1977, The Seattle Aquarium has brought the mystery and wonder of aquatic life to millions of residents, school groups and visitors of Seattle and Western Washington. Interactive exhibitry and a variety of educational programs aim to bring Aquarium visitors face-to-face with these creatures, and encourage an increased level of understanding of the delicate habitats these creatures call home. This "dual role" of serving as both visitor attraction and educational tool has brought national acclaim to Aquarium staff, and pride to a city so steeped in maritime history.

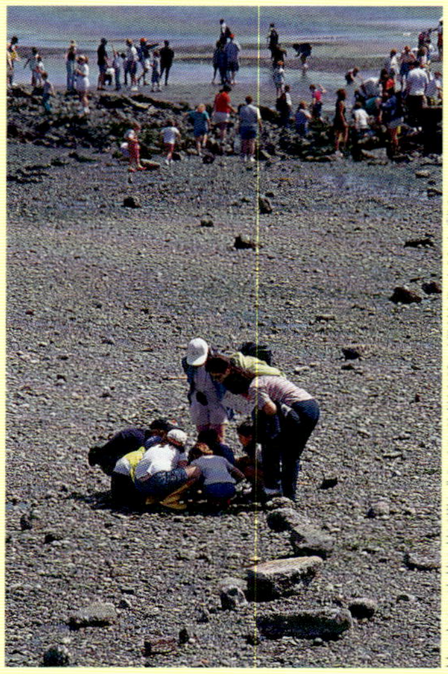

Courtesy of The Seattle Aquarium Society, Photo by Leo J. Shaw

On Alki Beach at low tide, the Seattle Aquarium education team helps children to better understand the aquatic life in Puget Sound.

The Seattle Aquarium is located on Pier 60.

Biological Excellence

Seattle Aquarium visitors have been able to witness a number of "firsts" in the aquarium industry. In-captivity births of the giant Pacific octopus, the sea otter and the tufted puffin have brought Aquarium biological staff renown among their peers. Behind the scenes, Aquarium staff members are regularly involved in the recovery and release of injured aquatic life found on local beaches and around the world.

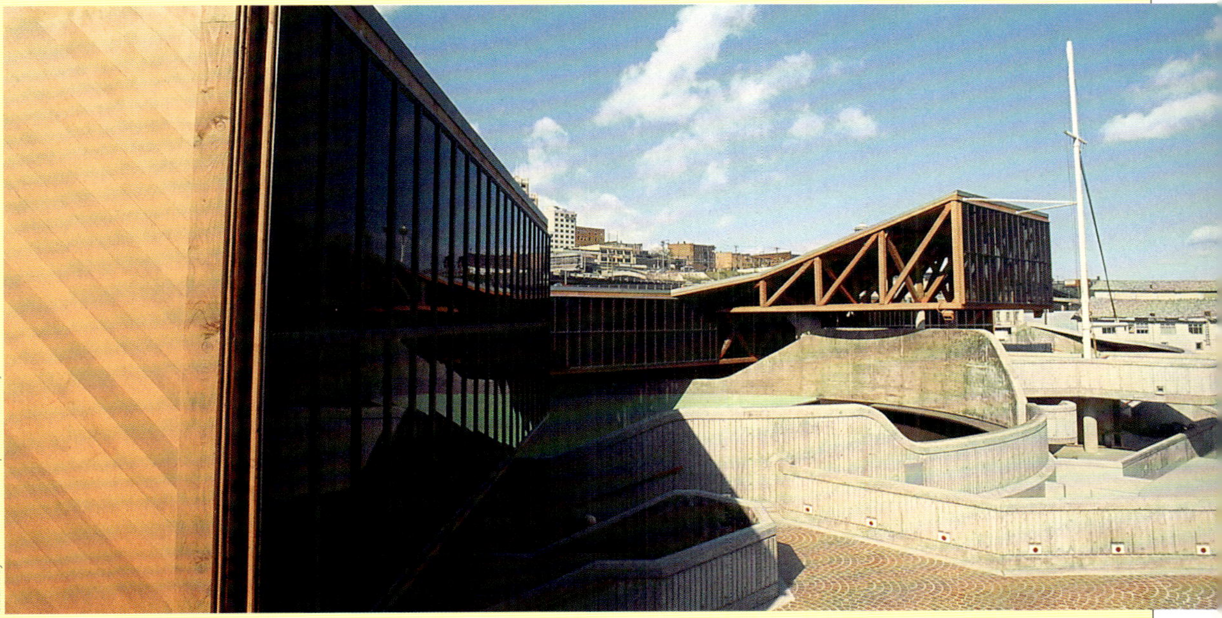

Courtesy of The Seattle Aquarium Society

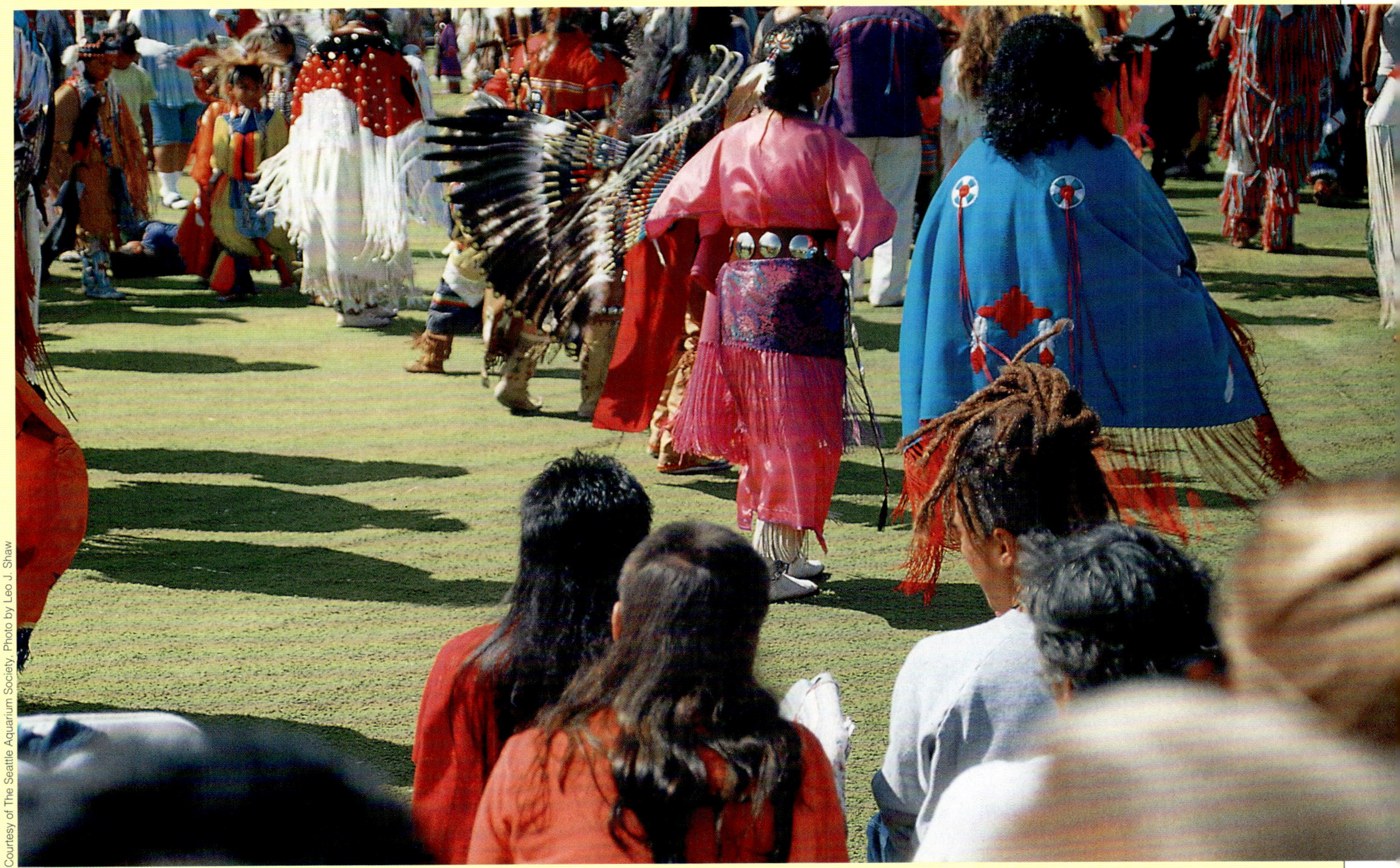

Courtesy of The Seattle Aquarium Society. Photo by Leo J. Shaw

The Seattle Aquarium and regional Native American Tribes sponsor the Salmon Homecoming celebration on the Seattle waterfront.

Young salmon produced at The Seattle Aquarium.

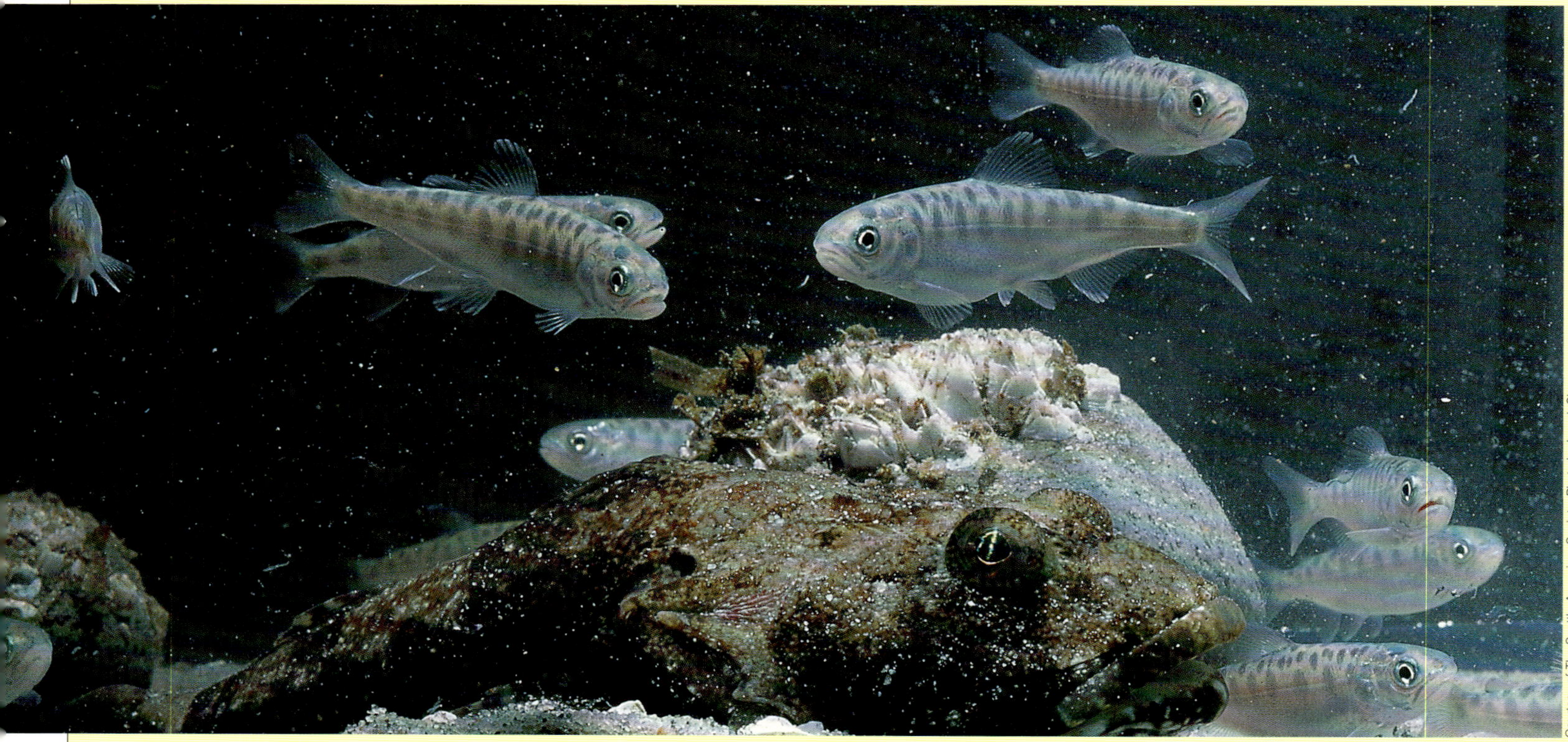

Courtesy of The Seattle Aquarium Society. Photo by Leo J. Shaw

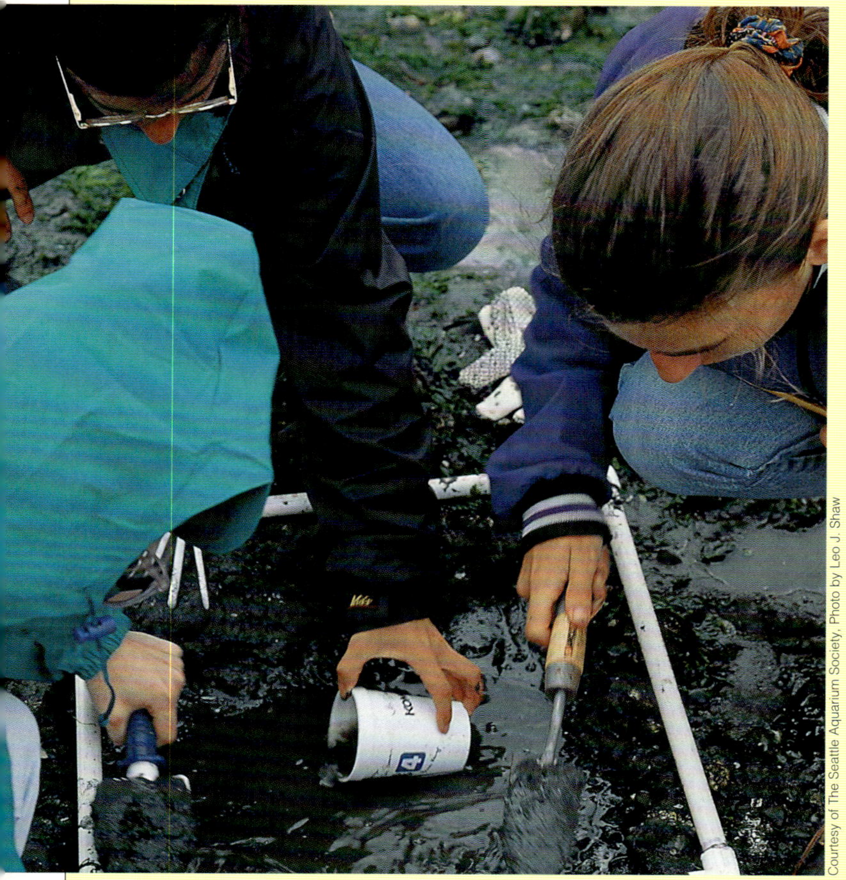

Courtesy of The Seattle Aquarium Society. Photo by Leo J. Shaw

The Seattle Aquarium education team works with the public on a survey on area beaches.

BRINGING VISITORS FACE TO FACE WITH NATURE

By giving visitors a taste of the natural habitat in which these creatures live, The Aquarium serves to teach child and adult alike about how unique these creatures are and how important it is to preserve the habitats in which they live. Outside viewing areas allow people to see local species of birds nest in realistic surroundings. Visitors can also view live salmon in various stages of development, as Aquarium staff raise and release almost 300,000 of the endangered fish each year into nearby Puget Sound. The 400,000-gallon Underwater Dome provides 360-degree views of fish, sharks, and eels swimming, feeding, and interacting as they might in the wild. The Discovery Lab exhibit provides anyone with the rare opportunity to safely touch and feel several species of marine animals, while learning about each organism and how it survives in the wild. Popular exhibits of sea and river otters, harbor seals, leafy seadragons and other creatures make a visit to The Seattle Aquarium a special treat for both young and old.

Visitors participate in Discovery Lab activities.

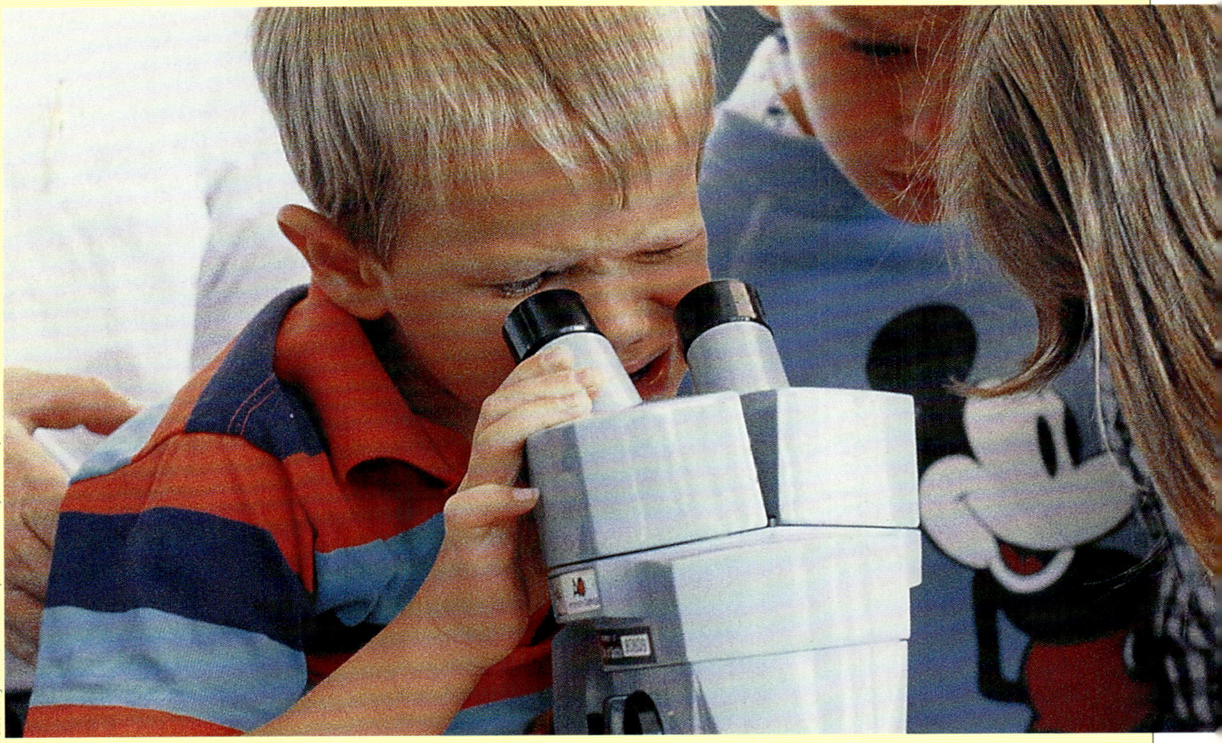

LOOKING FORWARD

Founded in 1981, the Seattle Aquarium Society (SEAS) has played an instrumental role in the continued growth of The Seattle Aquarium. Originally formed to coordinate and support The Aquarium's fundraising and membership efforts, SEAS has partnered with the City of Seattle build a new Pacific Northwest Aquarium, which would replace the current facility. This expanded structure will allow Aquarium staff to continue their efforts to inspire stewardship of the living world of water that surrounds us.

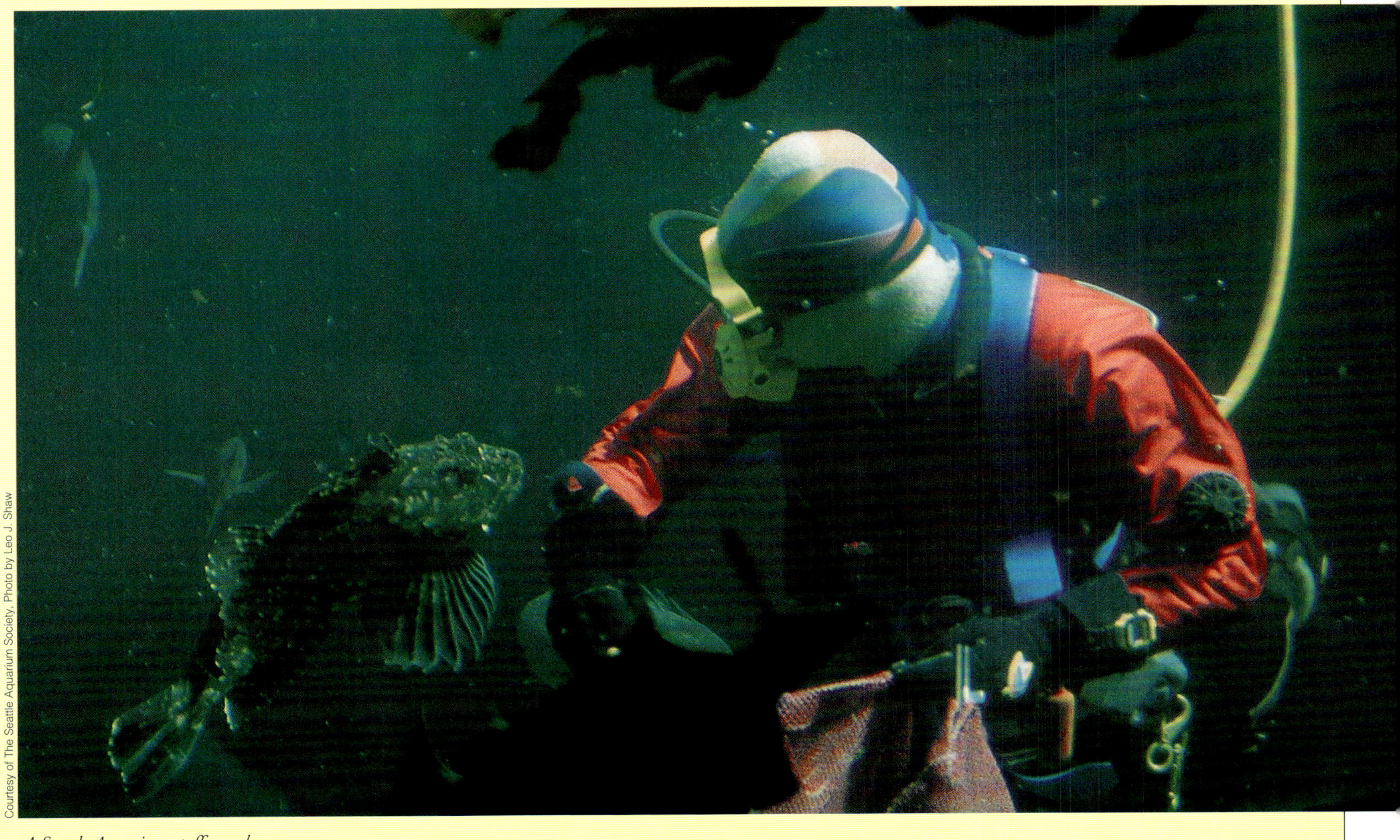

A Seattle Aquarium staff member does some underwater chores at the Underwater Dome.

Four Seasons Olympic Hotel

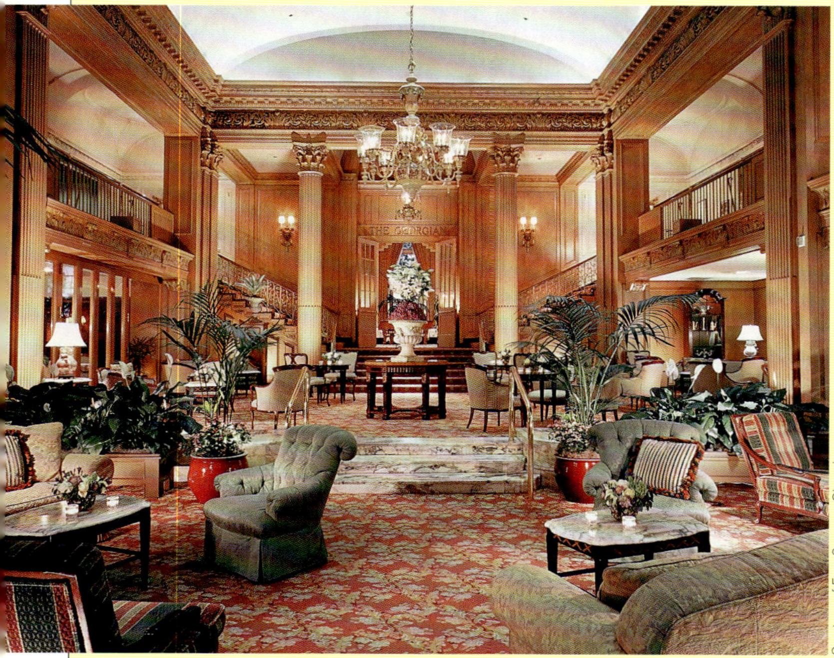

The lobby of the Four Seasons Olympic Hotel, with its original chandeliers and carved woodwork, remains true to the hotel's original 1924 construction.

The tattered pages of a copy of The Seattle Daily Times from 1924 tell the beginnings of a story, still true over three quarters of a century later:

In words of highest praise—praise for the indomitable spirit of the men who conceived and carried it through to completion, praise for the civic pride that made it possible, praise for the hands and minds that accomplished the artistry with which it is wrought—The Olympic was dedicated to the Queen City in a series of programs following the opening banquet last night.

It was obviously a celebration of the highest caliber when The Olympic was opened. Now Four Seasons Olympic Hotel, the beautiful building in the center of Seattle's downtown, still reflects the same degree of elegance and civic pride seen through the eyes of that newspaper reporter in 1924. A current publication describes Four Seasons Olympic as the "center of social life in the Seattle/King County area." Indeed, thousands upon thousands of current and past residents of the Seattle area can recite stories of senior proms, debutante balls, engagement parties, wedding receptions, anniversary celebrations, and civic galas from recent years or from distant memories. All were made that much more special because they took place at The Olympic.

Built on what was originally the site of the first campus of the University of Washington, Four Seasons Olympic has evolved from "the grandest inn west of Chicago" in 1924, to a fully restored, 450-guest-room hotel which has been lauded for its retention of the "old world charm" of its Italian renaissance architectural design. Listed on the national register of Historical Places, the hotel continues to receive national and international recognition. Some of the top national awards given to hotels have been added to Four Seasons Olympic's showcase annually.

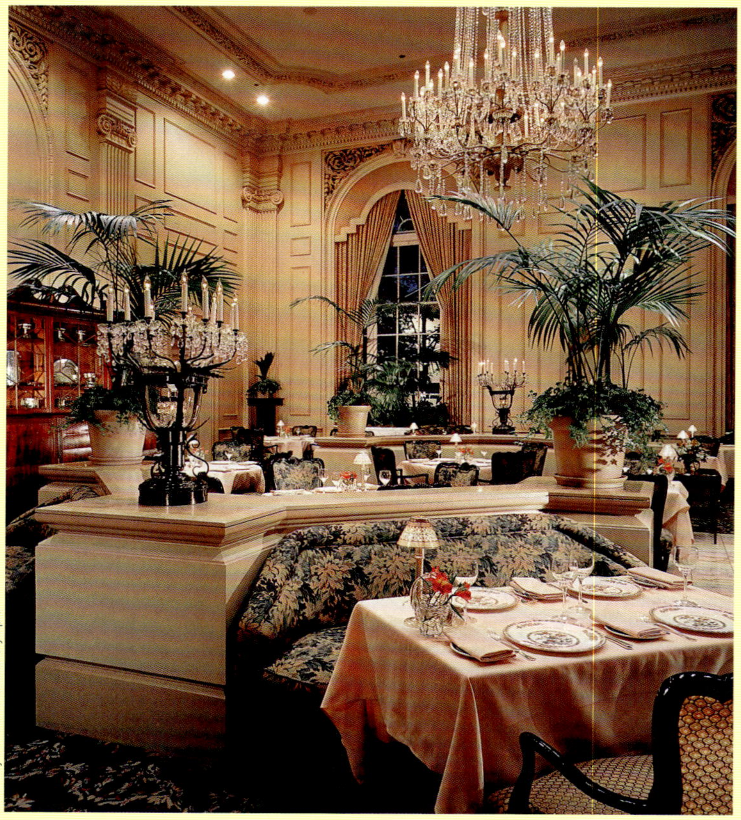

The Georgian is Seattle's premier dining room, featuring Northwest cuisine, Northwest wines, and world-class service.

From furnishings to state-of-the-art high-speed Internet service, the hotel's recent renovation ensures a stay that is both comfortable and productive.

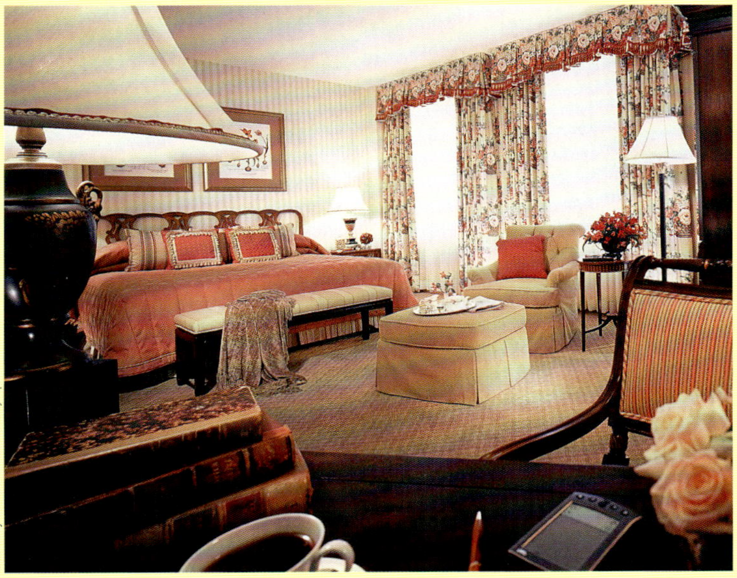

Courtesy of Four Seasons Olympic

Even with all these honors, today's management and staff continually look for ways to make every visitor's stay that much more memorable. Weekend guests are treated to warm cookies and milk at the time of their Sunday departure. Children find a bag of toys or complimentary cookies and milk awaiting them at check-in. Teens find popcorn, soda, and popular video games upon their arrival. For the business traveler, there are all the high-tech amenities that a modern executive could desire. Frequent guests have a personally monogrammed robe tucked away awaiting their every return.

Whether the visitor to Four Seasons Olympic is in town for an extended stay, an overnight business trip, or is a local resident dropping in for some fine dining, the elegance of the superbly appointed hotel leaves a lasting impression. A walk through the lobby, a brief visit to the arcade shops, or cocktails in the magnificent Garden Court, all bring a feeling of luxury and pampering. The hotel's chefs are recruited from among the world's finest, and the dining experience in any of the hotel's fine dining rooms will attest to their expertise.

The commitment of Four Seasons Olympic to service extends beyond the needs of hotel guests and into the local community. Numerous charity-driven functions and special events carry out that commitment such as "The Teddy Bear Suite,"and "Light Up A Child's Life" campaign recognized throughout the Northwest as an exciting holiday tradition that raises thousands of dollars each year for Children's Hospital. An annual chestnut roasting in front of the hotel features local government and business leaders as "celebrity roasters" and carries out the "old-world-charm" image while raising even more money for charity. The full list of events supporting local charity is too long to recite, and it keeps growing.

The 1924 "founding fathers" would be proud, indeed, if they could visit Four Seasons Olympic today. They would be following in the footsteps of six sitting United States Presidents, numerous foreign heads of state, and countless celebrities who have found the hotel's charm and luxury irresistible. At the 1924 opening gala, the President of the United Hotel Corporation, the original owners and builders of the hotel, said, "I want the Olympic to be an influence for good, to be a helpful factor in the development of those higher things in life not measured by material success." With all the luxury and all the amenities, Four Seasons Olympic Hotel has maintained that reputation and today's management continues the tradition and commitment to be much more than a fine hotel.

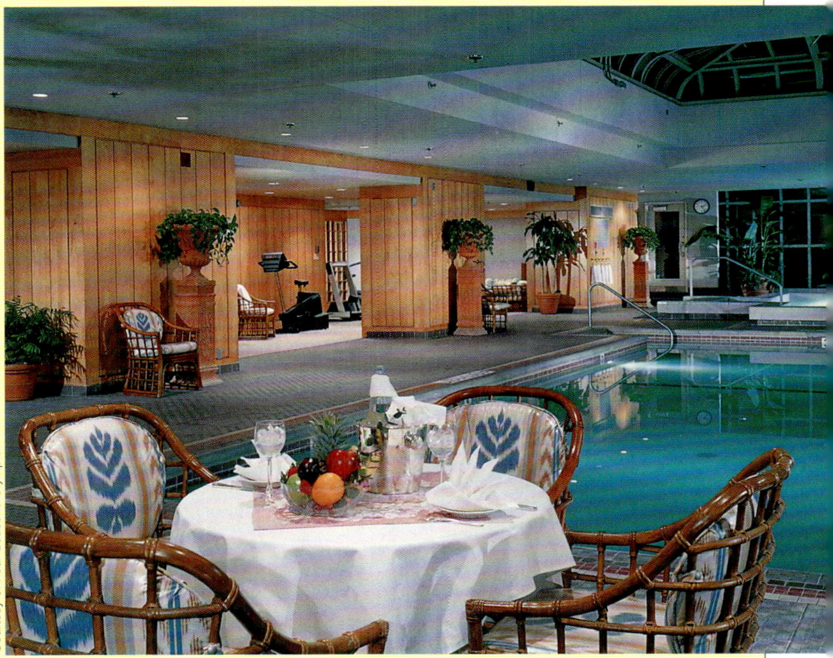

Courtesy of Four Seasons Olympic

The Health Club is fully equipped to help guests perfect the art of relaxation. The Four Seasons Olympic is always ready to outfit a guest who forgets to pack his or her running shoes or bathing suit, with the hotel's compliments.

Seattle Coffee Company

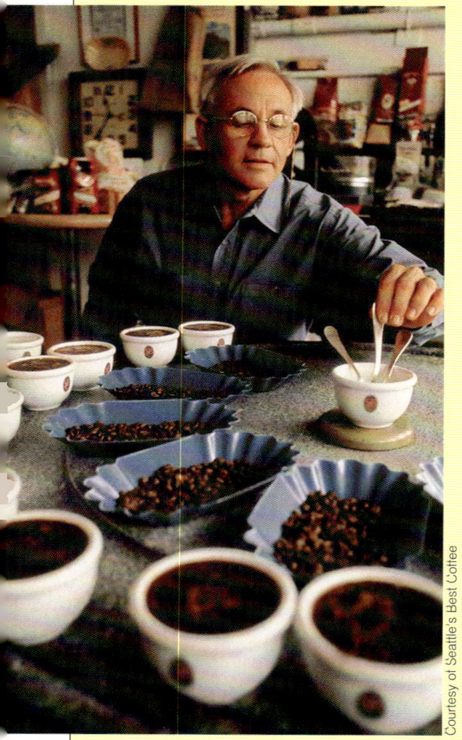

SBC founder Jim Stewart tastes several of the coffee company's many specialty roasts.

Once upon a time, on a Puget Sound island, two brothers started a small coffee business. This modest enterprise sparked the coffee revolution in Seattle. Ambitious and committed to quality, Stewart Brothers Coffee soon earned a local contest distinction of being the producers of "Seattle's Best Coffee." With a touch of inspiration, the entrepreneurs adopted the name "Seattle's Best Coffee"—conveniently, the SBC initials were already in their logo.

Similarly, in the hills of Perugia, Italy, traditional recipes for roasting and blending coffees were being perfected by another family, that of Umberto Bizzarri. In 1986, Umberto brought his family's recipes to the United States and opened his first Torrefazione Italia in Seattle's historic Pioneer Square.

Today, Seattle Coffee Company produces and promotes the two distinct brands, Seattle's Best Coffee and Torrefazione Italia. Seattle's Best Coffee had 81 retail units at the turn of the millennium and expects to total several hundred over the next five years. Torrefazione Italia operated 19 exclusive cafés in 2000 with plans for steady international growth in the years to come.

Seattle Coffee Company is an active and concerned member of the community and focuses its attention in two distinct directions. Seattle's Best Coffee is affiliated with the national Water Keepers Alliance, which stresses water quality—an important element in the coffee industry from growing to brewing. Torrefazione Italia has strong ties to the arts and is a benefactor of arts organizations in all the communities the cafés serve.

Jim Stewart, one of the founding brothers of SBC, is still the buyer of select coffee beans from premier growers throughout the world. In fact, Jim Stewart became a coffee farmer in Costa Rica in the early 1990s. This hands-on foundation of growing and harvesting top-quality, shade-grown specialty coffee beans is invaluable to his coffee buying responsibilities. However, when they do not meet the high standards he has adopted, Jim sometimes rejects certain beans, even from his own farm. These high standards include buying and roasting hand-selected, high-farmed arabica beans. The company also offers a line of shade-grown organic coffee as well as superior single-origin coffees including Kenyan, Kona, and Jamaican Blue Mountain.

Fortunately for coffee drinkers everywhere, Seattle Coffee Company offers fine-coffee lovers two unique experiences. With their firm family roots and commitment to quality, Torrefazione Italia and Seattle's Best Coffee will continue to have a worldwide impact on people's enjoyment of one the world's most favored beverages.

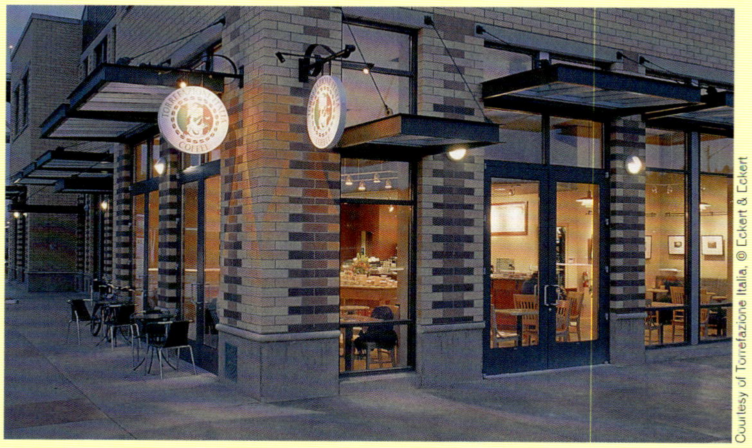

The warm interior of a Torrefazione Italia café beckons to the passerby.

Chateau Ste. Michelle Winery

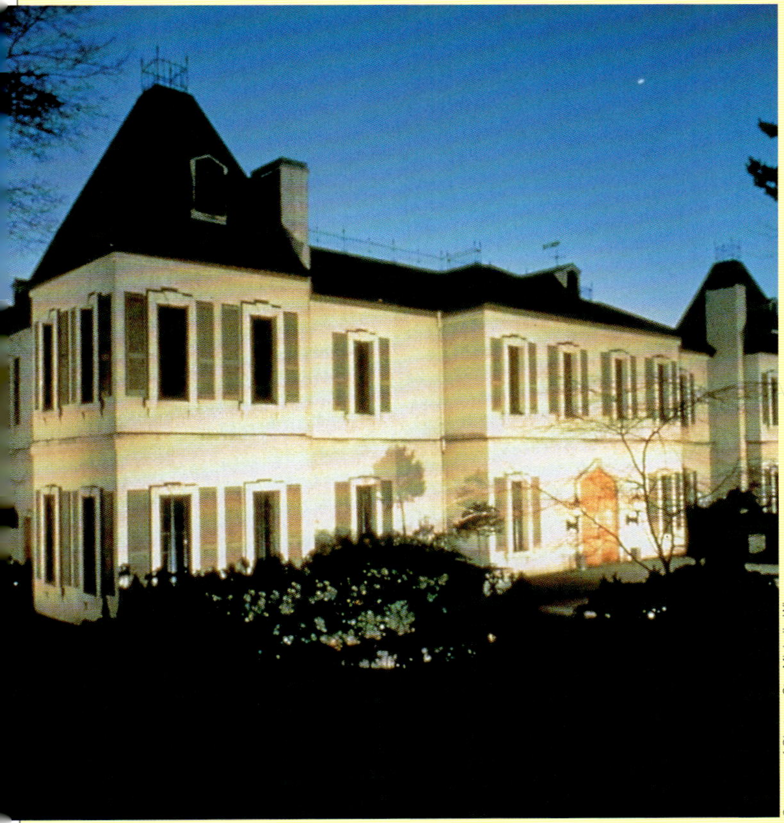

Courtesy of Chateau Ste. Michelle Winery

Chateau Ste. Michelle's headquarters are housed in a French-style chateau on the historic Stimson Estate in Woodinville, 20 minutes east of Seattle off Interstate 405.

What was once the 87-acre summer estate of Northwest lumber baron Frederick Stimson, is now the beautiful home of Chateau Ste. Michelle, a winery worthy of the title "Winery of the Year," an honor bestowed by *Wine & Spirits* magazine in 1996, 1998, and 1999. Chateau Ste. Michelle's King County winery was built in the mid-1970s, in the still-rural town of Woodinville, and it has since become a local institution. The business itself dates back to the 1930s, when it was established in the Columbia Valley of eastern Washington. The vineyards of the Columbia Valley are blessed with growing conditions that are similar to those found in the Bordeaux region of France.

Committed to crafting world-class wines of distinction, Chateau Ste. Michelle remains a limited-production winery, never compromising quality. As a result, Chateau Ste. Michelle has won national and international acclaim for its fine wines. In 2000, its Single Berry Select wine received a "97" rating, highest in Washington history.

The management and staff of Chateau Ste. Michelle take the winery's role as a local institution to heart by ensuring its commitment to the community. The winery is a major contributor to various non-profit organizations in the King County area. Each year, the winery hosts the Auction of Washington Wines, with the cooperation of many other state wineries. The proceeds from the auction go to Children's Hospital, and over the years, more than 10 million dollars has been raised.

The dramatic grounds of the Chateau are open year round to the public for tours and tastings. The grounds are also the setting for a series of summer concerts featuring top-name national and international acts. The net proceeds from the series fund the winery's charitable-giving program, which supports arts organizations such as the Pacific Northwest Ballet, the Bellevue Art Museum, the Seattle Symphony, and the Pilchuck Glass School.

Another of Chateau Ste. Michelle's contributions to the arts is in its growing collection of glass art, including the work of such masters as Dale Chihuly, Ginny Ruffner, William Morris, and Dan Dailey. The collection itself is a representation of the special link between glass and wine.

Chateau Ste. Michelle has a special aura about it. It is a quality that is reflected in the lovely grounds of the Chateau, in its dedication to the arts, and especially in the sensational wines that delight even the most particular of epicureans.

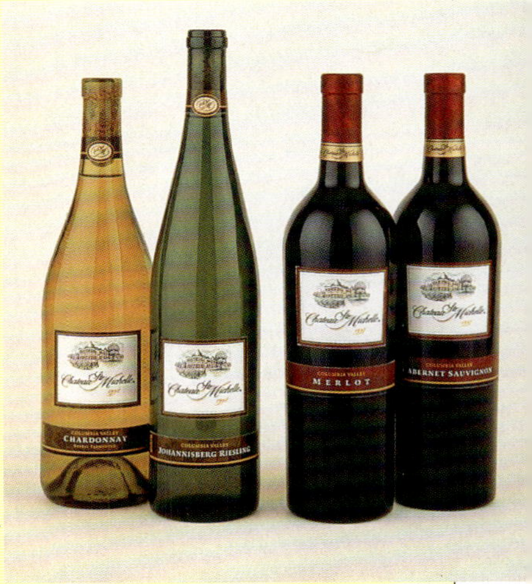

Courtesy of Chateau Ste. Michelle Winery

Visitors to Chateau Ste. Michelle can taste the award-winning wines in the gift shop, which is open seven days a week.

Aljoya Conference Center of Seattle

Aljoya Conference Center of Seattle, an executive retreat environment ten minutes from downtown Seattle, is surrounded by 18 acres of mature-growth cedar, maple, and alder trees. In this tranquil setting, meeting, lodging, and dining rooms are arranged around landscaped lawns, courtyards, walking paths, and a pond teeming with wildlife. Aljoya provides meeting facilities perfect for small group gatherings, creative thinking, and team building.

Built in the mid-'60s to house the Battelle Seattle Research Institute, the site has, over the years, played host to scholars, world-renowned scientists, and Nobel Prize winners. The property was purchased from Battelle in 1998, and the Conference Center was renamed Aljoya Conference Center of Seattle, in memory of the new owners' maternal grandmother. It was a fitting tribute to a family who had all lost their lives in the Holocaust.

Purchased again in 2000 by a private party, Aljoya Conference Center continues to be a meeting place and "think tank" for groups and businesses, attracting the best and the brightest, and remains dedicated to providing an ideal environment for adult learning. The Conference Center includes meeting rooms specifically designed for up to 100 guests, as well as 30 guest rooms, and a dining room featuring world-class cuisine. The Battelle Institute also remains on the property and is joined by the Talaris Research Institute, devoted to the study of early childhood learning.

Aljoya Conference Center of Seattle is managed by Columbia Hospitality. Columbia Hospitality also manages Bell Harbor International Conference Center, World Trade Center Seattle, and the Northwest Waterfront Inns.

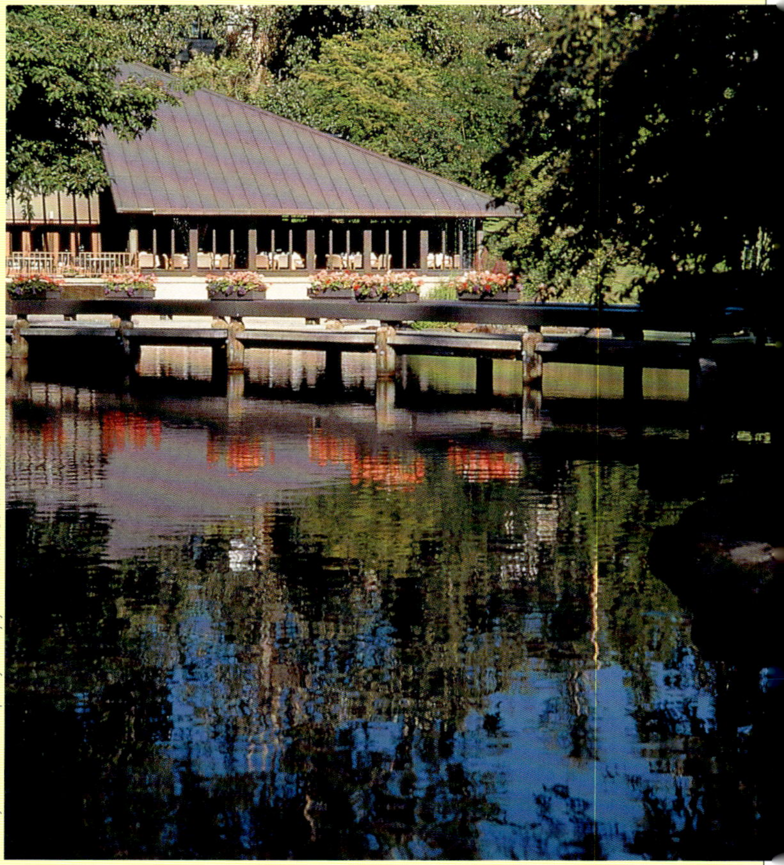

Courtesy of Columbia Hospitality and Aljoya Conference Center of Seattle

Eighteen acres of mature-growth cedar, maple and alder trees surround the Aljoya Conference Center.

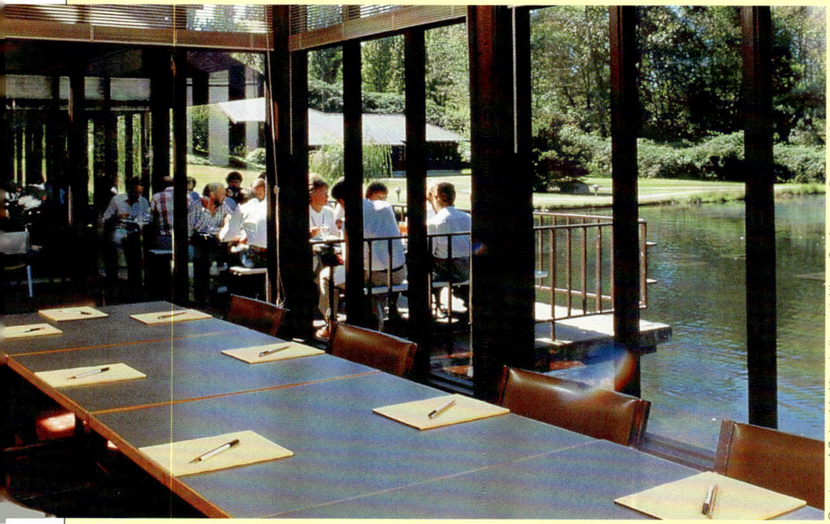

Courtesy of Columbia Hospitality and Aljoya Conference Center of Seattle

Aljoya Conference Center is dedicated to providing an ideal environment for adult learning. It is the perfect meeting place and "think tank" for small groups and businesses.

Bell Harbor International Conference Center

From U. S. presidents to leaders of the free world, when important meetings happen in Seattle, they happen at Bell Harbor International Conference Center. Bell Harbor offers over 36,000 square feet of flexible function space, including the new 10,000-square-foot International Promenade. For history-making occasions for up to 1,000 guests to events of a more intimate nature, Bell Harbor sets the stage for an inspired exchange of ideas and information.

When organizers are planning an event on an international scale, Bell Harbor is the only conference center on the West Coast with the built-in ability to interpret six languages. Designed to meet the requirements of the United Nations and the International Association of Conference Centers, the 300-seat Bay Auditorium includes six built-in simultaneous interpretation booths.

Located on Seattle's waterfront, Bell Harbor's spacious outdoor terraces and a large outdoor rooftop plaza offer a rare opportunity to step outside and enjoy the fresh sea air and warm summer evenings during receptions and special events.

Bell Harbor's Executive Chef and culinary team seek out only the freshest bounty of the season from the ocean waters and small farms of the Pacific Northwest. Regional delicacies—catered exclusively to the tastes of each group—are served in abundance, including salmon, shellfish, locally grown apples, Washington wines and of course, Seattle's world-famous coffee.

Bell Harbor International Conference Center is owned by the Port of Seattle and managed by Columbia Hospitality. Columbia Hospitality also manages Aljoya Conference Center of Seattle, World Trade Center Seattle, and the Northwest Waterfront Inns.

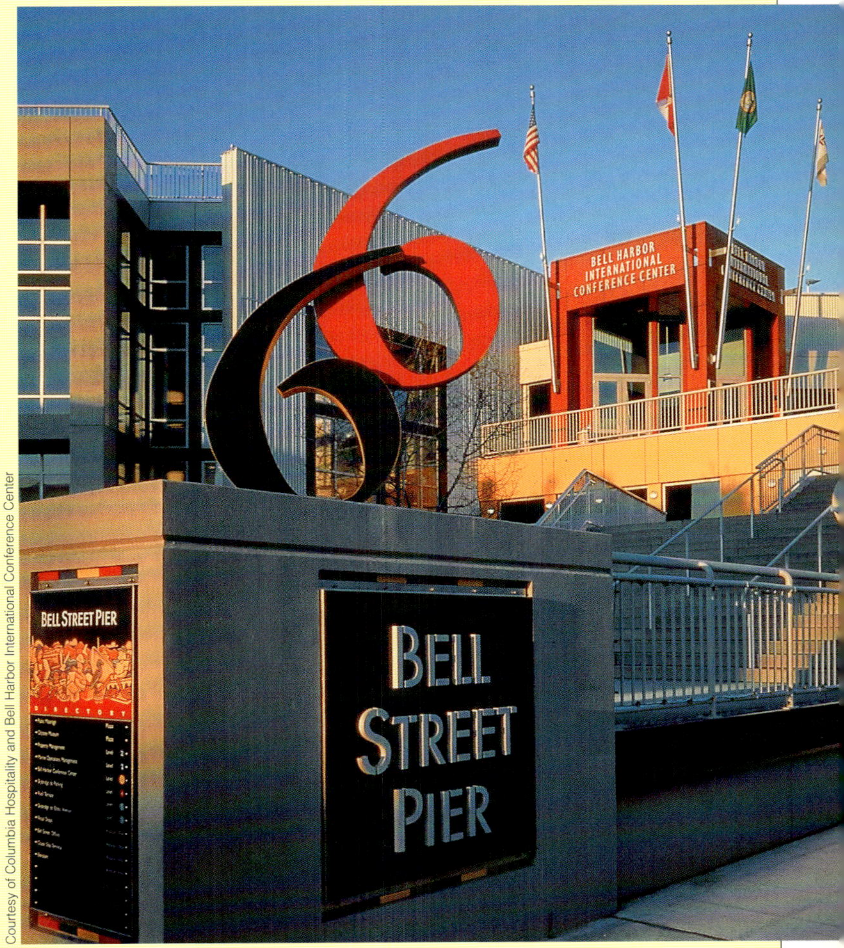

Courtesy of Columbia Hospitality and Bell Harbor International Conference Center

Located at Pier 66, Bell Harbor International Conference Center is an integral part of Bell Street Pier—an 11-acre neighborhood that has transformed downtown Seattle's waterfront into one of the most dynamic on the West Coast.

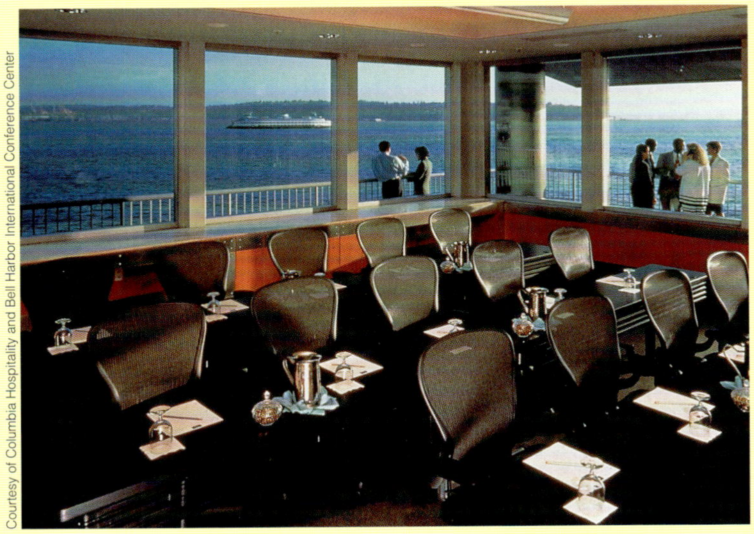

Courtesy of Columbia Hospitality and Bell Harbor International Conference Center

Overlooking picturesque Elliott Bay and the Olympic Mountain Range, the Cove conference room is just one of the many water-view rooms at Bell Harbor International Conference Center. Conference rooms are conveniently situated next to smaller breakout rooms, refreshment areas and a 4,000-square-foot wraparound deck.

Emerald Downs

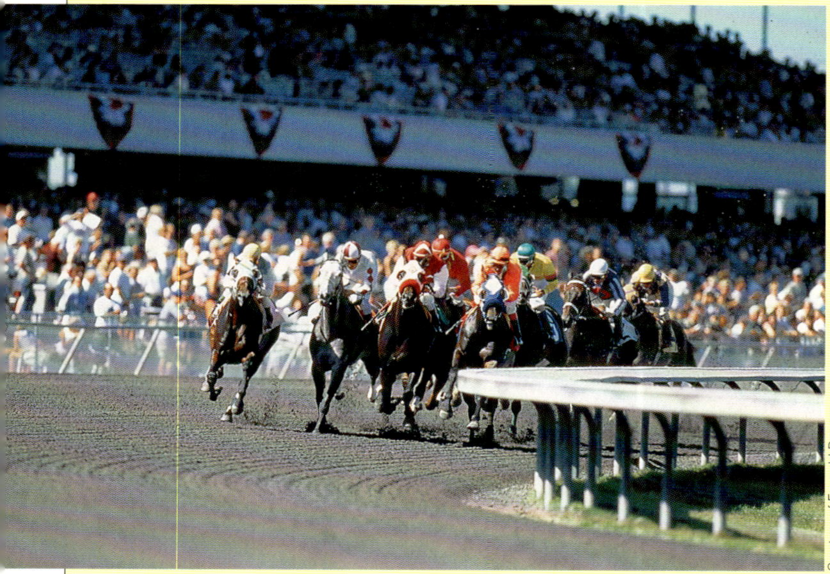

Courtesy of Emerald Downs

The $250,000 Longacres Mile is the racing jewel of the Pacific Northwest.

Emerald Downs, the beautiful new racetrack located just off Highway 167 in the lush Green River Valley, opened its first racing season on June 20, 1996. From the beginning, Emerald Downs has offered approximately 100 days of live racing each year, once again attracting top thoroughbreds, owners, breeders, and the betting public back to a regional track. Since 1998, Emerald Downs has operated year-round with the off-season filled by full-card simulcast coverage from major tracks throughout the country and around the world.

Emerald Downs exists today because it is a labor of love and largely the product of sheer determination on the part of one man: Ron Crockett. Ron and his investors, along with legions of supporters, fought to continue the legacy of thoroughbred horse racing in Western Washington. They fought and won.

Horses ran and people cheered at Longacres Race Track, a Northwest fixture for 60 years. And then in 1992, Longacres was lost. With its passing, many believed that thoroughbred racing in the region was also a thing of the past. Ron Crockett, a prominent horse owner and breeder, was determined not to let thoroughbred racing die in his community. He launched a drive to bring racing back to Western Washington. After securing a license to operate a racetrack in April 1992, Ron set his plans in motion. Four years later, his dreams were realized and Emerald Downs was born.

The popularity of thoroughbred racing in the Puget Sound region has reached exciting levels. In a typical live meet, Emerald Downs will draw approximately 600,000 patrons. Another 150,000 race fans attend the off-season simulcast sessions. Economic estimates suggest that the thoroughbred racing industry in Washington State, predominately focused at Emerald Downs, produces a combined direct and indirect annual contribution of over $337 million to the state's economy.

Emerald Downs is operated by Northwest Racing Association. As its president, Ron Crockett looks at the future as a new era in thoroughbred racing—and he does so with enthusiasm. "The real value for most of our patrons is in the enjoyment of an inexpensive, quality-entertainment outing that appeals to everyone," says Ron. "A day spent in our fun-filled park provides excitement and activities for the whole family." Top that off with a chance to win a little money and who can resist Emerald Downs?

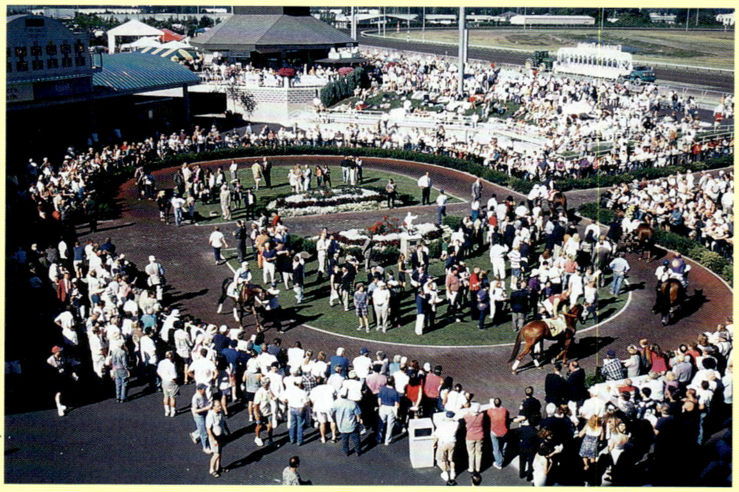

Courtesy of Emerald Downs

Thousands gather daily at Emerald Downs to participate in "the sport of kings."

The Bellevue Club

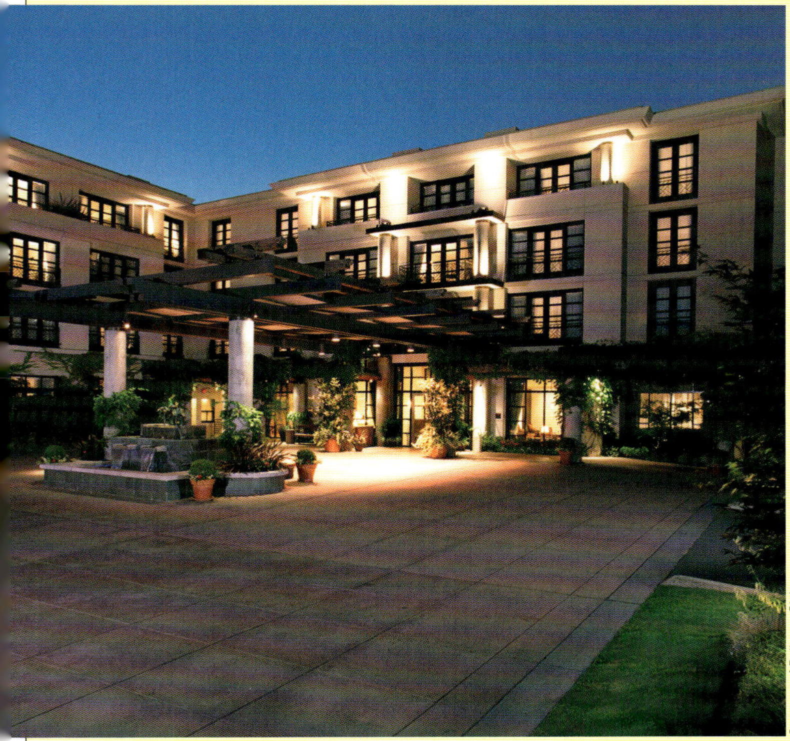

Courtesy of Bellevue Club

The award-winning Bellevue Club boasts warm and personal service, luxurious comfort, fabulous food, and a full-service spa.

Created in 1979 as a multi-purpose social/athletic club, The Bellevue Club has become a model of what a true community club should be. To say that the club is comprehensive in its programs and services is an understatement. The array of activities available to club members is both long and impressive.

Covering over nine acres, the club boasts over 220,000 square feet of space for tennis, fitness programs, gymnasium, swimming pool, restaurants, meeting rooms, and a hotel. In this space, between 12,000 and 13,000 members stay fit, dine in comfortable elegance, entertain guests, hold corporate meetings, and generally enjoy a beneficial social relationship with other club members and with the club staff.

The athletic portion of The Bellevue Club is, in itself, an amazing collection of facilities and programs. The tennis program operates on six indoor and five outdoor courts. The 50-meter swimming pool provides almost unlimited opportunity for lap swimming for fitness and for classes for all ages. Well-trained and highly qualified staff members are immediately available throughout the club to assist members in their efforts towards wellness, a major theme of the club.

Within the club, one will find the latest in sophisticated fitness equipment, high-tech media resources in the meeting rooms, and fiber-optic connections for business communications in the hotel rooms. In addition, one will find beautiful and interesting art and art objects.

The club's hotel is a member of the Small Luxury Hotels of the World and has earned both a four-star and a four-diamond rating. In one recent year, the hotel was ranked as the number one property among 250 hotels in its class. Added to The Bellevue Club in 1995, the hotel offers 64 luxury rooms and 3 suites. The club also offers three restaurants, from the upscale Polaris, to the casual The Sport Café and Ground Zero Espresso Café.

Not only does The Bellevue Club raise the mark for excellence in service, it sets the standard for the quality amenities it offers. It has earned its reputation as an exclusive and superior property. The Bellevue Club is committed to maintaining its high level of service to its members and guests and sustaining its standards well into the twenty-first century.

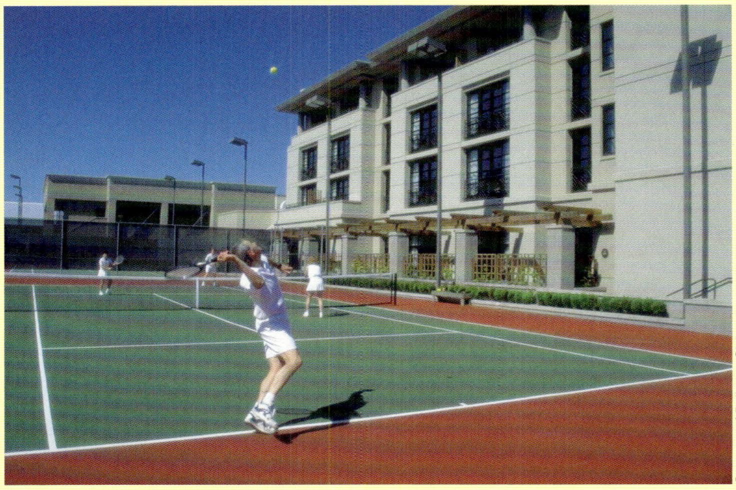

Courtesy of Bellevue Club

With indoor and outdoor tennis courts, an indoor running track, weight rooms, and a full-service spa, there is no need to leave the nine-acre facility.

The Seattle Symphony

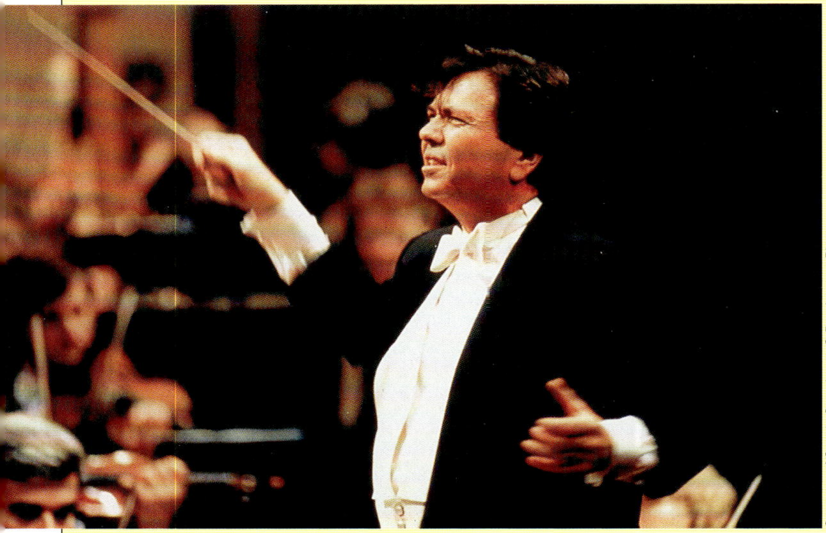

Courtesy of Seattle Symphony, © Dan Lamont Photo

Maestro Gerard Schwarz, Music Director of the Seattle Symphony, conducts the Orchestra in the acoustically superb Benaroya Hall.

The Seattle Symphony was founded in 1903, and is the oldest and largest cultural institution in the Pacific Northwest. With a roster of 90 musicians, the Symphony is the centerpiece of the vibrant classical music scene in Seattle and the Pacific Northwest. The Symphony performs in Benaroya Hall, widely acknowledged as one of the finest concert halls in the world. From September through July, the ensemble is heard live by more than 300,000 people annually in a schedule that includes 18 weeks of classical subscription *Masterpiece* concerts and a broad spectrum of other series including *Visiting Orchestras*, *Basically Baroque*, *Mainly Mozart*, *Music of our Time*, *The Boeing Distinguished Artists*, and *Light Classics*. In a lighter vein, the Symphony presents the *Seattle Pops* and *Popular Culture* series featuring major artists from popular, folk, jazz, and other genres. With an eye on future generations, the *Discover Music!* and *Tiny Tots* series reach new, young audiences.

Recognized for its daring programming and tradition of performing music by twentieth-century composers under the leadership of Maestro Gerard Schwarz, the Symphony is one of the world's most recorded orchestras. It is represented on more than 75 compact discs, including Grammy Award-winning and nominated compact discs devoted to music by Howard Hanson, David Diamond, and many other important American composers of the twentieth century.

On September 12, 1998, the Symphony held its inaugural concert in Benaroya Hall, its new state-of-the-art concert facility. Featuring the 2,500-seat S. Mark Taper Foundation Auditorium and the 540-seat Illsley Ball Nordstrom Recital Hall, the facility has been hailed for its clear, warm acoustics and the quiet elegance of its design.

Active in community programs and education, the Seattle Symphony presents an annual *U.S. Bank All Community Concert*, the entire proceeds from which go to eight pre-selected non-profit organizations. The Symphony offers many concerts and special programs for young people in the community including Arts-in-Education concerts, which bring classical music to 10,000 fifth-graders in back-to-back concerts each year.

Significant outreach efforts bring the Symphony and its individual musicians to classrooms throughout the region. In the spring of 2001, the Symphony will open a Learning Center in Benaroya Hall that will greatly enhance its educational programs for school children and adults.

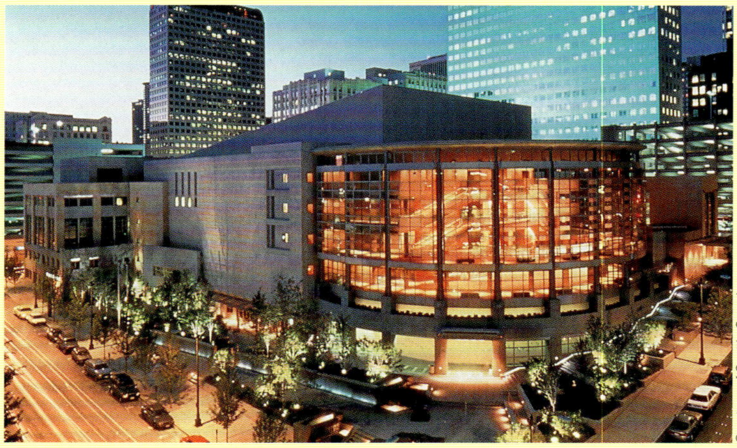

Courtesy of Seattle Symphony

Glowing in late summer twilight, Benaroya Hall, home of the Seattle Symphony, Gerard Schwarz, Music Director.

The Sorrento Hotel

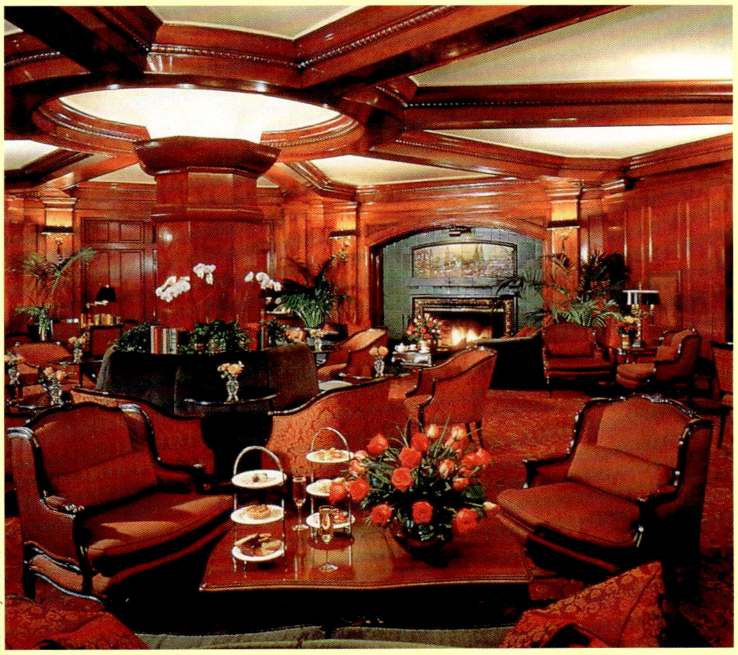

Courtesy of Sorrento Hotel

The Sorrento Hotel's Fireside Room is a perfect place to comfortably enjoy a drink or light dining. The walls are of Honduran Mahogany and the furnishings are both easy and elegant.

"World-renowned" is a term reserved for few landmarks in Seattle—the Space Needle is, of course, one of those. However, long before that notable structure was even conceived of for Seattle's 1962 World's Fair, a classic hotel that still graces the hill above the city's downtown area had earned that distinction. Designed in the Renaissance-era elegance of its Italian namesake, The Sorrento Hotel has charmed Seattle and its visitors since its completion in 1908.

From its beginning, the Sorrento has been a destination of the rich and famous, including the Vanderbilts and the Guggenheims. During the mid-century period, the prestigious, seventh floor "Top of the Town" restaurant became a popular destination in itself. Today, the hotel retains its reputation for excellent cuisine by way of the Hunt Club Restaurant, which has been named as one of Seattle's best and as one of the top ten restaurants in the United States.

After several modernizing renovations, the Sorrento has maintained its European refinement, while keeping pace with technology and changing patrons needs. In so doing, the hotel has broadened its reputation as one of the finest hotels anywhere. In one of the hotel's boldest moves, the original 150 rooms were renovated in 1981 to create 76 suites in their place. The plans carefully maintained the Sorrento's legendary elegance while providing more spacious surroundings for its guests. This broad stroke was a pioneering move that enhanced the hotel's popularity with its repeat guests and celebrities.

Another major change in the 1981 renovation was the conversion of the entire seventh floor into banquet facilities. A popular site for elegant events, each banquet room offers stunning views of Seattle's skyline, Puget Sound, and the distant Olympic Mountains.

Much of the charm of the Sorrento is captured in the details, including the smartly wrapped water bottle placed under the sheet at "turn down time" (called Chilly Spells by the staff) when the temperature dips. The details also complete the elegance of the Fireside Room, located directly off the hotel lobby. The walls are of Honduran Mahogany and the furnishings are richly appointed. It is the ideal place to enjoy the Sorrento's daily tea service.

The Sorrento Hotel is dedicated to maintaining its tradition of excellence. It is not surprising that patrons describe the Sorrento as having that highly sought-after, yet truly evasive quality of "subtle elegance." The praise is high, and well deserved.

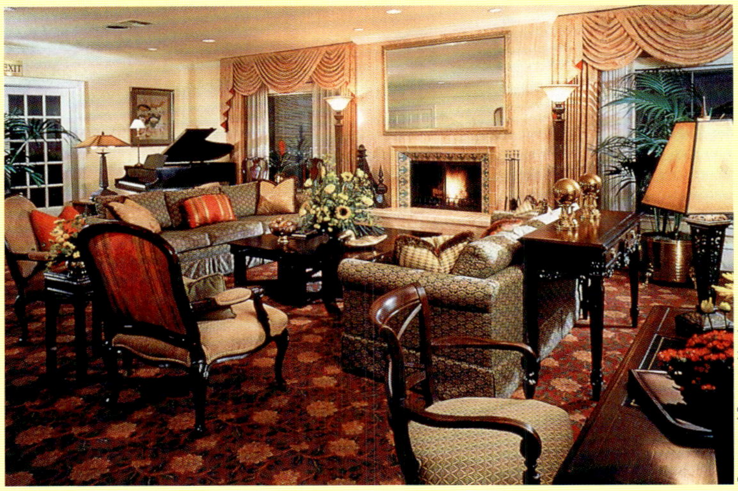

Courtesy of Sorrento Hotel

The Sorrento Hotel's elegantly appointed Penthouse Suite.

Burke Museum of Natural History and Culture

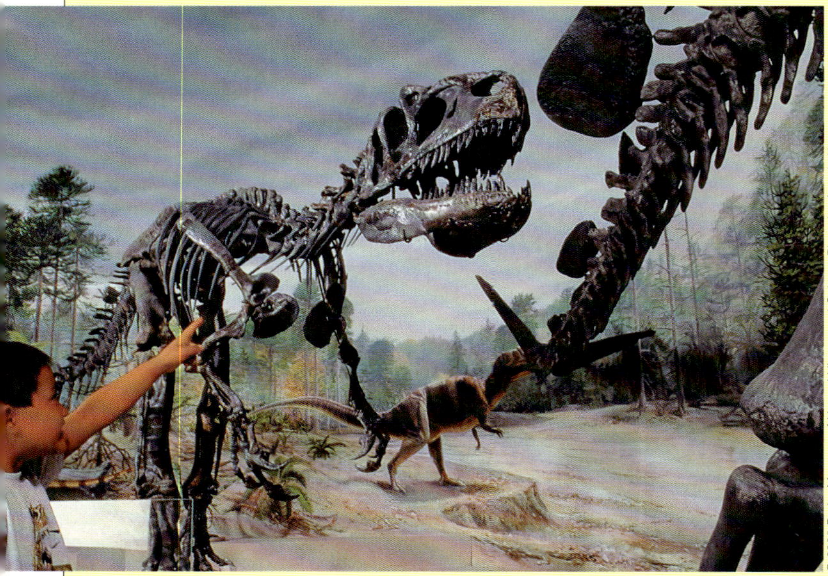

Dinosaur skeletons delight a young museum visitor.

—Where natural and cultural worlds come alive—
Home to Washington's only real dinosaur fossils and a world-renowned collection of Northwest Coast Native art, the Burke Museum of Natural History and Culture has thrilled and educated visitors for more than 100 years.

Founded in 1885 and designated Washington State Museum in 1899, the museum today holds nationally ranked collections in anthropology, geology, and zoology totaling nearly four million specimens. A vital education program reaches 120,000 children a year. Through exhibits, educational programs, and research, the museum promotes understanding of the natural world and of the cultural heritage of the region.

The Burke Museum is located just minutes from downtown Seattle on the northwest corner of the University of Washington campus and is accredited by the American Association of Museums. One can browse the Museum Store's fine selection of art and books and take a break at the Burke Museum Cafe.

Compelling Exhibits

Life and Times of Washington State
500 million years of geological history! Lethal lava, grinding glaciers, and rampaging reptiles—visitors can marvel at the forces that shaped Washington's landscape, and at the amazing animals that once lived here. Included are real dinosaur fossils, an Ice Age mastodon, and the giant ground sloth found at Sea-Tac Airport.

Pacific Voices
Living traditions....
This exhibit focuses on the lives of peoples from around the Pacific through their arts, ceremonies, and profoundly moving stories. Visitors can enjoy Native American art, and come to understand Chinese New Year and Laotian fire rocket festivals as observed here in Seattle.

Treasures at the Burke
From the world's third-largest topaz to rare Native American masks, the most beautiful and important treasures from the Burke's collections are on display.

Fascinating Programs

From Dinosaur Day to Native American Arts Celebration, from Thursday night lectures to family weekend activities, the Burke offers something special for everyone.

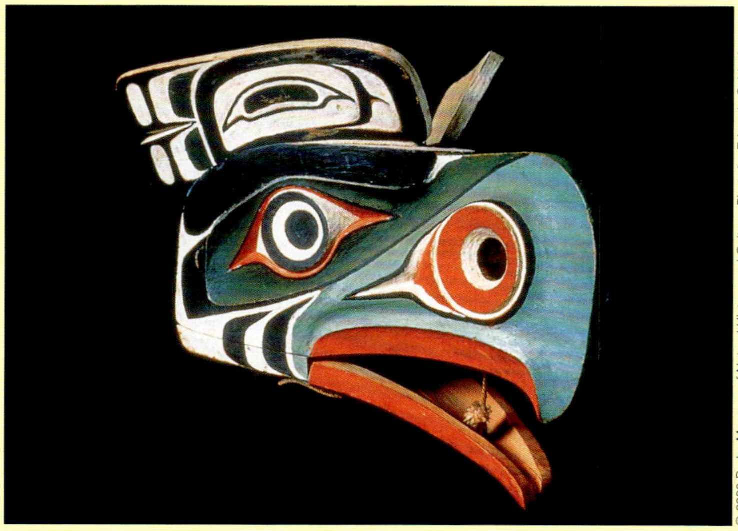

Thunderbird mask, Kolus.

Seattle Mariners

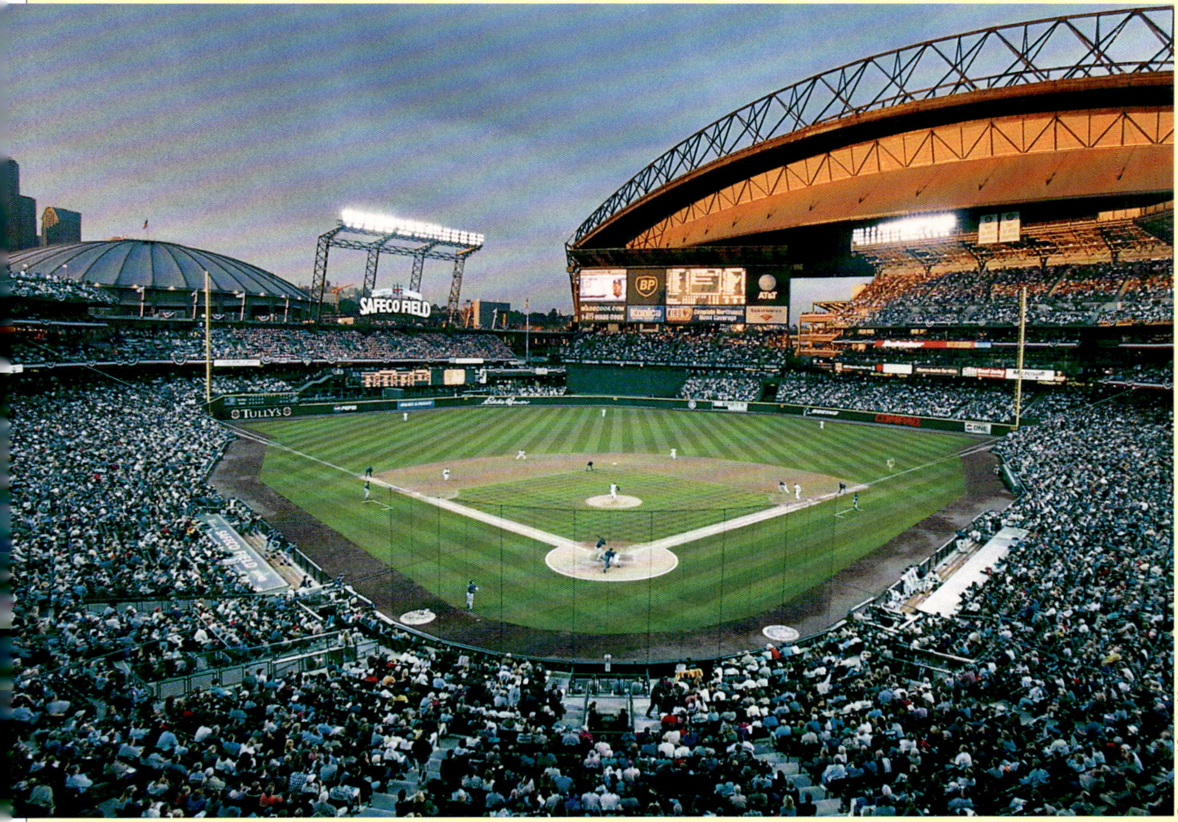

Courtesy of Seattle Mariners

SAFECO Field just before sunset on July 15, 1999, the ballpark's Inaugural Game.

The Pacific Northwest has a rich tradition of baseball—from the Negro League Seattle Steelheads and old Pacific Coast League Rainiers to the Major League Pilots and Seattle Mariners.

Seattle has been home to the Mariners since 1977. From its beginnings as a Major League Baseball expansion franchise playing in the Kingdome to the American League West Division Championships of the 1990s and the opening of SAFECO Field, the Seattle Mariners have come a long way. The Mariners now have taken their place as one of the premier teams in the game of baseball.

The Mariners' new home, SAFECO Field, combines the best of classic ballparks and the fan conveniences of modern stadiums. With a capacity of 47,000, SAFECO Field puts fans on top of the action on the field, and offers sweeping views of Puget Sound, the Olympic Mountains, and the downtown Seattle skyline. The first-of-its-kind retractable roof guarantees fans will stay comfortable and dry and games will be played despite the Pacific Northwest's changeable weather.

Led by CEO Howard Lincoln, the strong local ownership group is committed to fielding a competitive team and making a positive impact on the quality of life in the Pacific Northwest. Through the non-profit foundation Mariners Care, players, staff, and corporate partners donate time and millions of dollars to such worthy causes as Make-a-Wish Foundation, First Place School, Boys & Girls Clubs, and Big Brothers/Big Sisters.

With a fan base that draws from Alaska to Oregon, Idaho, and Montana, the Mariners are truly the Pacific Northwest's team.

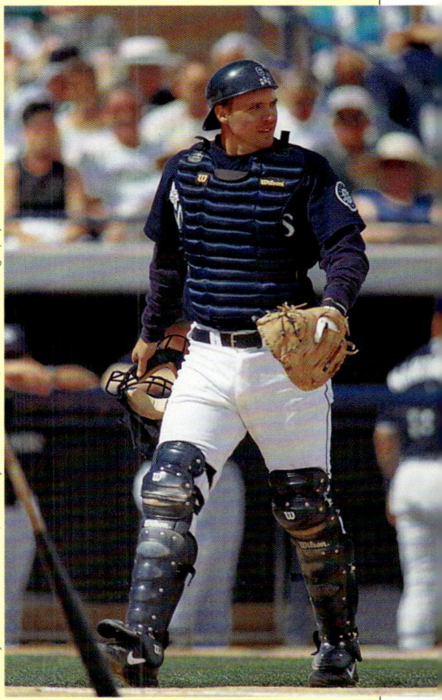

Courtesy of Seattle Mariners; Photo by Ben Vanhouten, Vanhouten Photography

Mariners catcher Dan Wilson makes his mark on and off the field. Wilson sponsors numerous charitable giving efforts and serves on the board of directors for Seattle's First Place School for children who are homeless or in transition.

The Museum of Flight

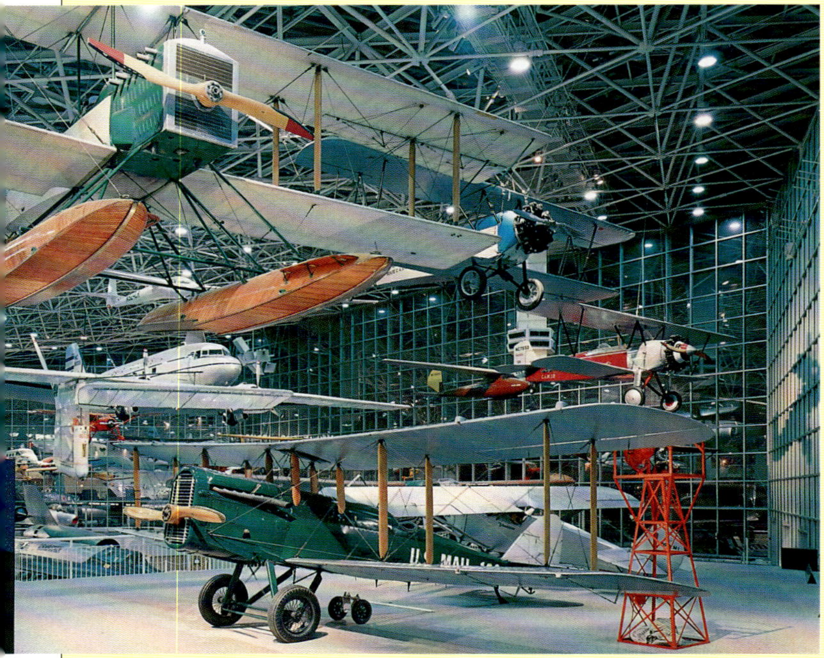
Courtesy of Museum of Flight. Photo by Steve Keating

The B&W seaplane exhibited in the Great Gallery at the Museum of Flight is a 1966 replica of a 1916 design. The B&W was the first airplane designed and built by Boeing.

The Museum of Flight is the largest air and space museum on the West Coast. With plans to more than double in size by 2003, this Seattle icon will become the largest independent, non-governmental flight museum in the world.

Currently welcoming more than half a million visitors and providing participatory programs for over 100,000 children and adults annually, the Museum of Flight is dedicated to educating the public in the history, science, and technology of flight—from the dawn of aviation to the Space Age. The world's first fighter from 1914, the only remaining Blackbird spy plane and drone, and the first U. S. presidential jet are just a few of the 100-plus authentic aircraft in the Museum's world-class collection.

In addition to providing a full range of on-site school and adult programs, the Museum of Flight travels the state with educational outreach programs, offers extensive teacher training courses, serves as a home base for the aviation and aerospace community, and hosts some of Seattle's most high-profile gatherings.

Founded in 1964 as the Pacific Northwest Aviation Historical Foundation, the Museum has been located on the southwest corner of Boeing Field/King County International Airport since 1983. Site of Seattle's first powered airplane flight in 1910, Boeing Field today is among the top dozen or so busiest airports in the country. It is home to Boeing flight test programs, Seattle's vital general aviation industry, and a big part of the reason why the Museum of Flight can offer visitors "an air show every day."

With its growing collection, constantly changing exhibits, extensive educational programming, and the lively activity in the air and on the ground, the Museum of Flight is truly a vital institution and one of Seattle's real "gems."

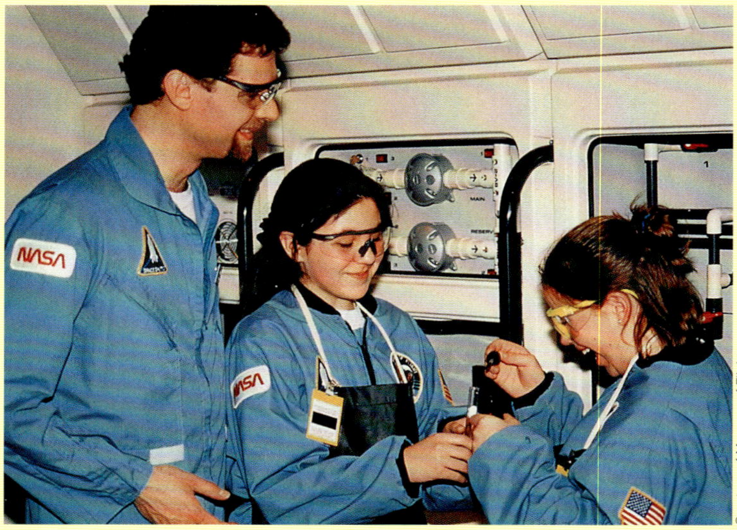

Courtesy of Museum of Flight

Children discover new things about astronauts in the Challenger Learning Center, a simulated space station environment at the Museum of Flight.

The Seattle Seahawks

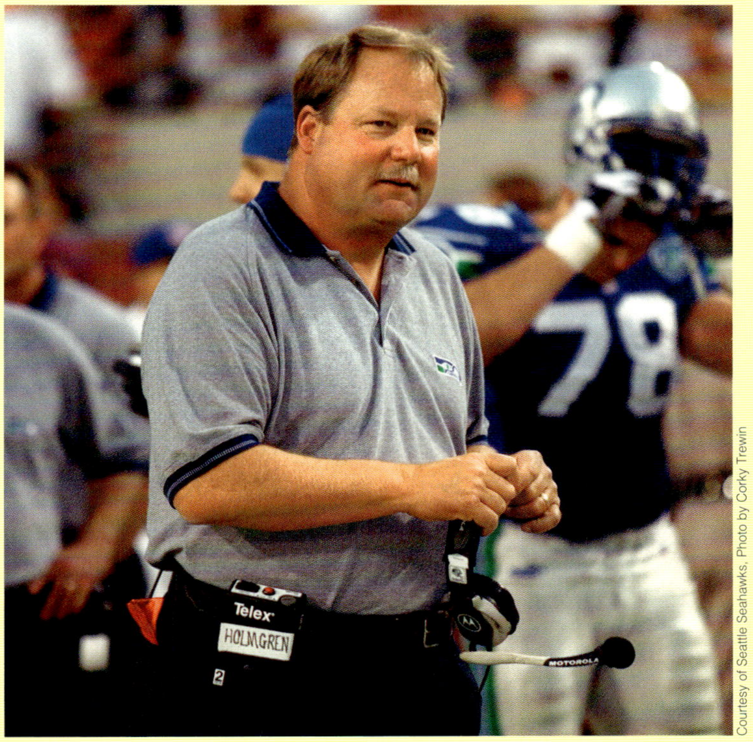

Head Coach Mike Holmgren smiles as he leads his team off the field after posting a victory.

The Seattle Seahawks, members of the National Football League, enjoy a tremendous regional following. As the NFL team of the Pacific Northwest, the Seahawks' loyal and passionate fans span Washington, Oregon, Idaho, Montana, Alaska, and British Columbia.

Many fine Seahawks players have entertained the fans over the years, including NFL Hall-of-Famer Steve Largent. Largent is renowned for his pass-catching abilities, as well as his off-the-field work with community causes. Seahawks "Ring of Honor" member Jacob Green has also served the community as a leading fundraiser with his annual golf tournament and auction, benefiting the Fred Hutchinson Cancer Research Center. Many other current and former Seahawks players devote countless hours to motivate children in schools, comfort hospital patients, and serve as celebrities for charitable fund-raising events. The Seahawks mascot "Blitz" and the Sea Gals also assist charitable causes and entertain thousands.

The NFL story in Seattle began in 1974, the year the city was awarded an expansion franchise. Two years later, the Seahawks played their first game in the Kingdome, which was home for 24 years. The team's early years were highlighted by the passing combination of Jim Zorn to Steve Largent, and by innovative play calling that led to exciting wins.

The Seahawks were an immediate fan favorite, with thousands of fans on the waiting list for season tickets. In recent years, fans were entertained by the big playmaking abilities of several Pro Bowl players, including Cortez Kennedy's defensive endurance, Shawn Springs' interceptions, Chad Brown's ferocious tackles, Michael Sinclair's quarterback sacks, and Walter Jones' consistent quarterback protection.

The Pacific Northwest almost lost its NFL franchise in 1996, before Seattle's own Paul Allen stepped forward and bought the team, pledging to keep the Seahawks in Seattle and help finance a new stadium. The new stadium, approved by the voters of Washington State in 1997, will also serve as the site for world-class soccer matches never before available to Seattle.

As the Seahawks soar into the twenty-first century, their future is full of promise. The "Mike Holmgren Era" is underway, and a fantastic new stadium will be home to the Seahawks beginning in the fall of 2002. Holmgren took the reins in 1999 as the Seahawks' Head Coach, General Manager, and Executive Vice President of Football Operations and promptly led the team to the AFC West Championship and the NFL playoffs. With strong leadership, a dynamic team, and committed fans, the Seahawks' future is as bright as the peak of Mount Rainier on a beautiful Pacific Northwest day!

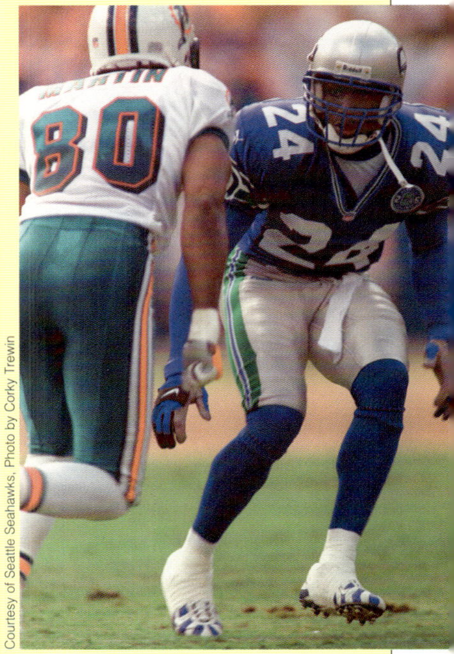

Opposing quarterbacks have avoided throwing the ball near Pro Bowl defensive back Shawn Springs since he came into the league in 1997. Springs is actively involved in numerous charitable causes throughout the Puget Sound.

Museum of History and Industry

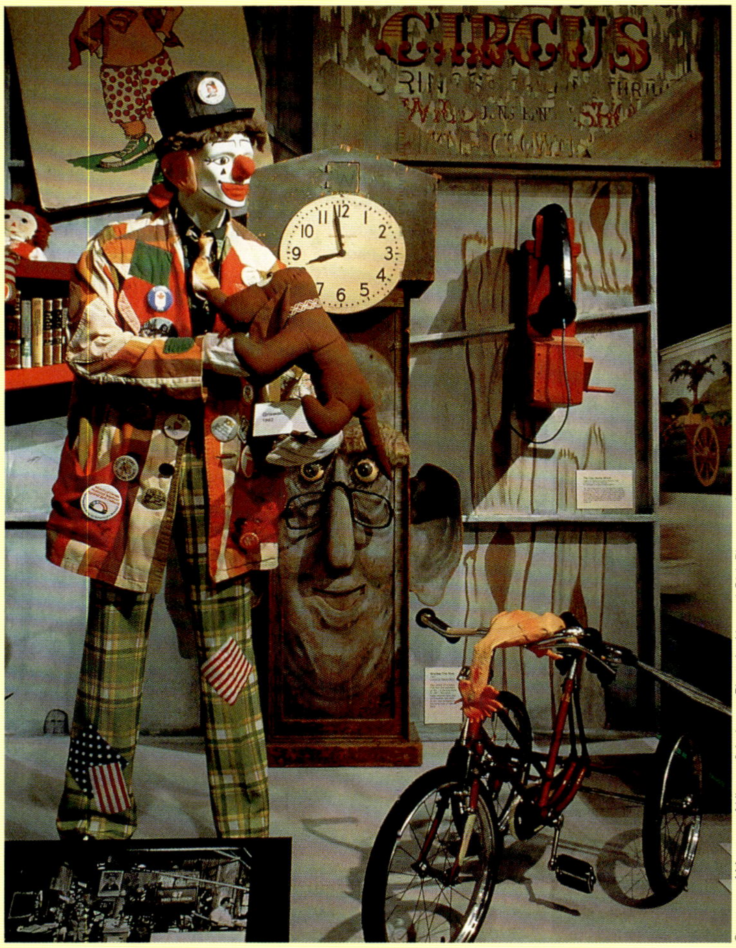

Courtesy of Museum of History & Industry, Photo by Howard Gisk Photographs

The JP Patches exhibit is a favorite attraction at the Museum of History & Industry. The artifacts evoke nostalgia for the golden age of local television.

Seattle's Museum of History and Industry (MOHAI) has grown to become the largest private heritage organization in Washington, attracting more than 60,000 visitors annually from the Northwest and beyond. The museum collects, preserves, and presents the rich history of the Pacific Northwest. MOHAI's engaging exhibits and programs have created an appreciation for the Northwest's diverse cultural, social, and economic history.

The idea of a museum to preserve and celebrate Seattle history was first discussed on November 13, 1911 when the first informal meeting of the Seattle Historical Society was held on the 60th anniversary of the landing of the Denny Party at Alki. The organization was officially founded three years later, and MOHAI opened on the shores of Lake Washington in the Montlake neighborhood on February 15, 1952.

The museum's collections—everything from ship wheels to evening gowns, gramophones to baby carriages, time clocks to crosscut saws, Boeing's first commercial airplane to the Slo Mo IV Hydroplane, Bobo the Gorilla to JP Patches memorabilia—give visitors glimpses of life in Puget Sound from the 1780s to the present day. The museum's library and archives, accessible via the internet, represent one of the most significant resources on Pacific Northwest history, containing 800,000 books, photographs, maps, and manuscripts. The library serves as a vital resource for regional media, historians, teachers, and students.

MOHAI presents special weekend family programs, encouraging parents and children to explore dance, music, storytelling, and crafts that bring history to life. History and nostalgia-themed merchandise is available in the museum gift shop.

The Museum of History and Industry is a private, not-for-profit educational organization dedicated to the collection, preservation, and exhibition of Seattle, King County, and Pacific Northwest history. The Museum of History and Industry is *supported by private contributions,* with additional funding from earned income, individuals, corporations, and foundations.

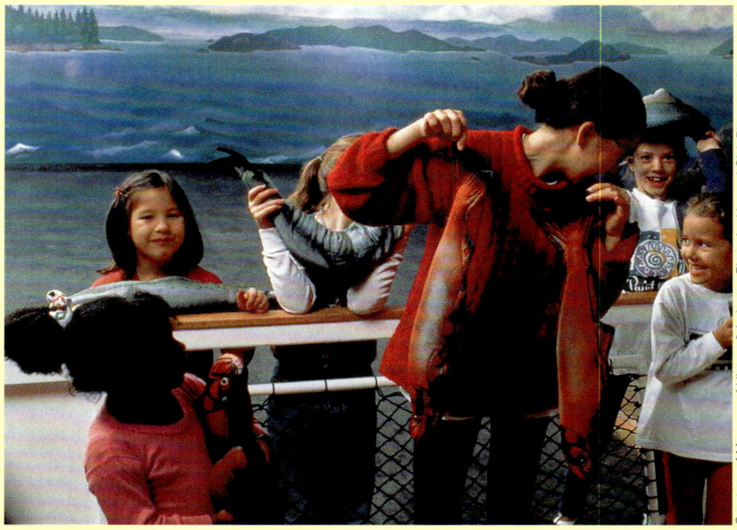

Courtesy of Museum of History & Industry, Photo by Howard Gisk Photographs

Children board a fishing boat in "Salmon Stakes," an exhibit with hands-on activities that are part of the fun at the Museum of History & Industry.

The Seattle SuperSonics

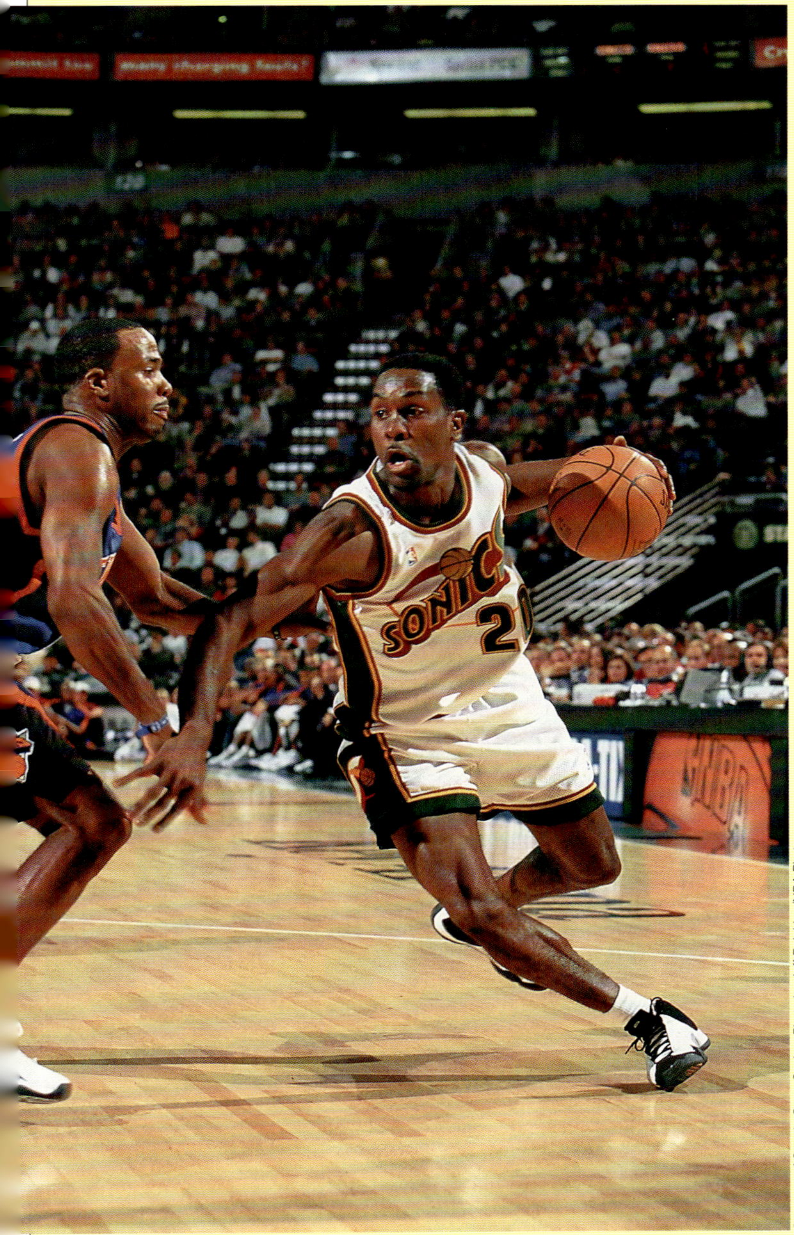

Courtesy of Seattle SuperSonics, Photo by Jeff Reinking/NBA Photos

Perennial All-Star and two time Olympic gold medal winner Gary Payton has established himself as one of the NBA's premier superstars.

One of the most popular franchises in the NBA, the Seattle SuperSonics marked their thirty-third season with the opening of the 2000-2001 season in late October. The Sonics consistently draw large audiences to KeyArena, the team's 17,000-seat home court located at Seattle Center.

After joining the NBA in the 1967-1968 season, the Sonics achieved the upper echelon of the league during two different decades. First, in the late 1970s, the Sonics were at the top of their game. Reaching the NBA Finals in two straight seasons, they won the crown in 1978-79 with an efficient team of interchangeable players led by Jack Sikma, Fred Brown, Dennis Johnson, and Gus Williams.

Seattle was resurgent in the 1990s and once again featured an unconventional lineup, a deep rotation, and an innovative array of defensive schemes. The Sonics' success was spearheaded by point guard Gary Payton—the team's co-captain and today's team leader. After finishing the 1999-2000 regular season with a 45-37 record, the Sonics entered the 2000 NBA Playoffs as the seventh seed in the Western Conference. They battled back from a two-game deficit to force a Game Five against the Utah Jazz in their first postseason round, but fell just short of a dramatic series comeback.

The Sonics returned to the 2000-01 season having acquired one of the NBA's 50 all-time greatest players in center Patrick Ewing. The team also re-signed 21-year-old sensation Rashard Lewis. In November, Sonics President and General Manager named former Sonics veteran Nate McMillan as the team's head coach.

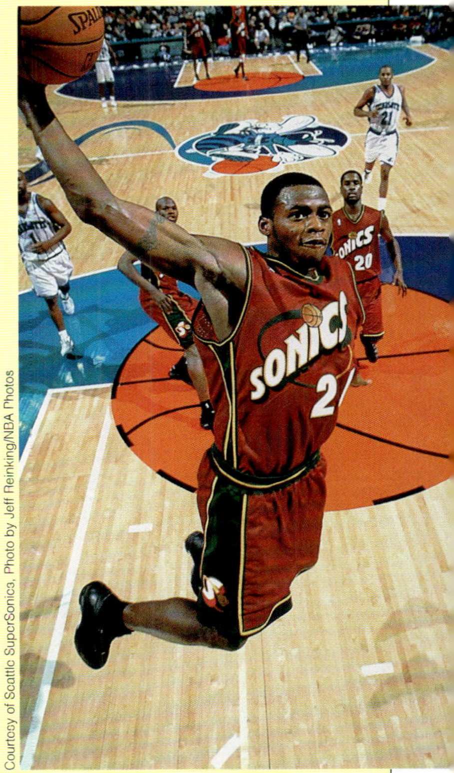

Courtesy of Seattle SuperSonics, Photo by Jeff Reinking/NBA Photos

Primarily a defense specialist for the Sonics in his rookie season, Desmond Mason joins Ruben Patterson and Rashard Lewis as three of the NBA's premier dunk artists.

King County Statistical Information

King County was organized in 1852 from Thurston County. It was originally named after William R. King, Vice President under Franklin Pierce; it was renamed in 1986, after civil rights leader Dr. Martin Luther King, Jr. The first settlements in the county were the donation land claims of Luther Collins, Henry Van Asselt, and Jacob Maple in September of 1851 in the Duwamish Valley area of present day Seattle. This settlement was followed in November by one led by David Denny and Leader Terry at Alki Point. The next year the Denny-Terry settlers moved to a better location for loading lumber on the east side of Elliot Bay and named the settlement Seattle after the friendly chief of the Duwamish Indians. The next year Henry Yesler set up the first steam sawmill on Puget Sound. King County grew and prospered during the late nineteenth and early twentieth centuries with the expansion of the shipping and lumber industries. It boomed again during and after World War II as an aircraft production and shipbuilding center. Today the county is the Pacific Northwest region's major manufacturing and shipping center.

Climate Seattle - elevation 14 feet:

Average	Jan	April	July	Oct
Max Temp	45.6	59.4	75.1	60.4
Min Temp	36.8	44.1	56.1	48.3
Mean Temp	41.2	51.8	65.6	54.4
Precipitation in inches	5.19	1.97	0.63	3.28

Average Annual Maximum Temperature: 60.0
Average Annual Minimum Temperature: 46.4
Average Annual Mean Temperature: 53.2
Average Annual Precipitation: 34.10 inches

Cities and Towns - Population 1996 Estimate

Algona	2,035
Auburn	36,130
Beaux Arts	285
Bellevue	103,700
Black Diamond	2,010
Bothell (part)	13,580
Burien	27,830
Carnation	1,540
Clyde Hill	3,015
Des Moines	23,020
Duvall	3,635
Enumclaw	10,260
Federal Way	75,240
Hunts Point	515
Issaquah	9,255
Kent	60,380
Kirkland	43,160
Lake Forest Park	12,480
Medina	3,085
Mercer Island	21,490
Milton (part)	800
Normandy Park	7,095
North Bend	3,070
Pacific (part)	5,395
Redmond	40,805
Renton	45,170
SeaTac	23,110
Seattle (County seat)	534,700
Shoreline	48,205
Skykomish	250
Snoqualmie	1,550
Tukwila	14,880
Woodinville	9,940
Yarrow Point	1,015

Area:

2,130.9 square miles
Ranking in state: 11th

Congressional Districts:

1, 7, 8, 9

Legislative Districts:

1, 5, 11, 25, 30-34, 36, 37, 39, 41, 43, 45-48

Principal Economic Activities:

Manufacturing
Shipping and Trade
Agriculture
Business Services
Shipbuilding
Fishing
Wood Products
Tourism

Source:
www.metrokc.gov/mkcc/Council_facts.htm#population

Key Players

Agilent Technologies
Heartstream Operation
2401 Fourth Avenue, Suite 500
Seattle, Washington 98121
Telephone: (206) 664-5000
Facsimile: (206) 664-5001
Web Site: www.heartstream.com

Aiphone Corporation
1700 130th Avenue NE
Bellevue, Washington 98005
Telephone: (425) 455-0510,
Facsimile: (425) 455-0071
Web Site: www.aiphone.com

Aljoya Conference
Center of Seattle
3920 Northeast 41st Street
Seattle, Washington 98105-5428
Telephone: (206) 268-7000
Facsimile: (206) 268-7001
Web Site: www.aljoya.com

ATL Ultrasound
22100 Bothell Everett Highway
Bothell, Washington 98021
Telephone: (425) 487-7000
Facsimile: (425) 485-6080
Web Site: www.atl.com

Aventail Corporation
808 Howell Street, 2nd Floor
Seattle, Washington 98101
Telephone: (206) 215-1111
Facsimile: (206) 215-1120
Web Site: www.aventail.com

Bank of America
National Direct Sales N. W.
P. O. Box 34477
Seattle, Washington 98124-9974
Telephone: 1 (800) 900-9000
Facsimile: (206) 358-0627
Web Site: www.bankofamerica.com

Bellevue Club
11200 Southeast 6th Street
Bellevue, Washington 98004
Telephone: (425) 455-1616
Facsimile: (425) 688-3456
Web Site: www.bellevueclub.com

Bell Harbor International
Conference
2211 Alaskan Way, Pier 66
Seattle, Washington 98121
Telephone: 1(888) 772-4422
Facsimile: (206) 441-6665
Web Site: www.bellharbor.org

The Boeing Company
P. O. Box 3707
Seattle, Washington 98124-2207
Telephone: (206) 655-2121
Web Site: www.boeing.com

The Bon Marché
Third & Pine Streets
Seattle, Washington 98181
Telephone: (206) 506-7000

Bullivant Houser Bailey PC
2400 Westlake Office Tower
1601 Fifth Avenue
Seattle, Washington 98010
Telephone: (206) 292-8930
Facsimile: (206) 386-5130
Web Site: www.bullivant.com

Burke Museum of Natural
History and Culture
University of Washington
Box 353010
Seattle, Washington 98195-3010
Telephone: (206) 543-5590
Facsimile: (206) 685-3039
Web Site: www.burkemuseum.org

Cadman
P. O. Box 97038
Redmond, Washington 98073
Telephone: (425) 867-1234
Facsimile: (425) 861-4046
Web Site: www.cadman.com

Chateau Ste. Michelle
One Stimson Lane,
P. O. Box 1976
Woodinville, Washington 98072
Telephone: (425) 488-1133
Facsimile: (425) 488-3340
Web Site:
www.stimson-lane.com

Children's Hospital and
Regional Medical Center
4800 Sand Point Way NE
Seattle, Washington 98105
Telephone: (206) 526-2000
Web Site:
www.seattlechildrens.org

Christensen O'Connor Johnson
Kindness PLLC
1420 Fifth Avenue, Suite 2800
Seattle, Washington 98101-2347
Telephone: (206) 682-8100
Facsimile: (206) 224-0779
Web Site: www.cojk.com

ConneXt
1301 5th Avenue, Suite 1900
Seattle, Washington 98101
Telephone: (206) 521-2100
Facsimile: (206) 521-2400
Web Site: www.connext.com

Data-Linc Group
2635 151st Place NE
Redmond, Washington 98052
Telephone: (425) 882-2206
Facsimile: (425) 867-0865
Web Site: www.data-linc.com

Department of Veterans
Affairs VA Puget Sound
Health Care System
1660 South Columbian Way
Seattle, Washington 98108
Telephone: (206) 762-1010
Facsimile: (206) 764-2250
Web Site: www.puget-
sound.med.va.gov

Documentary Book Publishers
615 Second Avenue, Suite 260
Seattle, Washington 98104
Telephone: (206) 826-4324
Facsimile: (206) 467-4301
Web Site:
www.sasquatchbooks.com

Economic Development
Council of Seattle &
King County
1301 Fifth Avenue, Suite 2400
Seattle, Washington 98101
Telephone: (206) 389-8650
Facsimile: (206) 389-8651
Web Site: www.edu-sea.org

Emerald Downs
P. O. Box 617
Auburn, Washington
98071-0617
Telephone: (253) 288-7000,
Facsimile: (253) 288-7010
Web Site: www.emdowns.com

Fisher Companies Inc.
600 University Street,
Suite 1525
Seattle, Washington 98101
Telephone: (206) 404-7000
Facsimile: (206) 404-7050
Web Site: www.fsci.com

Four Seasons Olympic
411 University Street
Seattle, Washington 98101
Telephone: (206) 621-1700
Facsimile: (206) 623-2271
Web Site:
www.fourseasons.com/seattle

GM NAMEPLATE
2040 15th Avenue West
Seattle, Washington 98119
Telephone: (206) 284-2200
Facsimile: (206) 284-3705
Web Site: www.gmnameplate.com

GREATER SEATTLE BUSINESS ASSOCIATION
2150 North 107th Street, #205
Seattle, Washington 98133
Telephone: (206) 363-9188
Facsimile: (206) 367-8777
Web Site: www.the-gsba.org

HARBORVIEW MEDICAL CENTER
325 Ninth Avenue
Seattle, Washington 98104
Telephone: (206) 731-3000
Facsimile: (206) 731-8605
Web Site: www.harborview.org

THE HIGHRIDGE CORPORATION
P. O. Box 260
Issaquah, Washington 98027
Telephone: (425) 392-0905
Facsimile: (425) 391-3654
Web Site: www.highridge.com

HUGH G. GOLDSMITH & ASSOCIATES, INC.
P.O. Box 3565
Bellevue, Washington 98009
Telephone: (425) 462-1080
Facsimile: (425) 462-7719
Web Site: www.goldsmithengineering.com

KIEWIT CONSTRUCTION COMPANY
4904 Lake Washington Boulevard NE
Renton, Washington 98056
Telephone: (425) 255-8333
Facsimile: (425) 255-9755
Web Site: www.kiewit.com

KING COUNTY DEPARTMENT OF TRANSPORTATION
201 South Jackson Street, KSC-TR-0815
Seattle, Washington 98104-3856
Telephone: (206) 684-1481
Facsimile: (206) 684-1224
Web Site: www.metrokc.gov/kcdot/

KING COUNTY EXECUTIVE OFFICE
KING COUNTY COURTHOUSE
516 3rd Avenue, Room 400
Seattle, Washington 98104
Telephone: (206) 296-4040
Facsimile: (206) 296-0194
Web Site: www.metrokc.gov/exec

KING COUNTY INTERNATIONAL AIRPORT
P. O. Box 80245
Seattle, Washington 98108
Telephone: (206) 296-7380
Facsimile: (206) 296-0190
Web Site: http://www.metrokc.gov/airport

KING COUNTY SHERIFF'S OFFICE
KING COUNTY COURTHOUSE
516 3rd Avenue, Room W-116
Seattle, Washington 98104
Telephone: (206) 296-4155
Web Site: www.metrokc.gov/sheriff

LAPLINK, INC.
18702 North Creek Parkway
Bothell, Washington 98011-8026
Telephone: (425) 487-5495
Facsimile: (425) 487-1284
Web Site: www.laplink.com

LYNDEN AIR FREIGHT
18000 International Boulevard, Suite 700
Seattle, Washington 98188
Telephone: (800) 426-3201, (206) 241-8778
Facsimile: (206) 777-7330
Web Site: www.skytrac.lynden.com

METROPOLITAN KING COUNTY COUNCIL
King County Courthouse
516 3rd Avenue, Room 1200
Seattle, Washington 98104
Telephone: (206) 296-1000
Facsimile: (206) 296-1098
Web Site: www.metrokc.gov/mkcc

MICROSOFT CORPORATION
One Microsoft Way
Redmond, Washington 98052
Telephone: (425) 882-8080
Facsimile: (425) 706-7329
Web Site: www.microsoft.com

MINOR & JAMES MEDICAL, PLLC
515 Minor Avenue, Suite 300
Seattle, Washington 98104
Telephone: (206) 386-9500
Facsimile: (206) 386-9605
Web Site: www.minorandjames.com

MUSEUM OF HISTORY AND INDUSTRY
2700 24th Avenue East
Seattle, Washington 98112
Telephone: (206) 324-1126
Facsimile: (206) 324-1346
Web Site: www.seattlehistory.org

MUSEUM OF FLIGHT
9404 East Marginal Way South
Seattle, Washington 98108-4097
Telephone: (206) 764-5720
Facsimile: (206) 764-5707
Web Site: www.museumofflight.org

NATIONAL OCEANIC AND ATMOSPHERIC ADMINISTRATION
1801 Fairview Avenue East
Seattle, Washington 98102
Telephone: (206) 553-7656
Facsimile: (206) 553-2246
Web Site: www.noaa.gov

NINTENDO OF AMERICA INC.
4820 150th Avenue NE
Redmond, Washington 98052
Telephone: (425) 882-2040

NORTHWEST AIRLINES, INC.
17900 Pacific Highway South, Suite 300
Seattle, Washington 98188
Telephone: (206) 433-3794
Facsimile: (206) 433-3568
Web Site: www.nwa.com

ONVIA.COM
1260 Mercer Street
Seattle, Washington 98109
Telephone: (206) 282-5170
Web Site: www.onvia.com

PCL CONSTRUCTION SERVICES, INC.
15405 Southeast 37th Street, Suite 200
Bellevue, Washington 98006
Telephone: (425) 454-8020
Facsimile: (425) 454-5924
Web Site: www.pcl.com

PENHALLEGON ASSOCIATES CONSULTING ENGINEERS INC. (PACE)
750 Sixth Street South
Kirkland, Washington 98033
Telephone: (425) 827-2014
Facsimile: (425) 827-5043
Web Site: www.paceengrs.com

PRECOR, INC.
20031 142nd Avenue NE
Woodinville, Washington 98072
Telephone: (425) 486-9292
Facsimile: (425) 486-3856
Web Site: www.precor.com

PRO2NET CORPORATION
1730 Minor Avenue, Suite 1900
Seattle, Washington 98101
Telephone: (206) 664-9000
Facsimile: (206) 664-7880
Web Site: www.pro2net.com

RealNetworks Inc.
P. O. Box 91123
Seattle, Washington 98111-9223
Telephone: (206) 674-2700
Web Site: www.RealNetworks.com

Seattle Aquarium Society (SEAS)
1402 Third Avenue, Suite 1000
Seattle, Washington 98101
Telephone: (206) 682-3474
Facsimile: (206) 682-0722
Web Site: www.seattleaquarium.org

Seattle Mariners
P. O. Box 4100
Seattle, Washington 98104
Telephone: (206) 346-4000
Facsimile: (206) 346-4350
Web Site: www.seattlemariners.com

Seattle's Best Coffee/ Torrefazione Italia
1321 Second Avenue, Suite 200
Seattle, Washington 98101
Telephone: (206) 624-8858
Facsimile: (206) 624-3262
Web Site: www.seabest.com/ www.titalia.com

Seattle Seahawks
11220 NE 53rd Street
Kirkland, Washington 98033
Telephone: (425) 827-9777
Facsimile: (425) 893-5072
Web Site: www.seahawks.com

Seattle SuperSonics
351 Elliott Avenue West
Seattle, Washington 98119
Telephone: (206) 281-5800
Facsimile: (206) 281-5839
Web Site: www.supersonics.com

Seattle Symphony
P. O. Box 21906
Seattle, Washington 98199-3906
Telephone: (206) 215-4700
Facsimile: (206) 215-4701
Web Site: www.seattlesymphony.org

The Seattle Times Co.
P. O. Box 70
Seattle, Washington 98111
Telephone: (206) 464-2111
Web Site: www.SeattleTimes.com

Sorrento Hotel
900 Madison Street
Seattle, Washington 98104
Telephone: (206) 622-6400
Facsimile: (206) 343-6155
Web Site: www.hotelsorrento.com

Sound Transit
401 South Jackson Street
Seattle, Washington 98104-2826
Telephone: 1 (800) 201-4900
Facsimile: (206) 398-5221
Web Site: www.soundtransit.org

Sverdrup Civil, Inc., A Jacobs Company
600 108th Avenue NE, #700
Bellevue, Washington 98004
Telephone: (425) 452-8000

Swedish Medical Center
747 Broadway
Seattle, Washington 98122
Telephone: (206) 386-6000
Web Site: www.swedish.org

University of Washington
University Relations, 400
Gerberding Hall, Box 351210
Seattle, Washington 98195
Telephone: (206) 543-2560
Facsimile: (206)543-5651
Web Site: www.washington.edu

University of Washington Medical Center
1959 N. E. Pacific Street
Seattle, Washington 98195
Telephone: (206) 598-3300
Web Site: www.washington.edu/medical/uwmc

URS Corporation
1501 4th Avenue, Suite 1400
Seattle, Washington 98101
Telephone: (206) 343-7933
Facsimile: (206) 343-0513
Web Site: www.urscorp.com

Valley Medical Center
400 South 43rd
Renton, Washington 98055
Telephone: (425) 228-3450
Facsimile: (425) 656-4202
Web Site: www.valleymedical.org

Virginia Mason Medical Center
1100 Ninth Avenue
Seattle, Washington 98101
Telephone: (206) 223-6600
Web Site: www.VirginiaMason.org

The Woodinville Weekly
P. O. Box 587
Woodinville, Washington 98072
Telephone: (425) 483-0606
Facsimile: (425) 486-7593
Web Site: www.nwnews.com

Biblicgraphy

Books:

Berton, Pierre. *The Klondike Fever: The Life and Death of the Last Great Gold Rush*, New York: Alfred Knopf, 1965, 99-130

Best Places Seattle, 8th Edition, Edited by Giselle Smith, Seattle: Sasquatch, 1999.

Book of Lists, 1999, Seattle, Puget Sound Business Journal. 1999

"Chapter 1: Overview of King County History," *King County Resource Protection Plan*, Department of Planning and Community Development, 1984.

Everything You Could Ever Want to Know About King County Park System and More, King County & Key Bank, 1999

Hidy, Ralph W.; Hill, Frank Ernest; Nevins, Allan. *Timber and Men: The Weyerhaeuser Story* (New York, 1963)

King County Heritage Resource Protection Plan, King County Department of Planning and Community Development, 1984

Klondike Gold Rush Official Map and Guide, Klondike Gold Rush National Historic Park, Alaska & Seattle, National Park Service, U.S. Department of the Interior

Unterberger ,Richard. *Seattle, The Mini Rough Guide*, London: Rough Guides LTD, 1998

Van Lindt, Carson. *The Seattle Pilots Story*, New York City: Marabou, 1993

Warren, James R., "A Century of Business", *Puget Sound Business Journal*, September 17, 1999

Web Sites:

http://sccdweb.sccd.ctc.edu/
www.5thavenuetheatre.org
www.acttheatre.org
www.ais.edu
www.amazon.com
www.atl.com
www.attachmate.com
www.aventail.com
www.bastyr.edu/
www.bcc.ctc.edu
www.boeing.com
www.bumbershoot.org
www.chmc.org
www.ci.seattle.wa.us
www.cityu.edu
www.connext.com
www.cornish.edu
www.costco.com
www.eddiebauer.com
www.elliottbaybook.com
www.emptyspace.org
www.federated-fds.com/divisions/bon
www.fhcrc.org/
www.highline.ctc.edu/
www.historylink.org
www.icos.com
www.immunex.com
www.intiman.org
www.kpcenter.org
www.laplink.com
www.mariners.org
www.medtronicphysiocontrol.com
www.metrokc.gov
www.metrokc.gov/airport/history>
www.metrokc.gov/parks/atlas/regtrails.htm
www.microsoft.com
www.nba.com
www.nintendo.com
www.nordstrom.com
www.nwbookfest.org
www.nwfolklife.org
www.onvia.com
www.overlakehospital.org
www.pan.ci.seattle.wa.us/business/tda
www.pathogenesis.com
www.pilchuck.com
www.plumcreek.com
www.pnb.org
www.portseattle.org
www.pro2net.com
www.pyramidbrew.com
www.realnetworks.com
www.redhook.com
www.rei.com
www.sct.org
www.seahawks.com
www.seattleantioch.edu
www.seattleartmuseum.org
www.seattlehistory.org
www.seattleopera.org
www.seattlerep.org
www.seattlesbest.com
www.seattlesymphony.org
www.seattleu.edu
www.sidewalk.com
www.starbucks.com
www.swedish.org
www.theparamount.com
www.titalia.com
www.urbantapestry.com/seattle/index.html
www.valleymed.org
www.vashonchamber.com
www.villagetheatre.org
www.vmmc.org/
www.wa.gov/esd/Imea/pubs/profiles/kingech.htm>
www.washington.edu/
www.washington.edu/burkemuseum
www.washington.edu/medical
www.washington.edu/medical/hmc/
www.weyerhaeuser.com
www.wnba.com
www.womadusa.com
www.xcyte.com
www.zymogenetics.com

Index

Page numbers in italics for photos

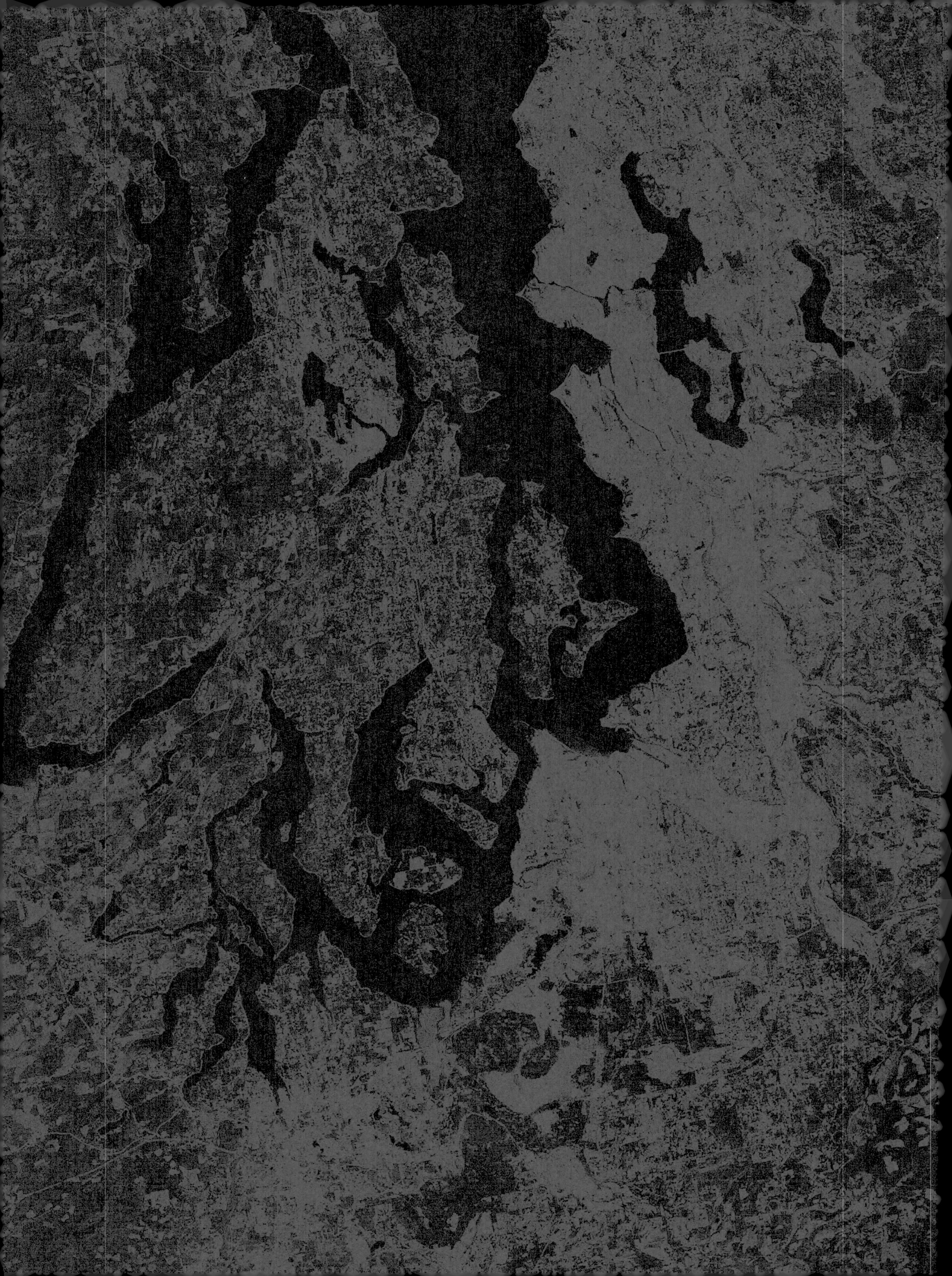